SOCIAL PROBLEMS

SECOND EDITION

George Ritzer
UNIVERSITY OF MARYLAND COLLEGE PARK

ORIGINALLY PUBLISHED AS
SOCIAL PROBLEMS
by Rodney Stark

RANDOM HOUSE
NEW YORK

To Mary

Second Edition
98765432

Published in the United States by Random House, Inc., and simultaneously in Canada by Random House of Canada Limited, Toronto.

Cover photo: "Rasalus," by James Brooks, courtesy of the Whitney Museum of American Art.

Library of Congress Cataloging-in-Publication Data

Ritzer, George.
Social problems.

Rev. ed. of: Social problems / Rodney Stark.
1st ed. [1975]
Bibliography.
Includes index.
1. Sociology. 2. Social problems. 3. United States—Social conditions. I. Stark, Rodney. Social problems.
II. Title.
HM51.R445 1986 361.1 85-30116
ISBN 0-394-35427-3

Manufactured in the United States of America

Text Design: Glen M. Edelstein
Cover Design: Ehn Graphics

The author is indebted to the following for permission to reprint copyrighted material: Table, "Replacement Ratios for Low, Medium, and High-Income Earners in Canada, The U.S., and Sweden, 1980," reproduced by permission of the Ministry of Supply and Services, Canada. Extract from John R. Coleman, "Diary of a Homeless Man," *New York Magazine,* 2/22/83 © 1983 by the author. Two figures, "Escalating Health Care Costs" and "Hospital Room Charges," reprinted by permission of The Conference Board, Inc. Extract from "A New Approach to International Economics," by Bernadet Madeuf and Charles-Albert Michalet in the *International Social Science Journal,* Vol. XXX. Copyright © 1978 by UNESCO. Reprinted by permission of UNESCO. Chart, "Population Growth from 8000 B.C. to the Present," from *The New York Times,* 10/6/81. Copyright © 1981 by The New York Times Company. Reprinted by permission. Extract from Peggy Reeves Sanday, "The Socio-Cultural Context of Rape: A Cross-Cultural Study," *Journal of Social Issues,* Vol. 37, No. 4, pp. 5–27. Reprinted by permission of the Society for the Psychological Study of Social Issues. Chart, from *Behind Closed Doors,* by Murray A. Straus, Richard J. Gelles, and Suzanne K. Steinmetz. Copyright © 1980 by Murray A. Straus and Richard J. Gelles. Reprinted by permission of Doubleday & Company, Inc.

PREFACE

This book is a dramatic revision of *Social Problems*, compiled and edited by Rodney Stark, and published by Random House in 1975. Although most of the text has been rewritten, I chose to work within the confines of the original text for several reasons. For one thing, Stark had used a format for organizing each chapter that was not only popular and extremely useful, but also similar to one that I had developed in sociological theory.[1] This format uses "levels of reality" to analyze the sources of each of the social problems discussed in the book. Although I have simplified the original schema by reducing it from five levels to three (individual, social psychological, and sociological), the basic pattern for analyzing the sources of social problems remains the same as the one used in the previous edition. In addition, I was comfortable with, and continue to employ in this edition, the basic structure devised for each of the chapters analyzing a social problem. That format involves dividing each chapter into three parts. Part One deals with a description of the problem. Part Two analyzes the sources of the problem using the levels of reality outlined above. Part Three analyzes a variety of responses to the problem under discussion.

Another attraction of the original text is that while Stark developed and defined the basic format, each chapter was written by an expert in the problem being analyzed. The result was that the substantive content of each chapter was of a much higher quality than is usually found in social problems texts. Coherence and continuity in the text was provided by the fact that each author wrote his/her chapter in accord with the structure developed by Stark. The distinguished set of authors associated with the original edition included Ronald L. Akers, Robert C. Atchley, James E. Blackwell, Katharine Briar, Scott Briar, Archie Brodsky, Howard S. Erlanger, Michael J. Hindelang, William Kornblum, Stanton Peele, Lynne Roberts, Rodney Stark, Marijean Suelzle, R. Jay Turner, and Rita Roffers Weisbrod.

Thus, I felt that in the original edition I had a book that I was comfortable revising because of its basic structure and one that was well worth revising because of the high quality of its content. However, the book was in need of substantial revision since it was written a decade ago and much has changed both in terms of social problems and the sociological study of those problems. The fact is that aside from the basic structure little remains from the original text. Most chapters have been substantially revised. Some chapters have been dropped. New chapters have been added. In other words, outside of the basic structure, this is in most senses an almost entirely new book, not a simple revision of an earlier edition.

I have done most of the writing and rewriting of this edition on my own. Following the pattern laid down in the original edition, however, several experts were recruited to write new chapters or, in one case, revise an existing chapter. The new chapters are Urban Problems, written by Richard Krannich of Utah State University; Problems in Health Care, written by Peter Conrad of Brandeis University; and Problems of the International Political Economy by Robert J. Antonio and Patrick Ackard of the University of Kansas. In addition, I have written new chapters on Family and Sexual Violence and Problems of the Economy and in the Workplace. Finally, Jill Quadagno of the University of Kansas wrote an almost total revision of the chapter on Aging and Ageism. Thus, of the sixteen chapters in this book, six are totally new chapters.

In many senses this is a collaborative effort involving not only myself, but also Rodney Stark, the authors of the chapters in the original text, the authors of new (or dramatically revised) chapters in this edition, as well as a slew of outside reviewers brought in by Random House to review the original edition and the components of this edition.

[1]George Ritzer, *Toward an Integrated Sociological Paradigm: The Search for an Exemplar and an Image of the Subject Matter* (Boston: Allyn & Bacon, 1981); *Sociological Theory* (New York: Random House, 1983).

Reviewers for the original edition by Rodney Stark were John Clausen, Travis Hirschi, and Wilson Record of the University of Washington, James McMillin of California State College at Bakersfield, and Larry Frye of St. Petersburg Jr. College, Florida. For this most recent edition there were both reviewers and consultants for individual chapters. The consultants were: Paul M. Roman of Tulane University, Norman Yetman of the University of Kansas, Toby Parcel of the University of Iowa, Riley Dunlap of Washington State University, James Blackwell of the University of Massachusetts at Boston, Erich Goode of SUNY at Stony Brook, Alan J. Lizotte of Indiana University, Charles Wellford of the University of Maryland, William C. Cockerham of the University of Illinois, Judith Wittner of Loyola University of Chicago, Kenneth Kammeyer of the University of Maryland, J. Ross Eshleman of Wayne State University, Jim Robbins of McGill University, Linda George of the Duke University Medical Center, Neil A. Weiner of the University of Pennsylvania, Scott Briar of the University of Washington, Arthur St. George of the University of New Mexico, and Professor Stanton Peele.

Reviewers for the second edition were: Ira M. Wasserman of Eastern Michigan University, Patrick M. Horan of the University of Georgia, James Orcutt of Florida State University, Barbara Johnston of North Hennepin Community College, Michael Grimes of Louisiana State University, William Feigelman of Nassau Community College, Robert Lovely of Indiana University Northwest, Vern L. Bengston of the University of Southern California, Walter E. Clark of St. Louis Community College, David L. Westby of Pennsylvania State University, Christopher Hurn of the University of Massachusetts, Camille Miller of the University of Virginia, Minta Littlejohn of Illinois Central College, Paul M. Roman of Tulane University, Rosamund Robbert of Western Michigan University, Joseph Schneider of Drake University, Paul Montagna of Brooklyn College, Paul Chalfant of Texas Tech, Kurt Tausky of the University of Massachusetts, Ray Rist of the Institute for Program Evaluation in Washington, D.C., David P. Aday of the College of William and Mary, Marvin Krohn of the University of Iowa, Raymond Bradley of the University of Minnesota, Larry Baron of the University of New Hampshire, James E. Rosenbaum of Northwestern University, Naomi Aronson of Northwestern University, Vicki McNickle Rose of Southern Methodist University, Irving Tallman of Washington State University, Hilary Silver of Brown University, and Donald Light of the College of Dentistry and Medicine of New Jersey.

In the end, however, this edition is my responsibility, as well as that of the new authors brought in to help with it. Rodney Stark has not been involved in this revision. The same is true of most of the authors in the first edition chapters, although in some cases they have served as reviewers for the current edition. Special thanks must be given to the people at Random House, especially Barry Fetterolf for suggesting this project and Sylvia Shepard for her enormous contributions as developmental editor for the book.

In many ways, this is a highly unusual text. The way in which the original edition was put together was innovative. This edition builds on those innovations, as well as the many talents utilized in the first edition. In addition, a number of new talents and ideas have been brought to bear on the second edition. The result, I believe, is a social problems text that is unlike any of its competitors.

George Ritzer

CONTENTS

I

Analyzing Social Problems

Aristotle: When one is running fast, it is hard to divert the whole body from its impetus in one direction to some other movement. 330 B.C.

Newton: Change of a body's motion is proportional to any force acting upon it, and in the exact direction of that force. 1687.

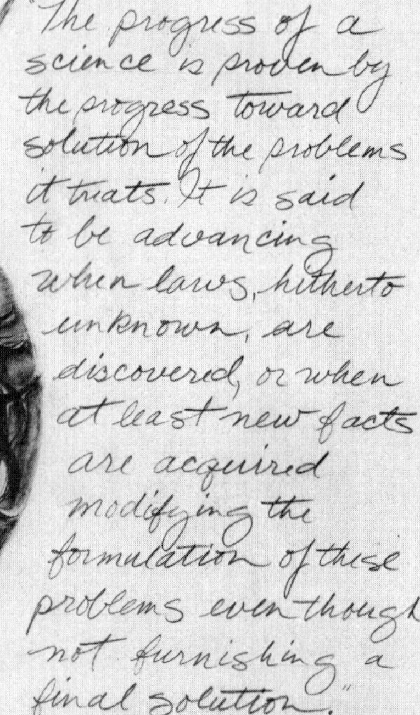

Einstein: Motion, time, and distance are not absolute but relative to moving frames of reference. 1905

Bruce M Dean

1 *Social Problems and Social Science*

We all know what social problems are, right? There is no question in our minds that the following *are* social problems:

__Supermarkets are robbed.

__Joggers are mugged in early morning runs through the park.

__Computer geniuses use their expertise to illegally transfer millions of dollars to their own accounts.

__United States Senators and Representatives take bribes from FBI agents posing as foreign officials.

__Presidents of the United States try to cover up illegal governmental activities.

__The city of Los Angeles chokes through a fifth consecutive day of a smog alert.

__An epidemic of AIDS (Acquired Immune Deficiency Syndrome) sweeps through the United States and panics its citizens.

__The unemployment rate approaches 20 percent for the black population as a whole and 50 percent for black teenagers.

__The likelihood of nuclear war increases as stockpiles of increasingly advanced nuclear weapons grow.

__The elderly struggle to survive by foraging through litter baskets.

__Achievement scores in public schools plummet.

__Heroin addiction begins to become a major problem not only in the lower classes, but in all social classes.

__Family violence, in the form of battered spouses, battered children, and incest victims, attracts greater public attention.

The list, of course, could go on and on, but little would be gained by adding to it. We all know that *these* are social problems, but does that mean that we always know what social problems are? Before answering this question you might be interested to know that not too many years ago narcotics abuse was *not* thought of as a social problem. During the late nineteenth century many patent medicines for sale in this country contained narcotics, and many Americans were as dependent on drugs as are today's drug addicts. For a long time no one considered this state of affairs a problem. Even after many people thought of drug abuse as a problem, it was not yet a *social* problem. It did not become one until people who regarded drug abuse as harmful began to organize and agitate that something be done about drug use. Beyond the case of drug abuse, you might be surprised by the following list of items that were *not* considered, at least at some point in recent history, to be social problems, or at least potential sources of social problems:

__The creation of the atomic bomb.

__The invention of the automobile.

__The migration of massive numbers of people to urban areas.

__The definition of a woman's place as being in the home.

__Racial segregation.

__The use of cocaine in Coca-Cola.

__Cigarette smoking.

__Population growth.

__Being overweight.

__Use of asbestos as a building material.

A new social problem, unknown prior to the 1980s, is Acquired Immune Deficiency Syndrome (AIDS). Here a gay organization seeks to mobilize people to urge the government to divert funds from warfare to health care for AIDS victims. (Bettye Lane/Photo Researchers)

With the hindsight of history, as well as recent scientific research, we now know that all the items on this list either produced social problems or are considered themselves to be social problems. To complicate matters further, we even have conditions that in the past were considered to be social problems, but which are now less and less likely to be viewed in this way. The best examples of this are in the realm of human sexuality. In the not too distant past there was a strong consensus in American society that the following were social problems: homosexuality, premarital sex, extramarital sex, and abortion. Although there is considerable variation in attitudes toward each, it is clear at least that a significant proportion of the population no longer regards these sexual issues as social problems. At the same time, a new social problem (AIDS), highly linked to human sexuality (especially homosexuality), has arisen in the 1980s. Thus, the question of what phenomena are (or are not) social problems is not as clearcut as it first appears. In order to be better able to answer this question we need a definition of social problems.

WHAT ARE SOCIAL PROBLEMS?

We may define *social problems* as *social conditions of which a significant proportion of the population is aware, defines as social problems, and sees in need of remedial collective action. These social conditions have causes and consequences at the individual, social-psychological, and/or sociological levels.*

1. *Social problems are social conditions.* By this, we mean simply that social problems involve a relatively large number of people, perhaps even society as a whole. Conversely, purely personal problems are *not* social problems.[1] An individual who suffers losses because of bad investment decisions is faced with a personal problem, but an individual who loses money in the stock market as a result of a stock market crash resulting from an economic depression is confronted by a social problem. In the case of a depression, the individual is not alone, but is one of many suffering from larger economic problems.

2. *Social problems are caused by individual, social-psychological, and/or sociological factors.* At the individual level, physiological and psychological abnormalities may cause people to become mentally ill, drug addicts, or criminals. Such individuals, especially taken together, cause social problems for large numbers of people, as well as for the society as a whole. At the social-psychological level we can say that people learn certain kinds of behaviors (for example, crime techniques, methods of drug use) from others and that these learned behaviors cause problems for the larger society. Also at the social-psychological level, it is possible to argue that groups of people, rather than individuals, often cause problems for society. In the area of crime, for example, juvenile gangs and organized crime cause society considerable difficulties.

Given the perspective of this book, the *most important* causes of social problems are to be found at the sociological level. Among other things, we can say that the nature of the American economy causes unemployment, the city causes many problems for those who live in it, and the system of social stratification has adverse effects on those who are at the bottom of that hierarchy.

Although we have discussed the individual, social-psychological, and sociological causes of social problems separately in this section, it is crucial that we understand that in most cases they are *all* involved in the causation of social problems. We need to be constantly attuned to the ways in which individual, social-psychological, and sociological factors *interrelate* to cause social problems.

3. *Social problems have individual, social-psychological, and/or sociological consequences.* Social problems generally have negative effects on individuals. It is individuals who suffer from crime, overpopulation, and ecological problems. Not every individual suffers from every social problem, but large numbers of individuals are affected by the various social problems discussed throughout this book. Social psychologically, we can say that relationships between and among people are adversely affected by social problems. Thus, the array of problems associated with city life forces many people to be wary and suspicious of each other. Similarly, the sexism and racism characteristic of our society affect the way males and females and blacks and whites relate to one another. As was true of causes, the *most important* concern in this book is the sociological consequences of social problems. We have in mind such issues as the impact of ageism on the older population, the effect of overpopulation on the economic well-being of a society, and the impact of high crime rates on the quality of life in society as a whole.

4. *A significant proportion of the population must be aware of the problem.* In order for a social problem to exist, a large portion of the population must be aware of the existence of the condition. This means that a social condition of which people are not aware is not a social problem even if that social condition has adverse individual, social-psychological, and sociological consequences. The public awareness that a problem exists is a necessary prerequisite to the final component of our definition of a social problem.

5. *A social problem must be so defined by a large portion of the population and seen as a condition in need of remedial collective action.* It is only when a large number of people are aware of the existence of a problem that they can define it as a social problem. And, in our definition, a social problem can only come into existence if it is defined as such by large numbers of people.[2] Thus, for example, cigarette smoking has always caused people health problems, but it did not become a social problem until it was so defined by large numbers of people. More recently, coffee drinking has begun to be defined as a social problem because of a growing awareness of the link between coffee drinking and various health problems.[3] To take one other recent example, wife-beating has gone on for ages, but is only now coming to be recognized as a social problem.[4]

It is often the case that some specific group must take the lead in defining a social problem and making the public aware of it.[5] However, it is also important to recognize that just because some group is successful in having something defined as a social problem, this does not mean that it will remain defined in this way. Efforts to define a problem may meet with initial success (as well as failure), but later developments may lead to the rejection of the idea that it is a problem.[6]

Most conditions that come to be defined as social problems have some basis in reality. People do not usually get upset over nothing or over mere imaginings.[7] It is more likely, for example, that people would call narcotics use a social problem if

For a social problem to exist, large numbers of people must be aware of the condition. Groups of people sometimes mobilize to raise the level of awareness of the population as a whole. In this case, a women's group seeks to make it clear that pornography is a social problem. (Jim Anderson/Woodfin Camp. & Assoc.)

the drugs did have some negative influence on the psychological states of individuals than if they did not.

However, it is possible for people to define a condition as a serious social problem even though there is little or nothing to support such a claim. For example, during the 1930s, Adolf Hitler and his Nazi party rose to absolute power in Germany partly on the basis of claims that the presence of Jews in German society constituted a severe social problem. According to Hitler, the Jews were a subhuman species dedicated to perverting and subverting the German people and were the cause of widespread social harm through their secret manipulation of the economic system (the Jew as capitalist), as well as through their efforts to incite revolution among the workers (the Jew as communist). By the time the Nazi reign ended, its leaders had murdered six million Jews in an effort to solve this "pressing social problem."

To understand how and why social problems arise, it is important to understand that objective social conditions may well differ from people's perceptions of them and that there is no direct one-to-one relationship between such conditions and the presence or absence of claims that a social problem exists. Harmful social conditions do not always become the focus of group assertions that something is wrong and needs righting. And, sometimes, such assertions are made on the basis of a wholly inaccurate perception of social conditions.

In addition to the issue of its definition, a social problem must be seen as a condition that can, at least potentially, be ameliorated or even eliminated by collective action. Thus, cigarette smoking has not only come to be defined as a social problem, but large numbers of people have undertaken actions to begin to cope with the problem. Among other things, we have health warnings on cigarette packages, restrictions on cigarette advertising, and limitations on smoking in certain locations.

THE SOCIAL CAREERS OF SOCIAL PROBLEMS

The issue in this section is what happens to a social problem once a group of people is aware of it and defines it as a social problem in need of solution. Malcolm Spector and John Kitsuse surveyed a variety of prominent social problems and found that there are a number of elements common to all.[8]

Stage 1: Agitation

Once some group of people defines a social problem, they direct their activity toward two goals: (1) convincing others outside the group that a problem exists and (2) trying to initiate action to improve conditions and to attack the alleged cause of the grievance.

To a considerable extent this initial stage is devoted to transforming "private troubles into public issues." However, not all, and perhaps very few, such attempts are successful. To be successful in convincing large numbers of people that a social problem exists, the complaining group must overcome or avoid a number of potential impediments such as making demonstrably false claims, adopting ineffective strategies, or arousing powerful opposition from groups with conflicting values or competing interests.

Claims

The extent to which a group correctly identifies a troublesome condition and its cause will greatly influence the group's course of action and its consequences. When a group has a clearcut sense of what is wrong and advocates specific action programs, it is more likely to succeed in its efforts and to alleviate conditions. When people are incorrect about what is bothering them or misunderstand the cause of the problem, they may still succeed in convincing others of their claim, but their success will be less likely. If a group wrongly assesses their problem, it may attempt to place responsibility inaccurately and call for irrelevant remedies. When groups with vague and misdefined grievances succeed in generating a social problem, the results are frequently harmful—for example, drug laws and programs that deepen the drug problem, criminal-justice systems that produce crime.

Power

Groups composed of the rich, groups that are very large, groups that are well organized, or groups accorded high social honor are more likely to succeed in getting sympathetic hearings for their grievances than small, poor, disorganized, or stigmatized groups. No matter how powerful the group, a critical task faced by all social movements attempting to define a social problem is to build up its strength. Typically, considerable effort is made in the beginning to enlist powerful supporters. However, efforts designed to increase the power of a movement also often serve to increase the extent of opposition.

Strategy

In the beginning, a major task in creating a social problem is to attract attention—to get society to listen. At any given moment, hundreds of groups with hundreds of messages are trying to get public attention. Most fail. All groups have a similar problem in strategy: to attract attention in a

Table 1.1 Life History of a Social Problem

STAGE 1: AGITATION
Victims of problem, interest group, or moral crusaders want public recognition of their problem. Factors related to success of group: 1. Claims should be clear, concise, and correct in analysis of social problem and remedy. 2. Power of group is dependent on money, social status of members, knowledge, and organization and skills. 3. Strategy to win public attention and support through changing norms or violating existing norms without offending public. 4. Competition between groups with opposing views must be overcome through conflict, cooperation, or compromise.
STAGE 2: LEGITIMATION AND CO-OPTATION
Legitimation: Official acknowledgment of problem. Co-optation: Official agencies define and take control of problem and choose "legitimate" spokespersons from groups making claims. Effects of Legitimation: Appointment of government commission may mean that members of protest group become only witnesses or spokespersons—could spell end of group control. Effects of Co-optation: Call on experts—government claims monopoly on understanding problem. Group may grow unexpectedly. Government often redefines problem and expands it. Possible outcomes: Cooling out protesting group, dispelling claim, supporting claim, or righting grievance.
STAGE 3: BUREAUCRATIZATION AND REACTION
Bureaucratic handling of problem not satisfactory to protest group—bureaucracy more interested in dealing with and processing complaints than in changing social conditions. Fate of problem may rest on organizational features of government agency and its ability to deal with the bureaucracy. Agency and bureaucracy may have interests at odds with those of protest group.
STAGE 4: REEMERGENCE OF MOVEMENT
Rejection by protest group of official response (or lack of government action). Development of new or alternative responses and institutions. Emergence of new concerns and search for new institutions to press claims more effectively. Emergence of social reformers and private reformers.

way that will not at the same time provoke outrage and opposition.

A common initial strategy for groups is publicly to violate norms they object to and to act instead according to norms they advocate as superior. Such norm violation attracts attention, but it is also likely to offend the public. There also is the danger that norm violation, once it is launched as a strategy for dramatizing and publicizing a social problem, tends to get out of hand: groups may turn to more serious norm violations and, therefore, may provoke increased public hostility.

Jerry Falwell, a leader of the conservative movement in the United States, has developed very effective strategies for attracting public attention to the conditions that he and his followers regard as social problems (for example, abortion). (Jill A. Cannefax/EKM-Nepenthe)

Competition

Social problems involve the claim by some group that an unacceptable state of affairs must be changed. A social problem is therefore likely to be vigorously opposed by groups that hold contrary moral conceptions or that have a vested economic interest in the status quo.

Successfully raising a claim to a wide level of social acceptance means overcoming opposing claims. The likelihood of success depends on three factors discussed previously: the relative power of proponents and their opponents; the clarity and accuracy of proponents' claims over those of opponents; and the adequacy of the adopted strategies and counterstrategies. In addition, the competition between proponents and opponents may, by itself, attract enough public attention to make a case that a social problem exists. When a group reaches the point of successfully creating serious controversy and receives a considerable amount of public acceptance of its claims, the developing social problem typically undergoes a major transformation.

Stage 2: Legitimation and Co-optation

The natural history of a social problem changes in two important ways when major social institutions, usually government agencies, recognize the complaining group and begin to respond to the group's claims. First, the group (and its problem) receives *legitimation,* or official acknowledgment. The claimants, who may earlier have been regarded as peculiar or un-American for speaking out strongly on a problem, are now treated as responsible and informed critics. Second, as government agencies enter the picture, they begin to take control of defining the problem and choosing its legitimate spokespeople. This process, a well-understood aspect of the behavior of large organizations, especially government bureaucracies, is called *co-optation.* Through co-optation, new interest or claimant groups are absorbed into the structure of an organization as a means of averting threats to the organization's stability.[9] The strategy is based on the principle, "let's not try to lick them, let's get them to join us." Often, opposition can be silenced or greatly reduced by putting the critics on the team, thus making them share the burden of responsibility for decisions and increasing their stake in supporting the organization rather than opposing it.

As we shall see, Stage 2 may result in a solution to the social problem and thus mark the end of the process; more typically, the problem is merely changed, and conflict over it renews.

Effects of Legitimation

Throughout Stage 1, a social problem ordinarily has only "unofficial" standing. The claimant group, although it may include high public officials in its ranks, is acting only in the capacity of private citizens in an effort to arouse public concern. But, if the movement is successful, it eventually attracts, or even forces, official notice.

Initially, official notice may be quite hostile. However, as official recognition is made more sympathetic (or initially takes a more sympathetic form), the protesting group and its claims will probably gain a higher standing than they had before.

Government, however, is likely to take action beyond simple acknowledgment of a problem. A common initial response is to appoint a commission or committee to investigate the nature and the extent of the problem and to suggest corrective measures. At this point, a protest group may find itself transformed into spokesperson and expert witness, thus increasing its legitimate recognition. Spector and Kitsuse note that just as legitimation may be the claimants' "finest hour," legitimation may also "represent the beginning of the end of control over the claims they raise."[10] This is so even though group spokespeople get to air their views before committees, for "they are cast in the role of providing information rather than defining and negotiating the nature of the problem."[11]

Effects of Co-optation

When the official career of a social problem begins, the unofficial protest group is likely to be phased out of the operation. When government becomes officially involved in a problem, it usually calls on "experts" other than spokespeople for the protest group—including experts representing opposition groups. Indeed, government often quickly develops its own staff of experts and then claims a monopoly on understanding the problem. At this point the protest group may find itself with many unexpected "allies" and fellow complainants, often because the scope of the problem expands as others attempt to share in the group's initial success.

The government may play a role in expanding the definition of the problem but, more often, it redefines the problem by narrowing the focus of the problem or diverting it. Whatever else happens, official action usually quickly overshadows the unofficial group, at least temporarily. What becomes of the social problem at this point substantially depends on the outcome of official co-optation of the issue.

One outcome is that the government may cool off the protesting group by simply taking note of its grievances and promising to study them. A second possibility is that results of a government study will (correctly or incorrectly) dispel the claims of the protest group as unfounded. Third, even when government investigation supports the claims of the protest group, the problem may still go untended and the group's effort may dissipate. The second and third possibilities make it clear that "commissions may be the burial ground of a great many social problems."[12] Fourth, the government may take effective action to remedy the grievances of the protesting group. Righting grievances is most common when the protesting group's claims are sharply focused, when the remedy is clearly recognized and feasible, and when the only significant opposition is based on values and morality, not on economics.

It would be wrong, however, to assume that when government co-opts a social problem, it either solves or buries it. Both results are relatively uncommon. A more common outcome is for the government to create some institutionalized means of dealing with the problem or, at least, of dealing with complaints about the problem. Government agencies and programs created in this way seem to take on a life of their own: after setting things in motion, the government finds it difficult to stop a line of action or to disband some agency. Thus, protest groups that have managed to get their problems translated into a government function have at least given some permanency to their quest for redress. But the question still remains whether redress will actually be forthcoming.

Stage 3: Bureaucratization and Reaction

During the first two stages in the career of a social problem, attention is focused on claims that there is a problem. Stage 2 ends when the grievances of the protesting group have been turned into a government function. During Stage 3, the fate of a social problem hinges on organizational features of government agencies and on the ability of those groups affected by government action to deal with government bureaucracy.

At one level, the interests of the government bureaucracy often conflict with the interests of the complainants. For example, actions taken by government agencies concerning a particular problem may have more to do with preserving the agency and the jobs of those who work in it than with solving the problem. The agency's policies may therefore move away from dealing with the problem to dealing with *complaints about the problem.* The question becomes not "What can we do to cure the condition they complain about?" but "How can we get them to stop complaining?"

As a result, it is not uncommon for agencies to come to treat protests as public-relations problems. The primary objective of many government agencies—widely regarded as engaging in solving social problems—is defusing complaints. Thus, the fate of claims concerning a social problem rests on the ability of complainants continually to monitor and renegotiate the thrust and character of government activities. If the complainants see that governmental actions are inappropriate, ineffective, or insincere, they must once again take on the task of mobilizing support and protesting the course of events. What happens next depends on how much success they have in accomplishing these tasks.

Stage 4: Reemergence of the Movement

Typically the problem persists through the first three stages and finally becomes a captive of government agencies; government policies and programs then become the target of growing disillusion and discontent by the original claimant group, new claimant groups, or groups that claim that the government programs themselves constitute a social problem. Whichever the case, during the fourth stage in the career of a typical social problem, we see a rekindling of concern about the social problem *and* opposition to existing programs and agencies that deal with the problem. Furthermore, the reemergence of the movement usually involves not merely opposition to these programs but a search for new institutions. Two different lines of development characterize this fourth stage. One line is toward the development of radically different institutions in the hope of finding *social,* or public, solutions that will benefit everyone. The second line is to withdraw from institutions altogether and seek *private,* limited solutions that benefit only group members.

Attempts to create new social institutions or radically to reform old ones in order to deal more effectively with a social problem confront most of the same difficulties already outlined in this chapter. For example, plans must be effective, strategies must be suitable, and the group must muster sufficient power and overcome opposition. But beyond these problems, the movement will once again encounter the dangers of being co-opted by government agencies, repeating the cycle of becoming a government undertaking. Sometimes, the movement succeeds in reshaping the goals and character of the co-opting government agency. On other occasions, co-optation greatly blunts the movement.

Spector and Kitsuse's four-stage natural history of the career of social problems makes it clear that social problems are preeminently a *political process* through which problems come to be publicly accepted as such and through which particular institutional responses to the problem are shaped and then reshaped.[13] "Political" in this context means, especially, that some group(s) sought to have a phenomenon recognized as a social problem while other group(s) resisted such recognition. The grievances and demands of one group to have a condition recognized as a social problem ordinarily impinge on the interests of other groups that strenuously resist having some state of affairs so recognized. For example, the drive by black leaders to have racism defined as a social problem was opposed by white supremacists. Similarly, the effort by feminists to have sexism thought of as a social problem was resisted by male chauvinists.

In addition to emphasizing the political aspects of social problems, another reason for devoting so much attention to the Spector and Kitsuse model is that it provides a systematic basis for understanding why it is so difficult to do something effective about social problems. When you have studied the institutional responses to particular problems treated in later chapters of this text, you will see that typically a variety of laws and massively expensive programs have been directed at every one of them. Yet the problems persist. Sometimes the laws and the programs have even made the problems worse. Throughout the book, many explanations are offered about why so many attempts to do good go wrong. In addition, many of the barriers to resolving social problems are inherent in the very processes (discussed above) through which social problems are socially defined and become the focus of public activity.

Some Additional Clarifications

Elite vs. Nonelite Definitions

Most social problems have been so defined by social movements organized and controlled by elite members of society, the leaders of our political, economic, scientific, educational, and religious institutions. These leaders, forming a wide array of coalitions, have successfully defined an enormous number of conditions as social problems: street crime, drug abuse, poverty, mental illness, pornography, prostitution, pollution, and the like. However, it should be borne in mind that there is a tendency for elite members of society to define the activities of lower-ranking members of society as the problems. One must also be alert to the results of efforts by nonelite members of society to define activities engaged in, or conditions caused by, elite members of society as social problems.[14] We can include the following under the heading of social problems attributable, at least in part, to elite members of society: governmental abuse of power, threat of nuclear war, dangers of nuclear power, occupational safety and health problems, excessive profits, and inequalities in the health care system. Thus, social problems are not just, or even most importantly, those defined by social movements spearheaded by elite members of society. Just as important, if not more important, are the problems caused by elite members of society and/or the various institutions they lead. Throughout this book we will be concerned with social problems as they are defined by *both* elite *and* nonelite members of society.

Focus on Problems, Not Social Movements

Although we view social problems as being the result of social movements, we do not intend to discuss the process by which various conditions come to be seen as social problems. Rather, we will examine the end results of these movements, the conditions that have been broadly defined as social problems.

Problems to be Discussed

As in any book, the author is imposing his views, at least to some extent, on those problems that are singled out for discussion in this book. For example, a number of people view "welfare cheats" as a serious social problem. While there are undoubtedly a number of people who cheat the welfare system, the author does not view this as the most serious problem in this area. Rather, the most serious social problem, by far, in this area is the system of social inequality and the high levels of poverty that it produces. It is this that is singled out for discussion and not the problem of welfare cheating. Although the author is exercising some discretion, the problems discussed in this book are those generally defined by both sociologists and the public as social problems.[15]

A SOCIOLOGICAL FRAMEWORK FOR ANALYZING SOCIAL PROBLEMS

Sociology is an extremely diverse field offering a wide array of theoretical approaches to every conceivable social issue.[16] Instead of starting out with this range of theories (many of which will be presented later in this chapter), we have chosen to begin with a very broad sociological framework that will be the basis for the analysis of *all* of the social problems covered in this book.

The basic premise of the approach to be used here is that the social world can be usefully and meaningfully organized in terms of several *levels of social reality.*[17] It is important to recognize immediately that the social world is not itself divided into various levels, but rather the levels are imposed on it by sociologists (and other social scientists) in order to make better sense out of it. In order to get an overall graphic sense of what we mean by levels of social reality, see Table 1.2.

At its most basic level, this is a model of the social world that runs from the most *microscopic,* or smallest scale, to the most *macroscopic,* or largest scale social concerns. Although this continuum could be divided into a number of more specific levels, we have decided to keep it simple by focusing on only three basic levels:

1. The individual (physiological and psychological) level.
2. The social-psychological (interpersonal and group) level.
3. The sociological (social structures, culture, society, and intersocietal relations) level.[18]

In most chapters, we will deal with each of these levels and their relationship to a social problem.

Each chapter will begin with a general overview of the problem(s) to be discussed. The heart of each chapter will be the second part, which deals with the causes and consequences of each social problem. It is this part that will be most informed by the levels of social reality schema outlined above. This schema will also be used, but much more loosely, in the final part of each chapter dealing with responses to social problems. In illustrating the levels of social reality approach in this introductory chapter, we will focus on the way it will be used in the causes and consequences portion of each chapter.

CAUSES AND CONSEQUENCES OF SOCIAL PROBLEMS

In some cases (for example, mental illness), we will begin our analysis of the causes and consequences of a social problem at the individual level and work our way up, while in others (such as ecological problems) we will proceed in the reverse order. It is in these and other ways that we will use our model flexibly, even creatively, throughout this book. Let us turn to each of the levels in the context of a discussion of the causes and consequences of social problems in order to make our discussion more concrete and to allow us to draw upon illustrative material from various social problems.

Individual Level

As was pointed out above, the individual level is subdivided into physiological and psychological sublevels.

Physiological Factors

Sociologists are rarely interested in physiological factors per se; they are the domain of biologists, physiologists, and the like. However, sociologists are interested in the effect of physiological factors on social behavior, as well as the reciprocal effect of social life on the physiology of human beings. Among the physiological factors of concern in this context are genetic predispositions, genetic abnormalities, physical characteristics, intelligence, racial and gender differences, hormonal factors, sexual needs, nutritional needs, and physical health. We will discuss such physiological factors in two ways. On the one hand, we will be concerned with the issue of whether these factors play a role in causing various social problems. On the other hand, we will have many occasions to discuss the effect of various macroscopic social problems on individual physiology. Let us look briefly at the physiological level in these cause-and-effect terms.

Physiological factors are often thought of as causes of various social problems. For example, many believe that criminals such as murderers have defective brains. Drug abusers are often thought to have a similar problem, as well as chemical imbalances in their bodies. Many believe that rapists are impelled by overwhelming sexual needs. Differences in the accomplishments of various races, and the two genders, are sometimes traced to physiological differences among and between them. There are many

Table 1.2 Levels of Analysis: Major Levels in the Analysis of Social Problems

LEVELS	APPROPRIATE QUESTIONS	A PARTIAL SYNOPSIS OF PRESENT CONCLUSIONS
INDIVIDUAL	Do physiological factors play a role in causing social problems?	Yes, although in general they are not of central significance.
	Do psychological factors play a role in causing social problems?	Yes. While more important than physiological causes, psychological factors are usually not of utmost importance.
	Do social problems impact on individual physiology?	Yes. Many social problems have powerful adverse effects on individual physiology.
	Do social problems impact on individual psychology?	Yes. Again the effect can be very strong.
SOCIAL-PSYCHOLOGICAL	Do social-psychological factors cause social problems?	Yes. We will discuss a number of social-psychological factors that play a role in causing social problems.
	Do social problems impact on the social-psychological level?	Yes. Social-psychological dimensions are negatively affected in various ways.
SOCIOLOGICAL	Do sociological factors cause social problems?	Very definitely. Throughout this book we will see how sociological factors are generally the most important causes of social problems.
	Are sociological factors affected by social problems?	Yes. Sociological factors are profoundly affected by social problems.

such beliefs about the causal role of various physiological factors in social problems, and we will have occasion at many points in this book to discuss them and to assess the evidence on their actual significance. Although we will see that physiological factors play a role in some social problems, in many others the evidence on the contribution of physiological factors to social problems is dubious at best. For example, the best thinking today on rape is that the rapist is not primarily impelled by sexual needs, but rather rape is a manifestation of sexism and an expression of power.

The evidence of the impact of social problems on individual physiology is far more clear and unequivocal. There is little doubt, for example, that poverty adversely affects the physical and mental health of poor people. The stress caused by various high-powered occupations causes heart disease and other maladies among holders of such positions. Inequalities in the health care system cause people to die from diseases that they otherwise might be able to avoid or survive. Excessive smoking, alcohol consumption, and drug use cause a wide range of physiological problems for those who engage in such behaviors. Ecological problems such as smog, chemical wastes, and nuclear wastes do immeasurable harm to the human physiology. And, of course, drunk drivers, murderers, soldiers, and nuclear weapons can inflict the ultimate physiological harm; they kill people.

Psychological Factors

As with the physiological sublevel, sociologists are not interested in the psychological sublevel in itself, but only as it relates to the other levels of social reality. The study of the psychological level as such is the domain of psychology, but sociology is open to insights from that field. There is some interest in the impact of physiology on psychology, but the main concern of sociologists, specifically those interested in the study of social problems, is the relationship between the sociological level (social structures, culture, society, and intersocietal relations) and psychological processes. Sociologists are *not* interested in the study of the psychology of specific individuals, nor are they concerned with individual psychotherapy. Rather, they are most concerned with the relationship between larger-scale social phenomena and psychological processes. Among the psychological processes to be discussed throughout this book are dependent personalities, antisocial personalities, psychoses, frustration, aggression, repression, scapegoating, authoritarianism, and many others.

As was true of physiological factors, in some cases we will be concerned with psychological dimensions as causes of social problems, while in others we will deal with the impact of social problems on psychological functioning. In still other instances, we will be concerned with the ongoing interaction between psychological factors and social problems. We can illustrate all of these relationships in the case of drug (and alcohol, which is a type of drug) abuse. On the one hand, there is some evidence that particular types of personalities, dependent personalities, are drawn to the use and abuse of drugs and alcohol. These types of people tend to become dependent on these substances, and it is they who often cause a wide range of problems for society. It is they who tend to become the skid row drunks who attract so much public attention and police surveillance. It is the dependent personalities who frequently become drug abusers who are unable to perform their public responsibilities and are often driven into the world of street crime in order to support their habits. Thus, the social problems associated with drug and alcohol abuse are seen as being caused, at least in part, by the personality problems of the people involved.

Social problems, in turn, impact on the personalities of the individuals involved. Substance abuse leads to a wide variety of psychological impairments. These drug- and alcohol-induced impairments make it increasingly difficult for the people involved to function in the "straight" occupational and social worlds. This, in turn, drives them further into the deviant subculture of drug and alcohol abuse, to crime to support their habits, and to other antisocial behaviors. Involvement in these subcultures makes it even more unlikely that such individuals will develop the psychological traits needed to function in "straight" society. Thus, dependent personalities and the drug and alcohol problems for which they are partially responsible, feed upon one another, which increases the difficulties for the individuals as well as the larger society. The same sort of thing could be said about the relationship between many psychological and social problems and we will analyze these relationships in many of the chapters in this book.

Social-Psychological Level

It is at the level of interpersonal relations and the social group that we get to the concerns of the sociologist proper, or at least those sociologists who consider themselves social psychologists.[19]

Social psychologists are interested in the entire array of interpersonal relations. Within the area of social problems, this leads to an interest, for example, in the ways that people are socialized (or learn) to be drug abusers, prostitutes, or criminals. We will also be interested in the process by which certain individuals come to be labeled by others as being one kind of deviant or another. Most generally, we will be interested in the relationship between the way people deal with and treat each other and the development or control of social problems. For example, we will need to examine the relationships between blacks and whites, minority groups and the majority group, males and females, police and the public, teachers and students, criminals and their victims, alcoholics and their families, mentally ill and their therapists, rich and poor, young and the aged. The list of such relevant relationships is virtually endless, but the point is that various types of interpersonal relationships are involved in many different ways in the creation, development, and attempted solution of all social problems. These interpersonal relationships are sometimes causes, sometimes consequences, and sometimes involved in a complex web of both causes and consequences.

It is not unusual for drunk drivers to injure or kill themselves and/or innocent bystanders. (Jill Cannefax/EKM-Nepenthe)

At the social-psychological level there is also a concern for the social group and its role in social problems. Social psychologists define a *group* as a small number of people who interact with one another over time and establish patterns of interaction, a group identity, and rules or norms governing behavior. We will be concerned with various types of groups in this book including gangs, families as arenas of conflict and violence, ethnic enclaves, and retirement communities. As is our pattern, we will be concerned with such groups as both causes and consequences of social problems. For example, a teenage gang in a lower-class community can be seen, at least in part, as a product of poverty, overcrowding, and other adverse living conditions. Such a gang, in turn, becomes a problem in itself, contributing mightily to the difficulties involved in living in such a community. Other groups are not in themselves causes of problems, but are created and maintained by social problems. For example, racism helps lead to the creation of racial enclaves, as well as the problems that often exist within them. Retirement communities are made necessary by the inability of Americans to integrate the elderly into the mainstream of society, and these communities are frequently wracked by a series of internal problems. The family is inherently neither cause nor consequence of social problems, although as it is now structured in the United States it seems to produce a number of problems including high divorce rates, battered wives and children, and even homicide. Thus, in a wide variety of ways, many different groups are involved in social problems.

Sociological Level

Moving toward the macroscopic end of the social continuum we encounter the larger-scale aspects of the social world, beginning with social structures and culture.

Youth gangs may be seen both as reflections of social problems in the larger society (for example, poverty) and as potential sources themselves of other social problems (for example, street crime). (Ed Lettau/Photo Researchers)

Social Structures and Social Problems

Social structures may be seen as sets of interrelationships that have a discernible form and/or shape. They have been created by people over time and have come to have a life of their own that exists, at least to some degree, apart from the individuals who make them up. A wide range of phenomena may be considered social structures. A large organization, especially one organized bureaucratically, may be thought of as a social structure, and this means that all of the following qualify as social structures: the federal government, state and local governments, the military, political parties, large corporations, labor unions, mental hospitals, prison systems, and police forces. In addition, even larger entities such as the economy, social stratification, urban areas, and even patterns of majority-minority relations can be thought of as social structures. Most of these structures are not problems in themselves, but they often create problems of a physiological, psychological, or social-psychological nature for the people who live within them. They also create problems for the larger society that we will discuss shortly. This is not to say that these structures produce only problems, because this is not so. They may have many positive consequences, but in a book on social problems our concern is with their negative consequences. The following is a list of a few of the problems created by a variety of social structures:

—The air pollution characteristic of modern urban life produces a variety of deleterious physiological consequences for individuals, such as emphysema and lung cancer.

—The unsafe working conditions in many factories produce a large number of occupationally related injuries and even deaths.

—Many of the goods produced by American corporations have adverse effects on the health of those who consume them. Examples include cigarettes, alcohol, automobiles with unsafe components, food products with hazardous additives, and many more.

—Many prison systems do a better job of allowing inmates to learn how to become more sophisticated criminals than in rehabilitating them.

—Collusion between the military and the defense industries allows for a massive expansion of weaponry, thus increasing the likelihood of warfare.

—The economy seems to require a large number of unemployed people.

—The system of social stratification operates in such a way that those at the top "stack the deck" in their favor and to the disadvantage of the poor who rank at the bottom of the stratification system.

The general point is that social structures of various types produce a variety of physiological, psychological, and social-psychological problems for the people who exist within them. In addition, these structures are apt to cause problems for the society as a whole. To take just one example, the military-industrial complex poses a threat to the very existence of society by making a nuclear holocaust increasingly likely.

Culture and Social Problems

Also toward the macroscopic end of the continuum are a series of culturally induced and/or relevant social problems. Basically, we can conceive of *culture* as the shared ideas of a community of people. Thus, we can talk of the culture of a society as a whole, as well as of a large number of subcultures within a given society. Among other things, a culture (or subculture) encompasses various types of ideas including knowledge, beliefs, values (desired ends), and norms (rules for achieving those ends). At one level, we can say that the culture of

American society as a whole creates conditions leading to social problems. For example, one of the major values of American society is success, especially economic success. However, while most Americans share this goal, many do not have access to legitimate means to achieve that end. Some people react to this situation by finding illegal means to achieve the end of economic success, such as stock swindling, computer theft, fraud, extortion, prostitution, drug dealing, purse snatching, burglary, shoplifting, and the like. In other words, the disjunction between cultural goals and legitimate means to those ends produces a number of social problems.

Other major cultural sources of social problems are the conflict between subcultures and the culture of the society as a whole, as well as among and between various subcultures. There is considerable evidence that various groups form subcultures whose ideas are at variance with those of the society as a whole. Among such subcultures would be those of heroin addicts, prostitutes, juvenile gangs, prison inmates, inmates of mental institutions, and many others. Problems often arise because these subcultures either reject conventional means to ends or even the ends themselves. Beyond that, problems arise because of conflict between one subgroup and another. For example, problems often arise because of a conflict between the values of juvenile gangs and those of the police who are supposed to control them. Similarly, social problems arise as a result of the conflict between subcultures formed by elderly Americans and those of younger Americans.

Society and Social Problems

At the more macroscopic end of the social continuum we come to society itself, as well as the relationships among and between societies. The importance of societal differences is shown, for example, in differences between societies in homicide rates. It is well known that murder is much more common in the United States than in many other societies, say Sweden, Japan, the Soviet Union, England, and France. What is it about American society as a whole that contributes to the high homicide rate? One factor is often thought to be the history of the Wild West and the resulting frontier spirit. This has led to a long-term romance in the United States with the gun and the gunfighter. Lionized by the movies, the gunfighter spirit continues to exist within American society. Americans have a continuing romance with the handgun, with the result that over 100 million handguns are in the possession of the public. In other societies there are laws and/or conventions against the possession of handguns. The result is that many more people are killed by handguns in the United States than in any other country in the world. It is a common finding in this country that people use handguns because they are there. Another societal factor is the higher level of poverty in the United States than in many Western European societies, as well as the greater level of deprivation associated with being poor in America. Other societies provide much better "safety nets" for their poor than does the United States. The result is that at least some poor people in the United States may be driven by need or despair to desperate acts. These societal level factors, and many others, contribute to the high level of interpersonal violence in the United States.

We might mention a few other examples of societal level factors and their role in social problems in America. For example, the high rates of geographic mobility among the American people have, along with a number of other factors, contributed to the undermining of the traditional extended family. Demographic trends such as the decline of the birth rate in the United States and the overall aging of the population have strained various social institutions such as the educational system (a decline in enrollments) and the Social Security system (growing demands for benefits from the system). The extraordinary need of the American population as a whole for energy of all kinds has placed tremendous ecological demands and strains on the world in which we live.

International Social Problems

In addition to problems at the level of society as a whole, there are also problems that are traceable to, and/or impact on, the international arena. Examples abound. The acid rain, which has been traced most importantly to a number of American factories and power plants, often falls on Canadian territory. The population problems of countries like Bangladesh and India reverberate throughout the world. Border wars between small countries like Iran and Iraq threaten to drag in the major powers. And, of course, the nuclear arsenals of the United States and the Soviet Union threaten the entire world. Thus, to tie together our most microlevel and most macrolevel concerns, international nuclear war threatens the physiological well-being of every person in this country and on the earth.

RESPONSES TO SOCIAL PROBLEMS

Part three of each chapter will be concerned with various responses to social problems. Although this section, too, will be informed by the levels of social reality approach, that approach will play a much less focal role than in the causes and consequences section of each chapter. In general, however, we can say that responses to social problems exist on the individual, social-psychological, and sociological levels. In addition, responses to social problems can also be differentiated in terms of whether they constitute efforts to prevent the problems from arising or attempts to deal with the problems once they have come into existence.

SOCIOLOGICAL THEORIES

Now that we have offered a coherent framework for analyzing social problems, we can present some of the diversity that characterizes sociology. Specifically, we will introduce you here to a number of the sociological theories that can be used to analyze social problems.

A *theory* is a set of ideas, usually expressed in the form of concepts, that is useful in understanding and explaining a broad range of social phenomena. Within sociology there are a number of important theories.[20] In fact, there are many more theories than the student requires to deal with the material discussed in this book. Thus, we will restrict ourselves to introducing only a few of the broad theories that exist within sociology as a whole. However, matters are made more complicated by the fact that there are a number of more limited theories within the sociology of social problems that are aimed at understanding and explaining a narrower range of social phenomena specifically relating to social problems. Thus, we will need to introduce, in addition, some of the more limited theories of social problems.

The rest of this book will be heavily influenced by the theories discussed in this section. However, the later material has been written in such a way that it can be read without constantly referring back to this section in order to understand what is being said. An understanding of the theories discussed here will give the reader a very broad sense of sociology, as well as a set of perspectives that will enhance the understanding of the main body of this book.

Structural Functionalism

Structural functionalism has been a dominant theoretical perspective in the social sciences, especially sociology and anthropology, for several decades.[21] Although somewhat less important today than it was in previous decades, structural functionalism continues to influence sociology as a whole, as well as the sociological study of social problems. Structural functionalists focus on the large-scale structures and cultural components of society and the functions that they perform within that society. When one wants to understand why some social structure (or cultural component) exists in society, one examines how it contributes to, or is sustained by, its relationships with other social structures (or cultural components).

Rather than talking about structural functionalism in general, we can illustrate it with a classic example from the work of the distinguished American sociologist Robert Merton.[22] Merton tried to understand why political machines (a social structure) existed for a long period in American history, even though they ran counter to democratic norms and values and often violated the law. Assuming society to be a system, as structural functionalists often do, Merton looked at what political machines did and attempted to demonstrate that such organizations made positive contributions to the needs of other parts of society that were not being adequately met in other ways. Merton discovered that political machines served several functions: they centralized political power to meet the demands of a variety of community subgroups; they gave lower-class groups personal assistance in the form of jobs, legal aid, food baskets, and so forth; they offered channels for upward social mobility for disadvantaged groups, especially poorer ethnic groups; and they offered protection for illegal services (such as gambling) that many members of the public desired. Consequently, Merton argued that in their day, political machines offered more means for resolving urban political tensions and social needs than did the available alternative political institutions.

Functional analysis seeks to explain social phenomena, especially social structures and cultural components, on the basis of their consequences for other parts of the system. It does not follow, however, that whatever one finds in society must have "good" consequences. Functionalists are quite aware that social systems can get out of kilter and that societies can become so misaligned that they break down. This is precisely the notion that underlies the functionalist analysis of social problems. Social problems, in the functionalist view, reflect failures or breakdowns in the social system. Functionalists use the term *dysfunction* to refer to instances in which one part of society is having negative effects on the other parts and thus on the operation of the system as a whole. For example, functionalists would say that conflicts between racial and ethnic groups are dysfunctional for political stability, or they might show that modern technology is producing pollutants that are dysfunctional for society as a whole.

In the functionalist view, social problems reflect *social disorganization:* something is going wrong within the system; it is not working as well as it could be, or should be; it is growing disorganized. A disorganized social system is one in which there are a number of social dysfunctions. As a result of disorganization within the system, people are often impeded in their ability to achieve their own objectives. The functionalist view stresses structural and cultural conditions as the causes of social problems. The claim that a social problem exists involves a technical judgment that something is basically wrong with the way the social system is operating.

This view of what causes social problems clearly indicates where the solution is to be found. Actions must be directed toward overcoming the disorganized features of a society. The dysfunctions must be reduced or eliminated and must be replaced with social arrangements without harmful effects or with less severe effects.

It is often charged that functionalist conceptions of social problems are fundamentally conservative; that is, they take for granted that a society ought to be preserved, and they regard social problems as symptoms of social disorganization, not as symptoms of an intrinsically wicked society. Critics sometimes claim that functionalist views tend to regard social unrest as a problem to be resolved by reform, not as the harbinger of a needed social revolution. The very tensions that functionalists would seek to relieve are the forces vital for producing the revolution: consequently, say the critics, functionalists are antirevolutionaries. Certainly, most functionalists do believe in reform rather than revolution. But reform is *not* a necessary consequence of the functionalist perspective. To notice that society is becoming increasingly disorganized is not necessarily to want to act to preserve it. Functionalism need not imply approval of an unjust and unfair society, let alone one that is corrupt and tyrannical.

Social Change

Social disorganization requires an explanation. How does it happen? What makes social systems get out of whack? Although structural functionalists have been notoriously weak in dealing with it, the answer is *social change*. Changes occur in social systems from two basic sources. Factors outside the system may cause it to undergo changes. Contact with a more advanced society may introduce rapid technological changes; war usually produces rapid change; famines or droughts cause changes. Changes can also be produced internally. A new invention (for example, robot technology) may lead to rapid changes in industry, which, in turn, may touch off changes in other parts of the system. Changes within the modern American family are decreasing fertility and are thus having considerable impact on the educational system that must grapple with the problem of shrinking enrollments. Throughout this book we shall be examining how the rapid change that characterizes modern industrial societies causes chronic problems of social disorganization. However, the study of social change is certainly not the exclusive concern of structural functionalists; indeed, it is conflict theory that is much more focally concerned with the study of social change.

Strain Theories

A more specific structural-functional theory of social problems is strain theory. Strain theories focus on the social forces that drive people to commit deviant acts. They begin with the premise that humans are fundamentally moral because they internalize many aspects of the culture, especially norms, and they want to obey the rules. To put it another way, through the process of socialization people develop a conscience. The argument is that human beings are profoundly sensitive to the expectations of others, and because others expect us to conform, we can only deviate at great psychic cost. In addition, strain theories assume that members of a society agree about what the norms are.

Having argued that people are fundamentally moral and are in agreement on the nature of morality, strain theorists confront an extremely difficult problem: What causes people to deviate? Strain theories argue that intense social pressures must be put on people to cause them to deviate.

According to Merton,[23] the source of this pressure is the discrepancy between goals and means: people are uniformly committed to the *goals* society tells them to desire, but they have unequal access to the *means* that are socially defined as legitimate for achieving these goals. Many people in society are thus subject to intense frustration of their socially legitimate desires, for example, to be successful, popular, and happy. By being born poor, black, homely, unintelligent, sickly, or otherwise disadvantaged, many people are severely handicapped in the race toward the goals that society tells them they ought to value and pursue. Because of the frustration in finding access to legitimate means for achieving goals, people sometimes turn to illegitimate means to achieve them and thus violate norms (deviate).

Figure 1.1 Merton's Strain Theory

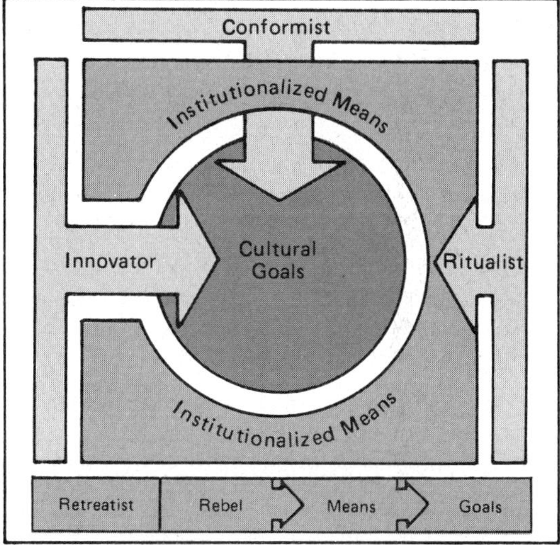

Strain theorists assume that because most people are in agreement about the goals of success, they will not deviate from norms unless they experience great strain in achieving those goals. The source of strain is unequal access to the means of achieving goals. Such strain may become so great that people retreat from society altogether, abandoning both its goals and means and turning instead to alcohol, drugs, or some other object of addiction.

Merton argued that people are of five basic types because they have five fundamental options in life: (1) A person can accept both the goals of society and the means defined as legitimate. Merton calls this type of person a *conformist.* (2) A person can accept the goals and reject legitimate means. Merton calls this type the *innovator.* (3) An individual can also be driven to reject the goals of society. When such a person nonetheless continues to adhere to legitimate means, Merton calls him or her a *ritualist.* (4) A person may reject both the goals and the means advocated by society and be classified as *retreatist* by Merton. (5) Finally, a person (the *rebel*) can simultaneously reject goals and means and substitute new goals and means to attain those goals. It is the retreatists and especially the innovators that are most likely to be deviants and to cause social problems.

There are a number of difficulties with strain theory. For one thing, while it seems to account well for deviance among the deprived members of society, it seems inappropriate for explaining deviance among those who have all the advantages. Nevertheless, the rich and successful are not immune from alcoholism, drug abuse, and becoming criminals. Furthermore, it is probably the case that most people are frustrated, but the vast majority of them do not engage in deviant behavior. Their seeming ability to ignore the strains in society is an embarrassment to the theory.

Subcultural Theories

Like strain theories, *subcultural* theories of deviance[24] begin with the assumption that human beings are fundamentally moral. But they go even further. They essentially deny that persons are capable of deviant behavior. How, then, can they account for the great numbers of acts that appear to deviate from, or to violate, social norms? They begin by denying that members of society agree about norms. Instead, they say that different groups within society are socialized into different sets of norms and that deviance is simply a judgment imposed by an outside group. Thus, what may appear to be deviant behavior is really conformity to a set of norms espoused by one group but rejected by another. Everyone conforms, but some kinds of conformity are frowned on and labeled as deviant by outsiders. When the outside group is more powerful, the behavior will be socially defined as deviant and perhaps punished.

The argument of subcultural theories is that society is not made up of a single uniform culture (a single set of norms, for example) but instead is a mosaic of different subcultures. In recognizing the existence of these subcultures, one sees that there is no deviance, only conflict among subcultures over which behavior shall be permitted.

The most basic problem with this theory has been its failure to demonstrate clearly that major types of deviant behavior do represent conformity to the norms of some distinctive subculture. For example, the overwhelming majority of alcoholics are members of groups that frown on alcoholism even though they permit drinking.

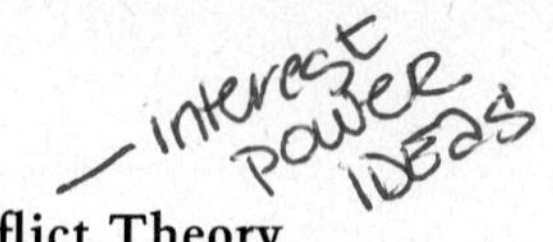

Conflict Theory

Like structural functionalism, conflict theory is a macro-oriented approach that focuses on large-scale social structures, as well as the society as a whole. However, instead of examining how various social structures affect the social system as a whole, conflict theorists tend to concentrate on the ways in which a society is organized to serve the interests of the small number of rich[25] and/or powerful[26] members of society at the expense of the many. From such basic differences in outlook as these flow a number of disagreements between functionalist and conflict interpretations.

One way of looking at the difference between conflict theory and structural functionalism is in their answers to the question: "Functional for whom?" Often, functionalists answer: "Functional for the society as a whole." In other words, they tend to see most social structures as functional for the larger society. In contrast, conflict theorists, following the lead of Karl Marx, answer: "Functional for the rich and/or the powerful." They stress the way in which all social structures—especially the economic structures—serve the rich and/or powerful at the expense of the rest of society.

Thus, conflict theorists tend to see an inherent conflict of interest within society. The "haves" are at constant odds with the "have nots." This ubiquity of at least the potential for conflict is what gives conflict theory its name. In contrast, structural functionalism tends to downplay the conflict that exists within society. To the structural functionalist, society is held together by consensus. That is, virtually everyone accepts the system more or less as it is. To the conflict theorist, no such consensus exists. Whatever harmony exists in modern capitalist society is derived from implied or actual *coercion* of the masses of people by those who control society. This order, however, is always seen as tenuous and subject to destruction by an uprising of the masses.

To the conflict theorist, the ultimate social problem is the capitalist system itself. It is, in their view, an inherently unequal system. Unlike structural functionalists, conflict theorists do not see this basic problem as being solved by a series of reforms. Since the conflict is built into the basis of the system, the conflict theorist believes that the only real solution lies in a total overhaul of the system. The unequal capitalist system needs to be replaced by a much more equitable social system in which the gap between the "haves" and the "have nots" is minimized.

To the conflict theorist, most of the more specific social problems stem in large part from the major problem of inequality within the system itself. Thus, high crime rates are traceable, at least in part, to the huge and unbridgeable gap between rich and poor. Environmental pollution is traceable to the greed of industrialists and their willingness to ravage the environment in the search for high profits. The high risk of war, especially nuclear war, is traced to the interests of the arms manufacturers, as well as the political leaders who are responsive to their needs and interests.

While most conflict theorists, especially those associated with the various branches of neo-Marxian theory, have focused on the problems of capitalist society, the ideas of at least some of them can be extended to communist and socialist societies. Some conflict theorists focus on differences in power and authority rather than on economic inequality. Such a theory can be applied at least as well to the Soviet Union as to the United States. In this view, social problems are seen as stemming from inequalities in the power and authority within society. Problems derived from such a source are just as likely to be found in contemporary communist as contemporary capitalist societies.

The criticisms of conflict theory tend to be mirror images of the criticisms of structural functionalism. Conflict theorists are accused of being fundamentally radical; of taking for granted that society is fundamentally flawed and in need of revolutionary change. They are seen as overlooking the possibility of reform and perceiving everything in terms of the need for social revolution. While such criticisms may apply to some Marxian-oriented conflict theorists, they do not apply to a number of more establishment-oriented conflict theorists.[27]

Although conflict theorists and structural functionalists disagree on many things, they do agree on the level of sociological analysis. That is, both theories tend to be macro-oriented, focusing on the large-scale structures of society, as well as society as a whole. They also tend to see the basic sources of social problems as lying at the macrolevels. To the structural functionalist, the source is social disorganization while for the conflict theorist it is the unequal structure of the society as a whole. It is extremely useful to examine the macrolevels, and we will do so throughout this book, sometimes using structural functionalism, at other times utilizing conflict theory, and at still other times using some combination of the two. However, as we saw earlier in this chapter, there is much more to sociology in general, and the sociological study of social problems in particular, than the study of macrolevel phenomena. We turn now to two other general sociological theories that focus on more microlevel phenomena.

Symbolic Interactionism

While the structural functionalist and the conflict theorist focus on the large-scale structures of society, the symbolic interactionist is primarily concerned with the more microlevel processes, especially interaction, that go on within those structures.[28] Symbolic interactionists are greatly concerned with individual actors; not any specific individual, but the individual as a general category. They assume that actors have minds that allow them to interpret and define their social worlds. Thus, actors are, at least potentially, seen as creators of their social world, rather than being determined by large-scale structures. People act and interact on the basis of their interpretations and definitions of the social world. It is this action and interaction that constitutes the primary concern of the symbolic interactionist.

As its name suggests, symbolic interactionism is not simply concerned with interaction, but with symbols as well. We may define a *symbol* as an object or word that stands for something else because those involved have agreed to such a meaning. Thus, for example, many words stand as symbols for some concrete entity. The word "book" is a symbol for the object that you are now reading. I do not literally need to show you a book in order for you to understand what I mean. When I use the word "book" an image of a book is likely to be conjured up in your mind. Similarly, physical objects can also be symbols for something else. For example, a police uniform is a symbol because it creates in our minds a set of common images including the law, society, power, a nightstick, a speeding ticket, an arrest, and many other things. The existence of symbols, as well as at least a general agreement on what they mean, allows people to interact with one another. Were it not for symbols, we would have to explain everything in enormous detail and show all sorts of objects in order to communicate what we mean. Symbols not only make interaction possible, all of social life is highly dependent on the existence of a body of symbols and generally shared symbolic meanings.

The idea of a symbol implies an actor with creative mental ability. First of all, it is people who create these symbols that allow social life to exist. Second, on a day-to-day level, we all need sufficient mental capacities to interpret and understand the symbols with which we are constantly coming into contact. In dealing with objects, and more importantly in dealing with other people, we must be able to interpret the symbolic meaning that is being communicated to us. Not only that, we must be able to formulate a reply or a reaction that takes the form of a series of symbols that will make sense to those with whom we are dealing.

Symbolic interactionism is primarily concerned with reflective action. It recognizes the existence of nonreflective behavior, but sees it as of secondary sociological importance. The actor is endowed with a mind; with the ability to engage in socially meaningful mental processes. On the basis of these mental processes, the actor engages in action and interaction, largely in groups. Actors are seen as filling roles in groups, but there is a tendency to see them not as responding passively to external expectations, but rather in creating their own role and the actions that are appropriate to it. The macroscopic concepts like social structure and society are far less important to the symbolic interactionist. They seem to be not much more than frameworks[29] within which the real stuff of social life—thought, action, and interaction—takes place.

In addition to being a general sociological theory, symbolic interactionism has helped spawn, and/or is related to, two more specific theories that apply directly to the study of social problems: labeling theory and differential association theory. Let us look briefly at these two theories.

Labeling Theory

The starting point for this line of thought is a denial that deviance is primarily found in the acts of persons identified as deviant.[30] Instead, in labeling theory, deviance exists in the eye of the beholder—in the way other people evaluate the acts of a particular person. Howard S. Becker, long associated with symbolic interactionism and a major proponent of labeling theory, put the argument this way:

> Social groups create deviance by making rules whose infraction constitutes deviance, and by applying those rules to particular people and labeling them as outsiders. . . . The deviant is one to whom that label has been successfully applied; deviant behavior is behavior that people so label.[31]

Similarly, Kai T. Erikson argues:

> Deviance is not a property *inherent in* certain forms of behavior; it is a property *conferred upon* these forms by audiences which directly or indirectly witness them. The critical variable in the study of deviance, then, is the social audience rather than the individual actor, since it is the audience which eventually determines whether or not any episode of behavior . . . is labeled deviant.[32]

Earlier in this chapter we emphasized that social problems are what people say they are. Similarly, labeling theorists often seem to be arguing that deviance is what people say it is. However, labeling theorists often do not understand that a social problem is *both* the claims that a problem exists and the objective conditions that may or may not warrant such claims. Many labeling theorists simply dismiss the act alleged to be deviant and focus on explaining why it is that some group defines some particular act as deviant.

Labeling theory begins with a set of symbolic interactionist assumptions about actors with creative minds constructing their own social realities. Among the things that we construct are our own self-concepts. We come to see ourselves as others define us, to respond on the basis of how others respond to us. Thus, if someone is labeled by others as bad, weird, a criminal, a drunk, a dope fiend, or a lunatic, the label may become a self-fulfilling prophecy and may lead that person to attempt to satisfy the expectations associated with that label. Thus, someone who is developing a slight drinking problem, or who is experimenting with drugs, may be pushed further into becoming an alcoholic or a drug addict by being treated like one by others. Labeling may also greatly impede efforts by alcoholics or drug abusers to reform. As we will see in upcoming chapters, labeling theory has been of some utility in helping us understand mental illness, drug abuse, alcoholism, and crime.

Labeling theory has been highly controversial and has come under severe attack.[33] In addition to underestimating the importance of objective acts, labeling theory is also unable to explain why people *first* engage in the kind of behavior that gets them socially labeled as deviant. Although the theory can outline a process by which a person who drinks may become an alcoholic under pressure of being labeled an alcoholic or by which a youthful offender may become a chronic delinquent through being labeled a delinquent by the police and the courts, the theory cannot explain why a person began to drink or why the youth committed the *initial* illegal act that led to arrest. Another symbolic interactionist theory has taken this question as its primary focus.

Differential Association Theory

In 1939, Edwin H. Sutherland, the American criminologist, first proposed a rigorous *differential association* theory of deviance. He began with the premise that all human behavior, whether piano playing, safecracking, or taking drugs, is learned through the socialization process in interaction with other people. Whether what an individual learns to do conforms to or violates social norms depends on who is doing the teaching or socializing. Fundamentally, Sutherland's argument comes down to keeping bad company. People learn to be drug addicts, alcoholics, or car thieves by keeping company with others who engage in or admire such behavior. The theory is called differential association because it attributes differences in behavior to differences in the groups with which people associate.[34]

Howard S. Becker, in addition to his identification with symbolic interactionism and labeling theory, also used a differential association approach in a classic study of marijuana smoking. He pointed out that people are introduced to marijuana smoking through their friends. In fact, people usually rely on their friends and do not buy their own supply of the drug until they have become relatively experienced marijuana smokers. Furthermore, people usually learn to detect and enjoy the effects of marijuana from their friends:

> The novice does not ordinarily get high the first time he smokes marijuana, and several attempts are usually necessary to induce this state. . . . If nothing happens, it is manifestly impossible for the user to develop a conception of the drug as an object which can be used for pleasure. . . . The ability to get high and to enjoy getting high are mainly socially determined.[35]

It is widely held in the drug culture that people who say they cannot get high have been improperly instructed in how to smoke and that people who say they did not enjoy their high did not smoke with persons they liked or trusted. Research by Erich Goode has confirmed the social nature of marijuana use.[36] Persons without friends who use the drug have little opportunity either to obtain the drug or to learn to like it.

Exchange Theory

Exchange theory is a sociological derivative of behaviorism in psychology.[37] Like symbolic interactionism, it is a micro-oriented

People must learn deviant behavior. For example, drug addicts may be introduced to heroin by their friends, and taught the techniques for using the drug, what the effects are, and that the effects are to be seen as pleasurable. (Rich Smolan/Stock, Boston)

theory. Together with symbolic interactionism, exchange theory tends to focus on the micro end of the social continuum while structural functionalism and conflict theory are much more oriented to macro-level phenomena. Although they tend to focus on a similar level of social analysis, there are important differences between symbolic interactionism and exchange theory. As we saw, symbolic interactionism is primarily concerned with the relationships among thought, action, and interaction. Great emphasis is placed on mental processes and the creativity of the actor. Exchange theorists tend to downplay the significance of the mind and human creativity. Instead of focusing on action, which implies prior mental processes, exchange theorists are mainly concerned with behavior, which implies little or no prior thought. In other words, symbolic interactionists are interested in reflective action while exchange theorists are mainly concerned with nonreflective behavior.

Exchange theory is built on the psychological principles of stimulus and response. In lower animals, a stimulus is applied (for example, food is put in a dog bowl), and a response is emitted (the dog begins to salivate in anticipation of eating the food). A similar set of processes is thought to exist among humans. People are likely to continue to perform behaviors that they have in the past found to be rewarding. For instance, if a person engages in shoplifting and is rewarded with prize goods, that person is likely to continue shoplifting. On the other hand, people are not likely to perform behaviors that have been painful or costly to them in the past. To continue with our shoplifting example, if the person is caught by the police early in his/her shoplifting career and suffers severe penalties, he/she is unlikely to continue a career as a shoplifter. Thus, the present behavior of people is seen as being determined by their history of rewards and costs. They continue to perform behaviors that have been rewarded in the past while they tend to cease those that have proven costly in the past.

There is little or no thought involved in emitting behaviors. Behaviors are seen as determined by the individual's history of rewards and costs. The individual does not think through each situation before acting. In a situation that is similar to past rewarding situations, the individual will almost automatically emit the behavior that has been rewarded in the past. In a situation that is similar to past costly situations, the individual is unlikely, in a fairly automatic way, to behave in a way that has proven costly in the past. When the exchange theorist considers mental processes it is most often with the view that they operate like a calculator. Potential rewards are weighed against costs, and a decision is made whether or not to emit the behavior in question. This, again, is a relatively automatic process lacking in the kind of creativity accorded the actor by symbolic interactionists.

Social-Learning Theory

Derived from exchange theory and behaviorism in general, as well as differential association theory, is social-learning theory.[38] Like exchange theory, social-learning theory is concerned with the issue of rewards and costs. But social-learning theory goes on to examine the social sources of the reinforcers that operate in the learning process. Differential association theory is incorporated to account for the sources of reinforcement: "bad" company reinforces drug taking or drinking; "good" company does not reinforce such behavior. For example, a college freshman may be initiated into drinking and intoxication by fraternity brothers who praise his ability to consume large amounts of alcohol and who reward him for regular appearances at the group's favorite tavern; they thereby establish him in a pattern of heavy and frequent drinking. What the social learners add to Sutherland's theory is a specific set of behavioristic principles through which the social situation shapes a person's behavior. The underlying learning theory proposition is that deviant behavior, such as drinking or drug taking, will be committed if, under similar circumstances in the past, it has been rewarded (reinforced) more frequently and consistently than conforming behavior.

PLAN OF THE BOOK

This chapter serves as a general introduction to the book, as well as a presentation of the overall framework and the sociological theories that will inform the rest of the book. The reader may wish some more aspects of the sociological perspective. If that is the case, a brief summary of basic sociological concepts may be found in Appendix A. In addition, Chapter 2 constitutes an introduction to basic sociological methods.

To conclude this chapter, it will be helpful to know how the remainder of the book is organized.

The problems dealt with in Chapters 3 through 16 are those about which Americans are presently complaining the loudest and toward which government is directing its greatest efforts. It is the public, not social scientists, who determine what a social problem is. We include a chapter on aging and ageism (not found in slightly older texts) because, very recently, the aged organized and succeeded in making their grievances a social problem. Similarly, there is a chapter devoted to problems in health care because of the mounting outcry from many groups about the spiraling costs of health care, as well as many other problems within the health care system.

This book is divided into four parts. Part One, *Analyzing Social Problems,* encompasses the introductory chapter that you are now completing and Chapter 2 on sociological methods. Part Two, *Deviant Behavior,* includes chapters on drugs and alcohol, mental illness, crime, and family and sexual violence. In Part Three, *Problems of Conflict and Inequality,* we deal with aging and ageism, majority-minority relations, gender inequality, and poverty. Finally, in Part Four, *Problems of Human Progress,* the focus is on problems in the economy and the workplace, in health care, and in the cities; population and ecological problems; and problems of the international political economy. Although we treat each of these problems in discrete chapters, bear in mind that most social problems are interrelated.

The purpose of this book is not to add more facts to your memory; it invites you to increase the scope and depth of your understanding of the social problems that currently beset your life and time.

SUMMARY

1. What is or is not a social problem is not always as clear as it might seem.
2. Social problems are defined as social conditions of which a significant proportion of the population is aware, defines as social problems, and sees in need of some remedial collective action. These social problems have causes and consequences at the individual, social-psychological, and/or sociological levels.
3. Once defined, social problems tend to have a patterned career involving four

Figure 1.2 Outline of the Book

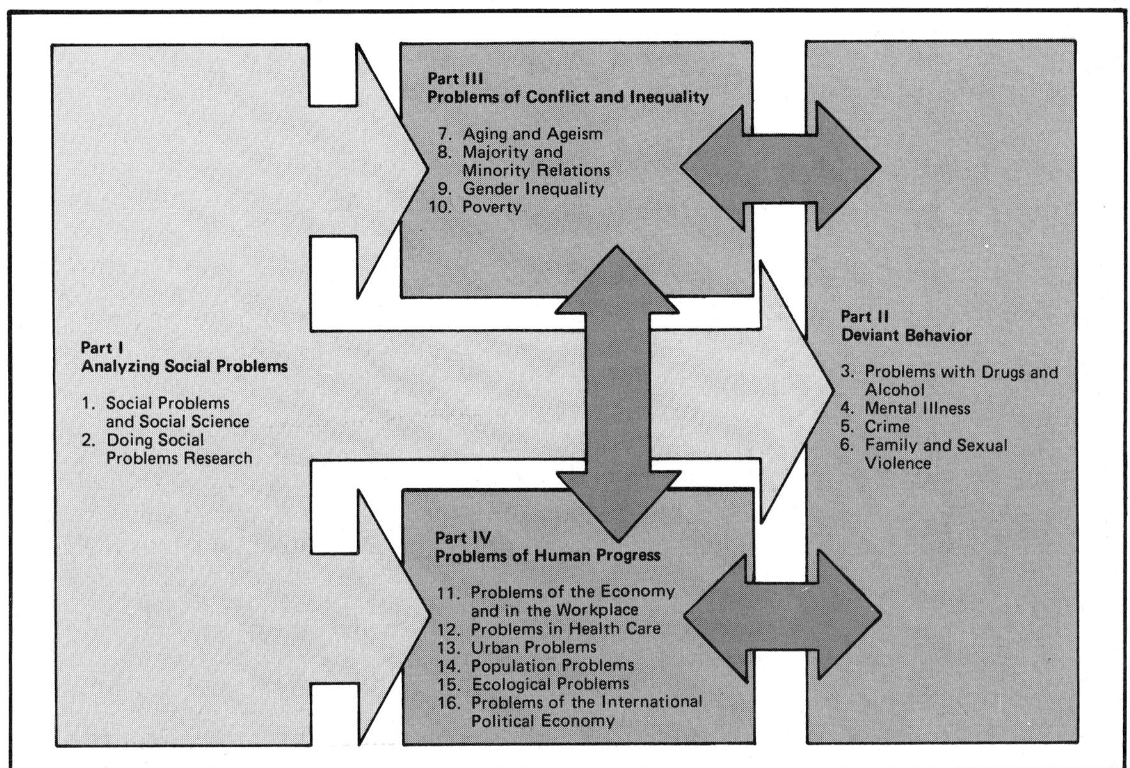

The analysis of social problems affects the social problems covered in Parts II, III, and IV. And because these problems are all interrelated, any given problem and its solution will affect other problems and their solutions.

stages: agitation, legitimation and co-optation, bureaucratization and reaction, and the reemergence of the movement.

4. The career of social problems demonstrates the politics involved in social problems, as well as the difficulties involved in doing something meaningful about them.
5. The book will focus on social problems defined not only by elite members of society, but nonelite members as well.
6. A sociological framework emphasizing *levels of social reality* will be used throughout this book. The major levels employed are the individual, the social-psychological, and the sociological.
7. The framework is illustrated in this chapter in a general discussion of the causes and consequences of social problems at each level. In the remainder of the book that framework will play a central role in the causes and consequences section of each chapter and a lesser role in the responses section.

8. A number of the theories utilized throughout this book are introduced in this chapter. One important general sociological theory introduced here is structural functionalism, as well as two more specific structural functional theories focally oriented to the study of social problems—strain theory and subcultural theory.
9. A second general theory introduced in this chapter and used throughout the book is conflict theory.
10. A third general theory is symbolic interactionism, which is introduced along with two derivative theories that focus on social problems—labeling theory and differential association theory.
11. The final general theory introduced here is exchange theory and it is discussed along with social-learning theory, which tends to be directed mainly at the study of social problems.
12. The chapter concludes with an overview of the book.

SUGGESTED READINGS

Walter Gove, ed., *The Labeling of Deviance: Evaluating a Perspective.* 2nd ed. Beverly Hills, Cal.: Sage, 1980. This book contains a series of essays outlining the nature, and major criticisms, of one of the most important theories specific to the study of social problems.

George Ritzer, *Sociological Theory.* New York: Random House, 1983. This is a basic text in sociological theory written by the author of this book. It deals in much greater detail with the theories discussed in this chapter.

Recent issues of the journal *Social Problems.* This journal is devoted to work on the kinds of social problems discussed throughout this book.

Malcolm Spector and John I. Kitsuse, *Constructing Social Problems.* Menlo Park, Cal.: Cummings Pub. Co., 1977. More work from the creators of the idea of the careers of social movements that is used prominently in this chapter.

FOOTNOTES

[1]C. Wright Mills, *The Sociological Imagination.* (New York: Oxford University Press, 1959).

[2]Helena Z. Lopata, "Social Construction of Social Problems Over Time," *Social Problems,* 31 (1984), 249.

[3]Ronald Troyer and Gerald E. Markle, "Coffee Drinking: An Emerging Social Problem?" *Social Problems,* 31 (1984), 403–416.

[4]Kathleen J. Tierney, "The Battered Woman Movement and the Creation of the Wife Beating Problem," *Social Problems,* 29 (1982), 207–220.

[5]Naomi Aronson, "Nutrition as a Social Problem: A Case Study of Entrepreneurial Strategy in Science," *Social Problems,* 29 (1982), 474–487.

[6]Richard A. Ball and J. Robert Lilly, "The Menace of Margarine: The Rise and Fall of a Social Problem," *Social Problems,* 29 (1982), 488–498.

[7]Howard S. Becker, *Social Problems: A Modern Approach* (New York: Wiley, 1966).

[8]Malcolm Spector and John I. Kitsuse, " Social Problems: A Re-Formulation," *Social Problems,* 21 (1973), 145–159.

[9]Philip Selznick, *T.V.A. and the Grass Roots* (New York: Harper Torchbooks, 1966).

[10]Spector and Kitsuse, *op. cit.,* p. 152.

[11]*Ibid.,* p. 153.

[12]*Ibid.,* p. 154.

[13]See also, Erich Goode, *Drugs in American Society* (New York: Alfred A. Knopf, 1984), pp. 12–14.

[14]David R. Simon and D. Stanley Eitzen, *Elite Deviance,* 2nd ed. (Boston: Allyn & Bacon, 1986).

[15]Robert H. Lauer, "Defining Social Problems: Public and Professional Perspectives," *Social Problems,* 24 (1976), 122–130; Jerry Jacobs, *Social Problems Through Social Theory: A Selective View* (Houston: Cap and Gown Press, 1983), pp. 28–29.

[16]George Ritzer, *Sociology: A Multiple Paradigm Science,* rev. ed. (Boston: Allyn & Bacon, 1980).

[17]Rodney Stark, *Social Problems* (New York: CRM/

Random House, 1975); George Ritzer, *Toward an Integrated Sociological Paradigm* (Boston: Allyn & Bacon, 1981); Jacobs, *op. cit.*

[18]In using the term "sociological" to describe this level, we do not want to imply that sociologists are uninterested in the social-psychological and individual levels. However, it is the macrolevel that is the most defining and distinctive interest of sociologists. Sociologists are interested in it, as well as in its relationship to the individual and social-psychological levels.

[19]There are also some psychologists who consider themselves social psychologists. The overlap between the fields of sociology and psychology is clearest in the case of social psychology.

[20]George Ritzer, *Sociological Theory* (New York: Random House, 1983).

[21]Jonathan Turner and Alexandra Maryanski, *Functionalism* (Menlo Park, Cal.: Benjamin/Cummings, 1979); Mark Abrahamson, *Functionalism* (Englewood Cliffs, N.J.: Prentice-Hall, 1978).

[22]Robert K. Merton, "Manifest and Latent Functions: Toward the Codification of Functional Analysis in Sociology." In Robert Merton, *Social Theory and Social Structure*, enlarged ed. (New York: Free Press, 1968), pp.73–138.

[23]Robert K. Merton, "Social Structure and Anomie," *American Sociological Review*, 3 (1938), 672–682.

[24]See, for example, Albert K. Cohen, *Delinquent Boys: The Culture of the Gang* (Glencoe, Ill.: The Free Press, 1955); Richard A. Cloward and Lloyd E. Ohlin, *Delinquency and Opportunity* (New York: Free Press, 1960).

[25]Karl Marx, *Capital*, Vol. I (New York: International Publishers, 1867/1967).

[26]Ralf Dahrendorf, *Class and Class Conflict in Industrial Society* (Stanford, Cal.: Stanford University Press, 1959).

[27]See, for example, Lewis Coser, *The Functions of Social Conflict* (New York: Free Press, 1956); Randall Collins, *Conflict Sociology: Toward an Explanatory Science* (New York: Academic Press, 1975).

[28]See, for example, George Herbert Mead, *Mind, Self, and Society* (Chicago: University of Chicago Press, 1934/1962); Herbert Blumer, "Society as Symbolic Interaction." In Arnold Rose, ed., *Human Behavior and Social Processes* (Boston: Houghton Mifflin, 1962); Joel Charon, *Symbolic Interaction: An Introduction, An Interpretation, An Integration* (Englewood Cliffs, N.J.: Prentice-Hall, 1979).

[29]Blumer,"Society as Symbolic Interaction," *op. cit.*

[30]Walter Gove, ed., *The Labeling of Deviance: Evaluating a Perspective*, 2nd ed. (Beverly Hills, Cal.: Sage, 1980).

[31]Howard S. Becker, *The Outsiders* (New York: Free Press, 1963), p. 9.

[32]Kai T. Erikson, "Notes on the Sociology of Deviance." In Howard S. Becker, ed., *The Other Side: Perspectives on Deviance* (New York: Free Press, 1964), p. 11.

[33]See Gove, ed., *The Labeling of Deviance: Evaluating a Perspective, op. cit.*

[34]Edwin H. Sutherland, *Principles of Criminology*, 4th ed. (Chicago: Lippincott, 1947).

[35]Becker, *The Outsiders, op. cit.*

[36]Erich Goode, *Drugs in American Society, op. cit.*

[37]See, for example, George Homans, *Social Behavior: Its Elementary Forms*, 2nd ed. (New York: Harcourt Brace Jovanovich, 1973); Peter Blau, *Exchange and Power in Social Life* (New York: Wiley, 1964); Peter Ekeh, *Social Exchange Theory: The Two Traditions* (Cambridge, Mass.: Harvard University Press, 1974).

[38]Ronald L. Akers, *Deviant Behavior: A Social Learning Approach*, 2nd ed. (Belmont, Cal.: Wadsworth, 1977).

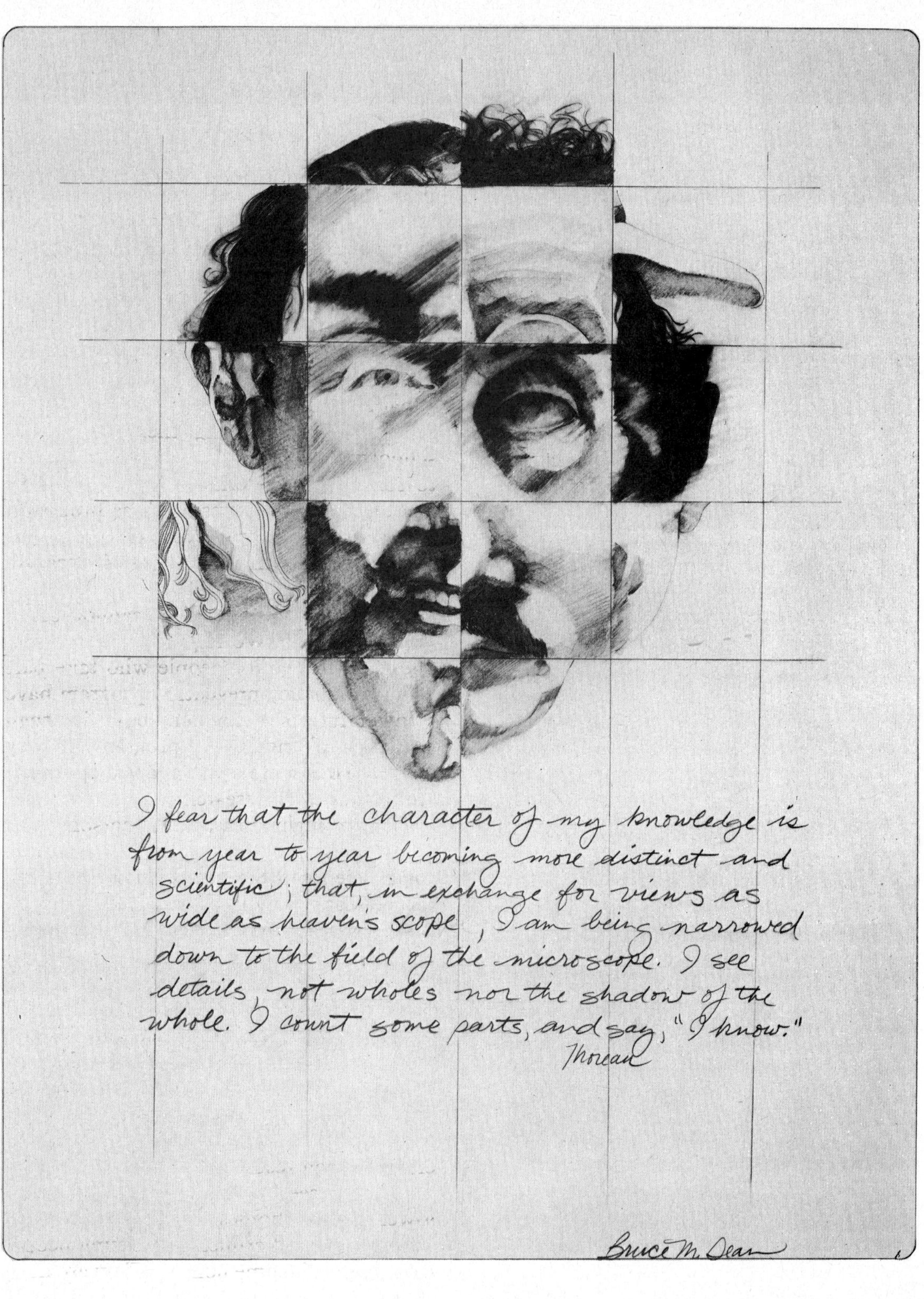
I fear that the character of my knowledge is
from year to year becoming more distinct and
scientific; that, in exchange for views as
wide as heaven's scope, I am being narrowed
down to the field of the microscope. I see
details, not wholes nor the shadow of the
whole. I count some parts, and say, "I know."
Thoreau
Bruce M. Dean

2 *Doing Social Problems Research*

In 1981 almost 1.4 million juveniles were taken into police custody.[1] Yet this enormous number of cases represents only the tip of the iceberg. Only a small proportion of criminal acts by young people ever become known to the police, and of these, only a much smaller proportion lead them to be taken into custody. Juvenile crime is a major fact of American life.

For decades, social scientists have tried to understand juvenile delinquency. What causes young people to commit crimes? What is the best way to deal with young offenders? Does sending them to reform school make them more likely or less likely to commit future crimes? To what extent do treatment programs, such as probation and counseling, or prevention programs, such as neighborhood youth activities, reduce juvenile crime?

Discussion or reflection cannot settle such questions. We require facts. For example, either young people who take part in a delinquency-prevention program have a lower rate of delinquent behavior than young people not in the program, or they do not. To assemble and analyze appropriate facts is to do research.

It is through research that persons who study social problems qualify to be called social scientists. Science consists of testing theories against appropriate and carefully gathered data, or evidence. Put another way, if a particular theory leads to the prediction that poverty causes young people to commit crimes, research is required to see whether the prediction is accurate. Someone must go out and collect data on the economic background of some appropriate group of young people and determine who among them has committed juvenile crimes. Then researchers must make comparisons to see whether young people from lower-income homes are more likely to have committed crimes than young people from higher-income homes. (They are not.)

Scientists conduct research in different ways and use specific methods for specific kinds of questions.

This chapter uses the subject of juvenile delinquency to provide examples of how social scientists conduct research. This chapter offers a behind-the-scenes view of several research methods directed at various central questions about delinquency. The purpose is to let you look over the shoulders of social scientists as they go about their business doing research on a major social problem.

The accounts are informal for two reasons: to let you see for yourself how research is done and to let you see that social researchers are not some strange and special breed of people. Like the rest of us, they are sometimes lazy, they blunder, they have good and bad luck, and they frequently have to compromise between practical demands and ideal research designs. The goal of the chapter is to help you understand basic research and analysis procedures. Instead of taking up these procedures as textbook principles, we let them emerge as tools that people who encounter real research use.

In this chapter we will focus on four major sociological methods—participant observation, natural experiment, survey research, and historical research. For each method we will discuss a classic piece of research that serves to illustrate at least some of the major aspects of each method. In addition, we will follow the discussion of each of these pieces of research with an analysis of a later effort to replicate (or repeat), at least in part, the original research effort.

GETTING BUSTED: PARTICIPANT OBSERVATION

Social scientists have developed a number of research methods. The method chosen depends on a particular researcher's skills and personality; some researchers relate well to people, others relate better to computers. In the final analysis, the nature of the problem determines the research method. Some questions are best answered by careful analysis of documents, such as court cases involving teenagers. Some are best answered by interviewing a randomly selected sample of persons. Other problems lend themselves to experimentation. However, certain kinds of questions are best answered by going out and actually observing what people do in real-life situations.

A number of questions about delinquency seem to require direct observation. For example, if we wanted to understand the extent to which delinquent acts are committed because of encouragement from other juveniles—who perhaps egg on a friend to steal something—we could gather accounts from young people who have been apprehended, but we could not be sure of their stories unless we, too, had been on the scene.

The fact that self-reports may not be accurate has long prompted sociologists to use the method of participant observation in studying delinquency. The social scientist witnesses the events he or she is attempting to study and carefully and systematically records these observations. Social scientists using this method usually have long-term interaction with the people they are studying.

Limits of the Method

Participant observation has obvious limitations. For one thing, the presence of observers can always change the behavior of those they observe. People who know that you are watching them are likely to behave differently in order to impress or deceive you. For example, teenage boys might commit more delinquent acts in order to show how tough they are, or they might decrease their delinquency in order to appear in a

seeing police-juvenile encounters, during nine months of concentrated effort they saw only seventy-six encounters. (This gives strong testimony to the futility of trying to conduct such a study by focusing on juveniles.) In ten of these encounters, the police let youths go so quickly that Piliavin and Briar saw no reason to include these cases in their primary analysis.

You might wonder what the police assigned to the juvenile bureau were doing during this nine-month period if they had only seventy-six encounters with juveniles. For one thing, they cruised assigned beats and essentially functioned as routine patrol officers; occasionally, they arrested adults for some offense. Most of the time, as with all policemen assigned to drive beats, they just rode around and frequently stopped for coffee. As all studies of policing report, it is mostly a boring, uneventful job.[4] Piliavin and Briar were trapped night after night in the backseat of a patrol car with little or nothing to do to pass the time, and they recall their months of observation as mainly a period of enforced boredom.

Encountering Juveniles

Nevertheless, their patience was rewarded. In time, they assembled enough data on juvenile-police encounters to shed light on the decision-making process. In every encounter, the police had several options. They could simply let the juvenile offenders go, or they could let them go after giving them an informal reprimand. They could also take them to the police station and do one of three things: give them an official reprimand and release them to a parent or guardian, cite them to appear in juvenile court, or arrest them and have them held in juvenile hall. The last two options placed the eventual disposition of the case in the hands of the courts.

Piliavin and Briar found, somewhat to their surprise, that the police were reluctant to take official action against youths, partly because they tried to avoid stigmatizing the youths with an official police record and partly because they lacked confidence in the effectiveness of correctional agencies and programs to achieve rehabilitation. The police believed that the juvenile justice and correctional processes were simply punishment, not treatment. Therefore, unless they confronted a juvenile whom they believed to be a serious and chronic offender, they were inclined toward leniency.

Factors in Decision Making

The fundamental problem the police had to resolve was to assess the juvenile offender's character. Should this offender be turned over for punishment or let go—is this a "bad" kid or simply an ordinary kid who has done something bad?

Character

According to Piliavin and Briar's observations, the police usually found little difficulty in assessing the character of offenders "who had committed serious crimes such as robbery, homicide, aggravated assault, grand theft, auto theft, rape, and arson."[5] The magnitude of such offenses confirmed their conclusion that the offender was a confirmed delinquent. However, even in a few instances involving serious offenses such as burglary and auto theft, the police let the juvenile go without court action. Furthermore, in over 90 percent of the cases, the infraction was minor and therefore did not help the police in assessing character.

A second major consideration in police decisions was the youth's record of previous offenses. The police ordinarily use a record as grounds for judging the youth to be of "bad" character and thus not an appropriate candidate for leniency. However, at the time they had to make a decision, the

While the police sometimes arrest juveniles, most police encounters with juveniles take less extreme forms. The police are reluctant to take official actions against juveniles because of the fear of stigmatizing youths and because of the lack of confidence of the police in the correctional process. (Peter Baylies/The Picture Cube)

police usually had no information about a juvenile's past record, or lack of one, unless one of the officers had had previous contact with the youth. (At the time of the study, juvenile records were not maintained in such a fashion that the police could call in and obtain information on records.)

Lacking such information and nearly always being confronted with juveniles whose offense was too minor to use as a gauge of character, the police mainly used cues that were derived from their interaction with youths. On the basis of these cues the officer made inferences about a youth's character.

Demeanor

The most important of these cues was demeanor—how the youth behaved during the encounter with the police. The critical element was how cooperative or uncooperative the youth was in dealing with the officers. As Piliavin and Briar reported:

> The cues used by police to assess demeanor were fairly simple. Juveniles who were contrite about their infractions, respectful to officers, and fearful of the sanctions that might be employed against them tended to be viewed by patrolmen as basically law-abiding or at least "salvageable." For these youths it was usually assumed that informal or formal reprimand would suffice to guarantee their future conformity. In contrast, youthful offenders who were fractious, obdurate, or who appeared nonchalant in their encounters with patrolmen were likely to be viewed as "would-be tough guys" or "punks" who fully deserved the most severe sanction: arrest.[6]

To check these conclusions, Piliavin and Briar wanted to compare the police dispositions of cases in which juveniles had been cooperative with those in which they had

Table 2.1 How Demeanor Affects Police Treatment of Juveniles

	YOUTH'S DEMEANOR		
SEVERITY OF POLICE DISPOSITION	COOPERATIVE	UNCOOPERATIVE	TOTAL
Arrest (most severe)	2	14	16
Citation or official reprimand	4	5	9
Informal reprimand	15	1	16
Admonish and release (least severe)	24	1	25
Total	45	21	66

Source: Adapted from Irvin Piliavin and Scott Briar, "Police Encounters with Juveniles," *American Journal of Sociology*, 70 (1964): 210.

been uncooperative. To prevent their own knowledge of how cases had been dealt with from influencing their judgments, Piliavin and Briar submitted their field notes, minus information on police actions, to a disinterested third person to classify. This independent classification is the basis for the data shown in Table 2.1.

It is easy to see that youths who cooperated with the police were likely to be treated leniently, to get off with only an admonishment or an informal reprimand—thirty-nine out of forty-five were treated leniently. But youths who were uncooperative, who were defiant or unrepentant, rarely received lenient treatment: two-thirds of them were arrested. These data powerfully confirmed Piliavin and Briar's hypothesis that demeanor determines police decisions about leniency.

Race and Demeanor

Piliavin and Briar also noticed that race seemed to play an important role in shaping the interaction between the police and juveniles. They believed their observations justified a conclusion that the police usually used race as a cue to character and behaved toward black juveniles in ways that made this a self-fulfilling cue.

First of all, they reported that of the ten juveniles inappropriately stopped and immediately dismissed by the police during the observation period (and dropped from the primary analysis), seven were black, but only a third of the youths police stopped for actual infractions were black. Thus, the proportion of encounters with blacks was high relative to the proportion who seemed to be guilty of wrongdoing. (Blacks made up 23 percent of the population of the city.) The police tended to be unduly suspicious of blacks. In one instance, after the officers stopped and questioned a black youth walking down the street and then let him go, they explained that they had been suspicious because: "He was a Negro wearing dark glasses at midnight."[7] In addition, eighteen out of twenty-seven officers interviewed openly admitted a dislike for blacks. They reported that blacks were more likely to commit crimes, to give officers a "hard time," and to show no remorse over their actions.

Piliavin and Briar argued that police attitudes lead to a process by which black delinquents are "manufactured." First, because of their belief that blacks are more likely than whites to be criminal, these officers did more patrolling in black neighborhoods than in white ones. Furthermore, the officers were much more likely to accost black youths simply because their skin color identified them to the police as potential troublemakers.

Because they are more likely to experience police investigation, even when innocent of wrongdoing, black youths are more likely than white youths to develop hostility toward the police. Furthermore, overexperience with police questioning reduces the importance of such encounters in the eyes of black youths; they begin to see them as routine. Both of these responses—hostility and unconcern—are the precise cues that the police use to judge character, to identify the serious delinquent. And so begins a vicious circle: the police become less lenient and thereby produce statistics showing that blacks are more likely than whites to have official records of delinquent behavior. And these statistics further reinforce the police in their belief that blacks are lawless.

Piliavin and Briar concluded that the police used their discretion to be lenient or tough on the basis of their perceptions of the offender. When the offense was petty—as was nearly always the case—they relied on demeanor and, indirectly, on race to make their decision. The police decision determines who will and who will not have a juvenile record; clearly, those who are cooperative and white are less likely to get their infractions recorded. Thus, if "nice" boys do not have records, it does not mean that they do not break rules.

Assessing the Study

One problem with these findings is that the study was limited to one police department and to relatively few cases. The researchers

A major issue in the study of police-juvenile contact is the degree to which the police discriminate against black (and other minority) juveniles. (Bobbie Kingsley/Photo Researchers)

have no way of showing that these findings can be generalized to other departments. But an even stronger objection can be raised against the findings.

It is logically possible that although police relied on race as a cue to character because they held racist views, race may have operated nonetheless as an accurate cue to delinquency. The distinction is subtle but significant. The police may, in fact, have accurately picked out the most serious delinquents—the chronic offenders—even though they misunderstood why race might be a valid cue. It is possible that the pressures of racism itself and ghetto existence serve to push a disproportionate number of black youths into delinquency. If so, then although the police are wrong in their understanding of the link between race and criminality, they may be accurate in regarding race as a cue to who is more seriously delinquent.

It is not our intention to assert that the above is true, but only to point out that it *could* be true. And we are not outlining this point to argue against Piliavin and Briar's premise that the police manufacture black delinquency rates but simply to clarify what additional evidence would be needed to make their argument more persuasive. We do this to demonstrate that one kind of research method more readily produces some kinds of evidence; other kinds of evidence require different methods of research.

Recall that neither the observers nor the police actually knew the past behavior of youths suspected of petty offenses. Piliavin and Briar's data simply cannot resolve whether race is a valid cue or whether the police manufacture black delinquency rates. To do that, different data are required. One would first need to know the actual delinquent behavior of representative samples of black and white youths. Then one would need to determine whether or not blacks are more likely than whites to acquire police records when both have committed the same offense. If so, then Piliavin and Briar are probably correct in asserting that the police manufacture black delinquency rates. The Richmond youth study reported later in this chapter brings precisely the needed data to bear on this question.

To conclude this discussion, let us reconsider what Piliavin and Briar did. As participant observers, their behavior differed significantly from everyday association with other people—for example, from what you do when you are with friends or in class. First, they systematically recorded all their observations as they occurred. They made efforts to pick out and note specific kinds of information—for example, the race of juveniles, the offense for which they were suspect, what they did and said, and what the police did and said. Furthermore, they took some pains not to delude themselves into believing what they wanted to believe. For example, they arranged to have an unbiased party—someone not associated with the study and unaware of their views—classify the youths as cooperative or uncooperative. It is precisely this care given to accuracy and to eliminating bias that qualifies social science as a science and makes it different from our common sense understanding of social life.

Police Control of Juveniles

Donald Black and Albert Reiss were involved in another participant observation study of the police that brought to light additional information about encounters between police and juveniles.[8] Undertaken a few years after the Piliavin and Briar research, this study was conducted in several cities in the northeastern part of the United States. A team of observers was employed and they "rode in scout cars or, less frequently, walked with patrolmen on all shifts on all days of the week for seven weeks in each city."[9] The researchers gave added weight to those times such as weekend evenings when police encounters with citizens are likely to be high in order to be sure that they observed enough of these encounters. Furthermore, they concentrated on those precincts where such encounters were likely to be high; that is, precincts in "lower socio-economic, high crime rate, racially homogenous residential areas."[10] Researchers used incident booklets and filled out one for each incident that the police noticed themselves or were requested to handle. They observed 5,713 such incidents, but this research was concerned only with the 281 cases that involved juveniles.

Black and Reiss differentiate between the two basic ways in which incidents initially come to the attention of the police: *citizen-initiated* (a citizen phoning the police to report an incident), or *police-initiated* (a police officer observing and acting upon a law violation), contacts. In their view, the mass media overemphasize police-initiated actions; in most cases the police act on the basis of initiatives taken by citizens: "The crime detection function is lodged mainly in the citizenry rather than in the police."[11] In fact, in their research on juveniles, if we exclude traffic violations, 78 percent were citizen initiated while only 22 percent were initiated by the police. They conclude: "it would seem that the moral standards of the citizenry have more to do with the definition of juvenile delinquency than do the standards of the policemen on patrol."[12]

Another conclusion drawn by Black and Reiss from their participant observation is that the overwhelming majority (95 percent) of transactions between police and juveniles involve minor matters. However, police encounters with black juveniles generally involve more serious violations of the law. Beyond this difference, black-white juvenile youth contacts with police follow roughly the same pattern. Black and Reiss conclude that their work shows no evidence of discrimination toward black youths by the police, but they recognize that their study is not focally concerned with that issue.

Most police-juvenile encounters (85 percent) do *not* culminate in arrest; in other words, about 6 in 7 cases do not become official delinquency statistics. It is in the decision to arrest that we find a high level of police selectivity. Police-black encounters lead to arrest in 21 percent of the cases, while only 8 percent of police-white encounters result in an arrest. And the greater likelihood of black arrest is not related simply to the fact that they are more likely to commit crimes. In addition, the likelihood of arrest is related to the severity of the offense; the more serious the offense, the more likely it is that an arrest will be made.

Complainants

Of great significance to Black and Reiss is the presence or absence of a complainant. When there is no citizen complainant involved, the differences between the races in the likelihood of arrest virtually disappears. However, when a complainant is involved, the differences are great. Interestingly, the complainants tend to be of the same race as the supposed delinquent. Black and Reiss conclude that it is the citizen complainants who are mainly responsible for the relatively severe dispositions of black youths and those complainants are themselves very likely to be black. Police officers are more likely to be lenient when they deal with black youths on their own initiative than when they are in the presence of complainants. Furthermore, as we saw earlier, when no complainant is involved, differences between black and white juvenile arrests virtually disappear. Although Black and Reiss acknowledge that most of the police they studied expressed racist attitudes, they feel that the evidence is that such racist beliefs did not explain the differences in arrests; the presence of a complainant did.

Not only is the presence of complainants important, but so are their preferences about the behavior of the police. In general, Black and Reiss found that white complainants are much more likely to prefer lenient behavior on the part of the police than black complainants. They also found a "quite dramatic" tendency for the police to comply with the preferences expressed by complainants. Since black complainants are more likely to prefer severe penalties, this has dire implications for black youths who commit crimes. Again, Black and Reiss take this as evidence that it is not police discrimination that accounts for race differences in arrests, because the white officers follow the same patterns of behavior for *both* white and black juveniles. As a result, they conclude that the complainant "often can play the role of judge in police encounters."[13]

Another interesting and important finding is that the police are no more likely to arrest a suspect in a situation in which they witness at least part of a crime than in situations in which all they have are citizen testimonies about what transpired. This fact is taken as strong evidence of the police use of discretion in deciding what to do about juvenile offenders.

Demeanor

Finally, Black and Reiss follow up Piliavin and Briar's concern with the demeanor of the suspect. First, they found that most juveniles are neither very respectful nor very disrespectful. Thus, the majority of arrests occur when juveniles are being reasonably civil to the police. The arrest rate in all cases was 16 percent, but it rose to 22 percent in the cases where youths behaved antagonistically toward the police. This seems to confirm Piliavin and Briar's conclusion, but the arrest rate is also 22 percent for youths who behave very deferentially.

Black and Reiss argue that there are two explanations (one methodological and the other substantive) for the major difference between their research and that of Piliavin and Briar: the high arrest rate for those who act very deferentially. Methodologically, they point to coding differences between the two pieces of research. Piliavin and Briar used only two codes, "cooperative" and "uncooperative." Black and Reiss used three codes, "very deferential," "civil," and "antagonistic." The first two of Black and Reiss's codes would have fallen into the "cooperative" category in the Piliavin and Briar research. Had they used the same coding system, Black and Reiss would have come to conclusions similar to those of Piliavin and Briar. Substantively, Black and Reiss argue that it is the juveniles

> who are and who know themselves to be particularly liable to arrest [who] may be especially deferential toward the police as a tactic of situational self-defense. After all, the notion that one is well-advised to be polite to policemen if one is in trouble is quite widespread in the community.[14]

In other words, the most guilty are also the most likely to be deferential. Because they are more likely to be guilty, they are more likely to be arrested even though they act deferentially. Indeed, the police may be even more suspicious of them because of the higher level of deferential behavior.

Black and Reiss's work serves to support some of Piliavin and Briar's conclusions and to extend and call into question others. One thing is clear; it is difficult with any single piece of participant-observation research to identify and record many of the most important variables. Hence, it is important to conduct a number of participant observations at different times and in different places.

DELINQUENCY TREATMENT: THE EXPERIMENTAL METHOD

As far back as written records go, human societies have distinguished between children and adults when punishing criminal acts.[15] Furthermore, child lawbreakers have always called forth strong social impulses to attempt their reform before it is too late. Common sense tells us that if only someone had intervened during the childhood years of adult criminals, had set them on the right path early on, much human suffering could have been spared.

All present-day probation and counseling programs for juvenile delinquents—juvenile homes and treatment centers, juvenile courts, and neighborhood delinquency-prevention programs—are motivated by this urge to save the young. But nagging questions have persisted. Which, if any, of these methods of dealing with delinquency is actually effective? And, if the methods are not effective, what should be done?

Clearcut answers to these questions require elaborate social experimentation. As we shall see, experimental programs may take a great deal of money and time, raise painful moral decisions, and bring disappointments to those who devote significant parts of their lives to making these programs work. Finally, simply to arrive at a clear answer in no way guarantees that social policies and practices will take such answers into account. One of the reasons we have chosen to begin with the Cambridge-Somerville experiment that began in 1937 and ended in 1945 (although the findings were intensively analyzed and reanalyzed for an additional twelve years) is to let you examine the process by which governmental and private policy makers and programs have held out against research evidence that refutes the basic premise on which they are operating.

The Cambridge-Somerville Experiment

In 1935, Ricahrd Clarke Cabot, a distinguished and wealthy New England physician and social philosopher, decided to do something about juvenile delinquency. He believed that delinquency could be deflected early in life if only the child could form a close and friendly relationship with an adult able to enrich the child's life and give the child effective guidance. He decided to create a program to try out his notions and to assess their effectiveness.

There was nothing particularly novel about Cabot's views. They reflected the views prevalent among the leading experts on child welfare at the time and, indeed, remain the dominant views today. What was novel was Cabot's willingness—and financial ability—to conduct a large-scale social experiment to find out whether a program conceived and carried out under optimum conditions could, in fact, save young people from delinquency.

Cabot launched his project in 1937. He selected two highly industrialized, economically depressed cities that were near Boston—Cambridge and Somerville—as the sites for the experiment. Next, he hired a staff and set to work; they selected 650 boys from Somerville and Cambridge for study. The boys' average age was eleven, still young enough, in Cabot's judgment, to respond to efforts to keep them from becoming delinquents.

The Experimental Design

Cabot wanted to know if participating in his delinquency-prevention program actually prevented delinquency. He therefore could not let all 650 boys participate. If he had, how could he have determined whether the proportion who committed delinquent acts was lower (or even higher) than it would have been if they had not participated? He could not. There would be no standard against which to compare the boys in his program.

Therefore, Cabot decided to split the boys into two groups. Half were recruited into the program; the other half were not. Later, records of program boys could be compared with those of nonprogram boys to see which group was less delinquent.

By May 1939, he had split the boys into two equal groups of 325, and the staff went to work to recruit those chosen for treatment into the program. When the counselors visited the boys' homes to recruit them, the parents often suspected them of being door-to-door salesmen, but they responded very favorably to the project once it had been explained to them. And well they might, for during the depths of the Depression, these poor families were offered a chance for their sons to receive free medical and dental care, special tutoring on their school work, interesting field trips, stays at summer camps, and other advantages far beyond what their families could afford. In fact, the counselors also helped the families secure welfare aid and other benefits. Overall, the project was designed to resemble the very best efforts made by progressive probation officers, family welfare agencies, and private groups such as the Big Brother Association. Each boy would have a personal counselor doing his best to help the boy cope with the world.

Sad to say, Dr. Cabot died of a heart attack in 1939 at the commencement of his project, but the project did continue. World War II soon brought difficulties: many of the original male counselors were replaced, often with women, so few boys had the same counselor throughout their participation in the program. Tire and gasoline shortages made transportation difficult for the counselors and cut down field trips. And, by the project's end in December 1945, many of the boys had entered military service.

The Results

Despite these limitations, the project was carried out. If the actual program was not as elaborate as Cabot's vision, it nonetheless equaled or surpassed government and private delinquency-treatment programs in actual operation both then and now. As William and Joan McCord[16] put it in their volume reanalyzing data from the project,

> the staff could look back with satisfaction at their record. A very large number of children had received social aid and some individual counseling averaging close to five years per boy. Furthermore, careful records had been kept. Thus, the Cambridge-Somerville project . . . stands as a unique event in the battle against delinquency.[17]

But what did the project actually accomplish? It demonstrated that its efforts to deflect delinquency were futile. Few sets of data in the history of social research have been analyzed so many times, so many different ways, and by so many different researchers; yet no significant differences have been found between boys in the program and those denied access to the program. In fact, about 40 percent of the boys in the program and those left out of the program were subsequently convicted of a criminal offense. Furthermore, boys in the program were convicted of approximately the same number of offenses as boys who were left out of the program.

At the time the original findings were reported, it was suggested that a "latent effect" might show up—that boys in the treatment program might turn out to be more stable adults and thus less apt to commit criminal offenses later on. But a follow-up study found that adult convictions for crimes were equally common among those who had been in the program and those who had not. Indeed, the only significant difference found was that those in the program, for some reason, were significantly more likely than those not in the program to be convicted of traffic violations as adults.

Having now gained a general picture of the Cambridge-Somerville experiment and its results, we can reexamine it in a more analytic fashion. All the critical elements of a proper experimental design are present. Figure 2.1 displays these elements, and the following discussion explains each one of them.

The Independent Variable

All experiments include at least one *independent variable* over which the experimenter has control. It is called independent because it is the factor that is thought to be the cause of something else. It is called a variable because this factor takes more than one value. If the independent variable were electric current, for example, it would be necessary for the experimenter at least to be able to switch it off and on.

In the Cambridge-Somerville experiment, the independent variable was the delinquency-prevention treatment program. The experimenters were able to manipulate, or control, it—they could decide which boys did or did not get included in the program. Boys who were assigned to be recruited into the program made up the ex-

Figure 2.1 The Experimental Design Used in the Cambridge-Somerville Delinquency-Treatment Program

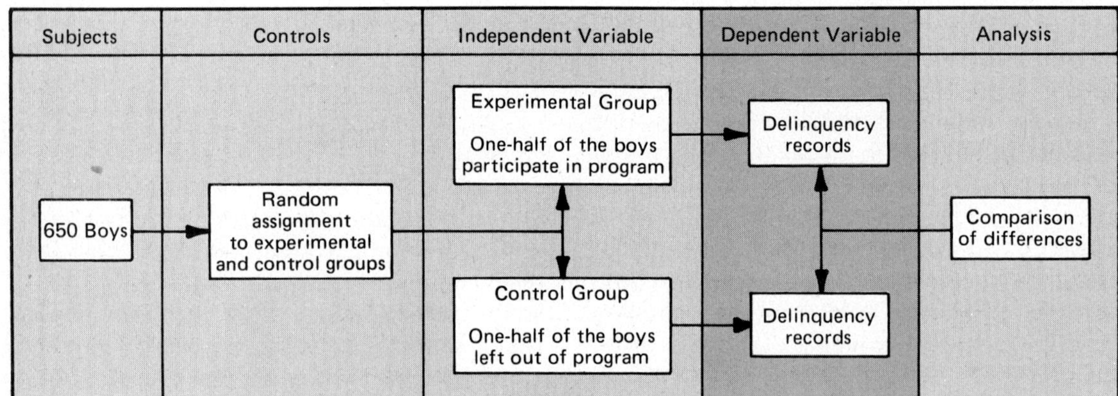

In the program, randomly assigning boys to be included or excluded from the program ruled out differences between the groups. If boys who participated in the program had been less likely to commit offenses than boys ignored by the program, there would have been substantial grounds to believe that the program was effective.

perimental group; they were to receive the experimental treatment. The other half of the boys were not recruited into the program. They made up the control group; they were the standard against which the experimental group was evaluated.

The Dependent Variable

The *dependent variable* is the factor that you expect the independent variable to affect—this factor is believed to be dependent on the independent variable. If your expectations are correct, you will find that changes in the independent variable are followed by changes in the dependent variable.

In this study, delinquency was the dependent variable, and it was defined and measured in a number of ways. The chief criterion was conviction for a criminal offense. Three years after the treatment program ended, official police and court records were secured for all 650 boys in the original group. As we have already reported, this study found that the independent variable had failed to produce any changes in the dependent variable. Boys in the program were as likely as those denied participation to have been convicted. It is clear that the program had no impact on delinquency whatsoever.

Controls

Experiments are designed to rule out the possibility that some factor other than the independent variable (and simple chance) could cause changes in the dependent variable. The experimenter uses *randomization* in assigning subjects to the experimental or control groups in order to rule out other possible causes. Whether a boy was recruited into the program or left out was determined randomly, in this case, by flipping a coin to decide what happened to each boy. If the experimenters had not used randomization to select boys for each group, they could not have been sure that unconscious biases or other unforeseeable factors were not operating to make differences between boys included in and excluded from the program. For example, "good boys" might have been disproportionately selected for treatment over boys who seemed dubious delinquency risks. Eventual differences in delinquency between the two groups might then have been a result of initial selection rather than of the treatment program. In fact, any group of 650 boys includes a great many differences: some are bigger, some are tougher, some are smarter, some are better looking, some get along better with their families, some do better in school, some are more religious. In an experiment it is important to equalize all such differences between the experimental and the control groups. The only way they should differ is in exposure or nonexposure to the treatment program. When assignment to the experimental or the control group is decided randomly, boys selected for study in both groups ought to be the same in all ways.

Statistical Analysis

Once an experiment is complete, the first step is to compare the experimental group with the control group on the dependent variable. If both score equally on the dependent variable, it is evident that the independent variable has failed to produce the expected effects. The experimenter must reject as false all predictions that the independent variable utilized in the experiment is a cause of the dependent variable. In the present instance, the results cause us to reject Cabot's hopes to create an enlightened program that could deflect boys from delinquency. Had the comparison of the experimental group and control group revealed a difference—with program boys less likely to commit crimes—then Cabot's expectations would have been borne out, provided that a second step in analyzing all these experimental results has been taken successfully.

We have pointed out that randomization is used to ensure that experimental and control groups are the same in all respects save receiving or not receiving the experimental treatment. But randomization does not absolutely guarantee that both groups will be the same in all respects. Instead, it simply makes it possible to compute the mathematical odds that any difference in the dependent variable found between the two groups is the result of the independent variable or the result of other differences between the two groups that occurred by chance during the random assignment.

The odds against such chance-produced findings in an experiment depend on two factors: the size of the experimental and control groups and the size of the difference found in the dependent variable. The larger the difference is, the less likely it could be produced by chance. The larger the experimental and control groups are, the smaller the difference required to discount chance findings. Obviously, the greater the number of times you flip a coin, the closer you will come to flipping heads exactly 50 percent of the time. It is equally obvious that small differences in the dependent variable are more likely to be the result of mere chance than are very large differences.

The usual way to compute these odds is to apply a test of statistical significance. As a rule of thumb, experimenters usually require that the odds be at least 20 to 1 against chance findings before they call the results statistically significant or put any trust in them. There was no need to worry about statistical significance in the Cambridge-Somerville experiment because no differences were found between boys in the experimental and control groups on such crucial matters as subsequent criminal convictions. When a difference is found, the next step is to turn to significance tests to compute the probability that the difference is the result of chance. You will recall that a difference did turn up in one comparison in the McCords's follow-up study—boys in the experimental group were more likely than those in the control group to have been convicted of a traffic offense after reaching adulthood. But this difference was in the wrong direction to offer any support for the program's effectiveness.

However, this finding does raise the question of significance. As is shown in Table 2.2, 16 percent of the boys who participated in the delinquency-prevention program had been convicted of traffic offenses, but only 10 percent of the boys excluded from the program had a record of such a conviction after age twenty-one. What is the probability that this represents a real difference between the two groups rather than simply a chance fluctuation? As is shown in the table, the odds are more than 20 to 1 that a finding this large could not occur purely by chance. Thus, if this study were repeated twenty times and if there were no real difference in the traffic behavior of the experimental and control groups, one would expect to find a differ-

Table 2.2 Differences in Traffic-Crime Convictions After Age 21

GROUP	PERCENT CONVICTED	
Experimental	16	
Control	10	$p < .05$

Source: Adapted from William McCord and Joan McCord, *Origins of Crime: A New Evaluation of the Cambridge-Somerville Youth Study* (New York: Columbia University Press, 1959).

ence of this size only once through chance. This is what is indicated by $p < .05$ in the table. The probability (p) that these findings are a result of chance is less than (<) 5 chances in 100 (.05), or 1 chance in 20.

Replication

A final guard against incorrectly accepting findings that are merely the result of chance or incorrectly rejecting real differences as mere chance is *replication*. In this case, replication involves the selection of a new group of boys, subjecting the experimental group to a delinquency-prevention program, and then comparing their eventual delinquency with that of boys in the control group. The odds of getting a difference resulting from chance twice in a row are relatively low. Furthermore, such replication is an excellent way to determine whether findings based on one population in a certain place at a certain time can be generalized to another population in a different place at a different time.

The Provo Experiment

While the Cambridge-Somerville Experiment was primarily concerned with the issue of delinquency *prevention*, the Provo (Utah) experiment, conducted between 1959 and 1965, was concerned with the *treatment* of repeat delinquent offenders.[18] A large number of the participants were candidates for reformatories, but in the experiment they lived at home and spent only a portion of each day at the program center. The program encompassed no more than twenty boys at a time, divided into two groups. The length of stay in the program was not predetermined; it depended on the progress of the boy and of the group to which he belonged. In general, boys spent between four and seven months in the program. The first phase involved intensive work programs and group meetings. The second phase followed release from this intensive program and involved an effort to maintain group support for the boy and to get the community involved in finding him employment.

Phase One

The Provo experiment eschewed formal structure. Boys were simply expected to appear every day, to work hard, and, if they wanted, to attend group discussions. This lack of structure was designed to make the boys uneasy and force them toward the group as a method of resolving their problems. When new boys arrived in the program, they received no formal instructions. This served to force them toward the peer group, and it is in that group that they learned the informal norms of the system. The peer group also played a key role in the group discussions, which had three main goals: "(1) to question the utility of a life devoted to delinquency; (2) to suggest alternative behavior; and (3) to provide recognition for a boy's personal reformation and his willingness to reform others."[19] The idea was to create an antidelinquent group with which the boy could identify instead of his previous identity with a prodelinquent group. For this to work, the boy had to become heavily and deeply involved in the group, and a variety of techniques were employed to be sure this took place.

The authorities also served to pressure the delinquents to change. However, their actions (and often inactions) were extremely subtle. For example, they provided little orientation or support, forcing the boy toward the peer group. They only took action when boys refused to get involved in the group or the group was unable or unwilling to take action. The authorities rarely told boys that they were in trouble, or what to do about it, if they were. The boys were left on their own to figure out the actions of authorities, as well as the alternatives open to them. The authorities did not supply counseling to help with such problems, with the result that the boys were forced back to the peer group. Thus, the main responsibility in the program was placed on the individual delinquents, and delinquent groups, *not* adult authority figures.

Another important component of the Provo experiment was involving delinquents in work programs. Rather than immersing them in an abstract educational program, the goal was to get them involved in actual work activities. Boys were employed in city and county parks, streets, and recreation areas in order to help them develop acceptable work habits.

Phase Two

The second phase of the Provo experiment was designed to maintain the two basic premises of the first phase—peer group support and employment. Following release from phase one, a boy continued to meet periodically with his old group. There were three objectives in such meetings: "(1) acting as a check on a boy's current behavior; (2) serving as a law-abiding reference group; and (3) aiding in the solution of new problems."[20] Efforts were also made to locate jobs for the boys.

Controls

As in the Cambridge-Somerville experiment, it was necessary to set up control groups to compare with experimental groups. The first step was for researchers to select those cases that were eligible for the study among those coming before the court. The court hearing was then held and for those judged guilty, the selection process continued. The judge then had to decide whether to incarcerate the boy or to give him probation. It was at this stage that the random selection process came into play. The judge was given two sets of numbered envelopes. One set of envelopes was for probation; the judge could assign a boy to either an experimental or a control probation group. The second set was for incarceration; a boy could be assigned, again, to either an experimental or a control group. Here is the way the procedure worked:

> Each set of envelopes contained randomly selected slips of paper on which were written either *experimental group* or *control group*. Assuming, for example, that the judge had decided he would ordinarily incarcerate a boy, he would then open the top envelope in the incarceration series. Depending on what was written on the slip in the envelope, he would announce his decision to the boy. If it said *experimental* group, the boy would be placed in the experimental program; if it said *control* group, he would be incarcerated.[21]

However, as is often the case in social research, the plan had to be altered in the face of realities. In this case, there were not enough cases for the experimental and control incarceration groups, in part because the judge was reluctant to recommend incarceration in juvenile cases. Thus, the researchers had to make two compromises. First, they "accepted all boys in the experimental program who would otherwise have been incarcerated, adding them to the few who had already been randomly assigned."[22] Second, they "took steps to choose a comparison group from the Utah State Industrial School, a group comprised of offenders from the entire state rather than the Provo court only."[23] The experimenters realized that the abandonment of randomization would lead to questions about their research, but the realities of the situation left them with no alternative.

The independent variable in this case is involvement in the two phases of the Provo experiment. The boys in the program made up the experimental groups and they were compared to the control groups that did not receive the experimental treatment. The dependent variable in this study of concern to us here is later involvement in criminal activities. The Provo researchers believed that those receiving the experimental treatment would commit fewer criminal acts. Unlike the Cambridge-Somerville researchers, the Provo researchers turned out to be right, at least in part.

Results

We need look at just a few of the results of the Provo experiment. One issue is the frequency of arrest in the four groups while the subjects were under supervision. The experimental group under probation had almost half as many arrests as the control group under probation. In other words, the experimental approach seemed to work quite well for those on probation. On the other hand, the experimental program for those who were to have been incarcerated did not work as well. This experimental group had a higher number of arrests than the incarcerated control group.[24] There were similar findings in the case of graduates of the program. LeMar Empey and Maynard Erickson conclude that "the experimental program was more effective than probation in controlling arrest frequency during exposure to the program" and that "the experimental program may have been almost as effective as incarceration."[25] Although the overall results are not all in the predicted direction, they do tend to support the efficacy of the approach taken in the Provo experiments. Thus, while there is little evidence that the Cambridge-Somerville program was successful, there is at least some experimental evidence supporting the approach taken in the Provo study.

The Struggle for Survival

It is worth noting that the Provo experiment, like the Cambridge-Somerville study, experienced a number of practical difficulties during its years of operation. Such problems are characteristic of experiments undertaken in the real world. It would be useful to look at the problems the Provo experiment encountered during its relatively short lifetime.

Although a community program to help delinquents had been in operation for several years, it is convenient to take a large grant from the Ford Foundation in the first half of 1959 as the start of the Provo experiment. The first year and a half of the study was fairly quiet and even optimistic. But, in the beginning of 1961, a new county commission was elected, and it was less favorably inclined toward the experiment and less willing to continue supporting it with a few thousand dollars in local funds. Furthermore, a budget deficit loomed, and the Provo experiment became the major target for reduction. There followed years of wrangling involving not only the county commission, but also the state government. The county commission contributed nothing after January 1963, and the state never contributed any money to the project. As a result, the Provo experiment did not live up to its commitment to the Ford Foundation to match its grant with local money. Nevertheless, the experiment was completed, in part because the staff accepted low salaries and, in part, because some aspects of the study were not completed. The funds for the study were finally exhausted in 1965, and efforts to keep the research going beyond that point failed.

The economic problems experienced in the Provo experiment are much more typical than the luxury of Cabot's private funding of the Cambridge-Somerville experiment. Field experiments are expensive and hard to support. One finds relatively few philanthropists like Cabot who are willing to invest their private fortunes in such work. Furthermore, such experiments often run into the kind of local problems experienced in Provo.

THE CAUSES OF DELINQUENCY: SURVEY RESEARCH

The Richmond Youth Study

In the spring of 1965, Travis Hirschi and the staff from the Survey Research Center at the University of California, Berkeley, administered a lengthy questionnaire to several thousand students, randomly selected from among the more than 17,000 junior-high-school and high-school students in the public school system of Richmond, California. The purpose of the study was to find out what causes juvenile delinquency.[26]

They spent more than a year designing and pretesting the questionnaire. Such caution is necessary partly because large-scale survey research, the method employed in this study, is expensive. If researchers ask the wrong questions, phrase them badly, or forget to ask something important, they may have wasted a large amount of the time and money allotted for the research. It simply costs too much to go back and ask questions again.

The Scope of the Method

In spite of these pressures, survey research is the only reliable procedure to follow to acquire certain kinds of information. If you want to know the distribution of some trait in a population—for example, delinquent behavior or religious beliefs—no other method suffices. If it did, nobody would pay the Gallup or Harris polling organizations many thousands of dollars to conduct a survey. Piliavin and Briar could not reckon what proportion of boys commit delinquent acts simply by riding around with the police—the police only encounter a small proportion of boys, even of boys who commit crimes. Indeed, simply by observing the police, Piliavin and Briar could not determine what proportion of boys at some time or other have run-ins with the police. To determine these proportions, one must examine the whole population of teenage boys, or a representative sample of them, and compute the percentage who have been picked up by the police, have committed a delinquent act, and so on.

By the same token, a search for the causes of delinquency does not lend itself to the experimental method. In order to find out what causes delinquency, social scientists could not take a group of children and try to manipulate their lives so that some would become delinquents; that would be both immoral and impractical. Furthermore, few of the independent variables in such a study could be created or manipulated experimentally. You cannot take people and recreate some of them as students and others as school dropouts. Nor could you raise some young people in close-knit families and deprive others of affection in a laboratory. These restrictions apply to most phenomena social scientists want to study, so researchers are forced to take people as they are and try to determine why they are that way. Clearly, the staff in the Cambridge-Somerville experiment could not study why 40 percent of the boys in their study became delinquents; they could only try to assess whether or not their prevention program made boys less likely to become delinquents. To show that aspects of young people's backgrounds and social circumstances relate to delinquency requires the kind of systematic data available only through a survey.

Hirschi's research design was guided by his intentions to test predictions about delinquency that follow from several competing theoretical traditions. The theories can largely be ignored here. The point to be made is that because Hirschi was testing particular theories, he had some clear notion of which data were relevant to his needs. You cannot gather all possible information about a sample of young people. Having a theory and knowing which arguments you plan to test clarifies what you need to know and ask.

Measuring Delinquency

One cannot explain delinquency without first measuring it. On what grounds are teenagers to be classified as more or less delinquent? It is well known that most delinquent acts are not detected; therefore, when you measure delinquency on the basis of official court and police records, you have several possible sources of substantial error. First of all, you may end up explaining not who commits delinquent acts but who gets caught for committing delinquent acts. Suppose out of 100 boys, 80 at one time or another steal an item worth more than $50 from a store. Suppose that only 5 of them are caught by the police. Assume also that you have IQ scores on all 100 boys. By comparing the IQs of the 5 caught by the police with the IQs of the other 95 without police records, you find that the 5 are not nearly as intelligent as the other 95. Not knowing that the uncaught group contains 75 undetected thieves, you might erroneously conclude that low intelligence causes boys to steal. But the truth might be that low intelligence is not related to stealing at all but only to getting caught.

Hirschi's strategy for measuring delinquency was to ask all teenagers in his sample to respond to six questions that would reveal commission of delinquent acts. The questions measured petty and grand larceny, auto theft, vandalism, and battery. The more frequently respondents reported committing these acts and the more of them they committed, the higher the respondents scored on delinquency. Eventually, Hirschi created a three-point measure of self-reported delinquency: those who had in the past year committed none of these acts, those who had committed one of them, and those who had committed two or more.

In addition to using this *self-report* measure of delinquency, Hirschi had his staff check the official police records for all boys in the sample and record all the official offenses for the past two years. (Most delinquency studies focus on boys only because boys are so much more likely than girls to commit delinquent acts.) Hirschi was now in a position to conduct a parallel analysis of delinquency using both self-report and official delinquency measures.

Data on Race and Delinquency

After all the questionnaires had been coded and fed into a computer, one of the first questions that Hirschi put to his data was the issue raised by Piliavin and Briar about police reactions to racial differences in juvenile offenders. Not only was this question an important one, but Hirschi's interest in it was heightened even further because Piliavin and Briar shared an office across the hall from his office.

The first thing Hirschi wanted to know was whether black and white teenagers differ in their involvement in delinquency. His first step was to divide his sample into whites and blacks. The result is shown in Example A.

The next step was to see how each group was distributed on the dependent variable, delinquency. Initially Hirschi used self-reported delinquency as his dependent variable. The results are displayed in Example B.

Example A

WHITE	BLACK
1,303 youths	828 youths

Example B

NUMBER OF DELINQUENT ACTS	WHITE	BLACK
None	730	422
One	326	207
Two or more	247	199
Total	1,303 youths	828 youths

Hirschi then compared blacks and whites to see which group was more likely to report committing delinquent acts. Looking at the raw numbers in Example B, it would be very hard to make such a judgment. Although it is true that the largest number (247) of boys who admitted to two or more delinquent acts during the year were white, they were also the largest group (730) who had committed no offenses during the year. The statistics reflect the fact that there are considerably more whites than blacks in the sample (and in the city of Richmond).

Percentage Conversions

When groups contain different numbers of people, they are hard to compare. The solution to this problem is to convert the raw numbers into percentages, which take account of size differences and make direct comparisons easy. You divide 730 by 1,303 to get the percentage of whites who denied committing any delinquent acts: 56 percent. Similarly, you divide 422 by 828 to get the percentage of blacks who denied committing any delinquent acts: 51 percent. The results of this division are shown in Example C.

Example C

NUMBER OF DELINQUENT ACTS	WHITE	BLACK
None	56%	51%
One	25%	25%
Two or more	19%	24%
Total	100%	100%

Reading across the table, you can see that there are only modest differences between blacks and whites in the proportions reporting delinquent behavior. Of whites, 56 percent denied any delinquent acts; of blacks, 51 percent. Exactly the same proportion (25 percent) of whites and blacks reported committing one delinquent act. Finally, looking across the bottom row in the table, you see that 19 percent of the whites and 24 percent of the blacks said that they had committed two or more such acts. Hirschi concluded that blacks were only slightly more likely than whites to have committed delinquent acts.

He next looked at responses to the question, "Have you ever been picked up by the police?" Again he created a percentage table so that he could compare black and white teenage boys. Here he found a slightly larger, but still modest, difference: 65 percent of whites and 57 percent of blacks said they had not been picked up by the police. Finally, Hirschi turned to his official measure of delinquency based on police and court records. Here he found a very substantial difference: 81 percent of the whites had no record of delinquency, but only 57 percent of the blacks had no record. These findings strongly implied that Piliavin and Briar were right—the police were responding differentially to black and white teenagers. Whites were only slightly less likely to admit offenses and nearly as likely as blacks to have been picked up by the police, but they were much less likely to have acquired an official record despite these similarities.

To make these differences clear, Hirschi computed a new table, as shown in Example D.

Example D

OFFICIAL RECORD	BOYS WHO ADMITTED BEING PICKED UP BY POLICE	
	WHITE	BLACK
Yes	45%	76%
No	55%	24%
Total	100%	100%

First, he selected only those boys who admitted they had been picked up by the police. Then, he separated them into blacks and whites. Finally, he computed the proportions of each group who had an official record of delinquency. As can be seen, the majority of whites who have been picked up by the police (55 percent) have no official record. In contrast, the overwhelming majority of blacks who have been picked up by the police (76 percent) do have an official record. These findings strongly suggest that when whites encounter the police, they are usually able to get off without a record. When blacks encounter the police, they typically do not get off without a record.

Although these findings offered confirmation of Piliavin and Briar's perceptions of how the police operate, the analysis can hardly stop here. Recall that in the Cambridge-Somerville experiment, boys were randomly assigned to the experimental and control groups. Randomization permitted control of all of the other possible causes of differences—besides differences created by chance—between those who participated in the program and those who did not. It established (within known probabilities) that both groups would be equal in terms of such factors as family background, attitudes, size, and all other potential sources of bias.

In experiments, the analysis of findings is complete when the initial comparison between groups has been made. The investigator then uses a simple statistical method to determine whether the size of the relationship found—for example, the differences between the proportions of blacks and whites who have been both picked up and have been given official records—is great enough to make it extremely unlikely to have been caused merely by chance. If the difference is significant, the experimenter then publishes the findings with considerable confidence that they are accurate.

Spuriousness

When survey research is the method used, one is not able to rule out other differences through random assignment. There is no way to randomly assign people to be black or white. Thus, black and white youths in Hirschi's study differ in many ways besides race. There is always the possibility that some of these other factors are responsible for the finding and that race has nothing to do with it.

This problem, over which most survey analysts lose sleep, is called spuriousness. When it can be demonstrated, in this example, that something other than race caused the differences in the proportions of official delinquency records, then it can be said that the relationship between race and record is spurious—there is no causal relationship between race and record.

There is nothing mysterious about the idea of spuriousness. It is part of ordinary common sense, and most of us use it all the time. For example, it is the case that the more fire trucks present at a fire, the greater damage the fire will do. Suppose someone told you that this proves that fire trucks cause fire damage. You would rightfully laugh out loud. It is obvious that both the number of trucks present at a fire and the amount of damage done is caused by the size of the fire. Big fires draw more fire trucks and cause more damage than small fires do.

Or, consider another example. Suppose someone told you that on the average, whites have larger bank accounts than blacks have, and that this shows that race differences cause differences in willingness to save money. You would undoubtedly dismiss such a claim as foolish because you would immediately see that the difference in the average size of bank accounts simply reflects the fact that the average income of blacks is lower than that of whites. We do not expect poor people to have as much money in the bank as rich people have, so willingness to save and race have nothing to do with the size of bank accounts, although race may have much to do with being poor.

In similar fashion, something other than race could be producing differences in the rate at which blacks and whites picked up by the police get official records. Indeed, many sociologists might suggest that the police are responding to social class, not racial differences. The argument could go as follows: The police believe that offenses committed by juveniles who come from lower-class homes more urgently require official action than do offenses committed by juveniles from middle- and upper-class homes. Therefore, it is not on racial grounds but on class grounds that the police discriminate.

How does one test such arguments? Social scientists use statistical controls to test for spuriousness. They try to remove the effect of factors that might be producing a spurious relationship. The principle involved is very simple. In the present example, Hirschi would simply compare the relationship between race and having an official record separately for boys of differing social-class backgrounds. For the sake of simplicity, let us suppose that it would be sufficient to divide boys who had been picked up by the police into two groups: those whose fathers were employed in blue-collar occupations and those whose fathers held white-collar jobs. Classifying boys by their fathers' occupations would create two tables out of the data in Example D—one for sons of blue-collar fathers, the other for sons of white-collar fathers.

Table 2.3 is a hypothetical illustration showing what would happen if social class, not race, were in fact the real cause of the differences that were found in official records.

Assume that simply by separating boys into two groups on the basis of their fathers' occupation, everyone in each group is now of the same social class. If within each occupation in the table, social class no longer varies, the social class differences have been controlled. If uncontrolled class

Table 2.3 Percentage of Boys with Records by Race and Fathers' Occupation

OFFICIAL RECORD	BLUE COLLAR		WHITE COLLAR	
	BLACK	WHITE	BLACK	WHITE
Yes	90	90	20	20
No	10	10	80	80
Total	100	100	100	100

differences had been the source of the original differences in official records between whites and blacks, then when social class is controlled, the original relationship ought to disappear. In other words, blacks and whites from equal family backgrounds ought to be equally likely to have official records if the argument being tested is true.

Notice that this is what has happened in the hypothetical table (Table 2.3). Among boys whose fathers have blue-collar occupations, 90 percent of both blacks and whites have official records. Among boys with white-collar fathers, only 20 percent of both blacks and whites have official records. Race makes no difference when class is controlled. If Hirschi had controlled for social class with these results, he would have had to reject the notion that the police respond differently to white and black juveniles. The apparent racial differences would simply have to be judged as an accident of the fact that blacks and whites differ in their social class, and we would have to say the original relationship between race and police records was spurious.

These results did not appear when Hirschi controlled for social class. Instead, he found that differences between blacks and whites remained little changed within each class. Regardless of class, the police seemed to single out blacks for official action. This finding increased Hirschi's confidence that his survey supported Piliavin and Briar's observations. He gained further confidence when other control variables, such as neighborhood, also failed to wipe out racial differences. This procedure is followed in all nonexperimental statistical analyses. Because differences cannot be removed through randomization, the analyst tries to exclude likely sources of spuriousness by systematically holding each possible source constant, as was shown in the hypothetical table. This procedure lacks the finality of experimental methods because possible sources of spuriousness are never exhausted, but it is the only possible way to study social phenomena that cannot be manipulated by experimental controls.

The method of analysis we have just examined is not limited to survey-research studies. It is the method used on all numerical data other than that obtained from an experiment. Whatever the source of nonexperimental numerical data, the question of spuriousness is always an urgent concern. Thus, in analyzing their data, social scientists always observe the same logical procedures that we have examined in order to control for possible sources of spuriousness.

The National Youth Survey

More recently, Delbert S. Elliott and Suzanne S. Ageton have sought to deal with the controversy over whether self-report surveys or police and arrest records are more accurate and reliable ways of studying the social correlates of delinquency.[27] As we have seen, the major difference here is that self-report studies tend to show no major differences in delinquent behavior by race (and class), while studies relying on official records report significant differences by race (and class). Elliott and Ageton focus on the problems involved in constructing the measures used in self-report research, as well as the procedures used in administering them. Their objective is to see whether the correction of these problems will lead to more consistent findings in self-report studies and official data.

Problems with Self-Reported Data Research

According to Elliott and Ageton, one set of problems relates to the way the research instruments in self-reported data studies are constructed. First, it is often claimed that many of the measures are unrepresentative; that is, they do not represent the entire range of delinquent acts. For example, trivial offenses like cutting classes tend to be overrepresented, while more serious offenses like sexual assault are often omitted. A second problem is the inclusion of overlapping items that leads to inaccurate estimates of frequency of offense. For example, an instrument may include both a "cutting class" and a "cutting school" item. A youth who cuts school is necessarily cutting class with the result that the student is likely to answer "yes" to both questions even though only one offense is involved. Third, the choice of responses given to subjects may cause problems. For example, the answer "three times or more" would be chosen by someone who shoplifted three times as well as someone who engaged in such criminal behavior hundreds of times.

A second set of problems involves the administration of the research instrument. One issue here is whether the respondent is anonymous or identified. Many believe that youths will not admit certain offenses if they are not guaranteed anonymity, but there is little scientific support for this view. It has been argued that the guarantee of anonymity may in fact be dysfunctional since respondents may then give careless or facetious answers. Related to this is the issue of whether to use interviews or questionnaires. Questionnaires allow for anonymity while interviews do not. Because it is more likely to be anonymous, it is believed (although there is controversy on this issue) that self-administered questionnaires yield more accurate responses than personal interviews.

A third set of problems revolves around the sampling designs and generality of the findings in self-report studies of delinquency. The major problem here is that these studies have been done on small and select groups of youths (for example, teenagers processed by a local juvenile court). These are rarely probability samples with the result that it is impossible to generalize accurately to adolescents in general. An additional problem here is that such studies have not been conducted on an annual basis with the result that it is impossible to identify trends or to make direct comparisons with standard delinquency data such as that found in the *Uniform Crime Reports.*

The Study

Elliott and Ageton attempted to deal with the problems described above in the *National Youth Survey* involving a national probability sample of 1,726 youths aged 11 through 17 in 1976. The youths were interviewed early in 1977 about involvement in delinquent behavior during 1976. The same procedure was followed in early 1978 about delinquency in 1977. This was to be repeated again in the early months of 1979, 1980, and 1981. This repeating of a study on the same group of people and on a regular basis over time is called a *panel study.* The data reported here are derived from the first phase of the study done in 1977 and dealing with delinquent behavior committed during 1976.

Elliott and Ageton took great care to deal with the three methodological problems usually associated with self-reported data (SRD) studies. On the problem of the representativeness of the offenses measured, they took care to develop a lengthy list of forty-seven items that they considered "more comprehensive and more representative of the conceptual universe of delinquent acts then [sic] found in prior SRD measures used in major, large-scale studies."[28] Great care was taken in getting information on the frequency of delinquent acts. Open-ended questions were asked and those who indicated that they had committed an act ten or more times were also asked to answer a closed-ended question on frequency (where a range of responses is preset rather than left totally to the respondent as in an open-ended question). Great care was also taken to avoid overlapping items. To yield a recall period of a year with reference points that are meaningful to young people, respondents were asked to report offenses committed "'from Christmas a year ago to the Christmas just past'."[29]

On administration issues, anonymity could not be guaranteed since the respondents would have to be restudied for five consecutive years. However, elaborate efforts were made to guarantee confidentiality, and the respondents received a certificate from the Department of Health, Education, and Welfare guaranteeing them that neither the data collected nor the interviewers could be legally subpoenaed. An interview was chosen over a self-administered questionnaire because Elliott and Ageton believed an interview would produce more accurate and reliable data and that the data derived would be similar to that produced by a self-administered questionnaire.

Finally, a national probability sample was used, and even after attrition the "participating youth appear to be representative of the total 11 through 17-year-old youth population in the United States."[30]

On the basis of this research, Elliott and Ageton derive findings and come to conclusions that more closely resemble studies based on official arrest data than on previous self-reported data studies. The most important finding is that in the Elliott-Ageton research there *are* significant differences in crimes committed by race and by social class. Blacks and those from the lower classes are significantly more likely to report committing various kinds of delinquent acts.

One of the major reasons for these differences appears to be the extended frequency ranges used in The National Youth Survey versus the more limited ranges employed in earlier studies, including the Hirschi study discussed above. Had they, too, used a limited range of frequency of offenses, Elliott and Ageton would have had findings similar to those of earlier self-report studies. The reason for this is that blacks and lower-class youths are disproportionately likely to commit a very large number of offenses. The use of an open-ended frequency response in this study allowed the researchers to pick up findings that eluded previous researchers because their response sets were limited to the low end of the frequency range. The authors also believe that the broader range of forty-seven offenses included in their study contributed to their distinctive findings. For example, previous self-report studies tended to exclude the more serious assault items, but these are the types of crimes that blacks are much more likely to engage in than whites. Thus, the omission of these kinds of offenses in previous self-report research tended to minimize racial differences in delinquency.

Elliott and Ageton are led to reject the conclusion of previous self-report studies that argued that the differences between races and classes are the result of processing biases by law-enforcement agents and are not traceable to behavioral differences between these groups. They tend to see at least "some" basis in the behavior of the offenders for the differences between races and classes in official processing. This, again, means that their results are more in line with official arrest data than data from most self-report studies. Furthermore, they argue that it is likely that it is the more frequent and serious offenders picked up in their study who are the ones who are likely to find themselves arrested and going through the official processing system. Past self-report studies tended to emphasize delinquents engaged in infrequent and not very serious acts. These were not the youths who were most likely to come into contact with the police; rather it is the delinquents who commit either very frequent or very serious acts who are most likely to come into official contact with the police. While Elliott and Ageton do not deny the existence of processing biases, they conclude that "it does appear that official correlates of delinquency also reflect real differences in the frequency and seriousness of delinquent acts."[31]

THE INVENTION OF DELINQUENCY: HISTORICAL RESEARCH

The final method to be discussed in this chapter is historical research. All of the methods discussed thus far involve collecting data on ongoing behaviors, but there are times when it is necessary to collect historical data. Obviously, if we want to know how something transpired in the past, or how some present structure came into being in the past, we need to gather information about the past. Gathering information about the past precludes the use of the methods discussed earlier in this chapter. For example, we cannot use participant observation, since such a technique requires that the researcher coexist with the people and/or events being studied. In many cases of historical research, the people involved in the past activities may be deceased, or at least no longer involved in those activities. In any case, it is certainly the case that the events and activities being studied are no longer taking place.

These same facts preclude real-life experiments of the type undertaken at Provo and Cambridge-Somerville, although it might be possible to simulate a past event in a laboratory experiment. Even if this were possible, however, it would only be a simulation and not a study of the historical events themselves. Finally, survey research may in some cases be used, but it is of only limited utility in historical research. If some of the people involved in a past event are still alive, we may want to survey them about past activities. However, depending on how far back we are delving, subjects' memories are likely to be hazy and, in most cases of interest, all of those involved are likely to be deceased. Thus, historical research requires a methodology different from any of those discussed up to this point.

The Child Savers

The specific work of primary concern in this section is Anthony M. Platt's *The Child Savers: The Invention of Delinquency.*[32] Originally Platt's doctoral dissertation, the text was written in the mid-1960s and was first published in 1969. It dealt with people and events that took place mainly in the latter part of the nineteenth century. Obviously, Platt had no first-hand experiences of the events and most, if not all, of the people involved must have been dead by the time Platt did his work. Thus, Platt could not be a participant observer, conduct field experiments, or do survey research on the events of interest to him. Instead he had to do historical research relying on such things as books, speeches, official documents, letters, diaries, and the like written during the period. The problem for the historical sociologist is how to make sense out of some past series of events on the basis of documents such as these. Further complicating matters is the fact that the researcher is often living in an entirely different era and may have difficulty understanding precisely what was taking place in the past. In addition, the researcher often approaches the past with points of view shaped by the era in which the researcher lives. This can make historical research more relevant to the contemporary scene, but it can also serve to distort findings about the past. In other words, contemporary concerns may cause the historical sociologist to come to distorted conclusions about the past. As we will see, this is one of the problems in Platt's research.

As is clear from the title, Platt is concerned with a group of people who came to be defined as "child savers." The child savers were a group of people who in the late nineteenth century helped to create programs and judicial and correctional institutions designed to handle "troublesome" youth. In Platt's view the origin of the modern idea of juvenile delinquency is to be found in the programs and ideas of the child savers. In other words, the child savers were, in Platt's view, responsible for inventing delinquency: "They brought attention to—and, in so doing, invented—new categories of youthful misbehavior which had been hitherto unappreciated."[33] In addition to analyzing the process by which the child savers created delinquency, Platt is interested in challenging the generally accepted, positive image of the child savers:

> The term 'child savers' is used to characterize a group of 'disinterested' reformers who regarded their cause as a matter of conscience and morality, serving no particular class or political interests. The child savers viewed themselves as altruists and humanitarians dedicated to rescuing those who were less fortunately placed in the social order. Their concern for 'purity,' 'salvation,' 'innocence,' 'corruption,' and 'protection' reflected a resolute belief in the righteousness of their mission.[34]

Platt is willing to grant the fact that many of the child savers may have had benign motives, but he feels that they had a variety of negative effects on adolescents, including diminishing their civil liberties and their privacy. Furthermore, although they were supposedly interested in protecting young people from the moral and physical dangers of modern society, they seemed to serve to aggravate such problems.

Instead of dealing with the child-saving movement in general, Platt chose to focus on the movement in Chicago, since it was in Illinois that the first juvenile court was founded in 1899. This decision, of course, served to make Platt's historical research more manageable, since he could focus on data dealing with a delimited geographic area rather than data on the nationwide child-saving movement.

The first task undertaken by Platt was to review the state of criminological theory at the close of the nineteenth century because that theory had a profound effect on the child-saving movement. The dominant view was that crime was a symptom of a pathology and that the pathology could be treated, at least in some cases, through a program of rehabilitation. While adult criminals tended to be seen as nonhuman and largely beyond rehabilitation, children could be treated if caught *before* they became adult, career criminals. Thus, adolescent criminal behavior was seen as "temporary and reversible."[35] In order to prevent them from developing into adult, career criminals, young people had to be isolated from adult criminals as well as the "brutish living conditions" in which they existed.[36] The reformatories were designed to perform these functions. They were often constructed in the country in order to rescue young people from the horrors of the city and return them to the supposedly saner and simpler life in the countryside.

While reformatories did succeed in these purposes, they had a variety of negative effects on adolescents. Young offenders were to be assigned to reformatories without a trial, without due process, and with indeterminate sentences. Within the reformatories, inmates were to be subjected to "military drill, physical exercise, and constant supervision," and they were to be taught "the value of sobriety, thrift, industry, prudence, 'realistic' ambition, and adjustment."[37] In other words, these young people were to be deprived of their civil liberties for an indeterminate amount of time and molded to suit an ideal image held by those middle-class individuals who created and maintained these institutions.

In addition to reformatories, Platt was interested in the creation of separate juvenile courts, or special tribunals "created by statute to determine the legal status of 'troublesome' children."[38] Although founded with supposedly humanitarian concerns, these courts went far beyond such concerns and brought under government control a series of activities that had previously been either ignored or dealt with informally, such as "drinking, begging, roaming the streets, frequenting dance-halls and movies, fighting, sexuality, staying out late at night, and incorrigibility."[39] As Platt saw it, the middle-class reformers behind the juvenile court movement were seeking to control behaviors associated primarily with lower-class youths. In order to achieve their objective of saving adolescents (primarily from themselves and their own actions), judges in these courts frequently handled the law in a very loose and informal manner.

Platt offers a series of conclusions about the child-saving movement that he feels contradicts popular images of it. The child savers did not, in his view, usher in new policies, but rather supported traditional policies. The child savers were middle-class conservatives who were trying to protect such things as parental authority and rural values from such perceived threats as urbanization, industrialization, and the influx of various immigrant groups. They operated on the assumption that adolescents were to be treated as dependents. While they had a set of paternalistic and romantic attitudes, these attitudes were clearly backed up by power and force. It was primarily the poor children from the cities who suffered the "experiences of control, restraint and punishment."[40]

Interestingly, in his 1977 introduction to the second edition of *The Child Savers,* Platt expresses some second thoughts about his conclusions that cast some light on the problems of historical research. As we said earlier, historical research is often undertaken from the perspective of the time in which it is done. Platt sees his work as a product of the 1960s, with its political militancy and radical consciousness. It is this that led him to see the child-saving movement in a new light, but it is also what, from his perspective in 1977, had led him somewhat astray.

Like others in the 1960s, Platt feels he was too prone to moralistic criticism, as well as to a naïve belief that the state can solve the problems he underscored. Furthermore, he feels he placed too much emphasis on criticizing the motivations and professional ambitions of the child savers. Instead, he now feels he should have placed this within a broader structural context and seen it as "part of a much larger movement to readjust institutions to conform to the requirements of the emerging system of corporate capitalism."[41] More specifically, the child-saving movement was one of a range of new forms of social control aimed at protecting the power and privilege of the middle and upper classes. Thus, by 1977 Platt retained his critical view of the child-saving movement, but now saw it as but a part of a wider movement to protect the interests of the capitalist system. If anything, this is a more far-reaching critique than the one Platt arrived at in his original work where he was inclined to restrict his criticisms to the people involved in the movement.

Reexamining the Invention of Delinquency

Platt's views were highly controversial. John Hagan and Jeffrey Leon saw them as part of a Marxian approach to social history.[42] Specifically, Hagan and Leon feel that the Marxian approach adopted by Platt (and others) biased his conclusions. They feel that "no evidence is provided that passage of juvenile court legislation resulted in an increase in the number of juveniles incarcerated, that the industrial elite benefited significantly as a result of this incarceration, or that the 'ruling class' played any direct role in the passage of this legislation."[43] Specifically, they accuse Platt of failing to prove that the sponsorship of societal elites caused the success of the child-saving movement. They seek to test out their assertions about the fallacies of the Marxian approach in an historical study of Canadian delinquency legislation.

In their historical analysis, Hagan and Leon draw on a number of data sources including

> historical accounts written by participants in, and observers of the child-saving movement; personal correspondence and accounts drawn from the archives of leading advocates of delinquency legislation; proceedings of conferences concerned with child welfare; reports of government commissions; legislative debates; and statistics drawn from the Toronto Juvenile Court.[44]

In addition, the authors relied heavily on the correspondence between the two leading advocates of delinquency legislation in Canada. They pick up the story of the child savers in Canada with the passage of two laws in 1857 and briefly describe legislation and legislative actions through the period of main concern to Platt and into the twentieth century.

One issue they address immediately is whether the founding of juvenile courts led to increased juvenile imprisonment. Toronto established a juvenile court in 1912, and in the preceding year 123 youths had been sent to industrial schools. In 1912, the first year of operation of the courts, the number declined to 71. More detailed data from later years on a variety of forms of institutionalization of juveniles indicates that at no time in the ensuing 40-year period "does the *total* institutionalized population exceed the number sent to industrial school alone in the year before court operations began."[45] In addition, Hagan and Leon found little evidence of interest in, or activity in behalf of, child-saving legislation by the industrial elite or the ruling class.

Instead of seeing the development of Canadian delinquency legislation in terms of class interests, Hagan and Leon see them more as the result of ongoing organiza-

Table 2.4 Uses and Limitations of Major Research Methods

The use and limitations of four research methods discussed in this chapter—participant observation, experiment, survey research, and historical. No single method is adequate in itself to answer all sociological questions. You may find it helpful to refer to this table as you read about various studies in subsequent chapters.

QUESTIONS	PARTICIPANT OBSERVATION	EXPERIMENT	SURVEY RESEARCH	HISTORICAL
Typical cost	Inexpensive (but much research time required)	Depends on equipment used, size of staff, and duration; can be very inexpensive but is occasionally very costly	Depends on sample size and whether questionnaire or interview is used (interview is generally more costly)	Inexpensive (but may take years to collect needed information)
Size of sample or group or number of subjects	Usually small	Limited by funds and time—usually small	Depends on size of population, funds and time—can be very large	Limited by availability of data that have survived
Type of interaction with subjects of study	Face to face—formal or informal	Face to face—formal or informal	If questionnaire used, indirect (by mail); if interview used, face to face but formal	Usually indirect; an exception would be oral history taken from survivors
Type of problem	Theory and variables generated in process of research—not controlled by researcher	Theory and variables known in advance and controlled by researcher	Theory and variables known in advance but not controlled by researcher	Theory and variables sometimes known in advance, more often generated in research—not controlled by researcher
Can the independent variable be manipulated by the researcher? (Can events be timed?)	No	Yes	No	No
How are the variables controlled?	Through testing and revision of the theory	By random assignment to experiment and control groups	Through statistical analysis	By comparison of different units in history
Can the results be generalized to a larger population?	Yes (only if groups have been selected randomly)	No (except when random sample is used)	Yes (by random selection of cases)	Possible, if more than one historical case has been used
Can it be used to find out the distribution of a variable (for example, age) in a population	No	No	Yes	Yes, if data are available for a population or a universe
Where does the research take place?	In the field: In limited area	In the lab or in the field	In the field: In extended area or several areas	Archives, libraries, communities where events occurred
Criteria for selection of groups, subjects, or cases	Nature of the study, availability	Convenience	Random sample from the population	Availability, theoretical significance

tional processes. They focus on how individual entrepreneurs can define issues and how these definitions can shape organizational direction. Thus, to them the key dynamic of delinquency legislation is to be found within the court organization. This intra-organizational perspective stands in contrast to the Marxian perspective that focuses on the way the upper classes shape organizational policy and direction. Operating with a different theoretical perspective, with a different data set, and in another country, Hagan and Leon come to very different conclusions than Platt about the history of the child-saving movement.

CONCLUSION

The purpose of this chapter has been to give you some insight into how research is done. As is evident, methods must be matched to what you want to find out. When you want to investigate particular social processes, such as interaction between the police and juveniles, the best method is to go out and see what is going on. When you are interested in causation and are able to manipulate the variable in which you are interested, such as who receives a particular form of help or counseling, the experiment is much to be preferred because its findings are unlikely to be spurious. When you want to know how some trait is distributed in a population and how one such trait is related to another, the appropriate method is to select a representative sample and use interviewers or a questionnaire to collect the data. When you are interested in past events, the appropriate technique is historical research. All of these methods have provided fundamental evidence on the social problems that are discussed throughout this text.

SUMMARY

1. This chapter is concerned with introducing the student to the major methods of doing sociological research.
2. The subject of juvenile delinquency is used to illustrate the various types of research.
3. The first research method discussed is participant observation. With this method sociologists witness the events they are attempting to study and carefully and systematically record their observations. Sociologists using this method usually have long-term interaction with the people they are studying.
4. The participation-observation method was illustrated by the study by Piliavin and Briar in which they spent nine months riding in police patrol cars observing police encounters with juveniles. Also used to illustrate this method was a study by Black and Reiss in which they, too, spent time with the police observing encounters between police and juveniles. Black and Reiss's work serves to support some of Piliavin and Briar's conclusions and extend and call into question others. One thing is clear—the study of any social issue requires a number of different observations at different times and at different places.
5. The second research method discussed was the experimental method. While in participation observation researchers have no control over the events they are studying, in the experiment researchers attempt to exert at least some control over what is being studied. Experiments involve at least one independent variable over which researchers have

control, a dependent variable that researchers expect the independent variable to affect, controls that are used to rule out the possibility that some factor other than the independent variable could cause changes in the dependent variable, statistical analysis comparing the experimental and control groups, and replication of the study to be sure that results are not the result of mere chance.

6. The experimental method was illustrated by two real-life experiments, the Cambridge-Somerville experiment on delinquency prevention conducted between 1937 and 1945 and the Provo experiment on delinquency treatment conducted between 1959 and 1965.

7. The third method discussed was survey research. Survey research involves the use of questionnaires to collect data, usually from a large number of respondents.

8. Two studies utilizing survey research were reported. The first, the Richmond youth study conducted by Travis Hirschi, studied junior-high and high-school students in an effort to uncover the causes of juvenile delinquency. Hirschi relied largely on the self-reports of those studied in determining whether a respondent was or was not a juvenile delinquent. The second study, by Elliott and Ageton, attempts to deal with the differences that are usually found between self-report surveys and data derived from police and arrest records. They show that by correcting certain problems in self-report research, results from this type of research can be brought more in line with official arrest data.

9. The final method discussed was historical research. In doing research on the past, one cannot use participant observation, experiments, or survey research. Instead one must do historical research, relying on such things as books, speeches, official documents, letters, diaries, and the like written during the period being studied.

10. To illustrate historical research, Anthony Platt's study of the "child savers" was discussed. The child savers were a group of people who, in the late nineteenth century, helped to create programs and judicial and correctional institutions designed to handle "troublesome" youth. Through his historical research, Platt felt he was able to cast new light on the child savers. Also discussed is an effort by Hagan and Leon to test out some of Platt's assertions in the context of the history of the child savers in Canada.

SUGGESTED READING

P. G. Hammond, ed., *Sociologists at Work: Essays on the Craft of Social Research.* New York: Basic Books, 1964. A number of well-known sociologists describe their research experiences.

Land Humphreys, *Tearoom Trade: Impersonal Sex in Public Places,* enlarged ed. Chicago: Aldine, 1975. An interesting and highly controversial piece of sociological research employing participant observation.

John P. Robinson and Robert Meadow, *Polls Apart.* Cabin John, Md.: Seven Locks Press, 1982. A look at survey research, especially political polls, with special attention to procedural errors that make such polls inaccurate.

William B. Shaffir, Robert A. Stebbins, and Alan Turowetz, eds., *Fieldwork Experience: Qualitative Approaches to Social Research.* New York: St. Martin's Press, 1980. A collection of essays on fieldwork research including many examples of participant observation.

J. L. Simmons and George J. McCall, *Social Research: The Craft of Finding Out.* New York: Macmillan, 1985. A short nontechnical introduction to social research aimed at the undergraduate student.

Darrell J. Steffensmeier and Robert M. Terry, eds., *Examining Deviance Experimentally: Selected Readings.* Sherman Oaks, Cal.: Alfred Publishing Co., 1975. Use of experimental methods to study deviance.

Arthur L. Stinchcombe, *Theoretical Methods in Social History.* New York: Academic Press, 1978. A complex and provocative view of the historical method from the sociological point of view.

FOOTNOTES

[1]Edmund J. Brown, Timothy J. Flanagan, and Maureen McCleod, eds., *Sourcebook of Criminal Justice Statistics—1982.* U.S. Department of Justice, Bureau of Justice Statistics (Washington, D.C.: U.S. Government Printing Office, 1984), p. 464.

[2]Travis Hirschi, *Causes of Delinquency* (Berkeley: University of California Press, 1969).

[3]Irvin Piliavin and Scott Briar, "Police Encounters with Juveniles," *American Journal of Sociology,* 70 (1964), 206–214.

[4]Albert J. Reiss, Jr., *The Police and the Public* (New Haven, Conn.: Yale University Press, 1971).

[5]Piliavin and Briar, *op. cit.,* p. 209.

[6]*Ibid.,* pp. 210–211.

[7]*Ibid.,* p. 212.

[8]Donald J. Black and Albert J. Reiss, Jr., "Police Control of Juveniles," *American Sociological Review,* 35 (1970), 63–77.

[9]*Ibid.,* p. 65.

[10]*Ibid.,* p. 65.

[11]*Ibid.,* p. 66.

[12]*Ibid.,* pp. 66–67.

[13]*Ibid.,* p. 72.

[14]*Ibid.,* p. 75.

[15]Wiley B. Sanders, ed., *Juvenile Offenders for a Thousand Years: Selected Readings from Anglo-Saxon Times to 1900* (Chapel Hill: University of North Carolina Press, 1970).

[16]William McCord and Joan McCord, *Origins of Crime: A New Evaluation of the Cambridge-Somerville Youth Study* (New York: Columbia University Press, 1959).

[17]*Ibid.,* pp. 4–5.

[18]LaMar T. Empey and Maynard L. Erickson, *The Provo Experiment: Evaluating Community Control of Delinquency* (Lexington, Mass.: Lexington Books, 1972).

[19]*Ibid.,* p. 10.

[20]*Ibid.,* p. 18.

[21]*Ibid.,* p. 25.

[22]*Ibid.,* p. 27.

[23]*Ibid.*

[24]Of course, the incarcerated control group was behind bars most of the time while the "incarcerated" experimental group was free because it was involved in the two phases of the Provo program.

[25]Empey and Erickson, *op. cit.,* p. 81.

[26]Hirschi, *op. cit.*

[27]Delbert S. Elliott and Suzanne S. Ageton, "Reconciling Race and Class Differences in Self-Reported and Official Estimates of Delinquency," *American Sociological Review,* 45 (1980), 95–110.

[28]*Ibid.,* p. 99.

[29]*Ibid.*

[30]*Ibid.,* p. 100.

[31]*Ibid.,* p. 107.

[32]Anthony M. Platt, *The Child Savers: The Invention of Delinquency,* 2nd enlarged ed. (Chicago: University of Chicago Press, 1977).

[33]*Ibid.,* pp. 3–4.

[34]*Ibid.,* p. 3.

[35]*Ibid.,* p. 45.

[36]*Ibid.*

[37]*Ibid.,* pp. 54–55.

[38]*Ibid.,* p. 137.

[39]*Ibid.,* p. 139.

[40]*Ibid.,* p. 177.

[41]*Ibid.,* p. xix.

[42]John Hagan and Jeffrey Leon, "Rediscovering Delinquency: Social History, Political Ideology and the Sociology of Law," *American Sociological Review,* 42 (1977), 587–598.

[43]*Ibid.,* p. 590.

[44]*Ibid.*

[45]*Ibid.,* p. 591.

II

Deviant Behavior

Can a man take fire in his bosom
and his clothes not
be burned?
Can one go on
hot coals and his
feet not be burned?
Proverbs 6:27,28
a
b
Bruce N. Dean

3 *Problems with Drugs and Alcohol*

Our basic concern in this chapter is with *psychoactive drugs,* including heroin, marijuana, cocaine, and alcohol. The defining characteristic of these drugs is the fact that they have some fairly *rapid, noticeable effect on the user's mind or emotions.* Not all drugs are psychoactive drugs. If you take vitamin C every morning in the belief that it will help maintain you in good health, you are not using a psychoactive drug; vitamins do not make you feel different immediately after taking them. On the other hand, if you smoke a marijuana cigarette or drink a shot of whiskey in anticipation of feeling better and/or more energetic, you *are* using a psychoactive drug. You feel the effects of marijuana and whiskey as soon as they stimulate your nervous system. It is generally agreed that psychoactive drugs *do* affect the nervous system, although it is important to remember that *there are major individual, situational, and cultural differences in the way people respond to psychoactive drugs.*

In discussing the use of psychoactive drugs we will try very hard to avoid the *chemicalist fallacy:* the assumption that a given drug has an invariable chemical effect on everyone who takes it.[1] Since the term *addiction* is often used to imply that drugs have inevitable effects on people, it has tended to fall into disfavor among some experts.[2] Among the efforts to clarify matters conceptually is Erich Goode's differentiation among physical, psychic, and behavioral dependency.

DRUGS: SOME BASIC DEFINITIONS

Types of Drug Dependence

Some drugs (for example, heroin) produce *physical dependence* because despite what the individual thinks, he or she develops a physiological need for the drug. Thus, physical dependence is traceable to the qualities of the drug itself. Other drugs, such as cocaine, produce mainly *psychic dependence,* or a pleasurable feeling that the individual wishes to renew whenever possible. Thus, psychic dependence is traceable mainly to the reaction of the individual taking the drug, and *not* the action of the drug itself. Psychic dependence can lead to *behavior dependence,* or the actual taking of a variety of steps to obtain and use the drug. Behavior dependence may even "become compulsive, repetitive and even destructive: the user will give up previously valued desirables, like money, health, a job, and marriage, just to continue taking the drug."[3] In coming to emphasize psychic and behavior dependence, sociologists are making the point that most often the user, not the drug, determines dependence. Also pointing to the fact that the chemistry of a drug can be of secondary importance is the fact that variations in use and response occur with any drug in different cultures and at different times.

When we use the term *addiction* in this chapter it will be restricted to the idea of physical dependence. Addiction generally involves tolerance, withdrawal, and a craving for a drug. *Tolerance* is the tendency for users to become increasingly accustomed to a drug, with the result that they require larger and larger doses to get the effect they seek from it.[4] Tolerance is commonly observed in alcoholics and heroin addicts.

When addicts cannot obtain a certain drug, they may go through a traumatic process called *withdrawal.* Symptoms of withdrawal from heroin, for example, resemble a severe attack of the flu, and may include sweating, shivering, vomiting, diarrhea, fever, sleeplessness, and alternate periods of frantic activity and total lethargy. The self-reports of addicts also convey a sense of their intensely felt malaise—a terrible yet indefinable feeling of ill-being. Symptoms comparable to these can be observed in the less severe agonies of someone breaking a cigarette habit.

Another indicator of addiction, which is more behavioral, is the addict's desperate single-minded *craving* for and pursuit of the drug when withdrawal distress occurs. When any motivation toward a single object becomes this strong, the intensity of other motivations decreases, and the person may lose all other interests.

Thus, despite the sociological emphasis on psychic and behavior dependence, there *is* evidence of physical dependence (addiction) created by some drugs. Thus, the properties of a drug are a good starting point for studying the significance that people have attached to different drugs. Once we know how a drug tends to affect the nervous system, we can trace the way in which different cultural and personal frameworks may modify this effect.

Types of Psychoactive Drugs

Psychoactive drugs ("controlled substances") are usually divided into five major categories: narcotics, depressants, stimulants, hallucinogens, and cannabis. (See Table 3.1 for a summary of information available about these broad types of drugs as well as many specific drugs.) *Narcotics* create a sense of euphoria in the user and also tend to cause drowsiness. The best-known narcotics are heroin, opium, morphine, and methadone. *Depressants* slow down the functioning of the central nervous system. This often results in a decline in anxiety and has a calming effect on the individual. Depressants also retard the action of a number of the body's organs. Among the drugs classified as depressants are barbiturates and a variety of other sedatives. *Stimulants* increase alertness and energize and excite the user. Natural stimulants include caffeine (in coffee, tea, and some colas), nicotine (in tobacco products, especially cigarettes), and cocaine, which is derived from the leaves of a South American bush. Amphetamines (collectively known as "speed" and most commonly found in diet pills) are synthetic stimulants.

What distinguishes *hallucinogens,* as the name suggests, is that they can cause hallucinations and distorted perceptions. Among the major hallucinogens are LSD, peyote, mescaline, and PCP ("angel dust"). Goode reports a number of experiences of people under the influence of hallucinogens, including the feeling of viewing movies with one's eyes closed ("eyeball movies"), simultaneous stimulation of several senses ("seeing" sounds), perception of reality as multileveled, seeing the world as in constant flux, a tendency to exaggerate things, emotional extremes, feeling of timelessness, and irrationalism.[5] Thus, the hallucinogens do not fit into any of the other categories because their effects are altogether different. In any case, categories of psychoactive drugs are merely suggestive, not definitive. As we have already pointed out, and will have more to say about later, different people in different social settings will have different experiences from the same psychoactive substances.

Finally, *cannabis* usually gives the user a sense of euphoria, serves to relax inhibitions, and is sometimes disorienting. The best-known varieties of cannabis are hashish and, most importantly, marijuana. At one time marijuana was considered an hallucinogen, but most experts now utilize a separate cannabis category, perhaps because marijuana is by far the most widely used illegal drug in the United States today. Some of the typical ways in which someone is affected by marijuana are: "a sense of one's mind wandering, a kind of stream of consciousness; a sensation that time is slowed down."[6] In short, marijuana often serves to enhance all sensations and activities.

PART I: THE PROBLEM

The most basic problem in this area is the large, and in some cases increasing, use and misuse of various drugs. In this section we will focus on the use of several of the drugs mentioned in Figure 3.1—narcotics (opium, especially heroin), marijuana, cocaine, and LSD. Along the way, we will also discuss alcohol, which is often considered a drug even though it is not listed in Figure 3.1. We want to see how usage patterns have changed and how prevalent the use of these drugs is.

Patterns of Narcotics Use

Opium

Opium in significant amounts was introduced in the United States in the 1850s by Chinese laborers on the West Coast. Other historical events, especially the Civil War, converged to lay the groundwork for an opium problem in the United States. The search by soldiers for painkillers led some of them to opium and the habit spread in some cases from those wounded in the Civil War to their families.[7] At this time, too, bottlers of popular patent medicines began to use opium as an active ingredient. Yet people still had no clear conception of opium addiction.

The two decades between 1890 and 1909 saw a dramatic increase in the amount of opium imported into the United States—greater, for example, than the amounts imported during the Civil War.[8] The increase coincided with the discovery in 1898 that heroin could be used as a painkiller; it could be produced by binding morphine (a derivative of opium) and acetic acid.

Table 3.1 Major Types of Psychoactive Drugs: Uses and Effects
This table summarizes available information about many commonly used psychoactive drugs.

	DRUGS	SCHEDULE	TRADE OR OTHER NAMES	MEDICAL USES	PHYSICAL DEPENDENCE
NARCOTICS	Opium	II, III, V	Dover's Powder, Paregoric, Parepectolin	Analgesic, antidiarrheal	High
	Morphine	II, III	Morphine, Pectoral Syrup	Analgesic, antitussive	
	Codeine	II, III, V	Codeine, Empirin Compound with Codeine, Robitussin A-C	Analgesic, antitussive	Moderate
	Heroin	I	Diacetylmorphine, Horse, Smack	Under investigation	High
	Hydromorphone	II	Dilaudid	Analgesic	
	Meperidine (Pethidine)		Demerol, Pethadol	Analgesic	
	Methadone		Dolophine, Methadone, Methadose	Analgesic, heroin substitute	
	Other Narcotics	I, II, III, IV, V	LAAM, Leritine, Levo-Dromoran, Percodan, Tussionex, Fentanyl, Darvon,* Talwin,* Lomotil	Analgesic, antidiarrheal, antitussive	High-Low
DEPRESSANTS	Chloral Hydrate	IV	Noctec, Somnos	Hypnotic	Moderate
	Barbiturates	II, III, IV	Amobarbital, Phenobarbital, Butisol, Phenoxbarbital, Secobarbital, Tuinal	Anesthetic, anticonvulsant, sedative, hypnotic	High-Moderate
	Glutethimide	III	Doriden	Sedative, hypnotic	High
	Methaqualone	II	Optimil, Parest, Quaalude, Somnafac, Sopor		
	Benzodiazepines	IV	Ativan, Azene, Clonopin, Dalmane, Diazepam, Librium, Serax, Tranxene, Valium, Verstran	Anti-anxiety, anticonvulsant, sedative, hypnotic	Low
	Other Depressants	III, IV	Equanil, Miltown, Noludar Placidyl, Valmid	Anti-anxiety, sedative, hypnotic	Moderate
STIMULANTS	Cocaine†	II	Coke, Flake, Snow	Local anesthetic	Possible
	Amphetamines	II, III	Biphetamine, Delcobese, Desoxyn, Dexedrine, Mediatric	Hyperkinesis, narcolepsy, weight control	
	Phenmetrazine	II	Preludin		
	Methylphenidate		Ritalin		
	Other Stimulants	III, IV	Adipex, Bacarate, Cylert, Didrex, Ionamin, Plegine, Pre-Sate, Sanorex, Tenuate, Tepanil, Voranil		
HALLUCINOGENS	LSD	I	Acid, Microdot	None	None
	Mescaline and Peyote		Mesc, Buttons, Cactus		
	Amphetamine Variants		2,5-DMA,PMA,STP,MDA, MMDA,TMA,DOM,DOB		Unknown
	Phencyclidine	II	PCP, Angel Dust, Hog	Veterinary anesthetic	Degree unknown
	Phencyclidine Analogs	I	PCE, PCPy, TCP	None	
	Other Hallucinogens		Bufotenine, Ibogaine, DMT, DET, Psilocybin, Psilocyn		None
CANNABIS	Marihuana	I	Pot, Acapulco Gold, Grass, Reefer, Sinsemilla, Thai Sticks	Under investigation	Degree unknown
	Tetrahydrocannabinol		THC		
	Hashish		Hash	None	
	Hashish Oil		Hash Oil		

*Not designated a narcotic under the CSA
†Designated a narcotic under the CSA

PSYCHO-LOGICAL DEPENDENCE	TOL-ERANCE	DURATION OF EFFECTS (IN HOURS)	USUAL METHODS OF ADMINISTRATION	POSSIBLE EFFECTS	EFFECTS OF OVERDOSE	WITHDRAWAL SYNDROME
High	Yes	3–6	Oral, smoked	Euphoria, drowsiness, respiratory depression, constricted pupils, nausea	Slow and shallow breathing, clammy skin, convulsions, coma, possible death	Watery eyes, runny nose, yawning, loss of appetite, irritability, tremors, panic, chills and sweating, cramps, nausea
			Oral, injected, smoked			
Moderate			Oral, injected			
High			Injected, sniffed, smoked			
		12–24	Oral, injected			
High-Low		Variable				
Moderate	Possible	5–8	Oral	Slurred speech, disorientation, drunken behavior without odor of alcohol	Shallow respiration, cold and clammy skin, dilated pupils, weak and rapid pulse, coma, possible death	Anxiety, insomnia, tremors, delirium, convulsions, possible death
High-Moderate	Yes	1–16	Oral, injected			
High		4–8				
Low						
Moderate						
High	Possible	1–2	Sniffed, injected	Increased alertness, excitation, euphoria, increased pulse rate and blood pressure, insomnia, loss of appetite	Agitation, increase in body temperature, hallucinations, convulsions, possible death	Apathy, long periods of sleep, irritability, depression, disorientation
	Yes	2–4	Oral, injected			
			Oral			
Degree unknown	Yes	8–12	Oral	Illusions and hallucinations, poor perception of time and distance	Longer, more intense "trip" episodes, psychosis, possible death	Withdrawal syndrome not reported
		Up to days	Oral, injected			
High		Variable	Smoked, oral, injected			
Degree unknown	Possible		Oral, injected, smoked, sniffed			
Moderate	Yes	2–4	Smoked, oral	Euphoria, relaxed inhibitions, increased appetite, disoriented behavior	Fatigue, paranoia, possible psychosis	Insomnia, hyperactivity, and decreased appetite occasionally reported

(continued)

Table 3.1 Major Types of Psychoactive Drugs: Uses and Effects (*Continued*)

The Controlled Substances Act sets forth the findings which must be made to put a substance in any of the five schedules. These are as follows (Section 202(b)):

Schedule I

(A) The drug or other substance has a high potential for abuse.
(B) The drug or other substance has no currently accepted medical use in treatment in the United States.
(C) There is a lack of accepted safety for use of the drug or other substance under medical supervision.

Schedule II

(A) The drug or other substance has a high potential for abuse.
(B) The drug or other substance has a currently accepted medical use in treatment in the United States or a currently accepted medical use with severe restrictions.
(C) Abuse of the drug or other substances may lead to severe psychological or physical dependence.

Schedule III

(A) The drug or other substance has a potential for abuse less than the drugs or other substances in Schedules I and II.
(B) The drug or other substance has a currenty accepted medical use in treatment in the United States.
(C) Abuse of the drug or other substance may lead to moderate or low physical dependence or high psychological dependence.

Schedule IV

(A) The drug or other substance has a low potential for abuse relative to the drugs or other substances in Schedule III.
(B) The drug or other substance has a currently accepted medical use in treatment in the United States.
(C) Abuse of the drug or other substance may lead to limited physical dependence or psychological dependence relative to the drugs or other substances in Schedule III.

Schedule V

(A) The drug or other substance has a low potential for abuse relative to the drugs or other substances in Schedule IV.
(B) The drug or other substance has a currently accepted medical use in treatment in the United States.
(C) Abuse of the drug or other substance may lead to limited physical dependence or psychological dependence relative to the drugs or other substances in Schedule IV.

Source: U.S. Department of Justice, Drug Enforcement Administration, "Controlled Substances: Use, Abuse and Effects" (Washington, D.C., U.S. Government Printing Office, 1979).

With opium (as heroin) now available in a convenient (and much more powerful) powdered form, it began to be used more widely, and the public therefore took more notice of it. In the first two decades of this century, physicians began to speak of addiction to opiates as a disease. In this period, organized medicine and pharmacy stopped classifying opiate addiction with habituation to alcohol, tobacco, and caffeine, and assigned it a significance of its own.[9] Once this distinction was made, public policy took a definite line outlawing the sale or use of opiates—without the wavering that we will see in the case of alcohol.

Heroin

It is heroin that has come to be considered *the* drug problem of the twentieth century, even though no more than 1 percent of the American population has ever used the drug.[10] Compared to the opium users at the turn of the century, modern heroin addicts tend to be younger, and more likely to be male, urban dwellers, lower in socioeconomic status, and members of minority groups.[11]

There are no exact figures, of course, on the number of heroin addicts, but one estimate puts the number at about one-half million Americans.[12] In New York City, which has a large portion of the nation's addicts, it was said in 1982 that "every indicator of heroin abuse is up."[13] The number of people treated for heroin overdoses in hospital emergency rooms increased almost 100 percent between 1978 and 1980.[14] Other indices of this rise in New York City include increases in arrests, robbery and burglary reports, detoxification admissions, overdoses, and overdose deaths. For the United States as a whole, deaths from heroin overdoses rose by 63 percent between 1980 and 1983.[15] Nor is an increase in heroin addiction restricted to the United States. The number of heroin addicts appears to be growing in Great Britain, with one estimate putting the number at 10,000 addicts in 1980.[16] And the heroin problem is not restricted to capitalistic societies, either. In 1970 there were only about 250 known heroin addicts in Yugoslavia, but by 1978 there were 5,678 registered addicts. It is estimated that there were actually ten times that number.[17] In spite of growing heroin problems in other societies, the United States still has far and away the largest number of heroin addicts in the world. About 8 billion dollars worth of heroin was sold in the United States in 1980.[18]

Patterns of Marijuana Use

Although marijuana use has a very long history,[19] the most dramatic changes have taken place in the last few decades. In the 18-to-25-year-old age group, only about 4 percent of the population had ever smoked pot in 1962, but 20 years later, in 1982, that figure had leaped to 64 percent.[20] It is estimated that about 53 million people had tried the drug at least once in their lives.[21] Retail sales of marijuana reached 24 billion dollars in 1980.[22] Marijuana grew in importance in the late 1960s and early 1970s with its popularity among students.[23] However, its popularity appears to have peaked.[24] For example, the percentage of high-school students who tried marijuana at least once in the preceding year peaked in 1978 and has been declining since.[25] One contributor to this decline may be the increasing belief among students that marijuana poses a "great risk" of harming them. In 1978, 35 percent of students expressed such a fear, but by 1981 that number had grown to 60 percent.[26]

Trends in Lifetime Drug Use for Sixth- and Eighth- through Twelfth-Graders, 1969–1981

Figure 3.1

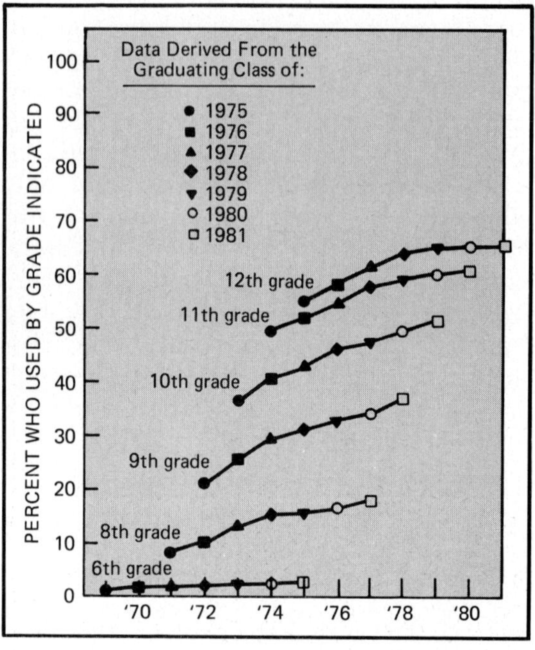

Figure 3.2

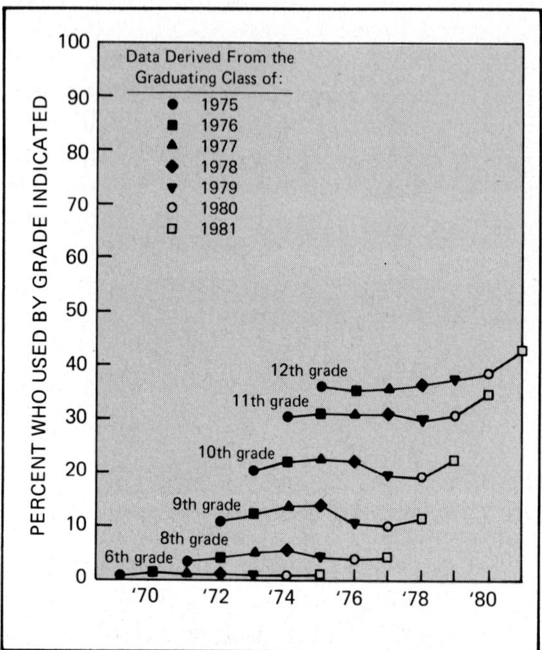

Figure 3.3

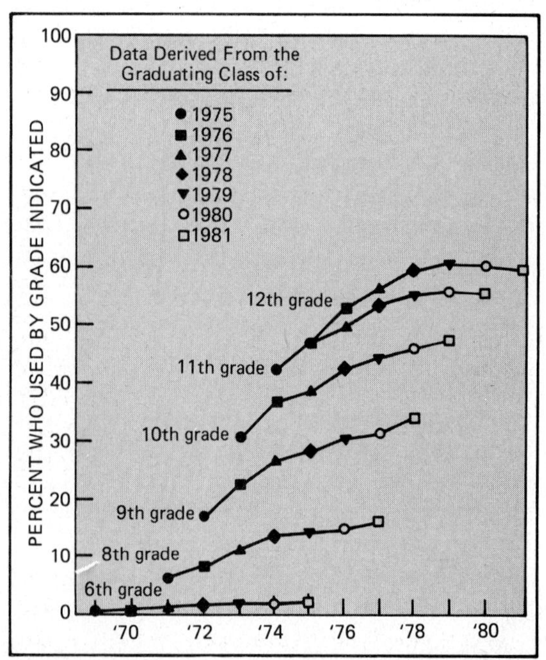

Figure 3.1 reports use of any illicit drug; Figure 3.2 reports use of any illicit drug other than marijuana; Figure 3.3 reports use of marijuana. In general, we can say that use of drugs among students in these grades is on the upswing. One exception is the slight decline in lifetime prevalence in use of marijuana among older students.

Source: Lloyd D. Johnston, Jerald G. Bachman, and Patrick M. O'Malley, *Highlights from Student Drug Use in America: 1975–1981* (Washington, D.C.: National Institute on Drug Abuse, 1981), p. 59.

Figure 3.4 Prevalence and Recency of Use

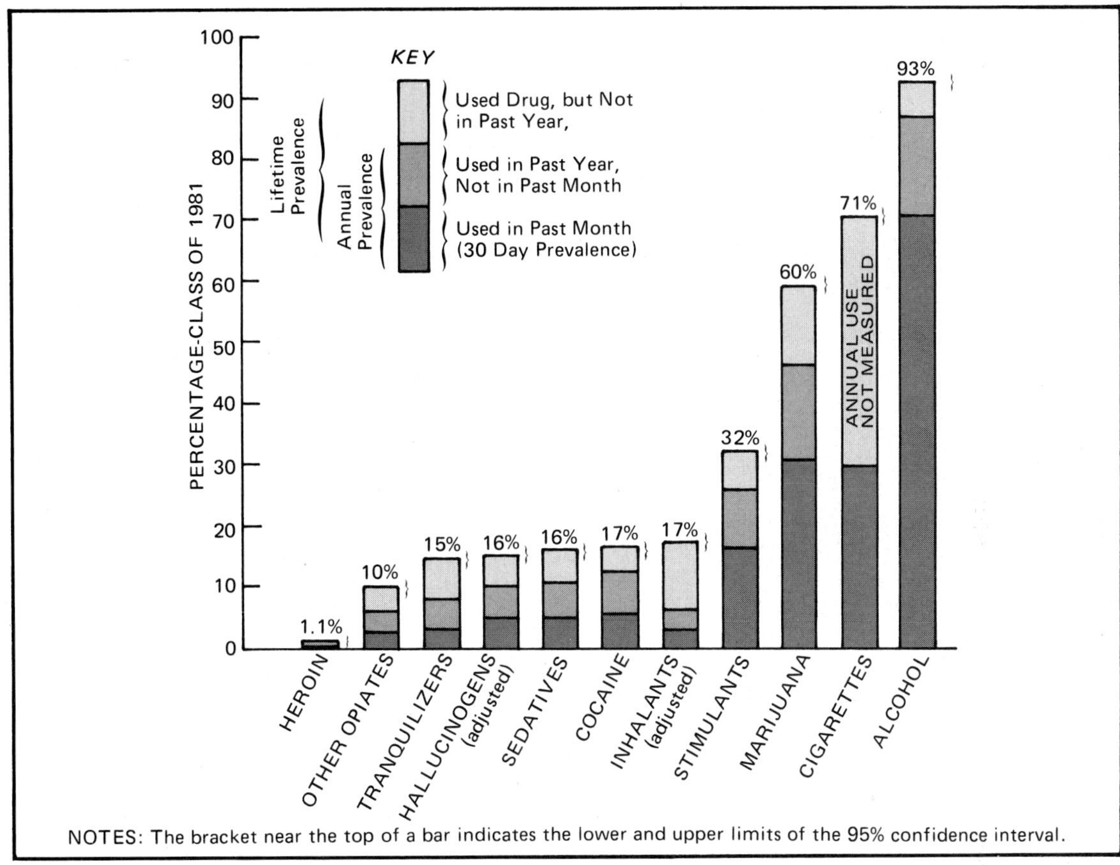

For the class of 1981 and in terms of lifetime prevalence, alcohol is the most used drug, while heroin is the least used. For these two drugs, as well as nine others, data are reported not only on lifetime prevalence but also on use in the last 30 days, in the last year but not the last month, and in one's lifetime but not in the past year.

Source: Lloyd D. Johnston, Jerald G. Bachman, and Patrick M. O'Malley, *Highlights from Student Drug Use in America: 1975–1981* (Washington, D.C.: National Institute on Drug Abuse, 1981), p. 59.

Patterns of Cocaine Use

While marijuana use may be declining, the use of cocaine seems to be increasing. While virtually unknown in 1962, cocaine use underwent what the Director of the National Institute on Drug Abuse called "an explosive increase,"[27] so that it was estimated that by 1982 about 22 million Americans had tried cocaine.[28] However, there is evidence that in the last few years the growth in cocaine use has leveled off.[29] It is widely believed that by 1980 dollar sales of cocaine were outstripping sales of marijuana,[30] 29 billion dollars in retail sales versus 24 billion dollars in sales for marijuana.[31] As many as 10 million Americans may be regular users.

Patterns of Alcohol Use

Alcohol has been a more constant feature of the American experience than has cocaine, marijuana, or opium (or heroin). In

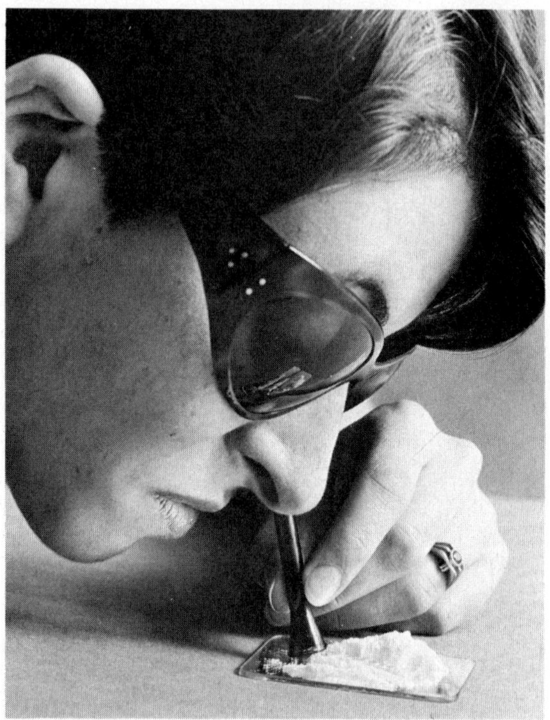

Marijuana use among young people grew dramatically in the 1960s and 1970s, but it appears to have peaked in the late 1970s and is now declining. The dramatic increase in cocaine use is more recent, but it too appears to have leveled off in the last few years. (Left, Ira Berger/Woodfin Camp & Assoc.; right, Tannenbaum/Sygma)

America, its use has always been accorded respectability within large sectors of the population, even when it was outlawed during Prohibition. Excessive drinking, severely frowned upon as it is, does not as readily inspire fear, loathing, and ostracism as does the slightest involvement with heroin, for example. Thus, change in alcohol use has been more gradual, and the differences in usage patterns, a matter of degree, not of kind.

Historical Background

Looking at the history of alcohol use in America, we see that the colonial era was characterized by near universal use of alcohol, with many persons drinking moderately, but steadily. By the middle of the nineteenth century, however, Americans had developed considerable *social ambivalence* about alcohol use.[32] There was *both* substantial heavy drinking in the working class and a strong sentiment for total abstinence among the upper, middle, and managerial classes. Thus, America had become polarized on the issue of alcohol use. This can be related to two opposing forces within American society: (1) the large cities and the frontier, both of which encouraged individual deviance and (2) the American heartland, which tried to impose a puritanical notion of sin on the nation. This inherent conflict led to an inability in American society to adopt a moderate attitude toward drinking. A byproduct of this ambivalence is a history of legal indecision about what to do about alcohol. Three separate waves of state prohibition laws occurred in which laws were passed and then repealed—the first in the 1850s, the second in the 1880s, and the third in the 1910s. The third wave culminated in the ratification of the Eighteenth Amendment in 1919 and the opening of the stormy period in American history known as Prohibition. Wide-scale violation of the law, coupled with the economic problems of the Great Depression, led ultimately to the repeal of the Eighteenth Amendment in 1933.

Recent Experience

Today, it is estimated that approximately 88 percent of all American adults (over 158 million people) have used alcohol at least once in their lives and about 61 percent have used it in the preceding month.[33] Since there is no totally accepted definition of an alcoholic, it is difficult to estimate how many people who drink are alcoholics. However, the most common estimate is that there are about 9 million alcoholics in the United States.[34] If numbers alone were the criterion, alcoholism would be considered almost twenty times more serious a social problem in the United States than heroin addiction.

The total drinking population has increased only slightly over the years. This increase seems to have come almost entirely from a rise in the proportion of women drinkers, for men continue to drink

While the alcohol consumption rate for males has remained fairly constant in recent years, the rate for females has increased. (Joseph Szabo/Photo Researchers)

at about the same rate. However, the rate of increase for alcoholism during the same period seems to have been somewhat sharper. One analyst, estimating the number of alcoholics from deaths caused by cirrhosis of the liver (believed to be a consequence of long-term, heavy drinking), estimates that there were about 3 million alcoholics in the United States in 1943, 5 million in 1956, 6.5 million in 1965, and, as we have seen, about 9 million today. The figures indicate that the percentage of the total American population who were alcoholics rose from 2.2 percent in 1943, to 3.35 percent in 1965, and to about 4 percent today.[35] It is interesting to note that the greater the temporal distance from Prohibition, the higher the percentage of alcoholics.

Patterns of LSD Use

LSD, or "acid" as it was called two decades ago, was *the* drug associated with the student, antiwar, drug culture of the 1960s. LSD is an hallucinogenic (or "psychedelic") that was taken to provide "a trip" that might include swirling colors and pulsating sounds. Unfortunately, for those who took LSD in the 1960s, a "bad trip" was not uncommon. There is evidence that LSD use has remained fairly stable over the last dec-

Table 3.2 Trends in Past Year Drug Use
This table provides information on the percentage of people in three age groups (12–17, 18–25, 26 plus) who have used various drugs in the preceding year. Data are provided for several years between 1972 and 1982. This allows us to examine change over time in drug use in the three age groups.

PAST YEAR USE, 1972–1982: YOUTH	USE IN PAST YEAR						Change:
	1972	*1974*	*1976*	*1977*	*1979*	*1982*	*1979–1982***
Youth: ages 12–17	(880)	(952)	(986)	(1272)	(2165)	(1581)	
Marijuana	x	18.5%	18.4%	22.3%	24.1%	20.6%	S
Hallucinogens	3.6	4.3	2.8	3.1	4.7	3.6	NS
Cocaine	1.5	2.7	2.3	2.6	4.2	4.1	NS
Heroin	*	*	*	.6	*	*	—
Nonmedical Use of:							
Stimulants	x	3	2.2	3.7°	2.9	5.6	§
Sedatives	x	2	1.2	2.0°	2.2	3.7	§
Tranquilizers	x	2	1.8	2.9°	2.7	3.3	§
Analgesics	x	x	x	x	2.2	3.7	§
Any Nonmedical Use	xx	xx	xx	xx	5.6	8.3	§
Alcohol	x	51	49.3	47.5	53.6#	47.3#	SS
Cigarettes	x	x	x	x	—	24.8	—
(Alternate Definition—Cigarettes)**					(13.3)	(14.2)	(NS)

*Less than .5%.
xNot asked.
xxSince questions on use of analgesics were not asked in surveys prior to 1979, the nonmedical use of any psychotherapeutic (including analgesics) could not be reported for these earlier years.
*1977 estimates based on split sample: N=623.
**In 1979, recency of cigarette use was asked only of those who had smoked at least five packs during their lifetime. In all other years, no such restriction was applied. For 1982, this version was calculated separately.
#In both 1979 and 1982, private answer sheets were used for alcohol questions; in earlier years respondents answered these questions aloud.
**Significance levels: SSS, .001; SS, .01; S, .05; §, .10; NS, not significant; §, significance test not performed (79–82 procedures not comparable).
Definitions of terms and categories used in this table are to be found in the "Key Definitions" section.
Source: Adapted from Judith Droitcour Miller, *et al., National Survey On Drug Abuse: Main Findings* (Rockville, Md.: National Institute on Drug Abuse, 1983), pp. 19–21.

Table 3.2 Trends in Past Year Drug Use (*Continued*)

PAST YEAR USE, 1972–1982: YOUNG ADULTS	USE IN PAST YEAR 1972	1974	1976	1977	1979	1982	Change: 1979–1982**
Young adults: ages 18–25	(772)	(849)	(882)	(1500)	(2044)	(1283)	
Marijuana	x	34.2%	35.0%	38.7%	46.9%	40.4%	SS
Hallucinogens	†	6.1	6.0	6.4	9.9	6.9	S
Cocaine	†	8.1	7.0	10.2	19.6	18.8	NS
Heroin	†	.8	.6	1.2	.8	*	—
Nonmedical Use of:							
Stimulants	x	8.0	8.8	10.4*	10.1	10.8	§
Sedatives	x	4.2	5.7	8.2*	7.3	8.7	§
Tranquilizers	x	4.6	6.2	7.8*	7.1	5.9	§
Analgesics	x	x	x	x	5.2	4.4	§
Any Nonmedical Use	xx	xx	xx	xx	16.3	16.1	§
Alcohol	x	77.1	77.9	79.8	86.6#	83.4#	S
Cigarettes	x	x	x	x	—	47.2	—
(Alternate Definition—Cigarettes)**					(46.7)	(41.4)	(S)
PAST YEAR USE, 1972–1982: OLDER ADULTS	**USE IN PAST YEAR 1972**	**1974**	**1976**	**1977**	**1979**	**1982**	**Change: 1979–1982****
Older adults: age 26+	(1613)	(2221)	(1708)	(1822)	(3015)	(2760)	
Marijuana	x	3.8%	5.4%	6.4%	9.0%	10.6%	NS
Hallucinogens	†	*	*	*	.5	.8	NS
Cocaine	†	*	.6	.9	2.0%	3.8	SS
Heroin	†	*	*	*	*	*	—
Nonmedical Use of:							
Stimulants	x	*	.8	.8	1.3	1.7	§
Sedatives	x	*	.6	*	.8	1.4	§
Tranquilizers	x	*	1.2	1.1	.9	1.1	§
Analgesics	x	x	x	x	.5	1.0	§
Any Nonmedical Use	xx	xx	xx	xx	2.3	3.1	§
Alcohol	x	62.7	64.2	65.8	72.4#	68.3#	SS
Cigarettes	x	x	x	x	—	38.2	—
(Alternate Definition—Cigarettes)**					(39.7)	(37.3)	(NS)

*Less than .5%.
xNot asked.
xxSince questions on use of analgesics were not asked in surveys prior to 1979, the nonmedical use of any psychotherapeutic (including analgesics) could not be reported for these earlier years.
†Not tabulated.
*1977 estimates based on split sample: N=750.
**In 1979, recency of cigarette use was asked only of those who had smoked at least five packs during their lifetime. In all other years, no such restriction was applied. For 1982, this version was calculated separately.
#In both 1979 and 1982, private answer sheets were used for alcohol questions; in earlier years respondents answered these questions aloud.
**Significance levels: SSS, .001; SS, .01; S, .05; $, .10; NS, not significant; §, significance test not performed (79–82 procedures not comparable).
Definitions of terms and categories used in this table are to be found in the "Key Definitions" section.

ade or so.[36] As one official of the Drug Enforcement Agency put it: "There is a whole new generation of kids growing up today who refuse to believe the horror stories the generation before them suffered with LSD."[37] In the last few years, for example, there has been an increase in those being admitted to hospital emergency rooms suffering from LSD-related problems. There is a perception that there is less LSD use today than there was in the late 1960s and early 1970s, but Goode argues that the only thing that has changed is that there is less media attention to the problem.

PART II: CAUSES AND CONSEQUENCES

Now we come to two central questions about those who abuse drugs of various types: Why do they do it? What are the consequences of their actions?

INDIVIDUAL LEVEL

Physiological Factors

The conventional wisdom is that sufficient dosages of a drug will have the physiological effects needed to invariably and permanently addict anyone. This is clearest in the case of a drug like heroin where the public tends to believe that a single injection will lead to a lifetime of enslavement. We know from experience that a single drink of liquor will not have the same effect, but many believe that if people consume enough liquor they will develop an addiction to it. A similar view exists on addiction to tobacco. Although there is some truth here, there is also a good deal of mythology. *In this section we will try to show that the physiological effects of drugs are relative, not fixed.*

For example, Norman Zinberg studied 100 hospital patients who, for at least ten days, required doses of morphine in stronger concentrations than addicts get on the street.[38] Once they were taken off the drug, only one patient felt any craving, and that was in response to actual physical pain. Zinberg's research with medical patients shows that addiction and withdrawal distress are *not* invariable physiological responses to the use of opiates.

Effect of Placebos

One important line of research on the relativity of psychoactive drug action is the study of the *placebo effect.* Such research has shown that the way people react to a drug is determined not only by what the drug *is* but also by what the drug *is presented to be.* In one study, morphine and a placebo (a substance that has no physiological effect) were administered under similar conditions to hospitalized patients suffering postoperative pain.[39] However, the patients were always told that they were getting morphine. A substantial minority of those studied were as satisfied with the analgesic effect of the placebo as with the morphine. For others, *neither* the morphine nor the placebo had any impact. Obviously, the physiological effect of a drug is affected by the way it is presented to people.

The Social Setting

Another factor affecting the impact of a drug is the social setting in which the drug is administered. In one study, two groups of subjects were injected with an energizing drug, but only one group was told what its effect would be.[40] After the injection, each subject was left in the company of a stooge (a paid assistant acting under the experimenters' instructions). Half the subjects in each group were given a happy, euphoric stooge, the other half an angry one. The group of subjects who were informed about the drugs' effects acted without regard to the stooge's behavior, but those who were not informed adopted the stooge's mood—whatever that was! Presumably, the stooge's behavior provided a model that permitted subjects both to act out and to account for the arousal they were feeling as a result of the drug. The experiment demonstrated that people are extremely susceptible to social influence when they have no explanation for the way they feel. It also

Table 3.3 Levels of Analysis: Drugs

LEVELS	APPROPRIATE QUESTIONS	A PARTIAL SYNOPSIS OF PRESENT CONCLUSIONS
INDIVIDUAL	Do drugs and alcohol create a physical dependency?	They do, but their effects are relative, *not* fixed.
	Can people control their dependency?	Through controlled use some people are able to lead relatively normal lives.
	Can people outgrow dependency?	There is considerable evidence that many people do outgrow drug dependency.
	Does drug abuse cause physiological problems?	There is considerable evidence that drug abuse causes physiological harm.
	Can drug abuse be the result of conditioned learning?	Yes, but we do not know why some who experience the positive effects become addicted while others do not.
	Do personality differences influence who does or does not become a drug addict?	Yes, personality factors are predisposing factors, but they are neither necessary nor sufficient conditions for substance abuse.
SOCIAL-PSYCHOLOGICAL	Does being labeled a drug addict lock people into such behavior?	It may, but many people eventually "mature out" of drug addiction. In addition, labeling theory tells us nothing about why people begin using drugs.
	Do people learn to be drug addicts through interaction with others?	Yes, but many who are exposed to the same learning process do not become drug addicts.

(continued)

Table 3.3 Levels of Analysis: Drugs (*Continued*)

LEVELS	APPROPRIATE QUESTIONS	A PARTIAL SYNOPSIS OF PRESENT CONCLUSIONS
SOCIOLOGICAL	Is social class related to the nature and type of drug use?	Yes, but it is erroneous to assume that drug (and alcohol) problems are restricted to the lower classes.
	Does culture affect the likelihood of drug abuse?	Yes. Not only does the larger culture affect drug abuse, but so does the nature of an individual's subculture.

demonstrated that the way people behave and the emotions they act out while on the drug depend both on what they think the drug does and on what is going on around them at the time.

Privileged Users

In another study, it was found that there are addicted physicians, with ready access to narcotics, who are able to successfully practice medicine.[41] Only rarely did their drug dependence get out of hand. These privileged, highly controlled users demonstrated that where the usual cycle (experienced by lower-class narcotics users) of limited availability, inflated prices, and poverty and crime is absent, narcotics *can* be taken as a regular part of a productive life.

Maturing Out

Another piece of evidence along these lines is the finding that lower-class heroin addicts begin to outgrow their addiction with the coming of adulthood,[42] with three-quarters becoming inactive by thirty-six years of age.[43] This regular pattern of outgrowing a heroin habit is called *maturing out.* The fact that most people outgrow a heroin addiction is strong evidence that there is much more to addiction than physiology. Were heroin addiction solely traceable to the drug's physiological impact, the coming of adulthood would not bring with it the end of heroin addiction for most users.

Paths Out of Addiction

Recently, Dan Waldorf and Patrick Biernacki have expanded on the simple notion of maturing out.[44] They see it as but one of several alternative paths from heroin addiction. A second is a change in situation from one where drug use was more appropriate to one where it was less appropriate (see the Robins research below). A third is retirement from the hard life of hustling associated with addiction at a younger age. Finally, an individual may move on to another drug such as cocaine or alcohol. These alternatives would presumably not be available to the individual if heroin addiction was explained solely by physiological factors.

The most persuasive study in this area is Lee Robins's *The Vietnam Drug User Returns.*[45] Studying a sample of returnees from Vietnam, Robins found that about one-third had used heroin in Vietnam, with about one-half of these considered addicted. Within a year of release, the returnees were interviewed, and urine samples were taken to obtain evidence on drug use. The major finding of this research is that there was a marked decline in narcotics use. The most dramatic decline was among frequent drug users. Most of the veterans who had been heavy users in Vietnam did not use *any* narcotics in the period between discharge and interview. Among the major reasons given for the decline in use were the expense of the drug, fear of addiction, and fear of arrest. The implication of this research is that heroin use and addiction is related to the situation; when the situation changes, use can drop dramatically. Extrapolating further, addiction to heroin is *not* determined solely by the drug, but by the combination of the drug and the social circumstances.

Range of Narcotics Use

Another demonstration of the lack of the overwhelming physiological effect of drugs is the fact that there is not a single type of narcotics use, but rather a continuum, or spectrum, of such use. Norman Zinberg and David Lewis divided their subjects into six groups, those who:

1. Rarely used opiates but adopted superficial features of the addict's life style.
2. Were addicted to the injection procedure, or ritual, rather than the drug.
3. Were addicted to a person associated with drug use rather than to the drug.
4. Were depressed and self-destructive and took the drug only to relieve the pain of living.
5. Used opiates regularly without developing tolerance or disrupting their lives (for example, doctors).
6. Showed the classical addiction syndrome—tolerance, withdrawal, compulsion, and craving.[46]

The basic point here is that opiate use does not have invariable and unchanging effects on people.

Alcohol and Physiology

The same point can, or course, be made about alcohol use. The concepts of controlled use and maturing out are even more commonly accepted for alcohol use than for opiate use. Normal drinking may be defined as the kind of nondependent, socially appropriate drinking that most drinkers engage in. Controlled drinking may be defined as the use of small, regular daily doses of alcohol in the context of a normal, productive life.[47] The evidence about the decreasing use of alcohol and alcohol rates with age suggests that maturing out applies to alcohol as well as to narcotics.[48] Data from 1982 indicate that alcohol use within the past month peaks in the 26 to 34-year-old age group (70.6 percent), while in the over-35 age category only 51.8 percent used alcohol in the past month.[49] Finally, there is growing attention to the fact that at least some people can resolve their chronic drinking problems on their own without formal treatment programs.[50]

Adverse Physiological Effects

The thrust of the above discussion is that there is little evidence that physiological factors are a major cause of drug abuse. However, that is not to deny the fact that excessive drug use can have a strongly negative impact on physiology. For example, the Drug Abuse Warning Network has collected partial data on nonfatal emergency room drug-related episodes and medical examiners' reports on fatal drug overdoses.[51] These data clearly show that drugs make people seriously ill and even kill a number of people. The biggest culprit, in terms of both emergency episodes and fatal drug overdoses, is alcohol used in combination with other drugs. Heroin is second in terms of fatal overdoses, while, surprisingly, minor tranquilizers are the second leading cause of emergency episodes. It is interesting to note that those drugs that the public worries least about, alcohol and minor tranquilizers, create the largest number of these problems.

Drug abuse can also have a variety of physiological effects on people that can cause them to do harm to themselves and others. This is nowhere clearer than in the relationship between drinking and driving. An individual who consumes as little as two ounces of liquor in an hour is likely to begin experiencing the familiar effects on motor performance: "clumsiness, an unsteadiness in gait, an inability to stand or walk straight, slurred speech."[52] It is generally estimated that as a result of such effects, alcohol is responsible for half of all highway deaths in the United States. Interestingly, alcohol consumption also seems to increase the likelihood that pedestrians will be involved in accidents. There is, of course, an increasing effort to crack down on those driving under the influence of alcohol, but the fact remains that many millions of people continue to drive while drunk, and over a million of them are arrested for it each year. Alcohol not only can kill those who consume too much of it, it can kill innocent bystanders as well.

In the preceding section we have discussed the relationship between drugs and physiological factors. Our main concern has been with the social-psychological and sociological factors that mitigate or even eliminate the role played by physiology in drug addiction. This is consistent with the trend away from looking at purely medical and physiological factors and toward an emphasis on social-psychological and sociological factors, as well as the psychological factors we are about to discuss. We will have more to say about social-psychological and sociological factors later in this chapter.

Psychological Factors

Clearly, physiological explanations of dependency, of getting and staying hooked, cannot adequately explain addiction. We must ask, on the one hand, what psychological factors lead some people to become addicted to drugs while others do not? On the other hand, we need to assess the psychological impact of drugs on different people.

Reinforcement and Addiction

Research on drug addiction and alcoholism in animals—including monkeys, pigs, and dogs—shows that animals turn into addicts and drunks when drugs and alcohol are regularly available to them.[53] This leads to the view that drug addiction and alcoholism are the result of *conditioned learning*. It is generally the case that people will repeat actions that are *reinforced;* that is, associated with pleasure or with the avoidance of pain. Through reinforcement (and the parallel process of *punishment*) people learn to engage in certain kinds of behaviors and not in others. To some extent, drugs and alcohol are directly rewarding. People (and many animals) rapidly come to experience the effects of drugs and liquor as pleasurable. Furthermore, people and animals quickly learn that taking the drug or consuming alcohol brings relief from the pain of withdrawal symptoms.[54] We will return to the idea of addiction as conditioned learning later when we examine methods of dealing with this problem, but it should be made clear that this orientation, while useful, suffers from incompleteness. In spite of recent efforts to integrate cognitive processes into our understanding of conditioned learning,[55] this approach tells us little about why some people who learn the positive effects of drugs become addicted while others do not. This brings us to the issue of the personality of the addict.

Personality Factors

Most people who try alcohol or drugs do *not* become addicted. To explain this fact, psychologists have long concentrated on finding distinctive personality traits that might be associated with becoming an addict. One major element is a person's self-concept. In one study, Richard Lindblad found a strong relationship between narcotic addiction and a negative self-image.[56] In other words, people who think less of themselves are more likely to be addicts. The issue, of course, is whether the negative self-image led the person to become a narcotics addict, or whether being an addict led to the poor self-image. Lindblad concludes from his study that the negative self-image came first, but his is not conclusive proof since it is not based on a longitudinal study. In fact, a recent and important longitudinal study of alcoholism by George Vaillant found personality problems did not contribute to the development of the problem.[57] This is clearly an issue in need of a great deal of additional research.

Stanton Peele has analyzed the dynamics of the addict's search for a specific experience through an addiction.[58] The addiction creates for the individual a relief from pain or anxiety and provides feelings of self-esteem, power, and control that are otherwise unavailable. In finding these essential psychological ingredients in the addiction, however, the individual loses the opportunity to derive fundamental satisfactions from normal life experiences, and is thus thrust back on the addiction in a deepening cycle of dependence. Addictive experiences can emerge not only with habitual drug use, according to Peele, but through other powerful involvements such as running, gambling, and even intimate personal relationships. Personality traits such as a negative self-image and an overreliance on external props characterize the addict. These individual dispositions pass through layers of social, situational, and cultural variables to determine whether—and to what particular personal involvement—a person becomes addicted. This approach serves as a transition to the next section on social-psychological factors and drug addiction.

In general, we can conclude on the personality factor, following Alan Lang, that there is no evidence that a "single, unique personality is a necessary or sufficient condition for substance use."[59] However, it may be that there are personality characteristics that predispose people to substance use and abuse.

SOCIAL-PSYCHOLOGICAL LEVEL

Labeling Theory

One of the main concerns of sociologists interested in the social psychology of drug addiction (and other forms of deviant behavior) is the process by which individuals come to be *labeled* as drug abusers.[60] Throughout our history we have created (and often changed) formal laws and informal rules about what is or is not considered a type of drug abuse that is harmful to the larger society. From a labeling theory perspective, there is nothing inherent in an act (smoking cigarettes, smoking marijuana, "shooting" heroin) that makes it an addiction of concern to society. Nor is there anything inherent in a particular drug that makes it an object of prohibition. Society labels certain drugs as harmful and others as acceptable. Similarly, we label certain people as abusers, while others are not so labeled. What defines drugs, and more importantly drug abusers, is the labeling process. Harmful drugs and harmful types of addiction are simply those that society says are harmful. There are a few objective conditions, however, that lead society to label some habitual drug users abusers while others escape such a label. For example, there are great differences between the impact of heroin and aspirin on the human being. It is the greater impact of heroin that leads society to label habitual users addicts while the regular user of the seemingly benign aspirin escapes such a label.

A basic premise of labeling theory is that people tend to come to see themselves as others see them, to respond on the basis of how they are responded to. Thus, if someone is labeled an alcoholic, a "junkie," or most generally a drug addict, the label may become a *self-fulfilling prophecy* and may lead the person to further live up to the expectations associated with such a label. Thus, someone who is developing a slight drinking problem or is experimenting with marijuana may be pushed further into becoming an alcoholic or a "pothead" by being treated like one by others. As the drugs are used more and more frequently, more and more people apply the label to the individual. At first, these labels are likely to be affixed informally by family, friends, and acquaintances. Later official agents such as police officers, judges, social workers, and psychiatrists may apply the label more formally and officially. In at least some cases, the drug abuser comes to be seen by virtually everyone around him or her, and even by him- or herself, as an abuser. Alcoholics or heroin addicts in the depths of addiction may come to organize their entire lives around that label. Such a label may also greatly impede efforts by addicts to reform. Once earned, such a label is very difficult to shed.

Differential Association Theory

While useful, a focus on the labeling of addicts is of only limited utility. For example, it does not explain why people take that first drink, or smoke that first marijuana cigarette, or inject that first ampule of heroin that *may* eventually lead them to be labeled an alcoholic or a drug addict. To understand that, we need to look at differential association theory, which, among other things, focuses on the *socialization* process whereby people *learn* to be addicts.[61]

All human behavior is learned, and whether what is learned conforms to or violates social norms and laws depends in large part on who is doing the teaching or the socializing.[62] The basic premise of differential association theory comes down to the idea that people who became drug abusers kept the company of drug abusers and learned the techniques of drug use from them.

This orientation was used in a classic study of marijuana smoking.[63] One basic point to emerge from this study is that people are introduced to marijuana smoking by their friends. In fact, people usually initially rely on their friends and do not buy their own supply of the drug until they have become relatively experienced marijuana smokers. Furthermore, people not only find out about and obtain the drug from their friends, but they also learn from them the ability to detect and enjoy the effects of pot. Later research has confirmed the social nature of marijuana use.[64] Persons without friends who use the drug have little opportunity to obtain the drug or to learn how to use it and to enjoy it.

The same principles clearly apply to the

use of narcotics and alcohol. Few people have taken up drinking entirely on their own; they at least started as social drinkers. Indeed, most people have to learn to enjoy the effects of alcohol—to experience the high as pleasant rather than as a loss of full faculties and to learn to pace their consumption so that they can maintain the high without becoming ill or passing out. In fact, most people even have to learn to like the taste of alcoholic beverages. Thus, novices and very occasional drinkers prefer mixed drinks that cover up the taste of liquor, wine, or even the creamy liqueurs that taste much more like candy than they do like liquor.

Introduction to narcotics is similarly social. New users must learn from others the proper preparation, dosage, and administration of the drug, including the use of a hypodermic syringe. Furthermore, as was the case with marijuana and alcohol, beginners must define the drug's effects as pleasurable. In one study, about 40 percent of the people who did not like their first experience with heroin learned to use and enjoy it despite an aversive first encounter.[65]

Both the labeling theory and differential association theory approaches to drug addiction credit the individual's social environment with a powerful role in causing deviant drug-taking and deviant drinking. But these approaches have little to say about the larger-scale question of what causes variations in the social environment. Why do only some people have friends who drink heavily, or shoot heroin, or smoke marijuana, or use cocaine and who are willing not only to introduce them to these substances but also teach them about these drugs and reward them for using the drugs on a regular basis? Why are some people who engage in these behaviors labeled as deviant drug users while others are not? These kinds of questions lead us to the macroscopic level of analysis.

SOCIOLOGICAL LEVEL

Social Stratification

The popular stereotype of alcoholics is that they are from the lower classes, even skid row. However, this image does not match the facts. According to one estimate, only 3 to 4 percent of America's alcoholics live in skid row circumstances.[66] Most observers argue that the vast majority of alcoholics are respectable, middle- or upper-class individuals who contain their habit within an orderly life.[67] Our distorted image of the alcoholic can be traced partly to the greater visibility of lower-class alcoholics and partly to our continued hesitation to label a higher-status problem drinker as an alcoholic.

There is some evidence that there has been an increase in drinking in the middle classes. In a well-known study published in 1945, John Dollard found that the middle class drank less than any other socioeconomic group—a reflection of the role of the middle class as the main exponents of traditional American values.[68] More recent evidence indicates that the middle- and upper-middle classes have come to be *more* likely to drink than the lower and working classes.[69] In fact, it is the increase in middle-class involvement with alcohol, along with the greater proportion of women drinkers,[70] that stand out as major contributing factors to the slight overall increase in the drinking rate.

While still primarily a lower-class problem, heroin addiction is becoming more common (although it still involves only a miniscule number of people) in the middle classes.[71] However, when they use heroin, the middle-class users tend to avoid the intravenous injections ("shooting") that they associate with the lower classes, crime, and death from overdoses. Said one nineteen-year-old who "dabbles" in heroin: "We're not skid-row junkies, we're respectable people."[72] Middle-class users are more likely to snort it like cocaine, dissolve it and inhale the vapors, or take it through a superficial injection in a muscle ("skinpopping").

Class differences in drug use are, of course, related to the cost of the drug. A heroin habit is expensive, but it can be afforded by a life as a petty thief. A cocaine habit is astronomically expensive, perhaps as high as $10,000 to $15,000 per week.[73] As a result, it is affordable by the very rich, those in the movie business, professional athletes, and other elite members of society.

Cultural Factors

Culture is another important factor at the sociological level. One important issue here is whether drinking is integrated into the life of a culture or is disruptive to the culture. For example, drinking is integrated into traditional Italian culture. Historically, Italians have thought of wine as a healthful drink and have not ascribed the psychological potency to it that Americans have. Thus, while they may consume a good deal of alcohol, it tends not to have a destructive impact on their lives. They tend not to become alcoholics in the (destructive) sense that we use the term.

Alcoholism that leads to self-destructive or antisocial behavior is more likely to occur in cultures or subcultures that have no prescribed social pattern of drinking. Such cultures consider drinking an individual pursuit and associate it to some degree with pleasure seeking or escapism. Among these cultures are those in which alcohol has been recently introduced, in which newly imposed legal controls have replaced traditional social regulations, and in which one social group has used alcohol to keep another group in subjugation. One of the best examples of this is the high rate of alcoholism among American Indians. The American Indians lacked a social pattern of drinking when alcohol was introduced to them by white Americans, in part to engage in exploitative commerce with them, but ultimately to keep them under control. This occurred at about the same time that their culture was being disrupted, and external legal controls were being imposed on them. A similar example is found among the Eskimos native to Alaska.[74] Before liquor was introduced by Russian settlers in the eighteenth century, the Eskimos had no intoxicating beverages of their own; consequently, they had no cultural and structural means of handling them. The result of introducing alcohol into such a normative vacuum has been to create a staggering problem with alcoholism among Alaskan Eskimos.

Subcultures

Another factor worth exploring briefly at this level is the role played by various subcultures in drug and alcohol use and abuse. For example, Greeley and his associates identified "different drinking subcultures" among a variety of ethnic groups.[75] Among other things, the norms and values of these subcultures influence a person's drinking behavior, as well as the propensity to develop drinking problems. Through socialization into various subcultures, people learn to drink, and some learn to become alcoholics. Vaillant comes to a similar conclusion in his massive study of alcoholism: "future alcoholics are more likely to come from ethnic groups that tolerate adult

Jews constitute one subculture in which moderate drinking is integrated into their way of life. Such integration serves to reduce the likelihood of alcoholism. (Hanna Schreiber/Rapho/Photo Researchers)

drunkenness but that discourage children and adolescents from learning safe drinking practices (such as consumption of low-proof alcoholic beverages at ceremonies and with meals)."[76] On the other hand, other subcultures tend to reduce the likelihood of drinking and alcoholism. In their study of how Jews avoid alcoholism, Barry Glassner and Bruce Berg identified four basic informal controls learned in the Jewish subculture: (1) alcohol problems are associated with non-Jews; (2) moderate drinking practices are learned at home in conjunction with religious ceremonies; (3) in adulthood, peer groups reinforce moderate drinking and punish those who drink too much; and (4) even in stressful situations Jews have learned a series of avoidance techniques that prevent them from beginning on the road to deviant drinking.[77]

PART III: RESPONSES

It seems clear that we have no singularly effective way of dealing with the various forms of drug addiction. In fact, some of our efforts seem to do more to exacerbate the problem and, in the process, create additional, even more serious, problems. Nevertheless, there are various efforts that have been tried at different levels and succeeded, at least for some people, for some time. We begin with more individual level responses and work our way toward responses at the sociological level.

INDIVIDUAL RESPONSES

There are a wide range of programs that attempt to deal with the physiological aspects of drug addiction and alcoholism. In this category we include efforts to give addicts the drug to which they are addicted, to give them substitutes for those drugs, or to put them through a process of behavior modification.

Heroin Maintenance

The United States has been characterized by a long-term effort to prohibit opiates, particularly heroin, but this has not been notably successful and has, in fact, created a whole other set of problems. In contrast to this, we have the British experience[78] in which the philosophy for years has been to treat the heroin addict as a patient and *not* as a criminal. Prior to 1968 any British doctor was permitted to prescribe heroin in order to allow an addict to continue to function in society.[79] Doctors in Britain were allowed to prescribe opiates as part of a gradual withdrawal cure, or to prescribe them indefinitely for addicts who upon withdrawal lose the capacity to live productive lives (some do lead productive lives while using stable doses of the drug).[80]

While heroin is still prescribed in England, it is only in very rare cases of hardened addiction. As the number of younger addicts began to grow in the late 1960s, England was forced to move away from heroin maintenance. Prescription of heroin created problems in England at a time when there were only a small number of addicts, and it is therefore unlikely to work in the United States with its vast heroin problem. It is feared that a program of heroin maintenance in the United States would lead more people to get hooked on the streets because they could count on a continuing supply at government clinics. Others raise a more fundamental objection: that heroin maintenance, although it is more humane than the present policy of prohibition, makes an addict permanently drug dependent and does not attack the individual and social problems of reliance on the power of drugs.[81]

Methadone Maintenance

To cope more humanely with the physiological problems of heroin addicts, England has moved in a direction that has also been used in the United States, *methadone maintenance.*[82] Resorting to such a maintenance program means conceding that the addict is so physiologically (and psychologically) habituated to the drugs that he or she cannot (or will not) live without them. Methadone is legally used as a substitute for heroin because addiction to methadone is considered less dangerous and more easily managed than heroin addiction. Unlike heroin, methadone does not lose its effect when taken orally, and using it in fruit juice eliminates injection—a major social ritual of addiction. Even when injected, it produces less of a "rush" than heroin and, perhaps most important, takes longer to wear off. It has to be administered once a day or every two days, instead of three or four times a day as is the case with heroin. For these reasons, methadone fits better into an orderly, controlled, productive life style than does heroin, and patients need not be hospitalized to be treated. It also produces "blockading"[83]—so high a level of tolerance for narcotics that the addict cannot obtain noticeable effect from any but a prohibitively large dose of illicit heroin.

There has been some indication that methadone maintenance can have encouraging results in helping addicts live orderly, law-abiding lives.[84] Among other things, there is evidence that while an addict is in methadone treatment there is a significant reduction in illegal opiate use and criminal behavior, as well as a less dramatic increase in employment.

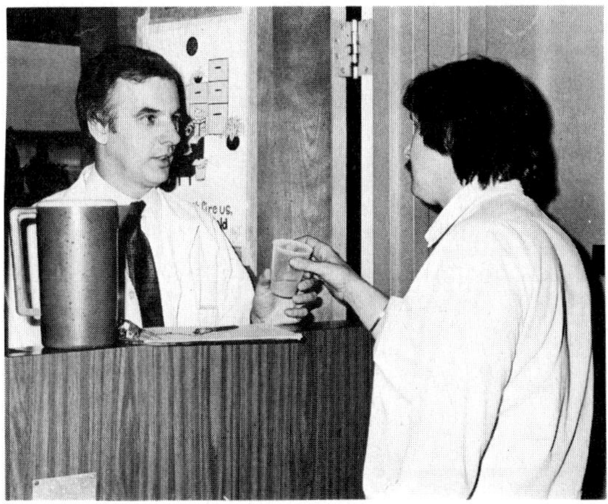

One highly controversial method of dealing with heroin addiction is methadone maintenance. (Martin M. Rotker/Taurus Photos)

Criticisms of Methadone Maintenance

There are however many critics of methadone maintenance programs, including the founders of these programs who later came to the conclusion that they were of only very limited utility.[85] In England, and later in the United States, methadone maintenance has been criticized on several grounds: users complain that methadone is *more* addictive than heroin; officials have found that it is not as easy to wean addicts away from methadone as was first hoped; methadone addicts must be detoxified (the elimination of active dependence on a drug through a program of supervised gradual withdrawal[86]) in the same way as heroin addicts; addicts may well remain on it for years, if not for the rest of their lives; some addicts have begun selling methadone illicitly on the streets in the same way they sell heroin;[87] and finally, and most importantly, methadone is just a substitute, it does nothing to alleviate the craving for a high.

There are other, more general, sociological critiques of methadone maintenance programs. For one thing, such programs cannot satisfy addicts who are drawn to the excitement of street life; these addicts will continue to seek illicit heroin even though its physiological impact may not be any greater than methadone's. Another criticism is that the success of some methadone maintenance programs is traceable not to the properties of the drug, but to the personal attention given addicts in such programs. Finally, one has to challenge the logic of treating one form of addiction with another. It does nothing to solve the root causes in the individual and the larger society of addiction, and it may also have the negative effect of fostering a view of new drugs as cure-alls for all sorts of problems. If methadone maintenance does work at all, its main advantage over heroin maintenance in the United States (and England) is that it is *legal*.

Behavior Modification

In the section on psychological causes we discussed the idea of conditioned learning as it applies to addiction. Derived from this idea is a therapy known as *behavior modification*, which attempts to find ways to reinforce (reward) new behavior patterns, such as avoiding drugs or alcohol.[88] Behavior therapists attempt to help the individual find new ways to respond to situations that previously prompted drinking or drug taking and reward these desirable new responses.

One way to make people stop taking drugs or drinking is to make them feel an aversion to the substance, to make drugs or alcohol seem disagreeable or offensive. *Aversive therapy* attempts to associate discomfort and unpleasantness with drinking and drug taking.[89] Alcoholics may be given drugs that cause them to become violently nauseated when they drink; the treatment may be continued even to the point at which seeing a bottle causes unpleasant feelings. For example, when a drug like disulfiram is administered regularly to patients, they cannot drink alcohol without experiencing nausea, vomiting, flushing, palpitations, and other unpleasant sensations. In addition, a drug that by itself produces nausea and vomiting (emetine and apomorphine) is administered along with alcohol so that the alcoholic will learn to associate liquor with the disagreeable effects of the emetic. Similarly, drugs and alcohol may be paired with an unpleasant stimulus, such as a mild electric shock, in an effort to condition an aversive reaction to drinking or drug taking. Both techniques have shown some promise in treating alcoholics and drug addicts.

Self-Help

One of the exciting new areas in dealing with drug and alcohol responses is the renewed interest in the ability of individuals to help themselves.[90] Barry Tuchfeld, for example, found that some people are able to resolve their alcohol problems on their own without the aid of organizations or therapists.[91] The work on the ability of people to limit their own drinking also points in the same direction, since this ability is intimately related to the capacity to resolve alcohol problems; in fact, it may be one of the major resolutions.[92] In a study of obesity and smoking, Stanley Schachter found that self-cures were relatively common occurrences.[93] Schachter cites the Robins research discussed earlier, as well as additional research, to show that people are also often able to cure themselves of heroin addiction. He concludes: "People can and do cure themselves of smoking, obesity, and heroin addiction. They do so in large numbers and for long periods of time, in many cases apparently permanently."[94] The seeming ability of people to help themselves is contrasted to the dismal success rates for most formal therapies. Schachter concludes that the difference in success is traceable to the fact that we are looking at one-shot therapeutic efforts versus lifetime efforts at self-help. In addition, formal therapeutic settings may attract unusually difficult cases and those settings may actually contribute to the problem rather than to help deal with it. Thus, at the individual level, there is a growing conviction among researchers that people may be able to help themselves, and may have in fact been doing so all along.

SOCIAL-PSYCHOLOGICAL RESPONSES

A range of approaches exists at the interpersonal and group levels in terms of dealing with drug abuse. For example, a wide range of psychotherapies has been used in order to try to help abusers cope with their problems. Another alternative, seemingly growing in popularity, is family therapy involving not only the drug abuser, but his or her family as well.[96] A variety of groups and organizations have been formed to help drug addicts and alcoholics, or to allow them to help themselves. Of this genre are a number of *therapeutic communities* throughout the United States. Such a community is defined "as a communal, residential, drug-free rehabilitation center in which drug addiction is treated as a personality disorder."[96] There is strict discipline in these communities and sometimes brutally honest exchanges among residents in encounter sessions.

Daytop Village

One example of a therapeutic community is Daytop Village in New York state. At Daytop Village the addict is seen as immature, lacking in self-confidence, and unable to handle stress. The goal is to destroy the personality structure that has resulted in addiction because it is seen as false and harmful.[97] The first step in the program is to break down what is considered an unhealthy self-image; only after addicts change their views of themselves can they admit their immaturity to themselves and to others.

Daytop is a peer-group community staffed largely by ex-addicts. It offers no gradual withdrawal or maintenance schedule and encourages the prospective residents to go through detoxification elsewhere. If addicts experience withdrawal after arriving at Daytop, they are shown no special consideration and are not excused from work. In fact, at Daytop communities one finds less severe forms of withdrawal symptoms than in jails and other environments that expect and accept these symptoms.[98]

Once the residents accept the community's authority, they go through a maturation process in which they take on progressively more responsible jobs and enjoy greater privileges. They are expected to model themselves after residents who have achieved a more advanced position than their own, and if they misbehave, they are punished with humiliating tasks and loss of privileges. Their development is monitored through intensive group therapy sessions. Finally, when they have shown sufficient maturity and have developed plans for living on the outside, they are considered prepared to reenter society—where they will not find the cooperative values and closely knit community support of Daytop.

There are also a number of nonresidential, self-help groups, such as Narcotics Anonymous, Pills Anonymous, and the best-known of them all, Alcoholics Anonymous. Begun in 1935 and now involving about 1 million problem drinkers, Alcoholics Anonymous (AA) is the model for all self-help groups.[99]

Alcoholics Anonymous

A world-wide, nonresidential voluntary association of local groups, AA has a single aim—to help its members stay sober through mutual support. It achieves this aim very effectively for a large number of people through a combination of group interaction and religious principles. All members of AA are on equal terms; it is a cooperative group with no leaders. Therapy takes the form of meetings, with open discussions for all members and more formal sessions in which speakers give inspirational accounts of their troubles with alcohol and of their redemption through AA. At the meetings, members have a chance to relate to people with the same problem in an atmosphere of mutual respect and candor. AA does not generally attempt any major restructuring of its members' lives and concentrates instead on conventional outlets such as hobbies and social activities. A beneficial psychological impact, especially on one's self-esteem, comes from participation in this kind of nurturant social setting.[100]

AA is primarily a male organization; only 4 percent of female alcoholics ever go to AA.[101] To solve this problem and to help the female alcoholics in the United States, a national self-help group, Women for Sobriety, was founded in 1975. Although it has some differences from AA based on the differences between the problems of male and female alcoholics, the similarities outweigh the differences. This is made clear in the following testimonial by one member: "I've made friends here with people who know exactly what I'm going through. Women alcoholics understand each other. I know I can count on these people forever."[102]

Al-Anon

One of the more recent developments in this area is the formation of groups to aid spouses, families, and friends of addicts.[103] The best known example is Al-Anon, the support community for those with close ties to alcoholics. They function in much the same way as AA, providing a group setting to air problems, hear that others have similar problems, and develop a support network. There is a great need for such groups. For example, children of alcoholics are more likely to be abused, victims of incest, neglected, exploited, and to attempt suicide.

MADD

Another, but very different, recent group effort to deal with an alcohol-related problem is Mothers Against Drunk Driving (MADD).[104] The specific concern of MADD is the carnage wreaked on the highways by drunken drivers. Enraged by the number of highway deaths and injuries that can be linked to drunken driving, MADD has raised public consciousness about this problem and led to police crackdowns on drunken drivers. The objective is not so much to help the alcoholic, but to prevent the alcoholic from hurting innocent people.

SOCIOLOGICAL RESPONSES

Moving to the more macroscopic levels, we encounter a range of other efforts to deal with the problem of drug abuse.

Changes in the Law

We have seen earlier in the chapter how, in the early 1900s, medical and public opinion began to turn against opiate use. This resulted in the Harrison Act of 1914 that restricted possession to certain registered individuals. This immediately cut off independent sources of supply, but left open the question of whether people could still obtain the drugs through a doctor's prescription. Some historians believe that the intent of the Act was merely to make the distribution of opiates more orderly by having it supervised by such responsible parties as physicians.[105] Here law enforcement officers came to the fore, and they interpreted the law otherwise and took action against physicians who prescribed opiates for people who were addicted. The United States Supreme Court upheld some of the convictions that were made in these cases, with the majority of the Justices interpreting the Harrison Act as prohibiting the prescription of opiates. In 1925, the Court reversed its position, but by then a pattern of law enforcement had been established, and public opinion had been conditioned to accept narcotic regulation as a legal, not a medical, question.

The enforcement of the Harrison Act came under the domain of the Narcotics Bureau of the U.S. Treasury Department. As time went on, the Bureau expanded its scope, gaining power and congressional support as it grew into a self-appointed moral crusader.[106] The change was a predictable instance of bureaucratic empire building; the agency was simply overstating the importance of its function. It is also worth noting that the American Medical Association (AMA) supported the Bureau and the objective of taking responsibility for narcotics control away from the individual physician and handing it over to the law-enforcement agents.[107]

The Narcotics Bureau and the AMA together nurtured public attitudes of intense fear and loathing toward opiates through a propaganda campaign that exaggerated the seriousness of the drug problem. False reports of a vast increase in opiate use were circulated, even though the number of addicts was, if anything, declining because of the severe restrictions on the drug. Official propaganda also fanned the public's contempt for opiate users by condemning them as degenerates and criminals. As a result, the drugs could only be taken in secrecy, and the use of such drugs could no longer be reconciled with middle-class respectability. Users risked being consigned to the lower ranks of society, and the new users would come mainly from these ranks.

In the aftermath of the crackdown on physicians, public-health clinics were set up in various cities for the benefit of long-time addicts whose supply was now cut off. This was America's only experience with heroin maintenance, and it was to be short-lived. The clinics could not survive in the climate of opinion created by the Narcotics Bureau. By the time the last clinic closed in 1923, the addict and the public were burdened with repressive attitudes and erroneous ideas about addiction that are only now beginning to be challenged.

Thus the law and various law-enforcement agents had a profound effect on the nature of heroin addiction in American society. They served to stigmatize the addicts and define them as people to be reviled by respectable society. This, in turn, led the addicts to apply similar negative labels to themselves The prohibition of heroin drove up the price and forced many addicts into a life of crime. When they were apprehended, many addicts ended up in prison where there was very little time or energy devoted to rehabilitation. The public was fed a series of myths about heroin addiction (one dose causes addiction, irreversible damage to the body). Perhaps most importantly, this created an atmosphere that would later lead to similar myths about other drugs such as marijuana and cocaine, and a similar public rejection of them.

The parallels between the long-term prohibition against heroin, and the relatively short-lived effort to prohibit alcohol, are striking. The Eighteenth Amendment did have some of the effects intended by those who supported the ban on liquor: drinking in America did, in fact, decline far below pre-Prohibition levels. Similarly, without the prohibition imposed by laws like the Harrison Act, drug use would probably be more widespread than it is today. It is clear, however, that the prohibition of drugs has not stamped out the drug problem any more than prohibition of alcohol stamped out drinking. The pusher is not hard to find today; neither was the bootlegger during the 1920s. When a significant number of people desire drugs or alcohol, and when these substances are illegal, there are immense profits to be made through illegal sales. As a result, dealers have a vested interest in creating a population of users. More generally, we can say that macro-level prohibitions cannot work when large numbers of individuals, impelled by their needs and desires, act to circumvent the law.

In fact, we can say that these macro-level prohibitions entailed great costs to society. The prohibition of liquor not only failed to dry up the flow of alcohol but also created and bankrolled gangster empires. Such legendary gang bosses of the 1920s as Al Capone were fundamentally beer barons—they grew immensely powerful through their control of bootleg liquor. This side effect led many to doubt whether society could afford to continue such a costly policy.

The prohibition of drugs has entailed even greater costs to society. The sale of outlawed narcotics goes a long way toward financing the empires of organized crime. The Attorney General of the United States reported that sales of illegal drugs were about 79 *billion* dollars in 1980, "about equal to the combined profits of America's 500 largest industrial corporations."[108] The high cost of illegal drugs has turned thousands of drug addicts into criminals. Estimates vary greatly, but all experts agree that drug addicts trying to feed their habits, which can cost as much as several hundred dollars a day, account for a staggering amount of crime.[109] Crime may or may not pay, but it *always* costs. In effect, in order to prevent endangering a relatively small number of drug addicts, we have passed laws that have led to crime that is a danger to the life and property of everyone.[110]

Decriminalization

Perhaps the most visible legal efforts are those undertaken by the police, who have actively sought to deal with the drug problem by arresting drug users and drug dealers. Although periodic drug busts attract a lot of media attention, they have not been notably successful, if one is to judge from the size of the drug business and the openness of drug sales and drug use. The activities of the police are, of course, related to those of the legislators who pass various laws designed to make and keep a number of drugs illegal. As a result of the failures of the law and the police, there are many who now argue for the decriminalization of various substances.

Most experts would, I think, argue for the decriminalization of marijuana.[111] Goode, for example, says: "What makes the most sense to me, then, is the decriminalization of marijuana in all states of the United States—the removal of all criminal penalties for the possession of small to moderate quantities of marijuana."[112] In fact, as of this writing, eleven states have already done this, and in the others the laws are fast becoming unenforced and unenforceable.

While most of those reading this book might see the merit of the decriminalization of marijuana, what of heroin? Surely, we cannot recommend its decriminalization too? Arnold Trebach has some interesting ideas on this. Although he does not

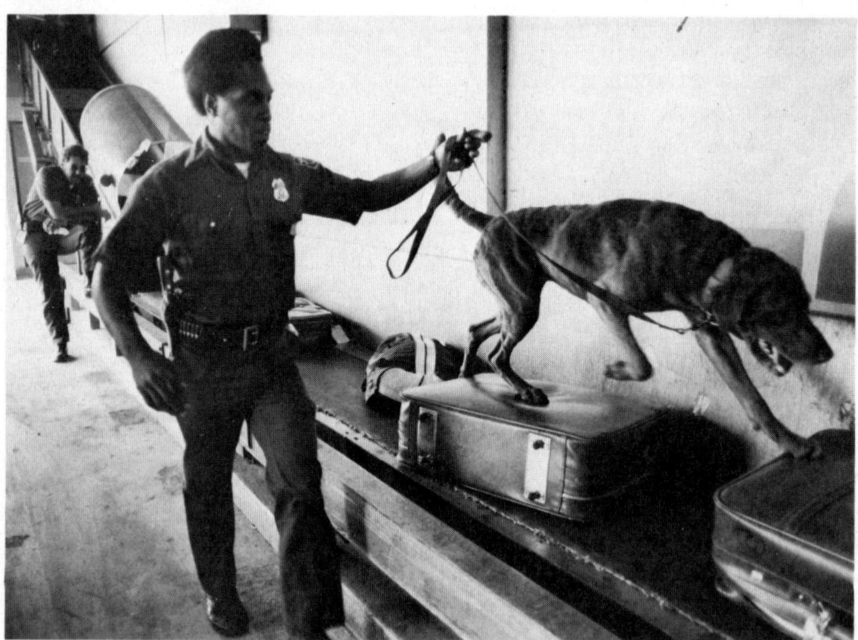

Although the government struggles to enforce the laws against drug importation, sale, and use, these efforts have not been notably effective. (Alan Reininger/Woodfin Camp & Assoc.)

support the unlimited legalization of heroin, he does want to see the laws against heroin loosened considerably. For example, he is in favor of dispensation of medical heroin to addicts. His view is that this "is their drug of choice, and many of them must have the drug in order to stay in treatment and out of agony."[113] He is also in favor of making heroin available to *all* patients under a doctor's care, not just terminally ill persons. Trebach argues that heroin is a wonderful painkiller and should not just be made available to, say, a terminally ill cancer patient, but also to a burn victim in great pain. Finally, he wants the law only to define the broadest possible limits and allow physicians and other therapeutic personnel to help heroin addicts with the widest array of possible tools. Thus, Trebach does not argue for decriminalization of heroin, but rather a humanization of legal restrictions on its use.

Living with Drug Use

Overall, Goode concludes: "Drug use is here to stay. . . . Addiction is a fact of American life. Heavy, frequent, compulsive, chronic drug use is also here to stay."[114] If Goode is right, and there is every indication that he is, then efforts to control drug abuse through laws and the police are doomed to failure. Goode comes to a realistic view of our future relationship with drugs:

> The only realistic approach to the drug problem is to develop methods, not to eliminate drug use or even to drastically reduce it, but to live with it and make sure that drug users do not seriously harm themselves and others.[115]

However, it seems highly unlikely, to put it mildly, that our nation is about to adopt a set of policies in accord with Goode's perspective. Rather, if we are to take presidential rhetoric seriously, we are moving in the opposite direction. In 1982, President Reagan "called for a major campaign against drug abuse in the United States." It is, in his view, "time for action," and among those actions, we must "brand drugs such as marijuana for exactly what they are: dangerous."[116] Thus, we seem to be continuing in the direction of a societal policy aimed at the clearly impossible goal of eradicating drug use.

SUMMARY

1. The focal concern in this chapter is dependence on an array of psychoactive drugs.

Part I: The Problem

2. The basic problem is the large, and in some cases increasing, use of various drugs. Of particular concern in this chapter are the usage patterns associated with narcotics (especially heroin), marijuana, cocaine, alcohol, and LSD.

Part II: Causes and Consequences

3. The physiological responses to various drugs have been shown to be relative rather than fixed; there are no invariable physiological responses to drugs.
4. Among the factors affecting the physiological responses to drugs are the social setting in which the drugs are taken and the status and position of the users.
5. There are also a variety of paths out of addiction, including simply outgrowing, or "maturing out" of, the addiction.
6. Also reflecting the relative response to drugs is the range of narcotics use from rare usage to the classical addiction syndrome.
7. While responses to drugs are variable,

it is clear that excessive drug use has adverse physiological effects on people.

8. Drug addiction can be the result of conditioned learning.

9. While there is no single personality complex invariably associated with drug abuse, it is clear that certain personality characteristics (such as a negative self-image) are linked to the development of drug dependency.

10. The labeling process is associated with drug use and drug abuse. The affixing of the label "addict" tends to become a self-fulfilling prophecy.

11. Differential association theory points to the importance of the socialization process in learning to be a drug user.

12. One's position in the social class system is related to the kinds of drugs one takes.

13. The culture and/or subculture in which one lives also has an impact on the kinds of drugs one uses as well as the impact those drugs are likely to have on an individual.

Part III: Responses

14. Among the responses at the individual level to drug abuse are heroin maintenance, methadone maintenance, behavior modification, and self-help, which can take a variety of forms.

15. At the social-psychological level, responses include various therapeutic communities (for example, Daytop Village) and nonresidential, self-help groups like Alcoholics Anonymous.

16. At the sociological level, the main responses have been laws designed to prohibit drugs of various types.

17. The historical evidence is that such laws do not work, with the result that there are strong reasons to support the decriminalization of marijuana and other drugs as well.

18. Whatever we do, it is likely that we are going to have to learn to live with drug use in our society.

SUGGESTED READINGS

Erich Goode, *Drugs in American Society*, 2nd ed. New York: Random House, 1984. A revised edition of a standard work summarizing sociological knowledge about drugs and drug use in the United States.

Lester Grinspoon, *Marihuana Reconsidered*, 2nd ed. Cambridge, Mass.: Harvard University Press, 1977.A basic source on various aspects of the marijuana problem.

Dan J. Lettieri, *et al.*, eds. *Theories on Drug Abuse: Selected Contemporary Perspectives.* Rockville, Maryland: National Institute on Drug Abuse, 1980. A collection of essays on a variety of sociological theories as they are applied to drug abuse.

Arnold S. Trebach, *The Heroin Solution.* New Haven: Yale University Press, 1982. Updated analysis of the British experience with the heroin problem.

George E. Vaillant, *The Natural History of Alcoholism.* Cambridge, Mass.: Harvard University Press, 1983. A recent and controversial study of the problem of alcoholism.

FOOTNOTES

[1]Erich Goode, *Drugs in American Society*, 2nd ed. (New York: Knopf, 1984) p. 6.

[2]Stanton Peele, "The Human Side of Addiction," *The U.S. Journal* (April 1981), 7; Goode, *op. cit.*, 1984. Complicating terminological matters is the fact that the term "drug abuse" has also come under attack. See: Norman E. Zinberg, Wayne M. Harding, and Robert Apsler, "What is Drug Abuse?" *Journal of Drug Issues*, 8 (1978), 9–35. We will have occasion to use both terms in this chapter, although we are cognizant of the problems with them.

[3]Goode, *op. cit.*, 1984, p. 21.

[4]Norman A. Krasnegor, ed., *Behavioral Tolerance: Research and Treatment Implications* (Rockville, Md.: National Institute on Drug Abuse, 1978).

[5]Goode, *op. cit.*, 1984, Chapter 6.

[6]Erich Goode, *The Drug Phenomenon: Social Aspects of Drug Taking* (Indianapolis: Bobbs-Merrill, 1973), p. 10.

[7]Lawrence Kolb, "Factors that Have Influenced the Management and Treatment of Drug Addicts." In Robert B. Livingston, ed., *Narcotic Drug Addiction Problems* (Bethesda, Md.: NIMH, 1958), pp. 23–33.

[8]John A. Clausen, "Drug Addiction." In Robert Merton and Robert Nisbet, eds., *Contemporary Social Problems* (New York: Harcourt Brace Jovanovich, 1966).

[9]Harris Isbell, "Clinical Research on Addiction in the United States." In Robert B. Livingston, ed., *Narcotic Drug Addiction Problems.* (Bethesda, Md.: NIMH, 1958), pp. 114–130. See also, Glenn Sonnedecker, "Emergence and Concept of the Addiction Problem." In Livingston, ed., pp. 14–22.

[10]Judith Droitcour Miller, *et al.*, *National Survey on Drug Abuse: Main Findings—1982* (Rockville, Md.: National Institute on Drug Abuse, 1983).

[11]On these changes see, John A. O'Donnell, *Narcotic Addicts in Kentucky* (Chevy Chase, Md.: NIMH, 1969); Clausen, *op. cit.*; Alan S. Meyer, ed., *Social and Psychological Factors in Opiate Addiction: A Review of Research Findings, Together with an Annotated Bibliography* (New York: Bureau of Applied Research, Columbia University, 1952).

[12]Thomas O'Toole, "Addiction Called No. 1 Health Hazard," *The Washington Post*, June 15, 1982, p. A6.

[13]*Ibid.*

[14]Nathaniel Sheppard, Jr., "Statistics Suggest U.S. Faces New Drug Abuse Problems," *The New York Times*, September 10, 1981, p. A18.

[15]Ronald Kessler, "Deaths From Heroin Use Increasing," *The Washington Post*, June 13, 1983, pp. A1, A21.

[16]Rita Dallas, "Drug Use Up Sharply in Britain as Key Therapy is Questioned," *The Washington Post*, September 3, 1981, pp. A33, A34.

[17]"Yugoslavs Alarmed by Sharp Rise in Drug Use," *The New York Times*, October 4, 1981, p. 13.

[18]Goode, *op. cit.*, 1984, p. 40.

[19]Ernest L. Abel, *Marihuana: The First Twelve Thousand Years* (New York: Plenum Press, 1980).

[20]Miller, *et al.*, *op. cit.*, p. 7. Bear in mind that many may have used marijuana once or only a few times.

[21]Goode, *op. cit.*, 1984, p. 42.

[22]Goode, *op. cit.*, 1984, p. 40.

[23]Miller, *et al.*, *op. cit.*

[24]Miller, *et al.*, *op. cit.*

[25]Robert Reinhold, "Student Abuse of Drugs Reported to Decline," *The New York Times*, February 25, 1982, pp. A1, A22.

[26]*Ibid.*

[27]Thomas O'Toole, "Sale of Cocaine Surges: Leaves 'Pot' in the Dust," *The Washington Post*, October 27, 1981, pp. A1, A7.

[28]"How Drugs Sap the Nation's Strength," *U.S. News and World Report*, May 16, 1983, p. 55.

[29]Miller, *et al.*, *op. cit.*, p. 8.

[30]"Cocaine: Middle Class High Time," *Time*, July 6, 1981, pp. 56ff.; Thomas O'Toole, "Sale of Cocaine Surges . . ." *op. cit.*

[31]Goode, *op. cit.*, 1984, p. 40.

[32]Abraham Myerson, "Alcohol: A Study of Social Ambivalence," *Quarterly Journal of Studies on Alcohol*, 1 (1940), 13–20.

[33]Goode, *op. cit.*, 1984, p. 42; Miller *et al.*, *op. cit.*, p. 71.

[34]Goode, *op. cit.* 1984, p. 72.

[35]Marty Mann, *Marty Mann Answers Your Questions About Drinking and Alcoholism* (New York: Holt, Rinehart and Winston, 1970). Latest figures derived from Goode, *op. cit.*, 1984.

[36]Goode, *op. cit.* 1984, pp. 165–166.

[37]Thomas O'Toole, "LSD Found to Be Regaining Its Popularity," *The Washington Post*, July 21, 1983, p. A7.

[38]Norman E. Zinberg, "The Truth is that Heroin Is Not a Drug of Pleasure," *The Boston Globe*, February 6, 1973, p. 20.

[39]Louis Lasagna, *et al.*, "A Study of the Placebo Response," *American Journal of Medicine*, 16 (1954), 770–779.

[40]Stanley Schachter and Jerome Singer, "Cognitive, Social and Physiological Determinants of Emotional State," *Psychological Review*, 69 (1962), 379–399.

[41]Charles Winick, "Physician Narcotic Addicts," *Social Problems*, 9 (1961), 174–186.

[42]Of course,some addicts do not survive to adulthood.

[43]Charles Winick, "Maturing Out of Narcotic Addiction," *Bulletin on Narcotics*, 14 (1962), 1–7.

[44]Dan Waldorf and Patrick Biernacki, "The Natural Recovery From Opiate Addiction," *Journal of Drug Issues*, 11 (1981), 61–74.

[45]Lee N. Robins, *The Vietnam Drug User Returns* (Washington, D.C.: U.S. Government Printing Office, 1974).

[46]Norman E. Zinberg and David C. Lewis, "Narcotic Usage 1: A Spectrum of a Difficult Medical Problem," *New England Journal of Medicine,* 270 (1964), 989–993.

[47]D. L. Davies, "Stabilized Addiction and Normal Drinking in Recovered Alcohol Addicts." In Hannah Steinberg, ed., *The Scientific Basis of Drug Dependence* (London: Churchill, 1969), pp. 363–373.

[48]D. Cahalan, *et al., American Drinking Practices: A National Survey of Drinking Behavior and Attitudes* (New Brunswick, N.J.: Rutgers Center of Alcohol Studies, 1969).

[49]Miller, *et al., op. cit.,* p. 73.

[50]Barry S. Tuchfeld, "Spontaneous Remission in Alcoholics," *Journal of Studies on Alcohol,* 42 (1981), 626–641.

[51]Cited in Goode, *op. cit.,* 1984, p. 44.

[52]Goode, *op. cit.,* 1984, p. 60.

[53]Abraham Wikler, "On the Nature of Addiction and Habituation," *British Journal of Addiction,* 57 (1961), 73–79; "Some Implications of Conditioning Theory for Problems of Drug Abuse." In Paul Blachly, ed., *Drug Abuse: Data and Debate* (Springfield, Ill.: Charles C. Thomas, 1970).

[54]Alfred R. Lindesmith, *Addiction and Opiates* (Chicago: Aldine, 1968).

[55]G. Terence Wilson, "Cognitive Factors in Lifestyle Changes: A Social Learning Perspective." In Park O. Davidson and Sheena M. Davidson, eds., *Behavioral Medicine: Changing Health Lifestyles* (New York: Brunner/Mazel, 1980) pp. 3–37.

[56]Richard A. Lindblad, *Self-Concept and Drug Addiction: A Controlled Study of White Middle Socioeconomic Status Addicts* (Rockville, Md.: National Institute on Drug Abuse, 1977).

[57]George E. Vaillant, *The Natural History of Alcoholism* (Cambridge, Mass.: Harvard University Press, 1983).

[58]Stanton Peele and B. K. Alexander, *The Experience of Addiction: A Unified Theory* (Lexington, Mass.: Lexington Books, (forthcoming); Stanton Peele, with Archie Brodsky, *Love and Addiction* (New York: Taplinger, 1975).

[59]Alan R. Lang, "Addictive Personality: A Viable Construct." In Peter K. Levison, Dean R. Gerstein, and Deborah R. Maloff, *Commonalities in Substance Abuse and Habitual Behavior* (Lexington, Mass.: Lexington Books, 1983) p. 218.

[60]Howard S. Becker, "The Social Bases of Drug-Induced Experiences." In Dan J. Lettieri, *et al.,* eds., *Theories on Drug Abuse: Selected Contemporary Perspectives* (Rockville, Md.: National Institute on Drug Abuse, 1980) pp. 180–190.

[61]Andrew M. Greeley, William G. McCready, and Gary Theisen, *Ethnic Drinking Subcultures* (New York: Praeger, 1978).

[62]Edwin H. Sutherland, *Principles of Criminology,* 4th ed. (Chicago: Lippincott, 1947).

[63]Howard S. Becker, *Outsiders* (New York: Free Press, 1963).

[64]See, for example, Erich Goode, ed., *Marijuana* (Chicago: Aldine, 1969).

[65]Isidor Chein, *et al., The Road to H: Narcotics, Delinquency and Social Policy* (New York: Basic Books, 1964).

[66]Mark E. Lender and James K. Martin, *Drinking in America: A History* (New York: Free Press, 1982), p. 102.

[67]Earl Rubington, "The Hidden Alcoholic," *Quarterly Journal of Studies on Alcohol,* 33 (1972), 667–683.

[68]John Dollard, "Drinking Mores of the Social Classes." In *Alcohol, Science, and Society* (New Haven, Conn.: Quarterly Journal of Studies of Alcohol, 1945), pp. 95–104.

[69]Lender and Martin, *op. cit.,* p. 178.

[70]*Ibid.*

[71]"Middle-Class Junkies," *Newsweek,* August 10, 1981, pp. 63–64.

[72]*Ibid.,* p. 63.

[73]"Kicking the Cocaine Habit," *Newsweek,* January 24, 1983, p. 50.

[74]Jay Mathews, "Curse of the North," *The Washington Post,* August 30, 1982, pp. A1, A4.

[75]Greeley, *et al., op. cit.,* p. 95.

[76]Vaillant, *op. cit.,* pp. 310–311.

[77]Barry Glassner and Bruce Berg, "How Jews Avoid Alcohol Problems," *American Sociological Review,* 45 (1980), 647–664.

[78]Arnold S. Trebach, *The Heroin Solution* (New Haven, Conn.: Yale University Press, 1982); Horace Freeland Judson, *Heroin Addiction: What Americans Can Learn From the British Experience* (New York: Vintage Books, 1974).

[79]Dallas, *op. cit.*

[80]Edwin Schur, *Narcotic Addiction in Britain and America: The Impact of Public Policy* (Bloomington: Indiana University Press, 1962).

[81]Henry Lennard, *et al.,* "The Methadone Illusion," *Science,* 176 (1972), 881–884.

[82]Dallas, *op. cit.*

[83]Robert Willette, ed., *Narcotic Antagonists: The Search for Long-Acting Preparations* (Rockville, Md.: The National Institute on Drug Abuse, 1975).

[84]See James R. Cooper, *et al.*, eds., *Research on the Treatment of Narcotic Addiction: State of the Art* (Rockville, Md.: National Institute on Drug Abuse, 1983).

[85]Vincent Dole and Marie Nyswander, "Methadone Maintenance: A Ten-Year Perspective," *Journal of the American Medical Association*, 235 (1976), 2117–2119.

[86]Dorynne Czechowicz, *Detoxification Treatment Manual* (Rockville, Md.: National Institute on Drug Abuse, 1978).

[87]James A. Inciardi, *Methadone Diversion: Experiences and Issues* (Rockville, Md.: National Institute on Drug Abuse, 1977).

[88]Roy Pickens, "A Behavioral Program for Treatment of Drug Dependence;" and Maxine L. Stitzer, George E. Bigelow, and Ira Liebson, "Reinforcement of Drug Abstinence: A Behavioral Approach to Drug Abuse Treatment." In Norman A. Krasnegor, ed., *Behavioral Analysis and Treatment of Substance Abuse* (Rockville, Md.: National Institute on Drug Abuse, 1979) pp. 44–54; 68–90.

[89]"Alcoholism: New Victims, New Treatment," *Time*, April 22, 1974, pp. 75–76.

[90]Stanton Peele, "Out of the Habit Trap," *American Health* (September/October 1983), pp. 42–47.

[91]Barry S. Tuchfeld, "Spontaneous Remission in Alcoholics," *Journal of Studies on Alcohol*, 42 (1981), 626–641.

[92]William R. Miller, "Controlled Drinking: A History and Critical Review," *Journal of Studies on Alcohol*, 44 (1983), 68–83; Stanton Peele, "Through a Glass Darkly," *Psychology Today*, April 1983, pp. 38–42; Glenn R. Caddy, Harold J. Addington, Jr., and David Perkins, "Individualized Behavior Therapy for Alcoholics: A Third Year Independent Double-Blind Follow-Up," *Behavior Research and Therapy*, 16 (1978), 345–362; David J. Armor, J. Michael Polich, and Harriet R. Stampul, *Alcoholism and Treatment* (Santa Monica, Cal.: Rand Corp., 1976); M. B. Sobell and L. C. Sobell, "Alcoholics Treated by Individualized Behavior Therapy: One Year Treatment Outcome," *Behavior Research and Therapy*, 11 (1973), 599–618. For a contrary finding on controlled drinking see, Mary L. Pendery, Irving M. Maltzman, and L. Jolyon West, "Controlled Drinking by Alcoholics? New Findings and a Reevaluation of a Major Affirmative Study," *Science*, 217 (1982), 169–174.

[93]Stanley Schachter, "Recidivism and Self-Cure of Smoking and Obesity," *American Psychologist*, 37 (1982), 436–444.

[94]Schachter, "Recidivism," p. 442

[95]Barbara Sowder, *et al.*, *Family Therapy: A Summary of Selected Literature* (Rockville, Md.: National Institute on Drug Abuse, 1979).

[96]Executive Office of the President, *Residential Drug-Free Manual* (Washington, D.C.: U. S. Government Printing Office, 1974), p. 1.

[97]Raymond M. Glasscote, *et al.*, *The Treatment of Drug Abuse* (Washington, D.C.: Joint Information Service of the American Psychiatric Association and the National Association for Mental Health, 1972).

[98]Norman E. Zinberg and John A. Robertson, *Drugs and the Public* (New York: Simon and Schuster, 1972).

[99]"Behind the Explosion in Self-Help Groups," *U.S. News and World Report*, May 2, 1983, pp. 33–35.

[100]Milton A. Maxwell, "Alcoholics Anonymous: An Interpretation." In David J. Pittman, ed., *Alcoholism* (New York: Harper & Row, 1967).

[101]Maria Riccardi, "SELF-HELP: Women Confronting Alcoholism," *The Washington Post*, September 1, 1981, p. B5.

[102]*Ibid.*

[103]Ann Corbett, "FOCUS: The Children of Alcoholics," *The Washington Post*, June 6, 1983, p. B5.

[104]"Is the Party Finally Over? Crackdown on Drunken Drivers Raises Hopes—and Doubts," *Time*, April 26, 1982, p. 58.

[105]Clausen, *op. cit.*, 1966.

[106]Rufus King, "Narcotic Drug Laws and Enforcement Policies," *Law and Contemporary Problems*, 22 (1957), 113–131.

[107]Kolb, *op. cit.*

[108]Nicholas Pileggi, "Drug Business," *New York*, December 13, 1982, p. 38.

[109]Gregory Austin and Dan J. Lettieri, eds., *Drugs and Crime* (Rockville, Md.: National Institute on Drug Abuse, 1976).

[110]Rodney Stark, *Police Riots* (Belmont, Cal.: Wadsworth Focus Books, 1972).

[111]Lester Grinspoon, *Marihuana Reconsidered*, 2nd ed. (Cambridge, Mass.: Harvard University Press, 1977), p. 367.

[112]Goode, *op. cit.* 1984, pp. 256–257.

[113]Trebach, *op. cit.*, p. 292.

[114]Goode, *op. cit.* 1984, p. 254.

[115]*Ibid.*

[116]*Federal Strategy for Prevention of Drug Abuse and Drug Trafficking: 1982* (Washington, D.C.: U.S. Government Printing Office, 1982).

"That Spring night I spent pillowed on your arm never really happened except in a dream. Unfortunately I am talked about anyway." Lady Suo

Bruce M Dean

4 *Mental Illness*

We may define *mental illness* as a serious failure to adapt mentally to external conditions that incapacitate a person in some ways. All societies have had to deal with people who show symptoms of madness or severe mental illness. Such symptoms vary widely. People may use speech that is out of keeping, muddled, or senseless. Or, they may engage in violent or self-destructive behavior. Some may hallucinate or see things that do not really exist. Others may withdraw into states of extreme depression or unresponsiveness. All societies, too, have taken some notice of less pronounced symptoms of emotional discomfort—anxieties, excessive fears, unhappiness, and the like. Although mental illness exists everywhere, societies have interpreted it and treated it in incredibly different ways. Our own society uses various methods to treat the mentally ill. Some persons receive drugs. Some undergo psychotherapy. Others are committed to mental hospitals. Some are treated through surgery. Recently, many have been released from the hospitals and allowed to make it on their own on the streets. There are still even a few who are exorcised to drive out evil spirits.

A wide range of disturbances have been labeled "mental illness" in our society. Indeed, in all modern societies, medical and social scientists disagree about what mental illness is, what causes it, and what cures it. This chapter cannot resolve the present debates. But it can clarify the disputes and provide a reasonable guide to what is known, what is only suspected, and what is still unknown about mental illness. How is it defined? How widespread is it? What factors probably play a part in causing it, and what factors do not? What treatment strategies seem at least promising?

PART I: THE PROBLEM

The symptoms of mental illness and the proportion of people who display those symptoms have been remarkably similar from one society and era to another. However, societies have differed greatly in their reactions to madness. Some societies have interpreted madness as a sign of special magical or religious powers. The ancient Greeks, for example, went for prophecies to the famous priestesses at Delphi, who were probably severely mentally ill.[1] In other societies the mentally ill were banished, tortured, or slain because they were thought to be evil or possessed by the Devil. Still other societies have pitied the mentally ill, and some have tried to cure them. The following is a very brief history of approaches to the mentally ill.

Historical Approaches

Ancient societies commonly regarded mental illness as a result of possession by devils or evil spirits. The sacred Hindu texts of India, for example, classified a number of forms of illness according to the demon that was thought to cause each.[2]

It was the ancient Greeks who were among the first to define madness in medical terms and to attempt to treat it. Hippocrates, who is generally honored as the father of medicine,[3] did not believe that mental illness had supernatural causes. He saw mental illness as stemming from natural causes such as physical disorders, conflicts within the personality, and external social pressures. Hippocrates' views prevailed throughout the Greek and Roman periods. As a result, the mentally ill were often treated with sympathy and kindness. Physicians advised people with mental problems to rest, to avoid excitement, and to seek a secure and comfortable environment.

During the Middle Ages, much of the knowledge gained by Greek and Roman civilizations was lost. Ignorance and superstition reigned. Demonic views of mental illness replaced the belief that madness had natural causes. Treatment therefore took the form of driving out the evil spirits through exorcism. Flogging, starvation, immersion in hot water, and burning were justified as ways to make the body inhospitable for the Devil. Hundreds of thousands of the mentally ill were tortured or put to death as witches or as devils in disguise.

Slowly, Western civilization rediscovered science and philosophy, and with that the notion that mad people were sick became popular again. In 1547, the monastery of St. Mary of Bethlehem in London was converted into a hospital for the insane. (People shortened the name to "bedlam," which became a common word for an insane asylum.) Hospitals for the insane were founded in various countries over the next few centuries.

These new institutions were an immense improvement over earlier practices, especially those of the Middle Ages. Yet conditions inside them more closely resembled prisons or zoos than hospitals. Inmates lived in filth and hunger. Many were kept in chains. The public bought tickets to view the antics of the "lunatics."

In 1793, a French physician, Phillipe Pinel, finally convinced officials to let him unchain some of the inmates in a Paris asylum. He gave these patients rooms and permitted them to walk around the hospital grounds. As a result, a larger number recovered and were released. Encouraged by the results, Pinel wanted to unchain all his patients. The president of France, looking at 300 inmates screaming and rattling their chains, said to Pinel, "Are you mad yourself that you want to unchain these animals?" But Pinel prevailed, and his reforms have influenced the treament of the mentally ill to the present time.

Mental Illness in the United States

The "father of American psychiatry" was Benjamin Rush (1745–1813),a contemporary of Pinel's.[4] The situation he confronted in colonial America in terms of its treatment of the mentally ill was far from an enlightened one:

> During the witchcraft delusions in Salem and elsewhere, the mentally ill were hanged, imprisoned, tortured and otherwise persecuted as agents of Satan. Regarded as sub-human beings, they were chained in specially devised kennels and cages like wild beasts, and thrown into prisons, bridewells and jails like criminals. They were incarcerated in workhouse dungeons, or made to slave as able-bodied paupers. . . . They were left to wander about stark naked, driven from place to place like mad dogs, subjected to whippings as vagrants and rogues.[5]

Although he himself had a number of primitive theories of psychiatric disorder, Rush did help pioneer humane treatment in American psychiatric hospitals. That cause was taken up by Dorothea Dix (1802–1887) in the mid-nineteenth century. Dix was appalled by the abusive treatment of insane persons and agitated for the reform of existing mental institutions. She also helped found a large number of more humane institutions. Ironically, despite her good intentions, Dix (and other reformers) contributed to the development of large mental institutions that served to separate the mentally ill from the rest of the population and to fill that population with a series of horrible ideas about the mentally ill. This problem continues to this day, although it has abated greatly in the last few decades.

Since the 1950s we have witnessed a process of *deinstitutionalization* among many mental patients.[6] This means that large numbers of people have been released from mental hospitals and allowed to live in halfway houses or even in the general community. This major change was made possible, at least in part, by the development and use of a wide range of drugs that are effective in dealing with various mental illnesses. Along with deinstitutionalization has come the development and increased use of community mental health centers. Instead of being locked away in mental institutions, people with mental problems can live in the community and periodically visit community mental health centers for drug treatment or psychotherapy.

The recent emergence of drug therapy and the resulting trend toward deinstitutionalization has *not* made the problem of mental illness less serious. It has simply shifted much of the problem from mental hospitals to halfway houses, community mental health centers, and the local community. It has also created a whole new range of problems as large numbers of people with severe mental problems are allowed to roam the streets. These people are often a problem not only to themselves, but also to the larger community. We will return to this issue in the last part of this section on responses to mental illness.

Approximately one out of every seven persons born in the United States will at some time in his or her life require professional help for emotional problems.[7] Bruce Dohrenwend estimates that the true amount of mental illness in the population may be even higher than that.[8] In spite of the fact that many millions of Americans are thought to be psychologically disturbed, and even though the problem has been studied intensively over the last century, we are not yet even sure what "mental illness" or "mental health" entails. Let us look at two definitions of mental illness.

Defining Mental Illness

Mental health and mental illness are defined in many ways. Although there are a number of others (for example, the statistical approach, which sees abnormal characteristics as simply those that are absent in most people[9]), we will focus here on the medical and the sociological approaches.

The Medical Approach

The medical model of mental illness, derived from physicians and psychiatrists, has become dominant in our society. This is part of a broader process that Peter Conrad and Joseph Schneider call "the medicalization of deviance."[10] It is not just mental illness that has come to be defined as a medical problem, but also such other forms of deviance as alcoholism, opiate addiction, and crime. The person with mental illness, like one with a physical illness, is seen as a *patient* who is *sick* and in need of *treatment.* In this approach, normality and abnormality are not defined statistically, but by the absence or presence of certain symptoms of disease. In this approach, mental disorder is seen as a *disease* that is caused by some inner (hereditary or biochemical) dysfunction in the individual. The *symptoms* of the disease are only external manifestations of the internal dysfunction. Treatment is based on the *medical model* in which the objective is to uncover and treat the inner disorder at its largely physiological source. Those who accept the medical model tend to trace mental problems to biological, genetic, physiological, or even biochemical sources. The basic idea is that if we can root out the cause, the symptomology of mental illness will disappear.

In recent years this medical model has come under attack by, among others, those who subscribe to a sociological model of mental illness. Among the most outspoken of the critics is Thomas Szasz, who argues that there is no such thing as mental illness, in the medical sense of the term.[11] Szasz recognizes that people have mental problems, but he rejects the idea that they are caused by some internal "disease" that needs to be cured. There are certainly people who have mental problems, but what they face is a series of social and ethical problems. To Szasz, people with mental problems suffer from what he calls "problems of living." These problems are not solved by institutionalization or by drugs. Their solution is in the social world in which we all live. It is the world, and not the individual, that needs "treatment."

The medical model has been extended to include various psychological and social factors. Such factors are seen by those who accept the medical model as producing a variety of changes *within* the individual. These changes, in turn, are seen as later manifesting themselves in a variety of symptoms, including the possibility of symptoms of mental illness. Thus, there is a tendency to see an analogy between physiological and psychosocial causes of mental illness. The analogy is extended to treatment where the objective is to root out the internalized manifestations of the original psychosocial causes. For example, childhood experiences such as severe parental conflict or poor adjustment to one's peers are seen as producing internal changes in the child that can later be manifest in mental problems of various types. The objective of therapy is to uncover and eliminate the internalized manifestations of the childhood experiences.

The Sociological Approach

As we have seen above in the discussion of Szasz, those who subscribe to a sociological approach to mental illness do not focus on problems within the individual, but rather on the causes of mental illness in the larger society. One variant of this is similar to some medical approaches in that psychological problems are traced to the individual's social relationships. For example, there is considerable evidence that one's position within the social class system is related to mental illness; specifically there seems to be more mental illness in the lower classes (that is, among the poor).[12] However, unlike the medical model, the focus remains on such social relationships rather than on the internal, psychological effects on the individual. The implication is that if we want to cope with mental problems, we need to change social relationships (for example, change the stratification system).

In another variant of the sociological approach, based on labeling theory, the focus is not on internal disorders, but on the social processes by which an individual is *labeled* as mentally ill.[13] What differentiates the mad from the sane is not some inner dysfunction, but rather the successful application of the label of mental illness. This shifts our attention from problems within the individual to the larger society and those who create and apply such a label. This approach also alerts us to the fact that the imposition of such a label can have an adverse effect on the individual, exacerbating, or even causing, psychological problems. We will have more to say about this variant of the sociological approach to mental illness later in the chapter.

Still another view is that it is society that is insane. It is the madness of society (as in the nuclear arms race) that makes people crazy. More extremely, it has even been argued that it is society, not a given group of individuals, that is mad. A major spokesperson for this point of view is R. D. Laing,whose views on this issue are that "individual madness [i]s the distorted reflection of a pervasive social and political madness."[14] In addition to treating the distortion in the individual, it is also necessary to alter the larger structural problems that lie at the root of the problem.

The medical and sociological models will inform much of the discussion that follows. While they are in some ways compatible, in others they are at odds, and that causes us problems in trying to assess the degree and nature of mental illness in society. In spite of the problems caused by these competing models of mental illness, it should be noted that there is now some effort to integrate them into a broader approach.[15] Although still in its infancy, this broader model has great promise for the future.

Categories of Mental Illness

Volumes have been written outlining the types of mental disorders recognized by psychiatry. However, in recent years the American Psychiatric Association has brought some order to this chaos by publishing a lengthy and definitive categorization of mental illness entitled *Diagnostic and Statistical Manual of Mental Disorders-III* (DSM-III).[16] We cannot begin to deal with all of the types delineated in DSM-III, but in order to understand mental illness as a *social* problem we need consider only a few general types of disorder.

A major distinction can be drawn between *organic* disorders known to be related to diseased or damaged brain tissue (brain damage, tumors, birth defects, and the like) and those for which no clear organic or physical cause has been shown. Problems that are not organic are called *functional* or *psychogenic* disorders. This means that the disorder is thought to be caused, at least primarily, by psychological or larger social factors. There is evidence that physiological, biochemical, and genetic factors may also play a role in some functional disorders. At present, however, the belief is that social and psychological factors have the clearest effect on these disorders. Three major functional disorders need to be distinguished: anxiety disorders, psychoses, and personality disorders.

Anxiety Disorders

There are generally three basic dimensions in *anxiety disorders*—feelings of tension and apprehension, behavior aimed at avoiding problematic situations, and such physiological reactions as increased heart rate and blood pressure.[17] Most of us under stress report similar symptoms, but they tend to go away when the stressful situation is over. Anxiety is a symptom of a mental problem only if it persists or keeps coming back over a long period of time and recurs even when there is no stressful situation to cause it. Those with anxiety disorders are usually able to get by—to hold jobs and fill roles in society—but their lives are fraught with worry, anxiety, and fear.

Within the general category of anxiety disorders there are three basic subtypes. The first is a *generalized anxiety disorder.* People with such a problem have a vague and general fear; they are unable to describe precisely what it is that is making them fearful. They are likely to be physically tense, to have physiological symptoms (for example, heart pounding), to be generally apprehensive, and constantly vigilant.[18] Second, are *phobic disorders,* which involve intense fears of specific (usually harmless) objects or situations as well as efforts to avoid them. Some of the most common phobias are fear of enclosed places (elevators, for example), fear of open spaces, and fear of heights. Third, are *obsessive-compulsive disorders.* An obsession is a recurrent thought while a compulsion is a recurrent action. These constitute disorders when the individual feels that these thoughts or actions are imposed on them; they feel powerless to control them. Obsessions and compulsions often occur together; hence the concept of obsessive-compulsive disorders.

Psychoses

A group of mental illnesses in which individuals manifest much more serious symptoms of mental illness than those who have anxiety disorders are called *psychoses.* Psychotics are very likely to suffer from emotional problems, to engage in a variety of bizarre behaviors, and to have difficulty functioning in the social world. They have a very hard time evaluating and relating to external reality. Their bizarre acts seem to be responses that are out of keeping with circumstances in the real world. We will discuss two broad types of psychosis: *schizophrenia* and the *affective disorders.*

Contrary to popular belief, schizophrenia does *not* mean "split personality." Such cases are called multiple personality and are quite rare in psychiatric history. The schizophrenic has one personality, and it is "split" only in the sense that feeling and thought are not integrated. In other words, feelings lead to inappropriate thoughts or thoughts lead to inappropriate feelings.

There is much disagreement on just what schizophrenia is and who is schizophrenic. However, there seems to be a consensus on the types of symptoms that are present in the disorder: (1) There are disturbances in the thought process and thought content—loose association, flight of ideas, and fragmented and senseless speech. (2) Schizophrenics show many problems in perceiving and in interpreting reality because they experience hallucinations and delusions. (3) They have trouble in interpersonal relationships including social withdrawal and isolation. One of the most defining characteristics of schizophrenia is a deterioration in comparison to previous levels of functioning. Family and friends of a schizophrenic are likely to say that the individual is "not the same" as he or she used to be.[19]

The *incidence* (rate at which new cases occur) of schizophrenia is not high. However, compared with other types of disorder, schizophrenia contributes very strongly to mental illness as a social problem in the United States. This is so because schizophrenia tends to be a chronic condition—people tend to suffer repeated episodes of illness—and because so many schizophrenics are found in mental hospitals. About 50 percent of all the beds in mental hospitals in the United States are occupied by schizophrenics. There are approximately 1 million actively schizophrenic people in the United States today.[20] Dohrenwend estimates that the number is actually much higher than that: 0.6 percent to 3.0 percent of the population under the ages of 60 to 65.[21] That would put the actual number of schizophrenics between 1 and 6 million. Such statistics give us a sense of the magnitude of the problem posed by schizophrenia.[22]

The other major form of psychosis comprises the affective disorders, which are marked by disturbances (usually extremes) of mood or feeling. Included are *mania, depression,* and *bipolar* (or *manic-depressive*) disorder. According to DSM-III, mania involves increased activity, elevated moods, hyperactivity, talkativeness, racing thoughts, inflated self-esteem, sleeplessness, easy distractability, and recklessness.[23] Depression involves feelings of dejection, unusual appetite, sleep disturbance, psychomotor retardation (excessive fatigue) and agitation (incessant movement), loss of pleasure or interest in usual activities, energy loss, feelings of worthlessness and guilt, difficulties in thinking, and recurring thoughts of death or suicide.[24] In the bipolar disorder, the first episode will take a manic form. Later the individual will alternate between manic, depressive, and normal periods.

Personality Disorders

Fundamentally, *personality disorders* are problems of inflexible and maladaptive personality traits that lead to impaired conduct. This is a very general category that can be clarified by discussing some of the subtypes within it. For example, *paranoid personality disorder* is characterized by an all-pervasive suspiciousness. It may take the form of feeling that one is being persecuted or involve delusional jealousy. However, the person with this disorder may well be able to function in the world, albeit with considerable difficulty. For example, it is very hard for someone with this problem to form lasting friendships. Those with *histrionic personality disorder* are prone to self-dramatization, such as fainting at the sight of blood and threatening suicide over a failed love affair. Then there is the *narcissistic personality disorder* in which the individual has an exaggerated sense of his or her own worth. While the personality disorders discussed to this point create more problems for the individuals themselves than for those they deal with, the same cannot be said about *antisocial personality disorder.* People with this disorder are unable to maintain consistent work behavior, are unable to be responsible parents or to maintain enduring relationships with sexual partners. Further, they are likely to reject social norms as well as laws, likely to disregard the truth, and likely to be irritable, restless, impulsive, hostile, and indifferent to those around them. In short, they may represent a genuine danger to others. These are frequently people who begin as juvenile delinquents and end up being adult criminals.

Because antisocial personality disorders

often involve conduct that society does not approve of, people are often tempted to use this category as an explanation for *all* criminal, delinquent, or other deviant behavior. But it is certainly not the case that all, or even most, deviant behavior is caused by antisocial personality disorder, or for that matter any mental illness. In fact, it is not even often correct to say that deviant behavior is irrational. Deviant acts may be very rational from the point of view of the people who commit them or the subculture to which they belong. For example, one need not be mentally unbalanced or incapable of feeling guilt in order to rob a bank, take drugs, or beat up a neighbor. People may have thought through such actions quite rationally, or simply learned these kinds of behaviors in their subcultures. In sum, deviant acts may well not be caused by underlying psychological problems at all.

Not only do we have a wide variety of mental illnesses, but we also have a number of different techniques for defining who has these mental problems and, more generally, who is or is not mentally ill. The result is that it is hard to determine the degree of mental illness within society as a whole. In spite of the difficulties, we must attempt to grapple with the problem of the magnitude of the problem of mental illness.

How Much Mental Illness?

How much mental illness is there in the United States? Answering this question is the task of a specialized branch of public health called *epidemiology*.[25] It is the study of the frequency and distribution of a disease within a geographic area or within a specific population.

Epidemiological studies of any disease employ two basic measures: incidence and prevalence. *Incidence* refers to the number of new cases occurring in a defined population group over a certain interval of time (usually one year). The *incidence rate* is the proportion of the total population under study that these new cases represent. *Prevalence* refers to the total number of cases existing within a defined population group at a specific point in time or over a specified interval of time. The *prevalence rate* is the proportion of the total population under study that these cases represent.

An additional distinction must be made between *treated rates* and *true rates*. True rates represent efforts to count *all* instances of disorder, whether treated or not. Although such rates are useful, our focus will primarily be on the *prevalence* (treated and true) of mental illness.

Treated Prevalence

From 1955 to 1972 there was roughly a 50 percent decrease in the number of residents in this country's mental hospital system.[26] The number fell from a peak of almost 559,000 inmates in 1955 to almost 276,000 in 1972. The number continued to drop dramatically until in 1979 there were slightly more than 140,000 residents in state and county mental hospitals.[27] It is estimated that in 1981 that number had dropped still further to 125,727, less than one-quarter of those institutionalized in 1955.[28] In other words, there has been a rapid and dramatic decline in the number of people in mental institutions over the last three decades. (There are signs, however, that that trend, while it continued into the early 1980s, is over, and we may see a leveling off, or even slight upturn, in the number of institutionalized mental patients. This can be traced to such things as the products of the Baby Boom between 1946 and 1961 reaching the age of greatest likelihood of institutionalization, the dislocations—such as the student and anti-Vietnam War protests—of the 1960s and

Figure 4.1 Inmates in Mental Institutions

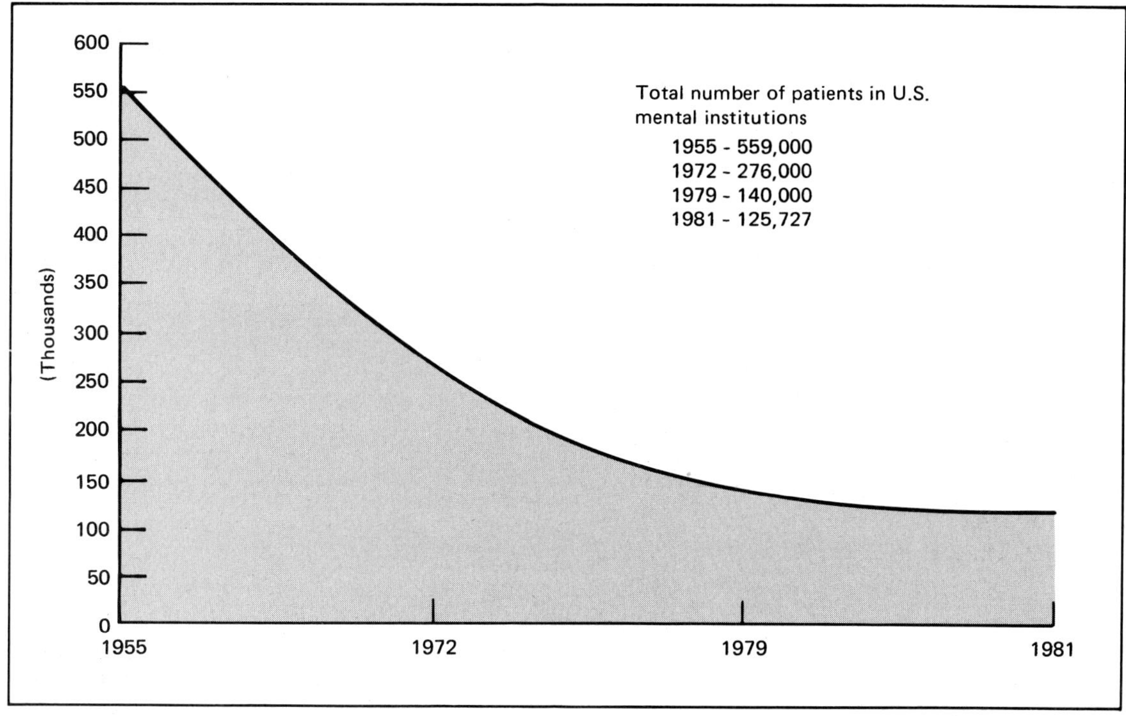

The process of deinstitutionalization is manifest in the striking decline in inmates in mental institutions.
Source: Survey and Reports Branch, National Institute of Mental Health. Unpublished data.

1970s, and the long-term adverse effect of heavy involvement with drugs that became much more common among young people during those years.)

Whatever may occur in the future, the issue here is how do we account for the dramatic decline in the number of mental patients between 1955 and the present? Have we, as a population, grown healthier mentally? Have we become so adept at treating patients that we can get them out of the hospitals cured of their problems? Unfortunately, there is little evidence to support such optimistic views about the drop in institutionalized mental patients. In fact, what has happened is, in large part, traceable to a change in our philosophy of treating mental illness. Basically, we have moved away, where possible, from treating mental illness on an inpatient basis to treating it on an outpatient basis in local hospitals, community mental health centers, short-term clinics, psychotherapists' offices, or not treating it at all and leaving disturbed people to their own devices on the streets.

Even though the number of hospitalized patients has decreased, the number of people who undergo treatment has increased. The increase is found in the number of people being seen on an outpatient basis by psychiatrists, psychologists, psychiatric social workers, and in community mental health centers. To take one example, in 1969 176,659 people were added to the population of those being treated as out-patients at federally funded community mental health centers. By 1979 that number had leaped dramatically to 1,222,305 outpatient additions.[29] New programs for the treatment of the mentally ill have been made possible because the number of mental health professionals has increased. For example, the number of psychiatrists almost doubled between 1963 and 1981 from 16,302 to 31,490. Membership in the National Association of Social Workers rose by 231 percent between 1960 and 1981 from 26,226 to 86,757. And the number of psychiatric nurses probably doubled between 1960 and 1980, increasing from about 25,000 to approximately 50,000.[30]

True Prevalence

The number of treated cases of mental illness is, of course, far lower than the actual number of such cases.[31] There are large numbers of people with one, or more, of the types of mental illness described above who are not visiting doctors, outpatient clinics, or are not institutionalized in mental hospitals. It is estimated that about 9 percent of the American population is being treated as mental patients in clinics or hospitals on an inpatient or outpatient basis. This, of course, leaves out all of those who are getting no help at all. This latter group may not get help because people are unaware that they have a mental problem, are unable to afford any kind of help, or are unwilling to admit they have a problem or, if they are willing to admit it to themselves, are not willing to admit it to others. The best estimate we have of the actual prevalence of mental illness is between 16 percent and 25 percent of the total population under 60 to 65 years of age.[33] This means that somewhere between 35 and 60 million people in the United States suffer from some type of mental illness. It has been estimated that the vast majority of these people, approximately 75 percent, have never been in treatment.[34] In the case of the more extreme psychotic disorders, perhaps as many as 45 percent have never received professional treatment. Even in the most extreme case, schizophrenia, it is estimated that as many as 20 percent have never been treated by a mental health professional. There is clearly an enormous gap between the treated and the true prevalence of mental illness.

The preliminary results of a recent large-scale study published by scientists at the National Institute of Mental Health (and already hailed as a "landmark in the development of American contributions to the psychiatric knowledge base"[35]) has contributed mightily to our knowledge of the prevalence rates of various mental disorders. The study, when it is finally completed, will ultimately encompass about 20,000 residents in five sites—Baltimore, New Haven, North Carolina, St. Louis, and Los Angeles. At the time of this writing, only data from Baltimore, New Haven, and St. Louis have been analyzed.

In one of the reports derived from this study, Robins, et al., analyzed the "lifetime prevalence" ("the proportion of persons in a representative sample of the population who have *ever* experienced that disorder up to the date of assessment"[36]) of 15 mental disorders listed in DSM-III. Lifetime prevalence was assessed by the use of a specially designed Diagnostic Interview Schedule (DIS). Table 4.1 reports data derived from this study on a number of mental disorders discussed previously in this chapter (as well as drug and alcohol abuse discussed in Chapter 3).

In this context we can only highlight a few of the major findings of this study. First, between 28.8 percent and 38.0 percent of the sample in the three cities experienced at least one of the 15 studied dis-

Table 4.1 Lifetime Prevalence Rates of DIS/DSM-III Disorders, Three Sites

Disorders	New Haven, Conn., % 1980-1981 N=3,058	Baltimore, % 1981-1982 N=3,481	St. Louis, % 1981-1982 N=3,004
Any of 15 Mental Disorders Covered	28.8	38.0	31.0
Anxiety Disorders*	10.4	25.1	11.1
Phoba	7.8	23.3	9.4
Obsession—Compulsive	2.6	3.0	1.9
Schizophrenia	1.9	1.6	1.0
Affective Disorders	9.5	6.1	8.0
Personality Disorder Antisocial Personality	2.1	2.6	3.3
Substance Use Disorders	15.0	17.0	18.1
Alcohol Abuse/Dependence	11.5	13.7	15.7
Drug Abuse/Dependence	5.8	5.6	5.5

Source: Adapted from Lee N. Robins, *et al.*, "Lifetime Prevalence of Specific Psychiatric Disorders in Three Sites," *Archives of General Psychiatry,* 41 (October, 1984), 952.

orders in their lifetimes. Second, the most prevalent lifetime diagnoses were "alcohol abuse or dependence, phobia, major depressive episode, antisocial personality, and drug abuse and dependence."[37] Third, when Robins, et al., analyzed their results by sex they found that males were significantly more likely to suffer from antisocial personality, alcohol abuse, and drug abuse while women were significantly more likely to suffer from major depressive episodes, agoraphobia (abnormal fear of open places), and simple phobia. Fourth, they found a higher prevalence of mental disorder among younger age groups than they had expected. Fifth, race proved *not* to be a significant factor as "differences between blacks and others in rates of psychiatric disorders are generally modest and rarely statistically significant."[38] Sixth, in terms of education one of the most important findings was that those who graduate from college tend to have fewer mental disorders than those who do not. We can anticipate continuing insight into the prevalence of mental disorders from this research study.

PART II: CAUSES AND CONSEQUENCES

An understanding of what *causes* mental illnesses, as well as their *consequences,* is needed to help us understand these age-old afflictions, to aid us in doing a better job of coping with them, as well as to help us know better how to prevent mental illnesses.

Mental illness has received a great deal of attention from social scientists. A massive body of research and theory is devoted to understanding this problem. As we will see, a great deal of work has been done at each level of analysis, but until we are able to deal with the entire range of questions raised by these different levels of analysis, we will not have a fully adequate sociology of mental illness. It is clear that there is no single cause for mental illness. Mental illness encompasses a wide array of psychological problems, and each one is the result of a complex set of causes.[39] Not only are there a multitude of causes of mental illness, but it is equally clear that mental ill-

Table 4.2 Levels of Analysis: Mental Illness

LEVELS	APPROPRIATE QUESTIONS	A PARTIAL SYNOPSIS OF PRESENT CONCLUSIONS
INDIVIDUAL	Is there a relationship between body chemistry and mental illness?	Yes. Certain chemicals have been linked to mental illness. Drugs have also been found to produce "model psychoses." However, much remains to be learned about the cause and effect relationship between biochemistry and mental illness.
	Can mental illness be inherited?	Genetic factors play an important role in mental illness, especially schizophrenia. However, we are a long way from sorting out completely the relationship between heredity and environment.
	Does psychoanalytic theory regard behavior disorders as the result (the symptoms) of intense inner conflicts?	Yes. Psychoanalytic theory sees the disturbed behavior of the mentally ill as symptoms of unresolved conflicts or imbalances in the personality system. To deal with the problem the basic inner conflicts must be resolved.
	Does learning theory regard the symptoms as the problem?	Yes. The goal is to learn how the inappropriate behavior of the mentally ill is learned and sustained and to alter behavior accordingly.
	What is the relationship between life-event stresses, personality, and mental illness?	Some people, with particular personality characteristics, are better able to deal with such stresses and are in a better position to ward off mental illness.

Table 4.2 Levels of Analysis: Mental Illness *(Continued)*

LEVELS	APPROPRIATE QUESTIONS	A PARTIAL SYNOPSIS OF PRESENT CONCLUSIONS
SOCIAL-PSYCHOLOGICAL	Does labeling theory deny that there is anything inherent in thought processes and behaviors that makes for mental illness?	Yes. To the labeling theorist, mental illness is a social role ascribed by other persons rather than achieved by the individual through thoughts and behaviors.
	What, then, to the labeling theorist differentiates the mentally ill from the mentally healthy?	The mentally ill, in contrast to the well, suffer from having been successfully labeled, as well as from various contingencies.
	How, to the labeling theorist, does a person who is labeled mentally ill know how to think and act like a mentally ill person?	We all have learned what it means to be mentally ill. Thus, when others treat a person as mentally ill, he/she already knows how to fill that role.
	How does labeling theory propose to "treat" mental illness?	Since the source of mental illness lies in society, it is society rather than the individual that is in need of treatment.
SOCIOLOGICAL	How does strain theory explain mental illness?	The mentally ill represent the retreatist response to the frustrations of failing to achieve socially valued goals.
	Is social class related to mental illness?	Yes. The lower a person's social class, the more likely it is that he or she will be diagnosed as mentally ill.
	Does social class cause mental illness?	Sometimes it seems to (social causation), but it is also the case that mental illness causes poverty (social selection).

(Continued)

Table 4.2 Levels of Analysis: Mental Illness (*Continued*)

LEVELS	APPROPRIATE QUESTIONS	A PARTIAL SYNOPSIS OF PRESENT CONCLUSIONS
	What is the relationship between class, stress, and mental illness?	The lower classes are subjected to more stress and those in it are less able to deal with it.
	What is the relationship between the family and mental illness?	There is a lower rate of mental illness among married people, but we do not know whether this is a result of social causation or social selection.
	Have the stresses of modern, industrial and urban societies produced an increase in mental illness?	Apparently not, as studies have not found changes over time or between rural and urban populations.

ness has a wide array of impacts on all levels within the social world.

One key in the relationship between the macro- and micro-levels and mental illness would seem to be the concept of *stress.* A number of studies have linked stress in the social world to psychological distress in the individual.[40] *Stress* may be defined as environmental conditions that cause anxiety, fear, frustration, and tension (psychological distress) in the individual. Strong linkages have been established between being in extreme situations, such as warfare, and mental illnesses. Somewhat less demonstrated is the relationship between stressful life events (for example, death of a loved one, loss of a job) and mental illness.[41] Efforts are also being made to link stresses caused by more macro-level phenomena—social classes, subcultures, society as a whole, the international arena—and mental illness. In other words, stress allows us to link macro-level phenomena to micro-level psychological distress. Stresses at the macro-level are linked to mental problems that are, in turn, linked to physical problems such as ulcers, high blood pressure, and heart disease. Although we are all subjected to stress and develop physiological and psychological symptoms as a result, we are *not* all likely to develop mental illness as a result of stress. We will have occasion to return to the issue of stress later in this part of the chapter.

INDIVIDUAL LEVEL

Physiological Factors

It is obvious that a variety of profound mental changes can be produced by physiological factors such as injury, physical disease, aging, and nutritional deficiencies. However, we will not deal with such physically induced mental illness in this chap-

Stress, including the pressures that may exist in one's occupation, has been linked to mental problems. (Mark Antman/The Image Works)

ter. Rather, our main concern is whether the severe functional disorders discussed above, such as schizophrenia, can be explained, in whole or in part, by physiological and biochemical abnormalities. We must also ask what role genetic factors play.

Biochemical Factors

Although we do not know the relationships definitely, there seems to be a link between biochemical changes in the body and functional mental illness.[42] As an example, low levels of two chemicals that serve as neurotransmitters, serotonin and norepinephrine, have been linked to depression.[43] As another example, an excess of dopamine has been linked to schizophrenia.[44] It is beyond the scope of this book to go into detail on the biochemistry of severe mental illness. Suffice it to say that linkages have been established between biochemical imbalances and mental illness and that we can anticipate that more such linkages will be discovered in the future. One thing we will need to unravel is the relationship between environmental stress, biochemical change, and mental illness.[45] There is a complex interaction among these phenomena.

This is pointed out in the fact that the medical and life histories, and even the diets, of psychiatric patients are very different from those of ordinary people. Most institutionalized schizophrenics, for example, eat an institutional diet, smoke incessantly, get little exercise, and have long histories of chemotherapies. Any of these factors can alter a person's biochemistry. Moreover, the extreme emotional and physical stresses associated with being mentally ill can also cause changes in biochemical functioning.[46] When researchers find peculiarities in the body chemistry of disturbed people, they must find ways to determine whether these peculiarities are related to the causes of the disorder, or whether they are effects of the people's emotional states or the situations they are living in. Although we are moving toward the view that biochemical changes are associated with severe mental illness, we are a long way from sorting out completely the cause-and-effect relationships involved in these changes.

Drugs and Model Psychoses

Another piece of evidence on the role of physiology in mental illness is the fact that certain drugs have been found to be effective with certain forms of disorder. For example, chlorpromazine usually reduces the disturbed behavior of a schizophrenic person, and lithium sometimes reduces the severity of depression. Again, however, the fact that drugs are effective in treating certain psychological disorders does not mean that chemical factors necessarily cause these disorders. Nevertheless, *chemotherapy,* or the use of drugs to treat disorder, has led many researchers to conclude that mental disorder could have a biochemical basis.

In addition to studying effects of drugs on certain symptoms of disorder, researchers have looked at drugs that create *model psychoses,* or artificial disorders. There are drugs like LSD and a mixture of cocaine and amphetamines that produce psychotic behavior that closely resembles schizophrenia.[47] This is another piece of evidence suggestive of the link between biochemical changes and severe mental illness.

Genetic Factors

Many experts suspect that biochemical sources of serious mental illness may be inherited. Whether or not this proves to be the case, the evidence is overwhelming that *genetic factors* play an important role in mental illness, especially schizophrenia. Thus, studies have found that 8 to 18 percent of children with one schizophrenic parent and 15 to 55 percent of those with two schizophrenic parents develop schizophrenia.[48] The best estimate at the moment is that "at least 40 percent of schizophrenic psychopathology is attributable to genetic factors."[49]

The best-known evidence on this linkage is provided by a series of studies conducted over a number of years on identical (single-egg) twins.[50] It was found that if one of the twins has schizophrenia, there is a strong, but not perfect, tendency for the other twin to also exhibit the disorder. Although this makes a strong case for genetics, it also powerfully makes the point that the impact of genetics is limited by environmental factors. Since the correlation between the twins is less than perfect, we can be certain that nongenetic factors play an important role in determining who becomes schizophrenic and who does not.[51]

The effort to separate hereditary from environmental factors has also involved the study of adopted children whose mothers were schizophrenic. These studies provide strong support for the idea that genetic factors contribute to schizophrenia.[52] Not even these studies, however, have provided clear evidence about the relative strengths of heredity and environment; nor have they been able to show just what it is that is inherited. It could be a specific vulnerability to schizophrenia, a more general vulnerability to mental disorder, a type of personality structure,[53] or even a certain biochemical make-up. What these studies *do* show, beyond any reasonable doubt, is that some genetic mechanism must be involved. However, it is also clear that genetic inheritance does not guarantee that a person will become mentally ill.

Psychological Factors

Why do some individuals fall prey to emotional problems while others, who face similar circumstances or have similar genetic make-up, do not? What impact do the various forms of mental illness have on individual personality? A wide array of psychologists, and other social scientists, have studied *personality* in order to try to answer these questions. Indeed, the view is widely held that whatever else mental health or mental illness may be, it surely involves the personality. A vast body of theory and research has been devoted to the analysis of the role of personality in mental illness. However, the major theorist, by far, associated with the role of personality in mental illness, indeed with the study of mental illness in general, is Sigmund Freud (1856–1939).[54]

Freud and Psychoanalytic Theory

Sigmund Freud is the father of *psychoanalysis* and *psychoanalytic theory.* Freud believed that the individual is acted on by internal and external forces. These forces produce tensions and conflicts within the individual. According to psychoanalytic theory, these conflicts underlie all symptoms of mental disorder. Symptoms are always expressions of some degree of failure on the part of the personality system.

Freudian theory also emphasizes the socialization process and the various stages a child goes through en route to adulthood. Each stage has its influence on the developing personality, and the mentally healthy adult has negotiated each of the stages and the psychic conflicts inherent in them. On the other hand, adults with mental disorders show symptoms that indicate which stage or stages produced conflicts that the individual was unable to resolve. Another objective of psychoanalysis is to allow the individual to return, at least in his or her mind, to that stage and cope with the unresolved conflicts.

It can be seen that Freudian theory has much in common with the medical model described earlier in this chapter. Symptoms are but superficial signs of unresolved inner psychic conflicts. Specific symptoms give clues to the underlying conflicts of the inner person. And, as in the medical model, the only way to intervene is to discover and treat the internal source of the symptoms. In this case, it is through painstaking psychoanalysis in which inner psychic conflicts are brought to the surface and are resolved by a strengthened ego (the rational aspect of the personality).

Most psychotherapists agree with the premise that personality disorders cause mental illness (although they may not agree with the specifics of Freudian theory). However, we are left with the question of what causes the personality disorder? It could be that biochemical and genetic factors predispose people to personality disorders. It is also certainly the case that larger-scale forces impinge on, and affect, the personality, in some cases causing the development of mental illness. Thus we cannot divorce personality problems from more microscopic and more macroscopic concerns.

Learning Theory

The psychoanalytic approach is certainly not the only effort aimed at understanding the psychology of mental illness. In order to give the reader a feel for the diversity of such approaches, we mention one other here—learning theory.

Unlike psychoanalytic theory, which attempts to explain all normal and abnormal behavior in terms of a single model of psychodynamic development, learning theory has no all-inclusive explanatory model. Therapists or clinicians who base their practice on learning theory try instead to discover how each patient has acquired inappropriate behaviors and which factors in the environment are currently maintaining them. They work with the hypothesis that abnormal behavior is learned in the same way as all other behaviors.

We can illustrate this approach with a classic experimental demonstration of how a person learns maladaptive behavior.[55] This is the case of a nine-month-old child who learned a phobia (irrational fear) of furry objects of all sorts. He had no fear of rats until the experimenters began to pair a loud noise with each presentation of a white rat. Soon the sight of the rat without the frightening noise was enough to cause a fear reaction in him. This fear rapidly generalized to all sorts of other furry objects such as rabbits and fur pieces, although no noise had been paired with them.

Thus, to the learning theorist, mental illness is a learned set of behaviors and is not traceable, as it is to the psychoanalyst, to inner conflicts. This leads to a different view of therapy. For adherents of the learning model, the symptom *is* the disorder, and to get rid of the symptom through "unlearning," or counterlearning, is to get rid of the disorder. Those persons holding the psychoanalytic position, on the other hand, argue that treating symptoms without getting at their internal source will only lead to the appearance of new symptoms.

Vulnerability to Stress

One of the latest areas of work in the study of the personality is the relationship between *life-event stresses* and the individual's vulnerability to and ability to cope with them.[56] Life-event stresses are events requiring change and adaptation in a person's life. Some of the most stressful life events include the death of a spouse, divorce, marital separation, a jail term, death of a close family member, personal injury or illness, marriage, being fired from one's job, marital reconciliation, and retirement.

It is clear that events in life are not equally stressful to everyone.[57] Some people, with particular personality characteristics and coping mechanisms, will be able to deal with stressful events or, more generally, with living in a particularly stressful life situation (for example, poverty). Others, with different personality characteristics and fewer coping mechanisms, would be unable to deal with similar events or situations. In general, we can say that the latter group is more likely to develop at least some forms of mental illness than the former group.

Death of a loved one is a life-event stress. People vary in the ability to cope psychologically with such stress. (Don Chidester/The Image Works)

SOCIAL-PSYCHOLOGICAL LEVEL

We have seen that different individuals respond differently to the same drugs, the same parents, the same environments. Obviously, personality has something to do with these differences. Beyond personality, it is clear that social experiences and processes play an important role. Such factors affect the onset, course, and duration of all behavior, including behavior that we consider disordered or reflective of mental illness. We could focus on a variety of social-psychological processes (for example, the process of being socialized into mental illness), but one such process stands out above all others in the social-psychological realm, and that is the process by which people come to be *labeled* as mentally ill. We have already encountered an application of labeling theory in the chapter on drugs; here we apply it to mental illness.

The Labeling Approach to Mental Illness

A basic premise of labeling theory as it is applied to understanding mental illness is that there is nothing inherent in thought processes and behaviors, in symptoms, that makes them reflective of mental illness. Rather mental illness is defined by the reactions and characterizations by others of certain thoughts and actions as symptoms of mental illness.[58] Thus, mental disorder is taken to refer not to a state or condition of an individual, or to his or her deviant behavior, but to the occupancy of a social role that is ascribed by other persons rather than achieved by the individual.

It is the work of Thomas Scheff that is most often associated with the analysis of the labeling of mental illness.[59] His basic thesis is that all societies tend to categorize and label norm violations as crime, sin, stupidity, and the like. After all these categories have been exhausted, there remain a number of forms of *residual deviance,* or forms of deviant behavior that cannot be included under any of the existing labels provided by society. Most of the symptoms that we generally associate with mental illness fall within this category. Society tends to lump all of these diverse symptoms under the label of mental illness. While it may be convenient for a society as a whole to have such a neat category for such diverse symptoms, it is often disastrous for the individual who is labeled as having such symptoms and therefore as being mentally ill. In Scheff's view, we all at one time or another experience these symptoms, including hallucinations, depressions, and withdrawal. However, most of us are not labeled mentally ill because of them. What differentiates the mentally ill from the mentally healthy, then, is largely reduced to a label.

Contingencies and Mental Illness

Since we all manifest these behaviors, what differentiates those who are labeled mentally ill from those who escape such labels? Erving Goffman's ideas are useful here; he believes what the mentally ill suffer from is *contingencies.*[60] If I am rich and hallucinate, I am likely to be labeled eccentric, but if I am poor and have the same hallucinations, I am much more likely to be labeled mentally ill. In the latter case, the person suffers from the contingency of being poor. Phyllis Chesler argues that another relevant contingency is whether one is a woman.[61] She contends that women are more likely than men, and in greater numbers than their percentage of the general population would predict, to end up as psychiatric patients. To take another example, if I have a loving spouse and I act in a bizarre fashion, my spouse is likely to protect me, but if my spouse detests me, he or she may want me labeled mentally ill and institutionalized. Other contingencies are frequency of bizarre behavior and whether that behavior tends to be manifest in public or in private. Thus it is contingencies like these, and not unusual thoughts and actions, that often differentiate those who are labeled mentally ill from those who are not.

Learning to Be Mentally Ill

Returning to Scheff, he argues that when deviant or bizarre behavior is denied or ignored, it tends to be temporary. That is, in many cases, if no one pays any attention to such behavior, it soon tends to go away. Trouble occurs when residual deviance is not ignored. Instead, it is labeled mental illness. This begins a process that results in making the temporary residual deviance relatively persistent. Instead of going away, it becomes fixed. All sorts of people come to label the person as mentally ill and the person comes to think of him- or herself in the same way.

This raises the question of how the labeled deviant knows what to do, knows how to play the role of "mentally ill" that other people have assigned. Scheff's answer is that all of us, beginning in childhood and through most of our lives, have learned, been socialized into, what is involved in being insane. When other people start to treat us as if we are insane, we know very well how to fill that role. Official agents and others begin to treat us in accord with the stereotype of someone who is mentally ill and we, in turn, begin to live up to that stereotype.

The "Myth of Mental Illness"

Another supporter of the labeling approach is Thomas Szasz, who is well known for his view that mental *illness* is a myth; it does not exist.[62] Szasz is cognizant of the fact that there are certainly people who have mental *problems,* but what they face is a series of social and ethical problems that are not caused by internal "disease" of an individual, as the term "mental illness" implies. Mental problems are not necessarily medical problems, so their treatment as an illness is not likely to help and can often hurt. A major liability of treating mental disorders as illnesses is that the individuals who are so identified come to be labeled as mentally ill. The application of such a label is likely to cause people even more problems; in fact, it can cause mental problems when none existed in the first place.

To Szasz, people with mental problems suffer from what he calls "problems of living." These problems are not solved by institutionalization or by drugs. Their solution is in the social world in which we all live. It is the world, and not the individual, that needs "treatment."

Criticisms of the Labeling Approach

There are a variety of criticisms of the labeling approach. In this section we will begin with a specific criticism of Szasz's perspective (as well as a response to it) and then move on to some general criticisms of the labeling theory of mental illness.

David Ausubel is one of the most important critics of Szasz's position.[63] He reflects the medical view that mental disorders are diseases of the central nervous system. Ausubel thinks psychiatric treatment is needed for those who are not able to cope with the realities of life.

But if mental disorders were exactly similar to physical illnesses, then we should expect from professionals a similar ability to diagnose the two types of problems. That is, we would expect a series of reliable observations and tests to determine whether one has pneumonia. Can the same thing be said for psychological problems? A study by David Rosenhan implies that it cannot, thereby calling into question the analogy between physical and psychological "illness."[64]

In Rosenhan's study, experimental subjects were sent to the admissions office of several mental hospitals and told to say they heard "noises." The only false information given by the subjects was their description of the noises (as well as their false names and vocations). Otherwise, they accurately described their other experiences, feelings, and interpersonal relationships. Despite this, *all* were admitted to a mental hospital and *all* were diagnosed as mentally ill. Once they were in the hospital they acted normally and said they no longer heard noises, but the hospital medical staff failed to uncover the fact that they were imposters. After stays in the hospital of from seven to as much as fifty-two days, all but one "patient" were diagnosed as having schizophrenia in remission. Could Rosenhan have designed a similar study in which his subjects claimed that they heard wheezing in their chests and then be treated and diagnosed as pneumonia patients? The answer would seem to be "probably not," thus casting considerable doubt on the idea that mental problems are classifiable illnesses.

The entire labeling approach to mental illness has been the subject of more general critical analysis. For example, several researchers have found mental illnesses like schizophrenia to be characteristic of a wide number of societies.[65] This indicates that there appear to be a number of things inherent in the behavior, rather than merely the label applied to that behavior, that lead it to be considered abnormal. Most recently, Raymond Weinstein has reviewed a large amount of the research done on patient attitudes and found very little support for the labeling approach.[66] However, even a critic like Weinstein believes that the labeling process does play some role, along with many other factors, in mental illness.

An understanding of the labeling of mental illness is useful as long as it is not taken too far. The labeling process is important, but only in conjunction with more microlevel physiological and psychological factors, as well as the more macrolevel factors we will discuss shortly. To put it another way, the labeling process is of utility, but *limited* utility, in understanding the development of mental illness. There are clearly many instances of the persistence of severe disorder although no label is affixed. There are also many instances in which disorder proves short-lived and the victim recovers quickly, even after having gone through the full labeling process. In addition, the fact that psychoses such as schizophrenia and manic-depressive reactions are found in all known societies suggests that purely social factors, such as those involved in labeling, are not the completely decisive factors.

SOCIOLOGICAL LEVEL

Strain Theory and Mental Illness

One of the most useful theories in dealing with mental illness is *strain theory,* especially the work of Robert Merton (see Chapter 1). In terms of Merton's types, the mentally ill represent the *retreatist* response to the frustrations of failing to achieve socially valued goals, such as success. The retreatist withdraws from the game of life, abandoning both the goals and legitimate means for attaining goals.

One of the major sources of strain leading to a retreatist response is the frustration associated with life in the lower classes. Is it therefore the case that the lower classes have a higher rate of mental illness?

Social Class

As was true of drugs, the evidence *is* that mental illness does fall quite disproportionately on the poor, the lower class.[67] While social class has been found to be strongly related to mental illness in general (when all forms and types are lumped together), of the specific types of mental illness, class seems only to be related to schizophrenia and personality disorder.[68] And, even here, the relationship is affected by a variety of other factors. It is important to understand that *this body of data implies neither that most disordered people are lower class, nor that most lower-class people can be regarded as disordered.* We can only say that there is significantly more mental disorder in the lower class than could be expected by chance alone.

One of the key debates here is whether this finding is the result of *social selection* or *social causation.* The social selection argument is that mental illness causes people to be economically unsuccessful. This hypothesis was first expressed in 1855 by Edward Jarvis, a New England physician and epidemiologist:

> Men of unbalanced mind and uncertain judgment do not see the true nature and relation of things, and they manifest this in mismanagement of their common affairs. They do not adapt the means which they possess or use to the ends which they desire to produce. Hence they are unsuccessful in life: their plans of obtaining subsistence for themselves or their families, or of accumulating property, often fail; and they are consequently poor, and often paupers . . . the cause of . . . their mental derangement lies behind, and is anterior to, their outward poverty.[69]

The logic of Jarvis's argument, and of the selection hypothesis, is that it is physiological or genetic factors, rather than social and environmental factors, that lead people to mental illness.

The social causation argument (which is consistent with strain theory) is essentially that it is the social and environmental factors involved in living in the lower classes that lead to a higher rate of mental illness. An early study of this genre done in the slums of Chicago in the 1930s concluded:

> In these most disorganized sections of the city and, for that matter, of our whole civilization, many persons are unable to achieve a satisfactory conventional organization of their world. The result may be lack of any organization at all, resulting in a confused, frustrated, and chaotic personality.[70]

At present, the question of selection versus social causation cannot be settled completely. It appears likely that both sets of factors play some as yet undetermined role in mental illness. If one has to choose among the two models, it seems, at least at the moment, that research favors the social causation model,[71] and therefore strain theory.

Class differences in responsiveness to stress are another aspect of the relationship between social class and mental illness. While recognizing the importance of class differences in exposure to stress, Ronald Kessler and Paul Cleary emphasize differences among classes in the way they respond to this stress.[72] Thus, while lower-class people are subjected to more stresses, they are also found to be "more responsive emotionally to the stresses they experience, even when these stresses are no more common among them than among persons who occupy higher social positions."[73] Thus, being in the lower classes is doubly disadvantageous—one is subjected to more stress and one is more likely to respond in a dysfunctional manner.

Family

Another important social structure in terms of its impact on mental illness is the family. No matter how mental health is measured, studies find a lower rate of mental illness among married people than among those who are unmarried.[74] We have the same issue on marital status that we had on social class, the question of social selection versus social causation. People who take the selection argument contend that the personal inadequacies of those who are later diagnosed as mentally ill cause them not to be selected for marriage, or, if they do marry, cause them to be divorced. The social causation interpretation takes the opposite view. It says that being unmarried puts people under stress (lack of sympathetic understanding, for example). And, such stress makes it more likely that they will become mentally ill. Furthermore, those who support this interpretation argue that marriage also gives some protection against treatment or hospitalization for married people who do become mentally ill; married people have families to care for them until they recover. In the end, we come to the same conclusion as in the case of social class—marital status is an important factor in understanding mental illness and both selection and social causation are involved in the relationship.

Figure 4.2 Cause-and-Effect Theories of Mental Illness

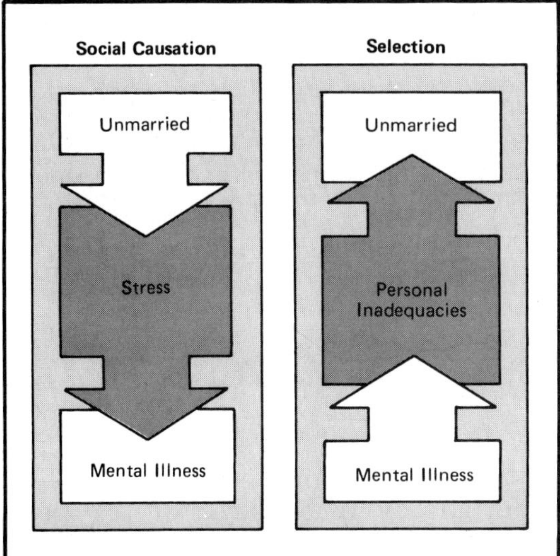

Does the stress of being unmarried cause mental illness? Or does being mentally ill cause people not to be selected for marriage? Social scientists who see stress as a major cause of mental illness argue that various social factors, including being poor, unmarried, or unemployed, produce stress and thus mental illness. Other social scientists see mental illness, however caused, as the major reason for personal inadequacies and social problems. They favor selection over social causation as an explanation of individual and social problems.

Modern Urban Society

A great many people are convinced that there is something fundamentally unnatural about life in modern urban societies. As proof that life has become too stressful, they contrast the complexity, the hectic pace, the impersonality, and the speed of contemporary social change to the tranquility of simpler times. The great increase in mental health practitioners and the expansion of facilities are often taken as proof that modernization has been purchased at a great psychic price—that, in effect, increasing numbers of persons are seen as breaking down under the stresses generated by society.

Obviously, many people do think that life used to be better than it is today; there is considerable nostalgia for the close interpersonal relations and the "timeless" customs of rural life. Many critics point out, however, that these notions of the past are badly biased. They omit the human suffering, the grinding labor, the uncontrollable diseases that killed as many as half of all the children born, the ignorance, and the bitter feuds of former days. But regardless of how one feels about the past, it is certain that life is now very different from the way it used to be. Have these changes included an increase in mental illness?

What evidence there is suggests that mental illness is not necessarily more common in modern urban life than it was in simpler settings. A number of studies have shown that some mental illnesses are more common in urban areas, whereas others are more likely found in rural areas.[75] Of course, it could be argued that this is not a true test since even rural life has become hectic and stressful in our society.

A more telling finding concerns a group called the Hutterites. These people have rejected modern ways of living and have successfully maintained isolated farming communities in various parts of the United States and Canada. Tightly knit family life goes on in these communities much as it did several centuries ago. The Hutterites do not have electricity or machines, and they adhere strictly to old-fashioned customs and dress. For a long time it was thought that they also were virtually immune to mental illness. However, studies have shown that rates of severe mental disorders are about the same among the Hutterites as among other Americans. The difference is that the Hutterites rarely seek treatment for their mentally ill members but instead care for them at home. Thus they do not become recorded cases of mental illness,[76] but being sheltered from modern life does not seem to offer them any protection against mental illness.

Perhaps the best-known study of the impact of modernization on mental illness was based on records of admissions to mental hospitals in Massachusetts from 1840 to 1940. The data revealed that there was no increase in hospitalization for psychosis during this century of rapid change from traditional rural to modern urban life.[77]

Upon reflection, it does not seem surprising that the evidence does not link mental illness solely with modern urban life. It is obvious that mental illness is not a new phenomenon; something in human existence was causing many of us to go mad long before there were freeways or two-martini lunches. This, however, is not to say that there are not characteristics of modern society that contribute to mental illness. Clearly, things like the threat of nuclear war, pressures in the work-world, economic inequality, and the rapid pace of modern life play a role in the etiology of mental illness.

PART III: RESPONSES

This section on responses will be divided among three broad issues. First, we will deal with the way that individuals may seek to cope with their mental problems. Second, we will discuss at least a few aspects of the mental hospital as a response to mental illness. Finally, we will deal with the alternatives to the mental hospital that have evolved in recent years as a result of deinstitutionalization.

Individual Responses

One of the most useful ways of thinking about individual responses to mental illness is to be found in Erving Goffman's work on stigma.[78] *Stigma* is a general concept standing for anything that can discredit an individual in the eyes of others. Clearly, mental illness is one type of stigma (another is any type of physical deformity). Goffman differentiates between two types of stigmatized individuals. The first type is the individual with a *discredited stigma* who "assumes his differentness is known about already or is evident on the spot." The second type is the individual with a *discreditable stigma* who assumes his stigma "is neither known about by those present nor immediately perceivable by them."[79] Although some people with mental problems may have a discredited stigma, most obviously have a discreditable stigma; their problem is not immediately obvious.

In Goffman's view the two different types of stigmatized people are confronted with fundamentally different problems. Since their stigma is known, discredited persons are confronted with the problem of managing tension during social contacts with normals caused by knowledge of their problem. On the other hand, discreditable persons must manage information so that others are prevented from learning of their stigma. The latter is the fundamental response open to the individual suffering from mental problems.

Managing information for mental patients basically comes down to concealing the fact that they suffer from mental problems. Under the broad heading of concealment, Goffman outlines a number of specific responses. Most generally, we can say that people with mental problems are likely to try to pass as normal. This means being cognizant of those actions that reflect psychological problems and trying to prevent them from occurring. Beyond that, people may seek to obliterate signs associated with mental illness, such as any evidence that they have been in mental institutions. People may use "disidentifiers"; things that indicate that they do not have mental problems. For example, sporting any symbol of long-term success in the social world—a college degree, a permanent job—would indicate to most normals that such people do not suffer from debilitating mental problems. People may also present themselves as less stigmatized than they actually are—such as a mental patient who passes as odd, daydreaming, or absent-minded. People with mental problems may enlist others (spouses, friends) to help keep their stigma secret. Most extremely, people with mental problems may avoid normals as much as possible in order to keep their stigma from them. They may find comfort among people with similar mental problems where they do not have to conceal their stigma.

Despite the array of devices open to them, people with mental problems are often not able to conceal those problems, and some of these people find their way into mental hospitals. The presumption is that since people cannot cope with their mental problems, perhaps the mental hospital can help them deal with their problems.

The Mental Hospital

For centuries the main approach to dealing with the seriously disordered was confinement in an insane asylum, or what in more recent times has come to be called a mental hospital.[80] The tendency was for these people to remain hospitalized for many years, if not a lifetime. Our objective in this section is not to present an exhaustive review of the strengths and weaknesses of mental hospitals. Rather, we will restrict ourselves to a narrow discussion of Erving Goffman's provocative thoughts on mental hospitals and mental patients.

Although Goffman has some thoughts on people who voluntarily enter mental hospitals, his main interest is in those who enter mental hospitals unwillingly, as a result of the actions of social control agents.[81] This is by far the most frequent route of entry into mental hospitals.

Once patients enter the mental hospital, they, in Goffman's words, get "caught up in the heavy machinery" of the mental hospital. They are almost immediately confronted with a massive assault on their self-image. A patient finds the therapeutic staff "arguing that his past has been a failure, that the cause of this [illness] has been within himself, that his attitude toward life is wrong, and that if he wants to be a person he will have to change his way of dealing with people and his conception of himself."[82] The humiliation of constantly being reminded that one is a failure is likely to intensify problems that already exist and to create new ones.

Yet individuals usually do not give up their identities easily. To protect themselves, they fabricate explanations of why they are in their present predicament (for example, due to a diagnostic mistake). Conditions, of course, belie such stories. Other patients are likely to ridicule the unreality of these sorts of statements. To make life easier for themselves, the staff in such institutions also point out to the patients that their stories are false. In so doing, they may be cutting the remaining threads that tie a person to normal mental health.

The construction of a case history record within the mental hospital is also part of the process of degrading and further destroying the self-image of the patient. One of the goals of the case history is to show that the person is sick, which justifies the original commitment and the continued hospitalization of the patient. The case history extracts from the life history of the patient those incidents that seem to be of symptomatic significance. While this information may be true, similar information could be uncovered about almost everyone.

The patient also is discussed publicly and, therefore, is further degraded. Public discussion of the patient occurs at various staff conferences and informal coffee breaks. Under this constant bombardment from all sides, the patient often finally gives up. "The patient seems to gain a new plateau when he learns that he can survive while acting in a way that society sees as destructive of him."[83] In other words, the only way many mental patients can survive is to affirm what everyone has been saying about them, that is, by behaving the way mentally ill people are "supposed" to behave.

Although we have emphasized some of the failures of mental hospitals in this section, it is clear that they have had, and continue to have, some successes. However, it is such failures, along with a number of other developments, that have led to the process of deinstitutionalization.

Deinstitutionalization

Over the past two decades, radical changes have occurred in the philosophy, as well as in the treatment, of mental illness. This change, which has been described as the "deinstitutionalization" of the mentally ill, involves a shift from treating seriously mentally ill patients in institutions to treating them within the local community.[84] As we saw at the beginning of this chapter, this has led to a massive decline in the number of institutionalized mental patients (see Figure 4.1).

One important factor in this change was the development of such psychotropic drugs as chlorpromazine (Thorazine), which made it possible to allow patients to leave the mental hospitals more rapidly and to continue to treat such seriously disordered persons in the community rather than in hospital wards. To go along with this, there has been a major expansion of community mental health centers of various types and a corresponding contraction in the significance of the mental hospital. Instead of remaining in a mental hospital, the seriously disordered person has been put on drug therapy and allowed to return to the community. There such people have a variety of alternatives, such as being treated during the day at a hospital and returning home at night, staying in "halfway houses" where they can live and be treated until they are ready to resume life on their own, living on their own and visiting community mental health centers for periodic treatment and evaluation,[85] or they may be left on their own to survive as best they can on the streets.[86] As one psychiatrist put it: "The streets are the mental asylums of the '80s."[87]

Legal Changes

A major new factor contributing to the process of deinstitutionalization is the change in mental health law since the early 1970s.[88] Changes in the law were motivated by abuses such as the case of a 19-year-old woman who was institutionalized in 1912 for, among other things, "a tendency to laugh and sing," laughing "at anything said or done," and having become "very voluble and will talk to anyone."[89] The doctors examining her thought the problems "only temporary" and attributed them to "bathing in cold water at menstrual period."[90] As of 1971, 59 years later, this woman was still a resident at a mental hospital.

Virginia Hiday enumerates a number of abuses in civil procedures undertaken by the state to commit people to mental hospitals, including perfunctory hearings of often less than five minutes duration, conclusory statements by medical and psychiatric personnel made on the basis of cursory examinations, rubber-stamping by judges, and defendants who were often not present at their hearings and frequently had no counsel or their counsels did a minimal job.[91] Abuses such as these led to increased interest in the civil rights of the mentally ill and to some changes in the commitment procedure. In general, the effect of these changes, at least in the short run, has been to reduce the number of involuntary admissions to mental hospitals. Thus, these legal changes are likely to contribute to the ongoing process of deinstitutionalization.

Problems with Deinstitutionalization

What started out as a humane program to allow hundreds of thousands of people to avoid the horrors of long-term, or even lifetime, incarceration has created a whole new set of perhaps even harsher problems for those who have been released from the mental hospitals. One of the factors in this is that most of the community mental health centers envisioned in the early 1960s were never built because money for them never materialized. Thus, for example, there was only one such center in all of Queens, New York in 1979, and that one had opened in 1977. Many areas have no community mental health centers at all. Not only are there not enough community mental health centers, but those that do exist are short on money, personnel, and research resources.[92] Without adequate community mental health centers, many people now feel that the mentally ill have simply been "dumped" onto the local community. The costs of supporting these people for years, if not lifetimes, in mental hospitals have been dramatically cut. Some feel that this was the real reason for the process of deinstitutionalization, rather than any great concern for the inhumanity of long-term incarceration.[93]

When they are cut loose from mental hospitals, often without fully realizing what is happening to them or what they are supposed to do, seriously disturbed people face a variety of problems. For one thing, they are likely to have little or no money. This leads many to lives in the rundown sections of our cities in cheap hotels, rooms, or worse, on the streets. There, they may forget about, or may have never fully understood, the community mental health centers. Often unable to care properly for themselves, they may suffer from malnutrition, sickness, and exposure. They are easy prey for the criminals who inhabit the same areas of the city. Cut adrift, they are likely to feel depressed and lonely, thus exacerbating their mental problems. Without supervision, they may forget to refill, or simply stop taking, their medications. Their symptoms are very likely to return with the result that they may end up either in the city's psychiatric wards for emergency treatment or in jail. Thus, in the name of

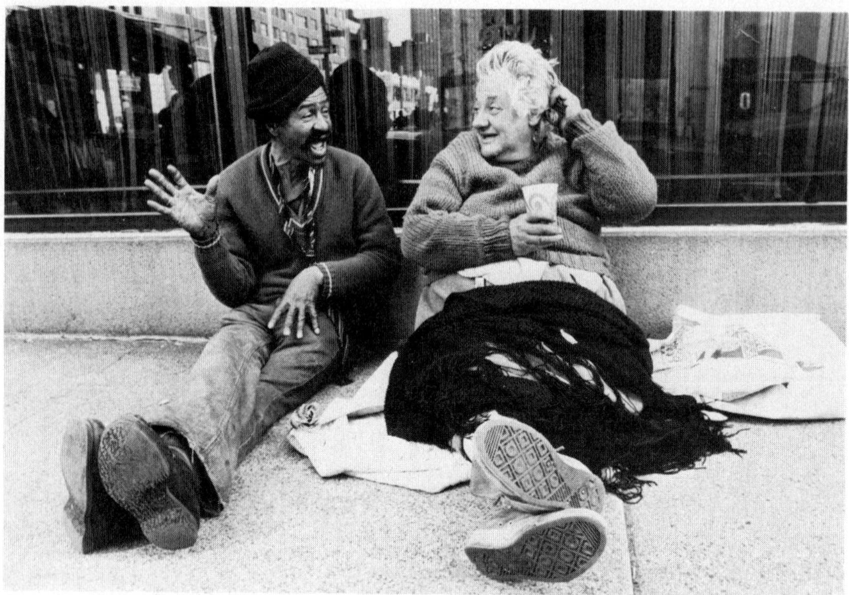

Many of those who have been released from mental hospitals have become the "street people" who seem increasingly common in urban areas. Life on the streets is hard on the street people and a cause of various problems for the larger society. (Jean-Marie Simon/Taurus Photos)

greater humanity, many former mental patients have been subjected to increasingly inhumane conditions.

In initiating the movement toward deinstitutionalization and community mental health, President John F. Kennedy enunciated some laudatory goals: "When carried out . . . reliance on the cold mercy of custodial isolation will be supplanted by the open warmth of community concern and capability."[94] But the fact that these objectives have not been attained was officially recognized less than two decades later when a panel reporting to President Jimmy Carter's Commission on Mental Health concluded that "it is now widely acknowledged that deinstitutionalization has, in fact, often aggravated the problems of the chronically disabled."[95]

Some Successes

It is tempting to judge the process of deinstitutionalization a total failure, but that would be too harsh a judgment. There are success stories in the movement from mental hospital to the community. There is, for example, the case of a paranoid schizophrenic who spent three years in St. Elizabeth's (a mental hospital) in Washington, D.C.[96] Among other things, he exhibited delusions of grandeur, believing himself to be "president of the world." He was released to a halfway house where, continuing on medication, he received counseling and job training. After two-and-a-half years, he was ready to seek a full-time job. He felt far more positive toward his experience in the halfway house than in the mental hospital: "At St. Elizabeth's . . . there's always someone to watch you, feed you. Here you learn to do for yourself."[97] Successes such as these have led observers like William Cockerham to conclude that "there have been significant successes" in the community mental health movement and that "[d]einstitutionalization is a desired process for many—including what may be a majority of mental patients."[98]

Improving Community Mental Health

Nevertheless, it is clear that a much better job must be done in the area of community mental health. Among the improvements needed are more, and better funded and staffed, community mental health centers. Greater care should be taken that those released from mental hospitals will be provided with adequate food, shelter, clothing, and medical care. Those who are released should receive more training in the coping skills needed to survive in the community. Support networks should be constructed and maintained in order to allow the released patient to continue to have the motivation to make it outside an institutional setting. Great care should be taken to be sure that the individual is able to break off dependent relationships with hospital personnel. Officials should also try to prevent those released from being thrust back into stressful family and social relationships. There should be better support and training of community personnel who will be involved with such ex-inmates. Finally, it must be realized that not all patients can be released to the community and that all concerned might be better off if some remained institutionalized. These are but a few of the things that can be done to improve the prospects of those who have been released from mental institutions.

Alternative Responses

Mental hospitals or community mental health centers are not the only alternatives available to us in dealing with those who are seriously mentally ill. There are more radical alternatives such as Judi Chamberlin's "patient-controlled" systems.[99] Chamberlin, a former mental patient herself, is critical of both mental hospitals and community mental health centers. She feels that both are heavily bureaucratized and professionalized systems in which people with mental problems are faced with distant experts who are anxious to label them as mentally ill. She urges the creation of alternative centers that involve ex-patients as well as the larger community, rather than "experts." These centers would focus on allowing ex-patients to reenter the community free of the label of "mental patient." Since professional experts, either in mental hospitals or community mental health centers, have a vested interest in maintaining and using this label, Chamberlin urges that they not play a role in these alternative systems. "Only by developing true alternatives can we prove that we can care for one another far better than psychiatry has 'cared' for its patients who have suffered under its control for too long."[100]

One other, of many, alternatives worth mentioning is the effort to increase the tolerance of family members of psychiatric symptoms. This is based on the fact that: *"Rehospitalization occurs when the ex-patient exhibits sufficient symptomatic behaviors that the family can no longer tolerate the ex-patient."*[101] It would clearly be beneficial to concentrate on increasing the family's tolerance of symptomatic behavior. Greater tolerance on the part of family members would enable more patients to remain in the community and out of mental hospitals. The assumption is that a caring and tolerant family environment would be better for most persons with mental problems than any professional and bureaucratized setting. At the minimum, remaining within the family, assuming the family is not a cause of the psychological problems, would increase the likelihood that outside services would be helpful.

In spite of such alternatives, it would appear that the dual problems of long-term institutionalization and massive deinstitutionalization are likely to be with us for the foreseeable future. On the one hand, we will need to keep large numbers of very seriously ill people in institutions for long periods of time. On the other hand, the economic and moral problems created by such institutionalization are likely to maintain the tendency toward deinstitutionalizing as many people as possible and as rapidly as possible. We must be prepared to confront the problems that this latter group poses not only to themselves, but also to the society around them.

SUMMARY

Part I: The Problem

1. All societies have had to deal with mental illness, or the serious failure to adapt mentally to external conditions that incapacitates a person in some ways.
2. The recent history of treating mental illness has involved the development of institutions to contain the mentally ill, the improvement of those institutions, especially in their ability to treat patients, and most recently the large-scale deinstitutionalization of the vast majority of mental patients.
3. These historical changes have not reduced the problem of mental illness, but have simply tended to shift it from mental hospitals to halfway houses, community mental health centers, and the local community.
4. Mental illness may be defined in various ways, but the two most important approaches are the medical model, which tends to see the source of the problem and the locus of treatment within the individual, and the sociological model, which sees the source of the problem and the arena of treatment in the larger society.
5. There are various categories of mental illness, the most important of which are the anxiety disorders, psychoses, and personality disorders.
6. It is difficult to get precise numbers on mental illness (although ongoing research is correcting this deficiency), but it is clear that it has increased dramatically. The drop in patients in mental hospitals has been more than offset by the dramatic increases in the number of people treated on an outpatient basis.

Part II: Causes and Consequences

7. At the physiological level, linkages have been made between biochemical and genetic factors and various types of mental illness. At the psychological level, it is clear that the personality of individuals, as well as their learned behaviors, are related to mental illness.
8. At the social-psychological level, it is clear that the labeling process plays a key role in mental illness. However, we must be careful to understand that labeling theory is only of limited utility in understanding mental illness.
9. At the sociological level, mental illness has been found to be related to the stresses of being in lower social classes, of being unmarried, and, more controversially, of modern, urban society.

Part III: Responses

10. As individuals, those with mental illness suffer, in Goffman's terms, from a discreditable stigma. As such, they are confronted with the problem of concealing information about their mental illness. Clearly, large numbers of the mentally ill are not able to conceal their stigma for very long or from very many people.

11. At least some of those who are unable to conceal their mental illness are likely to end up in mental hospitals. Although there are some successes, Goffman and others emphasize the degree to which such hospitals serve to foster rather than cure mental illness.

12. The failures of mental hospitals was one of the factors leading to deinstitutionalization, but there were others, such as improved medication, expansion of community mental health centers, legal changes that have reduced the number of involuntary admissions to mental hospitals, and the high costs of maintaining people in mental hospitals.

13. While there have been some successes, deinstitutionalization has created new problems, especially the fact that ex-mental patients have been left largely to their own devices to survive on the streets of our major cities.

14. One of the things that is needed, in light of deinstitutionalization, is a dramatic improvement in community mental health programs.

15. There are alternatives to mental hospitals and community mental health centers, such as patient-controlled systems. It might also be worthwhile to increase the tolerance of family members so that those with symptoms are kept out of bureaucratic and professional systems.

SUGGESTED READINGS

William C. Cockerham, *Sociology of Mental Disorder*. Englewood Cliffs, N. J.: Prentice-Hall, 1981. A solid, basic text summarizing sociological knowledge about mental illness.

Oscar Grusky, and Melvin Pollner, eds., *The Sociology of Mental Illness*. New York: Holt, Rinehart and Winston, 1981.

Thomas Scheff, *Being Mentally Ill: A Sociological Theory*. Chicago: Aldine, 1966. A near-classic of the labeling theory perspective on mental illness.

Thomas Szasz, *The Manufacture of Madness*. New York: Harper & Row, 1970. An important critique of the medical model of mental illness.

FOOTNOTES

[1]Gregory Zilboorg and G. W. Henry, *A History of Medical Psychology* (New York: Norton, 1941).

[2]Leonard P. Ullmann and Leonard Krasner, *A Psychological Approach to Abnormal Behavior*, 2nd ed. (Englewood Cliffs, N.J.: Prentice-Hall, 1975).

[3]There is some question now as to whether Hippocrates was really one person, or whether he stands for a number of people who received credit as one.

[4]Albert Deutsch, *The Mentally Ill in America: A History of Their Care and Treatment From Colonial Times*, 2nd ed. (New York: Columbia University Press, 1949), pp. 72ff.

[5]*Ibid.*, p. 53.

[6]Ellen L. Bassuk and Samuel Gerson, "Deinstitutionalizaton and Mental Health Services," *Scientific American*, 238 (1978), 46–53.

[7]President's Commission on Mental Health, *Report* (Washington, D.C.: U.S. Government Printing Office, 1978).

[8]Bruce P. Dohrenwend, "Summary and Conclusions." In Bruce P. Dohrenwend, *et al.*, *Mental Illness in the United States: Epidemiological Estimates* (New York: Praeger, 1980), pp. 150–157.

[9]Arnold Buss, *Psychopathology* (New York: Wiley, 1966).

[10]Peter Conrad and Joseph W. Schneider, *Deviance and Medicalization: From Badness to Sickness* (St. Louis, Mo.: C. V. Mosby, 1980).

[11]Thomas Szasz,"The Myth of Mental Illness," *American Psychologist*, 15 (1960), 113–118; *The Manufacture of Madness* (New York: Harper & Row, 1970); *The Myth of Psychotherapy* (New York: Doubleday, 1978).

[12]Bruce P. Dohrenwend and Barbara S. Dohrenwend, *Social Status and Psychological Disorder: A Causal In-*

quiry (New York: Wiley Interscience, 1969). The issue of social class and mental illness will be discussed further later in the chapter.

[13]Thomas Scheff, *Being Mentally Ill: A Sociological Theory* (Chicago: Aldine, 1966).

[14]James S. Gordon, "Who Is Mad? Who Is Sane? R. D. Laing: In Search of a New Psychiatry." In George Ritzer, ed., *Issues, Debates and Controversies: An Introduction to Sociology*, 2nd ed. (Boston: Allyn and Bacon, 1980), p. 86.

[15]Myrna M. Weissman and Gerald L. Klerman, "Epidemiology of Mental Disorders: Emerging Trends in United States," *Archives of General Psychiatry*, 35 (1978), 705–712.

[16]American Psychiatric Association, *Diagnostic and Statistical Manual of Mental Disorders*, 3rd ed. (Washington, D.C.: American Psychiatric Association, 1980).

[17]Richard Bootzin and Joan Acocella, *Abnormal Psychology: Current Perspectives*, 4th ed. (New York: Random House, 1984) p. 160.

[18]*Diagnostic and Statistical Manual of Mental Disorders, op. cit.*, p. 232.

[19]*Diagnostic and Statistical Manual of Mental Disorders, op. cit.*

[20]Bootzin and Acocella, *op. cit.*, p. 336.

[21]Dohrenwend, "Summary and Conclusions," *op. cit.*

[22]Although the number of schizophrenics is clearly high, there may be some overestimates here since there has been a tendency to use the diagnosis of schizophrenia as a catchall category for a range of mental problems that do not fit neatly into any other category.

[23]*Diagnostic and Statistical Manual of Mental Disorder, op. cit.*, pp. 208–209.

[24]*Ibid.*, pp. 213–214.

[25]Myrna M. Weissman and Gerald L. Klerman, "Epidemiology of Mental Disorders," *op. cit.*

[26]Bertram S. Brown, "A National View of Mental Health," *American Journal of Orthopsychiatry*, 43 (1973), 700–705; Bassuk and Gerson, *op. cit.*

[27]C. A. Taube and S. A. Barrett, eds., *Mental Health, United States 1983*, DHHS Pub. No. (ADM)83-1275 (Rockville, Md.: National Institute of Mental Health, 1983), p. 25.

[28]Survey and Reports Branch, National Institute of Mental Health, Unpublished data, private communication.

[29]*Ibid.*, p. 27.

[30]*Ibid.*, pp. 98–100.

[31]Darrell A. Regier, Irving D. Goldberg, and Carl A. Taube, "The DeFacto US Mental Health Services System," *Archives of General Psychiatry*, 35 (June 1978), 685–693.

[32]*Ibid.*, p. 693.

[33]Dohrenwend, "Summary and Conclusions," *op. cit.*, 1980. The Dohrenwends have done the best-known work in this area. See Bruce P. Dohrenwend and Barbara S. Dohrenwend, "The Problem of Validity in Field Studies of Psychological Disorder," *Journal of Abnormal Psychology*, 70 (1965), 52–69; *Social Status and Psychological Disorder: A Causal Inquiry, op. cit.*, 1969; "Class and Race as Status Related Sources of Stress." In Sol Levine and Norman A. Scotch, eds., *Social Stress* (Chicago: Aldine, 1970) pp. 111–140.

[34]Bruce Link and Bruce P. Dohrenwend, "Formulation of Hypotheses About the Ratio of Untreated to Treated Cases in the True Prevalence Studies of Functional Psychiatric Disorders in Adults in the United States." In Dohrenwend, *et al.*, *Mental Illness in the United States, op. cit.*, 1980, p. 147.

[35]Donald X. Freedman, "Psychiatric Epidemiology Counts," *Archives of General Psychiatry*, 41 (1984), p. 931.

[36]Lee N. Robins, *et al.*, "Lifetime Prevalence of Specific Psychiatric Disorders in Three Sites," *Archives of General Psychiatry*, 41 (1984), 949.

[37]*Ibid.*, pp. 952–953.

[38]*Ibid.*, p. 955.

[39]Weissman and Klerman, *op. cit.*

[40]Hans Selye, *The Stress of Life* (New York: McGraw-Hill, 1956); Hans Selye, ed., *Selye's Guide to Stress Research*, Vol. I (New York: Van Nostrand, 1980); Ronald C. Kessler, "A Strategy for Studying Differential Vulnerability to the Psychological Consequences of Stress," *Journal of Health and Social Behavior*, 20 (1979), 100–108; Ronald C. Kessler, "Stress, Social Status, and Psychological Distress," *Journal of Health and Social Behavior*, 20 (1979), 259–272; Ronald C. Kessler and Paul D. Cleary, "Social Class and Psychological Distress," *American Sociological Review*, 45 (1980), 463–478; Blair Wheaton, "Stress, Personal Coping Resources, and Psychiatric Symptoms: An Investigation of Interactive Models," *Journal of Health and Social Behavior*, 24 (1983), 208–229.

[41]Bruce Dohrenwend, "Sociocultural and Social-Psychological Factors in the Genesis of Mental Disorders," *Journal of Health and Social Behavior*, 16 (1975), 365–392.

[42]Eliot S. Gershon, *et al.*, eds., *The Impact of Biology on Modern Psychiatry* (New York: Plenum Press, 1977).

[43]Solomon H. Snyder, *Biological Aspects of Mental Disorder* (New York: Oxford University Press, 1980), p. 22; Hagop S. Akiskal and William T. McKinney, "Overview of Recent Research in Depression," *Archives of General Psychiatry*, 32 (1975), 285–305.

[44]S. H. Snyder, "Dopamine and Schizophrenia." In L. C. Wynne, R. L. Cromwell, and S. Malthysse, eds., *The Nature of Schizophrenia: New Approaches to Research and Treatment* (New York: Wiley, 1978), pp. 87–94.

[45]Akiskal and McKinney, "Overview of Recent Research in Depression," *op. cit.*

[46]David Rosenthal and Seymour S. Kety, eds., *The Transmission of Schizophrenia* (Elmsford, N.Y.: Pergamon Press, 1968).

[47]Solomon Snyder, *Madness and the Brain* (New York: McGraw-Hill, 1974).

[48]Herbert Weiner, "Schizophrenia: Etiology." In Harold Kaplan, Alfred M. Freedman, and Benjamin Sadock, eds., *Comprehensive Textbook of Psychiatry/III*, Vol. II, 3rd ed. (Baltimore: Williams and Wilkins, 1980), pp. 1121–1152.

[49]Herbert E. Lehman. "Schizophrenia: History." In Kaplan *et al., Comprehensive Textbook of Psychiatry/III, op. cit.*, pp. 1104–1113.

[50]The original work in this tradition is Franz J. Kallmann, *The Genetics of Schizophrenia: A Study of Heredity and Reproduction in the Families of 1,087 Schizophrenics* (New York: J. J. Augustin, 1938); for later research in this tradition see Margit Fischer, "Twin Studies and Diagnostic Issues in Schizophrenia." In Gershon *et al., The Impact of Biology on Modern Psychiatry, op. cit.*, pp. 261–270; Weiner, "Schizophrenia: Etiology," *op. cit.*, pp. 1124–1126.

[51]David Rosenthal, *Genetic Theory and Abnormal Behavior* (New York: McGraw-Hill, 1970).

[52]Rosenthal and Kety, *The Transmission of Schizophrenia, op. cit.*; Leonard L. Heston, "Psychiatric Disorders in Foster Home Reared Children of Schizophrenic Mothers," *British Journal of Psychiatry*, 112 (1966), 819–825; Seymour Kety, "Genetic Aspects of Schizophrenia: Observations on the Biological and Adoptive Relatives of Adoptees Who Became Schizophrenic." In Gershon, *et al., The Impact of Biology on Modern Psychiatry, op. cit.*, pp. 195–206; Weiner, "Schizophrenia: Etiology," *op. cit.*, p. 1136.

[53]Melvin Kohn, "Class, Family and Schizophrenia," *Social Forces*, 50 (1972), 295–313.

[54]Sigmund Freud, *Standard Edition of the Complete Psychological Works of Sigmund Freud* (London: Hogarth Press, 1953–1966).

[55]J. B. Watson and R. Rayner, "Conditioned Emotional Reactions," *Journal of Experimental Psychology*, 3 (1920), 1–14.

[56]William W. Eaton, *The Sociology of Mental Disorders* (New York: Praeger, 1980), pp. 58–59.

[57]Wheaton, *op. cit.*, 1983.

[58]Stephen P. Spitzer and Norman K. Denzin, *The Mental Patient: Studies in the Sociology of Deviance* (New York: Wiley, 1968).

[59]Thomas Scheff, "The Role of the Mentally Ill and the Dynamics of Mental Disorder: A Research Framework," *Sociometry*, 26 (1963), 436–453; *Being Mentally Ill: A Sociological Theory* (Chicago: Aldine, 1966).

[60]Erving Goffman, "The Moral Career of the Mental Patient," *Psychiatry*, 22 (1959), 123–142.

[61]Phyllis Chesler, *Women and Madness* (Garden City, N.Y.: Doubleday, 1972).

[62]Thomas Szasz, "The Myth of Mental Illness," *op. cit.*, 1960; *The Manufacture of Madness, op. cit.*, 1970; *The Myth of Psychotherapy, op. cit.*, 1978.

[63]David Ausubel, "Personality Disorder is Disease," *American Psychologist*, 16 (1961), 69–74.

[64]D. L. Rosenhan, "On Being Sane in Insane Places," *Science*, 179 (1973), 250–258.

[65]John Marshall Townsend, *Cultural Conceptions and Mental Illness: A Comparison of Germany and America* (Chicago: University of Chicago Press, 1978); Jane M. Murphy, "Psychiatric Labeling in Cross-Cultural Perspective," *Science*, 191 (1976), 1019–1028.

[66]Raymond M. Weinstein, "Labeling Theory and the Attitudes of Mental Patients: A Review," *Journal of Health and Social Behavior*, 24 (1983), 70–84.

[67]William C. Cockerham, *Sociology of Mental Disorder* (Englewood Cliffs, N.J.: Prentice-Hall, 1981).

[68]Bruce P. Dohrenwend and Barbara S. Dohrenwend, *Social Status and Psychological Disorder, op. cit.*, 1969; Bruce Dohrenwend, "Sociocultural and Social-Psychological Factors in the Genesis of Mental Disorders," *op. cit.*, 1975.

[69]Cited in Dohrenwend, "Sociocultural and Social-Psychological Factors in the Genesis of Mental Disorders," *op. cit.*, 1975, p. 371.

[70]*Ibid.*, p. 371.

[71]Blair Wheaton, "The Sociogenesis of Psychological Disorder: Reexamining the Causal Issues With Longitudinal Data," *American Sociological Review*, 43 (1978), 383–403.

[72]Kessler and Cleary, "Social Class and Psychological Distress," *op. cit.*, 1980.

[73]*Ibid.*, p. 476.

[74]Cockerham, *op. cit.*, 1981, p. 215; Lewis J. Sherman, *et al.*, "Prognosis in Schizophrenia, *Archives of General Psychiatry*, 10 (1964), 123–130; R. J. Turner, *et al.*, "Marital Status and Schizophrenia: A Study of Incidence and Outcome," *Journal of Abnormal Psychology*, 76 (1970), 110–116.

[75]Cockerham, *op. cit.*, 1981, p. 190.

[76]Joseph W. Eaton and Robert J. Weil, *Culture and Mental Disorders* (New York: Free Press, 1955).

[77]Herbert Goldhamer and Andrew W. Marshall, *Psychosis and Civilization* (New York: Free Press, 1953).

[78]Erving Goffman, *Stigma: Notes on the Management of Spoiled Identity* (Englewood Cliffs, N.J.: Prentice-Hall, 1963).

[79]*Ibid.*, p. 4.

[80]George Rosen, *Madness in Society* (Chicago: University of Chicago Press, 1968); Franz G. Alexander and Sheldon T. Selesnick, *The History of Psychiatry* (New York: Harper & Row, 1966).

[81]Erving Goffman, "The Moral Career of the Mental Patient," *Psychiatry*, 22 (1959).

[82]*Ibid.*, p. 133.

[83]*Ibid.*, p. 140.

[84]Bassuk and Gerson, *op. cit.*

[85]Leonard Stein and Mary Ann Test, "Alternative to Mental Hospital Treatment. I: Conceptual Model, Treatment Program, and Clinical Evaluation," *Archives of General Psychiatry*, 37 (1980), 392–399.

[86]Robin Herman, "Mental-Patient Release Program Leaves Many to Face Harsh Fate," *The New York Times*, November 18, 1979, pp. 1, 60.

[87]Alma Guillermoprieto, "Streets Called 'Asylums of the '80s' at Conference on Homeless," *The Washington Post*, April 26, 1984, p. D3.

[88]Virginia Hiday, "Sociology of Mental Health Law," *Sociology and Social Research*, 67 (1983), 111–128; David B. Wexler, *Mental Health Law: Major Issues* (New York: Plenum Press, 1981).

[89]Wexler, *op. cit.*, pp. 1–2.

[90]*Ibid.*, p. 2.

[91]Hiday, *op. cit.*, pp. 113–114.

[92]Bassuk and Gerson, *op. cit.*

[93]Andrew T. Scull, *Decarceration: Community Treatment and the Deviant: A Radical View.* (Englewood Cliffs, N.J.: Prentice-Hall, 1977). For a cost-benefit study of hospital-based versus community-based treatment that shows the economic advantages of the community approach, see Burton Weisbrod, Mary Ann Test, and Leonard Stein, "Alternative to Mental Hospital Treatment II: Economic Benefit-Cost Analysis," *Archives of General Psychiatry*, 37 (1980), 400–408.

[94]Lawrence K. Altman, "Release of Mentally Ill Spurring Doubts," *The New York Times*, November 20, 1979, p. B4.

[95]*Ibid.*, p. B1.

[96]Kenneth Bredemeier, "A New Life: Returning Mental Patients to the Community," *The Washington Post*, March 29, 1982, pp. A1, A4.

[97]*Ibid.*, p. A4.

[98]Cockerham, *op. cit.*, pp. 330–331.

[99]Judi Chamberlin, *On Our Own: Patient-Controlled Alternatives to the Mental Health System* (New York: Hawthorn Books, 1978).

[100]*Ibid.*, p. 220.

[101]James R. Greenley, "Family Symptom Tolerance and Rehospitalization Experiences of Psychiatric Patients." In Roberta Simmons, ed., *Research in Community and Mental Health*, Vol. I (Greenwich, Conn.: JAI Press, 1979), p. 358.

Rule a nation with justice. Wage war with surprise moves.
Become master of the universe without striving. How do I
know that this is so? Because of this. The more laws and
restrictions there are, the poorer people become. The sharper men's
weapons, the more trouble in the land. The more ingenious
and clever men are, the more strange things happen. The
more rules and regulations, the more thieves and robbers.
Therefore, the sage says: I take no action and the people
are reformed. I enjoy peace and people become honest.
I do nothing and people become rich. I have no
desires and people return to the good and simple life.
Lao Tsu
Bruce M. Dean

5 *Crime*

All human groups maintain some set of *norms*—rules about what members are expected to do and not to do under various circumstances. All groups impose considerable pressure on members to conform to their norms. And although such group pressure is effective enough to make people conform most of the time, no one has ever found a group so effective that everyone obeyed its norms all of the time. *Deviance*, as well as *conformity*, is a universal feature of groups.

Groups consider some forms of deviance relatively harmless and therefore make little effort to punish some instances of norm violation. They take other forms of deviance extremely seriously. Indeed, nearly all human groups have regarded some norm violations as so serious that they have made death the appropriate punishment.

As human societies became more complex, the enforcement of norms shifted from informal to formal procedures. Certain norms were enacted into legal codes, and the state assumed responsibility for determining guilt and assigning punishments. Thus, the concept of deviance applies to all norm violations, but crime applies only to deviance that is prohibited by law.

PART I: THE PROBLEM

The focus of this chapter is crime in the United States. Our basic thesis is that crime in this country is ubiquitous: as Daniel Bell once put it, crime is "an American way of life."[1] We will present the reader with a number of statistics to support this thesis. However, in spite of the mass of statistics, there are problems with all of the available methods of collecting data on crime.[2] Thus, in grappling with the dimensions of crime in America, we must also attempt to deal with some of the major ways of collecting information on crime as well as the problems associated with them.

Crimes: Definitions and Classifications

We may define *crime* as all behaviors and actions that violate the law and are subject to formally sanctioned punishment by the larger society.[3] One way of differentiating crimes is to distinguish between crimes against people and crimes against property. *Crimes against people* (or *violent crimes*) involve the threat of injury, or threat (or use) of force, against victims. Four major types of crime are usually included under this heading:

1. Murder and nonnegligent homicide (all willful homicides as distinguished from deaths caused by negligence).
2. Forcible rape (including assault to rape, threat of force, and attempted rape).
3. Robbery (stealing or taking anything of value by force or threat of force).
4. Aggravated assault (assault with intent to kill or to do great bodily harm).[4]

Property crimes do *not* involve the threat of injury, or threat (or use) of force, against victims; they are acts whose objective is to affect property unlawfully. The following are the major types of property crime:

5. Burglary (breaking or unlawful entry into a structure with the intent to commit a felony or theft; includes burglary attempts).
6. Larceny-theft (unlawful taking of others' property without force, violence, or fraud; excludes embezzlement and forgery).
7. Motor vehicle theft (theft or attempted theft of a motor vehicle).
8. Arson (willful and malicious burning or attempt to burn houses, buildings, vehicles, personal property, and the like of another person).[5]

The FBI calls all eight of the offenses listed above *index offenses.* They are also often called *street crimes,* a term we will use frequently throughout this chapter.

Another important way of differentiating crimes is on the basis of the ways in which they are handled by the criminal justice system. Here we may differentiate between felonies and misdemeanors. *Felonies* are the more serious crimes (for example, homicide, rape, and robbery) that are punishable by a year or more in prison. *Misdemeanors* are more minor offenses (drunkenness, shoplifting, and disturbing the peace) punishable by imprisonment for less than a year.

Most of our attention in this chapter will be devoted to street crimes. As a result of this focus, there are a variety of types of crime that will receive little or no attention in this chapter. In spite of the fact that they will not be discussed, it is important at least to mention some of the other major types of crime. A major social problem is *white-collar crime,* or crime usually committed by upper-status people in the course of their occupations, such as computer theft, embezzlement, consumer fraud, and bribery. Another type that has had considerable attention devoted to it as a result of Watergate and other scandals is *political crime,* or crime committed within or against the political system, such as illegal campaign contributions, "influence peddling," and terrorism. Then there is *organized crime,* or "those self-perpetuating, structured, and disciplined associations of individuals, or groups, combined together for the purpose of obtaining monetary or commercial gains or profits, wholly or in part by illegal means, while protecting their activities through a pattern of graft and corruption."[6] We usually think of the Mafia when we think of organized crime. Another important type of crime is *victimless crime.*[7] These are crimes in which it is difficult to identify a victim, since the participants choose to be involved in the activities, such as pornography and prostitution. Finally, there is *juvenile delinquency:* illegal or antisocial behavior on the part of a minor. There are, then, a large number of types of crime that we will not be able to deal with in this chapter. As the reader will see, we will have our hands full trying simply to deal with the complex topic of street crime in a single chapter.

Pornography and prostitution are included under the heading of "victimless crimes."
(Charles Gatewood/Stock, Boston)

Counting Crimes

Crime rates are fundamental to all discussions of crime in society and they are computed by dividing the number of crimes by the population size. (The result is ordinarily multiplied by 100,000 to avoid working with very small decimals, and thus we speak of crime rates per 100,000 persons in the population. In 1983, for example, it was computed that 8 homicides had occurred that year for every 100,000 Americans; the homicide rate was 8.0).[8] The possession of various crime rates allows us to address a number of important questions: Is crime increasing or decreasing? What are the effects of various laws or programs on reducing crime? What kinds of crime are occurring and how often? Few questions taken up in this book match these in terms of the extent of public anxiety, conflict, political exploitation, and pontification that they have produced over the last several decades. People everywhere fear to walk the streets; home-security appliances have enjoyed a bonanza market; politicians promise law and order; and prophets proclaim the doom of a society overwhelmed by criminality.

Despite this immense concern, the shocking fact is that until very recently (and to a lesser degree to this day) crime statistics were highly limited, inaccurate, and unreliable.[9] Thus it was often difficult to make more than an educated guess about the kind and amount of crime that occurred and about whether the amount represented an increase or a decrease from that of previous years.

Today, there are two main sources of data on crime in America. One is the annual *Uniform Crime Reports* compiled by the Federal Bureau of Investigation, which is a major source of *official crime statistics.* For many years this was the best source of data on crime, even though it had a number of problems.[10] Over the years many of those problems have been reduced or eliminated. More importantly, since the early 1970s it has been supplemented by the annual *Sourcebook of Criminal Justice Statistics* published by the United States Department of Justice. This sourcebook covers a number of areas that are not dealt with in the *Uniform Crime Reports*, especially *victimization statistics* derived from *The National Crime Survey* and information gleaned from *public opinion polls.* In the next several sections we will briefly review official crime statistics, victimization statistics, and information from public opinion polls.

Official Crime Statistics

The best-known crime statistics in the United States are those gathered from official law enforcement agencies and collated and published by the FBI as the *Uniform Crime Reports* (UCR).[11] Local police agencies send to the FBI monthly and annual summary reports on crimes in their jurisdiction; these provide the basis for the UCR statistics. There reports include data on the number of offenses discovered by or reported to these law enforcement agencies.

In 1983, the FBI indicated in the *Uniform Crime Report* that 12.07 million index criminal offenses were known to the police in the United States that year. Of these, about 10.83 million (about 90 percent) were *property* crimes—burglary, larceny, motor vehicle theft, and arson. Of the approximately 1.24 million *crimes against people,* approximately 19,000 were homicides, 79,000 were forcible rapes, 500,000 were robberies, and 640,000 were aggravated assaults.[12] Thus it is clear that the

Burglary is one example of a property crime. In addition to losing property, the victim is often affected by physical disruption and psychological trauma.
(AP/Wide World Photos)

vast majority of crimes in the United States are crimes against property and *not* crimes against people.

Urban-Rural Differences

Most crimes in the United States occur in urban areas. Even when we take into consideration the fact that a majority of the population lives in urban areas, it is still the case that crime is relatively more frequent in urban than rural areas. We will define an urban area as a Standard Metropolitan Statistical Area (SMSA), or "a county or group of contiguous counties which contains at least one city of 50,000 or more inhabitants." (For more on this see Chapter 13 on Urban Problems.) In 1983 SMSAs had a violent-offense rate of 627.2 per 100,000 (that is, there were 627.2 known violent index offenses for every 100,000 people living in SMSAs), whereas the comparable rate in rural areas was 161.2 per 100,000. The same year, cities had a property-offenses rate of 5,225.1 per 100,000, whereas the comparable rate in rural areas was 1,719.8 per 100,000. These figures underscore the extent to which the crime problem is disproportionately an urban problem. Violent crimes are about four times as likely to occur in cities than in rural areas, and the likelihood of property crimes in cities is about three times that in rural areas.

Historical Trends. Table 5.1 shows the recent trends in known offenses.

The upper half of the figure gives the *number* of known offenses for each category from 1960 through 1983; the lower half of the table gives the *rate* per 100,000 for known offenses for each category for the same period. The last row of the table reports the percent increase in the rate per 100,000 for each offense over the 1960 to 1983 period. For example, in 1960, the rate per 100,000 for murder and negligent manslaughter was 5.1, whereas in 1983 the rate was 8.3—an increase of 62.7 percent (3.2 divided by 5.1 = .627). More generally, the table shows an increase in violent crimes of about 229 percent and an increase in property crime of about 168 percent from 1960 to 1983. Of the individual offenses, robbery shows the greatest rate increase, while it is murder that shows the smallest rate increase from 1960 to 1983. The overall picture on crime during this period is discouraging, reflecting a broadscale increase in crime rates. However, we need to be cautious here since there is at least some evidence that there might have been more crime in the United States in the nineteenth century than there is today.[13] It is also interesting to note that there are some bright spots in the recent statistics, such as the relatively small increase in the homicide rate and the declining motor vehicle theft rate since 1980.

Although there certainly has been a dramatic increase in crime since 1960, the issue is more complex that it first appears. For example, the total number of index crimes was over 13 million in both 1980 and 1981, but dipped a bit below 13 million in 1982.[14] Crime *dropped* 3 percent in 1982 and in 1983 it dropped another 7 percent to 12.1 million[15] (see Figure 5.1). The biggest factor in this recent decline appears to be the aging of the post-World War II Baby Boom population into their 30s and beyond the most crime-prone 15- to 29-year-old category. In addition to the need to look more closely at very recent developments, it may also be that we have not taken a long enough time perspective on the crime problem. For example, as is evident in Figure 5.2, the homicide rate only recently surpassed the previous high rate achieved in 1933,[16] and as of 1983 has dipped below it once again. In one study, it was found that the rates for major crimes in Boston had declined between 1849 and 1950.[17] Another showed a general decline

Table 5.1 Estimated Number and Rate (per 100,000 Inhabitants) of Offenses Known to Police, by Offense, United States, 1960–1983.

	POPU-LATION[a]	TOTAL CRIME[b] INDEX	VIOLENT CRIME[c]	PROPERTY CRIME[c]	MURDER & NEGLIGENT MANSLAUGHTER	FORCIBLE RAPE	ROBBERY	AGGRAVATED ASSAULT	BURGLARY	LARCENY-THEFT	MOTOR VEHICLE THEFT
	Number of offenses:										
1960	179,323,175	3,384,200	288,460	3,095,700	9,110	17,190	107,840	154,320	912,100	1,855,400	328,200
1965	193,526,000	4,739,400	387,390	4,352,000	9,960	23,410	138,690	2.5,330	1,282,500	2,572,600	496,900
1970	203,235,298	8,098,000	738,820	7,359,200	16,000	37,990	349,860	334,970	2,205,000	4,225,800	928,400
1975	213,124,000	11,256,600	1,026,280	10,230,300	20,510	56,090	464,970	484,710	3,252,100	5,977,700	1,000,500
1980	225,349,264	13,295,400	1,308,900	11,986,500	23,040	82,090	548,810	654,960	3,759,200	7,112,700	1,114,700
1983	233,981,000	12,070,200	1,237,980	10,832,200	19,310	78,920	500,220	639,530	3,120,800	6,707,000	1,004,400
	Rate per 100,000 Inhabitants[d]:										
1960		1,887.2	160.9	1,726.3	5.1	9.6	60.1	86.1	508.6	1,034.7	183.0
1965		2,449.0	200.2	2,248.8	5.1	12.1	71.1	111.3	662.7	1,329.3	256.8
1970		3,984.5	363.5	3,621.0	7.9	18.7	172.1	164.8	1,084.9	2,079.3	456.8
1975		5,281.7	481.5	4,800.2	9.6	26.3	218.2	227.4	1,525.9	2,804.8	469.4
1980		5,899.9	580.8	5,319.1	10.2	36.4	243.5	290.6	1,668.2	3,156.3	494.6
1983		5,158.6	529.1	4,629.5	8.3	33.7	213.8	273.3	1,333.8	2,866.5	429.3
Percent increases:											
1960–1983		+173.3	+228.8	+168.2	+62.7	+ 251.0	+255.7	+217.4	+162.2	+179.0	+134.6

Source: 1960–1980 data from Edward J. Brown, Timothy J. Flanagan, and Maureen McCleod, eds., *Sourcebook of Criminal Justice Statistics—1983,* U.S. Department of Justice, Bureau of Justice Statistics (Washington, D.C.: U.S. Government Printing Office, 1984); 1983 data from U.S. Department of Justice, *Crime in the United States: 1983, Uniform Crime Records for the United States* (Washington, D.C.: U.S. Government Printing Office, 1984).

[a] Populations are U.S. Bureau of the Census provisional estimates as of July 1, except for the April 1, 1970 census and the April 1, 1980 census.

[b] Due to rounding, the offenses may not add to the total Crime Index.

[c] Violent crimes are offenses of murder, forcible rape, robbery, and aggravated assault. Property crimes are offenses of burglary, larceny-theft, and motor vehicle theft. Arson is omitted since data were only recently included.

[d] Crime rates calculated prior to rounding number of offenses.

Figure 5.1 Crime Index: 1962–1983

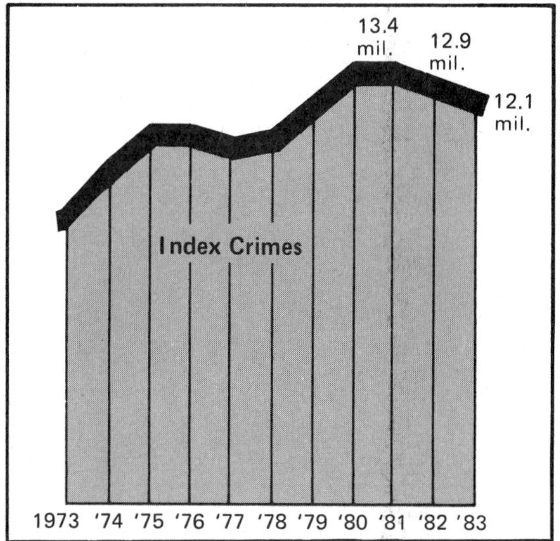

Overall, crime increased dramatically in the 1970s, but in the 1980s the crime rate has leveled off and even declined.

Source: U.S. Department of Justice, *Crime in the United States: 1983, Uniform Crime Reports for the United States* (Washington, D.C.: U.S. Government Printing Office, 1984), p. 43.

in urban arrest rates between 1860 and 1920.[18]

In spite of these caveats, it is clear that there is much more crime today than there was two or three decades ago. Sociologists have posited a number of explanations for this increase in crime, many of which focus on an array of social changes such as the increasing "stress on material success, the growing scale of modern social structure, pronounced urbanism, population heterogeneity flowing out of mass movements of foreign-born into the country in earlier periods, and other such occurrences."[19] A recent and interesting idea was offered by Murray Melbin, who argues that a major cause of the increase in crime is the increase in wakeful activity over more and more of the twenty-four-hour day; in other words, more and more nighttime is being used by larger numbers of people.[20] People are no longer tied to daylight activities as they were to a large degree before electric light. Melbin contends that the nighttime resembles such land frontier as the old West with, among other things, more lawlessness and violence. In other words, there is more crime, at least in part, because people are able to use more nighttime hours and because night is a kind of modern frontier.

Defects in UCR Statistics

As noted at the outset of this discussion, one cannot make firm statements about the level of offenses being committed on the basis of offenses reported in the UCR. One major difficulty is the variability of police detection of, and response to, events as crimes. As we have deployed more (or fewer) police more (or less) effectively, the number of crimes *known to the police* has increased (or decreased). Secondly, over time, victim *reporting behavior* often changes substantially. For example, rape was underreported in the past, but it is a crime that is more likely to be reported in the future as a result of increased consciousness of, and sensitivity to, the problem. In addition, the basic character of some offenses means that they are almost always better reported to the police than others. Homicide is usually reported; motor vehicle theft is consistently reported to the police, primarily because of insurance regulations. Thus, it is likely that increases since 1960 in the rates of these two offenses (homicide, 62.7 percent and motor vehicle theft, 134.6 percent) reflect *real* increases in offenses committed.

There are a number of other problems with UCR statistics. Over the years a small, but varying, proportion of police departments have not participated in the survey. This variation creates obvious problems in

Figure 5.2 Homicide Rate: 1900–1983

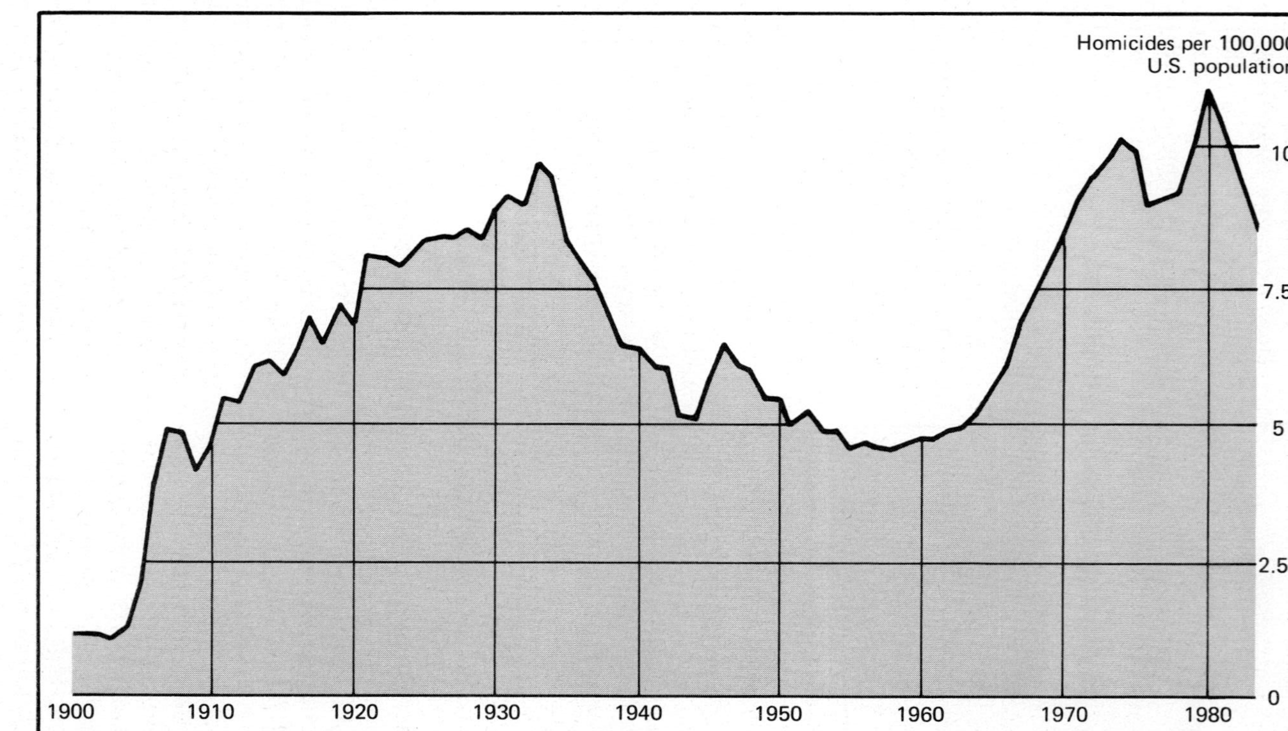

In 1980, the homicide rate was at the highest level in this century.

Source: 1900–1983: *Vital Statistics of the United States,* National Center for Health Statistics; 1983: U.S. Department of Justice, *Crime in the United States: 1983, Uniform Crime Reports for the United States* (Washington, D.C.: U.S. Government Printing Office, 1984).

comparing crime rates in one year to those in another. A second problem is that local authorities differ considerably in the *way* they classify offenses. For example, some reporting agencies would classify as robbery an incident in which a school child forced a classmate to surrender his lunch money; other agencies would not. A third source of error is primitive and inaccurate record keeping and reports that reflect a lot of guessing and faking. An additional problem stems from the fact that the local enforcement agencies frequently intentionally overreport or underreport crime, sometimes by changing the basis for classifying crimes and sometimes by falsifying the reports. Local pressures may make it expedient for the police or city hall to show by lower crime rates that they are winning the battle to control crime, or by higher crime rates that police need increased budgets or salaries.

An additional serious defect in the UCR statistics is that the FBI index offenses exclude a number of types of serious crime. For example, the index does not include consumer fraud or most kinds of corporate and white-collar crimes. The kid who steals a bike becomes a larceny statistic; the banker who embezzles millions of dollars does not. The index offenses also exclude trafficking in drugs, polluting the environment, violating civil rights statutes, fixing prize fights, running a gambling syndicate, running a house of prostitution, and molesting children.

But even if defects in the statistics and their classification were corrected immediately, UCR statistics would still not be completely reliable indicators of the actual levels of crime in the nation. Even perfect statistics would only tell us the number and kinds of *offenses known to the police.* An immense proportion of actual crimes never become known to the police, for some crimes are never discovered. When a gangland figure drops out of sight, the police may suspect that he has been fitted with cement overshoes and dumped in the river, but unless the body floats up or is otherwise discovered, no homicide will be recorded. Even when crimes are discovered, a great many of them are never reported to the police.

Victimization Statistics

Because of problems in UCR statistics, there is a need for other kinds of data on crime. One of the alternatives is the *National Crime Survey* conducted by the U.S. Bureau of the Census for the Bureau of Justice Statistics.[21] This survey, established in 1969, first conducted in 1972, and first reported in 1973, is based on interviews conducted in a representative sample of households in the United States. Instead of focusing on crimes known to the police, it obtains information "on the estimated number and rate of personal and household victimizations."[22] Nearly 132,000 people are interviewed twice a year for three years about crimes suffered by them in the preceding six months.

Crime Rates Based on Victim Reports

The results of a victim survey can easily be projected for the nation as a whole and then used to construct crime rates per 100,000 people. One of the earliest surveys of this kind occurred in 1967, and to no one's surprise it showed that there was substantially more serious crime committed in the United States than the UCR statistics showed. Overall, that victim survey uncovered about twice as much crime as FBI statistics revealed.[23]

Table 5.2 is based on the National Crime Survey for 1981 and it gives a clear picture of the relationship between crimes reported to the police versus those that go unreported.

Table 5.2 illustrates quite dramatically the fact that a large proportion of crimes, in fact about two-thirds of all crimes,[24] are *not* reported to the police. Among the crimes against persons, a majority of assaults and rapes are not reported to the police and an even greater percentage of personal larcenies go unreported. Of the household victimizations, a significant majority of larcenies are not reported to the police. Even in those crimes in which a majority are reported to the police, a very significant minority of all of them go unreported. While there is considerable variation from one crime to the other, the overall fact is that much crime of *all* types is not reported to the police. This means, of course, that official police statistics (which are the basis of the UCR) greatly *under*estimate the amount of crime in the United States.

Who Are the Victims?

One of the most important aspects of the victim survey technique is that it provides information about the characteristics of victims—an important area that is virtually ignored by the UCR. Generally speaking, victims of index crimes are more often male, nonwhite, and from lower socioeconomic groups; and they are more likely to be young, with many between the ages of sixteen and twenty-four. Interestingly, victims of crimes and those arrested for crime tend to share many of the same characteristics.

Table 5.2 Estimated Number of Personal and Household Victimizations, by Type of Victimization and Reporting to Police, United States, 1981

TYPE OF VICTIMIZATION	TOTAL		REPORTED TO POLICE		NOT REPORTED TO POLICE		DON'T KNOW WHETHER REPORTED	
	NO.	%	NO.	%	NO.	%	NO.	%
Personal Victims:								
Rape and Attempted Rape	178	100	99	56	74	42	5	3
Robbery	1,381	100	770	56	596	43	14	1
Assault	5,024	100	2,196	44	2,679	53	149	3
Personal Larceny w/ Contact	605	100	244	40	350	58	10	2
Personal Larceny w/o Contact	15,274	100	4,001	26	10,970	72	302	2
Household Victimizations:								
Burglary	7,393	100	3,775	51	3,506	47	112	2
Larceny	10,175	100	2,668	26	7,426	73	81	1
Vehicle Theft	1,439	100	959	67	468	33	12	1

Source: Edward J. Brown, Timothy J. Flanagan, and Maureen McLeod, eds., *Sourcebook of Criminal Justice Statistics: 1983.* U.S. Department of Justice, Bureau of Justice Statistics (Washington, D.C.: U.S. Government Printing Office, 1984), p. 307. Number in hundreds of thousands and rounded.

Problems with Victimization Statistics

However, we should be aware that while a welcome addition, victimization statistics themselves have problems. Wesley Skogan argues that there are problems with *both* police statistics *and* victimization surveys and that the latter, while useful, are not necessarily entirely accurate.[25] In a later work, Skogan outlines four basic kinds of errors in retrospective reports of experiences with crime.[26] First, respondents may not recognize that an incident in which they were involved was a crime. Second, they can forget about a criminal incident, or simply not tell the interviewer about it. Third, respondents may have inadequate or incomplete recall, or they may simply lie about an incident. Finally, the quality of the responses obtained is affected by the nature of the interview itself and such factors as the ease of the process and the cooperativeness of the respondent. While the above tends to underscore reasons for the underreporting of crime, another critic outlines some of the reasons why victim surveys may overestimate the amount of crime in America.[27] For one thing, respondents themselves may overreport crime by mistakenly interpreting incidents as crimes, incorrectly classifying incidents as crimes as a result of memory failures, and by outright fabrication. For another, the interviewers may be biased with the possibility that they may have an interest in reporting increases in crime in order to retain their jobs. Thus, they may classify a response as a crime when, in fact, no crime has occurred. Finally, those responsible for analyzing the responses obtained may incorrectly interpret them. The essential point is that there is reason to be cautious about victim statistics, indeed all statistics, but it should be borne in mind that victim statistics are an important development, especially when used in conjunction with data from police records.

Public Opinion Polls

A third source of data on crime comes from *public opinion polls.* Pollsters frequently ask randomly chosen samples of the American public what they believe about crime, how much they worry about it, and so on. Public opinion about whether crime is increasing or decreasing can be a vital source of information on crime as a social problem.

What the public believes, whether accurate or not, greatly shapes policies and determines which programs are possible. Furthermore, what the public believes frequently causes them to respond in ways that affect the crime rate. Thus, if the public believes there is a crime wave, they may alter their behavior in ways that influence the incidence of crime. For example, assaults and muggings necessarily decrease if everybody (out of fear of attack) stays off the streets (of course, this might cause an increase in family fights). Or, public beliefs about some action may cause its legal prohibition and thereby may increase crime by increasing those acts that will be counted as crimes. Similarly, crime could easily be decreased if public opinion led to the revoking of many criminal laws. Thus, what the public thinks has considerable impact on crime and crime rates.

Public Attitudes Toward Crime

Public perceptions of the extent of the crime problem—although they may be very inaccurate indicators of the amount of crime—may be quite useful in our understanding of the nature and the effects of the crime problem. The *Sourcebook of Criminal Justice Statistics* reports an array of such public opinion data.

The view expressed in the mass media is that not only is crime growing rapidly, but so is fear of crime. However, various public opinion polls dealing with a range of dimensions of public opinion on crime fail to show a consistent pattern of increasing fear of crime. Let us take two questions that yielded very different results. One question asked of respondents was: "Is there any area right around here—that is, within a mile—where you would be afraid to walk alone at night?" The percentage responding yes to this question has tended to increase over the years. In 1967, 31 percent of the respondents said there was such an area in their neighborhood and by 1975 that had jumped to 45 percent. However, in 1979 it dipped back to 42 percent, only to rise to 48 percent in 1982 and then to drop again to 45 percent in 1983.[28] Although the responses to this question generally conformed to our stereotype about increasing fear of crime, the results from another question did not. That question asked: "How about at home at night—do you feel safe and secure, or not?" Nineteen percent of the respondents in 1975 said that they felt unsafe in their own homes at night, but in 1977 that had dipped to 15 percent and it was only 16 percent in 1983.[29]

By presenting a mixed picture of public attitudes toward crime, we do not mean to minimize the public fear of crime of various types. However, the data show that the picture is not as one-sided as we are often led to believe.

PART II: CAUSES AND CONSEQUENCES

INDIVIDUAL LEVEL

Crime and Physiology

Theories of the causes of crime are as old as recorded history.[30] We begin our discussion of the role of individual-level factors in crime with a discussion of one of the major theories in the history of the field—the positive school. *The Positive School* was born in the work of Cesare Lombroso, an Italian physician, who published his epoch-making *Criminal Man* in 1876. In this and in subsequent publications, Lombroso and his followers put forth the notion that about one-third of all people engaging in criminal activity were "born criminals." Although born criminals were a numerical minority, they engaged in the most persistent and vicious crimes.[31] The positivists argued that born criminals were throwbacks to their more primitive ancestors. Applying the ideas of Darwinian biology, positivists saw born criminals as less evolved and more primitive than normal people. Born criminals had visible stigmata, such as abnormalities of the skull, overdeveloped jaws, flat noses, large ears, excessively long arms, high cheek bones, and other apelike traits. Although recognizing the importance of the environment, the positivists thought that little could be done to change born criminals or prevent their crimes. Since born criminals were not able to be helped, or to help themselves, Lombroso believed that they should be locked away in a decent environment in order to protect society.

Although the specific components of the original Positive School have been substantially discarded, the concern to explore the role of human genetics and physiology in causing crime remains in modern research activity.

From Lombroso's time to the present, it has been recognized that persons serving time in prison are, on the average, less intelligent than the general population.[32] Such evidence fails to establish, however, that persons with less intelligence are more likely to commit crimes than are persons with higher intelligence. Because less intelligent people could simply be more likely to get caught, comparing convicts with nonconvicts cannot resolve this matter. In

Figure 5.3 Crime Clock, 1983

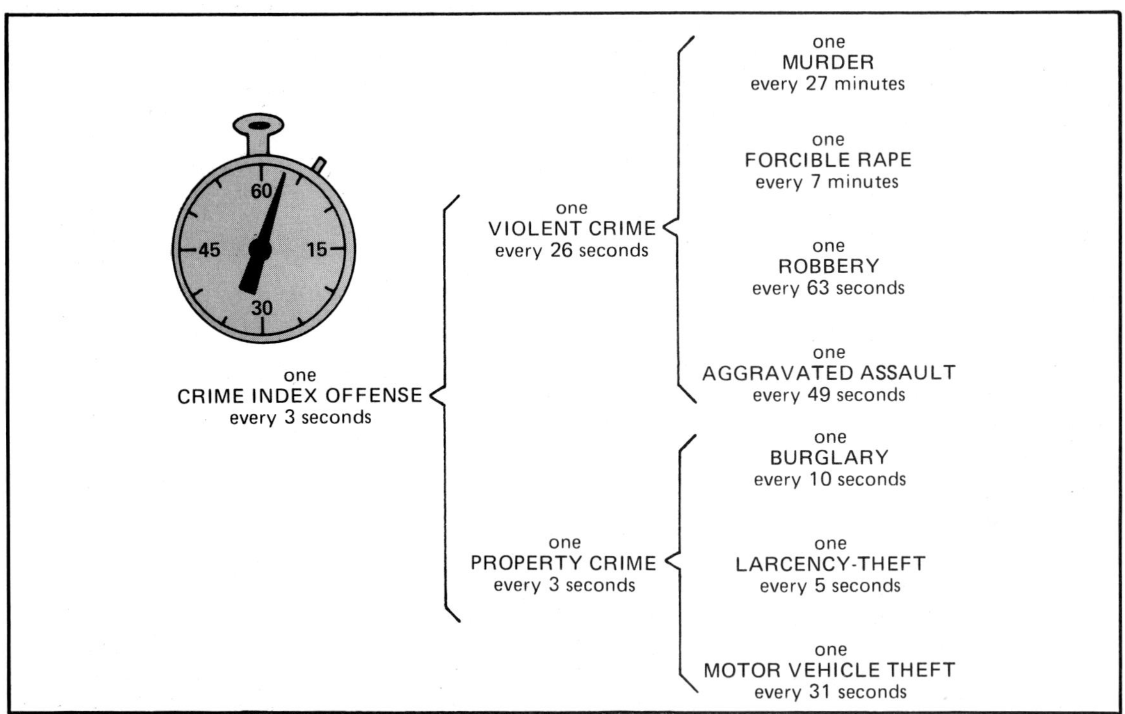

The crime clock should be viewed with care. Being the most aggregate representation of UCR data, it is designed to convey the annual reported crime experience by showing the relative frequency of occurrence of the Index Offenses. This mode of display should not be taken to imply a regularity in the commission of the Part I Offenses; rather, it represents the annual ratio of crime to fixed time intervals.

Source: U.S. Department of Justice, *Crime in the United States: 1983, Uniform Crime Reports for the United States* (Washington, D.C.: U.S. Government Printing Office, 1984), p. 5.

fact, it seems likely, also, that we are more inclined to arrest people who are less intelligent and to treat their behavior as criminal.

The only reasonable way to explore the relationship between intelligence and criminal behavior is to use data based on self-reported criminal actions. Unfortunately, self-report techniques have been limited mainly to studies of adolescents. Consequently, we do not know the role of intelligence in adult criminal behavior. But we do know that intelligence is negatively related to juvenile delinquency. For example, Travis Hirschi found that boys with high IQs were much less likely to report committing delinquent acts or to have police records than were boys with low IQs, and the relationship held for both black and white boys in his sample.[33] In a review of an array of research studies, Hirschi and Michael Hindelang argued that IQ was strongly related to juvenile delinquency.[34] Looked at in purely physiological terms, it is possible to argue that *some* delinquent behavior (and presumably some adult criminal behavior as well) results from a lack of intelligence. It can be argued that some

Table 5.3 Levels of Analysis: Crime

LEVELS	APPROPRIATE QUESTIONS	A PARTIAL SYNOPSIS OF PRESENT CONCLUSIONS
INDIVIDUAL	Is intelligence related to crime?	Low intelligence does seem to be correlated with street crime, but white-collar criminals are likely to be higher in intelligence. Bear in mind that intelligence is a result of *both* physiological and social factors.
	Does psychosis cause criminal behavior?	In rare instances, but persons convicted of crimes have no greater incidence of psychosis than the general population. In addition, the overwhelming majority of psychotics do not commit crimes.
	Is antisocial personality disorder related to criminal behavior?	Yes, but circular reasoning is built into the definition of the antisocial personality disorder since it involves committing a crime.
SOCIAL-PSYCHOLOGICAL	Does the labeling process—identifying someone as a criminal—cause subsequent law violation?	In some cases, but successful labeling does not always lead to subsequent criminal behavior. Most labeled juvenile delinquents do not go on to a life of crime.
	Is most criminal behavior learned?	Yes. Crime is learned by exposure to social groups that teach such behavior and reward those who exhibit it.
	Why do people become criminals in the place?	Many find it rewarding and the likelihood of being caught low.
SOCIOLOGICAL	Do changing social situations affect crime?	Definitely. For example, in recent years an increasing number of young people encountered more suitable targets with fewer guardians.
	Are the frustrations posited by strain theorists important causes of crime?	Probably not. Most assumed "frustrated" people do not commit crimes. Further, many who commit crimes would not appear to be "frustrated."

Table 5.3 Levels of Analysis: Crime *(Continued)*

LEVELS	APPROPRIATE QUESTIONS	A PARTIAL SYNOPSIS OF PRESENT CONCLUSIONS
SOCIOLOGICAL	Does a significant amount of crime reflect conformity to the norms of some subculture?	Some does, but most criminals accept the same general norms as the rest of society.
	Does the absence of strong bonds between the individual and society influence law violations?	Those with weak attachments, and hence little to lose, are more likely to commit crimes than those with strong bonds, and hence much to lose.
	Is social class related to crime?	There is great controversy here, but it is clear that those from the lower classes are more likely to be charged with street crimes. But bear in mind that poor people are *not* the only ones to commit crimes and that only *some* poor people commit crimes.

people break the law because they lack the mental capacity to correctly compute the benefits of breaking the law against the costs of detection. However, it should be remembered that we are dealing here with "street crimes," and as a result we are disregarding those offenses (such as many white-collar crimes) in which offenders may be systematically higher in intelligence.

It should also be pointed out that intelligence is only partly a physiological phenomenon. Studies have established that inheritance plays a significant role in determining intelligence. However, environmental factors such as poor nutrition, lack of early stimulation, and poor education also play important roles. Thus, some portion of the relationship between IQ and (street) crime reflects social, not genetic, factors.

Another physiological factor related to crime is an underactive autonomic nervous system. Among other things, this means that criminals, specifically those with antisocial behavior (see below), do not have adequate fear responses, are not able adequately to anticipate negative events emotionally, and show a very slow rate of fear dissipation.[35] Needless to say, work supporting the view that there is a biological basis for crime is highly controversial. Even those who make the case for biological factors are aware of the fact that they interact with an array of social factors such as family and education.

Crime and Psychology

Frequently, people who are accused of serious crimes—especially of serious violent crimes such as murder or rape—plead "not guilty by reason of insanity." Thus, the law recognizes that "mentally ill" persons should not be held accountable for their actions.

The underlying assumption in this link between the law and psychiatry is that the psychological make-up of individuals plays a major role in determining whether they commit crimes. Not all social scientists find this assumption convincing. Although some of them accept the idea that insanity pleas are sometimes justified—that, for example, a person may commit murder because of psychotic compulsions—many are uncomfortable with the idea that most crimes reflect personality disorders.

Psychosis

Severe mental illness—*psychosis*—is most frequently alleged in sensational crimes—mass murder, for example. In fact, people have a tendency to assume that anyone who commits an especially horrible crime must be insane. Why else would someone go on a murder spree, randomly killing total strangers? We may accept the idea that such crimes typically involve psychosis,[36] but these are highly unusual crimes. What about more usual varieties of crime?

Studies have shown that only a tiny proportion of persons sentenced to prison can be diagnosed as psychotic. Findings indicate that not more than 5 percent (and in many studies less than 1 percent) of persons were psychotic at the time of their admission to prison.[37] And, these percentages nearly match the estimates of the rates of psychosis for the general population, which indicates that convicted criminals are not disproportionately psychotic. Furthermore, the fact that a person convicted of a

Depicted above is John Hinckley (second from right in glasses and handcuffs), the man who attempted to assassinate President Ronald Reagan. Mental illness is often involved in such serious crimes, or at least there is an effort to plead "not guilty by reason of insanity."

(AP/Wide World Photos)

crime is diagnosed as psychotic does not necessarily mean that the psychosis *caused* the criminal behavior. Finally, the overwhelming majority of psychotics do not commit crimes. We can only conclude that psychosis plays only an extremely minor role in causing crime.

Antisocial Personality Disorders

The major focus of psychological analysis of criminal behavior has not been on psychosis, but rather on psychopaths, or those with antisocial personality disorders. We need not describe this disorder here since it has already been covered in the chapter on mental illness (see Chapter 4). However, we do need to underscore some of the problems with the use of this disorder to explain crime.

Although antisocial personality disorders undoubtedly play a role in causing some crime, the use of this category of disorder tends to involve a kind of circular reasoning. Specifically, the term "antisocial personality disorder" is used to *explain* the same behavior that was initially used to *define* the concept. For example, one of the basic characteristics of this type of personality is an early developing tendency to engage in socially disapproved behavior that continues into adulthood. Thus, crime is built into the definition of antisocial personality and it is, in turn, used to explain criminal behavior.

In addition to psychosis and antisocial personality disorder, many other personality traits have been studied as potential sources of crime. One of the most controversial recent studies is Samuel Yochelson and Stanton Samenow's effort to identify the distinctive thinking patterns of criminals.[38] On the whole, these efforts have been unsuccessful. As self-report studies have shown, most people have committed delinquent or criminal acts sometime during their lives. If this is so, it is futile to try to find an explanation of widespread behavior based on an alleged psychological abnormality, for, by definition, "abnormal" means "uncommon." It is true that the average person commits fewer criminal acts than the average person sent to prison. It is possible that some abnormal personality trait could help account for this greater frequency. So far, however, such a syndrome has not been definitively discovered.

SOCIAL-PSYCHOLOGICAL LEVEL

We now move beyond the individual to examine how elements in the immediate social environment influence criminal behavior. Our discussion will center around some of the major social-psychological theories that have been applied to criminal behavior.

Labeling Theory of Crime

Labeling theory usually ignores the issue of why an individual commits an initial, random criminal act, and begins with what happens to an individual after he or she has been labeled a criminal by him- or herself, by peers, and by law-enforcement agencies. Before we get to some of the things that happen to a person who has been labeled a criminal, it is important to underscore a point that we will deal with later in this chapter: that is, the likelihood of obtaining a criminal label is related to one's position in the social class system. Middle- or upper-class (high and middle income) people are far less likely to be labeled criminals than lower-class (low income) people when they commit the same, or similar, crimes. Our concern in this section, however, is not with factors related to the likelihood of being labeled a criminal, but with what is likely to happen to an individual who has been so labeled.

First, people labeled as criminal may find that the social stigma of the label limits their associations. They may be forced to associate with others who are similarly stigmatized. By being with others who are labeled lawbreakers, persons may find themselves in a social setting that encourages future violations. For example, by being labeled as a lawbreaker and getting locked up in jail or prison, a person is often instructed by other inmates in future criminal activities.

Second, labeling can increase criminality by increasing surveillance. Police, parents, associates, and teachers may keep a much closer watch on the behavior of people labeled as criminal. Therefore, such persons are much more likely to be detected in offenses than are persons not so labeled. For example, when certain kinds of crimes occur, the police often check out persons with a previous record of such offenses.

Third, people may come to accept their label and thus see themselves as criminals and act accordingly. Or, labeled persons may simply find they have less to lose from future transgressions because they see that they have already lost their good reputations.

Although the labeling process is useful in understanding crime, it is important to underscore its limitations. In particular, it is important to point out that successful labeling does not always lead to continuation along that line of criminal activity.[39] Most adolescents who are officially labeled as delinquents do not go on to a life of crime.[40] Indeed, most adolescents discontinue their delinquency around age sixteen.[41] Similarly, it is very rare for either juveniles or adults who are apprehended for shoplifting ever to be apprehended a second time for that offense.[42] In spite of these limitations, the labeling process can help us understand the high recidivism rates for adults convicted of serious crimes. Labeling can provide at best only a partial account of criminal behavior.[43]

Differential Association Theory

Criminal behavior is like all other behavior; that is, people learn it and learn to repeat it in appropriate situations.[44] Crime is learned by exposure to social groups that teach such behavior and reward those who exhibit those behaviors.

Many kinds of crime require considerable technique.[45] For example, in order to be more than a petty burglar, one must learn a good deal about locks and alarm systems—indeed, a whole repertory of entry techniques must be mastered. In addition, burglars must learn which things are worth taking, so they may have to learn about art, antiques, jewelry, and other valuables. Finally, they must learn where and how to sell what they steal. Obviously, many types of crime require instruction from others who have mastered the trade. Thus, we can be fairly sure that a good burglar, safecracker, forger, or hold-up person has a record of criminal associations. However, it is not clear that such associations turn him or her into a lawbreaker in the first place. It may be that such associations turned a petty or unexperienced criminal into a more skilled and serious offender only *after* the individual has already committed a first offense. Indeed, it is widely believed that much, if not most, tutoring in crime occurs in jail and in prison.[46] If so, then keeping company with other criminals will change an offender but will not create one.

While there is little doubt that people are taught, in varying degrees, how to be criminals, we are left with the issue of what causes people to move toward these endeavors in the first place. One answer may be that people may move into criminal activities because they find them more rewarding than conformity. When punishment is highly unlikely, as it is in many forms of property crime, people may be pulled toward it because of its rewards, or the absence of more acceptable means of earning a livelihood. And nonconformity may be directly rewarding, especially for teenagers. Illegal acts may offer thrills and excitement, and status as a "bad kid" may bring attention from straight peers. For example, teenage girls who experiment with prostitution already have discovered not only that it pays economically, but also that promiscuity attracts more attention than does conventional behavior.[47]

SOCIOLOGICAL LEVEL

We move now to various linkages between individuals and larger social structures and cultural forces. The thrust of the argument in this section is that there are a number of such linkages that tend to lead individuals to become criminals.

Social and Cultural Changes

There is an interesting sociological analysis by Lawrence Cohen and Marcus Felson that suggests that we should look at social and cultural changes, especially as they relate to the situational circumstances of crime.[48] Cohen and Felson focused on what they called *direct contact predatory violations,* or illegal acts in which someone takes or damages the person or property of someone else. In order for such crimes to take place, three minimal conditions must be met. First, there must be people who are motivated to be offenders. Second, there must be suitable targets for their activity. Third, capable guardians against such activities must be absent. There is much detail to their argument, but the essential point is that social changes since World War II have led to an increase in the crime rate. For one thing, the baby boomers reached their most crime-prone years during this period. This group encountered an increase in suitable targets for their criminal activities, especially easily moved, light-weight durable goods. And, there were fewer adult guardians in the home as more and more husbands *and* wives went to work leaving their homes, and their property, alone for long periods during the day. Clearly, we must look at such changing situational factors, as well as the characteristics of individuals likely to perpetrate crimes and those who are most likely to be crime victims.

Strain Theory

Another perspective on the macrolevel causes of crime is offered by strain theorists. One of the things they emphasize is that individuals are led to commit crimes because of the impact of social inequalities that allow them to overcome the bonds of conscience. People are seen as committing crimes in order to get rewards they cannot obtain through legitimate means. Another way of putting it is that the criminal accepts the goals society defines as desirable but lacks access to the means society defines as legitimate for attaining these goals. Faced with intense frustration, the individual engages in illegitimate methods for attaining goals.[49]

Strain theory runs into trouble because its concepts rely too heavily on people's frustration. The majority of those who, according to the theory, would seem to be subject to frustration are not particularly likely to commit crimes. A different kind of problem with strain theory is that the deviant behavior that it predicts would, in most cases, *not* relieve the intense frustration that people are supposed to be feeling. Although crime sometimes pays, for most criminals it usually pays very poorly. Finally, the theory, being fundamentally economic, is unable to account for crime committed by middle- and upper-class people who would not seem to suffer from frustration in the form strain theory describes.

Subcultural Theory

A related approach focuses on the relationship between individuals and the various subcultures that exist within society. All people try to conform to group norms, but conformity to the norms of one group may represent deviance from the norms of another. Crime represents conformity to subcultural norms that the rest of society has defined as criminal. We would not expect such criminals to express remorse, since they are conforming to the dictates of their consciences—they are behaving in the way their group has taught them to behave. A criminal subculture exists to some extent where the best safe-cracker, the slickest con man, the cleverest forger, or the toughest mob enforcer is held up by the group as a desirable model. It is true also that powerful elements in society sometimes outlaw behavior that some social group considers acceptable—for example, polygamy among the Mormons, gambling among the urban poor, and norms of personal and family vengeance among Appalachian mountain folk. Thus some crime is explained by the idea of criminal subcultures, but the fact is that most criminals come to accept the same general set of norms as the rest of society. Subcultural-deviance theories therefore cannot explain most crime.

Control Theory

Control theory does not assume that people are intrinsically moral or bound by conscience. Instead, it assumes that deviance is to be expected when people have little to lose by such behavior and that society is structured in such a way that some people have much and some have little to lose by crime.

The crucial element in control theory is that the source of morality and the pressures for conformity are in the *bond* that exists between the individual and society. Individuals will conform to society's norms to the extent that the bond between them is strong. When the bond between the individual and society weakens, the likelihood of norm violation increases. Hirschi argues that this bond has three major elements—attachment, commitment, and involvement.[50]

The most important of these bonds is *attachment,* or the ties of affection between an individual and other conventional persons—the degree of attachment is how much the person cares about others (and is cared about by them) and how much the person values others' feelings, opinions, and expectations. An individual who is strongly attached to others is likely to consider how his or her behavior will affect others and their attitudes, including their attitudes toward that individual. Unattached people lack such interpersonal stakes in conformity. Attachment is a powerful inhibitor of crime. For example, the more young people are attached to their parents, peers, or teachers, the less likely they are to commit delinquent acts.[51]

The second bond is *commitment:* the stake or investment an individual has in conformity. The more time and energy an individual invests in conventional activities (getting an education, building up a business, establishing a reputation for honesty and trustworthiness), the greater will be his or her stake in conformity to the norms. Thus, commitment serves as a bond between the individual and social norms

Figure 5.4 Bonds Between Individual and Society

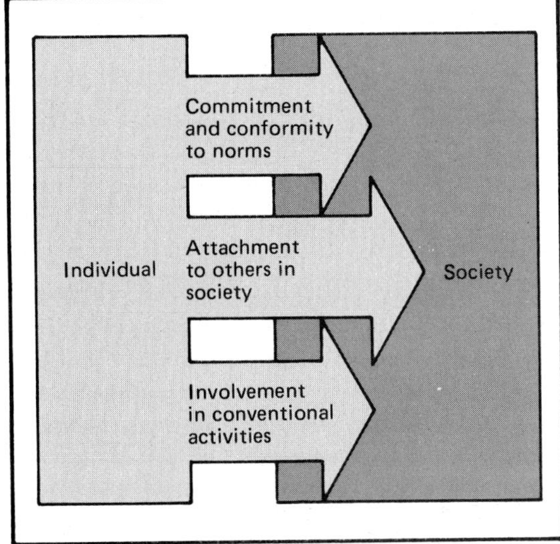

A depiction of the three elements that, according to control theory, bond the individual to society.

and represents *what the person has to lose* through deviant actions. As Hirschi pointed out:

> To the person committed to conventional lines of action, risking one to ten years in prison for a ten-dollar holdup is stupidity, because to the committed person the costs and risks obviously exceed ten dollars in value. . . .[52]

Thus, the more energy young people have invested in school performance and the more they hold high educational and occupational aspirations, the less likely they will be to risk their position by committing delinquent acts. By the same token, most adult crimes are committed by those with little stake in conventional forms of activity—street crime is overwhelmingly committed by persons with little to lose and for whom the fruits of crime at least seem worth the risks involved. Similarly, relatively successful and committed adults rationally assess costs and benefits when they commit crimes. They have much to lose and therefore usually commit only white-collar crimes that offer large gains. It would be irrational for a banker to stick up a liquor store, but it would not be so irrational for him to embezzle a million dollars.

A third aspect of the bond between the individual and society, *involvement,* is well expressed by the saying "idle hands are the devil's playground." Persons who are busy doing conventional things have less time and energy to devote to deviance than people who are idle. As Hirschi put it: "Many persons undoubtedly owe a life of virtue to a lack of opportunity to do otherwise. Time and energy are inherently limited."[53] Thus, while commitment involves the idea of losing investments as a result of criminal activity, involvement means simply that an individual lacks the time or opportunity to become involved in crime. It is obvious that attachment and commitment play a major role in determining involvement. People with families, people who work hard in school, or people who are busy establishing themselves in a career have much less chance of becoming involved in criminal activities than persons without such attachments and commitments.

Conflict Theory

Conflict theorists argue that crime is one of the inevitable byproducts of a society that is inherently unequal; one in which there are great disparities between the upper and lower classes, as well as between those who have power and those who do not.[54] Implied in this is the idea that poverty, as well as the unfairness and hopelessness associated with it, drives some people into committing street crimes.[55] Related to this is the belief that the laws of society are set by supporters of the upper classes and they serve to favor their interests and, conversely, to operate against the interests of the deprived members of society. What is and is not defined as criminal is thus rooted in social inequalities.

Although there has recently been considerable controversy over the issue of the relationship between social class and criminality, the consensus seems to be that social class *is* related to crime.[56] More specifically, persons charged with street crimes are disproportionately from the lower-income groups in society.[57] However, even with this reality, two qualifications should be kept in mind: (1) poor people are not the *only* people who commit crimes, and (2) only *some* poor people *do* commit crimes.

PART III: RESPONSES

AN OUTLINE OF THE CRIMINAL JUSTICE SYSTEM

Paralleling the complexity of the crime problem is an equally complex governmental response to it in the *criminal justice system.* The criminal justice system encompasses a wide array of institutions and officials such as police, prosecutors, judges, correctional officials, and parole officers.[58] At least a portion of the complexity of this system is caught in Figure 5.5, which describes the typical sequence of events in the criminal justice system:

Figure 5.5 What Is the Sequence of Events in the Criminal Justice System?

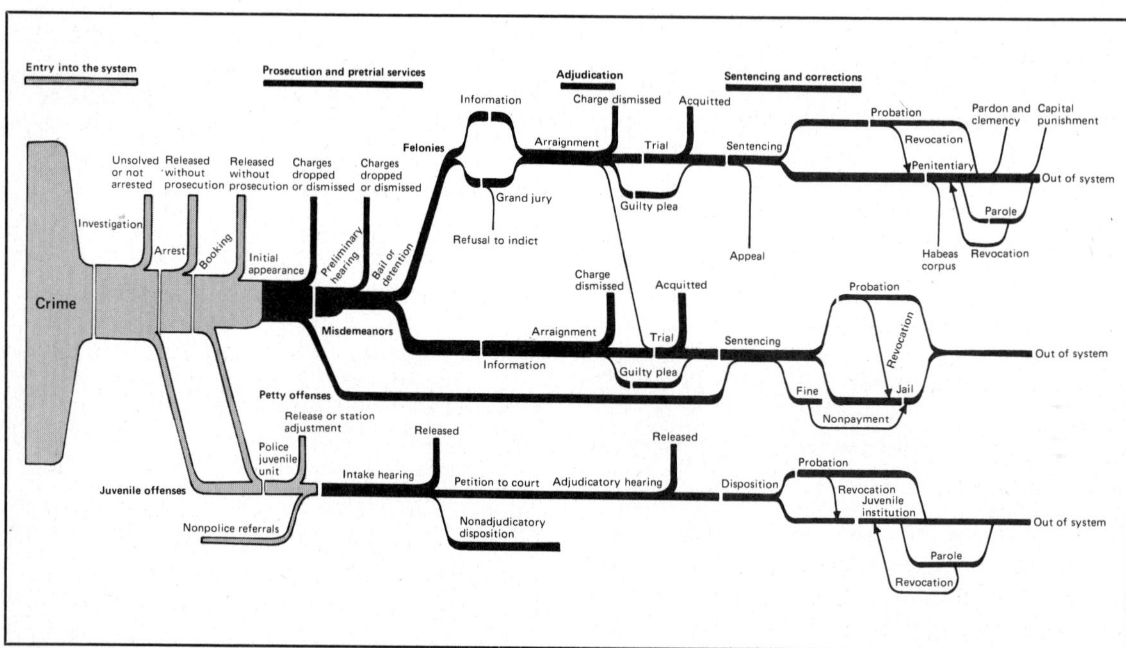

This chart gives a simplified view of caseflow through the criminal justice system. Procedures vary among jurisdictions. The weights of the lines are not intended to show the actual size of caseloads.

Source: Bureau of Justice Statistics, *Report to the Nation on Crime and Justice: The Data* (Washington, D.C.: U.S. Department of Justice, 1983), pp. 42–43; adapted from President's Commission on Law Enforcement and Administration of Justice, *The Challenge of Crime in a Free Society,* 1967.

Although we lack the space to go into them in detail, we can highlight some of the major steps in the criminal justice system as well as some of its major components:

1. *Police* identification and apprehension of a suspect. While some suspects are apprehended, most are not because a crime is never discovered or is not reported. Even in those cases in which a crime is discovered and reported, the police are often not able to identify or apprehend a suspect.

2. In those cases in which an arrest is made, the police provide information to a *prosecutor* who must decide whether or not to file formal charges. The prosecutor may decide not to bring charges or may drop them at a later point in the process.

3. If charges are filed, the suspect must be brought before a *judge* without unnecessary delay. The judge must decide "whether there is probable cause to detain the accused person."[59] In the case of minor offenses, a final decision may be made at this stage. In many areas, this initial appearance is followed by a preliminary hearing. Charges may be dropped or dismissed at either the initial or preliminary hearings.

4. With the arraignment of suspects, we move from the prosecution and pretrial phase to the adjudication phase. At the *arraignment* "the accused is informed of the charges, advised of the rights of criminal defendants, and asked to enter a plea to the charges."[60]

5. If the accused pleads guilty or *nolo contendere* (acceptance of a penalty without admitting guilt), and the plea is accepted by the judge, no trial is held, and the accused can be sentenced.

6. If the accused pleads not guilty, or guilty by reason of insanity, a trial date is set. Those accused of serious crimes are guaranteed the right to a *jury* trial.

7. The result of a *trial* may be "acquittal or conviction on the original charges or on lesser included offenses."[61]

8. After the trial, a defendant may *appeal* the case to an appellate court.

9. Following a guilty verdict (or plea), it is usually the judge who imposes a *sentence*.

10. Among the sentencing options open to judges are the *death penalty, incarceration, probation, fines,* and *restitution.*

11. If sentenced to prison, offenders may be eligible for *parole* after serving a portion of their sentences.

There is clearly a great deal more to be said about each one of these phases and components of the criminal justice system. However, we lack the space to go into the details of the operation of this system. Rather, our focus in this section will be on two of many problems associated with the criminal justice system. First, we will deal with the inequities that exist within this system. Second, we will deal with the correctional system and its basic failings.

IS THE CRIMINAL JUSTICE SYSTEM JUST?

Our focus in this section is on the conflict theory perspective of the criminal justice system. Conflict theorists generally argue that the criminal justice system tends to be biased against the least powerful[62] groups and persons in a society because the most powerful groups in society are able to structure it so that it generally operates to their advantage.[63] This thesis is probably best expressed in the title of a book on the topic: *The Rich Get Richer and the Poor Get Prison.*[64] Perhaps the best way to approach this topic is to examine the extent to which class interests (as opposed to the common interests of all citizens) have an influence on the criminal justice system.

Wealth, Power, and the Law

Perhaps the most fundamental charge that conflict theory can make against the legal system is that the rich and powerful create the laws, and as a result, many criminal statutes apply to acts that only poor people commit. As the French novelist, Anatole France, pointed out: "The law, in its majestic equality, forbids all men to sleep under bridges, to beg in the streets, and to steal bread—the rich as well as the poor."[65]

Furthermore, the historical record is filled with examples of the way powerful groups in societies have utilized the laws to increase or protect their privileged position. William Chambliss has traced the evolution of vagrancy laws from their origin in England in 1349.[66] He argues that vagrancy laws were used primarily to control labor and to protect the property of the rich. Because of a shortage of labor caused by the Black Death in the fourteenth century, vagrancy laws (which prohibited charity and idleness) were created to ensure landowners an adequate supply of labor at low wages. As the labor force grew over the next century, there was no longer a shortage of workers and the vagrancy laws were less and less strictly enforced. However, they were rewritten and enforced once again in the fifteenth century in order to control the highwaymen who were plaguing the growing commerce of the time. The English vagrancy and poor laws were instituted by the early American colonists to drive persons without visible means of support out of town. Chambliss argues that the history of vagrancy laws shows how extensively the legal system is used by the powerful to exploit the powerless.

In general, it seems clear that the legal system is unfair and tends to operate to the advantage of the well-off and to the disadvantage of the poor.

The Poor and Criminal Law

The poor and the powerless suffer from inequality under the criminal law. Law enforcement tends to be much less adequate in poor than in wealthy neighborhoods. This contributes to the fact that the poor are more likely to be victims of crime than the rich. The police simply do not respond as urgently or give the same quality of patrol in poor sections of town. On the other hand, when the police are out to apprehend a suspected criminal, they are far more likely to suspect and to apprehend poor people. This leads to the view held by poor people that they are being harassed by the police.

When the poor are accused under criminal law, they once again find themselves treated unequally; they lack the resources to obtain the quality of legal aid available to the middle and upper classes. All criminal defendants are entitled to legal counsel, but court-appointed lawyers or public defenders are not always drawn from among the ranks of the most skilled criminal lawyers. Furthermore, those defending the poor have neither the money for private investigators nor the time to prepare their cases carefully—advantages normally available to high-priced attorneys. As a result, the poor usually are not defended as well as the well-to-do, and they are more often convicted.

Another area of discrimination for the poor is over the matter of *bail.*[67] The fact is that the poor are far less able to afford or obtain bail than middle- and upper-class people. This means that more poor people must remain in jail until their cases are disposed of. People in jail are less able to play an active role in their own defense than those who are free on bail.

But inequality does not stop there. The poor are apt to receive longer and more severe sentences than are middle- or upper-class people convicted of the same or even more serious offences.[68] Thus, a poor person convicted of stealing a few dollars is likely to get a stiffer penalty than a business executive convicted of embezzling millions of dollars. A poor person who commits a murder is far more likely to be convicted than a corporate executive who makes a decision that ends up costing many people their lives.

This is well-illustrated by the case of the Ford Pinto.[69] The Pinto was produced even though Ford executives knew that its gas tank had a strong likelihood of exploding in a rear-end collision. In fact, hundreds of people *were* killed and injured in Pinto accidents, but the Ford Motor Company eventually won the court case against it. While the Ford executives escaped unharmed, it is interesting to compare their fate to that of William J. Rummel. On three separate occasions Rummel was convicted of crimes by Texas courts. His three convictions were for the following:

1. Forging a check for $28.36.
2. Obtaining $80 by fraudulent use of a credit card.
3. Taking a check for $120.75 in return for a false promise to repair an air conditioner.

Although none of these crimes involved physical injuries to the offended parties (physical injuries and deaths did occur in the Pinto case), these convictions all happen to be felonies, and under Texas law conviction for a third felony carries a mandatory sentence of life imprisonment. The constitutionality of the law was sustained by the Supreme Court. Thus, for crimes involving a *total* of $229.11, William Rummel faces life behind bars.[70]

Street Crime vs. White-Collar Crime

Much of the focus of the issue of unfairness in the legal system revolves around the differences in the handling of street crime versus white-collar crime. Poor people are highly unlikely to find themselves in a position to commit white-collar crime. They are not likely to have access to the corporate computer so that they can engage in computer crime. They are not likely to be in the offices of the Ford Motor Company and in a position to decide to go ahead with production of the Pinto. However, they *are* likely to be on the streets and committing crimes like shoplifting, purse-snatching, hold-ups, burglaries, and the like. The street crimes that the poor are likely to engage in are more likely to be punished, and to be punished more severely, than the white-collar crime characteristic of the middle and upper classes. It is thus in the interest of these classes to have light sentences attached to white-collar crime. Take the following quotation from a judge indicating his tendency to give preferential treatment to white-collar criminals:

> There is no getting away from the fact that the type of existence that jail provides is more hard on people who are accustomed to the better existence than it is on people who may not be fed as well in their homes as they are in jail. . . . It sounds as though you are penalizing poverty. There is no question that that is a fact. . . . I guess there is no getting away from the fact that the judge empathizes more with a white-collar person whose hardships you can understand, because a lifestyle is more like his or her own, than someone whose lifestyle you really can't understand.[71]

Street crime, on the other hand, represents a threat to the life and property of th well-to-do and may even reflect a rejec by the lower classes of the present of social inequalities. Thus, it is argued that the law is constructed to bear down hard on the lower classes.

THE CORRECTIONAL SYSTEM AND ITS FAILINGS

In the United States today, imprisonment is one societal response to criminality. Many do not realize that it is a relatively new phenomenon:

> Americans in the colonial period . . . fined or whipped criminals or put them in the stocks, or if the crime was serious enough, hung them; *they did not conceive of imprisoning them for specific periods of time.* (Italics added.)[72]

Since colonial times, the idea of imprisoning criminals has become widely accepted. In fact, the burgeoning prisons have become a problem in themselves. The population in American state and federal prisons in 1982 was approximately 412,000 prisoners.[73] By the end of 1984, the prison population had swelled to a record 463,866 inmates.[74] (See Figure 5.6 for a longer-term depiction of the number of persons in prison). Problems created by large increases in the prison population include high cost, overcrowding, and the increased likelihood of riots and prison breaks. We will return to the contemporary situation and its problems shortly, but first we need some more historical background.

Figure 5.6 What Are the Trends in Correctional Populations?

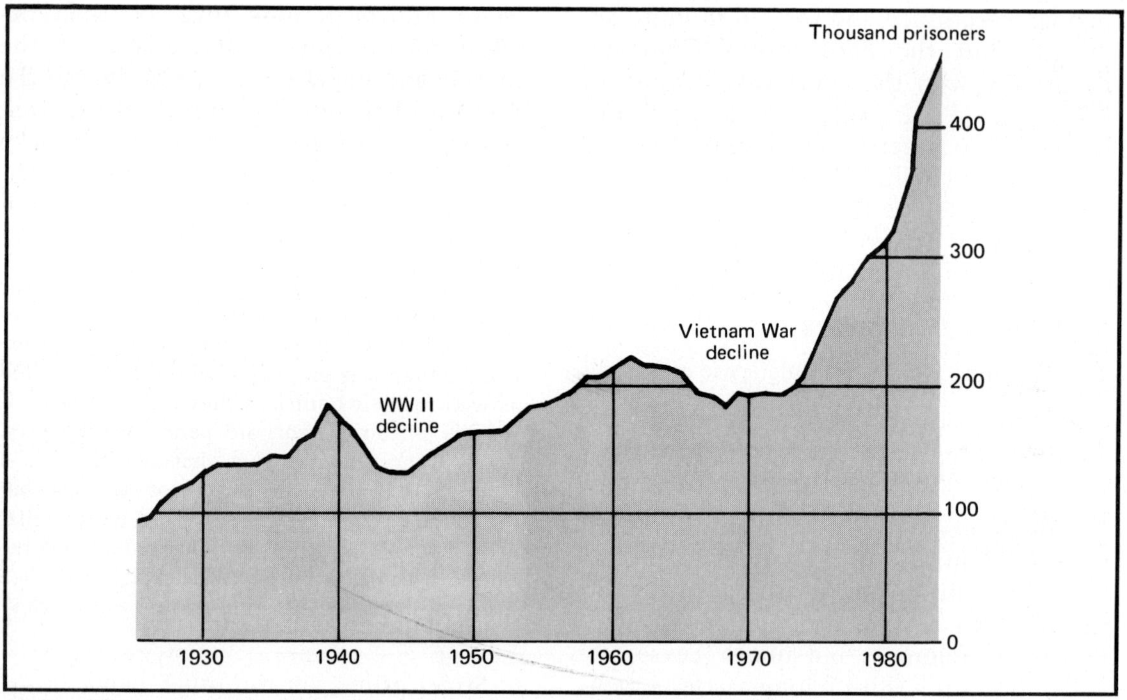

The number of persons in prison was 463,866 in 1984, an all-time high.

Source: Bureau of Justice Statistics, *Report to the Nation on Crime and Justice: The Data* (Washington, D.C.: U.S. Department of Justice, 1983), p. 81; Bureau of Justice Statistics, *Prisoners in 1984* (Washington, D.C.: U.S. Department of Justice, 1985), p. 1.

Retribution and Deterrence

Concepts of crime and punishment have changed over time. The criminal law replaced the earlier practice of private vengeance in retaliation for a wrong suffered. The punishments that the criminal law provided, however, did not do much more than take the right to execute vengeance from the individual who was wronged and give it to the state. The well-known principle of *lex talionis*—an eye for an eye—was widely practiced in many cultures. Under this system, murderers were typically killed, those who mutilated others were mutilated themselves, and so on. Other punishments such as flogging (used as recently as 1952 in Delaware) and the stocks were commonly used in the American colonial period.[75] One punishment popular in England and France was the transportation of convicts to penal colonies. Such punishments were primarily *retributive.* This rests on the idea that it is only through suffering that the criminal can atone for the offense committed and that revenge for a wrongful act is an appropriate societal response.[76]

In contrast, a number of social thinkers, as well as various contemporary economists interested in the issue of crime,[77] believe that crime can be prevented or deterred by the proper application of punishments. Although there is considerable controversy on this issue,[78] and it is difficult to unravel the effect of all of the relevant variables, the thrust of the evidence is that sanctions do deter crime.[79] Deterrence operates on two levels. First, *general deterrence* is achieved because the population at large is discouraged from committing crimes out of fear of punishment; and second, *special deterrence* is achieved because the individual offender who suffers punishment will be discouraged from committing future crimes.[80] Also relevant here is the effect of *incapacitation,* which isolates an offender from the larger society, thereby preventing any additional crimes, at least until release.[81]

Rehabilitation

The severe and cruel punishments of retribution ran against the humanitarian grain of the Quakers who inhabited Pennsylvania. In the latter seventeenth century, the Quaker Assembly decreed that imprisonment should replace all existing punishments for serious crime, except capital punishment for homicide. In the early nineteenth century, Pennsylvania built two penitentiaries (places for "penitence"). Under a system of completely separate confinement, prisoners had their own individual cells and exercise yards in which they spent the entire duration of their sentence without ever coming into contact with other inmates.[82]

Separate confinement served several purposes: it prevented inmates from influencing and educating each other; it provided them with a good deal of time to contemplate their deeds and become penitent; and it gave them ample time, space, and tools to work hard at and become proficient in such occupations as shoemaking, weaving, and tailoring.

These new methods for the *rehabilitation* of criminals were consistent with the views of the Quakers that all people, including criminals, had a share of the divine "inner light" that could be nurtured with appropriate treatment.[83] Their objective was to restore their "fellow creatures to virtue and happiness."[84]

Failures of Contemporary Responses

In the United States, especially during the past quarter century, rehabilitation has been the publicly avowed aim of impris-

While prisons clearly incapacitate people, they generally do not do a very good job of rehabilitating criminals.
(Owen Franken/Stock, Boston)

onment. Grand speeches have been made about rehabilitation, but few would be willing to defend the record of prisons as genuinely pursuing this aim. One recent report defines *rehabilitation* in the following way:

> Rehabilitation is the result of any planned intervention that reduces an offender's further criminal activity, whether that reduction is mediated by personality, behavior, abilities, attitudes, values, or other factors. The effects of maturation and the effects associated with "fear" or "intimidation" are excluded, the results of the latter having traditionally been labelled as special deterrence.[85]

In spite of a great deal of research on rehabilitation, little can be said definitively about it: "The entire body of research appears to justify only the conclusion that we do not know of any program or method of rehabilitation that could be guaranteed to reduce the criminal activity of released offenders."[86]

Recidivism

The high rate of recidivism, or prisoners who return to prison after their release, tends to confirm the failure of correctional facilities to do much rehabilitation. Although difficult to measure precisely, the best guess on the recidivism rate seems to be that about one-third of all those released from prison return to crime.[87] There is ample reason to believe that rather than rehabilitating offenders, our prisons, as they are now operating, may actually be debilitating offenders.

High Cost

Unfortunately, the mere custody of prisoners (let alone treatment) is very expensive. In 1979, local, state, and federal governments spent approximately $6 billion

Some correctional institutions have taken steps to teach inmates marketable skills, as the prisoners shown here learning how to use computers illustrate.

(Alan Carey/The Image Works)

for correctional activities. This approached a tripling of the $2.3 billion spent on such facilities in 1971.[88] Beyond correctional costs, the costs of police, courts, prosecutors, public defenders, and other services swelled the total cost of the justice system in 1979 to approximately $26 billion.[89]

Responses to the Failings of the Correctional System

From the time that prisons became widespread, some of their negative consequences have been recognized. Prisons are not only expensive but serve as classrooms for learning techniques of criminal trades and for making new criminal associations. It is not surprising, therefore, that very early in the history of prisons, attempts were made to divert convicted offenders from correctional institutions. During the 1950s and 1960s strong attempts were made to *reintegrate* the offender into the community through greater use of probation, parole, and referral to noncorrectional institutions. However, more recently, with a growing fear of crime and criminals, reactions have set in against the movement toward community corrections.

Probation

A sentence to community supervision, probation usually imposes conditions on the probationer, including periodic meetings with a probation officer. Modern probation efforts are said to date back to efforts of a Boston bootmaker who, on his own initiative, began to bail defendants out of jail in Boston's lower courts in the mid-nineteenth century. Shortly after the turn of the century, the use of probation began to accelerate, partly as a result of the juve-

Table 5.4 Total Justice Direct Expenditure and Percent Change, by Level of Government, Fiscal Years 1971 to 1979

YEAR	TOTAL	FEDERAL	STATE	LOCAL
	Amount (millions of dollars)			
1971	10,517	1,215	2,681	6,621
1972	11,732	1,502	2,948	7,281
1973	13,007	1,651	3,304	8,052
1974	14,842	1,859	3,900	9,092
1975	17,249	2,188	4,612	10,449
1976	19,681	2,450	5,204	12,027
1977	21,574	2,779	5,812	12,983
1978	24,132	3,122	6,688	14,322
1979	25,917	3,269	7,346	15,302
	Percent increase or decrease (−)			
1971 to 1972	11.6	23.6	10.0	10.0
1972 to 1973	10.9	9.9	12.1	10.6
1973 to 1974	14.2	12.6	18.0	12.9
1974 to 1975	16.2	17.7	18.3	14.9
1975 to 1976	14.1	12.0	12.8	15.1
1976 to 1977	9.3	13.4	11.7	7.9
1977 to 1978	11.9	12.3	15.1	10.3
1978 to 1979	7.4	4.7	9.8	6.8
1971 to 1979	146.4	169.1	174.0	131.1

This table provides information on the growth of direct government spending (federal, state, local) related to the justice system between 1971 and 1979. It shows a substantial increase in such expenditures at all governmental levels.

Note: Because of rounding, detail may not add to total.

Source: U.S. Bureau of Justice Statistics, *Justice Expenditure and Employment in the U.S., 1979.* (Washington, D.C.: U.S. Department of Justice, 1980).

nile-court movement, since putting juveniles on probation seemed a good way to supervise their behavior without exposing them to the harsh life of institutions. By 1925, every state provided for the probation of juveniles, but not until 1956 was this the case for adults.[90]

Conditions of probation often include the probationer's promise to obey all laws; to maintain steady employment; to support his or her family; to avoid criminal associates; not to drink to excess or enter bars or taverns; and to obtain approval before marrying, moving, driving, incurring debt, or traveling. In some jurisdictions, probationers must agree to let field agents search them and their premises at any time; narcotics users must agree further to medical tests for drug usage.[91] In addition, probationers are required to meet with their probation officers at specified intervals, depending on the individual probationer and the officer's work load.

Of the more than 2.4 million people

Table 5.5 Distribution of Expenditure for the Justice System, by Level of Government, Fiscal Year 1979 (Dollar Amounts in Thousands)

ACTIVITY	Amount				PERCENT DISTRIBUTION		
	ALL GOVERNMENTS[1]	FEDERAL GOVERNMENT[2]	STATE GOVERNMENTS	LOCAL GOVERNMENTS[1]	FEDERAL GOVERNMENT[2]	STATE GOVERNMENTS	LOCAL GOVERNMENTS[1]
Total justice system[3]	25,916,999	3,950,686	8,424,300	15,465,901	(X)	(X)	(X)
Direct expenditure	25,916,999	3,269,381	7,346,048	15,301,570	12.6	28.3	59.0
Intergovernmental expenditure	([3])	681,305	1,078,252	320,861	(X)	(X)	(X)
Police protection[3]	13,817,073	1,949,899	2,114,545	9,922,896	(X)	(X)	(X)
Direct expenditure	13,817,073	1,948,268	1,952,282	9,916,523	14.1	14.1	71.8
Intergovernmental expenditure	([3])	1,631	162,263	110,216	(X)	(X)	(X)
Judicial[3]	3,388,922	369,509	1,328,778	1,903,631	(X)	(X)	(X)
Direct expenditure	3,388,922	369,509	1,205,866	1,813,547	10.9	35.6	53.5
Intergovernmental expenditure	([3])	–	122,912	102,770	(X)	(X)	(X)
Legal services and prosecution[3]	1,650,739	275,897	455,133	958,088	(X)	(X)	(X)
Direct expenditure	1,650,739	265,898	430,337	954,504	16.1	26.1	57.8
Intergovernmental expenditure	([3])	9,999	24,796	4,428	(X)	(X)	(X)
Public defense[3]	595,198	240,232	125,973	239,066	(X)	(X)	(X)
Direct expenditure	595,198	240,232	116,041	238,925	40.4	19.5	40.1
Intergovernmental expenditure	([3])	–	9,932	1,916	(X)	(X)	(X)
Corrections[3]	5,996,332	392,589	3,777,292	2,198,172	(X)	(X)	(X)
Direct expenditure	5,996,332	353,961	3,486,474	2,155,897	5.9	58.1	36.0
Intergovernmental expenditure	([3])	38,628	290,818	77,715	(X)	(X)	(X)
Other criminal justice[3]	468,735	722,560	622,579	244,048	(X)	(X)	(X)
Direct expenditure	468,735	91,513	155,048	222,174	19.5	33.1	47.4
Intergovernmental	([3])	631,047	467,531	23,816	(X)	(X)	(X)

Shown is the breakdown of government (federal, state, local) spending on the justice system in 1979. Those funds are spent on police protection, the judicial system, legal services and prosecution, public defense, corrections, and so on. Also shown is the percentage of the total for each element of the justice system contributed by the federal, state and local governments. Overall, local governments account for 59 percent of direct expenditures to the total justice system.

– Represents zero or rounds to zero.
X Not applicable.
[1]Local governments data are estimates subject to sampling variation; see text for data limitations.
[2]Federal Government data are for the fiscal period beginning October 1, 1978 and ending September 30, 1979.
[3]The total line for each sector, and for the total Justice System, excludes duplicative intergovernmental expenditure amounts. This was done to avoid the artificial inflation which would result if an intergovernmental expenditure amount for one government is tabulated and then counted again when the recipient government(s) ultimately expend(s) that amount. The intergovernmental expenditure lines are not totaled for the same reason.
Source: U.S. Bureau of Justice Statistics, *Justice Expenditure and Employment in the U.S., 1979.* (Washington, D.C.: U.S. Department of Justice, 1980).

under some form of correctional care, custody, or supervision, over 1.5 million are on probation.[92]

Parole

After prisoners have served a portion of their sentences, they may be paroled. *Parole* involves conditional release from a correctional institution and from community supervision. The parolee's release and continued freedom in the community depend on conformity to the conditions of parole. Parole differs from probation in that it always applies to offenders who have served a portion of their prison sentences.

The decision to release prisoners on parole is usually made by a paroling authority—appointed by the governor of the state—with the recommendation of the institution in which the inmate was held. The conditions of parole are often similar to those of probation. Violation of these conditions during the term of probation or parole can result in imprisonment for the remainder of the sentence.

Parole is now the most common way of gaining release from prison. In 1976, over 70 percent of those released from U.S. prisons were released on parole.[93] There are approximately 300,000 parolees in the United States today.[94]

The Sentencing Reform Movement

Since the mid-1970s, and into the 1980s, there has been a sharp increase in actions by various states to reform the criminal justice system, in part by limiting the movement toward community corrections. A number of states have taken such actions as abolishing parole release for most offenders, establishing administrative guidelines for release decisions, and passing mandatory minimum sentencing laws. The latter reflects a reaction against the indeterminate sentences ("ten to twenty") common since 1900. The idea is to give the criminal a clear idea of exactly what penalty is to be imposed. This new attitude reflects a public and official commitment to try to take actions to deal with the crime problem by keeping criminals in the prisons longer. According to Alfred Blumstein and his associates, "the rehabilitative ideal began to crumble in the 1960s . . . and collapsed in the 1970s."[95] Two reasons are offered for this collapse. First, many people came to believe that rehabilitation does not do much to reduce later criminality. If rehabilitation did not work, then what was the legitimation for releasing prisoners before they had served their full term? Second, criticism arose over the abuse of the wide range of discretion available to those in programs like parole and probation. Instead of returning the criminals to the community, the emphasis in the 1980s has thus far been on incapacitating criminals, especially the career criminals who are responsible for such a large proportion of crime.[96]

In spite of the growth of the sentencing reform movement, its future is in doubt. That is, it is unclear how it will eventually come to relate to the earlier community corrections movement. While the public mood seems to point to a growing emphasis on sentencing reform, there is little positive sentiment for the higher tax rates needed to support an expanded prison system. (It now costs about $15,000 a year to feed and guard a prison inmate for a year.[97]) It seems likely that these cross-pressures will lead to the use of *both* types of programs in the future. That is, career criminals probably will find it harder to get out of prison, while others who pose less of a risk to the community will continue to be released through parole and probation. This tendency to release less threatening prisoners is likely to be enhanced by the increasing problems of crowding in American prisons. To relieve dangerous and inhumane overcrowding, prisons are increasingly likely to let such prisoners go before their sentences are completed. Also encouraging the idea of generally restricting prisons to career criminals are the dangers such prisons pose to less hardened offenders. The latter are likely to be preyed upon by career criminals and to be harassed, beaten, raped, and even murdered.

Because of continuing problems such as these, in coming years we can anticipate continuing interest in *diversion* programs in which the goal is to divert people from the criminal justice system and into a variety of community programs. This has been used most often with juvenile delinquents and to a lesser degree with adult misdemeanants, alcoholic offenders, and narcotics offenders. Diversion is one attempt to decriminalize some behaviors by reducing the emphasis on the use of the criminal justice system in such cases. It may well be that we tend to overcriminalize certain behaviors, especially among juveniles, and the interest in diversion programs reflects a move away from such an orientation. At the same time, we are also likely to see an increased effort to incapacitate career criminals.

SUMMARY

1. The focal concern in this chapter is crime, which is seen as a ubiquitous part of American life.

Part I: The Problem

2. There is a wide array of crimes, but this chapter focuses on *street crimes,* or what the FBI calls *index offenses.*
3. There is a flood of official crime statistics, but they are plagued by a series of defects.
4. Crime rates are higher in urban than rural areas.
5. Although there is some ambiguity, the general historical trend has been in the direction of a substantial increase in crime.
6. Official crime statistics have recently been supplemented by victimization data derived from the National Crime Survey. These data show that about two-thirds of all crimes are not reported to the police. Unfortunately, victimization statistics are also plagued by a series of problems that at times may cause overreporting of crimes and at other times the underreporting of crimes.
7. Data from public opinion polls indicate fear of crime, but it is not as pervasive or consistent as the mass media would have us believe.

Part II: Causes and Consequences

8. There is some evidence that intelligence is related to the likelihood of committing street crimes. Other physiological factors have been linked to crime, but relationships are questionable.
9. There is also evidence that crime is related to mental illnesses like psychoses, but again the linkages are tenuous.
10. Labeling theory seems useful in giving a partial explanation of criminal behavior.
11. Differential association theory helps us understand that a large amount of criminal behavior is learned in various settings and situations.
12. Various social and cultural changes have made crime increasingly likely.
13. Strain theory points to the fact that some people commit crimes in order to get the rewards they cannot obtain through legitimate means.
14. According to subcultural theory, some people become criminals by conforming to the norms of a criminal subgroup.
15. Control theory points to the nature of the bond between the individual and society as a major factor in crime.
16. To conflict theorists, crime is an inevitable by-product of a society that has great inequalities in wealth and power.

Part III: Responses

17. The criminal justice system is enormously complex, involving a large number of phases and many components—including the police, prosecutors, judges, juries, trials, appeals, sentences, and parole.
18. In many ways, the criminal justice system is unjust—favoring the rich and powerful over the poor and weak.
19. The number of inmates in prison has swelled to record numbers.
20. At least until very recently, the philosophy of the American correctional system tended to shift from retribution and deterrence to rehabilitation.

21. American prisons have never really done much rehabilitation,despite the lip service given it. One piece of evidence in support of this assertion is the high rate of recidivism.
22. During the 1950s and 1960s, in response to criticisms of the prisons, there were many attempts to reintegrate prisoners into the community through such programs as probation and parole.
23. Since the mid-1970s, however, a reaction has set in against these efforts to rehabilitate prisoners and reintegrate them into the community. This is the sentencing-reform movement which, among other things, has sought to limit paroles, pass mandatory minimum sentencing laws, and generally deal with the crime problem by keeping criminals in prison longer.
24. In the future, we are likely to see this sentencing reform movement coexist somewhat uncomfortably with the rehabilitation and community corrections movement. Basically, we are likely to see career criminals retained longer in prison, while those less likely to repeat their crimes will be released to the larger community.

SUGGESTED READINGS

Brown, Edward J., Timothy J. Flanagan, and Maureen McCleod, eds., *Sourcebook of Criminal Justice Statistics: 1983.* U.S. Department of Justice, Bureau of Justice Statistics. Washington, D.C.: U.S. Government Printing Office, 1984. A huge compendium of data on crime and criminal justice in the United States.

Gibbons, Don C., *Society, Crime, and Criminal Behavior,* 4th ed. Englewood Cliffs, N.J.: Prentice-Hall, 1982. A basic text on crime from the point of view of a sociologist.

Reiman, Jeffrey H., *The Rich Get Richer and the Poor Get Prison: Ideology, Class and Criminal Justice.* New York: John Wiley, 1979. Analysis of the social-class bias in the criminal justice system.

Silberman, Charles E., *Criminal Violence, Criminal Justice.* New York: Random House, 1978. A popular analysis of crime and the criminal justice system.

Vold, George, *Theoretical Criminology,* 2nd ed. Prepared by Thomas J. Bernard. New York: Oxford University Press, 1979. Summary of theoretical perspectives in sociology on the crime problem.

FOOTNOTES

[1]Daniel Bell, "Crime as an American Way of Life," *Antioch Review,* 13 (June 1953), 131–154; see also, Charles E. Silberman, *Criminal Violence, Criminal Justice* (New York: Random House, 1978), especially Chapter 2.

[2]Gwynn Nettler, *Explaining Crime* (New York: McGraw-Hill, 1974).

[3]Bureau of Justice Statistics, *Report to the Nation on Crime and Justice: The Data* (Washington, D.C.: U.S. Department of Justice, 1983), p. 2.

[4]U.S. Department of Justice, *Crime in the United States: 1983, Uniform Crime Reports for the United States* (Washington, D.C.: U.S. Government Printing Office, 1984).

[5]*Ibid.* Arson has just recently been added to the list and therefore statistics on it will not be reported in this chapter. It is also worth noting that there are unusual problems with the reliability of data on arson since both the police and the fire department may be involved in reporting statistics on this crime to the FBI.

[6]Bureau of Justice Statistics, *Report to the Nation on Crime and Justice, op. cit.,* p. 3.

[7]Edwin Schur, *Crimes Without Victims: Deviant Behavior and Public Policy* (Englewood Cliffs, N.J.: Prentice-Hall, 1965).

[8]U.S. Department of Justice, *Crime in the United States: 1983, op. cit.,* p. 7.

[9]Don C. Gibbons, *Society, Crime, and Criminal Behavior,* 4th ed. (Englewood Cliffs, N.J.: Prentice-Hall, 1982), p. 85.

[10]See, for example, John I. Kitsuse and Aaron V. Cicourel, "A Note on the Use of Official Statistics," *So-*

cial Problems, 11 (1963), 131–139; Marvin Wolfgang, "Uniform Crime Reports: A Critical Appraisal," *University of Pennsylvania Law Review,* 111 (1963), 708–738; Michael Hindelang, "The Uniform Crime Reports Revisited," *Journal of Criminal Justice,* 2 (1974) 1–17. Although Hindelang saw utility in the UCR, he felt that the problems with it at the time were "numerous, severe and varied."

[11]U.S. Department of Justice, *Crime in the United States: 1983, op. cit.,* p. 41

[12]*Ibid.*

[13]The President's Commission on Law Enforcement and Administration of Justice, *The Challenge of Crime in a Free Society* (Washington, D.C.: U.S. Government Printing Office, 1967), pp. 22–23; See also, Paul Boyer, *Urban Masses and Moral Order in America, 1820–1920* (Cambridge, Mass.: Harvard University Press, 1978); Silberman, *Criminal Violence, Criminal Justice, op. cit.*

[14]U.S. Department of Justice, *Crime in the United States; 1983,* p. 43.

[15]Ibid.,pp. 40–41.

[16]Bureau of Justice Statistics, *Report to the Nation on Crime and Justice, op. cit.,* p. 10.

[17]Theodore N. Ferdinand, "The Criminal Patterns of Boston Since 1849," *American Journal of Sociology,* 73 (1967), 84–99.

[18]Eric H. Monkkonen, *Police in Urban America: 1860–1920* (Cambridge: Cambridge University Press, 1981).

[19]Gibbons, *op. cit.,* pp. 240–241.

[20]Murray Melbin, "Night as Frontier," *American Sociological Review,* 43 (1978), 3–22.

[21]Robert G. Lehnen and Wesley G. Skogan, *The National Crime Survey: Working Papers. Volume 1: Current and Historical Perspectives* (Washington, D.C.: U.S. Department of Justice, 1981). Data from the National Crime Survey, along with much other information, are reported in Edward J. Brown, Timothy J. Flanagan, and Maureen McCleod, eds., *Sourcebook of Criminal Justice Statistics: 1983.* U.S. Department of Justice, Bureau of Justice Statistics (Washington, D.C.: U.S. Government Printing Office, 1984).

[22]Brown, Flanagan, and McCleod, eds., *Sourcebook of Criminal Justice Statistics: 1983, op. cit.,* pp. III–IV.

[23]Philip H. Ennis, *Criminal Victimization in the United States: A Report of a NORC Survey to the President's Commission on Law Enforcement and Administration of Justice* (Washington, D.C.: Government Printing Office, 1967).

[24]Bureau of Justice Statistics, *Report to the Nation on Crime and Justice, op. cit.,* p. 24.

[25]Wesley G. Skogan, "Measurement Problems in Official and Survey Crime Rates," *Journal of Criminal Justice,* 3 (1975), 17–32.

[26]Wesley G. Skogan, *Issues in the Measurement of Victimization* (Washington, D.C.: U.S. Government Printing Office, 1981).

[27]James P. Levine, "The Potential for Crime Overreporting in Criminal Victimization Surveys," *Criminology,* 14. (1976), 307–330.

[28]Brown, Flanagan, and McCleod, eds., *Sourcebook of Criminal Justice Statistics, op. cit.,* p. 197.

[29]*Ibid.,* p. 195.

[30]George B. Vold, *Theoretical Criminology,* 2nd ed. prepared by Thomas J. Bernard. (New York: Oxford University Press, 1979).

[31]Gina Lombroso-Ferrero, *Criminal Man* (Montclair, N.J.: Patterson-Smith, 1911).

[32]Paul Tappan, *Crime, Justice, and Correction* (New York: McGraw-Hill, 1960).

[33]Travis Hirschi, *Causes of Delinquency* (Berkeley: University of California Press, 1969).

[34]Travis Hirschi and Michael J. Hindelang, "Intelligence and Delinquency: A Revisionist Review," *American Sociological Review,* 42 (1977), 571–587.

[35]Sarnoff Mednick, "Human Nature, Crime, and Society: Keynote Address." In Fred Wright, Charles Bahn, and Robert W. Reiber, eds., *Forensic Psychology and Psychiatry* (New York: New York Academy of Science, 1980), pp. 335–348.

[36]While the layperson may think of a person who commits such a crime as insane, the law requires an independent standard in determining whether a criminal is insane.

[37]Edwin H. Sutherland and Donald R. Cressey, *Criminology,* 10th ed. (Philadelphia: Lippincott, 1978), p. 159.

[38]Samuel Yochelson and Stanton E. Samenow, *The Criminal Personality* (New York: Jason Aronson, Vol. I, 1976; Vol. II, 1977).

[39]Charles R. Tittle, "Labelling and Crime: An Empirical Evaluation." In Walter R. Gove, ed., *The Labelling of Deviance: Evaluating a Perspective,* 2nd ed. (Beverly Hills, Cal.: Sage, 1980), pp. 241–264.

[40]Bureau of Justice Statistics, *Report to the Nation on Crime and Justice, op. cit.,* p. 32.

[41]Hirschi, *Causes of Delinquency, op. cit.*

[42]Lawrence E. Cohen and Rodney Stark, "Discriminatory Labeling and the Five-Finger Discount," *Journal of Research in Crime and Delinquency,* 11 (1974), 25–39.

[43]Walter R. Gove, "Postscript." In Gove, ed., *The Labelling of Deviance, op. cit.,* pp. 264–269.

[44]Edwin H. Sutherland, *Principles of Criminology,* 4th ed. (Chicago: Lippincott, 1947).

[45]Peter Letkemann, *Crime as Work* (Englewood Cliffs, N.J.: Prentice-Hall, 1973).

[46]Ramsey Clark, "When Punishment is a Crime," *Playboy,* November 1970, pp. 100ff.

[47]Diana Gray, "Turning-Out: A Study of Teenage Prostitution," *Urban Life and Culture,* 1 (1973), 401–425.

[48]Lawrence E. Cohen and Marcus Felson, "Social Change and Crime Rate Trends: A Routine Activity Approach," *American Sociological Review,* 44 (1979), 588–608.

[49]Robert K. Merton, "Social Structure and Anomie," *American Sociological Review,* 3 (1938), 672–682.

[50]Hirschi, *Causes of Delinquency, op. cit.* 1969. A fourth element of control theory, *belief,* will not concern us here. For more recent work on control theory see Michael D. Wiatrowski, David B. Griswold, and Mary K. Roberts, "Social Control Theory and Delinquency," *American Sociological Review,* 46 (1981), 525–541; Ross G. Matsueda, "Testing Control Theory and Differential Association: A Causal Modeling Approach," *American Sociological Review,* 47 (1982), 489–504.

[51]Hirschi, *Causes of Delinquency, op. cit.,* 1969.

[52]*Ibid.,* p. 20.

[53]*Ibid.,* p. 21.

[54]Austin T. Turk, *Criminality and Legal Order* (Chicago: Rand McNally, 1969); Richard Quinney, *The Social Reality of Crime* (Boston: Little, Brown, 1970).

[55]David M. Gordon, "Class and Economics of Crime," *Review of Radical Political Economics,* 3 (1981), 51–75; Barry Krisberg, *Crime and Privilege: Toward a New Criminology.* (Englewood Cliffs, N.J.: Prentice-Hall, 1975).

[56]John Braithwaite, "The Myth of Social Class and Criminality Reconsidered," *American Sociological Review,* 46 (1981), 36–57. In addition to offering an overview of research on this issue, Braithwaite comes to the conclusion expressed in the body of the text.

[57]This conclusion has been experimentally supported by Richard A. Berk, Kenneth J. Lenihan, and Peter H. Rossi, "Crime and Poverty: Some Experimental Evidence From Ex-Offenders," *American Sociological Review,* 45 (1980), 766–786.

[58]Bureau of Justice Statistics, *Report to the Nation on Crime and Justice, op. cit.,* 1983, p. 44.

[59]*Ibid.,* p. 42.

[60]*Ibid.,* p. 43.

[61]*Ibid.*

[62]Although this is generally true, there are cases where the legal system operates to the detriment of the "haves" and against the "have-nots."

[63]Christopher Adamson, "Toward a Marxian Penology: Captive Criminal Populations as Economic Threats and Resources," *Social Problems,* 31 (1984), 435–458.

[64]Jeffrey H. Reiman, *The Rich Get Richer and the Poor Get Prison: Ideology, Class and Criminal Justice* (New York: Wiley, 1979).

[65]Anatole France. *Crainqueville.* Winifred Stephens (tr.). (Freeport, N.Y.: Books for Libraries, 1922).

[66]William Chambliss, "A Sociological Analysis of the Law of Vagrancy," *Social Problems,* 12 (1964), 67–77.

[67]Alan J. Lizotte, "Extra-legal Factors in Chicago's Criminal Courts: Testing the Conflict Model of Criminal Justice," *Social Problems,* 25 (1978), pp. 564–580.

[68]*Ibid.*

[69]Mark Dowie, "Pinto Madness," *Mother Jones,* September/October, 1977.

[70]"Life Term is Upheld in Theft of $120.75," *The New York Times,* March 19, 1980, p. A24.

[71]Cited in Kenneth Mann, Stanton Wheeler, and Austin Sarat, "Sentencing the White-Collar Offender," *American Criminal Law Review,* 17 (1980), 487.

[72]David Rothman, *The Discovery of the Asylum: Social Order and Disorder in the New Republic* (Boston: Little Brown, 1971), p. xiii.

[73]Brown, Flanagan, and McCleod, eds., *Sourcebook of Criminal Justice Statistics-1983, op. cit.,* p. 538 Bureau of Justice Statistics, *Report to the Nation on Crime and Justice, op. cit.,* p. 81.

[74]Bureau of Justice Statistics, "Prisoners in 1984" (Washington, D.C.: U.S. Department of Justice, April 1985), p. 1

[75]Harry E. Barnes and Negley Teeters, *New Horizons in Criminology,* 3rd ed. (Englewood Cliffs, N.J.: Prentice-Hall, 1959).

[76]Herbert Packer, *The Limits of Criminal Sanction* (Stanford, Cal.: Stanford University Press, 1968).

[77]See, for example, G. Becker, "Crime and Punishment: An Economic Approach," *Journal of Political Economy,* 78 (1968), 189–217; I. Ehrlich, "Participation in Illegitimate Activities: A Theoretical and Empirical Investigation," *Journal of Political Economy,* 81 (1973), 521–567; I. Ehrlich, "The Deterrent Effect of Capital Punishment: A Question of Life or Death," 65 (1975), 397–417.

[78]William J. Bowers and Glenn L. Pierce, "The Illusion of Deterrence in Isaac Ehrlich's Research on Capital Punishment," *The Yale Law Journal,* 85 (1975), 187–208.

[79]Alfred Blumstein, Jacqueline Cohen, and Daniel Nagin, eds., *Deterrence and Incapacitation: Estimating the Effects of Criminal Sanctions on Crime Rates* (Washington, D.C.: National Academy of Sciences, 1978), p. 47.

[80]Daniel Nagin, "General Deterrence: A Review of Empirical Evidence." In Blumstein, *et al., op. cit.,* pp. 95–139; Wolf Middendorf, *The Effectiveness of Pun-*

ishment, Especially in Relation to Traffic Offense (South Hackensack, N.J.: Fred B. Rothman, 1968).

[81]Jacqueline Cohen, "The Incapacitative Effect of Imprisonment: A Critical Review of the Literature." In Blumstein *et al., op. cit.*, pp. 187–243.

[82]Richard Korn and Lloyd McCorkle, *Criminology and Penology* (New York: Holt, Rinehart and Winston, 1959).

[83]Walter D. Lewis, *From Newgate to Dannemora: The Rise of the Penitentiary in New York, 1796–1848* (Ithaca, N.Y.: Cornell University Press, 1965).

[84]"What Are Prisons For?" *Time*, September 13, 1982, pp. 38ff.

[85]Lee Sechrest, Susan O. White, and Elizabeth D. Brown, eds., *The Rehabilitation of Criminal Offenders: Problems and Prospects* (Washington, D.C.: National Academy of Sciences, 1979), pp. 4–5.

[86]*Ibid.*, p. 3.

[87]Gordon Waldo and David Griswold, "Issues in the Measurement of Recidivism." In Lee Sechrest, *et al., op. cit.*, pp. 225–250.

[88]Brown, Flanagan, and McCleod, eds., *Sourcebook of Criminal Justice Statistics: 1983, op. cit.*, pp. 2–3.

[89]Bureau of Justice Statistics, *Report to the Nation on Crime and Justice, op. cit.*, p. 88.

[90]President's Commission on Law Enforcement and the Administration of Justice, *The Challenge of Crime in a Free Society, op. cit.*

[91]Frank Remington, Donald Newman and Marygold Melli, *Criminal Justice Administration* (Indianapolis: Bobbs-Merrill, 1969).

[92]Bureau of Justice Statistics, *Report to the Nation on Crime and Justice. op. cit.*, p. 74.

[93]Blumstein, *et al., op. cit.*, p. 56.

[94]Bureau of Justice Statistics, *Report to the Nation on Crime and Justice, op. cit.*, p. 74.

[95]Blumstein, *et al., op. cit.*, p. 64.

[96]Bureau of Justice Statistics, *Report to the Nation on Crime and Justice, op. cit.*, p. 34; Silberman, *Criminal Violence, Criminal Justice, op. cit.*, Chapter 3.

[97]"What Are Prisons For?" *Time, op. cit.*, p. 39.

Nobody's family can hang out a sign
"Nothing the matter here."
Chinese proverb

6 *Family and Sexual Violence*

The major concern in this chapter is violence committed within the family, especially wife and child abuse. We are also concerned with incest, a form of sexual violence that occurs within the family, and rape, which can occur both within and outside of the family context. Our concern, then, is with family and sexual problems, but it should be clear that there are many other problems within the family and sexual relationships that are not covered in this chapter. In other words, it is possible to define family and sexual problems far more broadly than they are defined in this chapter. Within the family, we could discuss such problems as the high divorce rate, the relationship between single-parent families and poverty, the large and increasing number of children born out of wedlock, and the like. Within the area of human sexuality there are a wide range of problems worthy of note including prostitution, pornography, and homosexuality. However, rather than dealing superficially with a number of family and sexual problems, we have decided to focus more narrowly on the *violence* that occurs within these domains.

Private Violence

Time magazine, in a cover story devoted to family violence and rape, combined the two under the general heading of "private violence."[1] Conveying the same theme, Murray Straus and his colleagues entitled their book on violence in the American family, *Behind Closed Doors.*[2] *Time* contrasts private violence to the far more visible public violence:

> What may be called public violence is as American as assassinations, mob wars and mass murders, the stuff of screaming headlines and periodic soul searching. What might be called private violence, what people who know each other, even profess to love each other, do to each

other, is a nightmarish realm only beginning to be forthrightly explored. Its particular horror stems from its violations of the trust upon which all intimate human relations depend: it is cruelly exercised on those nearest, most vulnerable, least able or inclined to defend themselves from their attackers.[3]

We have little difficulty thinking of wife abuse, child abuse, or incest as private violence, but what about rape? The common conception of rape is that it is a form of public violence committed by strangers against victims. However, the fact is that many rapes involve people who know one another. Thus, rape too may be considered a form of private violence.

We know comparatively little with precision about private violence. One exception is the most extreme form of violence, murder, and the fact that about one-fifth of all murders are of loved ones. However, exact figures on wife abuse, child abuse, incest, and rape are extremely hard to come by. The fact is that far more of these acts go undetected and/or unreported than find their way into official reports of one type or another. Many battered wives accept their condition as a part of their marriage and never report the offenses to anyone. Or, they may simply terminate the relationship, at least in part, because of the battering. Children are often too frightened, intimidated, or uncomprehending to report incidents of abuse or incest to anyone. Rape victims, especially when the perpetrator is known to them, are often unwilling to report an incident (and the rapist) to the police. Thus, the available official statistics grossly underestimate the true amount of private violence in the United States.

However, things are beginning to change. For one thing, there is much greater public attention to private violence today than there ever was in the past. In 1976 only 10 percent of the population considered child abuse a serious national problem, but by 1983 that figure had risen to 90 percent of the public.[4] Victims are much less likely to accept abuse idly, and perpetrators are much more conscious of the fact that their acts are more likely to be resisted and, if the resistance is unsuccessful, to be reported to the authorities. As a result of all of this, official statistics on private violence tend to be on the rise. However, these statistics are still a long way from accurately portraying the true extent of these problems.[5]

Abuse of Power

The underlying theme in this chapter is power, and its abuse within the family and/or sexual relationships.[6] We can define *power* as the ability to secure one's objectives, or to control the behavior of others, even against opposition. Wini Breines and Linda Gordon argue that we must look at the kind of violence discussed in this chapter within the broader context of power relationships.[7] Two of the most important aspects of this broader context are "gender and age structuring," which serve "as a source of power differences and personal tensions."[8] Traditionally, in our society males have had power over females, and parents have exercised power over children. The patterned ways that people hurt each other in our society often reflect "the power (or lack of it) that different family members hold in society."[9] Thus, in the family violence section of this chapter, we will be concerned with the violent manifestations of the power exercised by husbands over wives and parents over children. We will not be much concerned with forms of family violence (for example, siblings abusing each other, children abusing parents) that do not involve built-in power advantages possessed by abusers over their victims. Along the same lines, although incest can take a variety of forms, our main concern will be with the type that most involves abuse of power—father-daughter incest. Finally, we will discuss male rape of females as a manifestation of male abuse of their traditional power over females.

FAMILY VIOLENCE

It is certainly not commonplace to think of the family as an arena of violence. Most generally, we think of the family as the domain of love and affection. When we think negatively about the family, it is usually in terms of nonviolent conflict between husbands and wives, children and parents, and parents and grandparents.[10] In more recent years, however, there has been growing publicity about, and public awareness of, violence within the family. In fact, Murray Straus and his co-authors go so far as to say that "the family is society's pre-eminent violent institution."[11] Or, as Suzanne Steinmetz and Straus put it in the title of an early article on the subject, the family can even be seen as the "cradle of violence."[12]

PART I: THE PROBLEM

As is clear above, "we live in violent homes."[13] We can identify a variety of types of incidents that can take place in such homes, such as violence against wives (wife abuse), violence against husbands, violence against children (child abuse), violence between brothers and sisters, and violence against parents. However, since our underlying concern is violence as a manifestation of basic power differentials, we will focus on violence committed by husbands against wives, since this reflects abuse of gender differences in power. We will also deal with parental violence against children, since this is a reflection of abuse of generational differences in power. None of the other forms are manifestations of generally more powerful agents acting violently toward those with less power. While the other forms of family violence certainly occur, they do not occur as frequently nor can they be analyzed as well theoretically from the point of view of power as wife abuse and child abuse.

Violence Against Wives

Family violence is primarily a male problem. That is, although there is evidence of violence against husbands by wives,[14] the much more important problem is wife abuse.[15] Because of this, most public and sociological attention has been devoted to violence against wives,[16] and for good reasons. Among them are the fact that husbands are more prone to use the most dangerous and injurious forms of violence, their abuse is likely to do more damage, it is likely to be repeated more often, and a large number of such assaults are against wives who are pregnant. Violence by wives is more likely to be in self-defense, and wives are more likely to be locked into a marriage[17] and more dependent on their husbands.[18]

Based on their research, Straus and his colleagues concluded that in 16 percent of couples, one partner commits at least one violent act against the other partner every year. If one considers the entire length of a marriage, almost one-third of all couples will experience an act of violence at some time during their married lives.[19] Although these statistics may seem extremely high, they probably substantially *under*estimate the true extent of husband-wife violence, which may be as high as 50 percent, *or more.* Straus and his associates believe that among the reasons for this underestimation are the facts that in some families violence is so commonplace that it is not noteworthy, while in others violence is not

The problem of wife abuse has received increasing public attention in recent years. In a made-for-television movie ("Burning Bed"), Farrah Fawcett played a battered wife who ultimately felt compelled to kill her husband in order to put a stop to the abuse she continued to encounter.

(AP/Wide World Photos)

reported out of guilt and/or shame. In addition, the amount of violence is underestimated in their study because the study only included information on couples currently living together, thereby omitting past marriages that may have ended in divorce and may well have included a high level of violence.

The most common forms of violence against spouses were pushing, grabbing, or shoving; slapping; and throwing something at a spouse. The least common forms were beatings, threatening with a knife or gun, and actually using a knife or gun (see Fig. 6.1). Although the percentages involved in the latter forms are small, they add up to a very large number of people. Thus, it is estimated that in 1975 "*over 1.7 million Americans had at some time faced a husband or wife wielding a knife or gun, and well over 2 million had been beaten up* by his or her spouse."[20]

Although the statistics discussed above include both wife and husband abuse, the far more serious problem is violence committed against wives by husbands.

Parental Violence Against Children

Parental violence toward children (like wife abuse[21]) has a long history[22] and today is more common (if we include the milder forms) than violence by husbands against their wives. Straus and his coworkers report that over 70 percent of their respondents had used some form of violence at some point in their child's life. Predictably, the most common forms of violence against children were the milder forms

Parental violence against children is very common; although it is usually mild (for example, spankings), in a surprising number of cases it is quite violent.

(James R. Holland/Stock, Boston)

Figure 6.1 **Rate at Which Violent Acts Occurred in the Previous Year and Ever in the Marriage**

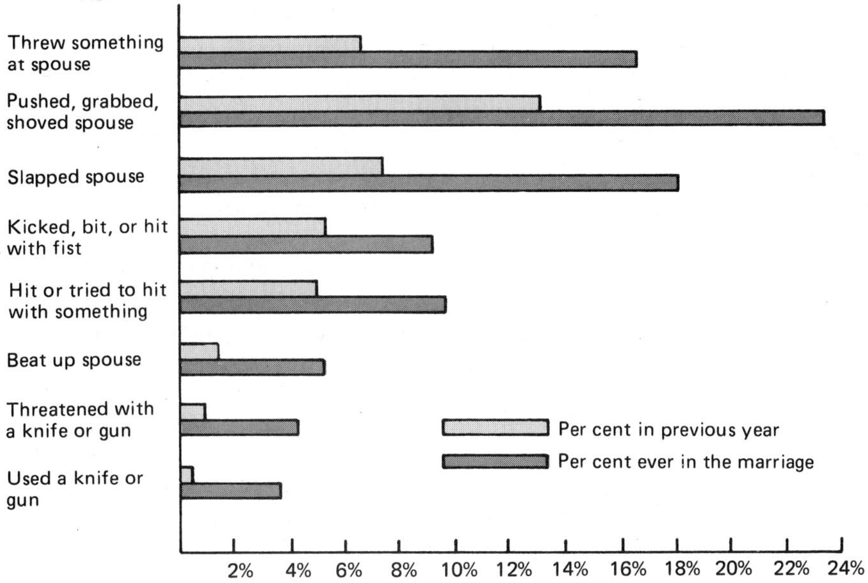

Threw something at spouse
Pushed, grabbed, shoved spouse
Slapped spouse
Kicked, bit, or hit with fist
Hit or tried to hit with something
Beat up spouse
Threatened with a knife or gun
Used a knife or gun

Per cent in previous year
Per cent ever in the marriage

2% 4% 6% 8% 10% 12% 14% 16% 18% 20% 22% 24%

Source: Murray A. Straus, Richard J. Gelles, and Suzanne K. Steinmetz, *Behind Closed Doors: Violence in the American Family* (Garden City, N.Y.: Anchor Books, 1980), p. 33.

such as slaps and spankings, pushing or shoving, hitting with an object, and throwing an object at a child. Nevertheless, a surprising amount of more dangerous forms of violence were found—"an astoundingly high number of American children who were kicked, punched, bitten, beaten up, threatened with a gun or a knife, or had a gun or a knife used on them."[23]

Although our focus in this section is on wife and child abuse, it is worth noting that there are other important forms of family violence. We close this discussion of the problem of family violence with a brief mention of violence between siblings and violence toward parents.

Violence Between Siblings

Somewhat surprisingly, violence between brothers and sisters is the most common form of family violence. Over 80 percent of children between three and seventeen years of age who have siblings at home engage in at least one violent act against a brother or sister in a typical year. Although much of this is of a minor nature, it was estimated that in 1975 19 million of these attacks were sufficiently severe that they would have been considered assaults if they had happened outside the family.

Violence Toward Parents

There is also a considerable amount of violence perpetrated by children against their parents. Claire Cornell and Richard Gelles estimate that almost 1 million teenagers commit a violent act toward one of their parents every year. Perhaps as many as 2,000 parents are killed each year by their children.[24] In addition, another half million elderly Americans over 65 years of age are attacked (beaten, punched, scalded, burned with a cigarette, etc.) by younger family members.

This, then, is the problem of family violence. We turn now to the causes and consequences of this social problem, specifically wife and child abuse.

PART II: CAUSES AND CONSEQUENCES

INDIVIDUAL LEVEL

There is some support for the idea that family violence is caused by, or is at least a correlate of, genetic or biological factors. There is, for example, evidence of a neurological and metabolic basis for explosive rage,[25] although such a basis fails to explain why that rage is vented toward a wife or a child. However, it is clear that family violence has a profound physiological effect on the victims. Clearly, there are wives and children who are battered, beaten, scarred, and even killed as a result of family violence.

The idea that family violence is caused by psychological factors would seem to have some credibility. For example, it seems clear that the aggression of the perpetrator is an important factor in family violence.[26] There is also evidence that a wife beater may be psychologically disturbed in one way or another.[27] Unfortunately, in the study conducted by Straus and his associates of family violence, the psychological make-up of those perpetrating family violence was not a major concern. However, in another work, Straus concluded that the rate of psychological problems in violent families is no higher than the rate in "normal" families.[28] Nevertheless, it is safe to say that we cannot exclude psychological problems in the perpetrator as a cause of family violence.

It is also unfortunate that Straus and his colleagues did not collect psychological data on the victims of family violence. However, there is a widely held view that psychological characteristics of victims, especially of spouse abuse, play a part in the assault.[29] That is, the victimized spouse may have psychological problems that attract and keep her or him in an abusive situation. One controversial concept here is Lenore Walker's idea of "learned helplessness."[30]

Walker's thesis is that as a result of rigid sex role socialization, women learn to be helpless. Consequently, when violence looms, they do not have the skills to deal with it or escape from it. Thus, the helplessness of the wife is seen as contributing to the husband's violence. Walker's ideas have come under attack, largely for seeming to blame the victim (the wife) for being battered.[31] In fact, in a later piece of research, Walker herself backtracks a bit on her concept of learned helplessness.[32] She now sees the concept as more "complicated" and in any case her data point toward placing more blame on the male perpetrator than on the female victim.

It is far clearer that family violence harms the psyche of the victims. For example, in one study, three-fourths of the battered women felt depressed as a result of the abuse.[33] It seems highly likely that victims of child abuse carry the psychological scars of such abuse with them throughout their entire lives.

Innocent bystanders to family violence may also suffer adverse consequences. For example, children exposed to the battering of their mothers by their fathers may experience present and future behavioral and psychological problems.

Table 6.1 Levels of Analysis: Family Violence

LEVELS	APPROPRIATE QUESTIONS	A PARTIAL SYNOPSIS OF PRESENT CONCLUSIONS
INDIVIDUAL	What is the evidence on the physiological causes and consequences of family violence?	There is some evidence that there is a physiological base for violence, but it does not tell us why it is aimed at family members. There is clear evidence that family violence has adverse physiological consequences.
	What is the evidence on the psychological causes and consequences of family violence?	Although the evidence is weak, we cannot exclude psychological problems in the perpetrator as a cause of family violence. There is clear evidence that family violence has negative psychological effects on victims as well as innocent bystanders in the family.
SOCIAL-PSYCHOLOGICAL	Is family violence learned?	Yes. There is a tendency for those who commit family violence to have learned it in their parents' home.
	What are other social-psychological causes and consequences of family violence?	For one thing, the nature of the history of the relationship between husband-wife and parent-child affects the nature of family violence. For another, family violence clearly has a profound effect on interaction within the family.
SOCIOLOGICAL	How does the structure of the family affect family violence?	There is a long list of basic characteristics of the family that help cause family violence. Among them are the sheer amount of time spent together, the intensity of family relationships, and the age and sex differences that are found within the family.
	What is the relationship between social stratification and family violence?	Although current evidence shows a higher rate of family violence in the lower classes, it is likely that the future will bring increasing revelations about such violence in the middle and upper classes.

(Continue

Table 6.1 Levels of Analysis: Family Violence *(Continued)*

LEVELS	APPROPRIATE QUESTIONS	A PARTIAL SYNOPSIS OF PRESENT CONCLUSIONS
SOCIOLOGICAL	What is the relationship between gender and age stratification and family violence?	The position of females at the bottom of the gender stratification system and children at the bottom of the age stratification system leaves them vulnerable to being victims of family violence.
	Does the nature of American culture play a role in family violence?	Yes. The wide range of ways in which American culture condones, even encourages, violence, is a cause of family violence.

SOCIAL-PSYCHOLOGICAL LEVEL

At the social-psychological level it is clear that *socialization* plays a major causal role in family violence:

> *Each generation learns to be violent by being a participant in a violent family* . . . . The more violent the grandparents, the more violent the couples in our study are as husbands and wives, and the more abusive they are to their children. The children of these couples, in turn, tend to follow the pattern of their parents.[34]

In various works, Straus places a great deal of emphasis on the learning of violence within the family context. He makes the point that physical punishment of children is virtually universal in American, and more generally Western, families. Of crucial importance are the unintended lessons of this punishment "which are so deeply learned that they become an integral part of one's personality and world view."[35] Straus enumerates four such unintended consequences of childhood punishment. First, the child learns to associate love with violence since it is likely to be the parents who will be the first to hit the child and to continue to do so throughout childhood. In other words, the child's primary love objects are the ones who commit the violence. Second, violence is used to teach children which dangerous things are to be avoided. This serves to imply to the child that it is morally right to commit violence on other family members. Third, the image is conveyed to the child that violence is justified in those circumstances in which something is considered truly important. Finally, the view is communicated that under certain circumstances (for example, stress, tension, anger) violence, although wrong, is still to some degree "understandable," or legitimate. In these and many other ways the child learns in the family both violence and the legitimations for its use.[36]

Needless to say, family violence impacts on the social psychology of the family. For one thing, violence inherently involves interaction between people—parents beating children, husbands attacking wives. For another, those types of violence clearly affect a wide array of family relationships and ultimately the structure of the family. Ongoing relationships among family members must be affected by violent incidents. And, of course, violence is likely to play a major role in the gradual dissolution and ultimately the destruction of the family through divorce.[37]

Recently, James Wiggins analyzed situational factors within the family leading to violence.[38] He argued that three factors elicited physical aggression by husbands against wives. First, aggression is likely to be elicited if the wife does not meet the husband's demands about a variety of things such as childbearing, sexual behavior, and money management. Second, a husband may become aggressive if the wife makes any demand at all of him, sometimes involving nothing more than questioning his opinions or actions. Finally, a husband may become more aggressive toward his wife if an outsider interferes with an assault on her. For her part, the wife usually reacts to such attacks by complying with the husband's demands or terminating her demands of him. The wife rarely responds with aggressive reactions of her own. Wiggins explains this aggression-compliance syndrome in terms of the history of the relationship between husband and wife: "The wife's repeated compliant reaction to her husband's aggression strengthens or reinforces his aggressiveness in future episodes. In turn, her compliance is strengthened or reinforced by its immediate effect—the avoidance or termination of his hostility."[39] The more general point here is that one must understand the history of the relationship between husband and wife in order to comprehend the nature of the violence that may exist between them. The same point applies to parent-child violence, indeed all other violent relationships within the family.

However, neither the causes nor the consequences of violence are restricted to the family. As Straus and his associates put it in terms of causes, "it would be a mistake to put the whole burden of violence on what is learned in the family."[40] While many of those who commit violence come from violent families, many others come from families that are not particularly violent. Thus, we need to look beyond the social psychology of family violence to the sociological level of analysis.

SOCIOLOGICAL LEVEL

The first thing to examine at the sociological level in terms of causes of violence is the basic structure of the family. Straus enumerates a number of structural factors that contribute to the high level of violence within the family.[41]

First, there is the fact that family members spend a great deal of time together. Although important, it should not be overemphasized since there are other groups (such as work groups) in which a great deal of time is spent, but there is comparatively little violence. Second, unlike most other groups that are highly focused, families cover a wide range of matters and activities. Thus, there are simply more matters over which conflict (and violence) can occur. Third, the much greater intensity involved in family relationships leads to a greater likelihood of violence. As Straus puts it:

> The failure of a work colleague to spell or to eat properly may be mildly annoying or more likely just a subject of derision. But if the bad spelling or table manners are those of one's child or spouse, the pain experienced is often excruciating.[42]

Fourth, the activities of one family member often impinge on those of other members. For example, the family member who fails to put anything away aggravates the neat member(s) of the family. Fifth, unlike most other groups, being a family member carries with it, at least implicitly, the right to influence the behavior of other family members. Thus, unhappiness over impinging activities are exacerbated by efforts to change the behavior of family members. Sixth, the family is a structure in which one finds both sex and age differences. Accompanying these differences are substantial cultural differences between sex and age groups, and these differences make "the family an arena of culture conflict."[43] A mild example is conflict over the type of music played on the stereo—a Beethoven symphony or a Bruce Springsteen album. Seventh, there is considerable sexual inequality within the family, and this has become a more important source of conflict and violence as a result of the women's movement. Women are now more conscious of the inequality, more angered by it, and more likely to do something about it. Eighth, the family is rather insulated from the rest of society, especially the social control and coping mechanisms that exist at the societal level. Thus, the family does not have recourse to these in time of conflict and violence. Ninth, family membership tends to be involuntary. This is certainly true of children and even, to some degree, of spouses who feel constrained to remain within the family. Thus when stress arises, family members do not have, or at least do not feel that they have, the option of leaving. Finally, there is a good deal of instability and stress built into the family. A large portion of this is traceable to the many changes built into the life cycle of the family—birth, maturation of children, aging, death.

Beyond all of these factors is Richard Gelles's argument: "A man beats up his wife because he can."[44,45] In other words, violence is more likely to occur in the family than at work or in school because the victims are always available and vulnerable, and the perpetrator is much more likely to get away with it. There are certainly other aspects of family life that could be linked to violence, but this list conveys the structural sources of violence within the family.

Social Stratification

Other structural aspects of American society are involved in family violence. One of great importance is the system of social stratification. There is evidence that violence is more likely in lower-class families; in families afflicted by poverty.[46] The basic premise is that poverty causes a number of stresses and strains for individuals. People react to these tensions in a variety of hostile and aggressive ways, including violence against family members. However, it would be a mistake to assume that wife and child abuse are restricted to the lower classes. It is likely that in the future, with increasing public attention to these problems, we will see an increasing number of revelations about the existence of family violence in the middle and upper classes.

Gender and Age Stratification

Two other structural aspects of American society need to be mentioned since they have played a central role in this analysis as well as in the problems of wife and child abuse. They are the stratification of society on the basis of gender and generational differences. R. Emerson Dobash and Russell Dobash embed their analysis of violence against wives within the history and structure of patriarchy—of male domination of females:

> The seeds of wife beating lie in the subordination of females and in their subjection to male authority and control. This relationship be-

tween women and men has been institutionalized in the structure of the patriarchal family and is supported by the economic and political institutions and by a belief system. . . .[47]

What such an analysis of patriarchy does is to place wife abuse squarely within the realm of the power of males over females. Similarly, it could be argued that not only is our society stratified on a gender basis, but also on an age basis. Thus, we can say that children stand at the bottom of the age-stratification system, and this leaves them vulnerable to abuse by the far more powerful adults. The position taken by Breines and Gordon is similar to the one being expressed here: "the social contexts of family violence have gender and generational inequalities at their heart."[48]

A Violent Culture

At a larger-scale level, we can point toward the United States as a society in which violence is a cultural norm.[49] There are a wide range of circumstances in which American culture not only condones, but encourages, violence (capital punishment, warfare, boxing). Many of the most notable of these norms apply to the family. For example, parents are expected to use force in order to deal adequately and appropriately with their children. The amount of violence allowed to parents is actually rather startling when you compare it to that allowed in other settings: "parents are permitted or expected to use a level of physical force for these purposes that is denied even prison authorities in relation to training and controlling inmates."[50] While the norms concerning violence toward children are explicit and even mandatory, similar norms concerning husband-wife relations are more implicit and taken for granted. The normative character of violence toward spouses, especially husbands toward wives, is expressed in commonly heard jokes, expressions, and ditties like the following:

A woman, a horse, and a hickory tree
The more you beat'em the better they be[51]

Again, we have not exhausted the role of culture in family violence, but rather merely suggested a few of the dimensions of its role in causing this violence.

PART III: RESPONSES

It is clear that dealing with family violence is no easy matter, nor is it likely to be one in the foreseeable future. The family is generally viewed as a safe haven in our society; one that is, and should be, generally free of outside interference. Problems have long abounded within families, but outside agencies have been loath to take any definitive action. However, the situation has begun to change in recent years. It is not that there is necessarily more family violence, but it is clear that there is much more attention to such violence. Hence the desire to act, as well as the number of such helping efforts, have increased in recent years. We will look at a few of the major responses by outside agencies, most of which have blossomed in the last few years, but first we need to examine how the victims, wives in particular, have tended to respond on an individual level to spouse abuse. We focus on wives, because childhood victims of family violence have comparatively few options open to them—given the extremely powerless position of minors within society.

Individual Responses

Rationalizations of Battered Wives

Because of the lack of support (at least until recently) from outside agencies, as well as the reluctance of wives to leave abusive spouses, battered wives have usually tried to rationalize their husband's use of violence. Kathleen Ferraro and John Johnson report six rationalizations employed by battered wives.[52] First, battered wives say they are willing to put up with the abuse in the hope of saving their husband from the problems that are causing his behavior. Second, the violence is blamed on some external source (for example, unemployment), and therefore the husband is absolved of responsibility for his actions. Third, women refuse to acknowledge that the violence has ever occurred and go on with their daily routines. Fourth, some women blame themselves, at least in part, for the violence. Fifth, a number of women may deny that they have any practical and/or emotional alternatives to their present marital situation. Finally, there is the view that the woman is enduring the abuse for some higher good such as religious conviction or commitment to the nuclear family.

Thus, women (and other abused family members) can respond to battering with a variety of psychological rationalizations. It is clear, however, that such rationalizations do not involve actions that get to the source of the problem, nor do they provide structural alternatives to the abusive family. Thus, there has arisen, especially in recent years, more interest in the actions that women can take, as well as in structural responses to the problem of family violence such as shelters for battered women.

Actions Open to Battered Wives

In general, we can say that action is more effective than psychological rationalization in dealing with the problem of wife beating (and child abuse as well). The six general types of actions identified by Lee Bowker are "(1) calling the police, (2) seeking professional counseling, (3) entering a shelter for battered women, (4) leaving home for good and seeking a divorce, (5) fighting back, and (6) convincing one's husband one's self, or with the help of informal support networks, to cease his assaultive behavior."[53] One of the issues of concern to Bowker in his research was what actions had worked best for his respondents in bringing the last incident of battering to an end. The most commonly mentioned responses were aggressive actions such as using threats and actively defending one's self. The next most common response was efforts to talk to members of informal support networks such as women's groups and friends. A number of respondents sought professional counseling by contacting social-service agencies. Finally, about 8 percent of Bowker's respondents sought a shelter to protect them from their husbands.[54]

In order to make use of these new shelters, wives must reject their rationalizations and come to view themselves as victims. In fact, these women's shelters help women see themselves as victims. Thus, the increasing consciousness of battered wives as victims and the increasing number of structural responses to this problem have fed off each other.

Sociological Responses

Shelters

Straus and his co-authors place great importance on the growth of women's shelters for victims of abuse by their husbands.[55] The first shelter was founded in England in 1971, and today Straus estimates that there are 500[56] of them in the United States and perhaps several thousand around the world. Shelters give women a place to go after they have been abused by their husbands or when they have managed to escape an impending assault. Thus shelters are obviously useful in the immediate situation, but they have longer-term utility as well. By being provided with physical, economic, and social support, women may be able to change their marriages so that future violent incidents are averted or ameliorated. Straus also sees such centers as symbolically important in stating that new standards are evolving concerning wife abuse. Finally, the fact that such centers now exist has likely reduced violence against wives by giving them the ability to threaten to leave home if violence occurs.

There is a similar need for shelters for children of abusive parents. However, far less headway has been made on such shelters than those for abused wives. The problem is that while abused wives can go to women's shelters on their own, children are much less likely to be able to take such action either because they are too young and/or too frightened. In any case, such shelters, since they are likely to be temporary homes for children, do not really cope with the cause of the problem—abusing parents.

Other Structural Changes

A number of other changes are suggested as ways of helping to reduce the problems

Day care centers for children give parents a break from constant contact with their offspring and therefore help reduce the likelihood of child abuse.

(Elizabeth Hamlin/Stock, Boston)

of family violence. More extensive availability of day-care centers would permit parents to have periodic breaks from dealing with their children. "The danger of child abuse is understandably great when a woman must stay with her child all day, every day, with no one to help."[57] An adequate nationwide system of day-care centers would provide such help. Changes are also needed in the child-welfare systems in order to provide better crisis intervention within families, to provide more support for families under stress, to do a better job of educating people to be better parents, and to provide longer-term and more continuous care for child-abuse cases. The police and the courts need to do a better job of dealing with domestic problems in general, and family violence in particular. Better family planning would help reduce the number of unwanted children, the type that is most likely to be the victim of child abuse. Finally, there is a need for improvements in individual, marital, and family therapy for both perpetrators and victims.

Cultural Change

There are many such concrete, programatic actions that can be taken to deal with the problem of family violence. However, such specific reforms are not likely to have much impact unless we begin to deal with the deeper, underlying causes of these problems. To do this, Straus and his co-authors suggest a series of steps to change some of the fundamental tenets of our cultural system. First, they suggest the elimination of the cultural norms that both legitimize and glorify violence within the family and in the larger society. In their view, the public is largely unaware of the degree and extent of violence within the family. They recommend a massive public awareness campaign to explain the extent of the problem, as well as its disastrous effects on the victims. Coupled with this, Straus and his associates suggest an assault on all forms of violence by stricter gun control measures, by elimination of violence committed by the state (for example, capital punishment), and by a reduction of the glorification of violence by the mass media, especially television. Second, an effort must be made to reduce or eliminate the kinds of stresses that lead to family violence. Along these lines, much needs to be done to eliminate unemployment, poverty, inadequate health care, and the like. Third, since abusing families tend to be isolated, there is a need to integrate them better into family and community networks. Fourth, since sexual inequality is at the heart of the struggle between men and women, efforts need to be made to create more equality between the sexes. Finally, building on the fact that violence tends to be carried from one generation to the next, it is critical to break the cycle of family violence. If we can stop one generation from believing in the physical punishment of its children, the next generation would be much less likely to use such techniques. Overall, then, there are things both of a general and a specific character that can be done to deal with the problem of family violence. Yet, such a nearly universal phenomenon, in one form or another, will clearly be extremely resistant to change.

As a transition to the topic of rape, we briefly address the problem of *incest*, which is a form of *both* family *and* sexual violence. That is, it is sexual violence committed within the family.

A NOTE ON INCEST

Incest involves sexual relations among immediate family members. We most often think of incest as involving intercourse, but a number of other forms of contact among family members can be categorized as incest, including "mutual masturbation, hand-genital or oral-genital contact, sexual fondling, exhibition, and even sexual propositioning."[58] Incest can involve a variety of different family members, but the one of greatest interest to us here is father-daughter incest. For one thing, it is the most commonly *reported* form of incest. For another, it is the form of incest that is most tied to our concern with power throughout this chapter. Judith Lewis Herman places the issue of father-daughter incest squarely within the power domain:

> Father-daughter incest is not only the type of incest most frequently reported but also represents a paradigm of female victimization. The relationship between father and daughter, adult male and female child, is one of the most unequal relationships imaginable. It is no accident that incest occurs most often precisely in the relationship where the female is powerless.[59]

This form of incest may be seen as one type of sexual victimization of children. David Finkelhor found in his research that most victimizers of children are males, and that males have a near-monopoly on sexual victimization. The predominance of male victimizers of children underscores in broader terms the theme of abuse of power.

Statistics on Incest

Needless to say, accurate data on incest are *extremely* difficult to obtain. In the case of father-daughter incest, the victim (the daughter) is highly unlikely to report the incident to the authorities. She may be unwilling to admit it to her mother, siblings, friends, or even herself. The father is certainly not likely to take the initiative and turn himself in to the authorities. Others in the family may be unaware of what is going on and even if they are aware, they, too, may be extremely reluctant to report the father. Thus, whatever official statistics we have on father-daughter incest are likely to be gross underestimates. At the same time, we can expect the number of reported incidents to grow as a result of the fact that incest is beginning to get more public recognition as a problem.

In their early work on human sexuality Alfred Kinsey and his associates concluded that .5 percent of the males they interviewed were involved in some form of incest.[60] The most common form of incest, by far, is brother-sister incest, with father-daughter incest considerably less likely to occur.[61] However, it is father-daughter incest that is far more likely to be reported than brother-sister incest (although it is *not* very likely to be reported either). It may be that brother-sister incest is less reported because it is considered by the participants more transient and experimental, and because it is less damaging psychologically to the victim. Other reasons for the lesser likelihood of reporting brother-sister incest is that it is not considered as taboo as father-daughter incest, it is likely to involve minors, and it does not create the explosive family situation that is often created by father-daughter incest. That is, the mother is highly threatened by father-daughter incest, whereas there is no parallel threat to the family in the case of brother-sister incest.

Incest Taboos

Almost all known societies have regarded incest as abhorrent and have instituted taboos against it.[62] The exceptions to the rule were generally instances in which members of royal families married each other in order to retain royal power. In the Egyptian, Incan, and Hawaiian royal families, marriages between immediate family members were made in order to keep the royal bloodline "pure" and to retain privilege and power in the family. There also is at least one documented historical period during which marriage between brothers and sisters, as well as fathers and daughters, occurred frequently among commoners. When the Romans ruled Egypt during the first to the third centuries A.D. such marriages were widely recorded. By allowing marriage between family members, Egyptians prevented family wealth and property from being confiscated by the Roman authorities through inheritance laws. However, modern American society is no exception to the rule of normative prohibition of incest. Despite the existence of such powerful opposing norms in our society and most others, incest has continued to exist. In general, people have refused to admit the existence of incest, but in recent years public attention to the issue has increased dramatically. This increase in attention has been spurred by spouse abuse, child abuse, and rape crisis centers that are uncovering unexpectedly large numbers of instances of incest.[63]

There are various explanations for the near-universal prohibition of incest. One, for example, is that incest would lead to inbreeding and inbreeding tends to produce an extraordinary number of physical and psychological defects.[64] The best known, however, is that of the world-renowned anthropologist Claude Levi-Strauss and his theory of marriage rules in general, and incest rules in particular.[65] In his view, if family members were allowed to follow their own inclinations, a large number of them would interbreed among themselves. If this were to occur, along with formal or informal marital relationships among the partners, each family would become a self-contained entity. The families in a population would become islands unto themselves, perhaps leading to populations with hundreds, or thousands, of separate social systems, each competing with the others. If a society is to be possible, there must be links, ties, and interconnections between and among families so that networks are formed that hold the many families together.[66] From this point of view, a society is possible only when there are rules that keep groups of families tied together, linked through the exchange of their children who, in turn, form new families.

In order for societies to exist, all people must evolve and formulate some rules or norms that will keep families from becoming "tight little island" fortresses. Families must achieve some degree of cooperation and interdependence with other families if the population is to be bound together in a larger social entity. The set of rules prohibiting incest and those promoting the exchange of marriage partners between families may be essential factors holding society together.

Nevertheless, in spite of the prohibitions against it, incest continues to exist. And, as revelations about its secret existence continue to be made, some have begun to wonder whether it really is taboo:

> It seems apparent, both by its incidence and by the noticeable absence of any sincere, widespread dread of retribution, that *incest is not truly a taboo.* Just a very, very long-lived, well-suppressed secret [italics added].[67]

A similar conclusion is echoed in a more academic source: "Incest this frequent is hardly tabooed."[68]

Incest and Patriarchy

The discussion about taboos against incest so far has been at a general level and does not differentiate among types of incest. One issue that it does not deal with is why father-daughter incest is so much more common than mother-son incest. If incest is taboo, it should be equally so for mothers and fathers. Judith Herman and Lisa Hirschman deal with this issue by tying it into the broader issues of power and patriarchy.[69] They argue that almost all societies have been dominated by men and that the incest taboo always involves "agreements among men regarding sexual access to women."[70] Since men traditionally create and enforce the rules, they are freer to break them. On the other hand, incest between mother and son is abhorrent to male-dominated society because it constitutes an affront to the power of fathers, and males more generally. Herman and Hirschman conclude that the incest taboo is asymmetrical because it is far less binding on fathers than mothers. Thus, patriarchy accords fathers more power to violate the incest taboo than mothers.

At this point in the chapter, this discussion of incest provides a bridge between the discussion of family violence and that of rape. Incest is *both* a form of family violence and, when it involves forced sexual intercourse, a form of rape. However, it is better to consider incest as a transitional problem and to discuss rape separately.

RAPE

The legal definition of rape is the "carnal knowledge of a female[71] forcibly and against her will. Assaults or attempts to commit rape by force or threat of force are also included; however, statutory rape (without force) and other sex offenses are excluded."[72] Based on this definition, a *known* (that is, reported to the police) forcible rape occurs every seven minutes. There were almost 79,000 known rapes in 1983, about the same number as occurred in 1982, but substantially higher than the 55,400 *known* rapes in 1974.[73] Known rapes have increased over 250 percent since 1960. We emphasize "known" here because it is widely believed that a large number of rapes are never reported to the police. Among the reasons for women not reporting rapes are "fears of retaliation by the rapist, his family, or friends; feelings of shame, guilt, or embarrassment; the desire to avoid publicity; the belief that nothing will be done; or the unwillingness to subject themselves to what has been termed 'the second rape'—the insensitive treatment they receive from some medical, law enforcement, and criminal justice systems."[74] According to one estimate, only 10 percent to 50 percent of all rapes are reported to the police.[75] If this is correct, the total number of rapes in the United States is somewhere between 150,000 and 750,000 per year. In fact, the National Crime Survey estimated on the basis of victim surveys that about 154,000 rapes and attempted rapes occurred in 1983.[76] This, too, is likely to be an underestimation, so we are certainly justified in estimating that well over 150,000 rapes are likely to occur in the United States this year.

The National Crime Survey has uncovered a number of factors about rape.[77] About two-thirds of rapes and rape attempts occur at night, with more occurring between 6 p.m. and midnight than between midnight and 6 a.m. Table 6.2 shows the places where rapes and attempted rapes of females occurred between 1973 and 1982. The largest number of completed rapes occurred at home, while the largest number of attempted rapes took place in the street or in a park, playground, parking lot, or parking garage. Rape victims are likely to be young, with over half between 16 and 24 years of age, and over three-quarters between 16 and 34 years old. Rapists are most likely to be strangers to the victim; a woman is twice as likely to be raped by a stranger than an acquaintance.

It should be pointed out that the legal definition of rape is greatly limited. The possibility of rape of males is omitted, as are oral or anal copulation involving female victims.[78] Inclusion of these types would further inflate the total number of rapes committed in the United States each year.

Table 6.2 Places Where Rapes of Females Occurred, 1973–82

	TOTAL	VICTIMS OF: ATTEMPTED RAPE	VICTIMS OF: COMPLETED RAPE
Number of victims	1,511,000	1,032,000	479,000
Percent of rapes occurring:			
Any place	100%	100%	100%
At home	27	24	35
Near home	7	9	4
Vacation home	2	1	3
On the street, or in park, playground, parking lot, or parking garage	39	43	31
In a commercial building	5	6	3
In an office	#	#	#
In school	2	2	#
Other locations	17	14	23

Too few cases in survey sample to obtain statistically reliable data.
Source: Bureau of Justice Statistics, "The Crime of Rape" (Washington, D.C.: U.S. Department of Justice, 1985), p. 2.

Some of the more recent state laws have included these types of actions under the heading of rape.

PART I: THE PROBLEM

Although rape is an age-old problem, there has been a boom in popular and academic concern about the problem since the early 1970s. Geis attributes a large portion of this increase in interest in rape to the women's movement,[79] in particular Susan Brownmiller's germinal work, *Against Our Will: Men, Women and Rape.*[80] Brownmiller's major contribution was to reorient our thinking about rape. Until that time (and to a large extent to this day) rape was considered a sex crime. That is, it was seen as an illegal expression of male sexuality. However, Brownmiller conceived of rape not in terms of sex, but rather in terms of *power.* That is, what men were expressing in raping females was "male domination over women by force."[81] Through rape, the male is demonstrating to women his superior strength and power; that he is dominant and she is vanquished. It has now become widely accepted that it is better to see power rather than sex as the major male motivation behind the crime of rape. As another author put it: "Rape is an aggressive act against women as woman . . . rape is the extreme manifestation of approved activities in which one segment of society dominates another. Rape is a ritual of power."[82] In short, this brings rape squarely within our broad concern throughout this chapter with the abuse of power.

One effect of this has been to move the attention of analysts away from the rapist and his sexual motives and toward a broader concern for rape within the entire constellation of power relations between males and females in society. In addition, it

Table 6.3 Levels of Analysis: Rape

LEVELS	APPROPRIATE QUESTIONS	A PARTIAL SYNOPSIS OF PRESENT CONCLUSIONS
INDIVIDUAL	To what degree is the rapist motivated by biological factors: his sex drive?	While sexuality plays a role, it is clearly subordinated to the power needs and the hostility of the rapist.
	To what degree is the rapist suffering from psychological problems?	It is very likely that the rapist suffers from some psychological dysfunction, but it is very unlikely that he is insane.
	What is the "rape trauma syndrome"?	This describes the acute and long-term physiological and psychological consequences of being a rape victim.
SOCIAL-PSYCHOLOGICAL	Is there any evidence that rape victims systematically bring rape upon themselves by the way they interact with the potential rapist?	No. For one thing, we know that rape is not a sex crime. For another, a woman is entitled to be seductive without calling forth the unwanted actions of a rapist. Finally, a woman should be able to say no to unwanted advances.
	What are the basic types of rape?	Rape can take various forms including anger, power, and sadistic rape. The best guess is that power rapes are the most common.
SOCIOLOGICAL	Can it be said that America has a "rape-prone" culture?	Yes. Cross-cultural evidence seems to indicate that American culture is one of those that is conducive to producing a rape-prone society. However, recent changes indicate that American culture may be losing many of its rape-prone characteristics.

(Continued)

Table 6.3 Levels of Analysis: Rape *(Continued)*

LEVELS	APPROPRIATE QUESTIONS	A PARTIAL SYNOPSIS OF PRESENT CONCLUSIONS
	How well have our various social structures and institutions coped with the problem of rape?	The evidence is that many agencies such as the courts, the medical profession, and the police have not done a good job of dealing with the rape problem.
	How is social stratification related to rape?	There is some evidence that rape perpetrators and rape victims come disproportionately from the lower classes. Along the same lines, rape has been linked by some to the individualism and exploitativeness of capitalism. Of course, it should be noted that rape is not restricted to the lower classes or capitalist societies.

has served to move us toward a concern for the impact of rape on the female victim. These will be our foci in the following section on causes and consequences of rape.

PART II: CAUSES AND CONSEQUENCES

INDIVIDUAL LEVEL

Physiological Factors

The first issue to be addressed (and largely dismissed) at the individual level is the degree to which the rapist is motivated by biological factors; by his sex drive. In a major study by A. Nicholas Groth entitled *Men Who Rape: The Psychology of the Offender,*[83] the sexual myth of the rapist is described: "he is frequently regarded as a lusty male who is the victim of a provocative and vindictive woman, or he is seen as a sexually frustrated man reacting under the pressure of his pent-up needs, or he is thought to be a demented sex-fiend harboring insatiable and perverted desires."[84] In line with the emphasis on power rather than sex outlined above, Groth debunks this myth and provides an alternate image of the rapist:

> Careful clinical study of offenders reveals that rape is in fact serving primarily nonsexual needs. It is the sexual expression of power and anger. Forcible sexual assault is motivated more by retaliatory and compensatory motives than sexual ones. Rape is a pseudosexual act, complex and multidetermined, but addressing issues of

> hostility (anger) and control (power) more than passion (sexuality). To regard rape as an expression of sexual desire is not only an inaccurate notion but also an insidious assumption, for it results in the shifting of the responsibility for the offense in large part from the offender onto the victim: if the assailant is sexually aroused and is directing these impulses toward the victim, then it must be that she has deliberately or inadvertently stimulated or aroused this desire in him through her actions, style of dress, or some such feature.[85]

Thus, while Groth does not totally eliminate sexuality from rape, it is clearly subordinated to power and hostility. This serves to affix blame on the male and the male subculture, rather than the victim, the female. In accord with this view, Beneke in his book, *Men on Rape*, argues: "rape (and violence against women generally) must be perceived, pure and simple, as a *man's problem* and one that results directly from the way men regard women in American culture."[86]

Psychological Dysfunctions

While Groth (and others) does not find sexual desire a major explanation of rape, he does conclude that rape is "always" the result of some sort of psychological dysfunction. While they do suffer from psychological problems, most rapists are not insane. Here is the way Groth describes the psychological problems of the "typical" rapist:

> His most prominent defect is the absence of any close, emotionally intimate relationship with other persons, male or female. He shows little capacity for warmth, trust, compassion, or empathy, and his relationships with others are devoid of mutuality, reciprocity, and a genuine sense of sharing.[87]

As a result of such emotional turmoil, the potential rapist is likely to grow desperate about his stressful situation and become fearful that it will destroy him unless he does something. Rape is one of the things that such a person might do under certain circumstances.

Although the psychology of the rapist is important, it is necessary to underscore the fact that the nature of the circumstances in which the potential rapist finds himself is of utmost importance. It is widely believed, and there is some evidence to support this belief, that a large number of men have the proclivity to rape.[88] Thus, a large number of men might be tempted to rape a drugged and naked woman whom they happen upon in the woods. However, very few men find themselves in such a circumstance and hence few actually carry out such an act. Furthermore, even if they did find themselves in such a situation, the laws against rape would serve to deter most men. It is also likely that men with the kind of psychological troubles described above can express them in a number of ways other than rape.

The Rape Trauma Syndrome

Among the most important concerns in recent years have been the physiological and psychological consequences of rape for the female victim.[89] In one of the earliest (1974) and best-known studies of this phenomenon, Ann Wolbert Burgess and Lynda Lytle Holmstrom argued that research up to that time had tended to overlook the victim of rape (and other sexual offenses). Their work helped open the floodgates, and there is, today, a voluminous literature on rape victims.[90] In their study of nearly one hundred victims, Burgess and Holmstrom labeled the impact on the victim the "rape trauma syndrome." This was defined as "the acute phase and long-term reorganization process that occurs as a result of forcible rape. This syndrome of behavioral, somatic, and psychological reactions is an acute stress reaction to a life-threatening situation."[91] They accept the view offered here that rape is not primarily a sexual act, but rather an act of power, aggression, and violence aimed against the victim, with sex as the specific weapon. Burgess and Holmstrom divide the rape trauma syndrome into an initial, acute phase and then a longer-term period of reorganization.

Burgess and Holmstrom found two basic types of reactions in the acute, initial period after the rape. About half the group expressed a strong reaction in which "feelings of fear, anger, and anxiety were shown through such behavior as crying, sobbing, smiling, restlessness, and tenseness."[92] The other half reacted in a controlled manner in which such feelings were concealed and the individual appeared calm. A wide range of somatic reactions were manifested over the first several weeks following an attack, including physical trauma such as bruises, muscle tension (for example, tension headaches), gastrointestinal irritability (nausea), and genitourinary disturbance (vaginal infections). A number of emotional reactions also ensued, including fear and self-blame for not having reacted differently to the attack.

The acute phase was characterized by disorganization, while the long-term reaction involved efforts at reorganizing one's life. A series of actions were often taken, including changing residences, obtaining new phone numbers and/or unlisted numbers, and turning to relatives and/or friends for support. A number of victims reported dreams and upsetting nightmares. A number of phobias or fears developed among many women, including fear of indoors (if raped inside a house), fear of outdoors (if assaulted outside), fear of being alone, fear of crowds (a man in the crowd might be an attacker), fear of people behind them, and fear of sex, even with their normal part-

Table 6.4 Injuries Received by Female Victims of Rape, 1973–82

	VICTIMS OF:		
	TOTAL	ATTEMPTED RAPE	COMPLETED RAPE
Number of victims	1,511,000	1,032,000	479,000
Percent of victims:			
Not injured	62%	71%	42%
Injured	38	29	58
Percent of victims receiving:			
Bruises, black eyes, and cuts	31	23	49
Internal injuries or knocked unconscious	4	2	10
Broken bones or teeth knocked out	2	#	3
Knife or gunshot wound	#	#	#
Other injuries	9	8	12

Victims of completed rape are more likely to be injured than victims of attempted rape. Also detailed in this table are the various types of injuries sustained by victims in both categories.

Note: As used in this table, "injury" means injury in addition to the rape or attempted rape itself. Percents for types of injury add to more than 100 because some victims received more than one type.
#Too few cases in survey sample to obtain statistically reliable data.
Source: Bureau of Justice Statistics. "The Crime of Rape" (Washington, D.C.: U. S. Department of Justice, 1985), p. 5.

Table 6.5 Medical Expenses of Injured Female Rape Victims, 1973–82

	TOTAL	VICTIMS OF: ATTEMPTED RAPE	COMPLETED RAPE
Injured victims[a]	580,000	303,000	277,000
Percent of injured victims with medical expenses	29%	15%	43%
Total medical expenses	$71,649,000	$13,601,000	$58,048,000
Median medical expenses	$104	$86	$115

Victims of completed rapes are almost three times as likely as victims of attempted rapes to have medical expenses associated with the assault, and their median costs are slightly higher.

Note: As used in this table, "injury" means injury in addition to the rape or attempted rape itself. Medians are computed only for those with medical expenses.
[a]Includes some victims who did not know the amount of their medical expenses.
Source: Bureau of Justice Statistics. "The Crime of Rape" (Washington, D.C.: U.S. Department of Justice, 1985), p. 5.

ners. Overall, Burgess and Holmstrom conclude that rape constitutes a crisis in most victims' lives.

In a follow-up study conducted five years later, Burgess and Holmstrom found that at least some of their subjects had *still* not recovered from the sexual assault.[93] A study of Philadelphia rape victims found that the kinds of adjustment problems that appeared immediately after a rape continued to be manifest a year after the rape had occurred.[94] However, at least one other study found greater recovery among rape victims.[95] In spite of such disagreements, there is no disputing the fact that rape has both short-term and long-term adverse consequences for the victim.

Other Adverse Consequences

Rape, of course, has adverse consequences beyond those suffered by the victim. For one thing, rape may well be a crisis for the victim's entire family.[96] This is particularly likely to be true for the victim's husband or boyfriend,[97] who must deal with his own feelings about the rape, as well as his difficulties in interacting with a rape victim—including the resumption of sexual relations. The victim may now be phobic about sex, and the husband and boyfriend may have problems having sex with a raped woman. Rape can also be seen as having adverse effects on women in general. The hundreds of thousands of rapes each year are not only harmful in themselves, but also for the fear they create in all women.[98] Beneke expresses this well:

> rape must be comprehended both in terms of the crime itself and the effect of its threat on women's lives. The ways in which the threat of rape alters the meaning and feel of the night and nature, inhibits the freedom of the eye, hurts women economically, undercuts women's independence, destroys solitude, and restricts expressiveness must be acknowledged as part of the crime.[99]

SOCIAL-PSYCHOLOGICAL LEVEL

Rape, of course, involves not only individual action and reaction, but also interaction between rapist and victim. There are four basic types of relationships between rapists and victims.[100] The rapist may be a total stranger whom the victim has never before encountered (the "classic" rape situation[101]). The rapist may also be a stranger who gains the confidence of the victim before raping her. The man who befriends a woman whose car has broken down would be an example of this type. Then there are the rapists who are acquaintances of the victim, but not well known to her. A man met at a bar in the same evening would fall into this category. Finally, there is the relationship in which the rapist is not only acquainted with the victim, but well known to her. This may involve a steady date or even a husband. In fact, there is growing attention to the problems of "date rape" and rape in marriage.[102]

One point to make early and emphatically is that there is little support for the idea that the victim brings the rape on herself.[103] It is difficult to defend the view that a woman by being seductive and provocative causes the rape. It is not against the law to be seductive, or to say no to the advances of a male, but there are laws against refusing to accept a no. In any case, as we have seen, the evidence is that rape is not a sex crime and therefore cannot be explained by female provocativeness.[104]

Types of Rape

Groth distinguishes among three basic types of rape—*anger* rape, *power* rape, and *sadistic* rape. Let us look at each, especially from the point of view of the interaction between rapist and victim.

In *anger rape* the rapist is expressing his pent-up anger and rage in a sexual assault. Such a rape entails an assault on the victim and physical brutality, often involving "grabbing her, striking her, knocking her to the ground, beating her, tearing her clothes and raping her."[105] Sex is not the primary motivation; rape is seen as an ultimate assault against the victim. In fact, such a rapist is not likely to report being aroused sexually during the attack. Furthermore, the act brings little sexual gratification to the attacker. It is the expression of anger that is found to be satisfying. Such rapes tend to be unplanned, spontaneous, and of short duration.

Anger rapes are likely to lead to considerable physical trauma to the victim. She is likely to have a number of visible injuries and to feel happy to have survived the attack. Although the physical impact of the rape is great, the psychological impact may be less severe than other types of rape. For one thing, the victim is happy to be alive and the sexual penetration is likely to be of secondary importance. For another, the visibility of her injuries leaves no question in the eyes of authorities that the victim has been raped. In less severe cases, authorities may wonder about false accusation or victim participation, but in anger rape there is virtually no question on such issues. However, the victim is likely to carry with her a greater awareness of her vulnerability in future situations.

The second type is *power rape*, in which the objective is not to hurt the victim, but rather to conquer her through sex. In this type of rape the sexual assault to the rapist "becomes a means of compensating for underlying feelings of inadequacy and serves to express issues of mastery, strength, control, authority, identity, and capability."[106] Unlike the anger rapist, the power rapist is likely to use only the amount of force needed to achieve his objective.

Finally, there is *sadistic rape*, which involves the fusion of anger and power. The sadistic rapist is angry at women and expresses his power over them by intentionally maltreating them. Such a rapist may take extreme actions against the victim, sometimes to the point of killing and mutilating her. While the actions of the anger rapist are unplanned, the sadistic rape is usually totally premeditated. It is also likely to take place over a longer time period with the rapist growing more frenzied as the event proceeds.

Overall, Groth's data show that power rapes are the most common (55 percent of the cases studied), with anger rapes second (about 40 percent of the cases), and sadistic rapes the least likely (5 percent). However, Groth gathered his data primarily from convicted rapists with the result that anger rapists were probably overrepresented in his study and power rapists underrepresented since there is less physical abuse and corroborating evidence in power rapes. As a result, he estimates that power rapes far outnumber anger rapes in society. It is also interesting to note that despite the great media attention to such cases, sadistic rapes make up a small proportion of the total number of rapes.

SOCIOLOGICAL LEVEL

The early feminist writers on the subject of rape tended to focus on the role of culture, especially American culture, in creating conditions conducive to a large number of rapes. A culture that subordinates women and places men in the dominant position is one that is also prone to violence against women,[107] especially rape. In a sense, the early feminists tended to think in terms of a "rape culture."[108] This idea is reflected in Susan Griffith's early and often-cited essay, "Rape: The All-American Crime."[109] In Griffith's view, even though rape is illegal, it is seen as understandable and even encouraged by our cultural system. Similarly, Nancy Gager and Cathleen Schurr write of a "rape-prone environment" in the United States in which women are seen as wanting "to be dominated and raped and . . . all males have the right to be sexually aggressive toward all females."[110] More recently, Martha Burt did research on the existence of rape myths within American culture.[111] She found that many Americans do believe many myths about rape (women unconsciously want to be raped, women provoke rape by such things as going bra-less, most rape victims are promiscuous).

Cross-Cultural Research

In trying to understand the role of American culture in rape, it would be helpful to compare it to the cultures of other societies. In that way we could see whether there really is something unusual about the American culture that leads to a higher rate of rape than in other societies. We do know that there is a higher rape rate in the United States than in a number of European countries, but problems with comparability of data make it difficult to draw any definite conclusions about the existence of more "rape-prone" cultural characteristics in the United States than in these other societies.[112]

Not surprisingly, since it focuses on culture, the best work in this area is the anthropology of rape.[113] Peggy Reeves Sanday examined a cross-cultural sample of 156 tribal societies. Her first conclusion is that rape is *not* a universal characteristic of humankind. That is, some societies are "rape prone" while others are "rape free." Sanday characterizes a rape-prone culture as follows:

> In all, men are posed as a social group against women. Entry into the adult male or female group is marked in some cases by rituals that include rape. In other cases, rape preserves the ceremonial integrity of the male group and signifies its status vis-à-vis women. The theme of women as property is suggested when the aggrieved husband is compensated for the rape of his wife by another man, or when an adulterous woman is gang raped by her husband and his unmarried compatriots. In these latter cases, the theme of

the dominant male group is joined with a system of economic exchange in which men act as exchange agents and women comprise the medium of exchange.[114]

In contrast, the rape-free culture is described by Sanday in the following manner:

> rape free societies are characterized by sexual equality and the notion that the sexes are complementary. Though the sexes may not perform the same duties or have the same rights or privileges, each is indispensable to the activities of the other. . . . The key to understanding the relative absence of rape in rape free as opposed to rape prone societies is the importance, which in some cases is sacred, attached to the contribution women make to social continuity.[115]

While interpersonal violence of all sorts is uncommon in rape-free societies, the converse is the case in rape-prone societies. Sanday concludes that it is not so much that the latter are prone to rape as they are prone to violence of all sorts, some of which is likely to take the form of rape. It would seem that America is closer to the description of a rape-prone society, but recent changes in relations between the sexes may indicate a movement toward the rape-free end of the continuum. If this continues to be the case, one would predict a decline in rapes in the United States in coming years.

The fact that rape varies enormously cross-culturally constitutes another critique of the idea that rape is inherent in male sexual needs. If that were the case, we would find rape to be universal and occurring in similar proportions across societies. It is not male biology, but rather the larger culture, which is a better explanation of rape. In particular, Sanday emphasizes a culture that includes "interpersonal violence, male dominance, and sexual separation."[116] In other words, it is such a culture that sanctions male power and male aggressiveness, and rape is one expression of that configuration of values. "Rape is not an integral part of male nature, but the means by which men programmed for violence express their sexual selves."[117]

Social Structures and Institutions

In addition to the culture, we also need to look at the relationship between larger social structures and institutions and rape. The thrust of much of the work on these structures and institutions has been to point out how ill-served rape victims are by various units within society, including the police, the medical profession, and the courts.[118] Surprisingly, it is the courts[119] and the medical profession that have come under more attack for their treatment of the rape victim than the police,[120] although the police too have been far from exemplary in their dealings with such victims. The entire law enforcement and judicial system is often indicted for doing an inadequate job of apprehending, convicting, imprisoning, and treating rapists. In addition to feeling that these institutions do an inadequate job of dealing with the problem of rape, there is also a similar view held of the people inhabiting the occupations and professions associated with these institutions. This frequently manifests itself in attacks on the prejudices against rape victims held by the police, physicians, nurses, psychologists, psychiatrists, social workers, lawyers, judges, and jurors.

Finally, we need to say something about the relationship between the structure of inequality and rape. Julia and Herman Schwendinger emphasize this factor in their work on rape: "Competitive and exploitative relations in capitalist societies generate an amoral individualism, and followers of this individualistic orientation, in all social classes, objectify and exploit people as things."[121] Since it is the economically, ethnically, and racially marginal

Table 6.6 Family Income of Female Rape Victims by Race, 1973–82

	PERCENT OF VICTIMS WHO WERE:		
	TOTAL[a]	WHITE	BLACK
Numbers of victims (in thousands)	1,511	1,228	265
Annual family income, of rape victims	100%	100%	100%
Less than $3,000	18	15	34
$3,000–$7,499	25	25	29
$7,500–$9,999	10	10	10
$10,000–$14,999	16	17	9
$15,000–$24,999	15	16	11
$25,000 and over	8	9	1
Not ascertained	8	8	6
Annual rate per 1,000 population	1.6	1.5	2.5
Less than $3,000	4.2	3.7	5.3
$3,000–$7,499	2.2	2.2	2.4
$7,500–$9,999	1.9	1.7	2.5
$10,000–$14,999	1.4	1.4	1.5
$15,000–$24,999	1.1	1.1	2.1
$25,000 and over	0.9	1.0	0.7
Not ascertained	1.3	1.3	1.7

Females in the lowest-income categories are more likely to be rape victims than those in the higher-income categories. This is true for both black and white victims, although the relationship between low income and rape is stronger for black females. Interestingly, the most rape-prone category overall is not the lowest income category (below $3,000), but the second lowest ($3,000–7,499).

Note: Percents may not add to 100 because of rounding.
[a]Includes "other" races not shown separately.
Source: Bureau of Justice Statistics, "The Crime of Rape" (Washington, D.C.: U.S. Department of Justice Statistics, 1985), p. 3.

members of society that are most likely to be exploited, this helps explain why they are also the most likely to be perpetrators (and victims) of rape.[122] Although there is a certain intuitive attraction to the idea that rape is related to the exploitative relations endemic to capitalism, the nature of these linkages needs to be explored in greater detail. Furthermore, we need more comparative work on the problem of rape in capitalist and noncapitalist societies.

PART III: RESPONSES

There are a variety of responses available at the individual, social-psychological, and sociological levels to the problem of rape.

Some of these, especially at the individual and social-psychological levels, have long been available. Others, especially those at the sociological level, are relatively recent innovations coming into existence with the rise in concern for the problem of rape during the 1970s. We will begin with individual responses and work our way toward more sociological responses.

Individual Coping Strategies

At the individual level are the various coping responses available to women before, during, and after rape. Women have used such responses since the first rape. What is different today is that women no longer have to rely solely on their own abilities to deal with the crisis. Nevertheless, the techniques open to the victim remain an important aspect of responding to a rape.

Burgess and Holmstrom analyzed individual coping strategies before, during, and after the attack.[123] Only a small proportion of victims had a sense, prior to the rape, that there was an impending danger. Once the victim realizes there is a definite danger of assault, the necessary coping responses involve efforts to avoid or escape the situation. A first step involves a mental assessment of alternatives available to them given the impending danger. Once the danger was manifest, the respondents were most likely to use an array of verbal strategies in order to try to talk the assailant out of the attack (for example, "My kids are in the next room"). Some of the respondents took physical actions such as attempting to flee the scene or resisting the attack. About a third of the respondents lacked any strategy whatever; that is, they froze with the onset of the assault. On the other side, about a third of the subjects employed two or more different strategies in their effort to ward off the attack.

Once the rape is underway, the victim has another set of coping responses available to her. There are a wide range of cognitive strategies such as concentrating on something else, focusing on survival, and observing the attacker(s) carefully for future identification. Verbal strategies include screaming loudly for help or trying to calm the assailant in the hope of avoiding injury. Some victims resisted physically, at least for awhile, but they tended to find it futile or dysfunctional in that it seemed to further arouse the attacker. A variety of psychological defenses were tried such as denying that the event was taking place. Finally, a number reported a series of involuntary physiological reactions. Said one victim: "I felt faint, trembling and cold . . . I went limp. I think he got scared and thought I was out."[124]

After the attack, the main objective is to escape the assailant. One tactic is to try to alert others to what has happened. The victim may also attempt to bargain with the attacker in order to gain her freedom by, for example, promising not to go to the police. Finally, the woman may have to free herself from the situation, and in order to do so she must keep calm and carefully survey the situation. Once free of the situation, the victim, of course, must find ways of coping with the aftermath of the rape.

Linda Williams has recently studied why so many rape victims do not report the crime to the police.[125] Her subjects were 246 female rape victims who had contacted a rape relief organization in Seattle, Washington. Of the 246 victims, 146 had reported the rape to the police, while 100 victims had not. Basically, Williams found that those victims who were involved in "classic" rape situations were more likely to report the crime. Specifically, those whose home was broken into, were attacked in cars, or were attacked or abducted in public; were attacked by strangers or acquaintances rather than friends;

were threatened with a weapon; were subjected to a high degree of force; and/or sustained serious injuries, were more likely to report the crime. It is in such classic rape situations that it was easier for the victim to convince herself and others that she was a "true victim." Conversely, the classic rape situations discourage a woman from blaming herself for the rape.

Social-Psychological Responses

In coping with the aftermath of rape, other people become involved. The family and friendship networks can be valuable aids in helping the victim cope with the aftermath of rape. For many, this informal aid will not be enough, and some sort of psychotherapy may be required.[126] But the need for outside help may well not stop with the victim; mates and families of the victims may also require therapy. As we have seen, rape is not only a crisis for the victim, but for other family members as well.

Sociological Responses

Rape Crisis Centers

The major innovation in dealing with rape at the sociological level is the development of *rape crisis centers* around the United States.[127] These centers are set up to deal with the immediate physical, psychological, and social problems, as well as the longer-term problems that rape victims can be expected to experience. Such centers, as well as other therapeutic agencies, are designed to assist the rape victim so that she is not left solely to her own coping devices. Rape crisis centers are usually staffed by volunteers who are often rape victims themselves or people close to such victims.

Rape crisis centers (and rape counselors) are recent creations that help victims deal with the short- and long-term problems stemming from the rape.

(Michal Heron/Woodfin Camp & Associates)

Such a background, as well as the day-to-day experiences of working in such centers, gives them great sensitivity to, and understanding of, the plight of rape victims. In addition to helping the rape victim, these centers also often play an important role in educating the community about the problem of rape.[128]

Increasing Institutional Sensitivity

Another of the recent changes in dealing with the rape victim is an increasing sensitivity in virtually all institutions to the nature of her problem. As we saw earlier, a number of agents, structures, and institutions have been less than totally sympathetic to the rape victim. In fact, Holmstrom and Burgess in their study of how law enforcement agencies, hospitals, and courts deal with rape concluded that they "often further victimize the victim."[129] In addition to outright prejudice and hostility toward rape victims, the day-to-day operations of these institutions may adversely affect the rape victim. The victim's feeling of being in a crisis often stands in stark contrast to the calm detachment of the bureaucrat or professional with whom she may be dealing. Since most of these agents are male, they have historically been inclined to side with the male attacker and see the victim as guilty, at least in some cases, of causing the attack by being too provocative. However, greater awareness of the rape problem and the difficulties facing the rape victim appear to have reduced the worst of these insensitivities. For example,

> Police treatment of rape victims in most cities reflects a new sensitivity. Recruits are given instruction on handling victims, and many forces have established special rape squads, with contingents of female officers. 'The old line that women ask for trouble just isn't heard any more,' observes . . . a . . . detective.[130]

Changing Rape Laws

One of the major changes in recent years is in the rape laws. For centuries, the laws seemed to imply that the woman was responsible for the rape. It was not enough to claim psychological trauma; women had to have physical injuries in order to demonstrate that they resisted the attack. "Defense lawyers were fond of using Balzac's celebrated statement on rape: 'One cannot thread a needle when the needle doesn't stand still.'"[131] Under pressure from those who supported the new conception of rape, which placed blame squarely on the shoulders of the male perpetrator, many states have reformed their rape laws to take many of the burdens off the female victim. One of the most important is Michigan's Criminal Sexual Conduct Law, which was signed into existence in 1974.

The Michigan rape law has four essential aspects.[132] First, there is a careful enumeration of degrees of criminal sexual assault with differential penalties associated with each. For example, penetration that results in physical injury is differentiated from penetration without physical injury. Previously, penetration without physical injury was not adjudged a crime, but it is now subject to a maximum penalty of fifteen years while penetration with physical injury can get the offender up to life in prison. Secondly, the victim is no longer required to demonstrate resistance to the rape. All that is required is evidence of force by the assailant. While consent may still be used as a defense in some cases, the victim is no longer required to risk her life in order to have a case against a rapist. Thirdly, legal protection against rape was extended to males and legally separated spouses. Finally, the Michigan law prohibits the use of evidence on the prior sexual conduct of the victim with anyone other than the accused rapist. Thus, the victim's past sexual history can no longer be used as evidence that she might have consented to the rape or that the credibility of her claims is to be questioned.

As a result of such changes in a number of states, victims are more likely to bring charges against rapists. They are less likely to be harassed and humiliated in the courtroom. In addition, juries have grown more sympathetic to the plight of the victim. Said one legal official:

> Juries used to be skeptical of rape victims . . . . They were always looking for some straw they might grasp to call it an orgy instead of rape. Now juries are quick to side with the complainant.[133]

The result of all of these changes is that there has been a general increase in the rate of convictions in rape cases. This is true in Michigan as well, but the new law has certainly not been totally successful. For example, criminal justice officials continue to adhere to the idea that only "real rape," rape committed by sexual psychopaths against strangers, should be prosecuted. Thus, the practitioners ignore the careful delineation of degrees of sexual assault outlined in the law. This clearly indicates that legal change, while important, is not enough. Changes in attitudes and practices are also necessary, but are likely to occur much more slowly.

Needed Changes in the Future

Although some changes in dealing with rape and rape victims have already taken place, much more remains to be done. We can close this section, and the chapter, with some of the policy recommendations made by Holmstrom and Burgess based on their study of the large-scale structures involved in dealing with rape.

First, there is the need to delegitimize rape, to make it absolutely clear that rape is unacceptable under *all* circumstances. This suggestion is made in light of the fact that it continues to be the case in the eyes of many that there are certain circumstances—the victim first accompanies the rapist willingly, the victim knew the assailant, the victim did not fight back—that continue to legitimize rape. Such legitimations must be eliminated so that all rapes are viewed as clearly and unequivocally unacceptable.

Second, there is the need for a long list of changes in the way bureaucracies and professionals deal with rape:

1. Special victim programs need to be developed within various institutions such as the police, hospitals, and courts. These programs should be staffed by specially trained people assigned to follow victims through the system. Those who work in such programs should not only aid victims, but also seek to change both short-run and long-term institutional procedures so that victims are better served by them.

2. Organizations involved with rape victims should systematically evaluate how their procedures affect victims, pinpoint problems facing victims, and institute appropriate changes.

3. There is a need for a rethinking of the "rights and obligations of persons in official positions as they deal with rape cases."[134]

4. Professionals must become even better sensitized to the plight of rape victims and better able to deal with them in a humane manner.

5. There must be movement away from keeping victims ignorant of the process in which they are involved. They must be provided with much more information and advice.

6. There also must be greater privacy for rape victims. As the situation now stands the entire incident, if not the victim's entire life, is exposed to public scrutiny.

7. More must be done to obtain and preserve information important to the case.

8. There is a need for greater continuity in the services provided to victims. For example, if the case drags on in the courts, there is likely to be a long succession of district attorneys involved in it. Each new DA starts from scratch and must learn again all there is to know about the case.

9. Then there is a need for greater cooperation and communication among the various professionals and organizations involved with rape victims.

10. Interminable delays must be ended and the various institutional responses speeded up.

Finally, Holmstrom and Burgess suggest various reforms in the criminal justice system. In their view, it is clearly not working well for rape victims. Among other things, they suggest (1) efforts to alleviate the suffering of victims within the court system, (2) compensation for rape victims, and (3) a general overhaul of the criminal justice system as it relates to rape.

Thus, there have been a number of efforts to try to respond to the problem of rape in America, but it is clear that we have just begun what will be a long-term process of reforming many aspects of the social system.

SUMMARY

1. This chapter is concerned with "private violence," that is, family violence (primarily wife abuse and parental abuse of children), rape, and, to a lesser extent, incest.
2. In addition to their largely private nature, the common theme that binds these three phenomena together is the systematic abuse of power by males and parents vis-à-vis females and children.

Family Violence

3. We live in violent homes in which there is a surprising amount of child abuse, wife abuse, and other forms of family violence.
4. Although physiological factors have not been shown to be important causes of family violence, it is clear that such violence has negative physiological effects on the victims.
5. There is a stronger case for a causal role for psychological factors, but it is unquestionably the case that violence has adverse psychological consequences for the victim.
6. It seems clear at the social-psychological level that people often learn to be violent in their own families. And family violence adversely affects social relationships within the family, perhaps helping to lead to the dissolution of many families.
7. Also at the social-psychological level, it is important to understand the history of the nature of the relationship between husbands and wives and parents and children in understanding the violence that exists between them.
8. At the sociological level, a number of characteristics of the family in our society contribute to violence within it.
9. Also at the sociological level, it is important to understand the role played

in family violence by social stratification, and gender and age stratification. Basically, we can say that the least powerful members of society are more likely to engage in family violence and to be victimized by it.

10. Finally, we underscore the role played by a violent American culture in the etiology of family violence.
11. Psychologically, the victims of family violence (especially battered wives) can rationalize the perpetrator's use of violence. While they may be psychologically useful, rationalizations do nothing to deal with the source of the problem.
12. More effective are a series of concrete actions open to victims (battered wives), such as calling the police, seeking counseling, leaving home for good, fighting back, seeking the help of informal support networks, or entering shelters.
13. The most important structural response has been the development of shelters, primarily women's shelters, for the victims of family violence.
14. In addition to responses already in place, it would be useful to take a variety of steps to reduce the causes of violence within the larger culture.

A Note on Incest

15. The focus is on father-daughter incest since it is most likely to be reported to the police and it is the type that most involves abuse of power.
16. There is growing evidence that incest occurs far more frequently than is commonly believed, and public awareness of it as a problem is growing.
17. Despite the fact that it exists, there have been cultural taboos against incest in virtually all societies throughout history. The major explanation for the taboo is that it prevents inbreeding and leads to alliances between families and larger groups.
18. The existence of patriarchy in most societies allows us to understand the far greater likelihood of father-daughter than mother-son incest.

Rape

19. There is also a growing consciousness of rape as a social problem and even the highest reported statistics are likely to be gross underestimations of the actual number of rapes occurring in the United States.
20. Male rape of females (which is the focal concern) is better seen as an abuse of power than an act motivated by sexual need.
21. Rape is not primarily a result of a male biological need for sexual gratification.
22. Although few rapists are insane, many suffer from some psychological dysfunctions.
23. The rape experience has profound physiological and psychological consequences for the victim (the "rape trauma syndrome").
24. At the social-psychological level, it is important to understand the nature of the relationship between rapist and victim.
25. Rape is more common in cultures (like that of the United States) in which male power and male aggressiveness are sanctioned.
26. Various structures and institutions in

American society have not in the past well served the needs and interests of rape victims.
27. There are a variety of actions a victim can take before, during, and after an attack.
28. After an attack, a victim may seek out the help of informal and formal social networks.
29. The major innovation in dealing with rape at the sociological level has been the development of rape crisis centers.
30. Rape laws have also been changed to make it easier for the victim to press charges and for the rapist to be convicted.
31. Many other things need to be done in order to help us cope better with the problem of rape.

SUGGESTED READINGS

Brownmiller, Susan, *Against Our Will: Men, Women and Rape.* New York: Simon and Schuster, 1975. A classic feminist work that analyzed rape as an act of power rather than sex.

Dobash, R. Emerson, and Russell Dobash, *Violence Against Wives: A Case Against Patriarchy.* New York: Free Press, 1979. An analysis of wife-beating that puts it in the broader context of patriarchy.

Finkelhor, David, *Sexually Victimized Children.* New York: Free Press. 1979. This book puts the problem of incest within the broader context of sexual victimization of children.

Groth, Nicholas, *Men Who Rape: The Psychology of the Offender.* New York: Plenum, 1979. An important study of the psychology of the rapist.

Straus, Murray A., Richard J. Gelles, and Suzanne K. Steinmetz, *Behind Closed Doors: Violence in the American Family.* Garden City, N.Y.: Anchor Books, 1980. An important piece of sociological research on family violence.

FOOTNOTES

[1]"Private Violence," *Time,* September 5, 1983, pp. 18–29.

[2]Murray A. Straus, Richard J. Gelles, and Suzanne K. Steinmetz, *Behind Closed Doors: Violence in the American Family* (Garden City, N.Y.: Anchor Books, 1980).

[3]*Time, op. cit.,* p. 18.

[4]*Ibid.,* p. 20.

[5]Patsy A. Klaus and Michael R. Rand, "Family Violence," *Bureau of Justice Statistics Special Report* (Washington D.C.: U.S. Department of Justice, April 1984).

[6]David Finkelhor, "Common Factors Of Family Abuse." In David Finkelhor, *et al.*, eds., *The Dark Side of Families.* (Beverly Hills, Cal.: Sage Publications, 1983), pp. 17–28.

[7]Wini Breines and Linda Gordon, "The New Scholarship on Family Violence," *Signs,* 8 (1983), 490–531.

[8]*Ibid.,* p. 529.

[9]*Ibid.*

[10]Randall Collins, *Conflict Sociology: Toward an Explanatory Science* (New York: Academic Press, 1975).

[11]Strauss, *et al., op. cit.,* p. 16.

[12]Suzanne K. Steinmetz and Murray A. Straus, "The Family as Cradle of Violence," *Society,* 10 (1973).

[13]*Ibid.,* p. 13.

[14]Richard J. Gelles, "Violence in the Family: A Review of Research in the Seventies," *Journal of Marriage and the Family,* 42 (1980), 878.

[15]R. Emerson Dobash and Russell Dobash, *Violence Against Wives: A Case Against Patriarchy* (New York: The Free Press, 1979), p. 20.

[16]Maria Roy, ed., *Battered Women: A Psychosociological Study of Domestic Violence* (New York: Van Nostrand Reinhold, 1977).

[17]Straus, *et al., op. cit.*, pp. 43–44.

[18]Debra S. Kalmuss and Murray A. Straus, "Wives' Marital Dependency and Wife Abuse," *Journal of Marriage and the Family*, 44 (1982), 277–286.

[19]Straus, *et al., op. cit.*, p. 32.

[20]*Ibid.*, p. 34.

[21]Dobash and Dobash, *Violence Against Wives, op. cit.*, pp. 31–47.

[22]Samuel X. Radbill, "A History of Child Abuse and Infanticide." In Ray E. Helfer and C. Henry Kempe, eds., *The Battered Child*, 2nd ed. (Chicago: University of Chicago Press, 1974), pp. 3–21.

[23]Straus, *et al., op. cit.*, p. 61.

[24]Claire P. Cornell and Richard J. Gelles, "Adolescent to Parent Violence," *The Urban and Social Change Review*, 15 (1982), 8–14.

[25]Frank A. Elliott, "The Neurology of Explosive Rage: The Dyscontrol Syndrome." In Roy, ed., *Battered Women, op. cit.*, pp. 98–109.

[26]Leonard Berkowitz, "The Goals of Aggression." In Finkelhor, *et al.*, eds., *op. cit.* 1983, pp. 166–181.

[27]Natalie Shainess, "Psychological Aspects of Wifebattering." In Roy, ed., *Battered Women, op. cit.*, pp. 111–119; M. Faulk, "Men Who Assault Their Wives." In Roy, ed., *op. cit.*, p. 119–126.

[28]Murray A. Straus, "A Sociological Perspective on the Causes of Family Violence." In M. R. Green, ed., *Violence in the Family* (Boulder, Col.: Westview Press, 1980), pp. 7–31.

[29]Shainess, *op. cit.*; John R. Lion, "Clinical Aspects of Wifebattering." In Roy, ed., *Battered Women, op. cit.*, pp. 126–136.

[30]Lenore Walker, *The Battered Woman* (New York: Harper & Row. 1979).

[31]Laurie Wardell, Dair Gillespie, and Ann Leffler, "Science and Violence Against Wives." In Finkelhor, *et al.*, eds., *The Dark Side of Families, op. cit.*, pp. 69–84.

[32]Lenore Walker, "The Battered Woman Syndrome Study." In Finkelhor, *et al.*, eds., *The Dark Side of Families, op. cit.*, pp. 31–48.

[33]Suzanne Prescott and Carolyn Prescott, "Battered Women: A Social Psychological Perspective." In Roy, ed., *Battered Women, op. cit.*, p. 84.

[34]Straus, *et al., op. cit.*, pp. 121–22.

[35]Murray Straus, "Social Stress and Marital Violence in a National Sample of American Families." In Fred Wright, *et al.*, eds., *Forensic Psychology and Psychiatry* (New York: Annals of the New York Academy of Sciences, 1980), p. 232.

[36]See also Wendy Schuman, "The Violent American Way of Life," *Parents*, 55 (1980), 66–70.

[37]Straus, *et al., op. cit.*, p. 17.

[38]James A. Wiggins, "Family Violence as a Case of Interpersonal Aggression: A Situational Analysis," *Social Forces*, 62 (1983), 102–123.

[39]*Ibid.*, p. 111.

[40]Straus, et. al., *op. cit.*, p. 122.

[41]Murray A. Straus, "Wife Beating: How Common and Why?" *Victimology: An International Journal*, 2 (1977–78), 443–458.

[42]*Ibid.*, p. 451.

[43]*Ibid.*, p. 452.

[44]Cited in "Private Violence," *Time, op. cit.*, p. 26.

[45]For more on this see, Richard Gelles, "An Exchange/Social Control Theory." In David Finkelhor, *et al.*, eds., *op. cit.*, 1983, pp. 151–165.

[46]Jessica H. Daniel, Robert L. Hampton, and Eli H. Newberger, "Child Abuse and Accidents in Black Families: A Controlled Comparative Study," *American Journal of Orthopsychiatry*, 53 (1983), 645–653.

[47]R. Emerson Dobash and Russell Dobash, *op. cit.*, pp. 33–34.

[48]Breines and Gordon, "The New Scholarship on Family Violence," *op. cit.*, 492.

[49]Mildred Daley Pagelow, *Woman-Battering: Victims and Their Experiences* (Beverly Hills, Cal: Sage, 1981), p. 21.

[50]Straus, "Wife Beating," *op. cit.*, 454.

[51]*Ibid.*

[52]Kathleen J. Ferraro and John M. Johnson, "How Women Experience Battering: The Process of Victimization," *Social Problems*, 30 (1983), 326–339.

[53]Lee H. Bowker, *Beating Wife-Beating* (Lexington, Mass.: D.C. Heath, 1983), p. 9.

[54]*Ibid.*, pp. 121–122.

[55]Straus, *et al., Behind Closed Doors, op cit.*, pp. 234–236. See also Murray Straus, "Societal Change and Change in Family Violence," Family Violence Research Program, mimeo., 1981.

[56]As of 1983, *Time* estimated that there were about 800 shelters in the United States. See, *Time*, "Private Violence," *op. cit.*

[57]Straus, *et al., op. cit.*, p. 227.

[58]David Finkelhor, *Sexually Victimized Children* (New York: Free Press, 1979), p. 84.

[59]Judith Lewis Herman (with Lisa Hirschman), *Father-Daughter Incest* (Cambridge, Mass.: Harvard University Press, 1981), p. 4.

[60]Alfred C. Kinsey, Wardell B. Pomeroy, and Clyde E. Martin, *Sexual Behavior in the Human Male* (Philadelphia: Saunders, 1948).

[61]P. H. Gebhard, *et al.*, *Sex Offenders* (New York: Harper & Row, 1965). See also David Finkelhor, *Sexually Victimized Children, op. cit.*, pp. 87–90.

[62]Russell Middleton, "Brother-Sister and Father-Daughter Marriage in Ancient Egypt," *American Sociological Review*, 27 (1962), 603–611.

[63]Sandy Rovner, "Facing the Aftermath of Incest," *The Washington Post*, January 6, 1984, p. D5.

[64]Gardner Lindzey, "Some Remarks Concerning Incest, the Incest Taboo, and Psychoanalytic Theory," *American Psychologist*, 22 (1967), 1051–1059.

[65]Claude Levi-Strauss, "Family." In Harry L. Shapiro, ed., *Man, Culture and Society* (New York: Oxford University Press, 1956).

[66]Robin Fox, *The Red Lamp of Incest*, (New York: Dutton, 1980), p. 215.

[67]Louise Armstrong, *Kiss Daddy Goodnight: A Speak-Out on Incest* (New York: Pocket Books, 1979), p. 272.

[68]Breines and Gordon, "The New Scholarship on Family Violence," *op. cit.*, 521.

[69]Judith Herman and Lisa Hirschman, "Father-Daughter Incest," *Signs*, 2 (1977), 735–756.

[70]*Ibid.*, p. 740.

[71]Although we focus on male rape of females, it is possible for females to rape males. See Philip M. Sarrel and William H. Masters, "Sexual Molestation of Men by Women," *Archives of Sexual Behavior*, 11 (1982), 117–131.

[72]U.S. Department of Justice, *Crime in the United States: 1983, Uniform Crime Reports for the United States*, (Washington, D.C.: U.S. Government Printing Office, 1984), p. 13.

[73]*Ibid.*, pp. 13, 43.

[74]Barbara J. Rodabaugh and Melanie Austin, *Sexual Assault: A Guide for Community Action* (New York: Garland STPM Press, 1981), p. 16; see also Nancy Gager and Cathleen Schurr, *Sexual Assault: Confronting Rape in America* (New York: Grosset and Dunlap, 1976), pp. 93–94.

[75]Timothy Beneke, *Men on Rape* (New York: St. Martin's, 1982).

[76]Bureau of Justice Statistics, "The Crime of Rape" (Washington, D.C.: U.S. Department of Justice, 1985), p. 1.

[77]*Ibid.*

[78]Rodabaugh and Austin, *op. cit.*, p. 7.

[79]Gilbert Geis, "Forcible Rape: An Introduction." In Duncan Chappell, Robley Geis, and Gilbert Geis, eds., *Forcible Rape: The Crime, The Victim, and the Offender* (New York: Columbia University Press, 1977), pp. 1–44; See also Vicki McNickle Rose, "Rape as a Social Problem: A Byproduct of the Feminist Movement," *Social Problems*, 25 (1977), 75–89.

[80]Susan Brownmiller, *Against Our Will: Men, Women and Rape.* (New York: Simon and Schuster, 1975).

[81]*Ibid.*, p. 209.

[82]Deena Metzger, "It is Always the Woman Who is Raped," *American Journal of Psychiatry*, 133 (1976), 405.

[83]A. Nicholas Groth, *Men Who Rape: The Psychology of the Offender* (New York: Plenum, 1979).

[84]*Ibid.*, p. 2.

[85]*Ibid.*

[86]Beneke, *op. cit.*, p. 169.

[87]Groth. *op. cit.*, p. 6.

[88]Neil M. Malamuth, "Rape Proclivity Among Males," *Journal of Social Issues*, 37 (1981), 138–157.

[89]Sedelle Katz and Mary Ann Mazur, *Understanding the Rape Victim: A Synthesis of Research Findings* (New York: Wiley, 1979).

[90]Ann Wolbert Burgess and Lynda Lytle Holmstrom, "Rape Trauma Syndrome," *American Journal of Psychiatry*, 131 (1974), 981–986. For more recent work on this issue see Diana E. H. Russell, *The Politics of Rape: The Victim's Perspective* (New York: Stein and Day, 1975); Sedelle Katz and Mary Ann Mazur, *op. cit.*; Thomas W. McCahill, Linda C. Meyer, and Arthur Fischman, *The Aftermath of Rape* (Lexington, Mass.: Lexington Books, 1979).

[91]Burgess and Holmstrom, *op. cit.*, p. 982; see also Malkah T. Notman and Carol C. Nadelson, "The Rape Victim: Psychodynamic Considerations," *American Journal of Psychiatry*, 133 (1976), 408–413.

[92]Burgess and Holmstrom, *op. cit.*, p. 982.

[93]Ann Wolbert Burgess and Lynda Lytle Holmstrom, *Rape: Crisis and Recovery* (Bowie, Maryland: Robert J. Brady Co., 1979).

[94]McCahill, Meyer, and Fishman, *op cit.*, p. 74.

[95]Dean G. Kilpatrick, Patricia A. Resick, and Lois J. Veronen, "Effects of a Rape Experience: A Longitudinal Study," *Journal of Social Issues*, 37 (1981), 105–122.

[96]Priscilla N. White and Judith C. Rollins, "Rape: A Family Crisis," *Family Relations*, 30 (1980), 103–109.

[97]Lynda Lytle Holmstrom and Ann Wolbert Burgess, "Rape: The Husband's and Boyfriend's Initial Reaction," *The Family Coordinator*, 28 (1979), 321–330.

[98]Stephanie Riger and Margaret T. Gordon, "The Fear of Rape: A Study in Social Control," *Journal of Social Issues*, 37 (1981), 71–92.

[99]Beneke, *op. cit.*, p. 170.

[100]Charles W. Dean and Mary deBruyn-Kops, *The Crime and Consequences of Rape* (Springfield, Ill.: Thomas, 1982).

[101]Linda S. Williams, "The Classic Rape: When Do Victims Report?" *Social Problems,* 31 (1984), 459–467.

[102]Karen Barrett, "Date Rape: A Campus Epidemic," *Ms.,* September 1982, pp. 42ff; Diana E. Russell, *Rape in Marriage* (New York: Macmillan, 1982).

[103]For the older, now-rejected view on this see Chapter 15, "Victim-Precipitated Forcible Rape." In Menachem Amir, *Patterns in Forcible Rape* (Chicago: University of Chicago Press, 1971).

[104]Dean and deBruyn-Kops. *op. cit.*

[105]Groth, *op. cit.,* p. 14.

[106]*Ibid.,* p. 25.

[107]Gager and Schurr, *op. cit.*

[108]William B. Sanders, *Rape and Woman's Identity* (Beverly Hills, Cal.: Sage, 1980), p. 29.

[109]Susan Griffith, "Rape: The All-American Crime," *Ramparts,* September 1971, 26–35. See also, Susan Griffith, *Rape: The Power of Consciousness* (New York: Harper & Row, 1979).

[110]Gager and Schurr, *op. cit.,* p. 3.

[111]Martha R. Burt, "Cultural Myths and Supports for Rape," *Journal of Personality and Social Psychology,* 38 (1980), 217–230.

[112]Sanders, *op. cit.,* p. 30.

[113]Peggy Reeves Sanday, "The Socio-Cultural Context of Rape: The Cross-Cultural Study," *Journal of Social Issues,* 37 (1981), 5–27; Susan A. Ritzer, *Rape: A Cross-Cultural Perspective.* Unpublished M. A. thesis, University of Kansas, 1975.

[114]Sanday, *op. cit.,* p. 15. For a discussion of a specific rape-prone culture see Robert A. LeVine, "Gusii Sex Offenses: A Study in Social Control." In Chappell, Geis, and Geis, *op. cit.,* pp. 189–226.

[115]Sanday, *op. cit.,* p. 18.

[116]*Ibid.,* p. 25.

[117]*Ibid.,* pp. 25–26.

[118]Lynda Lytle Holmstrom and Ann Wolbert Burgess, *The Victim of Rape: Institutional Reactions* (New York: Wiley, 1978); Sanders, *op. cit.,* pp. 30–32.

[119]Carol Bohmer, "Judicial Attitudes Toward Rape Victims." In Chappell, Geis, and Geis, *op. cit.,* pp. 160–169.

[120]Gary D. LaFree, "Official Reactions to Social Problems: Police Decisions in Sexual Assault Cases," *Social Problems,* 28 (1981), 582–594.

[121]Julia and Herman Schwendinger, *Rape and Inequality* (Beverly Hills, Cal: Sage, 1983), p. 204.

[122]Gary LaFree, "Male Power and Female Victimization: Toward a Theory of Interracial Rape," *American Journal of Sociology,* 88 (1982), 311–328.

[123]Ann Wolbert Burgess and Lynda Lytle Holmstrom, "Coping Behavior of the Rape Victim," *American Journal of Psychiatry,* 133 (1976), 413–418.

[124]*Ibid.,* p. 416.

[125]Linda Williams, *op. cit.,* 1984.

[126]Hannah I. Evans, "Psychotherapy for the Rape Victim: Some Treatment Models," *Health and Community Psychiatry,* 29 (1978), 309–312.

[127]Sharon L. McCombie, *et al.,* "Development of a Medical Center Rape Crisis Intervention Program," *American Journal of Psychiatry,* 133 (1976), 418–421; H. Elizabeth King and Carol Webb, "Rape Crisis Centers: Progress and Problems," *Journal of Social Issues,* 37 (1981), 93–104.

[128]Rodabaugh and Austin, *op. cit.,* p. 63.

[129]Holmstrom and Burgess, *The Victim of Rape, op. cit.,* p. 3.

[130]*Time,* "Private Violence," *op. cit.,* p. 29.

[131]*Ibid.*

[132]Jeanne C. Marsh, Alison Geist, and Nathan Caplan, *Rape and the Limits of Law Reform* (Boston: Auburn, 1982). See also Kenneth A. Cobb and Nancy R. Schauer, "Michigan's Criminal Sexual Assault Law." In Chappell, Geis, and Geis, *op. cit.,* pp. 170–186.

[133]*Time,* "Personal Violence," *op. cit.,* p. 29.

[134]Holmstrom and Burgess, *The Victim of Rape, op. cit.,* p. 266.

III

Problems of Conflict and Inequality

For eighty years I've
talked of east and west
What nonsense!
What's long/short
big/small?
There's no need of the
grey old man,
I'm one with all of
you, in everything
once through the
emptiness of all
Who's coming?
Who's going?
Kiyo-

7
Aging

Jill Quadagno
UNIVERSITY OF KANSAS

Why should college students be interested in the problems of aging? Of all the problems discussed in this book, the problems of old age are those you, personally, are least likely to escape; today most people do not die without becoming old. Further, this is not a problem you will face only in the future. We are all members of families and naturally have concerns about our own parents and grandparents. Aging is an issue, then, that confronts all of us in some way or another over the entire life cycle.

Old age is a fact of life in all human societies. All have some arrangements for dealing with it, but these vary tremendously from one culture to another. In some societies old age is glorified, and the heroes in folk tales, instead of being youthful or athletic, are old. The aged gain their prestige from their mythical abilities—for example, to control the weather, drive away famine, or change stones into bread. However, even when old age is glorified, distinctions are usually made between the useful period of life and the "helpless" stage. When the latter stage is reached by any person, he or she may be neglected and sometimes even "helped to die." As one old Hottentot woman told an anthropologist who found her abandoned in the desert:

> Yes, my own children, three sons and two daughters, are gone to yonder blue mountain and have left me here to die. . . . I am very old, you see, and am not able to serve them. When they kill game, I am too feeble to help with carrying home the flesh. I am not able to gather wood and make a fire, and I cannot carry their children on my back as I used to do.[1]

Although the practice of abandonment sounds harsh, even brutal to us, our own tendency to institutionalize large numbers of ill older people is not necessarily so different. It is the contemporary method through which societies handle those who are no longer able to contribute and who are perceived as a burden.

In modern industrial societies, the problem of what to do with the "old-old," those who are no longer able to care for themselves, has assumed critical importance. Because of recent advances in public health and medicine, life expectancy has greatly increased. Further, the most recent increases in life expectancy have occurred among those over the age of seventy-five, who are most likely to need physical care and attention. Never before has any human society had so many older people because never before have so many people lived so long. In this sense, the problems of aging are modern problems. It is also important, however, not to exaggerate the degree of disability among the older population. Most older people are not lonely or isolated, and most are sufficiently healthy to live independently with relative ease.

PART I: THE PROBLEM

Although there are very real problems associated with growing old (including reduced income, declining health, the loss of significant others, and the need to cope with new roles that are not always clearly defined), many of the issues often identified as problems are, in fact, not the direct result of aging. Rather, they are difficulties experienced by elderly people because of the kinds of solutions society has adopted to deal with increasingly larger numbers of people who live past retirement age. Many of these solutions are reflections of *ageism*—that is, systematic negative evaluations of older people that lead to job discrimination, disparaging public opinions about the skills and abilities of older people, and in general, innaccurate stereotypes. We will begin this chapter with a discussion of the actual problems that older people face, tempered by the awareness that many of these problems are created by the way society reacts to and evaluates them. For most older people, old age itself is not a problem; rather the problem is how we, as a society, deal with the changes that occur in later life.

Problems of Definition

Definition of Aging in Nonliterate Societies

In nonliterate societies there is no fixed way to calculate age on the basis of time, since the reckoning of a birthday depends on the existence of a calendrical system. In these societies the reckoning of age is most frequently done by the means of age categories. The classification of group members into age categories is called *age grading*. More specifically, age grading refers to the allocation of persons of different ages to given social roles. An example of age grading occurs among the Masai, where adolescent males form a group in which they remain throughout life, passing from junior warrior to senior warrior to executive elder to senior elder and, finally, to retired old man. In this particular case, the whole of public life is administered through age groups, and the social system is built around the process of aging in a highly integrated manner.[2]

Various criteria apply in determining when an individual enters a new age category. In many societies, an individual becomes an "elder" when he or she becomes the oldest member of a family. In other societies, a male may become an elder when he is no longer able to hunt. In Samoa, old age begins around age fifty, and some time between the ages of sixty and seventy the word *vaivai* is added to describe the individual, a word which means literally "weak in the body."

Definition of Aging in the United States

In the United States (and many Western nations), tradition has set a chronological age as the main criterion that we use, that is, age sixty-five. The reason why we tend to classify people over age sixty-five as old is because that is the age originally agreed upon by those who drafted the Social Security legislation in 1935 as the age at which people could become eligible to collect retirement benefits. The choice of age sixty-five was, even at that time, rather arbitrary. Some policymakers, concerned with the potential costs of pensions, argued that benefits should begin at age seventy. However, workers who witnessed substantial age discrimination against older workers advocated a much earlier retirement age, beginning at age sixty or even earlier. The result was a compromise of age sixty-five that had little to do with the actual needs of workers. The problem with this definition is that people who are labeled as old in terms of chronological age may be young in terms of numerous other criteria.

What other criteria do we use as indicators of age: one is physical appearance. Gray hair and wrinkles are clearly a sign of age. However, people age at different rates, and some people may have gray hair in their forties, while others may not be gray until they are in their seventies or eighties. The problem of defining old age becomes even more complex when we think of the many ways, in our youth-oriented society, that we are able to change our appearance to make oursleves appear more youthful. People use hair dyes and have face lifts that hide or erase the signs of normal aging, thus fooling us into believing they are younger than they really are.

Another criterion that we sometimes use to identify old age is the role a person plays. In our idealized view of grandparenting, for example, we view grandmothers as old women who bake cookies and knit sweaters for their grandchildren. While some grandmothers certainly enjoy these activities, many others are in their mid-forties or early fifties and are working full time in a variety of occupations. Similarly, we tend to see retirement from work as a criterion that defines an older person, and yet in many jobs people retire quite young. The most notable example is the military service, where a person can retire after twenty years of service. While many military personnel retire at forty or forty-five and then go on to build second careers, some remain permanently retired at a very young age.

Isolation, Neglect, and Abuse

Another problem in later life for some people is isolation. Due to their longer life expectancy, a considerable portion, more than forty percent, of all older women live alone.[3] Although most older poeple have children that they see at least once a month, some considerably more often, there are others who become isolated.

Many factors associated with aging shrink the social world of an older person and contribute to isolation. These include retirement from work, widowhood and other changes in family roles, and declining health. Each of these will be discussed in detail later in this chapter. However, isolation may also be a form of passive neglect, a term used to characterize situations in which an elderly person is left alone, forgotten by children or other close relations.[4] One study in which practitioners and professionals such as doctors, nurses, social workers, clergy, and morticians were interviewed, found that nearly all had had some firsthand experiences with passive neglect. In most instances the respondents felt that the families were simply too busy or too concerned with their own lives to pay adequate attention to dependent elderly relatives.[5]

Even more disturbing than passive neglect were the reports of both verbal and physical abuse, including such actions as intimidating, humiliating, or insulting elderly people or actually slapping, hitting, burning, or physically restraining them. Police officers, lawyers, and community health workers were most likely to have regular experiences with verbal abuse. Many of these respondents indicated that older dependent adults were treated in a manner that demolished personal dignity and self-worth and robbed them of a sense of independence. Experiences with physical abuse were rarer, but morticians, physicians, and medical examiners did note the presence of bodily marks and bruises that suggested physical violence unrelated to a single episode or a fall.[6] Passive neglect was seen to occur most often, followed by verbal and emotional abuse, active neglect, and finally physical violence. While it is difficult to determine how often these problems occur, the fact that so many professionals had witnessed some form of neglect indicates it is a problem that cannot be ignored.

Economic Difficulties

Retirement is usually associated with a significant drop in income that can lead to economic difficulties in old age. Although rates of older people living below the official poverty level declined dramatically from 35.3 percent in 1959 to 14.6 percent in 1974, in the late 1970s they began rising again as the economy deteriorated.[7] Furthermore, measurements of abject poverty through the official poverty indices fail to fully reveal the number of older people who face serious economic hardship. Accordingly, the Department of Health, Education and Welfare created the near-poor threshold, which is calculated at 125 percent of the poverty standards. In 1983 these income thresholds were $7,524 for older couples and $5,969 for older people living alone. Of those 65 and older, 25 percent, or 5.9 million people, had incomes at or below this alternative standard.[8]

Old age poverty is not evenly distributed among all members of the aged population but is disproportionately high for women and for members of minority groups. In 1981, only 8 percent of male heads of household over age sixty-five had incomes below the poverty level, compared with 15 percent of their female counterparts.[9] Because most of today's older women did not work outside the home, they are covered by Social Security or private pensions only through their husbands. Usually most private pensions do not contain provisions for widows' benefits, so when their husbands die, the income of most older women drops substantially.[10] For many widowed women, their deceased husband's Social Security check is their primary, if not their only, source of income. Further, women who did work and build up their own Social Security benefits typically had lower salaries on the average than men. Since the size of Social Security and private pension benefits is based on past earnings, elderly women receive smaller payments on the average than elderly men. Table 7.1 illustrates the difference in average benefits for men and women in 1982. Clearly, sex-based inequalities follow women into old age.

For aged members of minority groups the figures are equally striking; 38 percent of aged blacks and almost 31 percent of Hispanic aged were living at extreme poverty levels in 1982.[11] Old age poverty for minorities is a consequence of racism that results in exclusion from more desirable jobs earlier in life. Black workers face higher rates of unemployment than whites throughout the life cycle, and the jobs in

Old age poverty has forced some to attempt to survive on what they find by rummaging through garbage cans.

(Bernard Pierre Wolff/Photo Researchers)

which they are employed tend to be lower paying and to lack pension plans. The Social Security benefits that blacks receive are at the low end of the scale, because they are more likely to have worked at lower-paying jobs. Another problem is that people who are poor prior to retirement have fewer resources to compensate for low retirement benefits. Whereas white males often have Social Security, private pensions, and income from assets and interest payments, a high proportion of older blacks have only Social Security. Any supplementary income they receive is most likely to come from wages.

Many other modern nations have diverted a sufficient portion of their national wealth into old age benefits. In these na-

Table 7.1 Social Security Retirement Benefits by Sex, 1982 in Dollars

	AVERAGE MONTHLY BENEFITS	FULL BENEFITS	REDUCED BENEFITS
Males	$470	$528	$427
Females	362	433	332

Source: Statistical Abstract of the United States, *National Data Book and Guide to Sources* (Washington, D.C.: U.S. Bureau of the Census, 1984), p. 381.

tions, old age is not associated with poverty. A comparison of expenditures for income security programs in Western nations in Table 7.2 shows that the United States ranks lowest in total expenditures for income security programs.

Health and Medical Care

The geriatric population is the largest group consumer of health services in the United States. The elderly spend three times more money annually for medical services than do other adults. Older adults occupy one of every three hospital beds and require twice the number of hospital days relative to younger persons. Over 75 percent of the aged sees a physician yearly, and older people account for 2 out of every 5 general medical office visits; on the average an older person will see a physician 6.5 times in one year.[12]

One of the problems associated with the provision of health care to the aged is that the organization of health-care services is not geared toward the care of chronic illness. Instead the medical profession, on the whole, has been primarily oriented toward the treatment of acute illnesses for which there is a recognizable cure. This is partly a structural condition resulting from the way health-care services have developed in this country, since health care is concentrated in hospital settings rather than being oriented toward community-based preventive and rehabilitative care. In the final section of this chapter, we will discuss some of the recent solutions that have been adopted for improving health care for the aged.

A more subtle issue concerns the attitudes of health-care professionals toward their work. There is a widespread feeling among older people that most doctors are not interested in them, a perception that may be accurate given the ways that physicians are trained to define their work and their primary duties. One study of medical students found that a young physician's most important self-definition was as an active person who could respond quickly and that the greatest sense of satisfaction came from seeing a patient recover.[13] Quick solutions cannot be posed for chronic diseases, and it is difficult or impossible to define a patient with a chronic illness as cured. In addition, doctors are

Table 7.2 Total Expenditures for Income Security Programs as a Percentage of Gross National Product, Selected Countries, 1957–1977

	1957	1966	1977
Austria	13.5	18.5	22.2
Belgium	13.1	16.4	25.4
France	14.3	16.6	26.5
Germay, Federal Republic	16.6	18.4	26.5
The Netherlands	10.4	16.9	28.4
Sweden	10.5	14.5	30.7
Switzerland	7.6	8.9	15.5
United Kingdom	10.0	12.3	17.1
United States	5.0	7.7	13.7

Source: John Myles, *Old Age in the Welfare State* (Boston: Little Brown, 1984,), p. 17.

trained to recognize the symptoms of poor health rather than the eroding consequence of normal aging. For many reasons, then, physicians may find treating older people less satisfying.

PART II: CAUSES AND CONSEQUENCES

Why do these problems exist for older people? There are numerous reasons, ranging from the simple fact that biological aging does lead to deterioration to the complex influence of industrialization and massive social change.

INDIVIDUAL LEVEL

Physiological Factors in Aging

Even though, in our youth-oriented society, we may be told that creams can smooth away wrinkles and hair coloring can take ten years from our appearance, biological aging is inevitable, and all people must eventually accept the reality of biological change. Numerous physiological changes occur, and although they occur at different rates in different people, no one can escape the unalterable fact that we will grow old.

Everyone is aware that facial wrinkles, liver spots on the skin, and grey hair are associated with aging, but there are numerous other physiological changes, less visible, but more important in terms of functioning, that take place. Changes in the joints and decreased bone and muscle mass lead to stooped posture, reduced height, loss of muscle power, misshapen joints, and, eventually, limited mobility. Nerve cells are also lost during the aging process, a process that brings about a decreased capacity for sending nerve impulses to and from the brain. Vision, hearing, taste, smell, and touch are all affected. Changes in the gastrointestinal tract may produce digestive difficulties, and there is often a loss of cardiac muscle strength.[14]

Chronic Illness

These changes are all a part of normal aging; they are not symptoms of illness. Yet older people do suffer from higher rates of chronic illnesses than younger people, which explains why they consume such a large proportion of the health-care services in this country. Nearly half of all people over the age of sixty-five suffer from two or more chronic illnesses, such as heart disease, hypertension, osteoarthritis, rheumatoid arthritis, stroke with paralytic residuals, or diabetes.[15] Further, although older poeple are less likely to suffer from acute illnesses, when they do catch flu or get a cold, their average recuperation time is over twice as long as that for the population at a whole.[16]

The fact that older people suffer from multiple disorders causes some symptoms to be hidden from the untrained physician, leading to mistakes in diagnosis. For example:

> An older person with hyperthyroidism may appear apathetic, not hyperactive; tuberculosis may proceed in silence; appendicitis may occur without the characteristic abdominal tenderness . . ., without fever, and without an elevated white count. An older person may even have a heart attack without chest pain and may instead appear confused, disoriented, and seem like the victim of a stroke.[17]

Another problem associated with multiple chronic illnesses is that a person might be taking several medications simultaneously. This, in itself, can lead to drug misuse, since some combinations of drugs can have harmful side effects. Further, older people may also inadvertently misuse drugs, because of decreased vision or hearing. One study that examined the implica-

Table 7.3 Levels of Analysis: Aging

LEVELS	APPROPRIATE QUESTIONS	A PARTIAL SYNOPSIS OF PRESENT CONCLUSIONS
INDIVIDUAL	Is aging itself a cause of social problems?	No. Biological aging is inevitable, but it does not cause problems for people uniformly or inevitably.
	What are some physiological problems often caused by aging?	An increase in chronic illness and Alzheimer's disease are two of the most important physiological problems associated with aging.
SOCIAL-PSYCHOLOGICAL	Is retirement from work always a stressful role transition?	No. In fact, recent research has indicated that large numbers of people view retirement positively, not negatively.
	What are some of the adjustment problems involved in changes in family status?	Among the most important are the departure of the last child and grandparenthood.
	What are some of the problems involved in the transition to widowhood?	Grief, sudden shock, or the strain of dealing with long-term illness, and the loss of income.
SOCIOLOGICAL	How does American culture contribute to the problem of the aged?	Ageism is endemic to American culture and it is communicated through the mass media and other agencies.
	Is the work world structured so that it operates against the aged?	Yes. The aged are discriminated against in their work lives and this leads to greater problems with unemployment later in life.
	Does age-segregated housing inevitably operate against the aged?	No. However, there are places like welfare hotels that adversely affect the elderly.
	How have demographic changes affected the elderly?	The increasing number of aged people has greatly increased the problems of the elderly in our society.
	Is industrialization associated with an aging population?	Yes.

tions of drug misuse among older people found that the most serious problems were likely to occur when the individual was using two or more pharmacists or when two or more physicians were prescribing medications. This problem could be solved rather simply, perhaps by just having each physician and pharmacist review all medications with the patient.[18]

Alzheimer's Disease

One of the major medical problems that occurs most commonly in advanced old age is Alzheimer's disease, or as it is still often called, senile dementia. Alzheimer's disease is both organic and behavioral. Its organic indicators, which tend to be correlated with age, include neurofibrillary tangles and senile plaques in the brain.[19] Behaviorally, it is characterized by impaired memory orientation, judgment, and abstract reasoning. The afflicted individual may also lose the ability to communicate or to perform simple motor tasks.[20]

The state of the diagnostic art with respect to Alzheimer's disease is limited, because many of the behavioral changes, such as memory loss, may simply be signs of normal aging. Thus, no clinical diagnosis can be confirmed until a post-mortem examination has been made, and even then the findings may be subject to dispute, for symptoms of dementia may be present although pathological findings fail to reveal abnormalities in the brain. Conversely, an individual may have signs of Alzheimer's disease according to a post-mortem exam but not have manifested any behavioral abnormalities.

Given the diversity of potential symptoms and the lack of medical consensus regarding diagnosis, the definition of Alzheimer's disease tends to involve social factors that are equally as significant as are signs of actual biological deterioration. Because of the uncertainty of diagnosis, Alzheimer's support groups, established to help relatives deal with the burden of caring for aging family members, have tended to expand the definition of the illness to incorporate all symptoms that might be displayed by any relative of a support group member. As one nurse in one study of these support groups explained to a newcomer who was trying to understand the disease:

> "Who knows, in a few years we might come to realize that there are many types of Alzheimer's disease, like Type-A Alzheimer's, Type-B Alzheimer's, Type-C, like that. The more I see of this thing, the more I'm convinced myself that's the disease. Really, it shows up differently for everyone. . . ."[21]

Clearly, in this example, social and psychological definitions of aging are combined with physiological changes in a complex way.

SOCIAL-PSYCHOLOGICAL LEVEL

Role Transitions in Later Life

As a consequence of aging, people experience many changes in status that are stressful and can lead to isolation and depression. Among the transitions in this category are widowhood, retirement, and the loss of the parenting role. However, it is important to realize that even stressful transitions of later life need not inevitably lead to negative consequences for the individual. Aging involves losses that require adaptation, but these changes can bring opportunities as well as challenges, freedom as well as decrement.

Adjustment to Retirement

The transition from work to retirement would seem to be one involving stress and a sense of loss for numerous reasons. Work is not only a source of income but also a major source of personal status and identity. Work also provides a life routine that structures our use of time. Further, in the realm of work individuals may express creativity and obtain a sense of accomplishment. Of course, not all people find work interesting and exciting—for many work is simply a routine that must be performed to obtain income for other more satisfying activities—nonetheless work is a core activity for many people. The extent to which the transition to retirement is stressful is dependent on a variety of factors including social status variables, personal resources, personality characteristics related to coping skills, and socialization experiences.

One of the most important factors that affects the retirement process is the type of job from which an individual retires. In general, workers in high-status occupations, where there is likely to be more intrinsic job satisfaction, retire later than workers in low-status occupations. They are also more likely to report high levels of social adjustment after retirement than low-status workers.[22] This is most likely related to two other factors associated with satisfaction with retirement—income and health. Low life satisfaction is correlated with low retirement income, as is poor health. Since workers in high-status occupations are more likely to have higher incomes and better health after a lifetime of relative privilege than workers in low-status jobs,[23] it is not surprising that adjustment after retirement is also higher.

Personality predispositions also affect the adjustment to retirement. People in one study characterized as having an active mastery orientation to life in general were also likely to be most effective in mastering the challenge created by retirement. In contrast, more passive individuals who tended to constrict their life space were less able to exhibit positive adjustment. Overall, there is no single personality type associated with successful adjustment to retirement but several different styles that work well for different types of people.[24]

Socialization for retirement may be a formal or an informal process. Formal retirement socialization takes place through retirement preparation programs. Unfortunately, very few employers offer such programs, so that it is difficult to measure whether or not they are successful in helping people adjust to retirement. Only a small percentage of older persons have ever participated in a formal retirement preparation program.[25] More commonly, individuals prepare for retirement by beginning planning financially in their middle years and more directly by talking about it with family members and coworkers as the actual time nears. Sociologists refer to this as anticipatory socialization. For most people the process is an informal rather than a formal one.[26]

Although retirement may be stressful for some people, overall most studies indicate that the majority of older people have positive attitudes toward retirement. Even individuals who are forced to retire because of mandatory retirement regulations do not typically view retirement as stressful.[27] Thus, even though work provides a number of important elements in life, most people look forward to retirement and do not view it as a crisis.

Adjustment to Changes in Family Status

As individuals grow older, several changes occur in family structure. Children leave home to establish independent households of their own, grandchildren are added to the family group, and finally, one member of the marital dyad, usually the woman, becomes widowed. All of these transitions involve significant changes in family roles and relationships that could be stressful.

The phase of the life cycle that occurs when the last child leaves home is popularly called the "empty nest." Many early discussions of this topic hypothesized that this was a traumatic event for parents, particularly mothers. However, available research provides little support for the idea that the departure of the last child from home is stressful. Rather for many parents the empty nest appears to be a positive event that improves the marital relationship of the parents. Middle-aged spouses often feel a sense of increased personal freedom, as well as a sense of accomplishment in launching their children into an independent life style.[28]

Becoming a grandparent is a positive experience for most men and women and is associated with emotional self-fulfillment and a sense of biological continuity and renewal. However, grandparenthood is least satisfying for individuals who feel remote from their grandchildren. Increasingly, one of the sources of estrangement between grandparents and grandchildren is parental divorce. Over 60 percent of divorcing couples have at least one minor child. Divorce, then, affects not only the middle generation and their children, but also the relationship of the children to their grandparents.

What is the impact of divorce on grandparent-grandchild relationships? There is no single answer to this question, for it depends on a number of factors. One important issue is whether or not the grandparents are able to maintain friendly relations with their child's former spouse. When divorces are particularly unpleasant or hostile, it is often difficult for the grandparents to retain contacts, particularly if their own child was not awarded custody of the children. Even if they remain on friendly terms with their former daughter-in-law or son-in-law, they are likely to see less of their grandchildren after the divorce. Generally, maternal grandparents are in a much better position to maintain relationships with their grandchildren than paternal grandparents because women are more likely to obtain custody of children and because women are more likely than men to maintain kinship ties.[29] In fact, because daughters often turn to their parents for emotional and financial assistance after a divorce, the amount of contact these grandparents experience with grandchildren may increase. For example, in one instance from one study, a grandfather drove to California to collect his daughter and two small grandchildren, who temporarily moved in with the grandparents.[30] Thus, divorce alters relationships between grandparents and grandchildren in numerous ways, depending on who has custody of the children, how bitter the divorce is, and whether the grandparents are the maternal or paternal grandparents.

Adjustment to Widowhood

Eventually one partner in every surviving marriage faces widowhood. Of the more than 22 million people in the United States who are 65 years or older, almost one-half of the women and one-fifth of the men have lost their marital partners. With each additional year beyond age 65, the risk of having one's life partner die becomes greater. Since women, on the average, live almost 10 years longer than men, most of the widowed are women. There are four times as many widows as widowers.

The amount of warning that people get of impending widowhood varies greatly. In some instances, the partner is felled swiftly with no warning at all. When death occurs suddenly, personal grief may be compounded by lack of preparation. Some older women, for instance, have never taken any responsibility for the family finances. When their husbands die, they may not know what kind of life insurance was held, where financial records were kept, or even how to write a check.

In other cases, a terminal illness may last

for several months, allowing for some grief to occur in preparation for death and also for some real plans to be made to cope with the impending loss. In still other instances, death follows a long, lingering illness during which there is a great burden of physical care as well as high financial cost. Grief then becomes tempered by the strain of dealing with prolonged illness. The following quote from one study of widowhood indicates the tremendous psychological and emotional costs that are incurred by the surviving spouse and by other family members:

> We had a very hard time. My daughter and I had to help him with everything at the end—eating and everything. My daughter helped so much with him—she washed him, cleaned him. The nurses came every day but they were often in a rush so they often used to ask my daughter to take over. She would do everything.[31]

Regardless of the medical circumstances, widowhood is initially a devastating blow for most people. Several authors have described distinct phases of bereavement. It typically begins with shock, sometimes accompanied by denial of the death. The next stage is a period of intense grief, involving a searching for the lost person, leading to depression and apathy as the loss is accepted. The conflict in adjusting to the death of a close person is accompanied by the need to adapt to change but also to restore the past. The final stage is one of reorganization and of beginning again. Family and friends initally offer comfort to a bereaved widow or widower, but eventually the individual is left alone to cope with the process of readjustment.

A woman's grief may be compounded by the loss of some of her departed husband's retirement income, which may make her adjustment difficult on a practical, as well as an emotional, level. However, within a short time there are forces working to relieve her distress. The days of most older women were spent in caring for the home, in cooking, cleaning, and doing laundry—mundane tasks perhaps but chores that still shaped her existence. After her husband's death, these same tasks must still be performed, and these necessities help to reinstill a sense of order into her life. Chances are also high that at least some children and grandchildren live nearby, so she may rely upon family for support and continue to play the role of grandmother. Further, many new widows discover that their plight is shared by others, and it is relatively easy to gain membership into an informal support group of other widows.

The situation for widowers is more complex. Some research suggests that the emotional devastation experienced by men who lost their wives is often accompanied by extreme unreadiness for the role of widower. Many older men are almost totally dependent on their wives for even the simplest household chores, and widowed men who do not know how to cook may skip meals or eat poorly. The problems faced by older widowers are further compounded by the traditional definition of the man's role in society. Men are supposed to be independent and able to look after themselves. The masculine stereotype makes no provision for men to be old, infirm, and unable to cope. Thus, widowers are less likely than widows to receive financial support from children and are more likely to live alone.[32] On the other hand, older men are in scarce supply, and this makes them a valuable commodity. They are much more likely to remarry after widowhood than women, so the problems they face may be short-lived.

As more women enter old age with some labor force experience, and as more men share in household tasks throughout their lives, the problems of widowhood may change. The widowed of the future are likely to be quite different than those of the present.

SOCIOLOGICAL LEVEL

Ageism and Its Consequences

According to Jack and William Levin, authors of the book, *Ageism: Prejudice and Discrimination Against the Elderly:*

> For decades, there has been widespread acceptance of negative stereotypes about the aged involving references to their intellectual decline, conservatism, sexual decline, lack of productivity, and preference for disengagement. Though most such images are based on half-truths or outright falsities, they continue to be used to justify the maltreatment of the aged by American society.[33]

How is ageism perpetuated today within American culture? One way is through "common sense" observations. Everyday expressions such as "you can't teach an old dog new tricks" reflect a view that is negative and inconsistent with scientific knowledge. Yet these expressions are symptomatic of more deep-seated beliefs that are transmitted through a more all-encompassing process of socialization. "Ageism," according to the Levins, "is a cultural phenomenon whose acceptance is longstanding and crosscuts differences in age, region and social class. Ageism is passed from generation to generation by means of socialization. Children very early come to recognize age differences and to evaluate others based on their age."[34]

The mass media also socialize members of society to accept negative age stereotypes of older people. Virtually all analyses of the content of television programming show underrepresentation of older people in comparison to their numbers in the total population. For example, one study found that elderly prime-time TV characters comprised only about one-half their share in the general population.[35] Further, in many cases they were portrayed in a negative fashion. In another study only about 40 percent of older male and 10 percent of older female characters could be described in positive terms such as "good," "happy," or "successful." The number and proportion of males playing "bad guys" increased with age.[36]

Television is not the only mass medium that may perpetuate stereotypes about old people. Researchers have examined aging in literature, humor, letters to "Dear Abby," periodicals, advertising, poetry, and newspapers. Unfortunately, the cumulative picture painted of the elderly is one framed by ageism.

A study conducted by the National Council on Aging, which was published as a monograph entitled *The Myth and Reality of Aging,* indicated that these negative stereotypes are quite pervasive in society. The report was based on the results of an extensive poll conducted by the Harris organization, touching on many aspects of what it means to be old. Participants in the study were men and women of all ages, and the results are very revealing in terms of helping us to understand how most people in our society perceive aging.

Findings from the Harris poll confirm the idea that people have negative expectations of old age. However, in reality most older people do not conform to these stereotypes. Respondents were given a list of problems and asked if they thought most people over sixty-five had these problems. Then older people themselves were asked if they personally experienced these problems. A comparison between the problems attributed to "most people over sixty-five" by the public at large and the problems actually experienced personally by older people indicates the extent to which the public has a distorted view of what it is like to grow old. As shown in Table 7.4, in most cases, the discrepancy was enormous. What is striking in these findings is that people over sixty-five substantially agreed with those younger that these were problems for "most people over sixty-five." However, they did not see it as a personal problem. They considered themselves exceptions! Thus, both older and younger people have accepted what is apparently an inaccurate negative stereotype.

Age Discrimination in the Work World

One of the more concrete effects of ageism as a negative cultural evaluation of the aged is direct discrimination against both middle-aged and older people in the labor force. Typical ways that employers avoid hiring the older person are to declare that he or she is "overqualified," "unskilled," less in need of a job compared to a younger applicant, or less reliable and flexible. Discrimination on the basis of age is also blamed on the older worker's ill health, lack of education, or technologically obsolete skills. However, employment studies of older workers show that their attendance on the job is likely to be better than that of younger persons. Studies also show that older workers are less likely to change jobs and that their productivity compares favorably with that of younger workers in both blue-collar and white-collar occupations.[37]

Age discrimination in work leads to unemployment in later life, a problem that can have significant consequences for economic security in old age. Although rates of unemployment are lower for workers over age forty-five than for younger workers, the long-term consequences are often more serious. Older workers who become unemployed have greater difficulty in finding another job and thus have longer periods of unemployment. When they do find other work, they are likely to experience downward mobility in terms of occupation. The case history of one older unemployed man illustrates the negative conse-

Table 7.4 Problems That People Sixty-Five and Over Experience Compared with Problems Attributed to Them by the Public

	VERY SERIOUS PROBLEMS THAT THE ELDERLY EXPERIENCE	VERY SERIOUS PROBLEMS ATTRIBUTED TO MOST ELDERLY BY THE PUBLIC	NET DIFFERENCE
Fear of crime	23%	50%	+27%
Poor health	21	51	+30
Not having enough money to live on	15	62	+47
Loneliness	12	60	+48
Not having enough medical care	10	44	+34
Not having enough education	8	20	+12
Not having enough to do to keep busy	6	37	+31
Not having enough friends	5	28	+23
Not having enough job opportunities	5	45	+40
Poor housing	4	35	+31
Not having enough clothing	3	16	+13

Source: Louis Harris and Associates, *The Myth and Reality of Aging* (Washington, D.C.: National Council on the Aging, Inc., 1975), p. 31.

While many older women may knit sweaters for their grandchildren, others engage in a variety of surprising activities.

(Cary Wolinsky/Stock, Boston)

quences that can result from later life unemployment:

A 50-year-old man with a high school education lost his managerial position in an electrical machinery firm where he had been employed for 17 years. His annual earnings prior to his separation, which occurred between 1969 and 1971, were $13,000. In . . . 1971 this man reported 44 weeks of unemployment during the preceding 12 months but was then working as a sales clerk in a retail store. In 1973 he was doing clerical work for a farm machinery store, where his annual earnings were $8,500. Two years later he was unemployed and had worked only 22 weeks in the previous year, as a farm manager with earnings of $4,500. By . . . 1976 he had apparently given up; after 42 weeks of unemployment during the preceding 12 months he finally ceased looking for work. By this time his health, which had deteriorated over the preceding three years, prevented him from working entirely.[38]

In one sense, this man was fortunate, because his health problems may have made him eligible for disability benefits. Other older workers who become unemployed may use up their unemployment benefits and have no other recourse for financial support.

In 1967 the Age Discrimination in Employment Act was passed, prohibiting discrimination in employment for those aged forty to sixty-five, and in 1978 the protected age was extended to seventy. Although unevenly and often inadequately enforced, this act did provide some recourse for individuals who felt they were turned down for a job because they were too old. In a landmark case in 1971 the U.S. Court of Appeals ordered back wages for a 47-year-old woman who was refused employment:

Charges were first filed after a Labor Department investigation revealed that the employer, First Federal Savings and Loan Association . . . had noted on the woman's job application that she was "too old for teller." First Federal claimed its personnel interviewer had considered the job too strenuous for the woman because she was overweight; the Labor Department, however, alleged the woman was turned down because of her age, since the bank had considered hiring a younger girl of the same height but weighing twenty pounds more. The appeals court upheld the Labor Department's contention.[39]

Still, enforcement of this law is difficult, and there are numerous cases pending that never reach the courts. Of those who do manage to stay employed into their sixties, 85 percent will face mandatory retirement and at least 30 percent of these would like to continue working. Thus, older people face serious discrimination in the work force.[40]

Age Segregation and Housing for the Aged

In some instances by choice, in others as a matter of necessity, many older people live in age-segregated environments. Researchers have argued about whether age-segregated housing has positive or negative effects. Studies done in public housing projects or private retirement communities generally find that older people benefit from these environments. They are likely to enjoy better health, to have higher life expectancy, and to demonstrate higher levels of life satisfaction than do comparison groups who do not reside in housing for the aged.[41]

On the other hand, those who live in single room occupancy (SRO) hotels and rooming houses that are common in the blighted sections of cities do not fare so well. In one study of such a welfare hotel, isolation was the dominant feature. Most of the elderly residents avoided each other, a reflection of their desire for privacy and autonomy but also symbolic of their limited resources. The prime source of income for these SRO residents involved "hustling"—scavenging, peddling, pushing drugs, or shoplifting. Most residents had to go outside the hotel for food and routine health needs, and muggings in the area were frequent. Locked into this arrangement by poverty, ill health, and a desire to maintain independence, many of these older people planned to die there.[42]

Although research has tended to concentrate on those who live in age-segregated housing, in fact, approximately 90 percent of all people over age sixty-five live in age-integrated housing, mostly in their own homes. Unfortunately, much of the housing is substandard or deteriorating, which is problematic to the degree that reduced income and/or decline in physical strength preclude repairs necessary to offset this deterioration.[43]

The Impact of Industrialization and Population Aging

Many of the problems that are associated with aging today did not exist in the past. This is because the proportion of older people was substantially smaller, and they occupied an important position in society. Since the colonial era, massive structural changes that have occurred in the larger society have also affected the position of the aged.

In speaking of the past, we have to understand that until the late nineteenth century the American population was astonishingly youthful, certainly much younger than it is today. The median age of Americans in 1980 was over thirty; in 1790 it was barely sixteen.[44] Sixteen! That means that half the population was below that age.

The youthfulness of early American society can be attributed to high fertility—families produced large numbers of children. However, high mortality also meant that many of these children never reached adulthood. Largely because of the high death rates of infants and children, life expectancy was only thirty-eight. Few Americans survived to an advanced age. Less than 1 percent were sixty-five or older, compared to more than 11 percent today.

Literary evidence indicates that both deference and respect were associated with old age. As Samuel Dexter wrote in 1738:

> The honor we owe our parents and ancestors obligeth us to attend to that which our fathers have told us. Let us endeavor to recover that spirit of family government and authority which our fathers had; they ruled their houses well, and had their households in good subjection; children and servants knew their places and kept their distances.[45]

Older men maintained their authority in the family because they retained both possession and control of their land for a very long time—nearly to the end of their lives. In a largely agricultural society, this meant that children remained economic dependents long after they reached physical maturity. The dependency of youth gave older people a favored position within the extended family. Further, the goods that were made were produced in the household, not in factories. Both the manufacturing of crafts and farm work were occupations that older people could continue, long after they reached age sixty-five.

Of course, not all older people were revered or cared for securely within an extended family unit. Because of high mortality, some had no children left by the time they reached old age, while others who had never married were also left alone. Since there was no formal retirement system, like Social Security, the only source of economic support for the indigent aged was the poor law, an institution under which people could apply for relief through local authorities. Sometimes the poor law was lenient, and older people received a sufficient sum to survive, but often they received only a pittance, or, worse, were forced to enter the local almshouse.[46]

Beginning in the nineteenth century, our population began to age. The aging of a population is indicated by an increase in the median age and by a larger proportion of older persons. Table 7.5 shows the increased proportion of older people in the United States since the turn of the century.

Population aging is reflected in a changed age structure of a society. As Figure 7.1 shows, a "young" society has a pyramid-like shape, since most of the population is concentrated in the younger age groups. A society with an "old" age structure, in contrast, looks more like a rectangle. In general, less-developed nations tend to have a young age structure, as our country did earlier in our history, while industrialized nations exhibit the rectangular shape.[47]

What causes the age structure of a society to change? For the world as a whole, the factors that influence the age structure are fertility and mortality. For any single nation, migration may also be involved in the

Table 7.5 Population Age Sixty-five and Over in the United States, 1900–1980 (with projections)

YEAR	NUMBER (IN THOUSANDS)	PERCENT OF TOTAL
1900	3,099	4.1
1910	3,986	4.3
1920	4,929	4.7
1930	6,705	5.4
1940	9,031	6.8
1950	12,397	8.2
1960	16,679	9.2
1970	20,177	9.9
1980	25,551	11.3

Source: U.S. Department of Commerce, Bureau of the Census, *Current Population Reports* (Washington, D.C.: U.S. Government Printing Office, 1982), p. 121.

Figure 7.1 Population Pyramids for the United States, 1910 and 1970

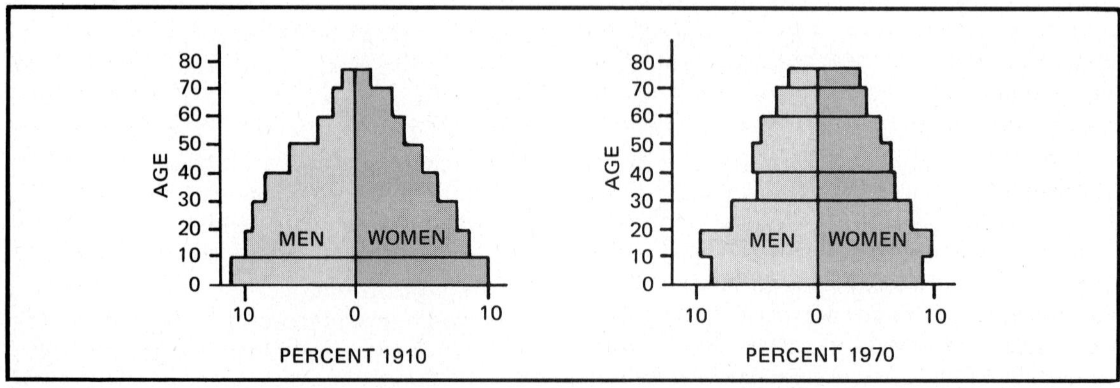

The United States in 1910 was a "young society," as reflected in its pyramid-shaped age structure, with most people in the younger age categories. By 1970 the United States looked more like an "old society" with a more rectangular-shaped age structure (people more equally distributed among the age categories).

Source: U.S. Bureau of the Census, General Population Characteristics, Final Report PC(1)-B1 United States Summary (U.S. Government Printing Office, 1972), p. 1-276.

aging of the population. The most important factor is a decline in fertility. A decrease in the birth rate decreases the number of young people and, therefore, increases the proportion of old. A decrease in the death rate may also affect the age structure of a society, depending upon the ages at which such mortality decreases occur. If mortality levels are reduced equally for everyone, then the age structure will remain the same. Most typically, mortality rates have been reduced for infants and young children first, leading to an immediate increase in the proportion of the young. However, this trend is usually accompanied by increases in life expectancy at later stages of the life cycle as well, contributing in the long run to an increase in the proportion of older people. When reduced mortality is combined with lower fertility, then the net result is an aging of the population.[48]

On a world-wide basis, population aging has been associated with industrialization. The reasons why are complex and have been the subject of numerous scholarly debates among demographers (those who study population processes). For our purposes, it is only necessary to note that this is true. However, it is important to understand more about industrialization, for the broad societal changes associated with economic change also have an impact on the lives of older people.

Prior to industrialization, we were a largely agricultural nation. Most people were employed in agricultural pursuits, as farmers or farm laborers. This meant that in later life, people could gradually reduce their work efforts, turning over portions of the farm to their children to run. Formal retirement was virtually unknown, and nonfarmers often performed part-time work, mowing grass, hauling grist to the mill, or doing minor repair work.[49]

As our nation industrialized, the number of people employed in agriculture declined, and young people increasingly found work in the burgeoning factories of the Northeast. The rise of factory production had important implications for the work and family life of older people. One aspect of the changing nature of work was that older farmers could no longer pass their skills on to their children since their children were engaged in new occupations for which the older generation was not trained.[50] Some researchers believe this contributed to a decline in the status of the aged.

Associated with the rise of factory production was the decrease in the demand for highly skilled workers who could make objects by hand. As factories speeded up the production process, the skills of older craftsmen became increasingly outmoded.[51] All of these changes led to increased retirement for older workers who were untrained for the new jobs and whose skills were less useful in a rapidly changing society.

PART III: RESPONSES

National, state, and local governments, as well as private organizations, have developed numerous programs to meet the diverse needs of the elderly. Some of these programs have been quite effective, while others have left many needs unmet.

Social Support Systems

Even though some older people are isolated and neglected, this is not the situation for most. Rather the majority of older people are embedded in social support networks made up of family and friends who provide services and emotional and financial support on an informal basis. For example, one study found that more than half of the older people interviewed had between eleven and forty people available to help them in their daily lives.[52] Further, this support is not one-sided; rather elderly people, for the most part, are engaged in reciprocal patterns of interaction in which they give as much as they receive. In fact, in friendship networks, the reciprocity of interactions is one of the central bonds. For example, in another study an eighty-nine-year-old widow named Louise managed to live independently in spite of severe health problems because of her reciprocal friendship network. She "brings cookies to one of the women on the floor, makes lunch for her visiting lady friends, and recently brought another floor neighbor part of the cake she had baked. She keeps in contact with her friends through the telephone and sending cards and handmade gifts on special occasions."[53] Another woman in the same study relied on friends to take her to church, take her grocery shopping, bring occasional gifts of food, and provide transportation. The extensiveness of her friendship network allowed her to distribute her dependence needs among them so that no one felt too burdened.[54]

Children also perform a variety of services, and older parents reciprocate through babysitting, loaning money, and helping in other ways. However, the relationship tends to become more one-sided when the elderly parent undergoes a health crisis. After a major illness, the child, usually a daughter, is likely to take on the role of caretaker, a transition which is often described as "role reversal." This can be stressful for the parent, who may become depressed about the loss of his or her independence and concerned about the decline in health. For example, one daughter tried to protect her mother from her own anxiety regarding her forgetfulness after she had undergone a stroke: "If there are plans that she's going someplace—there's a wedding or this or that—I tell her the date and everything. She gets very nervous that she's not going to remember it, even if I write it down. So I try not to tell her the day before because she gets very nervous about it. . . ."[55]

Children also experience stress, not only

in dealing with the new relationship to a parent but also because of the very real burdens on time and energy. For example, one woman visited her father in a nursing home, which was a half-hour drive away, for an hour four to five times a week even though she had a full-time job, two preschool children, and serious health problems of her own.[56] In spite of the heavy responsibilities children undertook, most did not portray themselves as burdened.

Now that significant numbers of middle-aged women are in the work world, the problems faced by the women described above are likely to multiply. Most studies indicate that children do feel a sense of responsibility for their aging parents and that family caretaking is one societal response that is quite common.[57] We will need to provide more formal support services to help families cope with these problems in order to ease the burden on middle-aged women who are increasingly likely to be pulled in many directions as dependent children, aging parents, and full-time jobs vie for their time and energy.

Political Involvement of the Elderly

Many older people take an active political role in working to benefit themselves and others. One reason why they are often successful when they mobilize politically is because, as a group, they tend to have high voting rates. Voting participation is lowest among those under twenty-five; it rapidly increases during the middle-age groups (fifty-five to sixty-four) and then gradually drops off.[58]

Older people do not usually vote on the basis of age-related issues. Rather they vote on the basis of income, occupation, education, or religion. However, when an age-based issue does arise,they have mobilized quite effectively. For example, in one area of Massachusetts: "Senior citizens. . . ., credited by some with killing the proposal for a new high school two years ago, this year waged a successful campaign to gain a Dial-A-Ride taxi service for the elderly."[59]

Much of this political activism takes place through age-based organizations. At present about ten groups are involved in national politics, more or less exclusively on behalf of the elderly. These include the National Council on Aging, the National Retired Teachers Association, and the National Caucus on the Black Aged, as well as the Gray Panthers, who have broader-based concerns than just those related to age.

Political groups such as the Gray Panthers are likely to grow increasingly active in coming years.
(Jean-Marie Simon/Taurus)

Public officials have begun to recognize the credentials of these groups, and they are increasingly being included in national policy processes.

Governmental Responses

As a result of the political activism of older people, as well as their increased needs, the number of formal services available to the aged have expanded enormously in the past twenty years.

The Older Americans Act

In 1965 the Older Americans Act, the single federal social-service statute designed specifically for the aged, was passed. The act established the Administration on Aging within the federal government, required states to establish state units on aging, and authorized state and community social-service programs. Among the numerous services funded under the Older Americans Act were homemaker services, transportation, congregate meals, nutrition education and counseling, and a foster grandparent program.[60]

Senior Centers

Under the stimulus of the Older Americans Act most communities have developed a variety of programs to help healthy older people remain active and involved in community life. Senior centers provide numerous services and activities, including music, handwork, educational programs, and general socializing. A few centers have professional staff members for such purposes. Most senior centers also attempt to participate in activities of the larger community by engaging in community-service projects, which are most often unpaid volunteer services. Many older people wish to be of use to the community and are willing to contribute their time and effort.

A problem is that only a tiny proportion (1 to 5 percent) of the older population frequents senior centers in most communities. Of course, many old people cannot attend because of transportation difficulties, disability, poor health, and so on. Yet even in those communities where an all-out effort to bring people in has been made, only a small percentage (usually less than 15 percent) of the older population has even set foot in senior centers, much less taken an active part in the program.

Foster Grandparents

The Foster Grandparent Program is an employment project designed specifically to provide employment for older workers. Foster Grandparents work twenty hours a week at the minimum wage in various child-care institutions. The program gives the older person both the satisfaction of providing a needed service and a needed income supplement. Despite the success of the program, it generally has a low priority for local funds and is kept alive only by federal support.

Budget Reductions

It is not only the Foster Grandparent Program that is threatened with a loss of funds. Federal funding for Older Americans Act expenditures have decreased significantly under the Reagan administration, from 993 million in 1981 to only 758 million in 1983. Other programs serving the aged have also experienced significant budget reductions.[61] Further, state and local governments, which are expected to pick up the costs of funding these programs through their own budgets, have experienced diminished revenues due to cuts in individual and corporate taxes. Thus, most states are unable to continue to fund these programs for the aged at the same level, and the response of many has been to reduce available social services for older people.[62]

The National Institute on Aging

For over forty years, advocates of biomedical, social, and behavioral research on aging attempted to place the issue of aging research on the public agenda of the nation. Initially, scientific inquiry into biomedical research issues and concerns about an increasing elderly population stimulated interest in the idea of a research center on aging. Later, changing social attitudes and issues surrounding the elderly gave significance to research on aging, as did the growth of age-based organizations and the recognition politicians gave to the potential of "gray power."[63]

Located within the National Institute of Health, the National Institute on Aging (NIA) supports a wide range of research, including health-related topics such as nutrition, Alzheimer's disease, bio-markers of aging, the impact of physical exercise on improving functioning—as well as more sociological topics such as the impact of an aging population on society, widowhood, and retirement. The founding of NIA represented a milestone in the development of gerontology as a scientific discipline and in the definition of aging research.

Social Security

The expansion of social services has been helpful in fulfilling the needs of older people. However, the most important government program has been Social Security, which helps to meet economic needs in later life.

Historical Background

At the dawn of the twentieth century there were almost no formal sources of economic aid for older people. Those forced to withdraw from active labor had only family, friends, charity, or, in the last resort, the poor law to rely upon. Aside from a few scattered pension programs for teachers, pension benefits paid by the federal government for veterans, and a few municipal programs, the government provided no source of old age security.[64]

In the early years of the century, several states began to investigate the feasibility of state pensions for the aged. In 1911 Arizona became the first state to establish an old age assistance plan but it was subsequently declared unconstitutional. Other states gradually followed, and by 1930 the majority of states had enacted old age pension laws. Most were ineffectual, because they were not mandatory, and only granted counties the right to pay out pensions to needy older people. If the county refused to tax itself for this purpose, then the aged had no recourse. In fact, few older people actually received any pensions under these laws.[65]

The Social Security Act of 1935

The onset of the Depression meant a crisis for those few state pensions that actually were in operation, and it soon became apparent that the federal government would have to intervene in the social welfare system. In 1935 after considerable debate in both houses of Congress, the Social Security Act was passed. The Social Security Act of 1935 was actually composed of two programs, although today most people are familiar with only one aspect of that act. First, there was an old age insurance title, funded by payroll taxes collected jointly from the employer and the employee. However, many older people during the Depression needed income immediately, and the insurance concept was based on the idea that you earned the right to receive an income in old age by contributions you made during your working life. This left many people who had not had the opportunity to contribute to the system with no source of income. The solution of policymakers was to add a second component to the program called old age assistance. Old age assistance was a joint federal-state program that guaranteed immediate relief to the needy aged. For years the two systems coexisted, and in fact, it was not until 1954 that more older people began receiving old age insurance than old age assistance.[66]

Financial Aspects

The original old age insurance program required a tax of 1 percent on the first $3,000 earned. Since that time the system has been expanded enormously to include dependents of workers, the disabled, and to finance Medicare. In order to fund these new programs, both the amount of taxable income and the percent of the tax have increased. In 1984 each worker paid 6.7 percent on the first $37,500 earned with employers contributing equal amounts.

The problem with financing old age insurance by this method is that it places a very heavy burden on low-income families. Over half the population pays more in payroll taxes than it does in federal income taxes. Even the very poorest, who have incomes so low that they pay no federal taxes, contribute a comparatively large proportion of their income in terms of the payroll tax. One solution that has been proposed to relieve the burden on workers is to take some of the money needed to finance Social Security out of general revenues, that is, out of the portion of the federal budget that is derived from income and corporate taxes. In fact, this was a solution supported by some of the original members of the committee who wrote the Social Security Act in 1935 and who anticipated a crisis by 1965.[67] However, the decision at that time was to only fund the system through payroll taxes, and since 1935 no one has been willing seriously to consider alternative sources of funding.

Major changes in the system were made in the early 1970s that reduced the problem of old age poverty significantly but also made the system much more costly. In 1972 benefit levels were increased substantially. This was not, by any means, the first time that benefits were raised, but in that year they were raised by a significant amount. The minimum benefit was increased by 54 percent and the maximum by 66 percent. However, between 1970 and 1973 the consumer price index rose by 23 percent, so that older people lost at least half of the gains they received.

The goal of Social Security is to replace a portion of a worker's preretirement wages up to a maximum percentage. In order to make income levels more equitable, the system provides a greater replacement of preretirement wages for low-income earners than for high-income earners. However, as Table 7.6 illustrates, the replacement ratios in the United States are not as generous as they are in some other western nations. In Sweden, for example, low-income workers in one-earner families receive a pension that is 110 percent of their preretirement income. Poor people in Sweden who retire actually *increase* their income. In contrast, in the United States low-income, single-earner families receive only 82 percent of their preretirement income. High-income workers also recieve significantly less back, but most people in this category have other sources of retirement income.

These replacement ratios are somewhat misleading, because they only apply to workers who receive their initial pensions at age sixty-five. A worker's benefits are reduced by up to 20 percent and his dependent's supplement by up to 25 percent if the worker applies for the initial benefit before reaching age sixty-five. In 1980, about 60 percent of all retired workers received Social Security benefits before age sixty-five.[68]

Table 7.6 Replacement Ratios for Low-, Medium-, and High-Income Earners in Canada, the United States, and Sweden, 1980.

	EARNINGS LEVEL BEFORE RETIREMENT		
	LOW	MEDIUM	HIGH
A. One-Earner Couples			
Canada			
a) With guaranteed income supplement	101	54	—
b) Without guaranteed income supplement	78	46	23
Sweden	110	80	54
United States	82	61	35
B. Single Earners and Two-Earner Couples			
Canada			
a) With guaranteed income supplement	59	33	—
b) Without guaranteed income supplement	52	30	15
Sweden	70	60	43
United States	56	41	22

Source: John Myles, *Old Age in the Welfare State* (Boston: Little Brown, 1984), p. 56.

Who retires early? Is it the more affluent people who, desiring more leisure time, move into luxurious retirement homes and travel around the world on cruise ships? Unfortunately, that portrait of the early retiree is inaccurate. Rather those who retire early are more likely to be in poor health, to have been unemployed for at least three years prior to retiring, and to be a member of a minority group.[69] Early retirement, for most older people, is not a matter of individual choice. Early retirees are forced out of the labor force due to poor health and unemployment. They take early and thus lower retirement benefits because they have no other source of income.

In the late 1970s fears arose that the Social Security system was going broke and might not survive. After much hysteria, and in the midst of tremendous publicity, the system underwent further revisions. Levels of taxation were increased, cost of living increases were delayed, and the age of eligibility for benefits was raised to sixty-seven for those who will reach old age in the twenty-first century. Not a very dramatic or even satisfactory solution in the minds of many observers, but one that mitigated public uncertainty and that generated additional revenues in the traditional way.

In spite of these recent improvements, we still have older people living below poverty level. In 1981, 93 percent of all people 65 and older were covered by or drawing annuities from Social Security.[70] However, policy, as we have seen, fixes the level of those benefits below poverty level for some people. As Table 7.7 shows, those older people who are living below poverty level receive most of their income from Social Security. To the extent that older people are poor, it is their retirement incomes that make them poor.

Table 7.7 Source of Income for People Aged Sixty-five and Over Living Below Poverty Level

Income Source	AGED LIVING ALONE* % RECEIVING INCOME FROM SOURCE		AGED FAMILY HEAD % RECEIVING INCOME FROM SOURCE	
	From Source	% of Income	From Source	% of Income
SS (Social Security)	88	77	84	67
SSI (Supplemental Security Income)	28	12	33	13
Dividends, Interest, Rents	37	4	31	3
Private Pensions	6	2	8	3
Earnings	5	1	25	10
Other Public Assistance	4	1	9	3
Other Programs	8	3	6	2
Number of Households	2.4 million		800,000	

*Or with nonrelatives
Source: *Social Security Bulletin, Annual Statistical Supplement* (Washington, D.C.: U.S. Government Printing Office, 1982), p. 136.

Private Pensions

Historical Development

The first private pension plans were introduced into American industry by the railroad and express companies in 1875, and since that time private pension funds have continued to grow. In 1940 only about 12 percent of the labor force was covered by private pensions, but by 1980 approximately 44 percent of wage-and-salaried workers in private industry received some type of job-specific pension, separate from Social Security.[71]

In the early years, pension programs were primarily used by employers as a means of keeping workers on the job. This was because the majority of company pension plans were discretionary, meaning that an employer had a moral rather than a legal obligation to pay the pension to the retired employee. Employees with pension benefits would hesitate to leave an employer, even if they were dissatisfied with wages, because then they would lose all of their pension benefits. Sometimes pensions were used by employers as a way to break up strikes. For example, in 1916 the weaving enterprise of Crompton and Knowles installed a liberal pension plan in the midst of a strike at their Worcester, Massachusetts and Providence, Rhode Island plants and announced that former employees would be given full credit for prior service if they returned to work.[72] Other companies threatened striking older workers with the loss of their pension if they refused to return to work as scabs.

Most early private pension plans were notoriously unstable and insufficiently funded, making them highly vulnerable during economic recessions. During the Depression of the 1930s, numerous companies went bankrupt, leaving their older employees with no protection against the vicissitudes of old age. However, these uncertainties in private pension funds continued long after the economy had stabilized. A 1972 study based on the examination of data from the Social Security Administration's "Retirement History Study" found that although 45 percent of recent retirees were covered by a pension on their longest or most recent job, 28 percent of the men and 45 percent of the women had never received a pension.[73]

In 1974 Congress passed the Employee Retirement Income Security Act (ERISA), which established minimum standards for regulating and supervising pension programs. The new regulations provided more protection for workers by guaranteeing that they would receive the pension benefits they had earned, and they also allowed workers to transfer pension benefits from one company to another. ERISA also required employers to allow all employees over the age of twenty-five to participate in a pension plan if they worked for the employer for one year. In addition, the act allowed employees in firms not covered by pension plans to establish their own Individual Retirement Accounts (IRAs), which are exempt from federal income taxes. While IRAs have been beneficial in allowing workers to save to their retirement with no tax penalty, they still tend to benefit the middle class more than the poor who need them most, since most low-income people do not have extra funds available to establish IRAs.

Because most private pensions have been designed as supplements to Social Security and personal savings, they tend to be quite low. Of 977 pension plans studied by the Bureau of Labor Statistics in the late 1970s, the median annual benefit for a male earner after 30 years of service was $2,720; a comparable female would receive $2,046; constituting a replacement ratio of 22 percent for men and 28 percent for women.[74] Those who are eligible for both a private pension and Social Security benefits are better off than those who rely solely on Social Security, but their pensions certainly do not make them wealthy.

National Health Insurance

The major step that has been taken toward improving health care occurred in 1965 when, after more than thirty years of strong opposition from the American Medical Association, a program of national health insurance for the aged was finally passed. There were two main components to this program, Medicare and Medicaid. Medicare, itself, has two different programs. Part A is a compulsory hospital insurance plan that primarily covers a bed patient in a hospital. Medicare will help pay covered services for a patient for up to 90 days of in-hospital care, for up to 100 days of extended care in a skilled nursing facility, and for up to 100 home health visits in a given benefit period. Part A also pays for such services as a semiprivate room, including meals and a special diet, regular nursing services, lab tests, drugs furnished by the hospital, and medical supplies and appliances furnished by the hospital.

Part B of Medicare is a voluntary medical insurance program, and an individual must pay a monthly premium in order to be eligible for coverage. Part B pays for a broad array of outpatient hospital services, doctors' services, home health benefits, and other medical supplies. Neither Part A nor Part B, however, pays for such things as routine physical examinations, foot care, eye or hearing examinations, eyeglasses, prescription drugs, false teeth, or full-time nursing care.[75] Medicare, then, leaves totally uncovered many major expenses of the aged, for it is not uncommon for an older person to spend $100 a month on prescription drugs alone.

Medicaid, in contrast, is not solely for the aged; rather it is a combined federal-state program of health care insurance that serves all of the indigent. Although older people comprise only about 15 percent of the Medicaid beneficiaries, they receive about one-third of its benefits, largely for nursing home care.

Since Medicaid (but not Medicare, except under limited conditions) does cover the costs of institutional care for the aged, it has served as a stimulus to the nursing home industry. Between 1963 and 1973 the number of nursing home beds increased by more than 100 percent.[76] In 1979 Medicare and Medicaid together contributed 52 percent of the nursing home bill in the United States, with most coming from Medicaid, and by 1980 40 percent of Medicaid payments went to the nursing home industry.[77] Medicaid further fosters institutionalization of the aged poor in that many services are only paid for if they are provided in an old age institution. In 1979 less than 1 percent of Medicaid outlays went for home health care services.[78]

Another problem with Medicaid is the widespread fraud and abuse that has been associated with it. Billings for clinical laboratory charges and prescribed medicines are often inflated, and charges reflect services that have been carried out only in part or not at all. For example, Medicaid is often billed by nursing homes for higher-priced, brand-name drugs, when lower-cost generic drugs are actually prescribed and used. Physicians sometimes misrepresent the kind of care they administer, so that Medicaid may be billed for 50 to 100 patients who were treated by the same physician in a single day. In fact, the patient received only a cursory visit and not an examination. These abuses have contributed to higher costs and resulting reductions in coverage.[79]

What is needed is a national form of health insurance that could effectively coordinate and regulate the disparate programs of economic support for health care. However, there is a great deal of political opposition to nationalized health care, and it seems unlikely to become a reality in the near future. If anything, we can expect further reductions in the services presently available due to the fiscal crisis created by a vastly mismanaged system.

Institutionalization

It is quite possible that improvements in medical care for the aged, specifically including increased emphasis on rehabilitative care in the community, could decrease the number of people who need to be institutionalized. However, the long-term trend over the past century, a trend that has accelerated in the past few decades, had been in the opposite direction, towards increased use of institutions as places of care for the aged. The fact that we, as a nation, are placing more older people in nursing homes means that we need to become increasingly vigilant about both the effects of institutionalization on the individual and the existing conditions in nursing homes.

Who gets institutionalized? The "typical" nursing home resident is white, female, widowed, aged seventy-nine, and has lived in an institution for 2.6 years.[80] The disproportionate number of elderly women in nursing homes (72 percent of the total population) reflects their predominance in the older population and the fact that greater life expectancy means that there are considerably more women over age seventy-five than men.

Nonwhites constitute only about 5 percent of the institutionalized elderly population. Several explanations have been posed regarding the low rate of institutionalization among minorities. One is that elderly nonwhites are more likely to reside in southern states where rates of institutionalization are low in general.[81] Others have argued that older minorities are denied access to nursing home care that they may require because of prejudice and discrimination, and that they are institutionalized in other types of facilities instead. For example, one study demonstrated that elderly blacks are more likely than whites to be found in state mental hospitals.[82]

The decision to institutionalize an older person is one that should be made with care. Most older people dread entering a nursing home, viewing it as a prelude to death. Their concerns are somewhat justified, for one-third of all nursing home patients die within their first year.[83] The average length of stay in a nursing home is 1.1 years. This is partly because very ill people enter nursing homes. However, illnesses are sometimes exacerbated by the treatment people receive once they are institutionalized. The following example illustrates how the emotional shock of institutionalization can increase the vulnerability of the patient to physical illness:

> One 83-year-old depressed lady was placed in a nursing home due to increasing inability to care for herself in her little apartment. . . . She became confused the first night when she was unable to find the bathroom, fell and suffered contusions on her head and arms. She remained awake all night, which disturbed her roommate. In the morning she was seen by a physician who prescribed Librium. Her gait became unsteady and she became confused and mildly disoriented. She thought that she was at home and that strangers had invaded the house and were stealing her possessions. In the afternoon she became agitated and began to abuse her roommate verbally and later physically. The physician was called and over the telephone he prescribed Thorazine. The patient's agitation finally subsided and gave way to psychomotor retardation, withdrawal from others, sullenness, increased time in bed and refusal to eat. Five hours after admission she was unable to be moved out of bed. . . . The patient was noted to be semi-comatose and dehydrated, and her skin was flushed. She was sent to a general hospital where she was found to have bronchopneumonia. She died within 36 hours after admission.[84]

Abuses like the kind reported above are unintentional and result from a lack of sensitivity to the individual. However, there is also, unfortunately, some evidence that intentional abuses do occasionally occur. This is most likely to happen when a nursing home is understaffed and where low-paid and poorly trained aides feel under pressure to get their necessary tasks done. Any patient who increases the work load by being unruly or more difficult faces a greater risk of incurring personal abuse, which might include such behaviors "as pulling a patient's hair, slapping, hitting or kicking, tightening restraining belts so that they cause a patient pain, pinching, or violently shaking a patient, throwing water or food on a pateint and terrorizing a patient by gesture or word."[85]

Many nursing homes have made sincere efforts to provide a high quality of patient care, to have ongoing activities that stimulate patients, and to be responsive to individual needs and desires. Still the process of institutionalization is, in itself, dehumanizing, whether it occurs in a nursing home, a mental hospital, or a prison, and the response of many patients is simply to retreat into their own private worlds.

Although all states have laws providing for the inspection and regulation of the quality of care in nursing homes, many are ineffective in improving institutional care. The reason for their ineffectiveness lies in the fact that the only sanctions that can be brought to bear against homes that violate state codes are license revocations. License revocation is a drastic measure that can have negative consequences for both the local community and for the residents of the nursing home. In most areas, there is a demand for nursing home care and the closing of any home poses serious problems in terms of where the patients go next. Thus, even when a home is determined to be negligent, judges are often reluctant to close a facility, especially when a nursing-home operator claims that deficiencies are being corrected.

While physiological aging is inevitable, some older people are quite capable of keeping up with much younger people. Shown here is two-time Boston Marathon winner Johnny Kelly, who still runs races in his mid-seventies.

(Bob Kalman/The Image Works)

Other problems in improving nursing home care stem from lack of effective public pressure, personal connections between nursing home operators and those responsible for supervising their regulations, which, in some instances, have led to blatant corruption, and general bureaucratic weariness.[86] Some researchers have proposed that facilities be made accountable, not just to state regulatory agencies, but to the community in which they are located. This could only be accomplished by direct community involvement. The problem is that at present there is not enough public knowledge or concern, and a community-based solution would have to involve a high degree of interest and awareness.

Innovations in Long-Term Care

There is another solution that gets away from our tendency to equate the need for long-term care with institutionalization and that is to provide alternative services that help to delay or avoid institutionalization. We have made some strides toward providing home health services that can help to keep people out of nursing homes.

Homemaker Services

One service developed to deal with some of these problems is homemaker-home-health services. Homemakers may help with laundering, shopping for and preparing meals, while home health aides provide such services as taking vital signs, giving baths, and assisting with physical therapy. Homemaker's services are not paid for by Medicare, but home health aides are.

Meal Programs

Another program that has helped to improve the nutrition of older people and to delay entry into nursing homes evolved from the Comprehensive Services Amendment to the Older Americans Act in 1972. This legislation generated a national program for one nutritionally planned hot meal a day five days a week, to people sixty years and over. The emphasis was on the establishment of congregate dining sites for the impoverished and isolated aged. Under this program transportation and escort services to the meal sites are also provided. The act also allowed communities to establish portable meals for the housebound elderly, and in many cities and towns, meals-on-wheels bring daily hot meals to older people who might otherwise have to be institutionalized.

Geriatric Day-Care Centers

A recent trend in the United States has been the development of geriatric day-care centers. Day care is available to older people who have some mental or physical impairment but who can remain in the community if supportive services are available. One type of day-care center is medical day care, which provides daily medical care and supervision either to individuals who may be recovering from acute illness but who no longer need to be hospitalized, or to chronically ill individuals who require continued nursing and other health supports. Another type of day-care center provides social activities for people who do not need health care services but who cannot remain home alone all day unsupervised. In these centers activities such as crafts, reading, and shows keep people busy and active.

Integrating Programs

In most communities services such as day care, meals-on-wheels, and nutrition sites have been available but highly decentralized. One agency is responsible for providing one service, another a different service, and so on. This means that help for the frail elderly has often been fragmented and resources underused. Recently a few communities have tried some innovative programs in which they have put together all available services for the aged under the jurisdiction of one coordinator. The intent has been to reduce the likelihood of institutionalization, as well as the high costs associated with nursing home care, and to increase independence for older people who need some help but who are capable of independent living. For example, the Wisconsin Community Care Organization (CCO) began a project that was funded jointly by the state Medical Assistance plan and a grant from the Kellogg Foundation. CCO sought to provide care for aged and disabled individuals in their own homes who might otherwise have become nursing home residents. Administrators coordinated services already available in the community and found that people who used their programs spent fewer days in the hospital and in nursing homes.[87] While fragmented services seem to have little impact since they tend to be underused, coordinated long-term care services do have the potential to provide alternatives to institutionalization for the frail elderly.

The Future for the Aged

It seems likely that the proportion of elderly persons will increase for a considerable time into the future. Because of the post-World War II Baby Boom, if our birth rate does not change dramatically, we will continue to see a rise in the aged population over the next fifty years. Those born during the Baby Boom will be passing through the postretirement ages between the years 2005 and 2030. The task of supporting and caring for these people will fall upon a relatively small group of adults born after 1965. The child- and youth-oriented economy and culture created by the Baby-Boom kids during the 1950s and 1960s is likely to be repeated in magnitude by an elderly oriented economy in the early decades of the twenty-first century.

In recent years, the public image of a retirement without debt or poverty has improved considerably. In addition, the future will bring an older population with a much higher average level of education, a much smaller proportion of foreign born, and a much smaller proportion who were reared on farms. These changes should reduce much of the current social distance between old people and people reared in different eras.

The prospects also look good for a more flexible definition of retirement. By 1990, some segments of the labor force, especially the service sector, will experience a labor shortage. The reason for this shortage is the decline in the birth rate at this time, which will result in fewer people to fill the jobs. The problem will no doubt be partly solved by allowing capable workers to stay on after the mandatory retirement age.

It is also very likely that older people will become more politically active. Their numbers will increase greatly unless reform in the retirement income system occurs, and this should encourage more political groups such as the Gray Panthers and win a broader base of support for old-age political movements. The older generation's power will also be enhanced by its increased educational achievements and by the greater cultural similarity of its members.

There may well be a shifting upward of the age people technically and legally become old. By 1990, age sixty-five will probably be even more inappropriate than it is today. Based on today's average level of functioning, age seventy-five is a more realistic point of demarcation. Yet sixty-five is so ingrained in our legal system and way of thinking that change can be expected to come only slowly.

The most significant change the future holds is probably in the public image of what it means to be an older adult. In the future, the older population is going to be more active and more visible. Such changes should soften considerably the harsh image many people hold of aging. If we can solve the economic problems, we may find that the social image will take care of itself.

SUMMARY

Part I: The Problem

1. It is not easy to define precisely old age and there is considerable variation from one culture to another in its definition.
2. Some older people in our society are isolated, neglected, and sometimes even abused.
3. Old age is often associated with a series of economic problems.
4. Health and medical care present the aged with a series of difficulties.

Part II. Causes and Consequences

5. The physiology of aging creates a variety of health problems for the aged such as increased chronic illness and Alzheimer's disease.
6. A variety of role transitions later in life cause problems for the aged. Among these role transitions are adjustment to retirement, changes in family status (e.g., the "empty nest," grandparenthood), and adjustment to widowhood.
7. The ageism endemic to our culture is

an important cause of problems among the aged.

8. The structure of the work world discriminates against the aged in a variety of ways.
9. Age-segregated housing for the aged can also cause them a range of problems.
10. A major demographic factor in the problem of the aged in our society has been the aging of the population as a whole.
11. Industrialization is related to the overall aging of the population.

Part III. Responses

12. Elderly people are involved in a range of informal support networks that help them cope with the problems of aging.
13. The political activism of the aged has helped them make a series of gains in their efforts to cope with the problems of aging.
14. The federal government has initiated a number of programs to help the elderly. The Older Americans Act of 1965 helped stimulate the development of Senior Centers and the Foster Grandparents Program. The National Insitute on Aging supports a wide range of research into aging.
15. The major federal response to the problem of aging, at least as far as economic matters are concerned, is Social Security. In spite of a number of reforms since its inception, the Social Security program is inadequate for the most vulnerable of the aged—women, minorities, the poor.
16. Private pension programs have also been instituted to deal with the economic problems of aging, but they too are riddled with problems.
17. Major steps toward coping with the problems of aging were taken with the development of national health insurance (including Medicare and Medicaid) for the aged. Although these programs are of great help, there is a need for a more coordinated and effective form of national health insurance.
18. The long-term trend has been to institutionalize more and more elderly people. Care should be taken in institutionalizing the aged since such a process can adversely affect the elderly, even to the extent of killing some of them.
19. Some of the recent innovations in caring for the aged include meals-on-wheels programs and geriatric day-care centers.

SUGGESTED READINGS

Butler, Robert, *Why Survive? Being Old in America.* New York: Harper & Row, 1975. This Pultizer-prize winning book is an eloquent and exhaustive analysis of the problems facing older people in American society today. However, it not only poses problems, it also explodes old myths and is jammed with recommendations for constructive change in every area.

Fischer, David Hackett, *Growing Old in America.* New York: Oxford Univerisity Press, 1978. This book is a highly readable historical account of the transformation in the status of the aged that occurred in the early nineteenth century.

George, Linda K., *Role Transitions in Later Life.* Monterey, California: Brooks/Cole, 1980. Another readable book in the Brooks/Cole series, this book provides an overview of the crucial role transitions in later life to retirement, widowhood, grandparenthood, the empty nest, and relocation.

Guillemard, Anne-Marie, *Old Age and the Welfare State.* Beverly Hills, California: Sage,

1983. For those interested in comparative studies, this book contains a series of articles regarding public policy issues for the aged in France, England, Italy, Germany, and the United States.

Hickey, Tom, *Health and Aging*, Monterey, California: Brooks/Cole, 1980. For those interested in health care, this book deals with such timely and crucial issues as long-term care, the social-psychological aspects of health, institutionalization, and solutions to the present health care problems that plague us.

Olson, Laura Katz, *The Political Economy of Aging*. New York: Columbia University Press, 1982. This book examines the role of traditional American institutions in fostering the social problems of old age in the United States. By describing five specific policy areas—health care, housing, social service delivery systems, and public and private pension funds—the author presents a detailed analysis of the major problems affecting the aged today.

FOOTNOTES

[1]Leo Simmons, *The Aged in Primitive Society* (London: Oxford University Press, 1945), p. 79.

[2]Jack Goody, "Aging in Nonindustrial Societies." In Robert Binstock and Ethel Shanas, eds., *Handbook of Aging and the Social Sciences* (New York: Van Nostrand Reinhold, 1976), p. 126.

[3]Arthur Schwartz, Cherie L. Snyder, and James Peterson, *Aging and Life* (New York: Holt, Rinehart and Winston, 1984), p. 213.

[4]Tom Hickey and Richard Douglass, "Neglect and Abuse of Older Family Members: Perspectives and Case Experiences," *Gerontologist*, 21 (1981), 172.

[5]*Ibid.*, p. 173.

[6]*Ibid.* , p. 173.

[7]U.S. House of Representatives, Select Committee on Aging, *Retirement: The Broken Promise* (Washington, D.C.: U.S. Government Printing Office, 1980), p. 7.

[8]"Characteristics of the Population Below the Poverty Level: 1983," *Current Population Reports*, 178 (1985), 60, 147.

[9]Anne Moss, "Social Insecurity: Pension Plans Shortchange Women," *Women's Political Times*, February 1983, p. 2.

[10]Beth Hess, "Aging Policies and Old Women: The Hidden Agenda." Paper presented to the American Sociological Association, September 1983, p. 5.

[11]Carroll L. Estes, "Fiscal Austerity and Aging." In Carroll Estes and Robert J. Newcomer, eds., *Fiscal Austerity and Aging* (Beverly Hills, Cal.: Sage, 1983). p. 31.

[12]Robert Butler, "Geriatric Medicine," *New York Journal of Medicine*, 9 (1977), 1470–1472.

[13]Howard Becker, Blanche Geer, Everett Hughes, and Anselm Strauss, *Boys in White* (Chicago: University of Chicago Press, 1961).

[14]Cary S. Kart, *The Realities of Aging* (Boston: Allyn & Bacon, 1981), pp. 54–55.

[15]E. L. White nd T. Gordon, "Related Aspects of Health and Aging in the United States." In *Colloquium on Health and Aging of the Population*, Vol. 3 (New York: Karger, 1969), p.38.

[16]Robert Atchley, *The Social Forces in Later Life* (Belmont, Cal.: Wadsworth, 1977).

[17]U.S. Dept. of Health, Education and Welfare, *Medicine and Aging* (Washington, D.C.: U.S. Government Printing Office, 1976) p. 79.

[18]Paul Raffoul, James Cooper, and David Love, "Drug Misuse in Older People," *Gerontologist*, 21 (1981), 146–149.

[19]Jaber F. Gubrium and Robert J. Lynott, "Alzheimer's Disease As Biographical Work." In Warren Peterson and Jill Quadagno, eds., *Social Bonds in Later Life* (Beverly Hills, Cal.: Sage, 1985).

[20]Rachel Filinson, "Chronic Illness and Care Provision: A Study of Alzheimer's Disease." In Peterson and Quadagno, eds., *op. cit.*

[21]Gubrium and Lynott, *op. cit.*

[22]Linda K. George, *Role Transitions in Later Life* (Monterey, Cal.: Brooks-Cole, 1980), p. 64.

[23]Karen Schwab, "Early Labor Force Withdrawal of Men: Participants and Nonparticipants Aged 58–63,"*Social Security Bulletin*, 37 (1974), 24–38.; Erdman Palmore, Gerda G. Fillenbaum, and Linda K. George, "Consequences of Retirement," *Journal of Gerontology*, 39 (1984), 114.

[24]George, *op. cit.*, p. 67.

[25]*Ibid.*

[26]Ann Foner and Karen Schwab, *Aging and Retirement* (Monterey, Cal.: Brooks/Cole, 1981), pp. 60–61.

[27]George, *op. cit.*, p. 60.

[28]George, *op. cit.*, pp. 82–83.

[29]Sarah H. Matthews and Jesse Sprey, "The Impact of Divorce on Grandparenthood: An Exploratory Study," *The Gerontologist,* 24 (1984), 41–47.

[30]*Ibid.,* p. 44.

[31]Ann Bowling and An Cartwright, *Life After a Death* (London: Tavistock, 1982), p. 36.

[32]Felix Berardo, "Survivorship and Social Isolation: The Case of the Aged Widower." In Jill Quadagno, ed., *Aging, the Individual and Society.* (New York: St. Martin's, 1980), pp. 259–279.

[33]Jack Levin and William C. Levin, *Ageism: Prejudice and Discrimination Against the Elderly* (Belmont, Cal.: Wadsworth, 1980).

[34]*Ibid,* p. 42.

[35]C. Aronoff, "Old Age in Prime Time," *Journal of Communication,* 24 (1974), 86–87.

[36]H. Northcott, "Too Young, Too Old—Age in the World of Television," *Gerontologist,* 15 (1975), 187.

[37]Foner and Schwab, *op. cit.,* pp. 26–27

[38]Herbert Parnes, Mary Hagen, and Randall King, "Job Loss Among Long-Service Workers." In Herbert S. Parnes, ed., *Work and Retirement* (Cambridge, Mass.: MIT press, 1981), pp. 79–80.

[39]Robert Butler, *Why Survive? Being Old in America* (New York: Harper and Row, 1975), p. 86.

[40]John Williamson, Anne Munley, and Linda Evans, *Aging and Society* (New York: Holt, Rinehart and Winston, 1980), p. 129.

[41]Frances Carp, "Impact of Improved Living Environment on Health and Life Expectancy," *Gerontologist,* 17 (1977), 242–250.

[42]Joyce Stephens, *Loners, Losers and Lovers: Elderly Tenants in a Slum Hotel* (Seattle: University of Washington Press, 1976).

[43]Charles Harris, *Fact Book on Aging* (Washington, D.C.: National Council on Aging, 1978).

[44]David Hackett Fisher, *Growing Old in America* (New York: Oxford University Press, 1978), p. 27.

[45]*Ibid.,* pp. 58–59.

[46]Jill Quadagno, "From Poor Laws to Pensions: The Evolution of Economic Support for the Aged in England and America," *Milbank Memorial Fund Quarterly,* 62 (1984), 417–446.

[47]Donald O. Cowgill, "The Aging of Populations and Societies." In Jill Quadagno, ed., *Aging, the Individual and Society* (New York: St. Martin's, 1980).

[48]Philip Hauser, "Aging and World-Wide Population Change." In Robert Binstock and Ethel Shanas, eds., *Handbook of Aging and the Social Sciences* (New York: Van Nostrand Reinhold, 1976), p. 64.

[49]John Demos, "Old Age in Early New England," *American Journal of Sociology,* 84 (1978), 245–287.

[50]Cowgill, *op. cit.*

[51]Jill Quadagno, *Aging in Early Industrial Society: Work, Family and Social Policy in Nineteenth Century England* (New York: Academic Press, 1982).

[52]Neena Chappell and Betty Havens, "Who Helps the Elderly Person: A Discussion of Informal and Formal Care." In Peterson and Quadagno, eds., *op. cit.*

[53]Margaret Roden, "The Independent Elderly: A Hidden Population." Unpublished Ph.D dissertation, University of Minnesota, 1984.

[54]*Ibid.*

[55]Lucy Rose Fischer, "Elderly Parents and the Caregiving Role: An Asymetrical Transition." In Peterson and Quadagno, eds., *op. cit.*

[56]*Ibid.*

[57]Elaine Brody, Pauline Johnson, Mark Fulcomer, and Abigail Lang, "Women's Changing Roles and Help to Elderly Parents: Attitudes of Three Generations of Women," *Journal of Gerontology,* 38 (1983), 597–607.

[58]Herman Brotman, "Voter Participation in November 1976," *Gerontologist,* 17 (1977), 157–159.

[59]Williamson, Munley, and Evans, *op.cit.,* p. 138.

[60]Carroll Estes, *et al., op. cit.,* p. 189

[61]*Ibid.,* p. 30.

[62]*Ibid.,* p. 142.

[63]Betty A. Lockett, *Aging, Politics and Research* (New York: Springer, 1983), p. 3.

[64]Anderw Achenbaum, *Old Age in the New Land* (Baltimore: John Hopkins University Press, 1978) p. 49.

[65]Jill Quadagno, "From Poor Laws to Pensions," *op. cit.,* p. 437.

[66]Paul Brinker, *Economic Insecurity and Social Security* (New York: Appleton-Century-Crofts, 1968), p. 60.

[67]Jill Quadagno, "Welfare Capitalism and the Social Security Act of 1935," *American Sociological Review,* 49 (1984), 632–647.

[68]Olson, *op. cit.,* p. 68.

[69]Schwab, *op. cit.*

[70]Olson, *op. cit.,* p. 59.

[71]Statistical Abstract of the United States, *National Data Book and Guide to Sources* (Washington, D.C.: U.S. Bureau of the Census, 1984) p. 385.

[72]William Graebner, *A History of Retirement* (New Haven, Conn.: Yale University Press, 1980), p. 132.

[73]G. Thompson, "Pension Coverage and Benefits, 1972: Findings from the Retirement History Study," *Social Security Bulletin*, 41 (1978), 3–17.

[74]Kart, *op. cit.*, p. 196.

[75]Tom Hickey, *Health and Aging* (Monterey, Cal.: Brooks/Cole, 1980), p. 148.

[76]Olson, *op. cit.* , p. 141.

[77]*Ibid.*, p. 142.

[78]*Ibid.*, p. 143.

[79]Hickey, *op. cit.*, p. 152.

[80]U.S. Department of Health, Education and Welfare, *Characteristics, Social Contacts and Activities of Nursing Home Residents*, DHEW Pub. No. (HRA) 77–1778 (Hyattsville, Md.: Public Health Services, 1977).

[81]B. Manard, C. S. Kart, and D. van Gale. *Old Age Institutions* (Lexington, Mass.: D. C. Heath, 1975).

[82]C. S. Kart and B. Beckham, "Black-White Differentials in the Institutionalization of the Elderly," *Social Forces*, 54 (1976), 901–910.

[83]Robert Butler, *Why Survive? Being Old in America*, *op. cit.*

[84]*Ibid.*, p. 89.

[85]Charles I. Stannard, "Old Folks and Dirty Work: The Social Conditions for Patient Abuse in a Nursing Home." In Jill Quadagno, ed., *Aging, the Individual and Society*, *op. cit.*, p. 513.

[86]M. A. Mendelson and D. Hapgood, "The Political Economy of Nursing Homes," *Annals of the American Academy of Political and Social Sciences*, 415 (1974), 95–105.

[87]Robert Applebaum, Fredrick W. Seide, and Carol D. Austin, "The Wisconsin Community Care Organization: Preliminary Findings from the Milwaukee Experiment," *Gerontologist*, 20 (1980), 350–355.

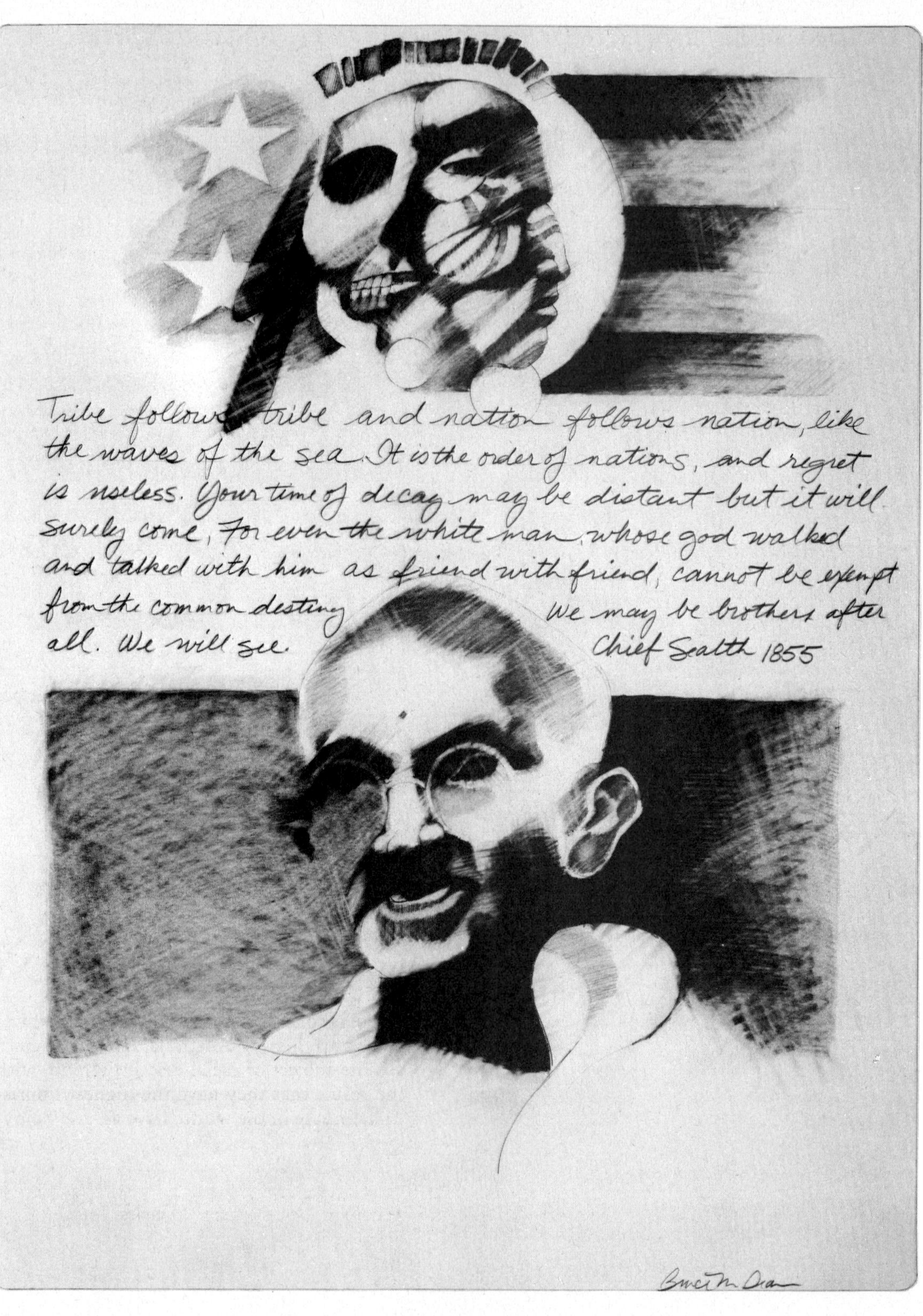
Tribe follows tribe and nation follows nation, like
the waves of the sea. It is the order of nations, and regret
is useless. Your time of decay may be distant but it will
surely come, For even the white man, whose god walked
and talked with him as friend with friend, cannot be exempt
from the common destiny. We may be brothers after
all. We will see.
Chief Sealth 1855

8 *Majority and Minority Relations*

The focus of this chapter will be relations, especially conflictive relations, between majority (or dominant) and minority (or subordinate) groups in the United States. Although we will discuss a number of minority groups and their relations to the majority group, our main concern will be with three minorities that continue, in varying degrees, to face severe difficulties in this country—blacks, Hispanics, and Native Americans (primarily American Indians). Of these three groups, the most attention by far will be devoted to black Americans. Black-white relations have been the most problematic minority-majority group relationship in the history of the United States.

It is important to make clear at the outset that majority-minority problems are not restricted to the United States; they exist worldwide. Note the following:

—In May 1985 racial rioting erupted again in Sri Lanka (formerly Ceylon), and almost 300 people were killed in a one-week period.[1] The struggle in this Indian Ocean nation is between the Tamils, a Hindu minority (about 11 percent of the population), and the Buddhist Sinhalese, who comprise 12 million (80 percent) of Sri Lanka's 15 million people. This was not the first such outbreak of violence between the two groups. An earlier eruption was caused by such things as the following anti-Tamil wall poster: "Your destruction is at hand. This is the country of us Sinhalese."[2]

—There is considerable friction between whites and aborigines in Australia. The aborigines are the subject of racial discrimination, with the result that they have the highest imprisonment rate in the *world,* have an unemployment rate six times the national average, are very poorly educated, and their health conditions are so bad that they have a life expectancy of twenty years less than nonaborigines.[3]

— In China, longstanding ethnic tension in one province has surfaced in the efforts of the Uighurs, a Turkic people of Muslim faith, to achieve greater freedom and autonomy. There is evidence of killings and beatings of both Uighurs and majority-group Chinese.[4]

— In Burundi, a tiny landlocked African country, violence erupted in the early 1970s between the minority group Hutu and the majority Tutsi. Although the Tutsi controlled the country, they made up only 15 percent of the population, with the minority Hutu comprising most of the other 85 percent. The Hutu rebelled against this domination, and in the process about 100,000 people, or 3.5 percent of Burundi's total population, were killed.[5] To put this in proper perspective, a comparable conflict in the United States would leave over 8 million people dead.

Clearly these examples illustrate the worldwide existence of majority-minority group conflict, and we have not even mentioned some of the best known examples such as the bitter, often deadly struggles between Catholic and Protestant in Northern Ireland and Jew and Arab in the Middle East.

PART I: THE PROBLEM

At the most general level our interest in this chapter is majority-minority relations in the United States. As we have already seen in the case of the Tutsi and the Hutu in Burundi, the terms "majority" and "minority" are not necessarily related to the numerical size of a group. The crucial variable in majority-minority relations is *power*[6]—the ability of one group to realize its goals and interests, even in the face of resistance. Power may be based on superior size, weaponry, technology, property, education, or economic resources of the dominant group. Power is not only important in establishing a system of majority-minority relations, but also in maintaining and perpetuating it.[7] Thus, a majority group is the one that possesses most of the power in a society while a minority group is one that is largely lacking in power. In analyzing majority-minority relations, we generally find ourselves dealing with either ethnic or racial groups.

Ethnicity and Race

An *ethnic group* is a social category that is socially defined on the basis of its *cultural characteristics.* Ethnic groups may differ in cultural characteristics as diverse as food habits, family patterns, sexual behaviors, modes of dress, standards of beauty, political orientations, economic activities, and recreational patterns. In American society, Chicanos, blacks, Jews, Filipinos, Poles, and white Anglo-Saxon Protestants can all be considered ethnic groups.

The terms "race" and "ethnicity" are often used interchangeably, but they should be distinguished. Ethnicity is determined by *cultural* characteristics; *race* refers to a social category that is socially defined on the basis of *physical characteristics.* A group of people is defined as a race by society when certain physical characteristics of the group are isolated and their importance as differentiating factors is emphasized. The crucial aspect of any definition of a group as ethnic or racial is that its characteristics are *socially defined.* Physical differences in themselve do not provide a basis for racial distinctions; the same group may be defined as a separate race in one society while in another no such distinction is made.

In many instances racial groups have ethnic characteristics as well. That is, racial groups have developed their own culture or subculture, come to share a common history or heritage, and come to think of themselves as having developed a consciousness of kind or a common identity. In American society, where they have been the largest and most clearly distinguished racial minority, blacks have developed at least some elements of a distinct subculture. The subculture is reflected by distinctive black music, language, religion, food, and dress. However, it should be borne in mind that black Americans have much more in common with the majority of Americans than they have distinctive cultural characteristics.

Intergroup Conflict

Our concern here, however, is not with racial and ethnic relations in general, but in *conflict* between majority and minority groups. Specifically, our concern is with *intergroup conflict,* which may be defined as conflict based on socially defined physical and cultural differences between groups. Religious, racial, ethnic, tribal, linguistic, or other differences have caused bitter conflict and have provided the basis for the subordination and exploitation of one group by another. Such conflicts have occurred in all modern societies. And they may, as we have seen, constitute one of the most serious internal problems of these societies today.

Prejudice and Discrimination

The differentiation between majority and minority groups does not necessarily create problems, although problems do ensue when majority group members develop prejudicial attitudes toward minority group members and also discriminate against them. *Prejudice* refers to a set of rigidly held negative attitudes, beliefs, and feelings toward members of another group. *Discrimination,* on the other hand, involves unfavorable treatment of individuals because of their group membership. Unlike prejudice, which is an attitude and an internal state, discrimination involves overt action or behavior. Our main concern in this chapter is discrimination, which may or may not result from prejudicial attitudes. Sometimes individuals who are not prejudiced find themselves in social situations that pressure or force them to act in a discriminatory manner. This is the problem of *institutional discrimination.* For example, realtors may not be personally prejudiced, but they may be compelled by their employers, as well as by the nature of their work, to discriminate against minority group members. Institutional discrimination will concern us at least as much in this chapter as *attitudinal discrimination,* or discriminatory behavior arising from prejudice.

Given the existence of prejudice and discrimination, both institutional and attitudinal, two issues need to be discussed. One is the set of policies open to the majority group in dealing with racial and ethnic minorities. The second is the range of responses to these policies available to the minority groups.

Majority Group Policies[8]

In the following discussion of majority group policies bear in mind that such policies are not mutually exclusive. That is, it is possible for the majority group to adopt more than one of these policies at the same time or at different times. Another point is that not all of these policies reflect hostility to minority groups, or at least they reflect a great range in the amount of hostility to minority groups. Since this is a book on social problems, we will begin with the most hostile policies and move toward more conciliatory ones.

Extermination

The most repressive dominant-group policy is *extermination,* or *genocide.* The objective of such a policy is to reduce substantially or eliminate the minority group. The most extreme and notorious example of extermination was the genocide practiced by the Nazis against millions of Jews and other "non-Aryans" (such as Gypsies). In American society, although it was never so formal or systematic a policy as was practiced by the Nazis, genocide was one of several policies employed by whites seeking to wrest control of the country's vast lands from the Indians. The slogan "the only good Indian is a dead Indian" was common among frontier whites who encountered Indian resistance to their continued encroachment. By the turn of the century the Indian population of the United States, in part as a result of genocide, had been brought to the point of virtual extinction. More specifically, the Indian population, which was estimated to have numbered about 10 million people at the time that Columbus discovered America, had dwindled to a few hundred thousand by the beginning of the twentieth century. To be fair, not all of these people had died in warfare with whites. More important than actual warfare in reducing the Indian population were European diseases such as smallpox, cholera, scarlet fever, and measles, which were fatal to large numbers of Indians, who had for centuries been insulated from the Old World and its diseases and so had little or no resistance to them. "Disease was the white man's strongest ally in the New World."[9]

Expulsion and Exclusion

The rationale of the policy of *expulsion* is the ejection of minority group members from the areas controlled by the majority group. Expulsion may be direct, that is, minorities may be forcibly ejected, or it may be brought about by indirect means such as harassment and persecution.[10] The policy of *direct expulsion* was at no time more pronounced in American history than during the nineteenth century, when increasing numbers of white settlers forced the Indians to move to areas west of the Mississippi River. *Indirect expulsion* occurs when harassment, discrimination, and persecution of a minority become so intense that the members "voluntarily" choose to emigrate. An excellent example of this is the flight of millions of Jews in the late nineteenth and early twentieth century from the pogroms of czarist Russia. A related policy is *exclusion,* where a host society refuses to permit another group entrance because this group is perceived as a threat. In this century, American immigration policies have served to exclude Asians, southern and eastern Europeans, and Africans from entering the country.

Caste

The policy of *caste* involves the exploitation of a social category that is denied equal participation in a society. A caste situation "depends on exclusiveness rather than exclusion."[11] Positions of higher prestige, power, and income are reserved exclusively for members of the dominant group. Unlike extermination, expulsion, or exclusion, a caste system accepts the existence of minorities but subjugates them and seeks to confine them to inferior social positions. The system of slavery in the South, and even the period after slavery, illustrates the caste system in operation in this country.

Assimilation

We now move to some of the less hostile majority group policies. The most typical response to ethnic minorities in the United States has been to seek their assimilation. *Assimilation* refers to a policy that seeks to achieve a homogeneous society by integrating or incorporating one group, usually a minority, into another group, usually the majority. It frequently involves *cultural as-*

similation, or the adoption by one group of the cultural values, beliefs, behaviors, and attitudes of another. *Social assimilation*, on the other hand, refers to the integration of social relationships between two groups. While today many minority groups have adopted the cultural characterisitcs of the majority, it is clear that many minority group members remain excluded from social organizations, jobs, neighborhoods, clubs, cliques, and friendship groups. Moreover, although there is considerable variation in rates of intermarriage among different ethnic groups, it is apparent that ethnic groups in the United States have not been fully assimilated in terms of marriage patterns.[12] Although most ethnic groups have not tended, at least socially, to assimilate to a large degree, the situation is even worse for racial groups such as American Indians and blacks. There remain strong cultural differences and social barriers between these racial groups and the majority of Americans.

Pluralism

Finally, *pluralism* refers to a system in which different cultures can coexist and be preserved. This policy is seldom advocated by majority group members, although it is sought by some minority groups. Pluralism is the most tolerant of the several policies we have considered, for it implies recognition of cultural equality among ethnic groups, not the superiority of one. It accepts cultural heterogeneity. Examples include such religious groups as the Amish and the Hutterites, who are culturally distinct and who have maintained their distinctiveness with a minimum of external interference from the larger society.

Minority Group Responses

How do minorities experience and respond to demands of the dominant group? The previous discussion has emphasized the role of the dominant group in setting the limits within which minority groups may function. Minorities, however, are not simply passive recipients of dominant-group policies; they actively respond in various ways to majority pressures for subordination. Sociologists have generally identified three general categories of minority group responses: acceptance, resistance, and avoidance.

Acceptance

This involves minority group acceptance of the majority group's definition of its subordinate status. Given the majority group's power, acquiescence may be necessary for survival. The southern caste system was for many years relatively stable because most blacks, at least on the surface, appeared to accept the elaborate system of racial etiquette and segregation. The most severe violence against blacks—lynchings and terrorism—was commited when blacks made, or whites thought they had made, an effort to reject the traditional passive roles ascribed to them. As we will see, blacks never fully accepted their situation, and over the last several decades most have come to reject such subservience completely.

Resistance

In fact it could be said that some blacks have always responded with *resistance* to the majority group's definition of their situation. Resistance may manifest itself in a variety of ways, including boycotts, strikes, legal action, political activity, nonviolent mass protest, and violence. Even during slavery, blacks resisted the domination of slaveholders by running away, damaging crops or livestock, and organizing slave revolts, but in recent years black Americans have participated in an increasingly wide range of forms of resistance. In fact, resistance by blacks (in the form of demonstrations, boycotts, legal challenges, and political action) served as a model for similar actions by other minority groups, such as American Indians and Chicanos.

Avoidance and Separatism

Finally, minorities may react with *avoidance,* in which they neither accept nor resist the dominance of the majority. Rather, they seek to set themselves apart from the majority and to keep contact to a minimum. Such a stance shields the minority group from prejudice and discrimination by the majority group and enables them to preserve their own culture and social institutions with minimal outside interference. Various minority groups (for example, the Irish) have practiced avoidance by refusing to give up their ethnic idenity to become "Americanized." The most extreme form of avoidance is *separatism,* in which there is little, if any, interaction with the majority. The impulse for separatism frequently has been generated by considerable conflict with the majority group and a desire to avoid a continuation of the discrimination or subjugation that a group has encountered.

Current Status of Minorities

We turn now to an examination of the current status of minority groups in the

Figure 8.1 Where Most Hispanics Live

Some 85 percent of the 14.6 million Hispanics counted in the 1980 U.S. census lived in these nine states. Mexican-Americans, the largest Hispanic group, are concentrated in the Southwest, particularly California and Texas. Most Puerto Ricans live in New York and New Jersey. Cubans are headquartered in Florida. The largest numbers of other Hispanic groups are found in California and New York.

Source: Cary Davis, Carl Haub, and JoAnne Willette, "U.S. Hispanics: Changing the Face of America," *Population Bulletin,* Vol. 38, No. 3 (Washington, D.C.: Population Reference Bureau, Inc., 1983).

Table 8.1 Total U.S. and Hispanic Population: 1950–1980 (Numbers in millions)

YEAR	TOTAL U.S. POPULATION	HISPANICS	HISPANIC POPULATION INCREASE IN PRECEDING DECADE	HISPANIC PERCENT OF U.S. POPULATION
1950	151.3	4.0	—	2.7
1960	179.3	6.9	2.9	3.9
1970	203.2	10.5	3.6	5.2
1980	226.5	14.6	4.1	6.4

Source: Cary Davis, Carl Haub, and JoAnn Willette, "U.S. Hispanics: Changing the Face of America," *Population Bulletin,* Vol. 38, No. 3 (Washington, D.C.: Population Reference Bureau, Inc.: 1983).

United States. Our primary focus will be on three minority groups—black Americans, Hispanic Americans, and Native Americans.

Demographics

Together, the three nonwhite American minority groups of main concern here numbered approximately 42.5 million people in 1980. We know that there were almost 26.5 million blacks and almost 1.4 million American Indians. We also know that there were slightly more than 14.6 million people who identified themselves as being of Spanish origin. However, some of those of Spanish origin may also have iden-

Table 8.2 U.S. Hispanic Population, by Type: 1980

TYPE	NUMBER (IN THOUSANDS)	PERCENT	STATES WITH LARGEST CONCENTRATIONS
Total Hispanic	14,609	100.0	California, Texas, New York
Mexican American	8,740	59.8	California, Texas, Illinois
Puerto Rican	2,014	13.8	New York, New Jersey, Illinois
Cuban	803	5.5	Florida, New Jersey, New York
Other Hispanic	3,052	20.9	California New York, New Mexico

Source: Cary Davis, Carl Haub, and JoAnne Willette, "U.S. Hispanics: Changing the Face of America," *Population Bulletin,* Vol. 38, No. 3 (Washington, D.C.: Population Reference Bureau, Inc., 1983).

tified themsleves as black and thus may have been counted twice.[13] Taking this into consideration, we can estimate that these groups comprise nearly one-fifth (19 percent) of the American population.[14] It should also be noted that each of these groups is growing far more rapidly than white Americans. Between 1970 and 1980 the white population increased by 6 percent while the black population grew by 17.3 percent, Hispanic Americans by 61 percent, and American Indians by almost 72 percent.[15] The growth of the Hispanic population is a result both of their tendency to have larger families than the national average and their substantial immigration into the United States in recent years.[16]

Economic Inequalities

Today the economic status of each of the three minorities we are considering remains considerably below that of white Americans. These minorities continue to experience discrimination, which occurs, for example, in trying to get a job, in pay, in promotion on the job, in fringe benefits, and in keeping a job.[17] Despite considerable government and private efforts to combat discrimination and eliminate inequalities, minority groups are still likely to be the last hired and the first fired.

In comparison with the dominant white group, blacks, Native Americans, and Hispanic Americans have the poorest jobs and are underrepresented in high-paying, high-status occupations. Because black Americans are the largest of these minority groups, we will restrict our analysis of economic discrimination to this group.

In 1982 the median income for all white families was $24,603, while it was $13,598 for all black families. Black family income was thus 55 percent of the white total.[18,19] More interestingly, rather than the status of blacks improving recently, between 1970 and 1980 black income actually *fell* from 61 percent of the white total to 57 percent.[20] We learn a good deal about black occupational status by looking at the occupations in which blacks are overrepresented. Blacks made up 11.2 percent of all employed persons in 1980, but were overrepresented in the following occupations (the percentage of blacks follows each occupation):

—household servants (53.4%)

—clothing pressers (40.4%)

—garbage collectors (34.8%)

—nursing aides and orderlies (28.8%)

—taxi drivers (25.3%).[21]

In other words, blacks tend to be greatly overrepresented in the lowest-status, lowest-paying occupations.[22] Conversely, blacks are underrepresented in some of the higher-paying and higher-status skilled and white-collar occupations. For example, in 1980 2.6 percent of engineers, 2.7 percent of lawyers, and 3.2 percent of physicians were black.[23]

The unemployment and underemployment rates for blacks also reflect the occupational situation facing this minority group and other nonwhite Americans. Over the years black unemployment has run at about twice the white unemployment rate. Thus, in July 1982, when the overall unemployment rate was 9.8 percent and the rate for whites was 8.7 percent, the unemployment rate for blacks was 18.5 percent, or 1.89 times the overall rate and well over twice the rate for whites. The unemployment rate for Hispanic Americans, while below that of blacks, was still 1.42 times the overall rate, or 13.9 percent. For black teenagers the unemployment rate was an astounding 49.7 percent (compared to 21 percent for white teenagers).[24]

Nonwhite minority groups are also very

There are many ethnic groups in the United States, and there is considerable diversity among them.
(Left, Bettye Lane/Photo Researchers; right, Jean-Claude Lejeune/EKM-Nepenthe)

likely to be underemployed, that is, working part-time, seasonally, or in jobs far below those for which they are qualified. The National Urban League computes what they call a "Hidden Unemployment Index" that includes those who are underemployed in part-time jobs because they were unable to find full-time jobs, as well as those who have become discouraged and given up looking for work. In 1983, the Urban League computes that about one-third of the black population fell into this category, more than double the number of whites in this group.[25]

What are the reasons for these disparities in income and occupational status? A major factor to be examined in this context is the role played by education and the educational institutions.

Discrimination in Education

The median education attained by the dominant white population in 1982 was 12.7 years for males (12.5 for females), while for blacks it was 12.2 for males (12.1 for females); for Hispanic males 11.5 (10.7 for females);[26] and for American Indians it was 12.2 years.[27] All of these figures are important because most social scientists believe that a strong relationship exists between income and education.[28] That is, those with higher levels of education are likely to earn more during their lifetimes and, conversely, those with lower levels of education are likely to earn less.

At least some of the problems of nonwhite minorities within the educational system, and therefore ultimately in the work world, are traceable to discrimination within educational institutions. Educational discrimination in various forms continues to exist despite the historic 1954 Supreme Court decision in the case of *Brown v. the Borad of Education of Topeka* that banned such discrimination in public education.

Because of the concentration of many minorities in ghettos, and the failure of various governmental levels to take decisive action against segregation, these minorities tend to be segregated in the school system. In almost every large American city, most blacks live in neighborhoods that are mainly black; Puerto Ricans, Cubans, Chicanos, and other Hispanics live, although to a lesser extent than blacks, in similarly segregated neighborhoods; and the Native Americans are concentrated in reservations. One of the most recent examples of this is the degree to which Miami, Florida, has come to be a Cuban enclave. It is estimated that close to half of the 350,000 residents of Miami are Cuban.[29] While once concentrated in the "Little Havana" section of the city, Cubans in great numbers have now fanned out throughout most of the city.

As a result of continued physical segregation due to housing patterns and the fact that such controversial social programs as busing for racial equality are today largely out of favor, racial isolation remains characteristic of our schools.[30] Present-day segregated schools, particularly those in the industrial Northeast, are often like segregated southern schools of the pre-1954 period. Blacks are likely to be housed in substandard buildings; the schools are sometimes overcrowded, and children may be forced to attend school in shifts; there are shortages of books, laboratory equipment, advanced technologies like computers, and other educational facilities. The top-quality teachers want to avoid, or to leave, these lower-status schools, with the result that the quality of teachers is often lower in schools that have predominantly minority student bodies.

Several characteristics of these schools tend to reduce the performance of nonwhite minorities. If teachers in these schools start out expecting less from their nonwhite students, that is precisely what they are likely to get. (The converse is also the case, but given general societal stereotypes, that is less likely to occur in schools with large minority populations.) This is the idea of the *self-fulfilling prophecy.*[31] It exists in terms of a teacher's expectations of a specific student and, more importantly for our purposes, for entire categories of students (for example, blacks, Hispanics, and Indians). If a teacher does not expect much of the students from such groups, then the students are likely to live up (or rather, down) to these expectations, no matter what their level of individual ability. The following dialogue illustrates the way teachers may learn to have lower expectations of minorities. It involves a new teacher's first piece of advice from a fellow teacher at an all-black high school in California:

> Jim, you ever work with these kids before? No, I admitted. I thought so. Well, now, the first thing is, you don't ever push 'em, and you don't expect too much . . . you take them as they are, not as you and me (sic) would like them to be. That means you find out what they can do, and you give it to them to do.[32]

Expectations such as these can clearly adversely affect the educational development of nonwhites.

A related characteristic of contemporary schools is the *tracking system.* In such a system formal tracks, or student career paths, are created; for example, high, medium, and low tracks. Students are placed into what is deemed the appropriate track on the basis of such factors as test scores, class performance, and/or teacher evaluations. Since nonwhites tend to perform less well than whites on all of these,[33] they are likely to find themselves being placed in lower tracks in disproportionate numbers. Being in a low track tends to be an institutionalized method of creating a self-fulfilling prophecy. Already defined as a poor performer by being placed in a lower track, the student in such a track comes increasingly to think of him- or herself as such a performer, and teachers, administrators, and fellow students reinforce that image on a regular basis. If students are not poor performers before they enter a lower track, they certainly will be after they spend some time in such an environment.

A good deal of light has been cast on the effects of teacher expectations and tracking by a well-known research study undertaken by Robert Rosenthal and Lenore Jacobson.[34] At "Oak School," the school they studied, all student were given IQ tests. At the beginning of the next school year, each of the eighteen teachers in grades one through six were given the names of students (about 20 percent of the population) who, researchers told them, could be expected to show dramatic intellectual growth in the coming academic year. These predictions were supposedly based on the students' IQ scores of the previous year. In fact, the names of the 20 percent had actually been drawn at random from the school population as a whole; there were *no differences* between them and the other students. As Rosenthal and Jacobson put it: "The difference between the special children and the ordinary children, then, was only in the mind of the teachers."[35]

The crucial finding in this research was that teacher expectations make a difference:

> After the first year of the experiment a significant expectancy advantage was found, and it was especially great among children of the first and second grades. The advantage of having been expected to bloom was evident for these younger children in total I.Q., verbal I. Q., and reasoning I.Q. The control-group children of these grades gained well on I.Q., 19 percent of them gaining twenty or more total I.Q. points. The 'special' children, however, showed 47 percent of their number gaining twenty or more total I.Q. points.[36]

Rosenthal and Jacobson's research was admittedly limited; it was only one study of a single school. Subsequent efforts to replicate their study at other schools have failed to produce such dramatic findings. Nevertheless, a variety of additional studies have supported the general notion that teacher expectations have an important effect on student performance.[37]

The existence of such mechanisms in grade schools and high schools contributes to the underrepresentation of blacks, Hispanics, and Native Americans in colleges and universities. Problems exist even prior to entry to college. While 39.3 percent of white high-school seniors in 1980 were in college preparatory programs, only 32.4 percent of blacks and 26.2 percent of Hispanics were in similar programs.[38] This is reflected in the college level attainments of these groups. For example, while 18.5 percent of whites have had four or more years of college education, less than half that many blacks (8.8 percent), and even fewer Hispanics (7.8 percent), have completed that much college.[39] While substantial differences remain, it should be borne in mind that educational differences between whites and nonwhites have in general been narrowing. For example, between 1965 and 1980 the number of black college students more than doubled.[40] There are today about 1 million blacks attending college.[41] The importance of a college education to blacks is pointed up by the fact that a *recent* black college graduate, on the average, earns *more* than a comparable white graduate.[42] However, overall, black college graduates do *not* earn more than their white counterparts. While still in those colleges, black students are highly unlikely to see many black faculty members. In 1980, less that 5 percent of all college and university faculty members were black.[43]

In 1954 about 90 percent of all black college students attended historically black colleges. Today, about 50 percent of all black college graduates come from these colleges, indicating their continuing importance to black Americans. However, such institutions have far less money to work with, and the educational qualifications of the faculty at these institutions are far lower than at America's major universities. Thus there are major problems with the quality of education being received by a large portion of black college graduates.[44]

These examples indicate that patterns of discrimination persist in the educational system three decades after the nation was ordered in the *Brown v. Board of Education* decision to move forward "with all deliberate speed" to wipe out the educational inequities of the past.[45]

Housing Discrimination

One of the chronic problems facing American society is discrimination in housing.[46] Residential segregation has widespread effects, for it follows almost naturally that within a segregated area all other institutions and most of the services are de facto segregated. Housing discrimination contributes greatly to intergroup conflict. Isolation by neighborhood prevents the intergroup understanding that might result from regular interaction between majority and minority groups. Isolation thus heightens group hostility and strengthens boundaries between groups.

Today, most minority groups are segregated residentially. About 50 percent of Native Americans in the United States live on 261 reservations scattered throughout the country.[47] Many of them live in substandard housing, generally without running water, electricity, or indoor toilets. The majority (approximately 85 percent) of Chicanos, Puerto Ricans, and Cubans live in the cities,[48] in *barrios* or *colonias*—segregated neighborhoods inhabited mainly by persons of Spanish origin. The dwellings are often deteriorating and overcrowded.

However, the housing patterns of black Americans reveal most dramatically the patterns of residential segregation[49] and housing discrimination. In the first place, the black population is largely an urban population. In fact, many major cities are now more than 50 percent black, including Gary, Indiana (70.8 percent), Washington, D.C. (70.3 percent), Atlanta (66.6 percent), Detroit (63.1 percent), and New Orleans (55.3 percent).[50] In 1980, while only 25 percent of the white population lived in central cities, 57.8 percent of blacks (and 50.4 percent of Hispanics) lived in such areas.[51] Typically, houses in the central city are older and more likely to be run down. Blacks are much less likely to be homeowners and more likely to be renters than whites. Blacks have only 7.2 percent of the homes in the United States that are owned, considerably less than their share of the total population. While 68.6 percent of whites own their homes, only 43.4 percent are homeowners.[52] On the other hand, 52.8 percent of black families live in rented housing, while this is true of only 29.8 percent of whites and others. Even when they are homeowners, blacks are more likely to own older and therefore presumably more rundown houses.[53]

In the last several pages we have been examining the problems confronted by minority groups within American society, specifically in the areas of economics, education, and housing. These, of course, are not the only areas in which minority groups experience problems. There is, for example, the *political arena* in which, despite some notable gains among the nations' mayors by blacks, minority groups continue to be greatly underrepresented. Although blacks comprise more than 11 percent of the total population of the country, only 1 percent of the nation's elected officials are black. Then there is *health care*, in which minority groups are not able to obtain the same quality care as members of the majority group.

Health Care

Although similar points apply to other minority groups, we will focus here on the health status of black Americans. On a variety of health/illness dimensions, blacks fare far more poorly than whites. For example, in terms of death from all causes, the death rate for black males in 1983 was 1,024.7 per 100,000, while for white males the rate was 701.8. Similarly, for black females the death rate was 571.5, while for white females it was 391.5.[54] For another, life expectancy for whites born in 1983 is 75.2 years, while for blacks it is 69.6 years.[55] For still another, in 1981 the white infant mortality rate was 10.5 per 1,000 live births, while for blacks it was 20.0.[56] Finally, as Table 8.3 shows, black males and black females have a much higher death rate on most specific causes of death than do white males and females.

A variety of factors are related to the relatively poor health of black Americans.[57] Health care is expensive, and given their relatively low incomes, black Americans are less likely to be able to afford it, or the insurance that helps reduce the cost. Because of the economic difficulties, black Americans get health care, especially of a preventive nature, far less frequently than white Americans. Medical services tend to be less available in black communities than in white communities. There are far fewer black physicians than white physicians. Blacks are much more likely to receive treatment in clinics or public hospitals, while whites are more likely to see private physicians and utilize private hospitals. For all of these reasons, and others, blacks (and other minority groups) receive poorer quality health care than white Americans.

The Family

Recently, concern has surfaced once again about the minority group *family*, especially the black family. Almost two decades ago, sociologist (and now U.S. Senator from New York) Daniel Patrick Moynihan expressed alarm about the dissolution of the black family.[58] In the late 1960s and through the 1970s Moynihan's ideas were rejected, in part because they were seen as placing the blame for black problems on blacks themselves. We have seen in this section, and will see throughout the chapter, that much of the blame lies with majority group prejudice and discrimination. However, placing the bulk of the blame on the majority group does not negate the fact that there are serious problems within the black family.[59] These problems are pointed up by the startling statistics that: "In 1965, when Moynihan pointed with alarm to the relative instability of the black family, one-quarter of all such families were headed by women; 15 years later, the figure was a staggering 42 percent."[60] Over half of black babies are now being born to unmarried women,[61] in comparison to 15 percent in 1959.[62] The likelihood of having a baby out of wedlock is nine times greater among blacks than whites.[63] William Julius Wilson claims that the problem is even greater in the inner cities. He cites data on families living in Chicago Housing Authority projects in 1980 that show that only 11 percent of them were husband-wife families and that 67 percent of black children in Chicago are born out of wedlock.[64]

The absence of a father is a serious problem for a variety of reasons, perhaps most importantly for economic reasons, since

Table 8.3 Age-Adjusted Death Rates for Selected Causes of Death, According to Race and Sex: United States, Selected Years 1950–83

(Data are based on the National Vital Statistics System)

RACE, SEX, AND CAUSE OF DEATH	1950[1]	1960[1]	1970	1979	1980	1981	1982[1,2]	1983[1,2]
	YEAR							
Black male			Deaths per 100,000 resident population					
All causes	1,373.1	1,246.1	1,318.6	1,073.3	1,112.8	1,067.7	1,045.5	1,024.7
Diseases of heart	415.5	381.2	375.9	314.1	327.3	316.7	—	—
Cerebrovascular diseases	146.2	141.2	124.2	77.9	77.5	72.7	—	—
Malignant neoplasms	126.1	158.5	198.0	221.8	229.9	232.0	—	—
Respiratory system	16.9	36.6	60.8	78.7	82.0	84.1	—	—
Digestive system	59.4	60.4	58.9	60.7	62.1	62.1	—	—
Pneumonia and influenza	63.8	70.2	53.8	24.2	28.0	26.4	—	—
Chronic liver disease and cirrhosis	8.8	14.8	33.1	30.3	30.6	27.3	—	—
Diabetes mellitus	11.5	16.2	21.2	17.0	17.7	16.8	—	—
Accidents and adverse effects	105.7	100.0	119.5	81.3	82.0	74.7	—	—
Motor vehicle accidents	39.8	38.2	50.1	33.7	32.9	30.7	—	—
Suicide	7.0	7.8	9.9	12.5	11.1	11.0	—	—
Homicide and legal intervention	51.1	44.9	82.1	70.1	71.9	69.2	—	—
Black female								
All causes	1,106.7	916.9	814.4	605.0	631.1	599.1	570.9	571.5
Diseases of heart	349.5	292.6	251.7	190.9	201.1	191.2	—	—
Cerebrovascular diseases	155.6	139.5	107.9	60.9	61.7	58.1	—	—
Malignant neoplasms	131.9	127.8	123.5	125.1	129.7	127.1	—	—
Respiratory system	4.1	5.5	10.9	17.4	19.5	20.1	—	—
Digestive system	40.2	37.5	34.1	35.0	35.4	34.5	—	—
Breast[4]	19.3	21.3	21.5	22.7	23.3	23.7	—	—
Pneumonia and influenza	50.4	43.9	29.2	10.9	12.7	11.3	—	—
Chronic liver disease and cirrhosis	5.7	8.9	17.8	13.3	14.4	12.7	—	—
Diabetes mellitus	22.7	27.3	30.9	20.8	22.1	21.3	—	—
Accidents and adverse effects	38.5	35.9	35.3	23.9	25.1	21.6	—	—
Motor vehicle accidents	10.3	10.0	13.8	8.7	8.4	7.7	—	—
Suicide	1.7	1.9	2.9	2.9	2.4	2.5	—	—
Homicide and legal intervention	11.7	11.8	15.0	13.9	13.7	12.9	—	—
Total[3]			Deaths per 100,000 resident population					
All causes	841.5	760.9	714.3	577.0	585.8	568.2	556.4	549.6
Diseases of heart	307.6	286.2	253.6	199.5	202.0	195.0	191.0	188.5
Cerebrovascular diseases	88.8	79.7	66.3	41.6	40.8	38.1	36.2	34.3
Malignant neoplasms	125.4	125.8	129.9	130.8	132.8	131.6	133.4	132.3
Respiratory system	12.8	19.2	28.4	35.2	36.4	36.6	37.7	38.1
Digestive system	47.7	41.1	35.2	33.1	33.0	32.5	32.1	31.8
Breast[4]	22.2	22.3	23.1	22.3	22.7	22.7	22.7	22.8

Pneumonia and influenza	26.2	28.0	22.1	11.2	12.9	12.3	11.1	11.2
Chronic liver disease and cirrhosis	8.5	10.5	14.7	12.0	12.2	11.4	10.4	10.4
Diabetes mellitus	14.3	13.6	14.1	9.8	10.1	9.8	9.2	9.8
Accidents and adverse effects	57.5	49.9	53.7	42.9	42.3	39.8	37.2	34.9
Motor vehicle accidents	23.3	22.5	27.4	23.2	22.9	21.8	19.6	18.1
Suicide	11.0	10.6	11.8	11.7	11.4	11.5	11.6	11.7
Homicide and legal intervention	5.4	5.2	9.1	10.2	10.8	10.4	9.7	8.2
White male								
All causes	963.1	917.7	893.4	738.4	745.3	724.4	709.7	701.8
Diseases of heart	381.1	375.4	347.6	276.8	277.5	268.8	—	—
Cerebrovascular diseases	87.0	80.3	68.8	42.9	41.9	38.9	—	—
Malignant neoplasms	130.9	141.6	154.3	158.7	160.5	158.3	—	—
Respiratory system	21.6	34.6	49.9	57.0	58.0	57.8	—	—
Digestive system	54.0	47.5	41.9	40.0	39.8	39.3	—	—
Pneumonia and influenza	27.1	31.0	26.0	14.4	16.2	15.6	—	—
Chronic liver disease and cirrhosis	11.6	14.4	18.8	15.6	15.7	14.8	—	—
Diabetes mellitus	11.3	11.6	12.7	9.3	9.5	9.3	—	—
Accidents and adverse effects	80.9	70.5	76.2	63.3	62.3	59.1	—	—
Motor vehicle accidents	35.9	34.0	40.1	35.5	34.8	33.4	—	—
Suicide	18.1	17.5	18.2	18.6	18.9	18.9	—	—
Homicide and legal intervention	3.9	3.9	7.3	9.9	10.9	10.3	—	—
White female								
All causes	645.0	555.0	501.7	402.5	411.1	401.4	395.1	391.5
Diseases of heart	223.6	197.1	167.8	131.3	134.6	129.8	—	—
Cerebrovascular diseases	79.7	68.7	56.2	35.9	35.2	33.1	—	—
Malignant neoplasms	119.4	109.5	107.6	105.7	107.7	107.2	—	—
Respiratory system	4.6	5.1	10.1	17.0	18.2	18.8	—	—
Digestive system	41.1	33.9	28.1	25.5	25.4	24.7	—	—
Breast[4]	22.5	22.4	23.4	22.4	22.8	22.8	—	—
Pneumonia and influenza	18.9	19.0	15.0	7.8	9.4	9.0	—	—
Chronic liver disease and cirrhosis	5.8	6.6	8.7	7.0	7.0	6.7	—	—
Diabetes mellitus	16.4	13.7	12.8	8.3	8.7	8.4	—	—
Accidents and adverse effects	30.6	25.5	27.2	21.6	21.4	20.2	—	—
Motor vehicle accidents	10.6	11.1	14.4	12.3	12.3	11.7	—	—
Suicide	5.3	5.3	7.2	6.3	5.7	6.0	—	—
Homicide and legal intervention	1.4	1.5	2.2	2.9	3.2	3.1	—	—

[1]Includes deaths of nonresidents of the United States.
[2]Provisional data.
[3]Includes all other races not shown separately.
[4]Female only.
NOTES: Age-adjusted rates are computed by the direct method to the total population of the United States as enumerated in 1940, using 11 age groups. For data years shown, the code numbers for cause of death are based on the then current *International Classification of Diseases,* which are described in Appendix II, tables IV and VI.
Source: National Center for Health Statistics, *Health, United States, 1984.* No. (PHS) 85-1232. Public Health Service (Washington, D.C.: U.S. Government Printing Office, Dec., 1984), p. 60.

Figure 8.2 Living Arrangements of Children Under 18: 1982

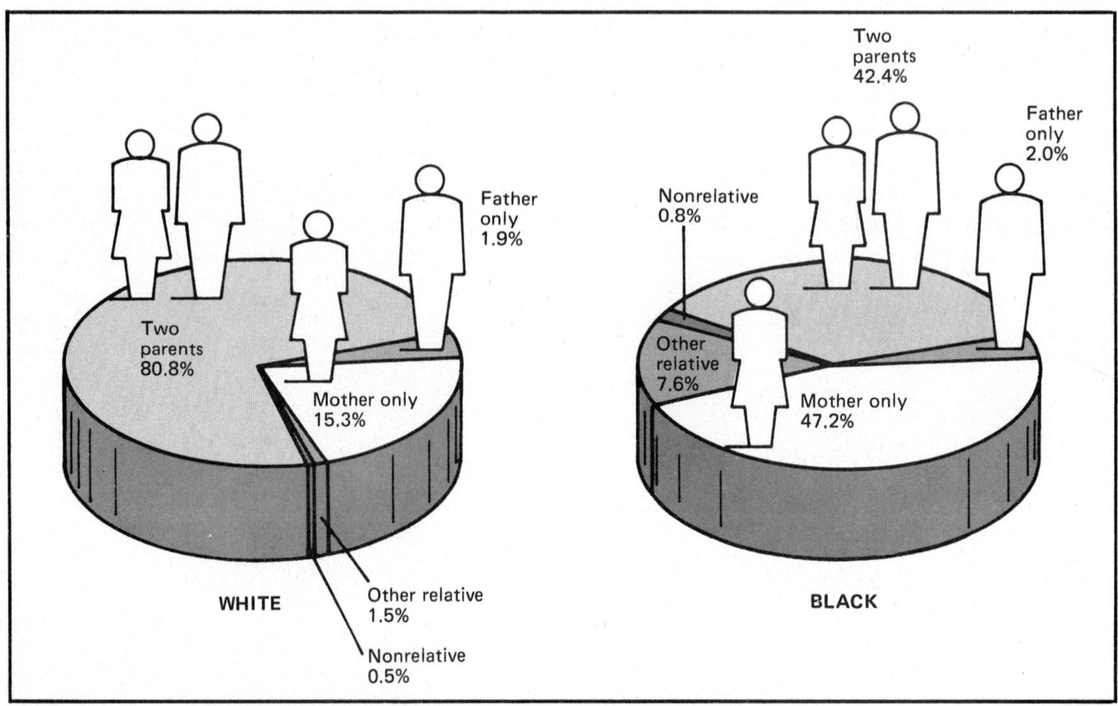

The problems of the black family are exacerbated by the fact that almost half of black children under 18 live with only their mothers. The same is true for only 15.3% of white children.

Source: U.S. Bureau of the Census, Current Population Reports, Series P-23, No. 130, *Population Profile of the United States: 1982* (Washington, D.C.: U.S. Government Printing Office, 1983), p. 15.

there is the absence of a man's income and because females on the average earn less than males. The median income for black female-headed families in 1980 was $7,425, while for black families with both parents present it was $18,593. In other words, black female-headed families had only 40 percent of the income of intact families. Thus, the absence of a father and poverty tend to go hand in hand. This problem, placed in more general terms, has come to be called the "feminization of poverty."[65]

Among other things, this poverty creates serious problems for the offspring of single-parent families, who are far more likely to be on welfare than children from intact families. Furthermore, throughout the rest of their lives, out-of-wedlock children will have to fight to overcome the handicaps created by their childhood circumstances. They are more likely to be unemployed, to engage in crime, and to suffer in a variety of other ways.

Wilson sees the enormous number of young blacks (and other minorities) in the ghettos as a significant cause of problems in the black community. For one thing, the black community tends to be young, and young people are more likely to get into trouble. Second, a large number of these young people come from female-headed families, with the result that they spend a good deal of their time without adult supervision. Third, young people are more likely to suffer economically, especially because teenagers, in particular black teenagers, are more likely to be unemployed. Finally, young women are more likely to have a child out of wedlock, to be the head of a new household, and to be on welfare. Thus, Wilson concludes: "much of what has gone awry in the ghetto is due in part to the sheer increase in the number of black youths."[66] Also important are ongoing economic changes that are actually reducing job opportunities traditionally open to urban blacks. The increasing youth of the black population, ongoing economic changes, *and* historic and contemporary discrimination are combining to create what Wilson calls a "black underclass."

Thus, problems for minority groups exist in every sector of society. The issue now is what are some of the major causes of these problems and in what ways do these causes impact on minority group members?

PART II: CAUSES AND CONSEQUENCES

Our objective in this section is to examine some of the major causes and consequences of majority-minority group conflict in the United States.

SOCIOLOGICAL LEVEL

An individual's thoughts and actions have little bearing on whether he or she will suffer for belonging to a racial, religious, or cultural group that is the object of prejudice and discrimination. Rather how such an individual will be treated is much more a function of the relationship between the majority group and the minority group. Beyond the relationships between these groups, the nature of the society as a whole makes a significant difference. For example, compared with the United States, Brazil has been relatively color-blind. As a consequence, blacks in Brazil historically encountered much less prejudice and discrimination than they have in the United States. Therefore, the search for the causes of intergroup conflict is best begun at the macrolevels, at the societal, cultural, and group levels. We will begin by examining these levels historically. One issue in the next section will be why certain intergroup conflicts have subsided while others have not. Our main concern will be with the role played by structural (institutional) and ideological (cultural) factors in shaping intergroup conflict. We begin with some of the cultural characteristics of the United States, specifically the bigotry built into American ideology.

Cultural Factors

American Ideology and Bigotry

On July 4, 1776, the leaders of the American Revolution signed the Declaration of Independence, the second paragraph of which begins:

> We hold these Truths to be self-evident, that all Men are created equal, that they are endowed by their Creator with certain unalienable Rights, that among these are Life, Liberty, and the Pursuit of Happiness.

Revolutionary lines such as these defied aristocratic traditions and committed the United States to a noble experiment with democratic institutions based on individual liberty and egalitarianism. There is no doubt that the founders of American democracy meant these sentiments, but it is also true that a number of them, *including* Thomas Jefferson, the person who drafted the Declaration of Independence, were slave owners.

This extraordinary contradiction was to

Table 8.4 Levels of Analysis: Majority-Minority Relations

LEVELS	APPROPRIATE QUESTIONS	A PARTIAL SYNOPSIS OF PRESENT CONCLUSIONS
INDIVIDUAL	What are the major sources of prejudice?	Prejudice has cultural (i.e., in ethnic and racial stereotypes) and structural (e.g., in competition between majority and minority groups) sources.
	Are there aspects of the personality that predispose an individual to prejudice?	Yes. Among others, displaced aggression (scapegoating), projection, and authoritarianism have been linked to prejudice.
	Are personality factors more important than sociological forces in understanding prejudice?	No. Most sociologists, not surprisingly, accord greater significance to cultural and institutional forces.
	What is the significance of the fact that blacks tend to score lower on IQ tests for understanding the role of physiology in majority-minority relations?	Although there are some who strongly argue for a genetic explanation of black-white IQ differences, most sociologists side with those who emphasize the role of social and cultural factors. More generally, most sociologists deemphasize the role of genetic and physiological factors in majority-minority relations.
SOCIOLOGICAL	Historically, did the American cultural commitment to equality encourage racism?	Yes. The contradiction between the ideal that "all men are created equal" and continued slavery led to the denial of the basic humanity of blacks.
	Do the cultural values of individualism work against minority groups in America.	Yes. Americans are inclined to blame the unsuccessful for their lack of progress.
	Has the effect of culture on minority groups been all negative?	No. American beliefs in equality and fair play have contributed to some progress for minority groups.

Table 8.4 Levels of Analysis: Majority-Minority Relations (*Continued*)

LEVELS	APPROPRIATE QUESTIONS	A PARTIAL SYNOPSIS OF PRESENT CONCLUSIONS
SOCIOLOGICAL	How does institutional discrimination operate against the interests of minority groups?	Inequalities in the day-to-day operations of many institutions (e.g., employment, jury selection, education) adversely affect minority group members.
	Have all minority groups been equally affected by sociological forces?	No. Because of their distinctive history, black Americans have suffered most from the negative consequences of sociological forces.

haunt and deform American society until this day and into the foreseeable future. In his monumental study of race relations in the United States, the Swedish economist, Gunnar Myrdal, identified the contradiction between our democratic cultural ideals and the oppressed situation of blacks as the "American dilemma."[67] How could a free people, committed to individual liberty, maintain a slave system and, when that system was dismantled, continue a system of exploitation and discrimination that held another people in bondage? Although some early citizens felt that they could not support this contradiction and became abolitionists, others tried to rationalize this contradiction. That is, they felt that their culture could not accommodate *human* slavery, but it could accept the enslavement of an inferior, less-than-human, race. Thus, many whites came to deny blacks their humanity and were therefore able to reason that the blessings of equality need not include them.

Ironically, aristocratic ideals, such as those held by the Spanish settlers in Latin America, did *not* necessitate the dehumanization of blacks, for slavery was perfectly consistent with their aristocratic views. The Spanish could easily think of humans as slaves and thus felt no moral pressure to dehumanize and stigmatize blacks (or white for that matter). Although slavery itself may have been as harsh under Spanish rule as in the American case, once freed, blacks did not bear the burden of being regarded as biologically inferior. It is a sad irony of their democratic ideals that Americans had to dehumanize blacks in order to condone slavery, and they could not regard the freed blacks as fully human.[68]

During the nineteenth and early twentieth centuries, following the Darwinian revolution in biology (and the popular idea of the survival of the fittest), a variety of biological doctrines of racial superiority came into vogue. These were eagerly seized upon by many white Americans to support "scientifically" their beliefs about black inferiority. As will be discussed later in this chapter, biological notions of black inferiority still linger, not only among the ignorant and intolerant, but also within seemingly respectable social-science circles.

A second irony of the American ideology is that the doctrine of individualism[69] has also worsened the plight of blacks, and other minority groups, in our society. The belief that each person is responsible for his or her own destiny has made many Americans deaf to pleas to aid disadvantaged groups. Thus, once blacks were freed, or formal discriminatory barriers removed, Americans tended to think that nothing further needed to be done, or should be done, to aid their progress. Instead, Americans are inclined to think that it is up to blacks to get ahead in life.[70] The belief is that if only blacks would work hard, they could get ahead.[71] Unfortunately, wanting to work hard is not enough, especially in recent years and particularly for blacks. That is, as we will see in Chapter 10, American society does not provide nearly enough jobs for all who want them and, moreover, blacks have faced particularly virulent prejudice and discrimination.

However, not all aspects of American ideology have worked against the efforts of minority groups such as blacks to achieve equality. The American belief in fair play and equality has been used by minority groups seeking a more equitable place in society. The fact that most members of the dominant group believe that society ought to be fair gives weight to such appeals. It was precisely for these reasons that enslaving and oppressing blacks put Americans in a moral dilemma. The treatment of blacks did violate deeply held moral values, and the resulting uneasy conscience of white America has played a large role in black progress.

We have concentrated in this section on how the culture of the United States has served to help subordinate and exploit black Americans. While this is the most extreme example of the oppression of minority groups in American society, many of the same general points apply to other nonwhite minorities, especially Indians and Hispanics. Ideas of racial superiority or inferiority, and the need for minorities to make it on their own despite the discrimination they have encountered, have also adversely affected them. While Hispanics have not suffered nearly to the degree that blacks have, it could well be argued that American Indians have suffered from the effects of even greater prejudice and discrimination. To take just a few examples, Indians are almost three times as likely as whites to earn less than $5,000 per year. When combined with Alaskan natives (mainly Eskimos), they have an alcoholism rate of almost eight times that of all others, a homicide rate 2.5 times the overall rate, and a suicide rate almost double that of everyone else.[72] They also have the highest school dropout rate and the worst housing and health of any minority group.[73] While a good portion of the problems facing Indians, and the other nonwhite minorities of concern in this chapter, is attributable to cultural factors, we also need to examine more structural reasons for the subordinate position of blacks, Hispanics, and Indians. In this context we will concentrate on the phenomenon of institutional discrimination.

Structural Factors

Institutional Discrimination

Over the centuries a number of large-scale institutions have evolved in the United States—large businesses, the government, labor unions, health establishments, school systems, and the like. Over the years, these institutions have developed a variety of ways of doing business, of handling their day-to-day affairs. While these practices were evolving, patterns of ethnic and racial discrimination were evolving with them. In many instances, these institutions were led and staffed by racists and reflected the racist ideologies of the time. Given minority group subordination caused by cultural and institutional forces, the essential point about institutional racism is that today the routine operations of these institutions, even when there is no overt prejudice, operate to the detriment of minority groups.

Institutional discrimination refers to the inequalities that are rooted in the normal operation of social institutions and organizations and have little relation to attitudes toward minority groups or the majority group's prejudices. It involves practices that appear to be neutral but that in reality have a negative impact on minority individuals and groups. If individual prejudice were somehow eliminated from American society overnight, the inequalities between nonwhite minorities and whites that have become rooted in the "normal" operation of existing institutions would remain. In other words, in many circumstances prejudice is no longer necessary to maintain racial inequalities; discrimination may occur even if members of the majority group have no intention of discriminating.[74]

Institutional discrimination is illustrated by the following examples, in which the normal functioning of a social system maintains inequalities between majority and minority.

Housing

Even if there were no individual prejudice among realtors, because blacks, Hispanics, and Native Americans are more likely to be unemployed, employed in low-status occupations, and to earn considerably less than the white majority, they are less likely to be able to purchase a home. Even when they can, it is likely to be in a poor neighborhood in which the quality of life and the quality of the schools is likely to have an adverse effect on the children.

Employment

An employer may be genuinely willing to hire individuals of all races. However, as is well known, many jobs are obtained on the basis of personal contacts.[75] Employers are likely to be white and to have comparatively few personal contacts with nonwhite minorities and, conversely, job-seekers among nonwhites are unlikely to have direct or indirect contacts with white employers. If minorities had been previously excluded from such informal contact networks, they would be unlikely to learn about a vacancy, let along be in a position to take advantage of an opening.

Jury Selection

Jury selection is supposed to be colorblind in most states, jurors being randomly selected from lists of registered voters. However, even with recent voter registration drives, minorities are less likely to be registered voters and therefore less likely to be selected for juries. Because their peers are underrepresented, this may mean that minority defendants may not get as fair treatment as white defendants.

Education

Because their schools are less well funded, and because the best teachers gravitate to other schools, black, Hispanic, and Indian students are not as likely to get as good an education as majority group students. With poorer education, minority group children face a series of problems throughout the rest of their lives. In the main, this means that they are not likely to qualify for high-paying, high-status occupations in the primary labor market. Instead, they are likely to be relegated to the unstable, low-paying, and low-status positions in the secondary labor market. (See Chapter 11 for a discussion of the dual labor market.)

Institutional discrimination is thus more subtle, more complex, and less visible than discrimination flowing directly from individual prejudice. Because it does not result from the motivations or intentions of specific individuals, it is highly impersonal. Nevertheless, it has discriminatory consequences for minority group members, just as does individual prejudice.

If ideology and institutional discrimination are the major macrolevel factors causing problems for minority groups, the issue is why these factors have continued to affect blacks, Indians, and Hispanics adversely, while some groups, for example, Jews, Japanese, and Italians, have been largely able to escape their adverse effects and move into the mainstream of society.

More Successful Minority Groups

In order to understand differences in status that are found among different ethnic groups in the United States, it is necessary first to see how minority groups typically have gained equality in the past. Then we will be able to see whether the position of blacks, Indians, and Hispanics is similar to, or different from, that of earlier groups and whether the same patterns for achieving equality can be used.

Although founded by settlers from various nations, the United States became an English-speaking nation. New settlers began arriving from non-English-speaking countries, and although they experienced some difficulties, many became acclimated and an integral part of American society. Later waves of immigrants tended to find it harder to make their way in the United States. For example, in the 1840s millions of Irish arrived, fleeing the infamous potato famine. The Irish found the going harder. They were unskilled, extremely poor, and Roman Catholic. They faced widespread hostility and discrimination.[76] Following the Irish, new waves of immigrants tended to pose severe problems for the belief that newcomers could find their place in American society by assimilating. Serious problems confronted Italians, Poles, Greeks, Czechs, Hungarians, Russians, Chinese, and Japanese. Differences in culture, religion, language, and, in some cases, race made assimilation more difficult for these minority groups. Extremely hostile sentiments were aroused in the dominant White Anglo-Saxon Protestant (WASP) society by the continued entry of these "different" people into the nation. On the West Coast, for example, people were alarmed by fears of the "Yellow Peril"—a vision of wave after wave of Asia's masses flooding the land and swamping WASP culture. (An image, by the way, that is being repeated today with warnings of swarms of Central Americans fleeing to the United States if revolutionary movements there are successful.) Following World War I this hostility led to laws limiting further immigration, but sizable numbers of people from these groups were already in the country. Most observers doubted that they would ever achieve economic parity or social acceptance. Yet most did.[77]

Several factors have played critical roles in the ability of some minorities to escape their subordinate position, while others have been less able to do so. One important factor seems to have been geographic concentration. Because of discrimination in housing, the need to settle near jobs in industrial centers, as well as a tendency to group together for mutual support, most new immigrant groups lived in urban neighborhoods. As a result, they were able to control their communities and maximize their political impact within delimited areas. The Irish in Boston and the Jews in New York (and, more recently, the Jews in southern Florida) are classic examples of this phenomenon.

A second factor in the ability of a minority group to succeed is the ability of that group to exploit population concentration in order to be able to control their local businesses (stores and shops, for example) and ultimately their own financial institutions, especially banks. This makes it possible to avoid discrimination by financial institutions controlled by the majority group.[78] At the turn of the century, a small neighborhood savings bank—the Bank of Italy—was vital to the economic progress of San Francisco's Italian community. By concentrating savings in its own bank, the San Francisco Italian community was able to fund its own members in acquiring and operating businesses. The ultimate success of this strategy is nicely told: after a few years this little bank changed its name to Bank of America, and it became the largest privately owned bank in the world.

A third vital factor in the fate of a minority group is its social-class characteristics. To progress, a group must, for example, have middle-class members trained in the professions, able to run businesses and financial institutions, and able to provide effective community leadership. Some groups arriving in America already had a sizable middle class, and their progress was relatively rapid (Jews, Cubans, Japanese, and currently Vietnamese). Others (Irish, Italians, Poles) have progressed more slowly because they had to build a middle class after they arrived.[79] Given these factors in the success of various minority groups, the issue now is why in light of this did not blacks, Hispanics, and Indian Americans achieve a similar level of success?

Black Americans

Let us begin with black Americans. Before getting to the three factors discussed above, it is important to underscore the fact that the virulent and long-running racism experienced by blacks exceeds by far anything experienced by any of the minority groups discussed above. Everything else must be considered in this context. No other minority group experienced slavery as well as the deeply ingrained racism that accompanied and followed slavery. These experiences have and continue to impose greater liabilities on blacks than on most, if not all, other minority groups.[80]

One difference between blacks and the more successful minority groups has to do with geographic concentration. Until World War I blacks were largely scattered throughout rural areas in the South.[81] During this period, other minority groups were congregating and developing economic security[82] and political muscle within the cities. With the war, blacks began to move to the cities. Thus they centralized *later* than other minority groups *and,* perhaps more importantly, they entered cities in which these groups had already gained good jobs and control over various power centers. It is not until very recently that blacks have begun to turn this around, at least politically, and gain, for example, mayoral positions in Chicago, Los Angeles, Atlanta, Detroit, and Philadelphia.[83]

A second liability confronting blacks has been their inability to gain control over their own businesses and financial institutions. Ivan Light offers some very useful insights into why this is the case.[84] For one thing, native-born proprietors were often unable to satisfy the distinctive consumer needs of racial and ethnic groups. When these groups arrived, they spoke little English, had their own culture, and needed stores to supply them with the ethnic foods and other services to which they were accustomed: "The special demands of ethnic consumers (for example, Lasagna noodles, Kosher pickles, won ton soup) created protected markets for ethnic tradesmen who knew about the things their countrymen wanted."[85] In contrast to most other racial and ethnic groups who had special consumer demands that kept the majority group out of those markets, blacks had few such distinctive demands. Therefore, whites were quick to open proprietorships in the black community. As a result, the black proprietor, in order to succeed, had to overcome severe competition from white entrepreneurs.

Many other minority groups came with, or were able to create, their own financial institutions that were used to nurture these indigenous business undertakings. We have already mentioned the notable case of the Italians in San Francisco. The best examples, however, are the "rotating credit associations" among a number of Asian groups. In these associations, each member makes a regular contribution, and the sum is then given out in whole, or in part, to each contributor on a rotating basis. Because black Americans lacked such a tradition, they had to rely on existing banks, which were generally owned and operated by whites. It is well known that these banks discriminated (and to some extent still do) against black loan applicants. Because they were more dependent on these banks, black proprietors were less likely to get the funds they needed to be successful.

Finally, we must mention the social class characteristics of black Americans. While there were always some middle-class blacks, most were prevented from rising to this position by slavery and the racism that persisted after its demise. As blacks urbanized in the 1920s, they generally lacked the businesspeople, the financiers, the teachers, and the professionals that they needed to succeed. To a large degree, blacks had to begin creating a middle-class base in the 1920s when they came to the cities. It is only lately that large numbers of blacks have been successful in moving into the middle class.[86] In fact, Wilson argues that class affiliation has now become more important than race in determining the life chances of blacks. The offspring of middle-class blacks now have a good chance of succeeding, but the same cannot be said for the vast black underclass discussed earlier in this chapter. Wilson concludes:

> [I]n the economic sphere, class has become more important than race in determining black access to privilege and power. It is clearly evident in this connection that many talented and educated blacks are now entering positions of prestige and influence at a rate comparable to or, in some situations, exceeding that of whites with equivalent qualifications. It is equally clear that the black underclass is in a hopeless state of economic stagnation, falling further and further behind the rest of society.[87]

Native Americans

All in all, the overwhelming problems faced by black Americans are traceable in part to the kinds of factors discussed above, but above all to the historical legacy of slavery and the persistence of racism. Similarly, Native Americans owe their present subordinate position to racist elements in American culture that defined good Indians as dead Indians, and led them to be hunted down, deprived of their land, and assimilated (forcibly, if necessary) into the white culture, thereby destroying their cultural core. While blacks suffered from too little geographic concentration, at least prior to World War II, American Indians have been *too* concentrated and in the wrong places. As we have seen, half of all Indians live on reservations controlled, administered, and heavily supported by the federal government. Furthermore, these reservations are in comparatively isolated rural areas. For these reasons, and because there are less than a million and a half of them in the

United States, Indians have not been able to develop the political clout of most other minority groups. The Indians have lived a highly impoverished existence with great dependence on federal monies of one sort or another. There are comparatively few businesses or financial institutions. The result is that Native Americans have a very weak financial base. Finally, and relatedly, the weak economic situation means that the middle class is comparatively small. For example, while about 53 percent of white families earn more than $20,000 per year, less that 32 percent of Indian families earn that much money.

Hispanic Americans

It is harder to generalize about the situation confronting Hispanic Americans since the category represents several very diverse groups. Mexican-Americans, or Chicanos, are heavily represented in the Southwest. While once a predominantly rural, agricultural population, Chicanos have tended to become concentrated in the *barrios,* or Chicano ghettos, of the Southwest. Up until now, however, Chicanos have tended to lack the business, financial, and middle-class base needed to exert considerable control over their environments. Puerto Rican immigrants have tended to concentrate on the east coast of the United States, especially in New York City, where about 1 million of the 1.5 million Puerto Ricans in the continental United States reside. Puerto Rican migration to the mainland was primarily among the impoverished loser strata of Puerto Rican society. Consequently, Puerto Rican immigrants are concentrated in blue-collar, semiskilled, and unskilled occupations. This means that they, like Chicanos, lack the businesspeople, the financiers, and, more generally, the middle class needed to exert greater control on their surroundings.

The case of Cuban migration provides a striking contrast to that of Puerto Ricans and Chicanos. The heart of the Cuban migration was made up of political refugees from Castro's communist revolution in Cuba. The early Cuban migration tended to be drawn primarily from the upper social and economic strata of Cuban society. Derived overwhelmingly from middle- and upper-class backgrounds, they brought capital, skills (financial, managerial, business, and educational) and entrepreneurial values that enabled them to prosper and achieve socioeconomic success with a speed—less than a generation—that is virtually unprecedented among American immigrant groups. In the twenty years since their main migration, Cubans have become a political and economic force in a number of American cities where they are heavily concentrated, especially Miami, Florida. Thus, Cubans have had the geographic concentration, the business and financial base, and the middle class needed to succeed in American society. This distinguishes them from other Hispanics, American Indians, and blacks and accounts for their distinctive history as a minority group in American society.

The most recent flood of Hispanic immigrants from such places as Haiti, El Salvador, Honduras, Guatamala, and a whole new wave from Mexico are largely from the lower classes and the peasantry. They tend to lack the capital, skills, and values that enabled Cubans (and other groups, such as Koreans and Vietnamese) to succeed in American society. The result is that they are likely to experience considerable difficulty in the coming decades.

INDIVIDUAL LEVEL

Psychological Factors

Prejudice: Cultural Sources

While prejudice is generally thought of as a psychological phenomenon, it has cultural and structural roots. The cultural

Figure 8.3 Immigrants by Continent: 1820–1979

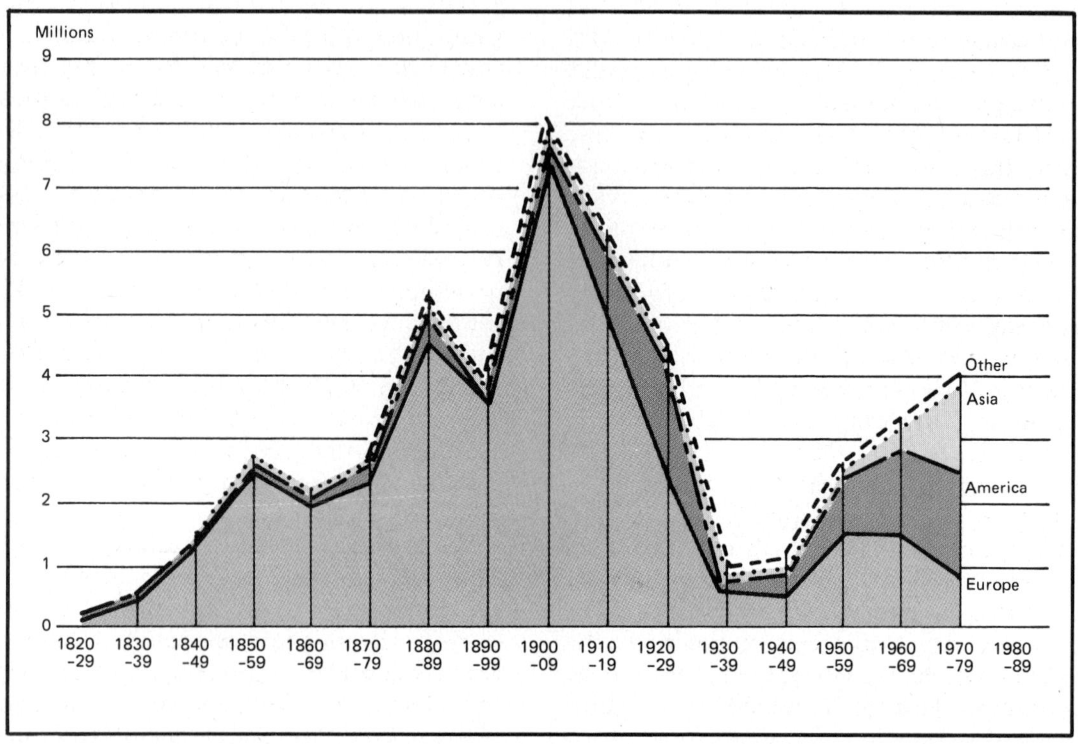

Shown here are the changing sources of immigration into the U.S., as reflected by the continental origins of the newcomers.

Source: U.S. Bureau of the Census, *Statistical Abstract of the United States: 1984* (Washington, D.C.: U.S. Government Printing Office, 1983), p. 89.

roots of prejudice are reflected in ethnic and racial *stereotypes.* Some of our stereotypes are: Germans are perceived as industrious, scientifically minded, and stolid; Irish are quick-tempered and extremely nationalistic; Jews are characterized as mercenary and intelligent; blacks are seen as musical, superstitious, and lazy. These stereotypes not only exist within the culture, but they are *learned* by people through the socialization process. In other words, one could easily say that people learn stereotypes about minority groups and more generally they learn whom to be prejudiced against and for what reasons.

Prejudice: Structural Sources

Prejudice can also be seen as having structural roots largely in the competition between majority and minority groups for jobs, political power, or social rank. Antagonism between white and black workers is frequently heightened when they compete for the same jobs. Prejudice toward blacks has been especially intense when they have been used as strikebreakers in labor disputes. Similarly, during the 1870s much of the anti-Chinese agitation in the Far West was led by labor unions, which regarded Chinese workers as an economic threat. Labor unions led the drive for exclusion of

Chinese immigrants. Their rhetoric emphasized Chinese racial inferiority and their congenital immorality.

Prejudice: Psychological Aspects

Although prejudice has cultural and structural roots and is learned social-psychologically, our main concern here is with the psychology of prejudice. As we have seen, *prejudice* refers to a set of rigidly held negative attitudes, beliefs, and feelings toward members of another group. Thus prejudice can be said to reside within the psychology of an individual. But where does prejudice come from? As we have seen, it can come from cultural and structural sources, and it is a learned phenomenon. But while these same sources exist for everyone, not everyone is prejudiced in the same degree. This leads to the perspective that there are *personality factors* that predispose some people to be prejudiced and others to be less prejudiced, or even to be completely lacking in prejudice. In other words, there are pathologies within personalities that lead people to be prejudiced.

One important psychological mechanism that is thought to lead to prejudice is *displaced aggression.* This idea emphasizes that prejudice is a manifestation of aggression, which is the inevitable outcome of frustration. Minority groups become convenient *scapegoats* for frustrations experienced by members of the majority group. People do not vent their aggression on just any available target. They most often direct it toward those whose capacity to fight back is limited—toward victims lacking in power. Minority group members are attractive targets for aggression because they are less able to fight back.[88] This may take the very individual form of unemployed white workers blaming blacks or Chicanos for their predicament, rather than blaming the owners or managers who may have laid them off. Such displaced aggression may be the result of more general forces as well. For example, the lurid anti-Semitic propaganda and the subsequent persecution of the Jews in Nazi Germany can be interpreted in part as a result of the frustrations experienced by the Germans after their defeat in World War I, when they suffered humiliation at the hands of the Allies.

Another psychological pathology related to prejudice is *projection,* or the tendency to attribute to others characteristics that individuals cannot admit they have themselves. Frequently, such tendencies are sexual in nature. In the South, sexual relations between white males and white females were inhibited by a puritanical code proclaiming the sexual purity of white women. As a result, white men found black females sexually attractive and established sexual liaisons with them. White men projected their sexual desire for members of a different race on black males and white females, for whom sexual relations with blacks were forbidden. Lynchings of black males for alleged sexual advances toward white women are seen by some scholars as the result of a projection of the white man's own repressed sexual desires.

Numerous psychological studies have also interpreted prejudice to be the result of a particular personality type—the *authoritarian personality.*[89] Such a personality is said to be found in individuals who, because of harsh and punitive forms of discipline during childhood socialization, become extremely rigid, conventional, insecure, conformist, and prone to identify with power figures. Authoritarian personality types are likely to be highly intolerant of group differences and prone to prejudices toward minority groups in general. Authoritarian personalities have also been found to be highly prejudiced against fictitious, nonexistent groups.[90]

Although they do not deny the importance of psychological factors, most sociologists see them as far less important than the large-scale social and cultural factors discussed earlier in this chapter. After his review of the importance of psychological and social-psychological factors in racial prejudice, Howard Ehrlich concluded:

> The primary causes of the transmission . . . and . . . maintenance of the ethnic prejudice in society are not to be found in the psychology of people or in the social psychology of their interpersonal relationships. It is to be found in the peculiar historical conditions and present political economic structure out of which intergroup relations develop and are sustained.[91]

Physiological Factors

Because race provides a prominent focus for intergroup conflict in the United States, it is clear that physiology plays an important role. Even though we emphasize the social definition of racial differences, physiological factors certainly play a central role in these definitions. Racism may be said to occur when biological differences between races are interpreted as evidence of the biological inferiority of some race.

Earlier in this chapter, we pointed out that racism was used to justify slavery and racial subordination, which directly contradicted the values of equality and freedom. By defining blacks as an inferior species, white Americans could justify their bondage. (The same device was used to explain and excuse the conquest of American Indians.) Notions that nonwhites were biologically inferior were held not only by southerners or slave owners but also by many northerners.[92]

For generations, the battle against racism has focused on establishing the common humanity and biological equality of all races. Today, crude biological doctrines of racial inequality are quickly discredited—only a few disgruntled hate merchants still warn about tainting white blood with black or claim that nonwhites are lower on the ladder of ascent from the apes.

Nevertheless, over the last two decades, a bitter controversy has raged in social science over claims that blacks, as a group, are genetically endowed with less intelligence than whites. Because some of these claims have been made by respectable social scientists, their potential impact on racial attitudes and public policy is considerable. These claims of genetic inferiority have outraged blacks and have been seized upon gleefully by white racists. Thus, it is essential to examine this issue.

For a long time it has been known that blacks achieve a somewhat lower average score on standard IQ tests than whites do. For nearly as long a time, it was generally assumed by social scientists that these differences meant nothing more than that blacks had been the victims of many cultural deprivations—poor education, poverty, the miseries of slum life, and the like. And, in fact, studies showed that some of these factors, when taken into account, reduced the differences between black and white average IQ scores. However, no study thus far has isolated enough environmental factors to account for all differences in IQ scores that occur between the races.

In 1969, in one of the most controversial works in recent years in the social sciences, Arthur Jensen, an educational psychologist, argued that there was clearly a significant genetic component to IQ and that even when environmental differences were taken into account, differences between the races would remain that could only be traced to genetics. Hence, he predicted that even when all traces of racism and disadvantage are rooted out of society, blacks would, on the average, still lag behind whites in terms of IQ.[93] While Jensen has been very cautious about conclusions to be drawn about his work, the same is not true of others with racist inclinations. They have drawn the conclusion from work like that of Jensen's that the principal causes of problems within the black community are genetically determined and that blacks with low IQs might be sterilized voluntarily in order to improve the overall population.[94]

Needless to say, the Jensen thesis has proven to be highly controversial and has been attacked on a variety of grounds. For one thing, as we saw earlier, race is a socially defined phenomenon, and this would lead us to be very dubious about any link to genetic factors. For another, in order to carry out comparative research on a scientific basis, "pure" racial groups are a necessity. However, it is difficult both internationally and in the United States to find such groups since both "white" and "black" groups have substantial admixtures of "blood" from the other group. In addition, in doing such research, it would be essential to control fully for environmental effects (for example, type of family life, type of education), and, given the tremendous class and cultural differences between blacks and whites, this would be virtually impossible. Then, it would be necessary to develop a genuinely culture-free intelligence test, a creation that most observers believe has yet to be achieved.[95] Finally, Jensen's work, and others of that ilk, are assailable on a variety of logical grounds for making a number of arbitrary and implausible assumptions.[96] It is hard at this point to support Jensen's position, but it is also impossible to dismiss totally the role of genetics in intelligence.

PART III: RESPONSES

We come now to the question of how, in the past as well as today, our various social, economic, and government institutions have responded to the existence of prejudice and discrimination. We will focus on the problems confronted by blacks, as well as national level and governmental efforts to destroy slavery and legalize racism. This is relevant beyond the case of the black minority, since a change in the legal status of black Americans generally meant improved status for all disadvantaged minorities. Where discrimination was banned by the government, it was banned against *all* individuals, regardless of race, color, or national origin.

Reconstruction Legislation

Following the Civil War, there was a flurry of civil rights legislation designed to transform former slaves into free persons and to grant them all the rights and privileges of citizenship. The Thirteenth Amendment (1865) freed all slaves who were not freed by President Lincoln's Emancipation Proclamation of 1863. The Fourteenth Amendment (1868) declared that former slaves were citizens and thus had the right to equal protection and due process under the law. The Fifteenth Amendment (1870) granted the new citizens the right to vote.

The Civil Rights Act of 1866 was the first federal law designed to protect the civil rights of American blacks. It not only declared that all persons born in the United States were citizens (with the notable exception of Native Americans), but also gave them the basic rights of all citizens (for example, to make contracts, to sue, to receive legal protection, to sell personal property). The law also called for equal punishment for crimes without regard to race or color. The Civil Rights Act of 1875 stressed social equality while the 1866 act had emphasized political equality. It guaranteed "full and equal" access to public accommodations, such as inns, public transportation, theaters, and amusement places. Blacks were permitted to serve on juries. It was to be almost a century later that Congress would pass another piece of civil rights legislation. Worse, for the next quarter century the principles set down by these laws were to be set aside.

Reassertion of White Dominance

During the last quarter of the nineteenth century, patterns of institutional racism became an established and integral part of American life. Those who opposed black equality enacted anti-civil-rights legislation (the "Jim Crow" system of legal segregation), which excluded blacks from positions of power, prestige, and privilege throughout the South. The legal power of the state was reinforced by vigilante groups, such as the Ku Klux Klan, which resorted to violence, terrorism, and, frequently, lynching, to intimidate blacks who sought to challenge white dominance or exercise their constitutional rights as citizens.

By 1896, the widespread attack against the equality of blacks was in full flower. In the case of *Plessy v. Ferguson* (1896), the Supreme Court upheld the principle of "separate but equal" as it applied to public transportation and facilities. There followed a rash of enactments of "separate but equal" legislation, which quickly extended the principle to all aspects of social and political life. Beyond that, a series of segregation laws was passed to discriminate further against and suppress blacks.

The Brown Case

The legal doctrine of "separate but equal" stood for more than a half century. However, in 1954, the Supreme Court declared the separate but equal principle unconstitutional. Although focusing on education, it dealt a death blow to all segregation laws and promised major changes in institutions, as well as in norms and values throughout society. However, the sweeping changes suggested by the 1954 decision were not implemented without an intense struggle. Public schools were closed and funds diverted to private schools, federal troops had to be called out to protect black children, and southern political leaders (among them Governor George Wallace of Alabama) made national reputations for themselves by trying to prevent some of these changes. By the end of the decade, Congress was to take legislative action to, among other things, protect voting rights and establish, and later extend the power of, the United States Commission on Civil Rights.

The 1960s

During the decade of the 1960s the federal government asserted itself in the area of human rights as it never had done before. The Civil Rights Act of 1964 outlawed discrimination in employment, as well as in such public places as hotels, restaurants, parks, hospitals, and the like. The 1965 Voting Rights Act (extended in 1983) banned previously existing literacy tests and other discriminatory tests for voters and gave federal examiners the power to protect voters' rights. Dramatic increases in black voter registration, in black voting, and in the number of blacks elected to office followed the enactment of the Voting Rights Act.

Race riots during the mid-1960s in cities like Los Angeles, New York, Washington, D.C., and Detroit, as well as the militancy of the civil rights movement, led to a shift in focus from the de jure discrimination in the South to de facto discrimination in the North and West. This shift led, at least in part, to federal legislation designed to address the existence of poverty in an "affluent" society. Examples include such programs as Head Start, the Job Corps, Medicare and Medicaid, school lunch programs, and many others. However, the election of Richard Nixon in 1968 ushered in a period of "benign neglect" in which comparatively little was done to improve the lot of the poor, deprived, and disadvantaged. In fact, with the Reagan administration strong efforts have been made to cut back and even dismantle many of the programs mentioned above.

Minority Power Movements

Paralleling, and in part contributing to, changes at the national level was the growth of various groups seeking in a number of ways to improve the status of blacks. Martin Luther King, Jr., and his nonviolent movement, was a powerful force until his assassination in 1968. King provided the groundwork for the development of more radical groups and black leaders. Among the most notable of these groups were the Student Non-Violent Coordinating Committee (S.N.C.C.) and the Black Muslims. The best-known leaders were Stokely Carmichael, Rap Brown, and Malcolm X. In thc 1960s, thcsc groups and leaders pushed for major changes in race relations in this country, and the federal government responded, at least in part. These black groups and leaders also served as models for other minorities. Subsequently, Chi-

Some blacks have adopted a militant response to their minority position in America. Pictured here (in 1982) are Moe and Mary Africa of the MOVE sect in Philadelphia. MOVE adopted a life style very different from that of most Americans. On May 14, 1985, the police tried to evict them from the building in which they lived, but a bomb dropped on the roof by the police led to a firestorm that killed five persons and set fire to sixty neighboring buildings.

(Mary D'Anella/Sygma)

cano power movements, "red power" movements, and even the Jewish Defense League—all modeled at least in part after black militant groups—sought to combat their minority status.

The 1970s and Into the 1980s

Blackwell has described this period as one marked by "stagnation and retrogression in economic and social progress among blacks."[97] One factor in this was a growing weakness in the black movement. During this period, it was torn by a series of internal schisms, and this sense of disarray was enhanced by a breakdown in some of its traditional alliances with groups in the white community. Another was a change in the political mood within the country. At one level this was seen in a series of Supreme Court decisions in the late 1970s (*University of California Regents v. Bakke; Fullilove v. Klutznick*) that seemed to temper various efforts to cope with past discrimination against blacks by the institution of affirmative action programs in which blacks were accorded some degree of preferential treatment.[98] At another, and more important, level a conservative shift in the United States culminated in the election of Ronald Reagan in 1980. With few political debts to the black community, and a commitment to get the federal government out of legislating such matters, Reagan did little to help black Americans in the 1980s. This political climate, as well as difficult economic times in the early 1980s, led to a loss of commitment by the population as a whole to the black cause.

SUMMARY

1. Majority-minority problems are found throughout the world.

Part I: The Problem

2. Power is the crucial factor in differentiating between majority and minority groups.
3. Our main concern is with the problem of intergroup conflict: conflict based on socially defined physical and cultural differences between groups.
4. Majority groups have a number of policies open to them in dealing with minority groups, including extermination, expulsion and exclusion, caste, assimilation, and pluralism.
5. Minority groups have a number of responses to majority group policies available to them, including acceptance, resistance, avoidance, and separatism.
6. Minority groups in the United States—Hispanics, Native Americans (Indians), and especially black Americans—suffer from a number of problems including economic inequality, inequality in education, housing discrimination, poor health and health care, and, particularly in the case of blacks, the deterioration of the family.

Part II: Causes and Consequences

7. American culture, from the beginning, had a built-in contradiction between democratic ideals and the oppression of the black minority.
8. The plight of black Americans was made worse by the ideology of individualism. This led to the view that if blacks were not getting ahead, they had only themselves to blame.
9. At the social structural level, we examined institutional discrimination, or the adverse effects on minorities of inequalities in the day-to-day operations of various large-scale institutions.
10. Institutional discrimination is illustrated in housing, employment, jury selection, and education.

11. We also explored the reasons why cultural and institutional factors continue to affect blacks, Indians, and Hispanics adversely, while Jews, Italians, Japanese, and others have been largely able to escape them. Among the factors discussed are geographic concentration of minorities, their ability to control local institutions, and the social class characteristics of the minority group. We examined the situation confronting blacks, Indians, and Hispanics in terms of these factors in order to better understand their continuing problems.
12. One of the major individual-level causes of problems for minority groups is prejudice. Prejudice is seen as being caused by an array of cultural, structural, and personality factors.
13. Although most biological explanations of racial inequality have been discredited, there is continuing controversy over the linkage between heredity and intelligence. Blacks score lower on IQ tests and some have argued that at least a portion of this difference can be explained genetically. A number of major criticisms have been made of this thesis, but the issue of a genetic factor in racial differences in intelligence refuses to disappear.

Part III: Responses

14. We surveyed the history of government efforts to deal with racism. We saw that a number of major changes were made between the end of the Civil War and the 1960s.
15. At the same time, minority power movements helped improve the position of cultural and racial minorities.
16. However, in the 1970s and 1980s, blacks and other minorities have experienced a period of stagnation and even retrogression.

SUGGESTED READINGS

Dinnerstein, Leonard, and David Reimers, *Ethnic Americans: A History of Immigration and Assimilation*, 2nd ed. New York: Harper & Row, 1982. A brief history of American immigration and assimilation.

Feagin, Joe R., and Clairece Booher Feagin, *Discrimination American Style: Institutional Racism and Sexism.* Englewood Cliffs, N. J.: Prentice-Hall, 1978. An analysis of the problem of institutional discrimination as it reflects not only racism, but also sexism.

Feagin, Joe R., *Racial and Ethnic Relations*, 2nd ed. Englewood Cliffs, N. J.: Prentice-Hall, 1984. A basic text in race and ethnic relations.

Wilson, William J., *The Declining Significance of Race: Blacks and Changing American Institutions*, 2nd ed. Chicago: University of Chicago Press, 1980. A highly provocative and controversial analysis of black Americans and social stratification.

Yetman, Norman R., ed., *Majority-Minority: Dynamics of Race and Ethnicity in American Life*, 4th ed. Boston: Allyn and Bacon, 1985. The most recent edition of a basic anthology on race and ethnic relations.

FOOTNOTES

[1]Anthony Davis, "Ethnic Conflict Spreading in Sri Lanka," *The Washington Post*, May 26, 1985, p. A21.

[2]Stuart Auerbach, "Racial Clashes Leave Bitter Legacy Marring Peace of Sri Lanka," *The Washington Post*, October 7, 1981, p. A11.

[3]William Branigin, "Australia's Aborigines Uneasily Straddle Racial, Cultural Divide," *The Washington Post*, November 3, 1981, pp. A16, A17.

[4]Michael Weisskopf, "Ethnic Conflict in Strategic Western Province Alarms Peking." *The Washington Post*, September 12, 1981, pp. A1, A25.

[5]Rene LeMarchand, "Ethnic Genocide," *Society*, 12 (1975), 50–60.

[6]James E. Blackwell, "Persistence and Change in Intergroup Relations: The Crisis Upon Us," *Social Problems*, 29 (1982), 325–346.

[7]Norman R. Yetman, ed., "Introduction: Definitions and Perspectives." In *Majority-Minority: Dynamics of Race and Ethncity in American Life.*, 4th ed. (Boston: Allyn & Bacon, 1985), p. 2.

[8]This section, as well as the next on minority group responses, is based on the work of my colleague, Norman R. Yetman. In addition, a number of his ideas may be found scattered throughout the chapter. For more of his thoughts, see the textual material in Norman R. Yetman, ed., *Majority-Minority: Dynamics of Race and Ethnicity in American Life*, 4th ed. (Boston: Allyn & Bacon, 1985).

[9]Wilcomb Washburn, *The Indian in America* (New York: Harper & Row, 1975).

[10]George E. Simpson and J. Milton Yinger, *Racial and Cultural Minorities: An Analysis of Prejudice and Discrimination*, 4th ed. (New York: Harper & Row, 1972), pp. 22–23.

[11]Edna Bonacich, "A Theory of Ethnic Antagonism: The Split Labor Market," *American Sociological Review*, 37 (1972), 547–559.

[12]Milton Gordon, *Assimilation in American Life: The Role of Race, Religion and National Origins* (New York: Oxford University Press, 1964).

[13]Andrew Hacker, *U/S: A Statistical Portrait of the American People* (New York: Viking, 1983), pp. 34–36.

[14]This number is probably an underestimation since there are many illegal immigrants—especially from Mexico and other Latin American countries—that may not show up in these figures. See David M. Reimers, "Post-World War II Immigration to the United States: America's Latest Newcomers," *Annals*, 454 (1981), 1–12.

[15]*Ibid.*

[16]James Fallows, "Immigration: How It's Affecting Us," *The Atlantic Monthly*, November 1983, pp. 45ff.

[17]David H. Swinton, "A Labor Force Competition Theory of the Labor Market," *American Economic Review*, 67 (1977), 400–404.

[18]James D. Williams, ed., *The State of Black America: 1984* (New York: National Urban League, 1984), p. 21.

[19]For comparison purposes, it is interesting to note that the position of Mexican-American families was not much better. In 1979, median family income for Mexican-Ameicans was less than $13,000, while it was close to $18,000 for non-Hispanic families. See Harry P. Pachon and Joan W. Moore, "Mexican Americans," *Annals*, 454 (1981), 111–124. However, it is Native Americans who are the worst off economically, lowest in income, and the least employed of all major minority groups. See Michael A. Dorris, "The Grass Still Grows, The Rivers Still Flow: Contemporary Native Americans," *Daedalus*, 110 (1981), 43–69.

[20]Williams *op. cit.*, p. 21.

[21]Hacker, *op. cit.*, pp. 128–129.

[22]William J. Wilson, "The Black Community in the 1980's: Questions of Race, Class and Public Policy," *Annals*, 454 (1981), 26–41.

[23]Williams, *op.cit.*, p. 177.

[24]Hacker, *op.cit.*, p. 123.

[25]Williams, *op. cit.*, p. 2.

[26]U.S. Department of Commerce, Bureau of the Census, *Statistical Abstract of the United States: 1984* (Washington, D.C.: U.S. Governmment Printing Office, 1983), p. 144.

[27]U.S. Department of Commerce, Bureau of the Census, *U.S. Summary*, PC 80-1-C1 (Washington, D.C.: U.S. Government Printing Office, 1980), p. 157.

[28]For a discussion of the general view, as well as some evidence against it, see Christopher Jencks, *Inequality: A Reassessment of the Effect of Family and Schooling in America* (New York: Basic Books, 1972), pp. 221–232.

[29]Edward Cody, "Florida's 'Havana'," *The Washington Post.* May 14, 1983, pp. A1, A4.

[30]Karl E. Taeuber, "Housing, Schools, and Incremental Segregative Effects," *Annals*, 441 (1979), 157–167.

[31]Doris R. Entwistle and Leslie A. Hayduk, *Too Great Expectations: The Academic Outlook of Young Children* (Baltimore, Md.: Johns Hopkins University Press, 1978).

[32]Cited in Charles Silberman, *Crisis in the Classroom: The Remaking of American Education* (New York: Random House, 1970), p. 84.

[33]See, for example, Jencks, *op. cit.*; "The Racial Gap in SAT Scores, " *Newsweek*, October 18, 1982, p. 110.

[34]Robert Rosenthal and Lenore Jacobson, *Pygmalion in the Classroom* (New York: Holt, Rinehart and Winston, 1968).

[35]*Ibid.*, p. 195.

[36]*Ibid.* p. 176.

[37]Sarane Spence Boocock, *Sociology of Education*, 2nd ed. (Boston: Houghton Mifflin, 1980).

[38]Hacker, *op. cit.*, p. 239.

[39]*Statistical Abstract: 1984*, pp. 37–41.

[40]Hacker, *op.cit.*, p. 247.

[41]Charles R. Babcock, "Federal Budget Cuts Cause Black Colleges Special Pain," *Washington Post*, October 3, 1981, p. A2.

[42]Wilson, *op.cit.* On the other hand, white male high-school graduates are likely to earn more than black

college graduates. Furthermore, even though the recent black college graduate may initially earn more than the white college graduate, the white college graduate is likely to outstrip him/her because of greater upward career mobility.

[43]James E. Blackwell, *Mainstreaming Outsiders: The Production of Black Professionals* (New York: General Hall, 1981).

[44]*Ibid.*

[45]In spite of continuing racial segregation, there are some outstanding schools with predominantly black populations.

[46]Juliet Saltman, "Housing Discrimination: Policy Research, Methods and Results," *Annals,* 441 (1979), 186–196.

[47]"America's Indians: 'Beggars in Our Own Land'," *U.S. News and World Report,* May 23, 1983, pp. 70–72.

[48]Thomas B. Morgan, "The Latinization of America," *Esquire,* May 1983, pp. 47ff.

[49]Wade Clark Roof, "Race and Residence: The Shifting Basis of American Race Relations," *Annals,* 441 (January 1979), 1–12.

[50]"Black Mayors of Major Cities," *The Washington Post,* April 24, 1983, p. A7.

[51]*Statistical Abstract: 1984.,* pp. 37–38.

[52]*Ibid.,* p. 753.

[53]Hacker. *op. cit.,* p.259.

[54]National Center for Health Statistics, *Health, United States, 1984.* DHHS Pub. No. (PHS) 85–1232. Public Health Service (Washington, D.C.: U.S. Government Printing Office, 1984), pp. 59–60.

[55]*Ibid.* p. 53.

[56]*Ibid.* pp. 53, 54.

[57]John E. Farley, *Majority-Minority Relations* (Englewood Cliffs, N.J.: Prentice-Hall, 1982), pp. 249–260.

[58]Daniel Patrick Moynihan, *The Negro Family: The Case for National Action* (Washington, D.C.: U.S. Government Printing Office, 1965).

[59]Wilson, *op. cit.*

[60]William Julius Wilson, "The Black Underclass," *The Wilson Quarterly* 90 (1984); see also William Julius Wilson, "The Urban Underclass, Social Dislocation, and Public Policy." In Leslie Dunbar, ed., *Civil Rights: Where Now and Where Headed* (New York: Pantheon, 1984). James D. McGhee, "A Profile of the Black Single Female-Headed Household." In James D. Williams, ed., *The State of Black America 1984* (New York: National Urban League, 1984), pp. 43–55.

[61]Judith Cummings, "Breakup of Black Family Imperils Gains of Decades," *The New York Times,* November 20, 1983, pp. 1, 56.

[62]Wilson, *op. cit.,* 1984, p. 90.

[63]*Ibid.*

[64]*Ibid.*

[65]*Ibid.,* p. 94.

[66]*Ibid.,* p. 97.

[67]Gunnar Mydral, *An American Dilemma: The Negro Problem and Modern Democracy* (New York: Harper & Row, 1944).

[68]Frank Tannenbaum, *Slave and Citizen: The Negro in America* (New York: Knopf, 1947).

[69]James R. Kluegel and Eliot R. Smith, "White Beliefs About Black Opportunity," *American Sociological Review,* 47 (1982), pp. 518–532.

[70]Howard Schuman, "Free Will and Determinism in Public Beliefs About Race." In Norman Yetman (with C. Hoy Steele), ed., *Majority and Minority: The Dynamics of Race and Ethnicity in American Life,* 3rd ed. (Boston: Allyn and Bacon, 1982), pp. 345–350.

[71]Gary Marx, *Protest and Prejudice: A Study of Belief in the Black Community* (New York: Harper & Row, 1967).

[72]"American Indians," *U.S. News and World Report, op. cit.,* p. 71.

[73]Charles R. Babcock, "Signs of Hope Rise in Indian Schools," *The Washington Post,* December 27, 1981, p. A1.

[74]Stokely Carmichael and Charles Hamilton, *Black Power: The Politics of Liberation in America* (New York: Vintage, 1967).

[75]Mary Corcoran, Linda Datcher, and Greg J. Duncan, "Most Workers Find Jobs Through Word of Mouth," *Monthly Labor Review,* 103 (1980),pp. 33–35. Graham Reid, "Job Search and the Effectiveness of Job Finding Methods," *Industrial and Labor Relations Review,* 25 (1972), pp. 479–495.

[76]Lawrence J. McCaffrey, *The Irish Diaspora in American* (Bloomington: Indiana University Press, 1976).

[77]Andrew Greeley, "The Ethnic Miracle." In Yetman and Steele, eds.,*op. cit.,* pp. 260–269.

[78]Ivan Light, *Ethnic Enterprise in America: Business and Welfare Among Chinese, Japanese and Blacks* (Berkeley: University of California Press, 1972). See also "Seller's Rush to Woo Hispanic Customers," *U.S. News and World Report,* August 8, 1983, pp. 42–43; "No Hurry to Reach Black Consumer," *U.S. News and World Report,* August 8, 1983, p. 43.

[79]Stephen Steinberg, *The Ethnic Myth: Race, Ethnicity and Class in America* (New York: Atheneum, 1981); Stephen Steinberg, *The Academic Melting Pot* (New York: McGraw-Hill, 1974).

[80]Stanley Lieberson, *A Piece of the Pie: Blacks and White Immigrants Since 1880* (Berkeley: University of California Press, 1980).

[81]However, it should be noted that blacks did develop a numerical majority in some areas, but they still did not achieve power commensurate with their numbers.

[82]Theodore Hershberg *et al.*, "A Tale of Three Cities: Blacks and Immigrants in Philadelphia: 1850–1880, 1930 and 1970," *Annals*, 441 (1979), pp. 55–81.

[83]However, it is problematic whether the power that black mayors possess today is comparable to the power of "ethnic mayors" of the past.

[84]Light, *op. cit.*

[85]*Ibid.*, p. 12.

[86]William J. Wilson, *The Declining Significance of Race: Blacks and Changing American Institutions*, 2nd ed. (Chicago: University of Chicago Press, 1980).

[87]*Ibid.*, p. 2.

[88]John Dollard *et al.*, *Frustration and Aggression* (New Haven, Conn.: Yale University Press, 1961). For a critical analysis of this idea, as well as many others associated with the psychology of prejudice, see Howard J. Ehrlich, *The Social Psychology of Prejudice* (New York: Wiley, 1973).

[89]Theodor Adorno *et al.*, *The Authoritarian Personality* (New York: Harper & Row, 1950).

[90]Eugene Hartley, *Problems in Prejudice* (New York: Kings Crown, 1946).

[91]Ehrlich, *op. cit.*, pp. 160–161.

[92]Thomas F. Gosset, *Race: The History of an Idea in America* (Dallas: Southern Methodist University Press, 1963).

[93]Arthur Jensen, "How Much Can We Boost IQ and Scholastic Achievement?" *Harvard Educational Review*, 39 (1969), 1–123; *Bias in Mental Testing* (New York: Free Press, 1980).

[94]Howard F. Taylor, *The IQ Game* (New Brunswick, N. J.: Rutgers University Press, 1980), p. 3.

[95]Norman Yetman, personal communication.

[96]Taylor, *op. cit.*

[97]Blackwell, *op. cit.*, p. 333.

[98]Charles Lamb, "Legal Foundations of Civil Rights and Pluralism in America," *Annals*, 454 (1981), pp. 13–25.

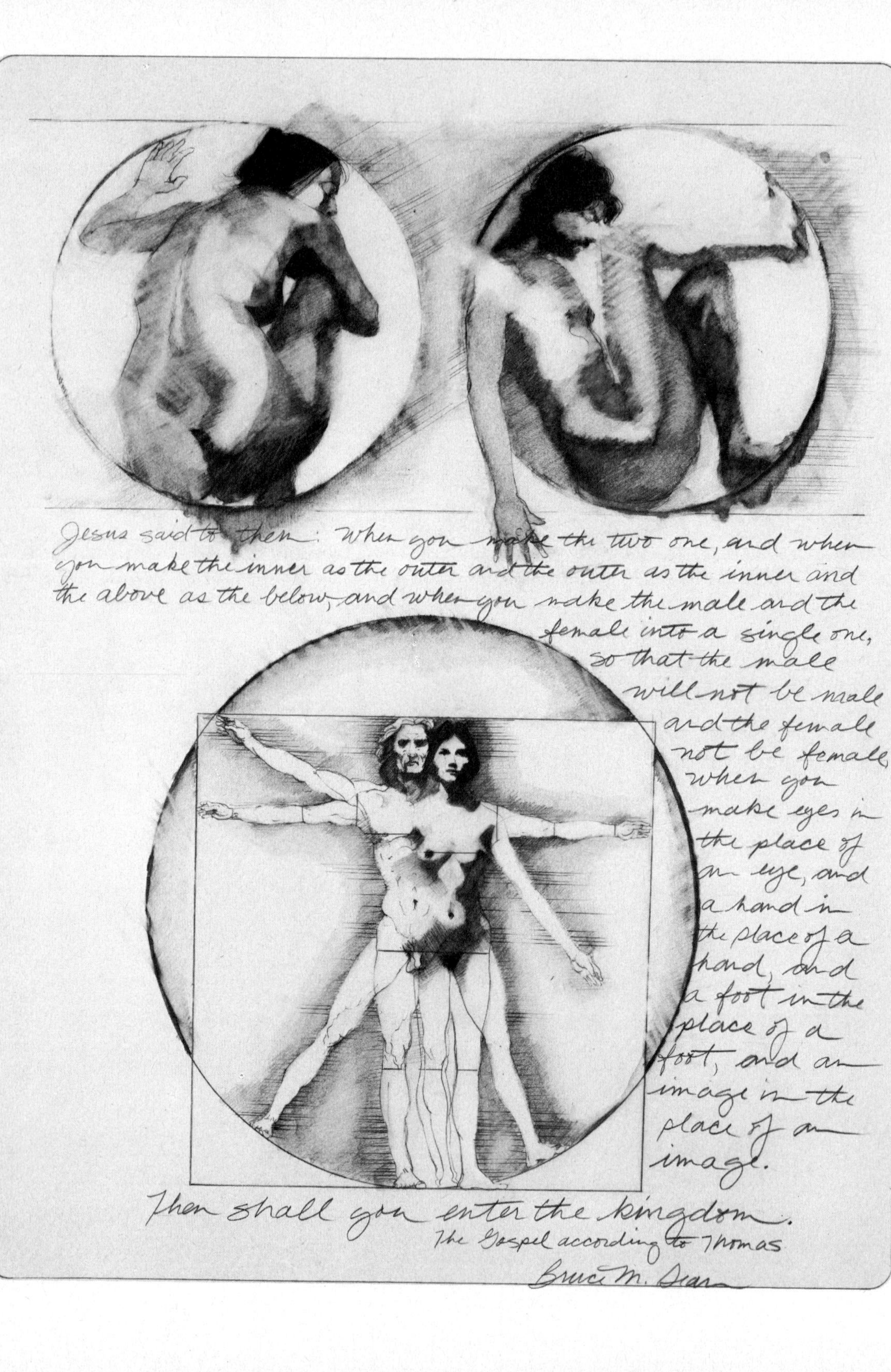
Jesus said to them: When you make the two one, and when you make the inner as the outer and the outer as the inner and the above as the below, and when you make the male and the female into a single one, so that the male will not be male and the female not be female, when you make eyes in the place of an eye, and a hand in the place of a hand, and a foot in the place of a foot, and an image in the place of an image.
Then shall you enter the kingdom.
The Gospel according to Thomas
Bruce M. Sears

9 Gender Inequality

Starting from such modest advantages as greater size and weight, as well as freedom from most of the burdens of pregnancy and child-rearing, males have exploited their initial physical advantages over females by gaining control over various social structures and the larger culture. With this control, they have been able to expand their power greatly while simultaneously limiting the amount of power available to females. Through the women's movement, at least in part, women have grown increasingly conscious of the inequality that exists within society; of the enormous power usurped by males and of the subordinate position to which women have been relegated. Women in large numbers are now attempting to rectify this imbalance by seeking, and in some cases beginning to attain, equality in all realms of the social world.

PART I: THE PROBLEM

In this section we will deal with some of the major dimensions of gender-based inequality in American society. We will see that in a number of important ways women are a subordinate group, denied equal status with men. (This is the case even though women outnumber men and represent more than 50 percent of the population.) We examine the changing conditions and grievances that gave rise to the modern women's movement. An examination of such conditions and grievances reveals the main contemporary features of sexual dominance.

INEQUALITY: THE CHANGING CONDITIONS

Social movements like the women's movement often arise when there is a growing discrepancy between the needs and aspirations of some group and actual (or perceived) social conditions. One well-known sociologist pointed out that women had not simply been standing still in terms of equality from the 1920s on—they had actually been losing ground.[1] Relative to men, the position of women had been deteriorating. And this deterioration ran headlong into, and in part motivated, the reemergence of a movement among women to improve their situation. As we will see, a number of changes combined to bring about a crisis over gender-based inequalities during the 1960s. Furthermore, these conditions, although continuing to change, exist to this day. While the women's movement is not as dynamic today as it was in the late 1960s and early 1970s,[2] it continues to be motivated by, and to impact on, these changing conditions. Changes in three major conditions will be considered: (1) changes in women's participation in the labor force; (2) changes in the duties of the wife-mother role; and (3) changes in educational achievement accompanied by continuing pay and status inequalities between men and women.

Women in the Labor Force

As Table 9.1 indicates, there has been a considerable increase in the proportion of women in the civilian labor force: women who do full-time or part-time work outside the home. In 1947, just 31.8 percent of the labor force was female,[3] but by 1970 it had jumped to 43.3 percent, and in 1981 it stood at 52.6 percent of the labor force.[4] The largest and most significant increases have been in the proportions of working wives. In 1947, 21.4 percent of married women held jobs; in 1970, more than 41.4 percent were working; and by 1982 that figure had further increased to 51.8 percent.[5]

Table 9.1 Participation Rates of Females in the Labor Force: 1960–1982

YEAR	PARTICIPATION RATE (PERCENT)
1960	37.7
1965	39.3
1970	43.3
1975	46.3
1980	51.5
1981	52.1
1982	52.6

Source: U.S. Department of Commerce, Bureau of the Census, *Statistical Abstract of The United States: 1984* (Washington, D.C.: U.S. Government Printing Office, 1983), p. 407.

Changes are even more marked among mothers. Some of the increase in the number of working mothers is accounted for by women entering the labor force after their children are grown, but more importantly there are also substantial changes among women with children still at home. Among women with children between the ages of six and seventeen, the proportion who work rose from 39 percent in 1960 to 49.2 percent in 1970; while in 1982 that number stood at 63.2 percent.[6] Mothers with children under the age of six more than doubled their participation in the labor force in the same period, from 18.6 percent in 1960 to 30.3 percent in 1970 and to 48.7 percent in 1982.[7]

These changes have created a number of strains that surfaced in the late 1960s and continue to be manifest to this day. Although we will discuss problems of the late 1960s and today together, it would be well to bear in mind that while these problems continue to be realities, they were much more exaggerated in the late 1960s when women, men, and larger institutions were less able and willing to deal with them.

Figure 9.1 Labor Force Participation Rates by Sex, 1950–1982

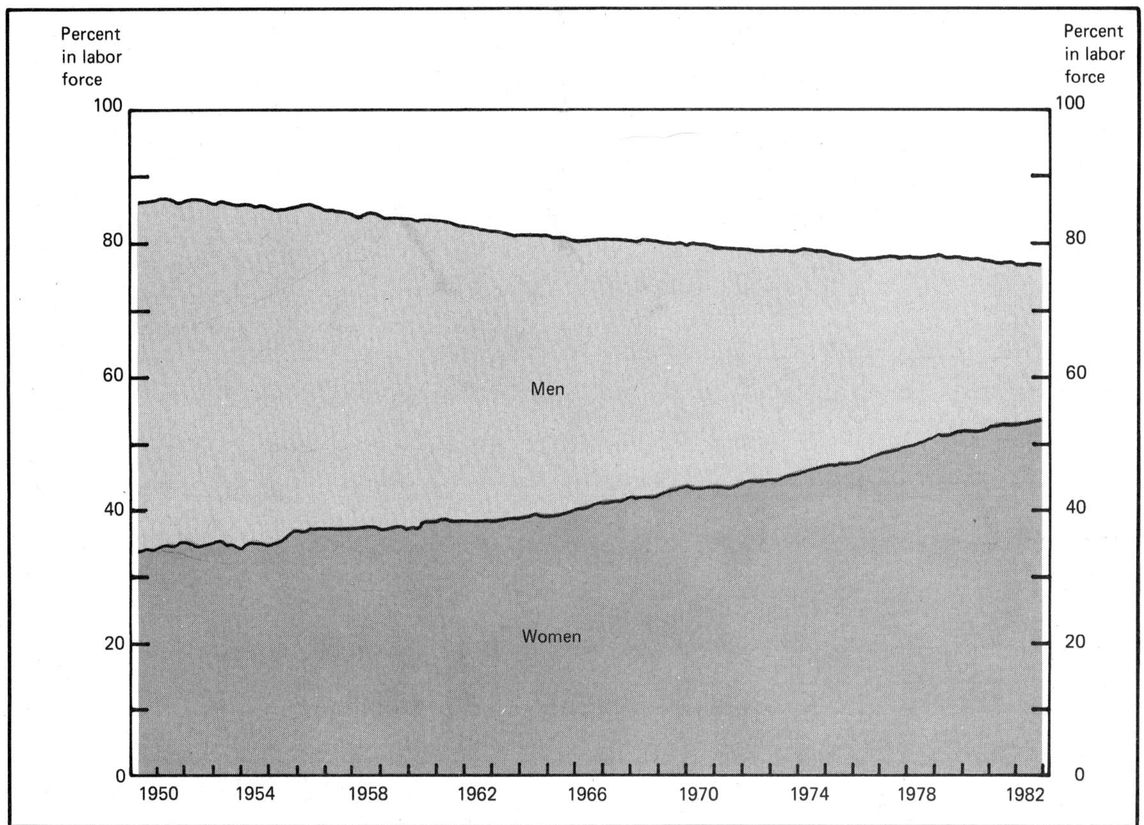

The number of women in the labor force grew dramatically during the years 1950–1982, while the participation rate for men declined slightly.

Source: U.S. Department of Labor, Bureau of Labor Statistics, *Women at Work: A Chartbook,* Bulletin 2168 (Washington, D.C.: U.S. Government Printing Office, 1983), p. 3.

Strains Confronting Women in the Labor Force

First, although increasing numbers of mothers with young children are working, child care is often expensive and difficult to find. Few employers are prepared to provide adequate day-care facilities, and private day-care centers, although they have proliferated, are out of the price range of many working mothers, especially those who are most likely to need them. Thus, while the percentage of children cared for in "group care centers" increased from 4.5 percent in 1958 to 14.6 percent in 1977, that is still a very small proportion of children of working mothers.[8] Second, although many husbands of working women undoubtedly help out with some domestic chores, such work is not defined as part of the role of husband and father, so most working women also continue to function as full-time "homemakers." Third, social disapproval of married women who work continues to run relatively high.[9] These and other pressures on working wives and mothers have come to be felt by more

Figure 9.2 Labor Force Growth by Sex, 1970s and Projected 1980s

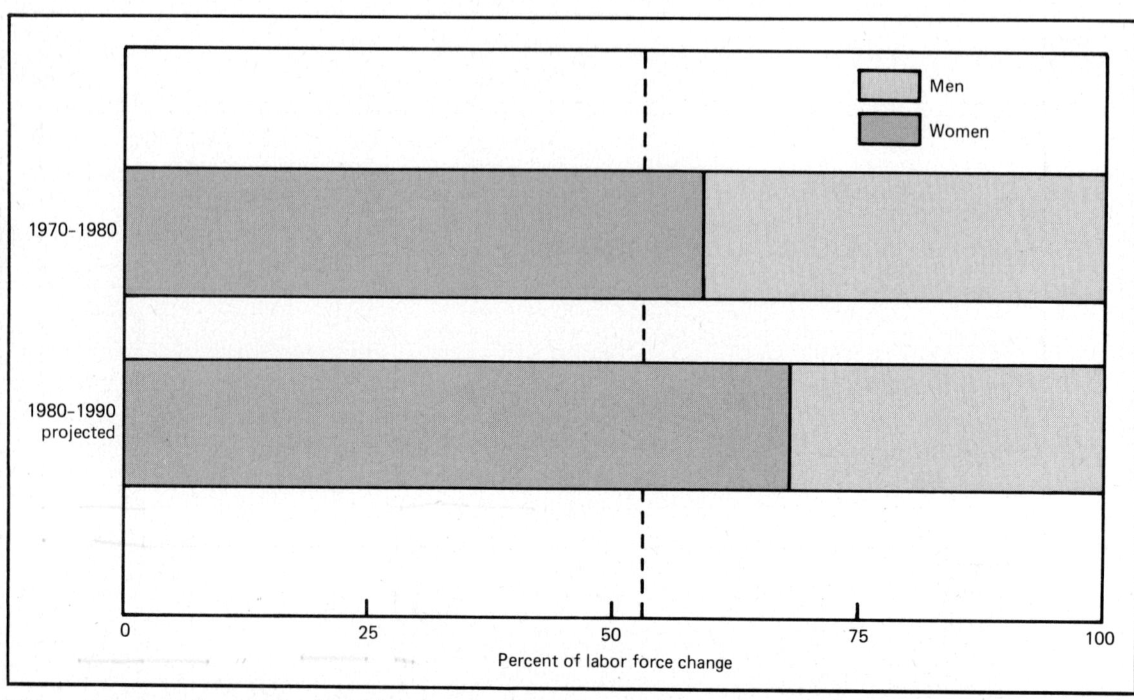

Women's share in the growth of the labor force is expected to increase in the 1980s.

Source: U.S. Department of Labor, Bureau of Labor Statistics, *Women at Work: A Chartbook,* Bulletin 2168 (Washington, D.C.: U.S. Government Printing Office, 1983), p. 15.

and more women who take jobs outside the home.

It is entirely possible that the majority of women who enter the labor force do so out of economic necessity. As we will see in Chapter 10 on poverty, about half of all people below the poverty line are in families in which the father is absent. In this group, women do not have the option of being supported by a man. And, to some extent, as we shall see shortly, the poverty of such families stems from the low wages paid women and the low-paying jobs open to them, as well as the tendency for women to be concentrated in the lowest-paying industries.[10] Among families with children under 18, 54.6 percent of wives whose husbands earn between $15,000 and $20,000 per year are in the labor force, while only 29.3 percent of wives whose husbands earn more than $50,000 work.[11] (These phenomena, taken together, reflect the "feminization of poverty."[12]) In many of these families, especially at the lower end of the income ladder, both the husband's and wife's incomes are required to maintain a modestly comfortable life style. Women in many of these families must choose between working and having their families do without many of the things that they want and need.

Thus, most of the women who entered the labor force in the last two decades did so because they needed to work for eco-

Figure 9.3 Labor Force Participation Rates of Women by Marital Status, 1962 and 1982

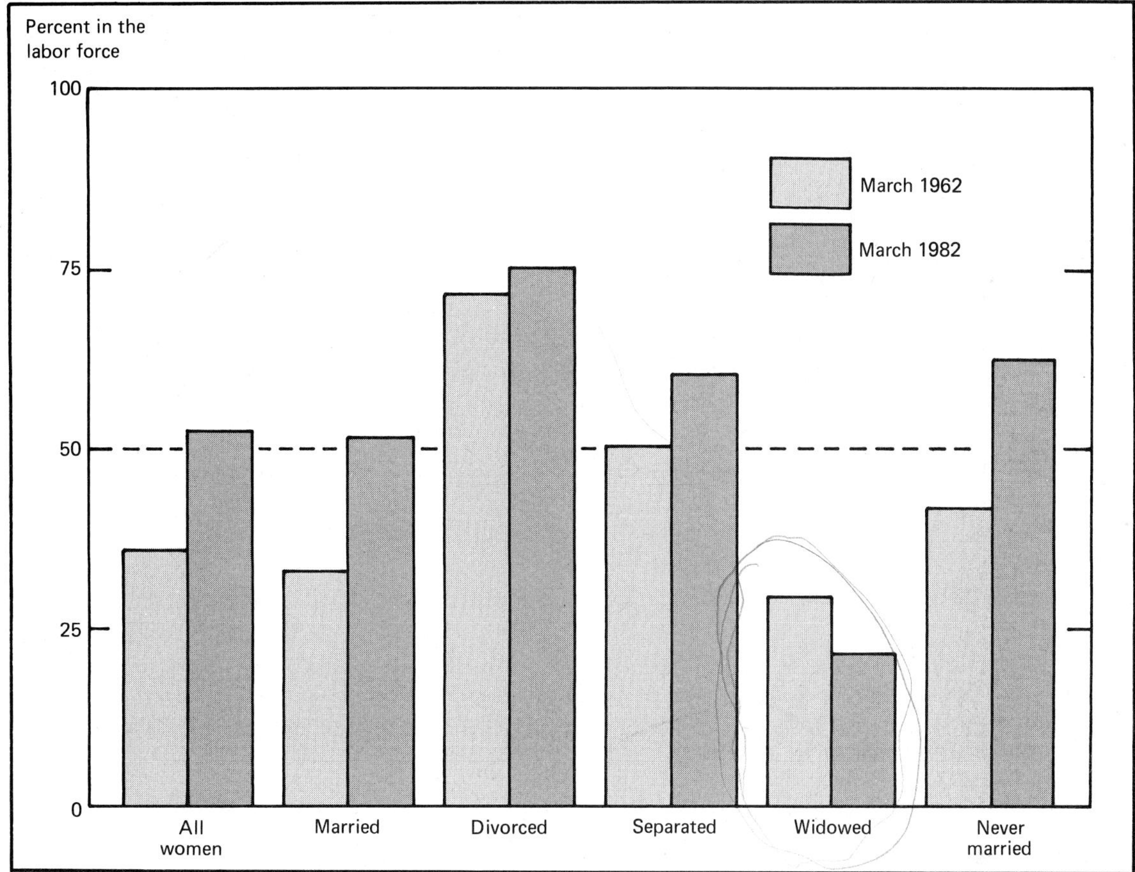

While this figure shows gains for women (except widows) in all categories of the labor force, the most striking gain occurred among married women—more than half are now in the labor force.

Source: U.S. Department of Labor Statistics, *Women at Work: A Chartbook,* Bulletin 2168 (Washington, D.C.: U.S. Government Printing Office, 1983), p. 23.

nomic reasons.[13] Of course, there were always women who worked not so much out of economic need, but because they wanted to work, to find fulfillment and satisfaction within the work world. As it has become more normative for women to work, more and more women are entering the labor force not because they absolutely must, but because they *want* to work.[14] It is difficult to envision anything but a continuation of this trend in the future. Now that the barriers are down, women who need to work *and* women who want to work will find their way into the labor force in increasing numbers in future years.

Historic Opposition to Women in the Permanent Labor Force

The American male establishment has been accustomed over the years to drawing

Figure 9.4 Children with Mothers in the Labor Force as a Proportion of All Children by Age of Children, 1972 and 1982

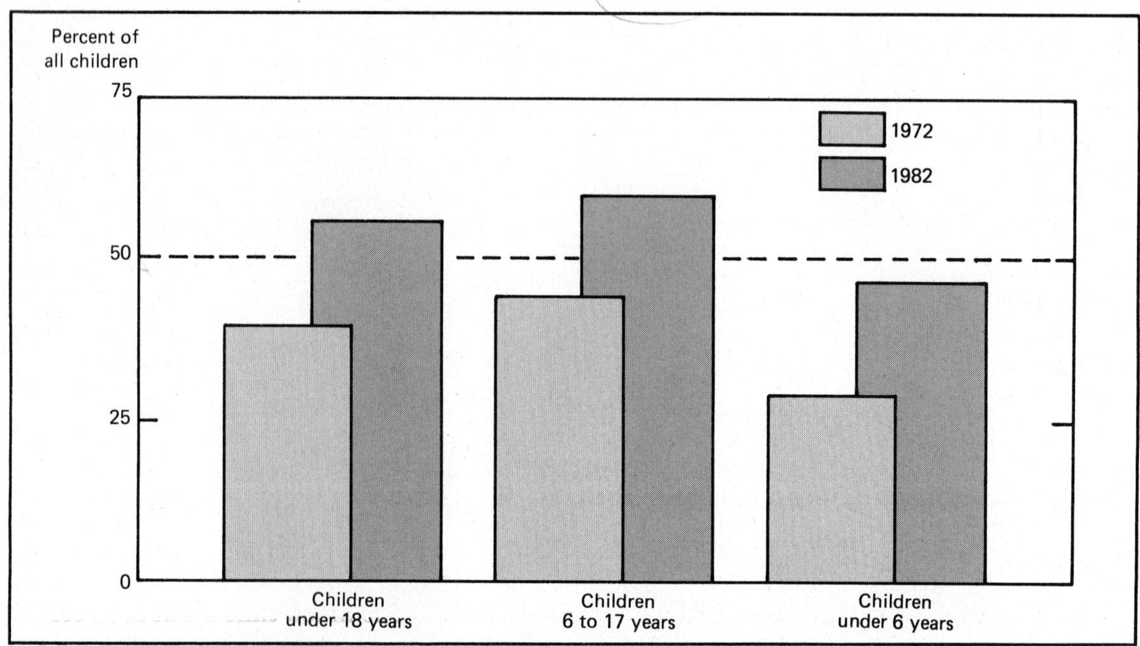

There has been a substantial increase in labor force participation among women with children of all ages.

Source: U.S. Department of Labor, Bureau of Labor Statistics, *Women at Work: A Chartbook,* Bulletin 2168 (Washington, D.C.: U.S. Government Printing Office, 1983), p. 21.

females into the labor force when they are needed and then dismissing them when they are no longer necessary. Now, however, more and more women will not leave the labor force so easily.

During World War II, as in previous wars, women reentered the work force in large numbers, with the active encouragement of spokespeople and propagandists from government and other social institutions, such as churches and schools. "Rosie the Riveter" became a popular symbol of women's capacity to fill traditionally male work roles. After the war, though, official voices (echoed by the media) pressured women to give up their jobs to returning veterans and to resume their former roles, so that men could find an America "just the way we left it." Through the 1950s and 1960s, and to some degree to this day, opinion leaders decreed that the maintenance of the American home was a woman's highest calling and greatest fulfillment. A good example is the *The Common Sense Book of Baby and Child Care* by Dr. Benjamin Spock. Spock played a key role in the widespread acceptance of the idea that children could not be healthy or intelligent without full-time attention from their mothers. During these decades there was an emphasis on the definition of marriage as an institution with an emotional base—romantic love between husband and wife was the cement. Traditionalists asked women to choose between family and work—and they clearly hoped and expected that they would choose family. However, in the 1970s and 1980s more women are unwilling or unable to make this choice—they want both! And why not? Males have both.

Changes in Wife and Mother Roles

As a result of changing sex roles, the decade 1970–1980 witnessed some interesting changes relating to women in the United States. For example, women tend to be marrying later. In 1970 the median age at first marriage for women was 20.8 years, while in 1980 it had risen to 22.1 years (a similar increase occurred for men).[15] To put it another way, in 1970 86.0 percent of all women had been married at least once by age 25 but in 1980 that number had dipped to 71.6 percent.[16] The later age of first marriage seems to indicate a greater propensity on the part of women to postpone marriage in order to complete schooling and/or to at least get a good start in their careers. A related trend is a decline in the percentage of children born to women under 25 and a doubling of the percentage of first births accounted for by women over 30.[17] In spite of these trends, by their mid-thirties most women are done with the demanding and time-consuming care of small children. And those who have their children later are probably often prepared to put their infants in the care of others early so that they can return to work. Thus, by their middle to late thirties most women have the opportunity, the desire, and the need to find something to do to fill their time. In addition, the average life span has increased, with a woman born in 1980 having a life expectancy of 77.5 years (it was 54.6 years in 1920).[18] This means that most women have over forty years of life ahead of them by the time their youngest child begins school. All of these changes leave women with more time to devote to the labor force and to developing and maintaining an occupational career.

The Myth of Less Housework

In this context, it would be useful to discuss the widely held myth that as a result of various labor-saving devices (washers, driers, dishwashers, and so on), American women spend less time on housework than they used to, as well as less time than women in other countries. The evidence does *not* support either of these positions.[19] For one thing, since the 1920s, there has been relatively little change in the number of hours devoted to housework. While there is some evidence that in very recent years there has been some decline in these hours, the decline has not been dramatic. For another, women in the United States spent about as much time on housework as women in other nations *without* the labor-saving devices. One reason for this anomaly may be that some so-called "labor-saving devices" actually *create* work. For example, a combination electric and microwave oven may actually lead to more cooking, or the presence of a washer and drier may lead to cleaning clothes more often. Since labor-saving devices do not mean less housework, women continue to be likely to do the housework. *And* since more women have entered the labor force, this means that women often now find themselves in the position of holding down *two* full-time jobs; one at the workplace and the other in the home.

The Myth of Increasing Divorce

Another myth related to the changing place of women in society is that this has contributed to an increase in the divorce rate. The idea is that newly liberated women are more likely to be dissatisfied with traditional marriage, indeed marriage in general, and that as a result they are more likely to seek the dissolution of marriage through divorce. Of course, there are a number of other factors associated with the presumed increase in the divorce rate,[20] including declines in mate selection by the extended kin, in the patriarchal ideology that allowed the husband to keep the family together on *his* terms, in the ideal that marriage is forever, as well as increasing belief in the importance of personal happiness. Another of the structural changes that seems to make divorce more feasible today are recent reforms in the divorce laws.[21] Divorce has generally been obtainable only through adversary proceedings, in which one partner must accuse the other of adultery, desertion, mental cruelty, or the like, before a divorce can be granted. Some states have abolished the adversary proceedings and now allow couples jointly to claim irreconcilable differences. As the legal formalities of divorce are diminished, then perhaps divorce becomes easier and therefore a more frequent option.

In spite of all of these reasons to expect an upswing in the divorce rate, the evidence does *not* indicate such an increase. If we take a long enough perspective and go back to the 1920s, the divorce rate has risen. However, the increase has not been linear, and the divorce rate has actually declined in the 1980s. The increase began in the 1930s and lasted until the 1940s.[22] Then it declined through the 1950s only to begin climbing again in the 1960s. This upward trend continued until the late 1970s, when it leveled off. It is the increase that occurred in the 1970s that led many people to talk in terms of an increase in the divorce rate, an increase that seemed to coincide with the growing strength of the women's movement.

The counterintuitive evidence of the 1980s, at least to this writing, is that the divorce rate has *declined* modestly thus far in this decade. During the first two months of 1984, 180,000 couples obtained divorces. This was 3,000 fewer divorces than were obtained in the first two months of 1983. In percentage terms (per 1,000 population), the divorce rate was 4.7 for the first two months of 1984, while it had been 4.9 for the comparable period in 1983.[23] For the twelve-month period ending February 1984, there were 1,175,000 reported divorces, 13,000 fewer than for the twelve-month period ending February 1983. This constituted a 2 percent decline in the divorce rate.[24] These are obviously not striking declines, but what makes them so interesting is that they occurred during a period in which a variety of forces seemed to be pointing toward an increase in the divorce rate. It is obviously too early to tell how long this trend will continue and how much lower the divorce rate will go. The key point here, however, is that changing sex roles (as well as other social changes) have not led to an increase in the divorce rate up to this point in the 1980s.

Occupation and Education

For many years the educational attainments of females lagged far behind those of males. Women were more likely to be urged to leave school, get married, and raise a family. The lag in educational level, in turn, had an adverse effect on women's occupational opportunities. However, as in many areas, the gap between men and women in terms of educational attainment is narrowing. For example, in the academic year 1972–1973 men accounted for 58.8 percent of all those enrolled on a full-time basis in colleges and universities, while women accounted for only 41.2 percent. By 1981–1982, the gap between the sexes had narrowed dramatically, with men account-

Figure 9.5 Divorce Rates: United States, 1925–1982

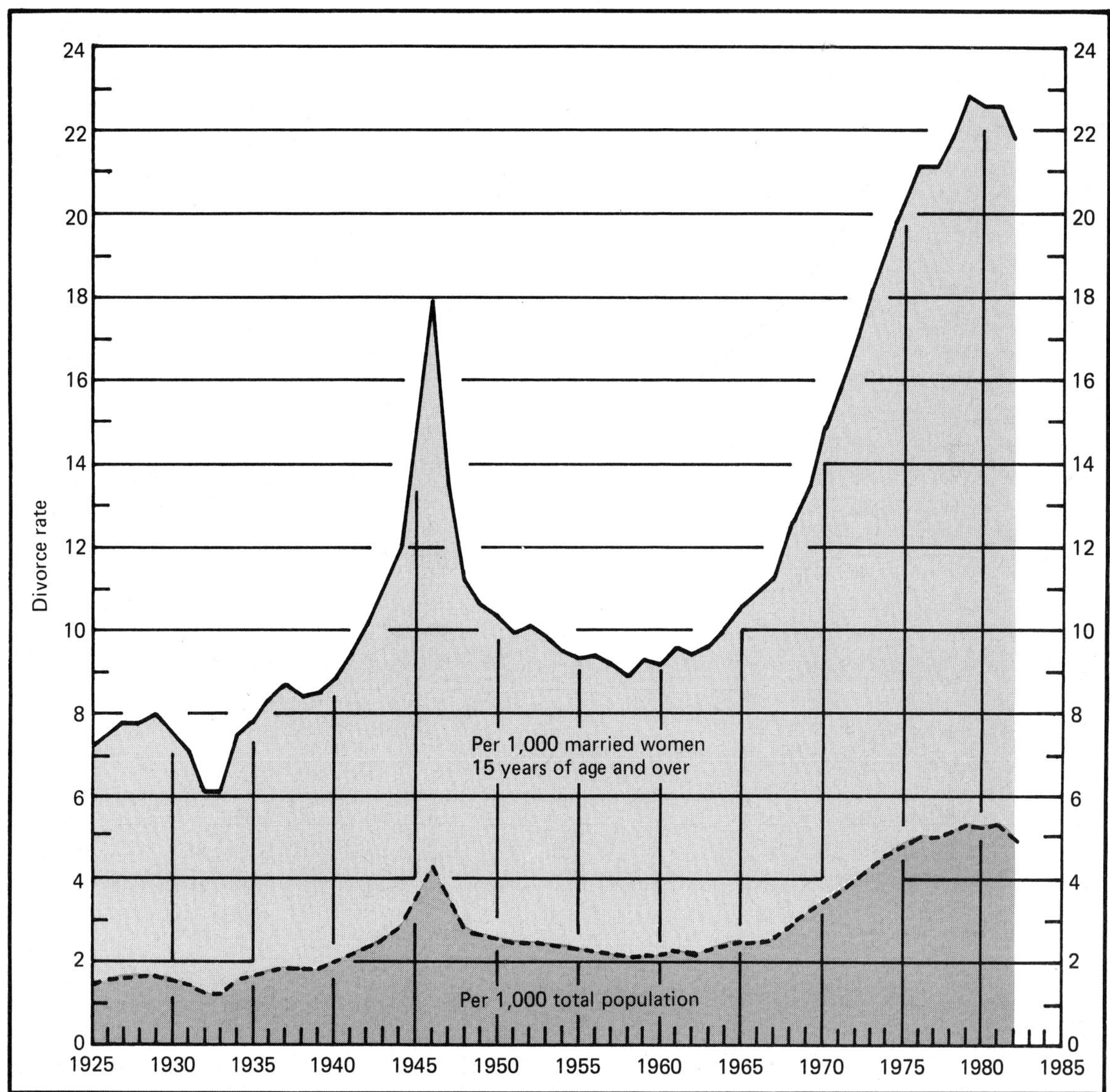

Although the divorce rate shows a long-term increase dating from the 1950s, a slight decline has been in progress since the late 1970s.

Source: "Advance Report of Final Divorce Statistics, 1982," *Monthly Vital Statistics Report* 33 (Feb. 28, 1985), p. 2.

Figure 9.6 Divorce Rate per 1,000 Population

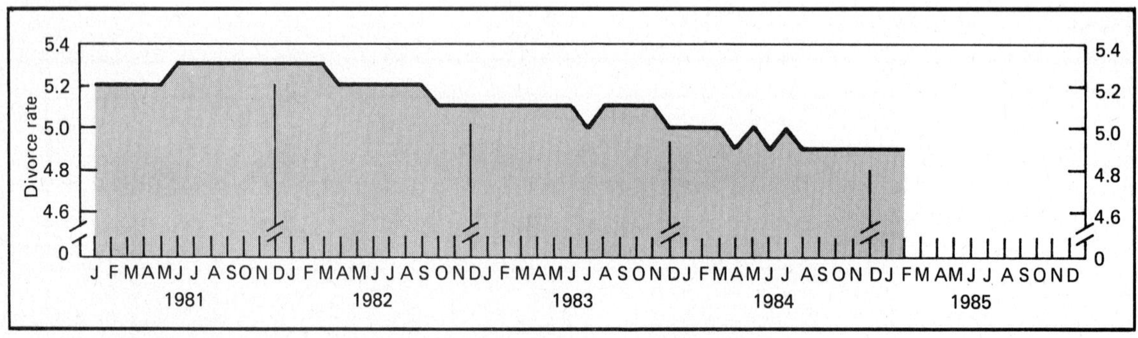

A pronounced downward trend in the divorce rate continued into the 1980s.

Source: National Center for Health Statistics, "Births, Marriages and Deaths for February, 1985," 34 (May 28, 1985), p. 3.

ing for 51.6 percent and women 48.4 percent of the college population.[25] Women are also earning an increasing number of professional and advanced degrees. In 1966 women earned only 4.5 percent of first professional degrees, but in 1979–1980 that had risen to 24.8 percent. Women earned about a third of all Master's degrees in 1966, and by 1979–1980 that had grown to 29.7 percent.[26] This narrowing of the ed-

Women are earning more and more college, professional, and advanced degrees. The educational gap between males and females has narrowed considerably.

(Bernard Pierre Wolff/Photo Researchers)

ucation gap augurs well for the occupational prospects of women in the future. At present, however, there are still major occupational differences between men and women.

Income Differences Between Males and Females

In 1960 the mean income of males was $4,617, while for females it was $1,861. In other words, males on the average earned more than 2.5 times the income of females. By 1981 the average incomes had been greatly inflated and, surprisingly, the differences between males and females had *not* been reduced as much as one might believe. The mean income of males was $16,515 in 1981, while for females it was $7,440: a multiple of a bit less than 2.5.[27]

These figures are affected by the fact that women are more likely to be employed on a part-time basis than men. If we consider only full-time year-round workers, the median income figures in 1981 were $20,260 for men and $12,001 for women; full-time working women earn 59.2 percent of male earnings.[28] While there were 442,000 men who earned $75,000 or more from full-time work, there were only 12,000 women in this category; in other words for every 1,000 men earning over $75,000 per year there were only 27 women. At the opposite

Figure 9.7 Usual Weekly Earnings by Sex, 1967–1982

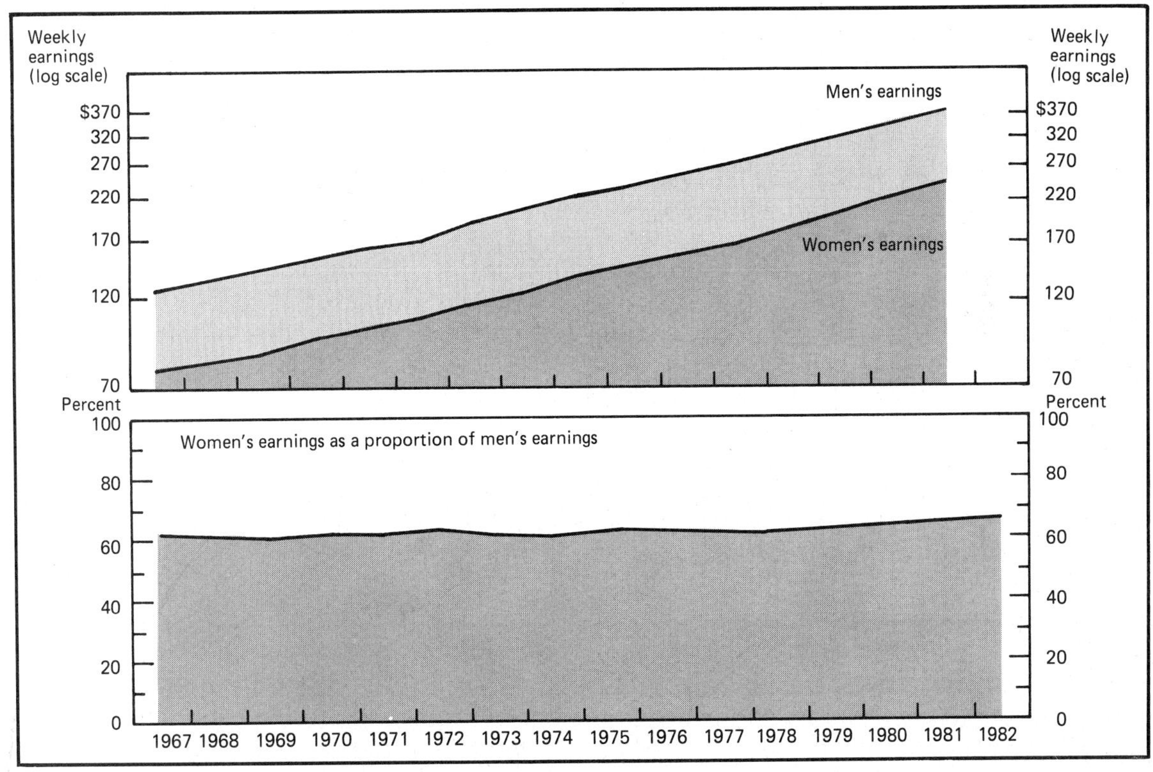

Women's earnings continue to average about 60% of male earnings.

Source: U.S. Department of Labor, Bureau of Labor Statistics, *Women at Work: A Chartbook,* Bulletin 2168 (Washington, D.C.: U.S. Government Printing Office, 1983), p. 29.

end of the spectrum, more women earned $15,000 per year or less than men.[29]

The great disparity between male and female income tends to hold no matter what the occupational category or educational level. Thus female professionals earn 66.4 percent of what their male peers earn, while in clerical occupations that percentage is 60.3 percent. In terms of educational level, women with five or more years of postsecondary education earn 65.4 percent of the earnings of comparably educated males, while among those with less than any high-school education females earn 62.6 percent of males. There are a lot of specific numbers here, but they all add up to continued substantial income differences between males and females at all income levels. As Janet Norwood puts it: "On the average, therefore, whether college graduates or high school dropouts, women earned about 60 cents for every dollar their male counterparts were paid."[30]

Underrepresentation of Women in High-Status Occupations

Another of the problems that continues to face women in the work world is the distribution of women in various occupational categories. Most notable here are the strides made, and the gaps that remain, in the higher-status, higher-paying occupational categories. For example, in the professional and technical category women made up 40.2 percent of the population in 1970, and by 1981 that proportion had grown to 44.7 percent.[31] In the category of managers and administrators, women made greater strides, but they had (and have) a greater distance to go—16.6 percent of managers in 1970 to 27.4 percent of that catetory in 1981.[32] Since there are several million more women than men (due to longer life expectancy), and women therefore account for more than 50 percent of the population, this means that women are underrepresented in the professions and greatly underrepresented among managers. However, these general categories tend to conceal some other dimensions of discrimination against females. For example, within the professional category women tend to be concentrated in such lower-status, lower-paying "semi-professions" as nursing (97.4 percent of nurses were women in 1970; 96.8 percent in 1981). Similarly, 70.4 percent of grade- and high-school teachers were women in 1970; 70.6 percent in 1981. On the other hand, women are underrepresented in such higher-status, higher-paying professions as medicine (8.9 percent of doctors were female in 1970; 13.8 percent in 1981), the law (4.7 percent of lawyers and judges were women in 1970; 14.0 percent in 1981), and engineering (1.6 percent of engineers in 1970 were female; 4.3 percent in 1981).[33]

Overqualified Women Workers

We have seen that women have nearly achieved educational equality with males, but their occupational position, while improving, continues to lag significantly behind that of men. By the mid-1960s, and to a great extent to this day, there were and are a large and growing number of women whose status in terms of educational attainment was far higher than it was in terms of income and occupational prestige. This means that they often found themselves in positions for which they were overqualified. Women who had come, during the process of achieving college degrees, to see themselves as intelligent and socially valuable were often assigned boring tasks, were denied authority, and were frequently expected to be office servants—to make the coffee, tidy up the office, run personal errands for the boss, and massage his ego. Worse yet, they often had to accept significantly lower pay than men, and sometimes lesser job titles, for identical work. The proportion of women attending college has continued to increase, and, therefore, so has the number of women caught in statuses that are inconsistent with their level of educational achievement. These were precisely the kind of women who were likely to be drawn into more active involvement with the women's movement.

Given the problems discussed in this first section, we turn now to an analysis of the major causes and consequences of such problems.

PART II: CAUSES AND CONSEQUENCES

This chapter began with the observation that male dominance is as old as the human species. Although there is cross-cultural evidence of wide variation in the activities performed by males and females,[34] the fact remains that most societies have developed a system of sex stratification with males tending to be dominant over females. We now turn to a discussion of the major causes of inequality between the sexes. We begin at the individual level with a discussion of the role of physiological factors in inequality between the sexes. Later we turn to a discussion of social-psychological and, most importantly, sociological factors in this inequality.

Much of our concern in this part of the chapter is with inequality in the division of labor. As far back as we have knowledge, human societies have to some degree displayed a division of labor so that not everyone in society performs the same set of tasks. In early history, most of this division of labor was quite informal. However, over the centuries we have moved to a more formally defined division of labor. In addition, as societies have become more complex, the division of labor has come to reflect increasing specialization. That is, more and more tasks become the special responsibility of a few members of society.

There are some good reasons for the evolution of a highly specialized division of labor. Larger societies have more tasks to perform, and many of them tend to grow more complex. It becomes necessary to ensure that there are people to handle each of these responsibilities. In addition, many of these tasks come to require highly specialized skills and/or training. It is less and less possible to think of generalists handling a wide array of these tasks; they are simply likely to lack the needed skills and training. It could also be argued that by dividing tasks societies grow more efficient, which means those societies that develop the most sophisticated means of specializing tasks are likely to be more productive and to enjoy a competive advantage over those that do not. These basic ideas on the division of labor are fundamental to understanding the following discussion of the causes of inequality in gender stratification.

INDIVIDUAL LEVEL

In this section we will examine the roles of physiological factors in the sexual stratification associated with the division of labor. This is a highly controversial issue, and we will alternate between assertions about physiological factors and criticisms of such assertions.

Physiological Factors

The Conventional Anthropological View

We begin with conventional wisdom among anthropologists about the origins of gender inequality. In a small, primitive society, the vital task of having babies could only be assigned to women.[35] (By the way, with the advent of "test tube" babies this

Table 9.2 Levels of Analysis: Gender Inequality

LEVELS	APPROPRIATE QUESTIONS	A PARTIAL SYNOPSIS OF PRESENT CONCLUSIONS
INDIVIDUAL	What is the traditional anthropological view on the role of physiological factors in the origins of gender inequality?	Males began with a series of slight physiological advantages that they exploited in gaining for themselves the preeminent positions within society.
	What are the criticisms of the traditional anthropological view on physiology?	Male dominance is not inherited, the destinies of the sexes were not settled in ancient times, and culture is more important than biology in determining the relative positions of males and females.
	What is the position of modern biosociologists on gender inequality?	Modern biosociologists see a role for genetic and biological factors, but they leave an important place for social and cultural factors.
	Are modern biosociologists free of criticism?	No. It is felt even they have used biological differences incorrectly to explain and often justify male dominance.
	Even if we admit that biological factors play some role in gender inequality, have changes in the modern world reduced the imperatives of biology?	A number of recent developments (e.g., the various reasons for the declining number of pregnancies) have all but eliminated the biological bases of gender inequality.
SOCIAL-PSYCHOLOGICAL	Is gender identity established early in life?	Yes. Once established, it is virtually irreversible.
	What is the major mechanism by which gender identity is learned?	It is through the socialization for sex roles that children learn to think of themselves as boys and girls.
	What are the stereotypes into which boys and girls are socialized?	Boys are socialized into instrumental personality traits while girls are socialized into expressive personality traits.
	What are the social-psychological consequences of sex-role inequality?	Among the wide-ranging social-psychological consequences are gender differences in expressiveness and in interaction patterns.
SOCIOLOGICAL	Is sexism built into the social structure?	Yes. Sexism permeates schools, work settings, and all other social structures.
	Is male dominance reinforced by the educational system?	Yes. The educational system serves to insure that the sexes learn their respective sex roles. Since males have occupied a position of dominance, this education serves to reinforce their position.

Table 9.2 Levels of Analysis: Gender Inequality *(Continued)*

LEVELS	APPROPRIATE QUESTIONS	A PARTIAL SYNOPSIS OF PRESENT CONCLUSIONS
SOCIOLOGICAL	Does the work world operate in terms of male dominance?	Yes. Despite some improvements, females continue to operate at a disadvantage within the work world. Among the problems facing females are barriers to obtaining needed credentials, lack of sponsors, lack of role models, institutional sexism, occupational sex segregation, sexual harassment, and difficulties in handling critical career-testing points.
	Has American culture played a role in gender inequality?	Yes. Sexism exists within American culture and it has served to support male dominance and female subordination.

seeming inevitability is no longer inevitable.) And, because there were no such things as baby formulas and bottles, only women could be assigned the task of feeding infants. Of course, once the infant was weaned, it would have been possible to turn it over to the man to raise. However, given the very high infant mortality rates (perhaps as many as one-half would die before the age of five) in premodern societies, once a woman had weaned one infant it was not unusual for her to become pregnant again so that the society could maintain or increase its population. Frequent pregnancy tended to undermine the health of women, and although life expectancy was short for everyone in a primitive society, it was shorter for women. Few women lived much beyond the end of their fertility.

Thus, in considering the division of labor in primitive societies, it is argued that it is not even necessary to take account of the fact that men (on the average) are larger and stronger than women in deciding who will be warriors or hunters. It is only necessary to recognize that most adult females will be pregnant, nursing an infant, or both, a good deal of the time. In premodern societies tasks were divided according to this biological state of affairs. The other tasks assigned to women tended to be work that was compatible with the focal responsibilities of pregnancy and child rearing. Thus, women tended to work in or near the home. This left to the males the tasks requiring absence from home and freedom from caring for children.[36] It should be emphasized that this is a general characterization of the divison of labor within primitive societies and that there was considerable variation from one society to another in precisely how men and women divided the tasks.[37]

Thus, males began with a series of slight initial advantages (the need for females to stay close to home and babies, the males' greater size and strength) that they were able to exploit in gaining for themselves the preeminent positions within society. Males took control over such responsibilities as hunting, defense, and offense.[38] As a result, males could claim the important responsibilities of hunter and defender. If females refused to recognize the greater importance of these positions, males always had greater strength and later the control over the weapons to buttress that power. Thus, physical differences gave males an initial advantage, an advantage they exploited and developed into a system of structured inequality.

As society over the centuries shifted from subsistence agriculture to industry, male dominance of the powerful positions in society expanded. The family gradually ceased to be the site of economic production. Jobs were increasingly found outside the home in workshops and factories. Yet most women were still tied to the home and the manufacture and maintenance of infants. Thus, it was the men who could and did venture out of the home and into the work world. As long as women were unable to seek positions away from the family, they remained economic dependents lacking in substantial power. Furthermore, so long as the social role of women is confined to the family—so long as a woman is economically dependent on a male and has no outside resources of her own to sustain her—she is very vulnerable to the physical domination of males as well. Thus, the evolution of modern industrial society, at least until the last few decades, has tended to make women more dependent on men for their survival. The result of this dependency was dominance for males and subordination for females. In other words, the result was a system of sex-based inequality.

Criticisms of the Conventional Anthropological View

In recent years a number of feminist anthropologists have come to question the view outlined above, arguing that it reflects the biases of male anthropologists.[39] For one thing, they argue against the view that women have "an unchanging biological role."[40] More specifically, they reject the idea "that female reproductive roles made women different from and complementary to men and guaranteed both the relative passivity of women in human history and the relative continuity of 'feminine' domains and functions in human societies."[41] They also argue that male dominance is not inherited,[42] that the destinies of the sexes were not settled in ancient times,[43] and that it is culture far more than biology that determines the relative positions of males and females.[44] Sherry Ortner and Harriet Whitehead are perhaps clearest on this point: "What gender is, what men and women are, what sorts of relations do or should obtain between them—all of these notions do not simply reflect or elaborate upon biological 'givens,' but are largely products of social and cultural processes."[45] The orientation of this chapter is in accord with the views of the feminist critics. Although we have begun this section with the issue of the physiological bases of gender differences, we will ultimately make our way to the far more important role played by social structure and culture in these differences.

The Biosociological View

Another group, biosociologists, have also made a controversial contribution to our understanding of the physiological differences between males and females. Alice Rossi, for example, enunciates a biosociological position on gender differences, but it is one that leaves an important role for social and cultural factors:

> A biosocial perspective does not argue that there is a genetic determination of what men can do compared to women; rather, it suggests that the biological contributions shape what is learned, and that there are differences in the ease with which the sexes can learn certain things.[46]

To take a specific example, Rossi argues that biological factors play a crucial role in the mother-infant relationship. For one thing, males only have an innate sexual orientation to women, while females are innately oriented sexually to males *and* they have an innate reproductive orientation to their young. For another, the immaturity of the human infant makes for a great need for bonding between the infant and mother. Rossi makes a number of other points on this issue, and others, but the key point is that biology plays a role in gender-role differentiation.

Criticisms of Biosociological Arguments

While Rossi is making a strong point on biology here, it is important to bear in mind that most biological differences (real and imaginary) between the sexes have been used incorrectly to explain and often justify male dominance. For example, it was long believed that because of their hormones and other biochemical features, women were naturally more emotional, more submissive, more passive, and otherwise less qualified than men to deal with responsible positions in life. In their exhaustive review of the literature on this issue, Eleanor Maccoby and Carol Jacklin found little support for the idea that these are female personality characteristics. For example, they conclude that "the term 'passive' does not accurately describe the most common female personality attributes."[47] Instead, such personality traits have more to do with such sociological issues as the way boys and girls are socialized, the roles they are asked to perform, and the social structures and cultural values that they encounter. We will turn to these issues shortly.

The Declining Imperatives of Biology

Before we do, we need to take another look at the imperatives of biology, this time in the context of modern society. *If* biology explained a good portion of the early destiny of females, and that is certainly not an uncontroversial assertion, biological factors no longer play anything like the role they once did. A number of recent developments have all but eliminated the biological bases for differentiation and inequality between males and females.

For one thing, it is no longer the case that women are doomed to a cycle of incessant pregnancy, child-rearing, and early death. In modern industrial society women now have fewer pregnancies, and the average woman is done with dealing with infants by her mid-thirties. There are several important reasons for this change. First of all, infant mortality has been so greatly reduced that, instead of half the infants dying, only a small percentage now die. Thus women no longer need to have a great number of children in order to be sure that a few will reach adulthood. Second, children are now much more of an economic burden than an asset. Until recently, children were an important source of labor, especially for farm families. Very few American families now live on farms and even those who do are more likely to rely on modern technology than on their children. Certainly, urban families are not aided economically by having many children. Indeed the reverse is the case; children are an enormous economic burden to the modern family. Third, children have not only become a burden to families in industrialized societies, but in nonindustrialized societies they have become a problem to the societies themselves. In the majority of those societies, many of the familial reasons for having many children continue to exist (high infant mortality, need for child labor), but for the society as a whole rapid population growth has become an intolerable problem (see Chapter 14). These less industrialized societies simply lack the resources to support their burgeoning populations. Fourth, contraception has made it possible to separate sexual behavior and reproduction so that women can avoid incessant pregnancy. Furthermore, the increasing popularity of contraceptive techniques controlled by women (for example, the diaphragm, the pill, sterilization-tubal ligation) has given them the power to decide whether or not they want to become pregnant. Then there is the greater acceptability of abortion as a method of terminating an unwanted pregnancy. Finally, even when they do bear children, modern mothers do not need to stay at home and care for them. Bottles and nursing formulas make it possible for anyone to provide for an infant. There is greater acceptance of women having children and then leaving the bulk of the rearing to others. There are more alternatives (although still far from enough) open to mothers of young children (day-care centers, nursery schools) that allow them to have children and to earn a living for themselves, if that is what they want and/or need to do. All of these things have served to increase the power of females and reduce the power of males.

In consequence, in part, of many fewer pregnancies, adult female mortality has greatly decreased. Women now live a good deal longer than men. For the first time in history, females have a life not bounded or shortened by the biology of reproduction. This, in turn, gives the modern woman much more flexibility in deciding how to live her life than her predecessors.

SOCIAL-PSYCHOLOGICAL LEVEL

At the social-psychological level, we are most generally concerned with the interaction processes by which the social meaning of being male or female emerges. Sex can be viewed as a "social label, an instance of social classification."[48] Although biological factors form the basis of these definitions, they do not determine their nature or extent. The definition of being male or female is determined early in life by the differences in the way others respond to male and female infants, as well as the way others designate sex through the use of verbal labels. Gender identity (a recognition of one's sex and an acceptance of those things typically associated with that sex) is not simply a result of the way others react to children; children play an active role in their own gender development. For example, children may attempt to structure interactions so that they validate their gender identities. Furthermore, the child's self-evaluation intervenes between the evaluations by others and the behavior of the child.

Although there are many interactional processes involved in the acquisition of gender identity, our main concern at the social-psychological level will be *socialization* (the process by which a person learns and generally accepts the ways of a particular social group or society) for *sex roles* (the particular behaviors that are expected of males and females). We are especially interested in the childhood socialization through which children learn to think and act as boys and girls. The importance of childhood socialization is underscored in the small number of cases where children identified at birth as one gender are later found to be of the opposite gender. In most cases children socialized into the "wrong" gender ended up thinking and acting like someone of the sex to which they were (erroneously) assigned rather than as one from their sex of birth. Thus the babies erroneously designated and reared as boys "thereafter thought of themselves as boys, played with boys' toys, enjoyed boys' sports, preferred boys' clothing, developed male sex fantasies, and in due course fell in love with girls."[49] The reverse was true for erroneously designated females: "they preferred marriage over a career, enjoyed domestic and homemaking duties, and saw their future fulfillment in the traditional woman's role."[50] The implication of this research is that socialization is more important than biology; at the minimum it shows that biology can be affected and modified by the socialization process.

Social-Psychological Causes of Sex-Role Inequality

Childhood Socialization

Socialization for sex roles plays a causal role in sex-role inequality in that we tend to socialize children into stereotypical male and female characteristics. In these stereotypes, males are thought to possess *instrumental personality traits* involving, among other things, the belief that they are better leaders, more objective, aggressive, independent, active, dominant, competitive, logical, scientific, calculating, tough, strong, and unsentimental. On the other hands, females are thought to possess *expressive personality traits* such as being sympathetic, sensitive, compassionate, concerned about others, artistic, esthetic, followers, and more moral.

In understanding socialization for sex roles in our society, we must recognize that most parents have these stereotypes in mind when they are raising their children. In general, if parents are socializing girls, they want them to end up with expressive personalities; if they are socializing boys, they want them to have instrumental personalities. This is accomplished, in part, by parents rewarding children when they think and act in accord with the stereotypes. Conversely, parents are likely to punish children whose thoughts and actions are inconsistent with these stereotypes. A little boy who likes dolls is usually shamed out of that preference, for example. In general, boys are rewarded (or at least benignly tolerated) when they are rough and aggressive. On the other hand, girls are more often rewarded for being gentle, quiet, and "ladylike." Parents, however, are generally more willing to tolerate "tomboy" behavior in their daughters than they are willing to accept "feminine" behavior in their sons. Some observers have reasoned that this is true because "male type" behavior is valued more highly in our society. Perhaps this is why it seems more tolerable when a girl behaves like a boy than when a boy behaves like a girl. At least, the reasoning goes, the "tomboy" female is aspiring to a "higher-status" position, while the boy who is more "feminine" is actually "lowering" himself. Perhaps this is why young girls can more successfully deviate from the traditional sex role. They cannot safely do so, however, much beyond the age of ten or eleven.

Besides acquiring appropriate sex-role behavior through rewards and punishments from parents (and others), children also acquire sex roles as a result of the organization of the ideas and experiences they have encountered in early life.[51] Children develop a sense of self, a sense of who they are, from interacting with other persons. They learn that they are boys or girls because they are so identified by parents as well as other children, teachers, and the like. "The boy in effect says, 'I am a boy, therefore I want to do boy things,' therefore the opportunity to do boy things (and to gain approval for doing them) is rewarding."[52] The same applies, of course, to girls. This sense of gender is already a part of most children's understanding by the age of three and is firmly fixed by the age of five or six. Through the early years of socialization, children tend to value things that are the same or similar to those things they already know and like. A girl, for example, learns that she is a girl. Through the experience of early social rewards and punishments, and by listening and observing, she learns some of the things that are generally associated with being a girl. She learns to value certain games, toys, and nurturant behaviors, because they are consistent with being a girl. Thereafter the girl will look for, and find more interesting, activities that are associated with her already accepted female-like behavior. The same process occurs for boys.

Recently, Nancy Chodorow has illuminated one aspect of this process of sex-role socialization.[53] Focusing on mothering, Chodorow argues that it is the division of labor within the nuclear family that reproduces the gender division of labor in the next generation. Thus, in fulfilling their roles as mothers, women produce in their daughters both the capacities and the desire to mother. However, the nature of their (as well as the father's) relationship to sons systematically curtails and suppresses the need and capacity to be nurturant. Thus, while daughters are prepared to take their nurturant roles of wife and mother, sons are socialized to play a less affective role in the family and to concentrate on the more impersonal world of work. The socialization that occurs within the family tends to reproduce and perpetuate traditional female and male sex roles.

Although there are problems with overly restrictive sex roles, there is utility in the fact that most children do learn their gender identity early and that this identity is virtually irreversible. One could envision a wide array of social problems arising from gender confusion, with greater sexual problems in society, as well as more stress and strain on the family. However, our problems do not stem from gender confusion, but from sex-role definitions that are too narrow and restrictive. This is particularly true of females because the sex-role attributes they learn are not only narrow but also not highly esteemed. On the other hand, while males learn different, but similarly narrow sex roles, their sex-role behavior tends to be very highly rewarded. In other words, males who manifest instrumental personality traits are more highly rewarded than females who demonstrate expressive personality traits.

Social-Psychological Consequences of Sex-Role Inequality

Up to this point in this section, we have dealt with some social-psychological causes of sex-role inequality. But once in existence, sex-role inequality also has social-psychological consequences. For one thing, as Jack Sattel has argued, boys are generally socialized to be inexpressive; unable to show such things as affection, tenderness, and emotion.[54] However, Sattel goes further and contends that inexpressiveness is a characteristic that males need throughout their lives in order to exercise power. People in powerful positions need to appear impassive and unemotional, and that is what males learn during the socialization process. Furthermore, inexpressiveness can also be used as an interactional tool in order to exercise power, especially over females who are often forced to "draw out" the inexpressive male. Finally, inexpressiveness helps maintain power by allowing the male to conceal his areas of ignorance.

Another example of the social-psychological consequences of sex-role inequality is in its impact on conversational interaction. In a study of such interaction, Pamela Fishman found that women devote much more attention to insuring the continuation and success of interaction than men.[55] Among other things, women ask more questions to keep interaction going and are supportive while males are talking. Men, in contrast, are much less active in trying to maintain interaction. They are likely to make statements and then sit back and rely on others, particularly females, to draw out the implications of their pronouncements. Thus, males tend to exercise the power within conversations while females are assigned the task of trying to keep the interaction going. There is work here, but since it is the work that females do, it tends to be hidden and devalued.

SOCIOLOGICAL LEVEL

We may define *sexism* as the belief that one sex is inherently and innately superior to another. Sexism is often used to rationalize or justify a sexually organized social order. Sexism is acquired by boys and girls during childhood socialization and is reinforced over the years as they come into contact with various social structures. In this section we will examine how the school and the work world encourage and sustain the stereotyped sex roles that the family has instilled in children.

The Schools

The educational system is an institutional way of ensuring that each generation of children is trained in the ways of the society. Among the things the child learns, or rather continues to learn, are the nature of society's sex roles.[56] If the schools, their curricula, and their personnel manifest sexism, then children are likely to emerge with stereotyped views of male and female sex roles. Since most schools have been organized in this way, children have generally left the educational system with a series of sexist attitudes and beliefs. Although we will focus on some dimensions of sexism in the schools in this section, bear in mind that sexism has been reduced in many educational systems. And there is at least some evidence that exposure to a nonsexist school system can reduce sex-role stereotyping.[57]

Books

One of the foci of those who have studied the perpetuation of sexism in the schools is the treatment of males and females in children's books and textbooks. Most of these studies were done in the early 1970s, and since then many of the worst stereotypes have been eliminated. However, as we will see, more recent research shows a continuation of at least some of these problems. The generalizations that follow hold for pre-1970s books, but in at least some cases they continue to be true to this day.

Even in the preschool years, picture books for children show males and females in different ways.[58] When boys are pictured, they are often shown doing active, industrious, and adventurous things. Girls are shown in more passive, unproductive, and generally inconspicuous postures. Boys are the "doers." Girls are the passive supporters. (These are the forerunners of the instrumental and expressive dimensions of traditional sex roles.) In a recent study, Eleanor Ashton has shown that exposure of preschoolers to sex-stereotypic picture books affects their behavior.[59] Specifically, children who read a sex-stereotypic story were more likely to choose a sex-stereotypic toy to play with. Conversely, children exposed to a nonstereotypic book were more likely to play with nonstereotypic toys.

First-grade textbooks pick up where preschool books leave off and stress stereotypes of female inferiority (and male superiority). The following excerpt from a first-grade reader of a few decades ago illustrates the kind of sexism that appeared, and to some extent continues to appear, in school books. In this story of Janet and Mark, Janet tries on her new skates and falls down:

"Mark! Janet!" said Mother
"What is going on here?"
"She cannot skate," said Mark.
"I can help her.
I want to help her.
Look at her, Mother.
Just look at her.
She is just like a girl.
She gives up."

Mother forces Janet to try again,

"Now you see," said Mark.
"Now you can skate.
But just with me to help you."[60]

In one 1971 study, textbooks in use in the second through the sixth grades in California were examined.[61] It was found that in 75 percent of the stories, the main characters were male. Stories about females were not as long as those about males. Only about 20 percent of story space was devoted to females, and only 15 percent of the illustrations depicted women or girls.

Since the early 1970s many people have called attention to the prevalence of sex-role stereotyping in children's books and textbooks, but there is evidence that steps were not immediately taken to rectify the problems. A 1975 study, for example, showed that sexual (and racial) stereotypes continued to prevail in twenty widely used reading series.[62] Another study in the same year indicated that sex-role stereotyping continued to be common in children's books.[63] The most recent (1981) research available on this issue indicates that not as much has changed as one might expect.

Change occurred in the frequency of female pictures and characters, *not* in role portrayal and characterization. Therefore, young children who read books similar to those sampled are likely to encounter more pictures of females and female characters, *but their roles continue to be expressive, nonsignificant, and stereotyped.*[64]

Curricula and Teachers

In addition to the story books and textbooks, the school curricula and the teachers also tend to reinforce traditional sex roles. Only after a series of legal decisions in the last two decades has there been an effort to provide exactly the same educational and recreational opportunities for boys and girls in the schools. As recently as 1970, seventy-seven courses in the New York City schools were listed as "technical courses restricted to males."[65]

Although legislation now generally prohibits courses and activities limited to one gender, the teachers, counselors, and administrators can still informally influence students. This influence may be subtle, even unconscious, or it may be direct: "You had better leave the hard sciences alone and take home economics instead."

School Sports

Another area of discrimination against females, although it has undergone great change in recent years, is sports. For generations girls were forced into the role of onlookers while boys honed their athletic skills and in the process developed self-confidence, the ability to deal with stress, and the ability to work cooperatively on a team. Not only had girls been excluded from boys' sports, but they were not in most cases offered any worthwhile women's sports programs in most school systems. Great changes were set in motion in 1972 with the passage of Title IX of the Education Amendments Act, which required schools that receive federal funds to offer equal opportunities to males and females. Among other things, this led to a big boom

Women have made major gains in school sports, but female sports are a long way from rivaling male sports.

(Alice Grossman/The Picture Cube)

in women's athletics and much more attention to women's interscholastic teams. For example, the number of women in interscholastic high-school sports increased by 527 percent between 1971 and 1979; female participation in intercollegiate sports doubled; and many more women received athletic scholarships.[66] Although great strides have been made, women's sports continue to lag far behind those of their male counterparts.

College

Education for submission continues in college. College textbooks, again until very recently, almost always used the word "man" to mean the human race. Although terms and phrases such as "Urban Man," "Man and Society," or "Economic Man" are meant to include women, both male and female students tend to take them literally to mean *man.*[67] Little wonder that female students tend to feel excluded from significant activities suggested by such subjects as the "History of Man." As a minority group, women have been excluded from significant roles in that history, and that seems to be confirmed and reinforced by such titles.

One of the most significant problems noted among college women is that they are subjected to confusing and contradictory messages. In a study published just after World War II, it was found that such women were simultaneously expected to do well in school, but not to do so well that they lose their feminine qualities and overshadow "eligible" young men. In other words, doing too well in school might jeopardize chances of a good marriage.[68] This finding was replicated, at least in part, in a study conducted three decades later among college students who certainly would have been affected by the women's movement. Basically, it appeared that women were still getting the same kinds of mixed messages that female college students had been getting for decades.[69]

The degree to which college-age women have tended to lack confidence in the ability of women has been demonstrated in various ways. In one particularly interesting and revealing study,[70] a booklet was put together containing academic articles. The *same* articles were attributed to a male author in one set of booklets and to a female author in the other set. The different sets were then given to samples of college women to rate. Half the sample saw the male-authored set and half the female-authored set. In every case, the women rated the male-authored articles as more important and their author more competent. This is another reflection of the degree to which women are educated by the schools to accept their subordinate status.

Work

The sexism within the educational system has, as we saw earlier in this chapter, an adverse effect on the occupational chances of women. They are likely to enter the work world with a series of liabilities in comparison to males. But once they enter the work world, women encounter a wide range of additional barriers that make it much more difficult for them to succeed occupationally. An enormous number of such problems exist, but to give the reader a feel for them we will discuss a few in the next few pages.

Barriers to Obtaining Credentials

Success in an increasing number of careers is dependent upon specialized training and advanced degrees. However, women are likely to encounter sexism that tends to discourage them or even prevent them from obtaining the needed credentials.[71] For example, to succeed in academia it is virtually mandatory to have a Ph.D., but women have had to overcome the sexism of their male professors in order to get the degree. While it is less likely than a decade or two ago, female graduate students may still hear comments like the following from male faculty members:

"A pretty girl like you will certainly get married; why don't you stop with an M.A.?"

"You're so cute. I can't see you as a professor of anything."[72]

Lack of Sponsors

In addition to the education one receives, graduate and professional schools are important because it is there that one is likely to find a *sponsor,* or someone who has "made it" in an occupation and who is able and willing to help a newcomer succeed.[73] The problem for females has been that most successful people in many professions were males, with the result that they were much more inclined to sponsor male rather than female newcomers. Without a well-placed sponsor to help a career along, especially in its early stages, it is very difficult to succeed occupationally.

Lack of Role Models

A related problem, but with a slightly different flavor, is the lack in the past of successful *role models* for females. Role models, in this sense, are people who have succeeded in an occupation and who serve as a model to be emulated by newcomers to the occupation. Since so few women had succeeded in many high-status occupations, most of the successful models were men. It was clearly far easier for male rather than female newcomers to accept and emulate these successful men. In fact, the comparative lack of successful females led young women to the opposite conclusion that occupational success was unlikely or even impossible.

Institutional Sexism

In Chapter 8 we discussed the institutional racism that exists throughout society; the concept of *institutional sexism* applies equally well to women. By institutional sexism we mean that the day-to-day operations of our large-scale social structures operate to the detriment of females. Thus males need not have sexist attitudes or overtly engage in sexist behavior for females to experience sexism in the work world. We mentioned, for example, the inadequacy of child-care facilities that operates to the detriment of female workers far more than of male workers. Within employing organizations, recruitment, hiring, training, promotion, and the like may all function in such a way that females are discriminated against even though it may be that none of the individuals involved is overtly sexist.[74] Thus, a recruiter may have in mind a set of characteristics needed for a job without realizing that these are characteristics that are far easier for males to acquire than females.

Occupational Sex Segregation

Another, even more important, dimension of institutional sexism in the work world is the *sex segregation* of occupations.[75] This means that certain occupations have been traditionally assigned to women, while others have been reserved by and for men. Women are concentrated in a relatively few occupations (schoolteacher [70.6 percent female], nurse [96.8 percent], secretary [98.6 percent]) with relatively low pay, power, and prestige.[76] Males, on the other hand, hold most of the high pay, power, and status positions (physician [13.8 percent female], lawyer [14.0 percent], business executive [27.4 percent]) for themselves.[77] The achievement-oriented woman, even in the absence of overt sexism, is still stymied by the structure of the work world. She is likely to find it difficult to get into all but a few occupations and even then will have restricted mobility within them. The achievement-oriented woman does not have the same opportunities available in the work world as similarly oriented men.

Heidi Hartmann has examined the question of the roots of the system of occupational sex segregation.[78] Her basic premise is:

> Job segregation by sex . . . is the primary mechanism in capitalist society that maintains the superiority of men over women, because it enforces lower wages for women in the labor market. Low wages keep women dependent on men because they encourage women to marry. Married women must perform domestic chores for their husbands. Men benefit, then, from both higher wages and the domestic division of labor. This domestic division of labor, in turn, acts to weaken women's position in the labor market. Thus, the hierarchical domestic division of labor is perpetuated by the labor market, and vice versa.[79]

Hartmann sees this division of labor as the combined product of capitalism and patriarchy.

Hartmann sees *patriarchy*, or "the hierarchical relation between men and women in which men are dominant and women subordinate,"[80] as preceding capitalism historically. In patriarchal systems, men controlled[81] the labor of women (and children) through a system of personal control. However, with the advent of capitalism and its large-scale economic units, such personal control was no longer adequate. What was needed in capitalism were more indirect and more impersonal methods of control. But Hartmann does not see capitalist control replacing patriarchal control in the modern world. In the name of maintaining the patriarchal system, men have acted in a variety of ways to keep women in a subordinate position. Thus, Hartmann writes of "the continuing interaction of two interlocking systems, capitalism and patriarchy," both maintaining occupational sex segregation (as well as the hierarchical domestic division of labor).[82]

Sexual Harassment

One of the forms of occupational sexism that has gotten a great deal of publicity in recent years is *sexual harassment.* While sexual relationships do develop between people at work,[83] and the dividing line between a sexual relationship and sexual harassment is sometimes difficult to draw, it is important to make the distinction. One of the keys to sexual harassment is that it involves *unwanted pressure* for sexual activity. Furthermore, the harassed are often denied the choice of being involved. Sexual harassment also involves a situation of unequal power; one person is in a position to impose his (or her) will on the other. It may be that sexual harassment, like rape, is more an expression of power and dominance than of sexuality.[84] We most often think of sexual harassment as involving superiors and subordinates, but it can also involve coworkers as well as clients. Finally, although both sexes can be either harasser or harassed, males much more often harass females.

Sexual harassment is *not* a new phenomenon.[85] For many years, the more vicious forms of sexual harassment were largely ignored by the public. Today, however, the harmfulness and unfairness of sexual harassment have achieved a high level of public awareness.

Sexual harassment is a problem in itself, and it is a problem because a woman's occupational success may hinge on accepting unwanted sexual overtures from male superordinates. Sexual harassment can take a variety of forms. Mild forms include the use of words, verbal jokes, or suggestions that are unwanted and unpleasant for the recipient. The most extreme forms involve physical force or rape. Between these extremes is a wide range of other actions, including leering and ogling, accidentally brushing someone's body, friendly pats, squeezes and pinches, quick kisses, and indecent propositions with the threat of job loss.[86]

Women encounter sexual harassment throughout their lives and long before they enter the work world. Some of the harassment may adversely affect their career prospects.[87] There are, for example, male professors who are willing to swap good grades in classes for sex with their female students.[88] (There are a few cases of female professors making the same overtures to male students.)

Once in a career, women often face similar kinds of situations in which success is tied to accepting unwanted sexual overtures. The following is the case of a female broadcast journalist:

> [She] was pushed against a wall and French-kissed by the defendant . . . alleged to be acting as agent of the company. . . . In the face of her repeated rejection, [he] allegedly said that "the only way a woman would succeed in broadcasting was to 'play the game'" . . . she took all reasonable steps to terminate his sexual advances, but was discharged for her refusals.[89]

Even more startling is the following example, since it involves President Lyndon B. Johnson. William Gulley, an aide to Johnson, reported that when Johnson was president, he recruited three beautiful women, promising them jobs after they had finished secretarial school.

> When they'd graduated and were working in the White House, he decided to take the youngest

and prettiest of them on a trip with him as a "supplemental secretary." When he sent for her the first night she picked up her notebook and pencil and went to his bedroom, but when she realized she was expected to take more than dictation from the President, she ran out of the room in a flood of tears.

Later that same night I sent an unmarked plane out to get her and bring her back to Washington. She was transferred to the Executive Office Building, and she never set foot in the White House again.[90]

While women have traditionally had few options in such situations, they have increasingly taken recourse in lawsuits and various collective efforts.

Testing Points

Finally, we might mention a problem that involves the fact that in most careers the most critical period is the decade after one leaves school and enters the work world. The most critical *testing points* are likely to occur in these years.[91] These are the tasks that if successfully handled virtually guarantee at least some measure of career success. The problem for females is that these are the years that women are most likely to be bearing children and taking time off to have them, and in most cases, to raise them as well. This means that they may miss, or may be less well prepared for, these testing points. This, in turn, means that their future career prospects will be dimmer than those of their male peers. Knowing this, many women try to do it all—wife, mother, worker, and so on—they try to be *superwomen.*[92] The problem is that this places impossible demands on the women who try to live up to the superwoman model, while for other women it is a source of a sense of their own inferiority. Said one "superwoman": "I always have 5 million things left to do. . . . It's a guilt trip that I'm not as much of a mother as I could be."[93] However it works in a specific case, the superwoman mythology is likely to have an adverse effect on women's career prospects.

Cultural Factors

Sexism also exists in the American culture, including its basic definitions of "male" and "female." Male dominance has been supported by a complex set of values and beliefs that view true femininity as unsuited for taking on responsibility outside the home. Manly characteristics have been the ones considered necessary for holding such important positions.

Historical Roots

These values and beliefs did not originate in American society. American settlers brought with them the legal, religious, and political expectations that had kept women subordinate in the Old World.[94] Under English common law, for example, women suffered "civil death" upon marriage: they could not sign contracts, had no title to their own earnings or property (even when it was their own by inheritance or dowery), and had no rights to their children in the case of legal separation. The religions of the newcomers to America led to the view that women had special virtues of modesty, meekness, compassion, and piety that helped fit them to their proper role of motherhood.

While it is true that sexism can be traced to long before the founding of America, it was in the early American experience that many of the stereotypes that continue to be applied to modern women were first developed. For example, in the late eighteenth and early nineteenth centuries a "cult of domesticity" developed in which women were urged "to be wives and mothers, to nurture and maintain their families, to provide religious example and inspiration, and to affect the world around them by exercising private moral influence."[95] These stereotypes underwent change and extension in the later nineteenth[96] and twentieth centuries,[97] but the key point is that sexism has a variety of distinctive roots in American history.

Contemporary Manifestations

Sexism permeates contemporary culture. Adult women are frequently called "girls"—a practice analogous to calling an adult black man "boy." Advertising, adult and children's literature, and most social institutions have actively promoted a view of women as narcissistic, silly, weak, headachy, emotionally unstable, and generally competent only to judge the whiteness of the wash. The titles "Miss" and "Mrs." categorize women according their marital status, but men are referred to as "Mr." whether they are married or not. Although for this reason "Ms." has grown in popularity, most women are still referred to by either "Miss" or "Mrs."

Because sexism permeates the culture and is passed down in the socialization process, women as well as men tend to learn to be sexist by acquiring sexist ideas and beliefs. Women are frequently harsh judges of other women whose behavior deviates from role-prescribed behavior, and of course, it is mostly mothers who socialize their daughters into traditional feminine roles.

The cultural pressures on women to be seen as attractive by men is both produced by and supportive of male dominance. The pressures to be attractive to men divide women by making them rivals and also making them dependent upon men: it is men who decide which women are attractive. This tends to reduce women to being *sex objects.* Opposition to such views of women have surfaced in attacks on such cultural forces as *Playboy, Penthouse,* and *Hustler,* which encourage men to treat a woman's body as a commodity.

PART III: RESPONSES

In the previous section we have detailed the ways in which sexism is produced and sustained through the culture, various social structures, the socialization process, and individual thought and action. Above all, these processes have affected and been part of the unequal division of labor between males and females. Equality between the sexes depends on changing this inequality in the division of labor, as well as the structures and processes that sustain it. In this section we will examine some of the recent efforts to change the divison of labor, but before we do so we need a brief summary of the history of the women's movement, which can be seen as a response to the problem of sexism in general, and more specifically, to the inequality within the divison of labor.

A Brief History of the Women's Movement

This is not the first time in our history that there has been a profound awareness of sex-based inequality as a social problem[98] To understand the present women's movement, it would be instructive to look briefly at the rise and decline of a previous phase that ran from the nineteenth century through the end of World War I. We will focus on the United States, although a parallel movement evolved in Great Britain.

The Early Years

The earlier phase of the feminist movement began, in the United States at least, with women who were active abolitionists (for example, Elizabeth Cady Stanton [1815–1902]), or were inspired by the abolition (antislavery) movement. The discrimination, both legal and social, that they experienced as women working in that movement awakened them to the need for a women's movement. They were struck by the parallels between the situation confronting women and the condition of slavery. Their involvement in the effort to free the slaves provided them with insights into, and ideas for solving, the problems of women. However, females were not always welcomed by male abolitionists. Female representatives to an international antislavery conference in 1840 were refused seats—an occurrence that serves to remind us (as it did them) that social issues can be very narrowly defined. Such treatment led them to establish (at a conference held in Seneca Falls, New York, in 1848) a movement for the emancipation of women.

There was, of course, concern about women's rights prior to this time. Elite female members of society had expressed interest in this issue for years, and by the 1830s these concerns had been extended to middle-class women's groups.[99] In some experimental communes of this period, equality of the sexes was often attempted in all spheres—socially, in work, intellectually, and sexually.

As was to be true in later wars, women took on more importance in the labor force during the Civil War as they supported the war effort and filled jobs vacated by men who had gone to war. After the Civil War, the "woman question" was widely debated. Many adherents of the women's movement expected that when the right to vote was granted to blacks (*male* blacks) it would be extended to women as well. They were disappointed by the Fourteenth Amendment because it gave the vote only to black males.

In these early years of the movement, women's primary tactics were agitating and propagandizing to awaken attention to the injustices they suffered. At first, the feminists faced strong opposition and ridicule. Amelia Bloomer (1818–1894) and others who, in the mid-nineteenth century, tried to do away with the restrictive steel-ribbed and whalebone corsets simply earned abuse and the lasting derogatory term "bloomers" for wearing more comfortable clothing.

In the second half of the nineteenth century, when there was widespread concern about education, many women's colleges were founded. Despite much social opposition, even graduate education and training in such professions as medicine and law were opened—although only to exceptional women.

From 1868 to 1870, the National Woman Suffrage Association published a weekly newspaper, *The Revolution,* with the motto: "Men, their rights and nothing more; women, their rights and nothing less!" Feminists turned their attention to a great number of issues, including reforms in education, dress, industrial working conditions, religion, marriage, and divorce laws. By the turn of the twentieth century, they also concerned themselves with peace, prohibition of liquor, and economic legislation.

By the time the women's movement entered its second generation, toward the end of the nineteenth century, many of its leaders were educated and professional women, whereas formerly many had been housewives. While earlier leaders had called for a "new morality" and a radical rethinking of the family (Stanton identified domestic slavery as the source of women's oppression), many of the new generation of feminists had quite orthodox views on issues other than suffrage. The country had in the meantime changed from an agrarian to an industrial society, and the change brought great concern with the evils and ills of city life. Great waves of immigrants reached America, only to suffer in the filth of the cities. Women such as Jane Addams (1860–1935), who might have concentrated their attention on narrowly defined feminist issues, were drawn instead into a broader concern for social work and efforts at social reform. These reform efforts encompassed not only sexism, but also other problems such as poverty and racism which, of course, also impacted on women.

During the early twentieth century, the attention of the women's movement tended to shift toward a concern for winning the right to vote.[100] During World War I women were once again drawn into the labor force to help "make the world safe for democracy," yet they still were not entitled to share in that democracy. Late in 1919, after lobbying, demonstrations, and picket lines that resulted in the jailing of militant women, and with the reluctant support of President Wilson, the vote was finally granted women by the passage of the Nineteenth Amendment. However, women failed to win the broader social reforms they had sought.

With the right to vote, feminism tended to subside and become submerged beneath a number of other events and issues—the Depression, World War II, the atom bomb, the "Cold War," and other issues. But feminism had never completely disappeared and by the early 1960s it had begun to reemerge and was soon to become stronger than ever.[101]

The Modern Women's Movement

The rebirth of the women's movement received an impetus in 1960 when President Kennedy set up the President's Commission on the Status of Women.[102] This was followed by the development of state commissions in each of the fifty states. The women who served on these various commissions formed an embryonic communications network since they had many opportunities to meet and keep in touch with each other. They also shared the common experience of an increased realization that women were still thoroughly denied rights and opportunities.

In 1963 Betty Friedan published her important book, *The Feminine Mystique,* which helped to crystallize the feelings of many women about their status in society.[103] In 1964 the Civil Rights Act was amended to include sex discrimination, thus committing the federal government to insuring women's rights. In 1966 the National Organization for Women (NOW) was formed, with Betty Friedan as its first president. NOW was formed with the goal of bringing "women into full participation in the mainstream of American society now, assuming all the privileges and responsibilities thereof in truly equal partnership with men."[104] NOW, as well as several other formal women's organizations established during this period, developed great skill in public relations. They used the media to make a large part of the population aware of the women's movement and women's problems. However, these organizations were not very effective in organizing the mass of women, or in bringing about many of the changes they sought.

During the late 1960s, younger, less establishment-oriented, often radical women began to participate actively in the women's movement. They saw women's problems as being primarily political in nature and as being best solved by organizing large numbers of women in order to gain increased power. In the late 1960s, this led to the formation of a number of independent women's organizations in various American cities. By this time, the anti-Vietnam war, student, and black civil rights movements were in full swing and many activist women believed in those causes and were actively involved in them. In fact, there was a tendency to see all of these movements as of one piece with the women's movement; a gain in one was seen as a gain for all of these causes. However, women soon discovered that not everyone shared their concern for women's problems. The following illustrates the dawning of one such realization:

> At the University of Washington, an SDS [Students for a Democratic Society] organizer was explaining to a large meeting how white college youth established rapport with the poor whites with whom they were working. He noted that sometimes after analyzing societal ills, the men shared leisure time by 'balling a chick together.' He pointed out that such activities did much to enhance the political consciousness of the poor white youth. A woman in the audience asked, 'And what did it do for the consciousness of the chick?' . . . After the meeting, a handful of enraged women formed Seattle's first group.[105]

It was instances like these that led to the independence of many women's groups in the 1970s and their more single-minded focus on issues directly related to women.

The Equal Rights Amendment

A major focus of the women's movement in the 1970s and early 1980s was the Equal Rights Amendment (ERA). The amendment was passed by Congress in March 1972 and would have become the twenty-seventh amendment to the Constitution had it been ratified by thirty-eight states. After a vicious, ten-year battle the supporters of ERA failed, at least for the moment (an effort to revive it in the House of Representatives failed in late 1983), in obtaining the necessary number of state ratifications. Had ERA been accepted, it was anticipated that it would have portended even more massive changes toward the goal of sexual equality in employment and in all other areas in which women had encountered restrictions. For all of the hostility it engendered, and its ultimate failure, ERA was surprisingly benign in its basic provisions:

> Section 1. Equality of rights under the law should not be denied or abridged by the United States or by any State on account of sex.
>
> Section 2. The Congress shall have the power to enforce by appropriate legislation the provisions of this article.
>
> Section 3. The amendment shall take effect two years after the date of ratification.

Had it been ratified, it would have nullified the many state laws that at present treat men and women differently. For example, not only would employers have been required to hire and promote men and women on an equal basis, but they would not have been permitted to give women any benefits that were not also provided for men—including rest periods and maternity leaves—or in any other way to make distinctions on the basis of sex. The amendment would also have wiped out divorce laws that favored women. Many women, especially those who chose to fulfill traditional female roles, were threatened by these aspects and implications of the amendment. These women, along with a large number of traditionally oriented men, formed a powerful coalition that was able to prevent ratification of ERA within the allotted ten year period.[106]

The Women's Movement in the 1980s

In spite of the failure to ratify ERA, the women's movement has had, and continues to have, successes. In general areas such as the work world, females have made considerable strides in recent years. Women's organizations have grown more visible and more powerful. NOW is a national force and its membership in 1982 had risen to 220,000.[107] More specifically, the 1980s have brought the important appointment (at least symbolically) of the first female Supreme Court Justice and the 1984 nomination by the Democratic party of a woman for Vice President. Yet there is a long list of changes still to be made in politics, work, education, and the family. Complicating

In spite of considerable effort by the women's movement, the Equal Rights Amendment was not ratified by enough states in the allotted period of time.
(Jean-Louis Atlan/Sygma)

matters for the women's movement is the strength of various opposition groups such as Phyllis Schlafly's Eagle Trust Fund, right-to-life groups, and fundamentalist religious groups. The conservative political climate of the early 1980s has also had a negative effect on the women's movement. Finally, there is at least some questioning by younger feminists of the gains and future direction of the women's movement. Friedan, for example, writes of hearing "undertones of pain and puzzlement, a queasiness, an uneasiness, almost a bitterness that they hardly dare to admit."[108] This prompts Friedan to argue for the need to move on to the "second stage" of the women's movement. The objective is to move beyond fighting against the "old structure of unequal, polarized male and female sex roles" and toward the second stage of "the restructuring of our institutions on a basis of real equality for women and men."[109] The women's movement of the middle and late 1980s is likely to be different from its immediate predecessor, but it is nevertheless likely to continue to play a visible, vocal, and important role in American society.

Instead of continuing to discuss the women's movement in general, it would be useful to look at some of the changes in the division of labor aided, at least in part, by that movement. In the process, we will also encounter some of the major problems in this area that still need to be overcome.

Changing the Division of Labor

In spite of some recent gains, women are still consigned to less powerful, less prestigious, and lower-paying positions within the division of labor. Until sex no longer plays a role in the division of labor, women will not achieve equal status. Thus, an end to all hiring and promotion practices that foster a sexual division of labor is a central demand of those opposed to sex-based inequalities.

Legal Approaches

One word, inserted in the Civil Rights Act of 1964 at the last moment in the hopes of stalling passage, has had an important effect on the division of labor in the work world. In Title VII of the Act, intended to prohibit job discrimination against nonwhites, the word "sex" appears. Thus, the act forbids employers to take account of "race, color, religion, sex, or national origin," when hiring or promoting workers. Subsequent court decisions have held that the Civil Rights Act makes it unlawful to bar women from such jobs as airline pilot or telephone installer, or to bar men from such jobs as airline steward or telephone operator.

Indicative of the changes forced by legal decisions is that newspaper want ads were forced to cease indicating sex restrictions on jobs or using sections called "Jobs for Men" and "Jobs for Women." It was not too long ago that jobs such as secretary, receptionist, and telephone operator appeared only in the women's jobs section, while jobs such as machinist, executive trainee, and the like appeared only in the men's job section. Many ads even stated specifically that applicants had to be male or female.

In addition to changes brought about by changes in the law, law suits have also produced a reduction in sex segregation in the workforce. But, as we have already seen, the division of labor within the labor force, while improving, remains highly sex segregated. This means that such formal efforts to end sexual restrictions in employment practices have not, and will not by themselves, end a sexual division of labor—and certainly not rapidly.

Affirmative Action

The government, under pressure from the women's movement, has not merely taken legal action to end discrimination in employment practices, it has also sought to encourage the more positive policy known as *affirmative action.*[110] Such programs are not simply designed to end discrimination, but also involve positive steps to increase female (and other minority) representation until it reflects their representation in the general population. This means that the ultimate objective is an occupational system in which there is *no* discrimination on the basis of sex. This, of course, is a very ambitious goal and there is a long way to go before it can even be approached.

In the 1980s, under the Reagan administration, there has been much less emphasis on programs like affirmative action. However, opposition to such programs certainly predates the Reagan presidency. For example, through the middle and late 1970s, the conservative New Right opposed not only feminism in general, but also the ERA, abortion, and most importantly in this context, affirmative action, which the New Right saw as "reverse discrimination."[111] For another, various corporations through the 1970s undermined, purposely or accidently, government efforts to implement affirmative action programs. There is the case of American Telephone and Telegraph (AT&T), which in the early 1970s was called by the Equal Opportunity Employment Commission (a government agency) "the largest discriminator against women in the U.S."[112] However, simultaneous to its being forced to undertake an affirmative action program, AT&T also embarked on a series of major technological changes. The result was that while some women did improve their positions in the organization, more were forced to leave the organization as a result of technological change. Thus, affirmative action programs were undermined intentionally and unintentionally by political action groups, various corporations, and, in the early 1980s, the President of the United States.

Day-Care Centers

One structural change needed to help eliminate sexism in the workplace is the establishment of many more formal child-care facilities. We have seen some growth in this area, again in large part because of pressure from the women's movement, but much more is needed. Not only are there not enough child-care centers, but those that do exist tend to be of poor quality and very expensive. The absence of child-care facilities may well prevent many women from working. The poor quality of many of the available choices may force some women to choose to stay at home rather than to place their children in such circumstances. And the high cost may make it economically irrational for women to work until their children can enter public school. All of these things, of course, are likely to affect the woman's occupational aspects adversely.

The United States lags far behind most other industrialized nations in having a national child-care program. The day-care centers in the Soviet Union serve about 13 million children. Sweden provides child care for children through the ninth grade. In addition, the government will pay 90 percent of a parent's salary so that either the mother or father can stay home for a year and care for the children. These programs reflect a great commitment in both of these countries, as is the case in many others, to the full equality of the sexes.[113] The United States needs such a commitment, as well as the funds, to set up a child-care system that approaches those of other countries. In addition to government efforts, corporations must do more to set up day-care centers for their own workers.[114]

Comparable Worth

One of the hot new areas in the search for ways to create more equality in the division of labor is "comparable worth."[115] Equal pay for equal work has been mandated by federal law since 1963, but this does not directly affect a large proportion of female workers because they are found in a small number of predominantly female occupations. The advocates of comparable worth argue that even though men and women may do different work, they may do work that is of comparable value to their employer and therefore should be equally rewarded. If women are in jobs that are comparable to those of men but are not rewarded in a like fashion, this is just another form of sex discrimination, and legal recourse is available to them.[116] This issue is just beginning to be raised and we will need to wait and see whether it has any significant effect on reducing the gap between male and female income.

Changes in the Family

Substantial changes in the occupational situation facing women cannot come about without substantial changes in the structure of the family. In fact, it is likely that continued progress in the work world will bring about needed changes in the structure of the family. Until they do, the typical family is likely to prevent women from succeeding occupationally. For those who do succeed in spite of the family, there is likely to be considerable guilt, frustration, and pressure to take on the role of superwoman. Various changes are underway in the traditional family that promise to make

The advances made by women reached a new peak in 1984 when Geraldine Ferraro was the Democratic candidate for vice-president.

(A. Tannenbaum/Sygma)

it easier for women to succeed occupationally, or to put it another way, that will produce a kind of family that is compatible with a woman who is a success in her chosen field. Included here would be later marriages, having children later, having fewer (or no) children,[117] sharing more family responsibilities with the husband, and leaving much of the care of children, even infants, to others. More radically, more temporary, nonmarital relationships with men, remaining single, or even surrogate mothers might be even more useful in helping women succeed occupationally.

How Far Have We Come?

We close this chapter with a brief assessment of progress in the area of sex-role inequality with special reference to the work world. However, rather than discussing this issue in general terms, we will focus on more specific occupational categories—women in law, female executives, and female clerical workers.

Women in Law

The number of women in law quadrupled between 1972 and 1982 (3.8 percent to 15.4 percent). Even more promising is the fact that in 1960 women received only 2 percent of all law degree, but in 1981 that proportion had leaped to 32 percent.[118] While charting these and other gains, Cynthia Epstein in her recent study, *Women in Law,* has also uncovered continuing problems for the female lawyer.[119] For example, she found that women lawyers are disproportionately likely to do the kind of legal work that is consistent with traditional sex roles—"family and government law, public interest and defender work."[120] And these are the areas in law that are likely to be less rewarded economically and to be lower in professional prestige. Thus, women have made significant progress in law, but they still have a considerable distance to go.

The Female Executive

As was pointed out early in this chapter, women have also made strong gains at the managerial level and now more than one-fourth of all managers are female. However, the situation here, as it is in general, "is at once discouraging and promising."[121] Linda Brown points to a number of areas of continuing problems for females in management. For one thing, female managers tend to cluster in certain fields like health administration and restaurant, bar, and cafeteria management. For another, females in business/industrial management tend to be much more likely to be middle-level rather than top managers. In addition, female managers are far less likely to be found in higher pay brackets than male managers. In spite of these and other continuing problems, Brown is hopeful about the future. It is at entry-level managerial positions that women have made their major gains in recent years and those women will begin to make their way into top management positions in fifteen to twenty-five years.

The Female Clerical Worker

Clerical work is an area in which females have traditionally been overrepresented. This continues to be the case to this day. Thus, in contrast to the case of females in law and business management, there has been little progress in reducing sex-role inequality within clerical occupations. Furthermore, there are ongoing social changes that are in the process of greatly lowering the status of these occupations. Thus, instead of improvement in this area of the occupational world, females are experiencing a diminution in their position.

The changes taking place here involve technological developments in the office such as the coming of the word processor and the increasing use of typing pools. What these changes succeed in doing is "degrading" and "deskilling" clerical work.[122] The skills now needed by the clerical worker are more mechanical, narrower, and of a lower level than those needed by clerical workers in the past. In addition, management has tended to move toward more extensive control over the work of clerical workers. For example, the work of a word processor can be overseen directly and continuously by a supervisor watching a monitor. This greater control, as well as the decline in the skills needed, has tended to degrade clerical work. This is a particularly great problem for women since they represent such an overwhelming majority of these workers.

The image conveyed by the three specific types of occupations discussed above is consistent with the overall situation of women in the labor force. There has been progress, yet many inequalities remain. But, as the case of the clerical workers makes clear, women cannot afford to congratulate themselves for gains already made and concentrate solely on solidifying and expanding upon those gains. There are also ongoing forces of varying kinds that may well come to pose new threats to the position of women in the work world. These new and impending problems will need to be attended to while previous gains are maintained and built upon not only in the work world, but in all of our social structures and institutions.

SUMMARY

Part I: The Problem

1. In a number of important ways, women are a subordinate group in American society denied equal status with men.
2. Although there have been improvements in women's position in the labor force, a number of problems and strains remain.
3. Some of the problems associated with the roles of wife and mother have been reduced, while others continue to exist much as they have in the past.
4. The gaps in the educational sphere between males and females have narrowed dramatically, but despite this change women continue to be discriminated against (for example, in income, representation in high-status occupations, and in being overqualified for their positions) when they leave school and enter the occupational world.

Part II: Causes and Consequences

5. At the physiological level, the conventional anthropological view is that the need for females to bear and raise children, as well as their lesser physical strength, has given them a disadvantage vis-à-vis males. Males capitalized on these slight initial advantages and erected an unequal society in which they took the preeminent positions.
6. The conventional anthropological view has been criticized by feminists who have argued that male dominance is not inherited, the destinies of the sexes were not settled in ancient times, and cultural factors are far more important than biological factors.
7. More recently biosociologists have revived the idea that there are important physiological differences between males and females that help account for their differential status within society. This view, too, has come under severe criticism.
8. Even if we accept the highly controversial arguments in favor of the importance of biological factors in the origin of inequality between the sexes, the fact remains that ongoing changes have reduced and perhaps even eliminated many biological imperatives.
9. At the social-psychological level, the differential socialization for sex roles plays a key role in causing sex-based inequality. At the same time, this inequality has a series of social-psychological consequences such as that impacting on the nature of conversation for males and females.
10. At the sociological level, schools are one of the social structures that play a causal role in creating and sustaining sexism. This sexism may be found in primary and secondary schools: in schoolbooks, the school curriculum, teacher attitudes and behaviors, school sports, as well as in various ways at the college level.
11. Also at the sociological level, the structure of the work world operates against women. Among the structural barriers are impediments to gaining needed educational credentials, lack of sponsors, lack of role models, institutional sexism, occupational sex segregation, sexual harassment, and liabilities in dealing with crucial testing points.
12. Finally at the sociological level, the culture of the United States is permeated by sexism and this serves to create and sustain sex-based inequality.

Part III: Responses

13. The main focus of this section is a brief history of the major response to the problems discussed in this chapter—the women's movement.
14. Women have made some gains as a result of the women's movement as well as other responses to the gender inequality discussed throughout this chapter.
15. The chapter concluded with some of the gains made by women within the divison of labor, as well as some of the continuing problems.
16. Three occupations were examined to illustrate the gains made, as well as those still to be made, by females. Specifically, we discussed the current situation facing women in law, executive-level positions, and clerical work.
17. In the coming years, women will need to deal with new and impending problems while maintaining and building upon previous gains.

SUGGESTED READINGS

Berch, Bettina, *The Endless Day: The Political Economy of Women and Work.* New York: Harcourt Brace Jovanovich, 1982. A useful overview of the position of women in the work world.

Chodorow, Nancy, *The Reproduction of Mothering: Psychoanalysis and the Sociology of Gender.* Berkeley: University of California Press, 1978. This is a difficult, controversial, and highly esteemed analysis of gender from a psychoanalytic point of view.

MacKinnon, Catherine A., *Sexual Harassment of Working Women.* New Haven, Conn.: Yale University Press, 1979. A legal analysis of the problem of sexual harassment of females on the job.

Ryan, Mary P., *Womanhood in America: From Colonial Times to the Present.* New York: New Viewpoints, 1975. Useful historical background, which must be supplemented with information on recent developments.

Weitzman, Lenore, *Sex Role Socialization: A Focus on Women.* Palo Alto, Calif.: Mayfield, 1979. An analysis of the critically important problem of the socialization for sex roles among females.

FOOTNOTES

[1]Alice S. Rossi, "Equality Between the Sexes: An Immodest Proposal." In Robert J. Lifton, ed., *The Woman in America* (Boston, Mass.: Houghton Mifflin, 1965), pp. 98–143. For the view that women had been standing still see Edward Gross, "Plus Ça Change . . . ? The Sexual Structure of Occupations Over Time," *Social Problems,* 16 (1968), pp. 198–208.

[2]For a discussion of this see "Young Feminists Speak for Themselves," *Ms.,* April 1983, pp. 43ff.

[3]Bettina Berch, *The Endless Day: The Political Economy of Women and Work* (New York: Harcourt Brace Jovanovich, 1982), p. 5.

[4]U.S. Department of Commerce, Bureau of the Census, *Statistical Abstract of the United States: 1984* (Washington, D.C.: U. S. Government Printing Office, 1983), p. 407.

[5]*Ibid.,* p. 413.

[6]*Ibid.,* p. 414.

[7]*Ibid.*

[8]Andrew Hacker, *U/S: A Statistical Portrait of the American People* (New York: Viking, 1983), p. 164.

[9]Nancy E. McGlen and Karen O'Connor, *Women's Rights: The Struggle for Equality in the Nineteenth and Twentieth Centuries* (New York: Praeger, 1983), p. 217.

[10]Donald J. Treiman and Heidi I. Hartmann, eds., *Women, Work and Wages: Equal Pay for Jobs of Equal Value* (Washington, D.C.: National Academy Press, 1981); Janet Norwood, "The Female-Male Earnings Gap: A Review of Employment and Earnings Issues" (Washington, D.C.: U.S. Department of Labor, Bureau of Labor Statistics), Report 673, September 1982, p. 2.

[11]Hacker, *op. cit.,* p. 134.

[12]William Julius Wilson, "The Black Underclass," *The Wilson Quarterly* (1984), pp. 88–99.

[13]U.S. Department of Labor, Office of the Secretary, Women's Bureau, "20 Facts on Women Workers." Washington, D.C., 1982.

[14]According to the U.S. Department of Labor, 9.7 million of the 14 million working mothers in 1982 worked "to supplement low family incomes." This means that over 4 million working mothers in the labor force are not there as a result of economic duress. U.S. Department of Labor, Office of the Secretary, Women's Bureau. "Economic Responsibilities of Working Women" (Washington, D.C.: November/December 1982), p. 3.

[15]Hacker, *op. cit.*, p. 104.

[16]*Ibid.*

[17]*Ibid.*, p. 58.

[18]*Ibid.*, p. 64.

[19]Berch, *op. cit.*

[20]John H. Scanzoni, *Sex Roles, Life Styles, and Childbearing: Changing Patterns in Marriage and Family* (New York: Free Press, 1976).

[21]Arthur J. Norton and Paul C. Glick, "Marital Instability in America: Past, Present, and Future." In George Levinger and Oliver Moles, eds., *Divorce and Separation: Context, Causes and Consequences* (New York: Basic Books, 1979), pp. 6–19.

[22]Andrew Cherlin, *Marriage, Divorce, Remarriage* (Cambridge, Mass.: Harvard University Press, 1981), p. 22.

[23]National Center for Health Statistics, "Births, Marriages, Divorces, and Deaths for February, 1984," *Monthly Vital Statistics Report*, vol. 33. no. 2 (Hyattsville, Md.: Public Health Service, May 23, 1984).

[24]*Ibid.*

[25]Hacker, *op. cit.*, p. 149.

[26]U.S. Department of Labor, Office of the Secretary, "Equal Employment Opportunity for Women: U.S. Policies." Washington, D.C., Table 17.

[27]U.S. Department of Commerce, *Statistical Abstract: 1984, op. cit.*, p. 469.

[28]Hacker, *op. cit.*, p. 149.

[29]Hacker, *op. cit.*, p. 148.

[30]Janet Norwood, "The Female-Male Earnings Gap: A Review of Employment and Earnings Issues." (Washington, D.C.: U.S. Department of Labor, Bureau of Labor Statistics, Report 673, September 1982), p. 2.

[31]Norwood, *op. cit.*, p. 8.

[32]*Ibid.*

[33]*Ibid.*

[34]George P. Murdock and Caterina Provost, "Factors in the Division of Labor by Sex: A Cross-Cultural Analysis," *Ethnology*, 12 (1973), pp. 203–225.

[35]Ernestine Friedl, *Women and Men: An Anthropologist's View* (New York: Holt, Rinehart and Winston, 1975).

[36]Roy G. D'Andrade, "Sex Differences and Cultural Institutions." In Eleanor E. Maccoby, ed., *The Development of Sex Differences* (Stanford, Cal.: Stanford University Press, 1966); George P. Murdock, *Social Structure* (New York: Macmillan, 1949).

[37]Friedl, *op. cit.*

[38]Gerhard Lenski and Jean Lenski, *Human Societies: An Introduction to Macrosociology*, 4th ed. (New York: McGraw-Hill, 1982), pp. 125, 174.

[39]Michelle Zimbalist Rosaldo, "Woman, Culture and Society: A Theoretic Overview." In Michelle Z. Rosaldo and Louise Lamphere, eds., *Woman, Culture and Society* (Stanford, Cal.: Stanford University Press, 1974), pp. 17–42; Michelle Zimbalist Rosaldo, "The Use and Abuse of Anthropology: Reflections on Feminism and Cross-Cultural Understanding," *Signs*, 5 (1980), pp. 389–417: Ruby Rohrlich-Leavitt, Barbara Sykes, and Elizabeth Weatherford, "Aboriginal Women: Male and Female Anthropological Perspectives." In Rayna R. Reiter, ed., *Toward an Anthropology of Women.* (New York: Monthly Review Press, 1975), pp. 110–126.

[40]Jane Collier, Michelle Z. Rosaldo, and Sylvia Yanagisako, "Is There a Family? New Anthropological Views." In Barrie Thorne and Marilyn Yalom, eds., *Rethinking the Family: Some Feminist Questions* (New York: Longmans, 1982), p. 32.

[41]*Ibid.*, p. 31.

[42]Kathleen Hough, "The Origin of the Family." In Reiter, *op. cit.*, p. 58.

[43]Lila Liebowitz, "Perspectives on the Evolution of Sex Differences." In Reiter, *op. cit.*, pp. 20–35.

[44]Ann Oakley, *Sex, Gender, and Society* (New York: Harper Colophon, 1972), pp. 146–147.

[45]Sherry B. Ortner and Harriet Whitehead, "Introduction: Accounting for Sexual Meanings." In Ortner and Whitehead, eds., *Sexual Meanings: The Cultural Construction of Gender and Sexuality* (Cambridge: Cambridge University Press, 1981), p. 1.

[46]Alice Rossi, "A Biosocial Perspective on Parenting," *Daedalus*, 106 (1977), pp. 1–31.

[47]Eleanor Emmons Maccoby and Carol Nagy Jacklin, *The Psychology of Sex Differences*, Vol. 1 (Stanford, Cal.: Stanford University Press, 1974), p. 355.

[48]Spencer E. Cahill, "Reexamining the Acquisition of Sex Roles: A Social Interactionist Approach," *Sex Roles*, 9 (1983), 2.

[49]Leonore Weitzman, *Sex Role Socialization: A Focus on Women* (Palo Alto, Cal.: Mayfield, 1979), p. xxii.

[50]*Ibid.*

[51]L. Kohlberg, "A Cognitive-Developmental Analysis of Sex-Role Concepts and Attitudes." In Eleanor E. Maccoby, ed., *The Development of Sex Differences* (Stanford, Cal.: Stanford University Press, 1966), pp. 82–173.

[52]*Ibid.*, p. 89.

[53]Nancy Chodorow, *The Reproduction of Mothering: Psychoanalysis and the Sociology of Gender* (Berkeley: University of California Press, 1978).

[54]Jack Sattel, "The Inexpressive Male: Tragedy or Sexual Politics?" In Rachel Kahn-Hut, Arlene Kaplan Daniels, and Richard Colvard, eds., *Women and Work: Problems and Prospects* (New York: Oxford University Press, 1982), pp. 160–169.

[55]Pamela Fishman, "Interaction: The Work Women Do." In Kahn-Hut *et al., op. cit.*, pp. 170–180.

[56]Weitzman, *op. cit.*

[57]Sally A. Koblinsky and Alan Sugawara, "Nonsexist Curricula, Sex of Teacher, and Children's Sex-Role Learning," *Sex Roles*, 10 (1984), 357–367.

[58]Lenore J. Weitzman *et al.*, "Sex Role Socialization in Picture Books for Preschool Children," *American Journal of Sociology*, 77 (1972), pp. 1125–1150.

[59]Eleanor Ashton, "Measures of Play Behavior: The Influence of Sex-Stereotyped Children's Books," *Sex Roles*, 9 (1983), pp. 43–47.

[60]Cited in Virginia Kidd, "'Now You See,' said Mark," *The New York Review of Books*, September 3, 1970, pp. 35–36.

[61]Marjorie U'Ren, "The Image of Woman in Textbooks." In Vivian Gornick and Barbara K. Moran, eds., *Woman in Sexist Society: Studies in Power and Powerlessness* (New York: Basic Books, 1971), pp. 281–225.

[62]Gwyneth E. Britton, "Danger: State Adopted Texts May be Hazardous to Our Future," *The Reading Teacher* (1975), pp. 52–58.

[63]John Warren Stewig and Mary Lynn Knipfel, "Sexism in Picture Books: What Progress?" *The Elementary School Journal*, 76 (1975), pp. 151–155.

[64]Richard Kolbe and Joseph C. LaVoie, "Sex Role Stereotyping in Preschool Children's Picture Books," *Social Psychology Quarterly*, 44 (1981), p. 373 (italics supplied).

[65]Weitzman, *op. cit.* 1979, p. 37.

[66]Kathy Sawyer, "Women Students Make Big Gains in U.S. Schools," *The Washington Post*, October 18, 1981, pp. A1, A11.

[67]Joseph W. Schneider and Sally L. Hacker, "Sex Role Imagery and Use of the Generic 'Man' in Introductory Texts: A Case in the Sociology of Sociology," *American Sociologist*, 8 (1973), pp. 12–18.

[68]Mirra Komarovsky, "Cultural Contradictions and Sex Roles," *American Journal of Sociology*, 52 (1946), 184–189.

[69]Weitzman, *op. cit.* 1979.

[70]Philip Goldberg, "Are Women Prejudiced Against Women," *Transaction*, 5 (1968), 28–30.

[71]Randall Collins, *The Credential Society: An Historical Sociology of Education and Stratification* (New York: Academic Press, 1979).

[72]Ann S. Harris, "The Second Sex in Academe," *AAUP Bulletin*, 56 (1970), 85.

[73]George Ritzer and David Walczak, *Working: Conflict and Change*, 3rd ed. (Englewood Cliffs, N.J.: Prentice-Hall, 1986).

[74]Rodolfo Alvarez *et. al.*, eds., *Discrimination in Organizations* (San Francisco: Jossey-Bass, 1979).

[75]Valerie K. Oppenheimer, *The Female Labor Force in the United States* (Berkeley: University of California Press, 1970).

[76]Francine D. Blau, "Women in the Labor Force: An Overview." In J. Freeman, ed., *Women: A Feminist Perspective* (Palo Alto, Cal.: Mayfield, 1975); 1981 statistics on women in various occupations from Norwood, *op. cit.* 1982, p. 8.

[77]Norwood, *op. cit.*, p. 8.

[78]Heidi Hartmann, "Capitalism, Patriarchy, and Job Segregation by Sex," *Signs*, 1 (1976), Part 2: pp. 137–169.

[79]*Ibid.*, p. 139.

[80]*Ibid.*, p. 138.

[81]This emphasis on the importance of control is derived from Harry Braverman, *Labor and Monopoly Capital: The Degradation of Work in the Twentieth Century* (New York: Monthly Review Press, 1974).

[82]Hartmann, *op. cit.*, p. 139; For later work by Hartmann on the domestic division of labor, see Heidi Hartmann, "The Family as the Locus of Gender, Class, and Political Struggle: The Example of Housework," *Signs*, 6 (1981), pp. 366–394.

[83]Patricia Linenberger, "What Behavior Constitutes Sexual Harassment?" *Labor Law Journal*, 34 (1983), 238–247.

[84]Susan Brownmiller, *Against Our Will: Men, Women and Rape.* (New York: Simon and Schuster, 1975).

[85]Catharine A. MacKinnon, *Sexual Harassment of Working Women* (New Haven: Yale University Press, 1979), p. 176.

[86]*Ibid.*

[87]Donna J. Benson and Gregg Thomson, "Sexual Harassment on a University Campus: The Confluence of Authority Relations, Sexual Interest and Gender Stratification," *Social Problems,* 29 (1982), pp. 236–251.

[88]Noel Epstein, "When Professors Swap Good Grades for Sex," *The Washington Post,* September 6, 1981, pp. C1, C4.

[89]Cited in MacKinnon, *op. cit.*, p. 75.

[90]Bill Gully (with Mary Ellen Reese), *Breaking Cover* (New York: Simon and Schuster, 1980), p. 57.

[91]Ritzer and Walczak, *op. cit.*

[92]"The Superwoman Squeeze," *Newsweek,* May 19, 1980, pp. 72ff.

[93]"The Superwoman Squeeze," *op. cit.*

[94]Eleanor Flexner, *Century of Struggle: The Women's Rights Movement in the United States* (Cambridge, Mass.: Harvard University Press, 1959).

[95]Nancy F. Cott, *The Bonds of Womanhood* (New Haven, Conn: Yale University Press, 1977), p. 8.

[96]Nancy F. Cott, ed., *Root of Bitterness: Documents of the Social History of American Women* (New York: Dutton, 1972).

[97]Mary P. Ryan, *Womanhood in America: From Colonial Times to the Present* (New York: New Viewpoints, 1975).

[98]Ryan, *op. cit.*

[99]Carol Andreas, *Sex and Caste in America* (Englewood Cliffs, N.J.: Prentice-Hall, 1971).

[100]Waltraud Ireland, "The Rise and Fall of the Suffrage Movement," *Leviathan,* 2 (1970), 4–7.

[101]Jo Freeman, *The Politics of Women's Liberation* (New York: McKay, 1975).

[102]Lois W. Banner, *Women in Modern America: A Brief History* (New York: Harcourt Brace Jovanovich, 1974).

[103]Betty Friedan, *The Feminine Mystique* (New York: Norton, 1963).

[104]Jo Freeman, "The Origins of the Women's Liberation Movement," *American Journal of Sociology,* 78 (1973), p. 799.

[105]*Ibid.*, p. 801.

[106]Jane O'Reilly, "The Big-Time Players Behind the Small-Town Image," *Ms.*, January 1983, pp. 37ff.

[107]Nancy E. McGlen and Karen O'Connor, *op. cit.*, p. 30.

[108]Betty Friedan, *The Second Stage* (New York: Summit Books, 1981), p. 15.

[109]*Ibid.*, pp. 40–41.

[110]Jennie Farley, *Affirmative Action and the Woman Worker* (New York: AMACOM, 1979).

[111]Linda Gordon and Allen Hunter, "Sex, Family and the New Right," *Radical America,* 11 (November 1977/February 1978), pp. 9–25.

[112]Cited in Sally L. Hacker, "Sex Stratification, Technology and Organization Change: A Longitudinal Case Study of AT&T." In Kahn-Hut *et. al.*, *op. cit.*, p. 249.

[113]"The Superwomen Squeeze," *op. cit.*

[114]Jura Koncius, "Day-Care at the Workplace: New Fringe Benefit Pays Off for Parents and Employers," *The Washington Post,* March 24, 1982, pp. Md.1, 4.

[115]Benson Rosen, Sara Reynes, and Thomas A. Mahoney, "Compensation, Jobs, and Gender: Should a Female Nurse Make as Much as Male Truck Driver?" *Harvard Business Review,* 61 (1983), 170–190.

[116]Clarence Thomas, "Pay Equity and Comparable Worth," *Labor Law Journal,* 34 (1983), 3–12; John B. Golper, "The Current Legal Status of 'Comparable Worth' in the Federal Sector," *Labor Law Journal,* 34 (1983), 563–580.

[117]Jean Veevers, *Childless by Choice* (Toronto: Butterworths, 1980).

[118]U. S. Bureau of the Census, *Statistical Abstract of the United States: 1984, op. cit.*, pp. 419; 170.

[119]Cynthia Epstein, *Women in Law* (New York: Basic Books, 1981).

[120]*Ibid.*, p. 381.

[121]Linda Keller Brown, "Women and Business Management," *Signs,* 5 (1979), p. 268.

[122]Evelyn Nakano Glenn and Roslyn Feldberg, "Degraded and Deskilled: The Proletarianization of Clerical Work," *Social Problems,* 25 (1977), pp. 52–64.

'What a pretty kite the beggars children fly high above their hovel
Issa
Bruce McLean '74

10
Poverty

It is true that the poor have always been with us, but they have not always received the same amount of attention. For most of human history the vast majority of people have been poor. Poverty did not seem to be a problem since so many people were poor; poverty was simply taken for granted. In America, the Great Depression was a watershed in our thinking about poverty. Centuries of economic progress capped by the boom period of the 1920s led to economic success for large numbers of people and, perhaps more importantly, to the assumption that most, if not all, Americans would share in the economic boom. It was the bursting of this bubble that made the Depression of the 1930s such a critical event. Many who had never experienced poverty, and never expected to, were suddenly poor. Others, who had hoped to move out of the lower classes, had their hopes dashed. In response to the outcry from both of these groups, the government put into effect its first significant poverty programs, including many elements of the welfare system that are still in operation today.

Consciousness of poverty as a social problem waned during World War II, as almost everyone returned to work in order to support the war effort. The economic boom fueled by military needs continued after the war as pent-up consumer demand kept the economy humming at a high level. Americans quickly achieved, and as quickly took for granted, a standard of living and a national affluence unparalleled in the history of the world.

For a time in the late 1940s and into the 1950s, hardly anyone seemed to notice that not all Americans were sharing in the national bounty. The poor seemed nearly invisible—for they were mainly hidden from the eyes of the affluent majority—in depressed rural areas such as Appalachia, in racial and ethnic ghettos of the large cities, and in run-down hotels and rooming houses that sheltered the aged. However, the richest nation on earth was about to look again, and it was to find millions of impoverished Americans in its midst.

Several events coalesced in the late 1950s to reawaken interest in the poor. The civil rights movement had begun to gain momentum in this period, and a disproportionate number of blacks were poor. The black population knew the harsh realities of poverty, for discrimination and the long legacies of racism had kept blacks from participating in postwar prosperity. (It is important to remember that most poor people were and are *white;* blacks are simply overrepresented among the poor.) The civil rights movement did, and continues, to bring attention to the problem of poverty. Another factor was the primaries leading up to the 1960 presidential election campaign, especially the West Virginia primary. West Virginia had a very large poor population, and it also turned out to be pivotal to John Kennedy's chances of obtaining the Democratic nomination and ultimately the presidency. Kennedy seemed to "discover" poverty during the primary and through him the public was exposed to poverty in the United States. Kennedy's concern about poverty was reinforced by the appearance in 1963 of Michael Harrington's *The Other America,* an exposé of poverty that had a profound effect upon American society. Poverty became a central issue to the Kennedy administration and later to the Johnson administration.[1] In fact, Lyndon Johnson declared a "war on poverty" in which the objective was "to end poverty in this generation." Unfortunately, the Vietnam war intervened, and attention and money was diverted from the war on poverty to the war in Southeast Asia. Poverty was *not* ended in the 1960s and 1970s; it remains with us to this day. In fact, with the decline in the last decade of many of this nation's traditionally strong industries (notably autos and steel), what has been called the "deindustrialization of America,"[2] there is concern that poverty may be an even greater problem in the future than it has been in the past. At the same time, with the swing toward conservatism reflected in the presidential elections of 1980 and 1984, the federal government evinced less interest in solving the problem of poverty, at least through federal programs. The legacy of the 1960s, however, is that we remain conscious of poverty and we are not likely to lose sight of this problem in our midst.

PART I: THE PROBLEM

Relative and Absolute Poverty[3]

Obviously, poverty is a relative concept. For example, a famous German sociologist, George Simmel (1858–1918), made the point that the poor are not simply those found in the bottom rung of society, but that poverty is found in *all* social strata.[4] If people in the upper classes have less than their peers (for example, fewer yachts, a Mercedes Benz but not a Rolls Royce), they are likely to *feel* poor in comparison to them. Although we may be able to see how the concept of poverty applies to these people, it is very difficult to think of them as poor. However, it is not difficult for us to think of a welfare family from rural Mississippi as being poor. Yet such a family would be unimaginably well-off in comparison to a similar family in Calcutta, India, where some people literally live, raise their children, sleep, and die on the streets. Similarly, that poor Mississippi family today lives a better life than most quite well-to-do families did in preindustrial times.

Yet for all of that, we do not live hundreds of years ago, or in Calcutta today. We live in a society that takes for granted many gains in the quality and security of life. We do not expect people to have to set up housekeeping on the street or to die at a young age of what now would be considered minor ailments (as they did in preindustrial times) in order to qualify as being poor in contemporary America. Nevertheless, even today's poor in the United States suffer from hunger, inadequate shelter, and premature death. For purposes of discussion it is necessary to formulate an adequate working definition of American poverty.

The most widely used definition of poverty in the United States is based on the idea of *income sufficiency*—the amount of money needed to purchase the basic necessities of life. Although there are several standards that might be used to determine what level of income is sufficient, the measure used by the Social Security Administration has become the official government index of poverty.

The Poverty Index

One way of estimating the extent of poverty in this country is the poverty index. The index utilizes U.S. Department of Agriculture estimates of the costs of a minimal food budget, adjusted to the size of the family. The per person daily food budget is then multiplied by three to determine the approximate level of funds needed for *all* other living costs—housing, clothes, medical care, heat, light, and other necessities. Thus, in 1982 the index classified as poor all families of four with an income of less than $9,862.[5] This means that 34.4 million Americans were below the official poverty line, up from the less than 32 million people below the poverty level in 1981. That means that 15 percent (it was about 14 percent in 1981) of the total population was officially poor in 1982.[6]

Criticisms of the Poverty Line

However, this number, as striking as it is, is assailable on various grounds. For one thing, this method of calculating the poverty line is highly arbitrary. There are clearly many families a few dollars, or even a few thousand dollars, above the official poverty line who are by virtually any standard (food, shelter, and the like) poor, but who are not so classified officially. For another, these statistics are based on data collected by the Census Bureau, and the poor are well known to be underrepresented in those statistics. The Census Bureau is unable to find many poor people and, for their part, the poor often do not want to be found by *any* government agents. Problems are also created by the fact that there is only one overall national standard and it does not take into account regional and/or rural-urban differences. Clearly our family in rural Mississippi would live better (but *not* well) on $9,862 a year than a similar family in Chicago. Finally, the index, although readjusted annually, is absolute, not relative. Thus, while we can ascertain the number of poor people in this way, it tells us nothing about the gap between the poor and the rich. In looking at poverty we need to examine not only income insufficiency, but also the degree of *inequality* in society.[7]

Recent Changes in Poverty Levels

There is, in fact, evidence that the gap between those at the bottom and the top has been widening rather than narrowing; it could be said that the poor are relatively worse off today than they were several decades ago.[8] This has been made worse by welfare programs and income tax changes

Figure 10.1 Percent of Persons Below Poverty Level: 1970–1982

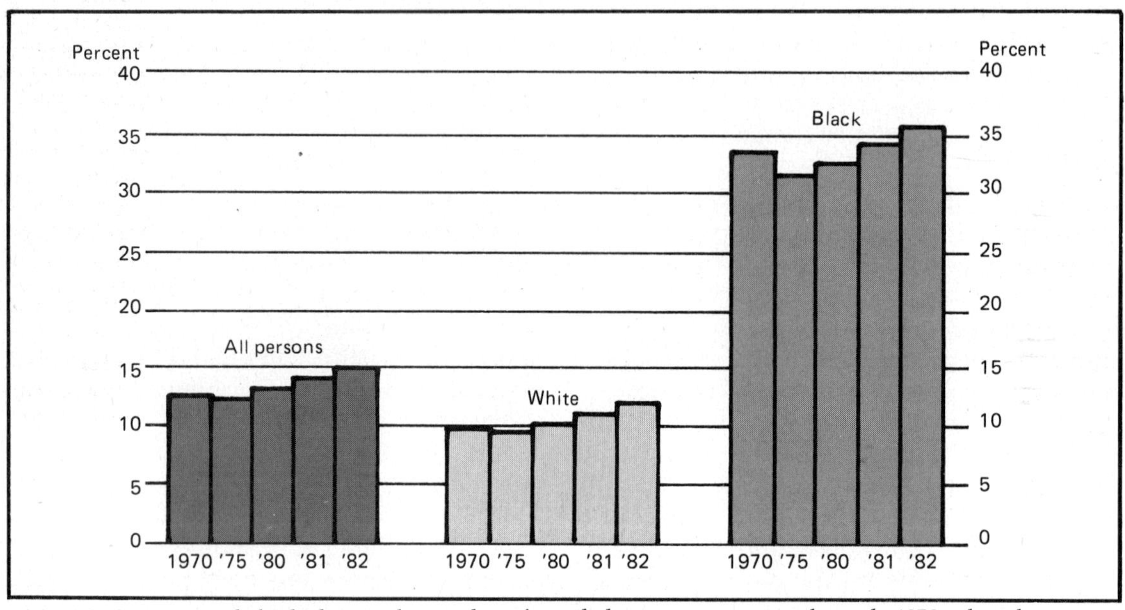

Although there was a slight decline in the number of people living in poverty in the early 1970s, there has since been a steady rise in their numbers. Note that while blacks are more likely to be poor, whites constitute a majority of those living below the poverty line.

Source: U.S. Bureau of the Census, *Statistical Abstract of the United States: 1984.* (Washington, D.C.: U.S. Government Printing Office, 1984), p. 444.

in the 1980s that have disproportionately hurt the poor[9] and aided the well-off and thereby further widened the gap between rich and poor.[10] One observer, Paul Blumberg, sees this as just the beginning of a long-run process that will see the decline of the American economy and a corresponding increase in poverty and inequality.[11]

For a long time, Americans congratulated themselves on the decline of officially measured poverty in the United States. In 1959, the first year in which comparable data were collected, 39.5 million people, or 22.4 percent of the population, were below the poverty line. Those figures declined steadily until 1973 when they reached low points of 23 million people, or 11.1 percent of the population. The major decline in the number of officially defined poor occurred during the middle 1960s when the poverty programs initiated by the Kennedy and Johnson administrations were in full-scale operation. Those figures remained fairly stable through the 1970s with conservative Republicans and a conservative Democrat in the White House. But with the combination of even more conservative policies and a strong recession, they began to rise in the early 1980s. Thus, as we have seen, in 1982 the poverty figures were 34.4 million people, 15 percent of the population.[12] Overall, then, we can say that official poverty is on the rise again and that official figures are underestimated. Clearly, poverty is a social problem of considerable importance and significance.

Who Are American's Poor?

The tendency of most middle- and upper-class Americans is to think of the poor as the "dregs" of society, as the most disreputable members of society.[13] When we think of the poor we tend to visualize skid row winos, "bag women," able-bodied adults who prefer welfare to working, and the like. However, the reality is that the poor do not fit our stereotypes. For one thing, it is important to make clear that there are large numbers of *working poor;* that is, people who earn so little from their work that their income is below the federal poverty line. In the next several paragraphs we will deal with some groups that you might be surprised to find among the most likely to be poor. Although there are some winos, some bag women, and even some able-bodied, nonworking adults in some of those categories (and they may contribute to the poverty of others), they represent only a very small proportion of poor Americans.

Children

Of the nearly 32 million poor Americans in 1981, over 11 million, or more than one-third, were under 16 years of age. Nearly 4 million more were between 16 and 21. If we consider the latter age group, or even most of it, children, then the percentage of

Figure 10.2 Number of Related Children Under 18 Living in Families Below the Poverty Level, by Type of Family: 1969, 1979, and 1981

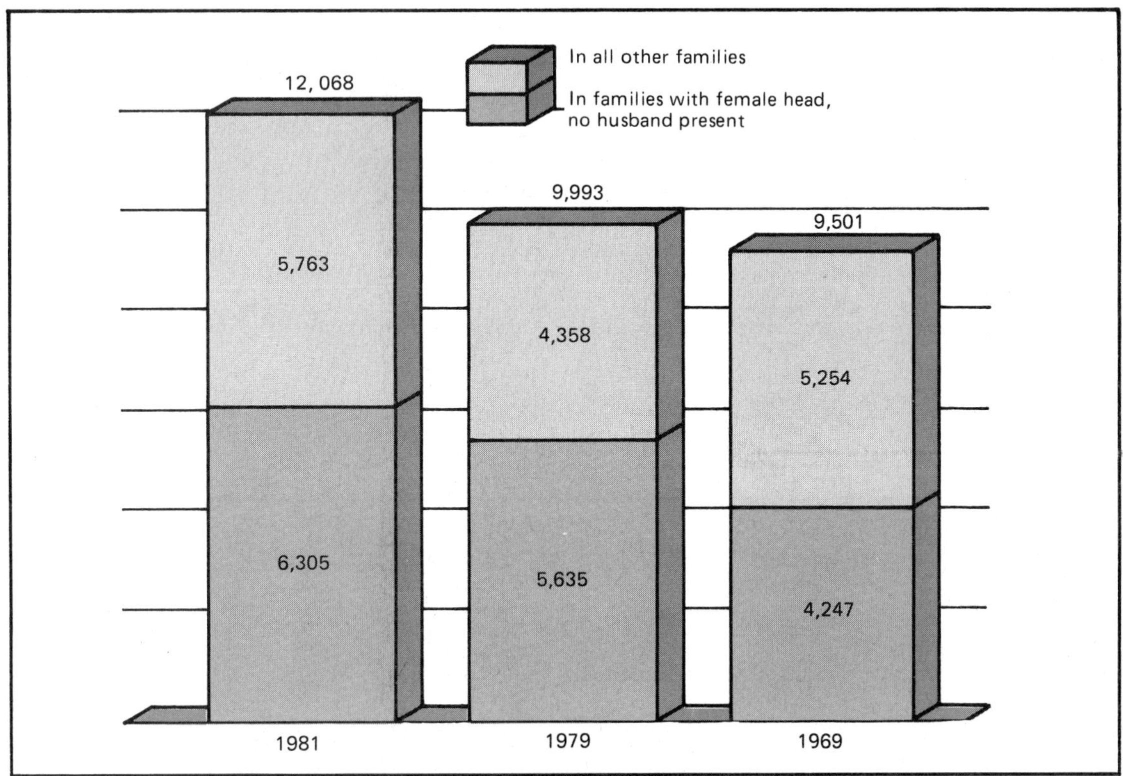

There has recently been a large increase in the number of children living below the poverty line. More than half of these children are from households headed by females, with no father or husband present.

Source: U.S. Bureau of the Census, Current Population Reports, Series P–23, No. 130, *Population Profile of the United States: 1982* (Washington, D.C.: U.S. Government Printing Office, 1983), p. 35.

poor people who are children ranges between 40 and 50 percent. To put this another way, over 20 percent of children under 16 are poor and over 36 percent of those under 21 years of age suffer from poverty.

The Aged

Almost 4 million Americans aged 65 and older are poor; another roughly 12 percent of the poor are accounted for by the aged. Putting this in other terms, over 15 percent of all old people are poor. It is also worth

Figure 10.3 Poverty Rate of Persons 60 and Over, by Living Arrangements, Sex, and Race: 1981

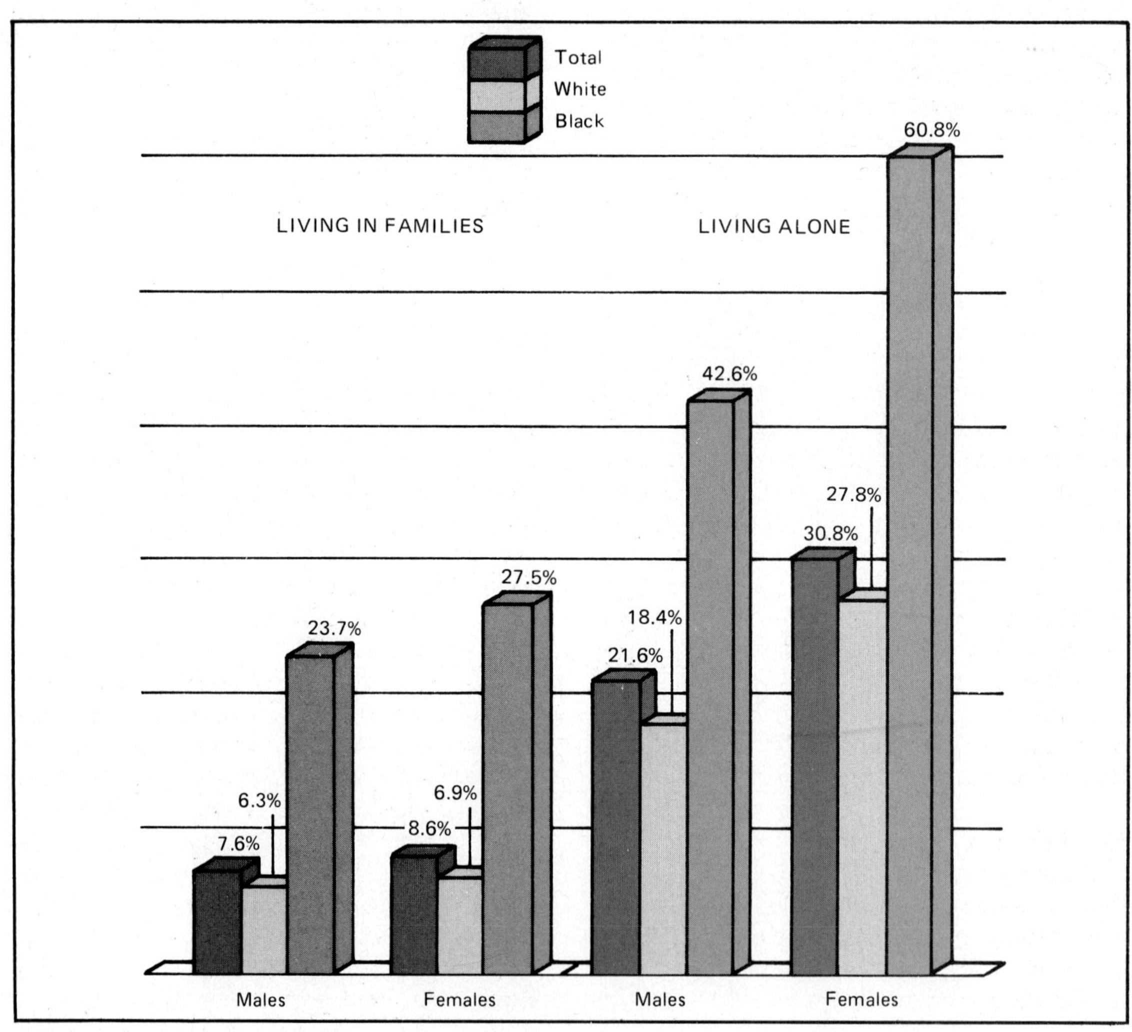

Older people who live alone are more likely to live below poverty level. Elderly blacks (male and female) are about twice as likely to experience poverty in their later years.

Source: U.S. Bureau of the Census, Current Population Reports, Series P–23, No. 130, *Population Profile of the United States: 1982* (Washington, D.C.: U.S. Government Printing Office, 1983), p. 37.

noting that another 10 percent of the aged stand just above the poverty line, and their eonomic position is, at best, shaky.[14] Recently, the idea that a disproportionate number of the elderly are likely to be poor has come under attack. It is argued that when we include Social Security income, realize that the elderly pay a lower tax rate (in part, because income from Social Security is tax-exempt), and recognize that elderly households tend to contain fewer persons, the elderly are in terms of per capita, after-tax income better off than the population as a whole.[15] Although there is some merit to this argument, we will continue to operate with official government statistics, which put about a quarter of the elderly below, or just above, the poverty line.

Fatherless Families

The poor are concentrated in fatherless families. About half of all the poor are found in families in which the husband is absent. In this group are many of the children and some of the aged discussed above. But there are also many adult women who are unable to work because of the demands of a family without a husband, or, if they are able to work, are unable to earn enough to move above the poverty line. It is worth noting that this is a *growing* problem, since only about a quarter of the poor came from female-headed families in 1959 and that percentage has about doubled in little more than two decades.

Handicapped

Although exact numbers are hard to get, there is some evidence that those with severe handicaps—the blind, deaf, and crippled—are more likely to be poor than the nonhandicapped population.[16]

Black Americans

Over one-third of all blacks are poor, while only a little more than one in ten whites are below the poverty line. Blacks are greatly overrepresented among the poor. However, the white population is much larger than the black population. As a result, the vast majority of poor people are white. Approximately two-thirds of the poor are white (21.6 million), while well under one-third are black (9.2 million). Nevertheless, the sociologically most important point here is that blacks are overrepresented among the poor.

Barriers to Simple Solutions

In addition to being surprising in itself, this profile of poverty in the United States shows how difficult it will be to come up with simple solutions to the problem. Many people argue that the poor are simply lazy and that if they would go out and find work, poverty would be eradicated, or at least greatly reduced. From the above profile, it is clear that there are a number of problems with this view. First of all, many of those included in the groups discussed above are unable to work. Most of the children under 16, old people over 65, and the handicapped simply cannot or should not work. Second, it is not clear that it would be either cheaper or advisable to send the mothers of fatherless young children out to work when the costs of child care and the needs of the children are taken into consideration. Thus, whereas some people are poor for lack of employment, or because their employment does not pay a living wage, a great many poor people are unemployable rather than unemployed. In short, jobs cannot help poor people who are unable to take them.

There is another important point to be made here. Even if all of these people wanted, and were able, to work, we must remember that the United States already suffers from an enormous unemployment rate. Most of the poor are not now counted

Figure 10.4 Percentage of Persons Living Below the Poverty Level, by Race and Spanish Origin: 1969, 1979, and 1981

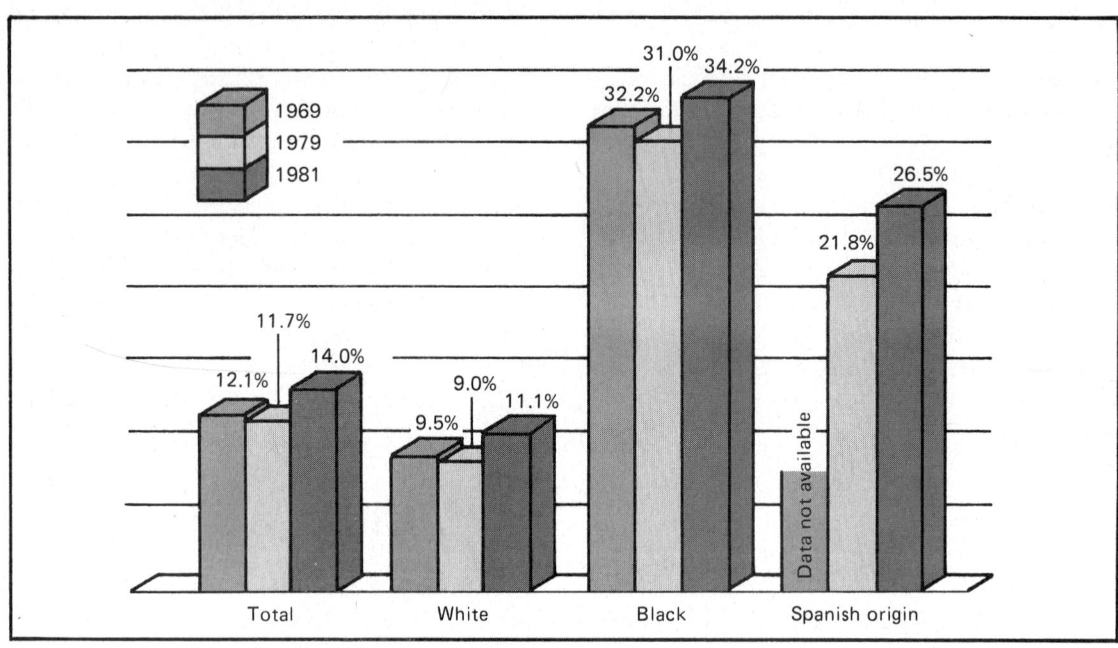

The poverty level among Hispanics is currently closer to that of blacks than whites.

Source: U.S. Bureau of the Census, Current Population Reports, Series P–23, No. 130, *Population Profile of the United States: 1982* (Washington, D.C.: U.S. Government Printing Office, 1983), p. 34.

In addition to the groups discussed in this chapter, there is a large number of rural poor.

(Susan Kuklin/Photo Researchers)

as unemployed because, in the main, they are not seeking work. Were the young, the old, the infirm, and the female heads of household to enter the workforce, they would find little more than millions of other poor people ahead of them who are also looking for work. To put it another way, were these people to look for work, the vast majority would end up unemployed and right back where they started from. Thus, what we as a society must confront is a vast population that is largely unable to work, and even if they were able to work, we as a society could not provide nearly enough jobs for them.

All of this is not to say that there are not lazy, shiftless adult males (and females) among the poor. They are there and they contribute to poverty not only by not seeking work themselves, but also by fathering children and then deserting the mothers and leaving them the burden of supporting the family. However, our anger toward them should not blind us to the fact that the vast majority of poor people are the victims of adverse circumstances that are far beyond their control. The vast majority of the poor among children, old people, the handicapped, and female heads of households did not create their situation and are virtually powerless, on their own, to change it.

PART II: CAUSES AND CONSEQUENCES

The thrust of the argument in this part of the chapter is that the causes of poverty are traceable primarily to the inter- and intrasocietal levels. This orientation leads us to a focal concern with economic inequality both on an international and an intranational (specifically intra-American) basis; that is, economic disparities between and within nations. The structures and the dynamics at these macrolevels are the major causes of poverty in the United States, as well as throughout the world. After we describe these macrolevel causes, we will trace their impact on the microlevels, the social psychology, the psychology, and the physiology of poverty. In other words, the main contention in this section is that poor people are generally the *victims* of larger forces. As you will see, the argument presented here stands in contrast to the position taken by most lay people about poverty. Their inclination is to see poor people as the cause of their own situation. Our perspective is that the conventional wisdom is a version of "blaming the victim" for his or her problems.[17]

SOCIOLOGICAL LEVEL

It is the thesis of this section, indeed this chapter, that poverty is built into the basic structure of capitalism. Before getting to a discussion of the nature of capitalism, a few points of clarification are needed. First, capitalism does not have exclusive rights to poverty; there is poverty in the socialist world as well. However, to keep the discussion to manageable lengths, we will concentrate on poverty in the capitalist world. In any case, the United States is best described as a capitalist society, so a discussion of the relationship between capitalism and poverty is most relevant to a book aimed at an American audience. Second, given the existence of poverty throughout the history of the world, the limited resources in the world today, and its burgeoning population, poverty may be endemic to human existence, at least into the foreseeable future. In other words, at least at the present time, *no* system—capitalist, socialist, or any other—may be able to do much about the problem of poverty.

Table 10.1 Levels of Analysis: Poverty

LEVELS	APPROPRIATE QUESTIONS	A PARTIAL SYNOPSIS OF PRESENT CONCLUSIONS
SOCIOLOGICAL	How is the capitalist world-system related to the problem of poverty throughout the world?	We are much more likely to find poverty in the exploited peripheral areas of the world system than in the dominant core areas.
	What is the Marxian theory of poverty?	According to Marx, there is a tendency in capitalism to move toward a smaller and smaller number of well-to-do capitalists and a larger and larger number of impoverished workers.
	Is poverty inevitable in capitalism?	No. Many capitalistic Western European nations have developed social welfare programs that have greatly limited the problem of poverty.
	How do government policies affect poverty?	The government can take a variety of actions that can serve to increase or decrease the level of poverty in society.
	Is racism related to poverty?	Yes. Discrimination keeps a disproportionate number of blacks below the poverty line.
	Is sexism related to poverty?	Yes. We have even begun to think in terms of the "feminization of poverty".
	Is ageism related to poverty?	Yes. Many people become poor when they grow old.
	How is the family related to poverty?	Problems within the family (e.g., broken homes) can lead to poverty. Conversely, poverty can create problems within the family.
	Does poverty have any positive functions?	Yes, a number. In fact, if we hope to do away with poverty, we must find alternative rewards for those who benefit from poverty.
	What is the relationship between American culture and poverty?	The American ideology of individualism has led its people to tend to blame poor people for their poverty (e.g., they are lazy) rather than to blame the larger system.
SOCIAL-PSYCHOLOGICAL	Does poverty cause some people to be labeled as disreputable?	Yes, at least in the United States. Some poor people are thought of as disreputable for specific reasons (e.g., the able-bodied person who refuses to work). However, it is not uncommon for many Americans to think of all poor people as disreputable.
	Can poverty be learned?	Yes. Poor people are taught that they are poor and how a poor person is supposed to behave.

Table 10.1 Levels of Analysis: Poverty (*Continued*)

LEVELS	APPROPRIATE QUESTIONS	A PARTIAL SYNOPSIS OF PRESENT CONCLUSIONS
INDIVIDUAL	Are there psychological factors that lead some people to be poor?	Yes, but it is likely that only a very small percentage of poor people are poor as a result of psychological liabilities.
	Does mental illness cause poverty?	Perhaps, but it is even more likely that poverty causes mental illness.
	Are there physiological factors that cause poverty?	Yes, or at least the social definitions of those physiological factors. Among them are race, age, gender, and physical handicaps.
	What is the relationship between poverty and intelligence?	Some people may be doomed to a life of poverty by low intelligence, but a much larger number have their intelligence limited by a life of poverty.
	How is poverty related to physical health?	Because of inadequate food and nutrition, the poor are more likely to suffer from ill health. Furthermore, the poor are likely to get lower-quality medical care.
	How is poverty related to mortality?	There is evidence that poverty is related to lower life expectancy.

The Capitalist World-System

One of the most useful perspectives for explaining differences among various capitalist countries on a variety of dimensions, including poverty, is the world-systems theory developed by Immanuel Wallerstein.[18] Before we get to Wallerstein's argument, we need to supplement our earlier discussion of poverty in the United States with a discussion of poverty in a country that has a very different place in the world-system—Brazil—as well as some generalizations about economic differences around the world.

The Example of Brazil

Like most capitalistic countries, Brazil, is characterized by extreme differences between a small number of wealthy people and a vast number of poor people. Emblematic of these differences, and of the desperation of the poor, is the practice of poor Brazilians selling not only their blood, but also parts of their bodies, such as their corneas and their kidneys.[19] Advertisements are taken out in the classified sections of newspapers by poor people interested in making such sales. One such ad read: "Cornea for sale . . . Please call working days."[20] The price for the cornea: about $40,000. Other such ads contain phrases like "financial problems," "best offer," "urgent," "good health," "perfect vision," and "young."[21] Thus parts of human bodies are being sold in Brazil the way used cars or stereos are marketed in the United States. The sale is seen by a poor person as a way of making ends meet, or even as a method of crawling up from the bottom of the heap. As one man who placed an ad for his cornea said: "It's very simple—on one side you have the man who has money but no vision, and on the other side is me: vision, but no money. . . . The more people think about it, the more normal it will become."[22] This represents an extreme form of poverty, an extraordinary degree of economic inequality, and an inhumane exploitation of the poor by the rich. (As this chapter is being written efforts are under way to create a similar market for human "parts" in the United States.)

Brazil and the World Economy

Another dimension of the Brazilian situation leads us out of the intranational domain and into the international realm. Long before the poor of Brazil were selling parts of their bodies, they were selling their blood in order to survive. Commercial blood banks in Brazil are usually found in impoverished areas and they offer donors about $3.00 and a bowl of soup for a pint of blood. A large amount of this blood appears to be reprocessed and then shipped to wealthy countries like the United States and West Germany. Thus, the poor of Brazil are not only being exploited within their own country, but throughout the world. As one Brazilian doctor put it: "Brazil is today the largest exporter of blood in the world. . . . We are selling our blood at banana prices to the industrialized countries."[23]

Rich Nations, Poor Nations

There has long been an awareness of a split in the capitalistic world between the rich and poor countries, the developed and the developing countries, the North-South split, or in Wallerstein's terms, the core versus the periphery (and semiperiphery). In general, we can say that today there are a relatively small number of countries led by the United States, with West Germany and Japan also notable, that have dominated the world economy and thereby collected a disproportionate amount of the world's wealth. More generally, it is the world's northern hemisphere that contains most of the wealthiest countries, while most southern hemisphere countries have been relegated to the status of developing nations. As in the case of the blood of poor Brazilians, a great deal of the success of the developed countries is based on their ability to exploit the developing countries. Although there are many other factors involved in the relative poverty of developing countries, there is no dispute over the fact that there are enormous disparities between the rich and poor nations.

Although there are many more people in developing than developed nations, they have less of almost everything. Specifically, developing nations have about 75 percent of the overall population, but only about 21 percent of the gross national product, 25 percent of export earnings, 22 percent of military expenditures, 16 percent of expenditures for public education, and only 9 percent of public health expenditures.[24] Life expectancy in developed nations is 72 years while in developing nations it is only 56 years. One in 50 infants in developed nations die before their first birthday, while it is 1 in 10 in developing countries.[25] There is no question that there is enormous inequality both within and between nations. But why is this the case? It is here that we find the utility of Wallerstein's world-systems theory.

World-Systems Theory

The modern world-capitalist system is based, in Wallerstein's view, on economic domination. There is a geographical international division of labor within the modern world-system—the core, the periphery, and semiperiphery. The *core* geographical area dominates the world economy and exploits the rest of the system. The *periphery* consists of those areas that provide raw materials to the core and are heavily exploited by it. The *semiperiphery* is a residual category that encompasses a set of regions somewhere between the exploiting and the exploited areas. The key point here is that to Wallerstein the international division of exploitation is defined not by state borders but rather by the economic division of labor in the world.

In his historical analysis, Wallerstein details a shift from political (and thus military) dominance within what he calls the "world empire" to economic dominance within the "world-system." Wallerstein sees economics as a far more efficient and less primitive means of domination than politics. Political domination is very cumbersome, whereas economic exploitation "makes it possible to increase the flow of the surplus from the lower strata to the upper strata, from the periphery to the center, from the majority to the minority."[26] In the modern era, capitalism has provided a basis for the growth and development of a world economy; this has been accomplished without the aid of a unified political structure. Capitalism can be seen as an economic alternative to political domination. It is better able to produce economic surpluses than the more primitive techniques employed in political exploitation.

The solidarity of capitalism is ultimately based on its unequal development around the world. Different parts of the capitalist world came to specialize in different specific functions—breeding labor power, growing food, providing raw materials, organizing industry, and, today, developing advanced technologies. Moreover, each of the three parts of the international division of labor tended to differ in terms of major type of labor and mode of labor control. The core had free labor in the form of wage workers, skilled craftsmen, managers, and entrepreneurs (and, today, high-tech specialists); the periphery had forced labor in the form of slaves and the like, and the semiperiphery was characterized by peasant sharecroppers. Wallerstein argues that the key to capitalism on a world scale lies in a core dominated by a free market for highly skilled workers and a coercive labor market for less skilled workers in peripheral areas.

The core areas began with small initial advantages that they used as the basis for developing greater advantages later on. Among these advantages is the greater economic success of the core areas. The core areas, in general, have grown progressively richer while semiperipheral and, especially, peripheral areas have grown poorer, at least relative to the core areas. Thus we are much more likely to find poverty in the latter regions than in the core areas, especially the United States. Nevertheless, there is poverty within the United States, and in order to understand that we need to move from the international arena to an analysis of American society.

Poverty and the American Economy

Some of the basic tenets of Marx's original theory[27] provide a starting point for understanding the existence of poverty within the United States, indeed in *any* capitalist society. Marx's theory explains many things about capitalist society, but we will focus on its relevance for understanding poverty in America. However, capitalism today is very different from the capitalism of Marx's day. Thus, after we briefly deal with Marx's theory, we will need to look at some of the more recent work by neo-Marxists on modern capitalism. In addition, we will need to supplement the conflict theory of poverty offered by neo-Marxists with a structural-functional view of poverty.

Marxian Theory

For Marx, the notion of social class is crucial to an understanding of capitalism and many things about capitalist society, including poverty. Social classes are determined by their relationship to the means of production (tools, machines, raw materials, and so on). Fundamentally, Marx believed that the industrial societies of the mid-nineteenth century were divided into two basic classes: the *bourgeoisie* (or the capitalists), who owned the means of production, and the *proletariat* (or the workers), who had to sell their labor time to the bourgeoisie. The entire capitalist system was based on a simple premise: the owners had to exploit the workers in the sense that they were able to get more for what the workers produced than the workers were paid to produce it (the profits of capitalism). The dynamics of capitalism, especially the competition among capitalists, led them to develop even better methods of exploiting the workers and thereby paying them less and less for more and more production. The capitalists who survived and succeeded were those who were best able to exploit their workers. Marx's view was that this process led to a situation in which a smaller and smaller number of very wealthy capitalists ruthlessly exploited an increasingly large number of ever-poorer workers. Thus, to Marx, capitalism was characterized by a dynamic that steadily pushed more and more people to and below the poverty line.

Neo-Marxian Theory and Modern Capitalism

Although Marx's theory illuminated much about early capitalist society, it is in need of massive overhaul if it is to be applied to modern capitalist societies like the United States. Various neo-Marxian theorists have tried to adapt Marx's original insights to the realities of contemporary capitalism. We cannot go into this complex subject here,[28] but we can highlight at least a few of the basic points made by neo-Marxists about the causes of poverty in modern capitalist societies.

Poverty Is Not Inevitable in Capitalism

Few modern societies accept the inevitability of poverty. In earlier times in human history—prehistoric times, the Dark Ages, the preindustrial era—it seemed impossible to hope to feed and clothe everyone adequately. But the staggering gains in productivity that resulted from industrialization have made it feasible to provide a decent minimum standard of living for entire populations. Indeed, some industrial nations (the Scandinavian countries, for example) have virtually eliminated poverty in the absolute sense; that is, almost everyone has a decent standard of living even though some people have more money than others do. Demonstrably, then, it *is* possible to overcome poverty. Yet the United States, the richest nation on earth, has failed even to come close to eliminating poverty of the kind that dooms people to hunger, cold, suffering, and hopelessness.

Most Western European countries, while primarily capitalistic in orientation, have been able to develop an array of social welfare programs that have served to make the problem of poverty much less severe than it is in the United States. The fact is that on the average, Western European countries spend more than 25 percent of their gross national product (GNP) on social welfare programs (many of which relate to the poor) while the United States spends about 13 percent of its GNP on such programs. In dollar terms, Sweden, which has one of the most elaborate social welfare programs in the world, spends about $3,900 per capita while the United States spends about a third of that amount.[29] The result of this kind of expenditure is that the kind of grinding poverty we find in the United

States is largely absent in most of Western Europe. Thus, capitalism need *not* produce poverty if society is willing to devote a considerable amount of its resources to preventing it and mitigating its worst effects. To be fair, however, it should be noted that the recessionary times of the early 1980s have led Western European countries to question their ability to devote so much money to social welfare programs.[30] In fact, we are beginning to see a significant reduction in sums devoted to these programs,[31] but it is unlikely that Western European countries will, if they can possibly avoid it, allow poverty to reach the levels and depths that it has been allowed to reach in the United States. This begins to take us from a structural explanation of poverty to the role of culture in this problem. Western European societies with capitalistic economies have made great efforts to soften the problem of poverty while the United States has not. Since the structure of capitalism cannot fully explain these differences, it would be useful to look at the role of cultural factors in accounting for them.

Given the success of some Western European societies in coping with poverty, the question is why, with its great wealth, does poverty remain a major problem in America? One obvious answer is that the United States has been much more closed than Western European countries to integrating a range of socialistic programs into their essentially capitalistic economies. But rather than belaboring the well-known resistance of the United States to socialistic programs, we will look at some of the structural factors in the United States that contribute to the existence of poverty.

Poverty and Other Structural Factors in the United States

Government Economic Policies

One might guess that the objective of any government would be to seek to attack poverty by, among other things, attempting to eradicate unemployment. However, there is little to support this view, at least as far as the recent history of the United States government is concerned. At one level, this is not so surprising since the government is likely to be responsive to the interests of the business leaders and investors who dominate the capitalist economy. And, as Marx argued (see Chapter 11 for a discussion of this issue), capitalists have a vested interest in maintaining a significant level of unemployment in order to provide them with a readily available pool of workers to be drawn upon during economic upturns. At another level, and more importantly, there is a belief held by many economists and government leaders that full employment causes inflation and, therefore, the way to control inflation is to maintain or even increase levels of unemployment. Full employment causes inflation by putting money in the hands of more workers and by allowing workers to demand and get higher wages. The latter is the case because owners must meet such demands because there is no pool of unemployed workers to take the place of existing employees. This national policy of dealing with inflation by increasing unemployment has been illustrated best in the government's policies in the early 1980s.

In 1980, the inflation rate was 13.5 percent and the unemployment rate was 7.1 percent.[32] In 1982 the inflation rate had dipped to 6.1 percent while the unemployment rate had risen to 9.7 percent.[33] Now there are many factors involved in such a change, but one of them, probably *the* most important, was the governmental policies designed to lower inflation by slowing the economy down, thereby, among other things, increasing unemployment.[34] Through such policies as restricting the money supply, the Reagan administration was able to bring inflation down, but in slowing down the economy it contributed to the rise in unemployment. What this means is that the prosperity of the majority was paid for by the suffering of the poor. It is their unemployment that is used to keep the economy in tune. While jobs are far from the complete answer to poverty, it is certainly the case that lower unemployment would translate into fewer people below the poverty line.

Racism

We have dealt with the problem of racism in depth in Chapter 8. Suffice it to say here that racist attitudes, as well as the institutions that operate in a racist manner, have served to contribute to high rates of poverty among most groups of nonwhites, especially blacks. As we have already seen, the proportion of blacks below the poverty line is in percentage terms three times greater than the proportion of whites below that line. The poverty of blacks, and other nonwhites, is traceable to two basic factors: (1) because of *past* discrimination and poverty such minorities tend to lack the education, background, experience, training, and job skills that could help pull at least some of them out of poverty; (2) because of *continuing* discrimination, even when these minorities have the needed abilities, they continue to face barriers to rising above the poverty line.

Sexism

In recent years there has been increasing attention to the "feminization of poverty."[35] As we have seen, this is best reflected in the rapidly growing number of fatherless families below the poverty line. Females are not only represented in the ranks of the poor as heads of fatherless families, but also as members of minority groups, the aged, children, and the handicapped. A number of forces are contributing to the high level of poverty among women. For one thing, the high divorce rate often leaves many women alone to handle a growing family. The demands of children make it difficult for many of these women to work, at least on a full-time basis. Second, the growing number of children born out of wedlock often leaves women, often very young women, alone to raise the children. They often find it difficult even to get started in the work world, let alone to succeed there. Third, welfare policies tend to favor female-headed families with the result that the man may leave, even be urged to leave, in order to allow the family to qualify for greater public assistance. (For more on the issue of sexism see Chapter 9.)

Ageism

The fact that about 15 percent of those over 65 years of age are poor, and another 10 percent rank just above the poverty line, does not mean simply that poor people live to become elderly, but it reflects more the fact that many people become poor when they grow old. Less than half of the civilian work force was covered by a pension plan in 1980,[36] and many of those covered by pension plans find that in the end they collect far less than they anticipated.[37] It is also the case that the benefits derived from Social Security are rather meager. In 1981, the average Social Security benefit for all retired men amounted to $4,880. Interestingly, and reflective of sexism, is the fact that the average retired woman in that year received only 69.7 percent of the benefit paid to men, or $3,403.[38] The poverty line in 1981 for a single person 65 years of age and older was $4,359, which means, assuming (unrealistically in many cases) *no* additional income, that a single man above 65 on Social Security would be just above the poverty line while a single woman would be considerably below. All too frequently, getting old in the United States means becoming poor. (For more on aging and ageism see Chapter 7.)

We turn now to one last structure, the

family, and its role as both a cause of poverty and the consequences that poverty has for the family.

Family

The family, in particular problems within the family, contributes to poverty in various ways. Broken families headed either by males or females can contribute to poverty, although this is certainly more likely to occur in female-headed families. Poverty is also a much more likely outcome in the case of unwed women with children. Another link between the family and poverty is fertility: large families are in much greater risk of poverty than are small ones. For example, the poverty line for a family of nine or more persons is about double that of a family of four.[39] This means that a family of nine in 1981 had to earn well over $19,000 simply to reach the poverty line.

Conversely, poverty can contribute in a variety of ways to problems within the family. The difficulties involved in surviving below the poverty line are likely to place great stress on the family unit. For one thing, lack of adequate income is likely to lead to more acute marital problems in poor families than in middle- or upper-class families.[40] For another, various welfare programs may literally force the man to leave the family because welfare payments would be higher without him. Poverty produces other problems for the family unit such as a greater likelihood of physical and mental illness.[41] Ultimately, these and other pressures resulting from poverty lead to a higher rate of marital dissolution in the lower classes than in other social classes.[42] Economic problems contribute to the higher rate of marital dissolution not only by creating problems for the family, but also because husbands and even wives have less to lose economically if their marriage breaks up. On the other side of the spectrum, middle- and upper-class couples may stay together because they do not want to jeopardize their community standing and careers by separating and divorcing. But our central point here is that poverty creates extraordinary marital problems for lower-class families.

Two things should be evident from the above discussion. First, all of the macro-level causes of poverty are interrelated and second, many of the social problems discussed in detail in this book (ageism, sexism, racism, unemployment, and others) are deeply implicated in the problem of poverty.

The Functions of Poverty

Throughout this section most of our insights have been derived from conflict theory, especially Marxian and neo-Marxian variants of conflict theory. However, structural functionalists also have useful ideas on poverty and we would be remiss if we did not present at least one example of such an approach, Herbert Gans's work on the functions of poverty.[43]

Using Robert Merton's model of structural-functional analysis (see Chapter 1), Gans recognized that poverty is far more dysfunctional than functional. However, most of us concentrate quite naturally on the dysfunctions of poverty. In focusing on the positive consequences (functions) of poverty, Gans was reasoning that the continued existence of an impoverished segment of society suggested that such a group must be useful to some other group(s). If we can understand which groups are gaining from poverty and in what ways, we might be able to help do away with poverty by providing those groups that benefit with alternative sources of rewards.

Gans outlined four general functions of poverty: economic, social, esthetic, and political. Poverty serves an *economic* function by providing a group of people who perform society's dirty work, usually because they have no choice. The poor work for low pay, and do dangerous work or work that is considered undignified and menial. Another economic function of poor people is the way they provide a kind of economic subsidy to the rich. Poor people cost less to employ, so the rich may use the money saved in wages for other purposes. Third, a whole series of occupations owe their existence to the poor. Examples include police officers, penologists, welfare workers, many lawyers, and even loan sharks. Finally, poor people purchase goods and use services that otherwise would go unused; incompetent physicians, for example, find a clientele in economically depressed areas.

The poor also perform several positive *social* functions. First, they serve to show what the societal norms are. Although it is doubtful that they deviate from norms more often, they are more easily labeled as deviant because their poverty makes them vulnerable to many agents of social control (including police and courts). If middle-class and poor youths commit the same deviant act, it is far more likely that the poor youth will be labeled a juvenile delinquent. The poor also perform the valuable function of enabling society to maintain its values, such as hard work, honesty, and accomplishment. We see most clearly what our values are when some people violate them. Second, by giving charity to the "deserving" poor, the upper classes can demonstrate their concern, pity, and altruism. Third, affluent people can live vicariously by imagining that the poor engage in and enjoy more uninhibited sexual, alcoholic, and narcotic behavior. Fourth, the poor provide a reference point to which other groups can compare themselves and derive the satisfaction of ranking higher in the system of social stratification. Finally, because the poor are denied adequate education and other advantages, they cannot rise in the stratification system. This makes it easier for people in other economic categories to do so.

The poor perform two major *esthetic* functions. First, they have historically provided the labor and the excess capital to allow societies to produce their most impressive achievements. The Egyptian pyramids, for example. were constructed by the poorest classes of Egyptian society. Second, the poor often provide esthetic products for those above them in the stratification system. A good example is New Orleans jazz, which has been adopted by the middle and upper classes, but was originally a product of poor blacks.

The poor perform some major *political* functions. First, they provide an issue for various political groups. The Left rallies around the poor and seeks to develop government programs to aid them, while the Right often attacks the poor with such political epithets as "welfare chiselers." Second, the poor take the burden for change and growth in the society as a whole. The poor build the cities and are then forced to move out in the name of "progress," when programs such as urban renewal are implemented. At another level, the poor have often provided a large share of the human cost of the growth of a country's international power. The poor fight the wars initiated by society's upper classes. The poor contribute to the stability of the political system by not participating actively in the political arena. If they were active, they might well push for social revolution.

Gans's analysis of poverty suggests that if we really want to do away with poverty we must *find* alternatives to the variety of functions currently being performed by the poor. Instead of the poor doing society's dirty work, Gans suggests that we automate at least some of this work. Instead of creating occupations for the problems of only the poor, Gans suggests that we find other useful activities for social welfare workers; for example, they could help ulcer-ridden executives rather than skid row bums. If we hope to do away with poverty, we must find alternatives for the many benefits now derived from the existence of poor people in society. Those who profit from the existence of poor people would be more likely to accept and institute improvement of the condition of the poor if they knew their own gains would continue from other sources and in other ways.

Thus structural functionalism, or at least Gans's version of structural functionalism, shares with conflict theory a desire to do away with poverty. However, while conflict theory generally envisions the need to overthrow society completely, structural functionalism sees much more modest reforms of the existing system as the answer. Gans's search for functional alternatives to poverty may be seen as an example of the latter approach.

In this section we have examined a number of social structural causes of poverty. However, it is also the case that cultural factors, in this case in the United States, are implicated in the problem of poverty.

The Role of American Culture

One of the defining characteristics of American culture is an ideology of individualism. The individual is valued above all else; in particular, the individual is placed before the interests of the collectivity. In addition, there is belief in individual effort; regardless of one's social position, the individual can succeed through his or her own efforts. At issue here are the philosophical and social origins of this ideology of individualism.

The American colonies were being settled as two major revolutions were taking place in their primary point of origin, European society. The first was the *egalitarian* revolution that attacked the traditional privileges of aristocratic rank determined by birth. The other was the *industrial* revolution that changed the nature of work and the character of the economy. The factory owners and industrialists soon emerged as a new class with the wealth to demand political rights and power formerly accorded only the aristocracy. The battle cry of this new class was egalitarianism—belief in the equality of all persons regardless of social rank. The American colonies were frequently settled by people attracted to this new ideology. In addition, the new nation was overwhelmingly Protestant, and Protestantism strongly reinforced the doctrines of individual responsibility: individuals were expected to be captains of their own soul and to behave so as to ensure their own salvation.[44]

The virgin wilderness of America reinforced these beliefs. Land was easily available to anyone who wanted to take it, and it seemed that anyone could succeed beyond the wildest dreams of the European masses. Thus everyone *ought* to become successful, for it seemed that to be poor could not be blamed on the system but only on defects of personal character. The beliefs in social equality and individual responsibility nurtured the creation of a nation of individualists. In the nineteenth century, the French philosopher-sociologist, Alexis de Tocqueville, caught the essence of this emerging cultural value: "It is strange to see with what feverish ardor the Americans pursue their own welfare, and to watch the vague dread that constantly torments them lest they should not have chosen the shortest path which may lead to it."[45]

Inherent in the American ideology of individualism, competition, and success is a basic reluctance to take responsibility for others. Many Americans believe that *both* success *and* failure (particularly poverty) are *individual matters.* Success is seen as the result of hard work while poverty is the product of sinful laziness. As a result, it strikes most Americans that welfare or guaranteed incomes—the kind of welfare programs popular in Western Europe—provided by the taxes of hard-working citizens, are unfair rewards for laziness.

The fact that the American economy was amazingly successful from the earliest colonial times only served to confirm everyone's beliefs that motivated individuals can look after themselves and that others—who complain that they are "trapped" in poverty—are merely unmotivated, or lazy. Even with today's economic problems, the United States remains, by far, the world's economic giant. Because so large a proportion of Americans are so well-off[46] and because they look back on a long-term and relatively rapid improvement in their circumstances, they find it difficult to comprehend poverty. Even large numbers of Americans who are not successful tend to blame themselves for their failure and not the system.[47]

In sum, the major macrolevel explanations of poverty are the structures of capitalistic society and the cultural idealization of individualism. Capitalism, by its very nature, doomed large numbers of people to poverty, and the cultural value system led society to blame the poor for their plight and to do comparatively little to help them. While such global forces are important in understanding poverty in America, there are other, less macroscopic, forces at work in the genesis of our problem with poverty.

SOCIAL-PSYCHOLOGICAL LEVEL

Given the great emphasis on social and cultural factors as the main *causes* of poverty, our discussion in this section and the next will focus on the social-psychological and individual *consequences* of these macrolevel causes. In this section we will examine how the immediate social circumstances of the poor conspire to keep them in poverty. We examine the consequences of the stigma of poverty—of living in a social situation where those around you are poor and of how, to some extent, people learn to live with poverty and, in so doing, learn to behave in ways that tend to keep them poor. Although we will be getting at the role the poor play in their own poverty, bear in mind that by far the main responsibility for poverty lies with the larger structural and cultural forces we have been discussing to this point.

The Stigma of Disrepute

To be poor in an affluent society is to be discredited. After all, in an economy where the overwhelming majority of people are quite prosperous, what kind of person fails so woefully? As we have seen, the widespread American outlook of individualism, reinforced by the nation's extraordinary economic success, encourages the view that people are personally responsible for their own poverty. And this theme of personal responsibility is manifest in the thinking of the nonpoor, as well as in that of the poor.

In discussing the stigma of poverty we return to the idea of the *labeling* process outlined in earlier chapters. In this context, the argument is that the label that is attached to poor persons by others in society has profound, largely negative, consequences for the self-conceptions of poor people and thus for their behavior. But not all poor people are affected in the same way by their label; they are not all equally stigmatized. Some wear poverty with honor; some are condemned as slothful and shiftless and tend to internalize such an image of themselves.

Our main concern here is for what have been called the "disreputable poor."[48] In David Matza and Henry Miller's view, it is not poverty per se that is the social problem, but the application of a disreputable label to the poor: "Disrepute is the pathology of poverty. Above all it is a *social* pathology, which is to say that disrepute is the imputation of stigma that goes along with being subemployed."[49] This is not to say that being cold and hungry is not a problem in itself, but these derivatives of poverty might not be allowed to exist were it not for the distaste that the rest of society holds for the poor. Furthermore, many of the pathologies that are associated with poverty such as crime, delinquency, illegitimacy, drug addiction, and mental illness are associated much more with the disrepute of the poor than with the objective conditions of being poor.

Poverty that is associated with apparent idleness and indolence is a primary basis of disrepute. The stigma is given to persons who, though able-bodied, remain habitually unemployed or who work only very irregularly. Also stigmatized are the poor who end up in prison, thereby relegating family members to even greater and longer periods of poverty. Women who have a succession of illegitimate children whom they are unable to support, and whom no one else is willing to support, are another group likely to be stigmatized. Finally, a range of behaviors among the poor such as drug addiction, violence, and crime are likely to bring disrepute. There is a disturbing tendency on the part of many people to label *all* poor people as disreputable. Thus innocent children, handicapped persons, and the elderly might well find themselves lumped together with the lazy, the promiscuous, and the criminal. However, we will continue to operate as if a clear distinction is made between the deserving and the disreputable poor.

This family is being forced to undergo the humiliations of life in a public shelter.

(A. Tannenbaum/Sygma)

It is mainly for the disreputable poor (but for many deserving poor as well) that all interactions with others, especially with official agents and agencies, are likely to be a series of humiliations and degradations. In this context, it is interesting to recount part of the story of John R. Coleman, a former college president who decided to spend ten days on the streets of New York as a "homeless man."[50] There is a wide consensus that "street people" are a growing problem in all major American cities.[51] In Washington, D.C., it is estimated that there are between 1,000 and 4,000 such drifters.[52] Coleman reported that on one of the particularly cold nights that he was on the streets, over 4,500 people sought warmth, food, and shelter in New York City's refuges, and this represents only a small percentage of the city's homeless. Among other things, there are many homeless people who refuse to avail themselves of such city services. One of the reasons for this reluctance is the humiliation and degradation they suffer in such settings.

Early in his journey, Coleman came upon a man living on a heated grate on the city streets. The man said he had been living this way for about twelve years, but when he was asked whether he ever went to the city shelters, he replied: "I couldn't take that. I prefer this anytime."[53] The obvious question is: why would a man (in fact, many men) prefer to sleep on a city grate on a cold night rather than go to a warm room in a city shelter? Coleman was to discover the answer for himself when he went to a shelter a few nights later. First, we have Coleman's description of the humiliations involved in eating dinner:

> It was time to get into line to eat. This meant crowding into what can only compare to a cattle chute in a stockyard . . . A man with a bullhorn kept yelling at us to stand up and stay in line . . . At the appointed hour, we were released in groups of 20 or 30 to descend the dark, filthy steps to the basement eating area. The man with the bullhorn was there again, clearly in charge and clearly relishing the extra power given to his voice by electric amplification. He insulted us collectively and separately without pause, but because his vocabulary was limited it tended to be the same four-letter words over and over . . . . The shouting and the obscenities didn't stop once we had our food. Again and again we were told to finish and get out. Eating took perhaps six minutes, but those minutes removed any shred of dignity a man might have brought in with him from the street.[54]

Coleman had similarly humiliating encounters with the welfare establishment (as well as the desperate and sometimes dangerous users of these facilities) and, as a result, ultimately came to the same conclusion as many other homeless people: "I was finished with the public shelters."[55]

One of the best-known sources of humiliation and degradation for the disreputable poor is their interactions with the welfare agents. For example, the social welfare system often insists that people reveal details about their private lives. If the caseworker asks about a recipient's sexual activities, an answer is required, on pain of losing welfare aid. Indeed, anything that is discrediting in the lives of the poor is apt to become public knowledge. For example, the family fights of the poor are disproportionately likely to become official police statistics.

The disreputable poor must face a contemptuous world. But sometimes, it becomes even more difficult to face themselves. If, in so doing, they come to accept their stigma, or label, by accepting it, they may seal their fate. They may come to accept themselves as moral lepers and may act accordingly. Indeed, at least some of their tendency to engage in deviant behavior may be traceable to the fact that they see themselves as the kind of people who do such things and, in any event, have very little to lose by doing them.

A major inducement to accepting (and obtaining) the stigma of disreputability is to be surrounded by others who are disreputable. In most cities there are areas where disreputable persons are concentrated (the worst areas are often called "skid row"). To be identified as living in such an area is almost an admission of disreputability. It is in such areas that people learn, if they have not already learned, how to be poor; to think and act the way a poor person is supposed to. The following is a description by a sharecropper mother of the need she felt to teach her children that they were poor:

> [M]y girl came home and said the teacher made them say that everyone here in the country of America is born equal, and we're all the same. Well, I didn't say a word. I was preparing their

supper, and I kept on thinking to myself, and I asked myself how I could let my children believe that, when that's not the way they're going to live. So, I called my girl over, and the other children too; and I told them there is the white man and the black man, and the rich man and the poor man . . . and there's the ones who have got a say and the ones who don't. That's what I told them, and you know what, I had them repeat it to me, out loud, and they did; and I told them they should listen to what they just said, and they'd better keep repeating to themselves, saying it, until the end of their lives, like we all do.[56]

Not all *socialization* to be poor is so blatant, indeed most of it is much more indirect, but the fact remains that people *are* taught that they are poor and how a poor person is supposed to behave.

Perhaps the worst learned response to poverty is to accept it as inevitable. Many poor people feel helpless, apathetic, and trapped. Once they learn such attitudes, they tend not to make either personal or collective attempts to solve their problems or to protest their "fate." Although it is true that in the last few decades the poor have been demonstrating a bit more political energy, it is far less than they are capable of displaying. Although it is hard to ignore starvation and sleeping on grates in the city, it could be argued that the greatest curse of poverty is that it saps the spirit.

INDIVIDUAL LEVEL

This discussion of the sapping of the spirit brings us to the role of psychological and physiological factors in poverty.

Psychology

Our view is that psychological factors play only a limited role in causing poverty. It is certainly true that some people are poor because they lack an achievement drive, or because they are unable to defer gratifications in order to obtain long-term goals, or because they have a range of other psychological liabilities. However, the bulk of the discussion up to this point has pointed to the weakness of such an argument. The children, the aged, the handicapped, and female heads of households are not in the main poor because of their psychological problems. In general, they are in fact powerless to alter their situation. Furthermore, the structure of American society (for example, the built-in unemployment) dooms large numbers of people to poverty no matter how achievement-oriented they may be or how able they may be to defer gratification. There are doubtless some people who are poor because of an array of psychological liabilities, but they make up a very small percentage of the total number of poor people.

A rather intriguing factor in poverty is mental illness. As we have seen in Chapter 4, there is certainly a link between poverty and mental illness, especially schizophrenia. However, what we have been unable to unravel is whether mental illness causes poverty or whether the adverse living conditions of the poor cause a higher incidence of mental illness. While it is clearly true that mental illness causes some people to be poor, it is likely that many more cases of mental illness are caused by poverty.

Physiology

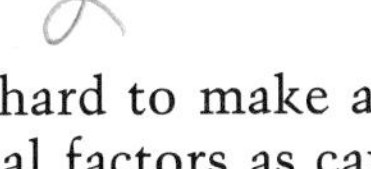

While it is hard to make a strong case for psychological factors as causes of poverty, the same is not true of various physiological factors. There are a number of physiological factors that make it much more likely that one will end up being poor:

— If you are born *black*, you have a greater likelihood of being poor.

—If you are *young*, there is a greater likelihood of poverty.

—If you are *old*, poverty is a greater possibility.

—If you are a *woman*, poverty is more likely.

—Being physically or mentally *handicapped* is likely to be linked to poverty.

It is crucial to remember that it is not these physiological characteristics, but rather the way those with these characteristics are treated by the larger society, that increases the likelihood of poverty. Of course, none of these factors predestine one to poverty. There are many black, young, old, female, and/or handicapped people in the middle and upper classes. However, one's chances of being poor are enchanced by being in one or more of these categories. And there are other physiological factors such as obesity, homeliness, and the like that may make it more likely that an individual will become poor.

Poverty and Health

Turning from physiological causes to consequences, the poor are likely to suffer from inadequate food and poor nutrition, and this has a variety of adverse physiological effects on them. Because of the mother's inadequate nutrition, poor children are more likely to be smaller at birth, to die in infancy, and to have birth defects. Such children start life behind middle- and upper-class children and they may never catch up. This inability to catch up is supported by poorer nutrition throughout the life cycle. In brief, poor nutrition adversely affects poor people and makes it likely that they will remain poor.

Although chronic physical illness can lead to poverty, the much more likely linkage is that poverty serves to make it more likely that people will become ill. Inadequate nutrition, clothing, and shelter are important causes of poor physical health among the poor. Even when they think they may have a physical problem, ignorance or lack of knowledge of available treatments may prevent them from visiting a physician. The poor are more likely to try home remedies suggested by family or friends. Often it is only after such efforts have failed and their physical condition has deteriorated that they seek professional medical help. The poor also face barriers even when they do seek medical care. There are fewer physicians available in poor areas than in the more affluent areas of the city or suburbs. When they find a doctor, the poor are less likely to have the health insurance that today is a virtual prerequisite to obtaining quality medical care. Lack of finances forces the poor who seek medical care to use public health facilities, which often do not provide the same quality care as private medical facilities. Private care is more often available to the middle and upper classes, who can pay for it.[57] In virtually every way, medical care of the poor is inferior to that received by the middle and upper classes.[58]

Poverty and Mortality

Physical illness is, of course, linked to mortality. In general, there is evidence that poverty is related to a lower life expectancy.[59] And that, in turn, is related to cause of death. Because of poorer living conditions, lack of information, and lack of access to medical resources, the poor are more likely to acquire certain diseases and to die from preventable or treatable diseases. The poor are also more likely to die as a result of homicide,[60] state executions,[61] and warfare.[62]

Thus, physiology is related to poverty, partly as a cause, but mainly in the fact that poverty has a variety of physiological effects on the individual.

PART III: RESPONSES

In light of the many interrelated factors that combine to create poverty and are, in turn, affected by poverty, we now attempt to assess some of the ways in which the United States has tried to cope with the problem of poverty. Given the continuing large number of poor people, larger than most other developed nations, the underlying theme of this section is why, and to what extent, these responses to poverty have failed, or in some cases even worsened the problem. Along these lines we need to address why, in recent years, the United States has been doing *less* rather than more about poverty.

Most of the responses to the poverty produced by capitalistic America (and in most of Western Europe as well) can be seen as efforts to adopt elements of socialism *without* accepting a wholesale transformation from capitalism to socialism. This means, specifically, that over the years the government, mainly the federal government, has sought in various ways to ameliorate the worst problems associated with poverty in a capitalistic society. The feeling mounted, especially during the Great Depression, that the capitalist market system was not able to deal with such problems. Thus, socialistic measures were put into place to *support* the capitalistic system rather than to replace it.

The Origins of the Welfare System

It is useful in understanding the American case to backtrack to the enactment of the Poor Law in England in 1601.[63] In fact, there is even evidence today that there is some revival of interest in some of its provisions.[64] One of the essential provisions of the Poor Law was the establishment of workhouses where the poor lived and worked. The law stipulated that the wages to be paid in these workhouses would be less than those received by the lowest-paid worker in the village or town. Such low pay, it was hoped, would keep the poor from seeking the workhouse and public support as a way of life. It was assumed that if wages paid in the workhouses were ample, there would be no incentive for the poor to leave them and become independent. In many areas being poor was treated as a crime.[65]

The Colonial Era

Interestingly, the early colonial attitude in America was very different from the British perspective.[66] The colonists tended to adopt a hostile and punitive attitude only toward the poor from other areas, vagabonds, and beggars. When the colonists built workhouses, and they did so surprisingly rarely, they built them primarily for the unwanted poor from outside their communities. As to their own poor, the colonists adopted a very benign position. They sought to support the poor in their own households, or in houses in the community. They rarely sent poor people from the community to such institutions as almshouses or workhouses. Thus, the colonists made a crucial differentiation between the deserving and the undeserving poor.

From the Civil War to the Depression

During and after the Civil War, private charity organizations expanded. Their operating assumption tended to be that assistance should be given to the poor not simply on the basis of their need but rather in such a way as to increase their self-sufficiency. By 1900, relief through private agencies had all but replaced public relief in the United States. This voluntary relief system reinforced strong American views against government intervention in this area. Many critics blamed government intervention in England for the perpetuation of poverty in that country. Private relief was seen as the preferred alternative that would reduce the costs of poverty.

By the end of the 1920s, however, private relief agencies were overwhelmed by the number of poor people, and the federal government was forced to intervene. The need accelerated greatly with the deepening of the Depression. However, support for the idea of protecting people against economic insecurity did not come immediately. In the early Depression years it was acceptable for the government to provide food for livestock but not for unemployed persons. The American idea that individuals should look after their own welfare held on until 1935, when the Social Security Act was passed.

The Social Security Act

As we saw in Chapter 7, the Social Security Act established two separate systems for providing economic security. One system introduced the principle of social insurance, in which persons were required to contribute to the plan and thus had a "right" to receive benefits. The second system involved public assistance and required no contribution. Benefits were to be paid by the federal government according to the ability of the destitute to demonstrate need. The use of federal funds was a new practice, but public assistance was not a new concept; rather, it represented an evolution of the Poor Law of England and a shift of responsibility from private charities to public agencies. The public assistance program was intended to be only a residual measure to meet the temporary emergency needs of the poor.[67] It was assumed that in a reasonably short time as the nation recovered from the Depression, the need for this program would wither away. However, this did not turn out to be the case and public assistance programs grew enormously in the ensuing decades.

Although the largest and most problematic program is the social insurance program, which is what we ordinarily think of when we mention Social Security, we will omit discussion of it here since it has already been discussed in Chapter 7 on aging and ageism. Our concern here is with the recent history and current status of various social assistance programs instituted by the federal and, in some cases, state governments.

Recent Developments in the Welfare System

Until the Reagan administration's efforts to rein in the growth of social welfare expenditures, the absolute amounts had been growing at a rapid rate (but bear in mind that inflation was very high during this period). For example, the costs of welfare programs to all levels of government had risen from about $146 billion in 1970 to approximately $428 billion in 1979, a rise of almost 200 percent in nine years. Of the total, the federal government paid for 53 percent of all social welfare costs in 1970, but by 1979 that had grown to almost 62 percent. By 1979 welfare expenditures

Figure 10.5 Federal Income Security Programs

Information is provided here concerning amount of payments and number of recipients for six federal programs, including Medicaid, Food Stamps, and Aid to Families with Dependent Children.

Source: U.S. Bureau of the Census, *Statistical Abstract of the United States: 1984* (Washington, D.C.: U.S. Government Printing Office, 1984), p. xxii.

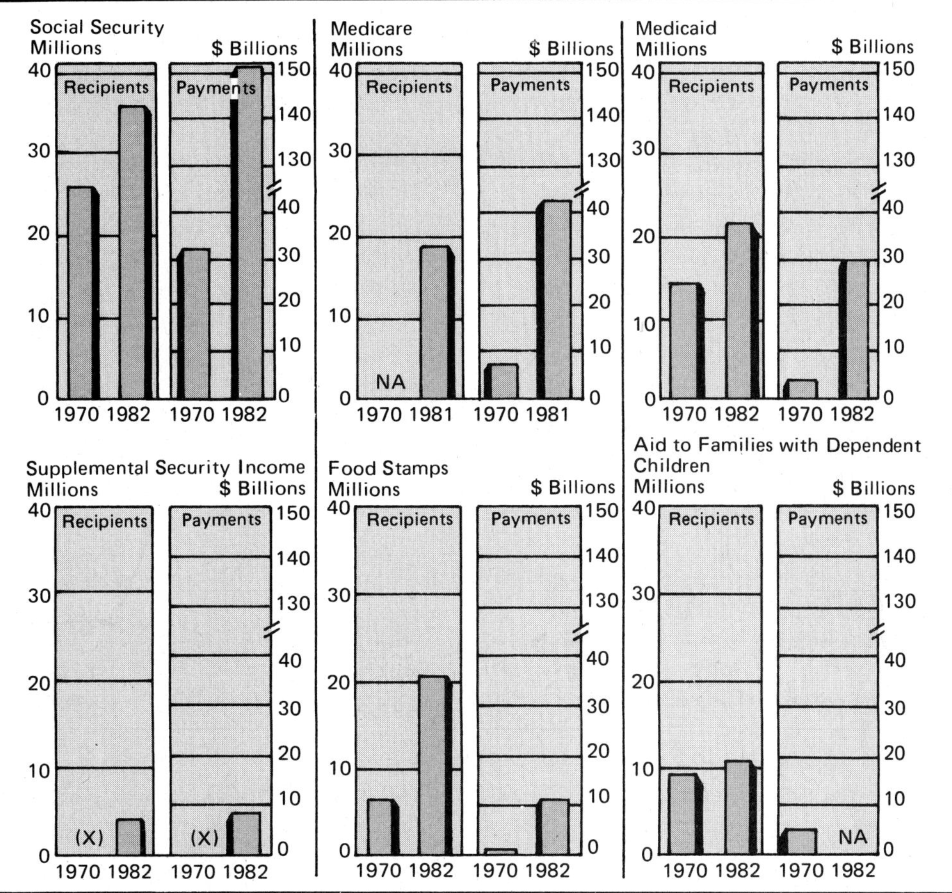

Subject	Unit of measure	1960	1970	1975	1980	1982	Average annual percent change 1960–70	Average annual percent change 1970–75	Average annual percent change 1975–82
Social security—									
Recipients	Millions	14.8	26.2	32.1	35.6	35.8	5.9	4.1	1.6
Payments	$Bil.	11	32	67	120	156	11.0	16.0	12.9
Medicare—									
Recipients[1]	Millions	(X)	[2]9.4	13.0	18.0	[3]18.7	(X)	[4]8.4	[5]6.3
Payments	$Bil.	(X)	7.1	15.6	35.7	[3]43.5	(X)	17.0	[5]18.6
Medicaid—									
Recipients	Millions	(X)	14.5	22.2	21.6	21.9	(X)	8.9	-.2
Payments	$Bil.	(X)	4.8	12.3	23.3	29.9	(X)	20.7	13.5
Supplemental Security Income—									
Recipients[6]	Millions	(X)	(X)	4.3	4.1	3.9	(X)	(X)	-1.6
Payments	$Bil.	(X)	(X)	5.9	7.9	9.0	(X)	(X)	6.2
Food stamps—									
Recipients	Millions	(X)	6.5	19.2	22.0	20.3	(X)	24.3	.8
Payments	$Bil.	(X)	.6	4.4	8.7	10.2	(X)	51.5	12.8
Aid to families with dependent children—									
Recipients	Millions	3.1	9.7	11.4	11.1	10.5	12.1	3.4	-1.2
Payments[7]	$Bil.	1.0	4.9	9.2	12.5	[3]13.0	17.1	13.7	[5]5.9

NA Not available. X Not applicable. [1]Represents persons served. [2]1971 data. [3]1981 data. [4]Change, 1971-75. [5]Change, 1975-81. [6]Federally administered payments only. [7]Federal costs.

amounted to 18.5 percent of the GNP and 55 percent of the federal government's budget.[68] It was in the context of this rise, and a deep-seated American hostility to such welfare programs, that we should see the Reagan administration's efforts to moderate this growth. Let us look at some of the specific programs.

The School Lunch Program

This program was created on the basis of revelations about children coming to school hungry and being unable to afford to buy lunch. Although in existence for some time, the federal school lunch program grew rapidly after amendments to the National School Lunch Act in 1970. These reforms were prompted by a 1967 report of the Field Foundation that concluded:

> Wherever we went and wherever we looked we saw children in significant numbers who were hungry and sick, children for whom hunger is a daily fact of life, and sickness in many forms, an inevitability. The children we saw were more than just malnourished. They were hungry, weak, apathetic.[69]

The amended law mandated that free lunches be given to children from families below the poverty line, while all school lunches were to be subsidized to some degree. These changes led to an enormous growth in this program from almost $600 million in federal subsidies in 1970 to over $3 billion in such subsidies in 1980. In 1980, about 27 million students in elementary and secondary schools availed themselves of the subsidized lunch program.[70] In this area, the Reagan administration intended to spend in 1983 about 50 percent less than the sum projected by the previous administration.[71] There is no doubt that there were abuses in this program such as wasted food and parents lying about their financial situation so that their children would qualify for free lunches, but there is also little doubt that it prevented many children from going hungry at lunch time.

Food Stamp Program

The food stamp program was begun on a pilot basis in 1961[72] and did not become a nationwide program until 1971. In 1962 only about 150,000 people received food stamps at a cost to the government of just over $14 million. By 1980 over 22 million people received stamps at a total cost to the government of over $11 billion. The Reagan administration hoped to be able to remove almost 1 million people from the

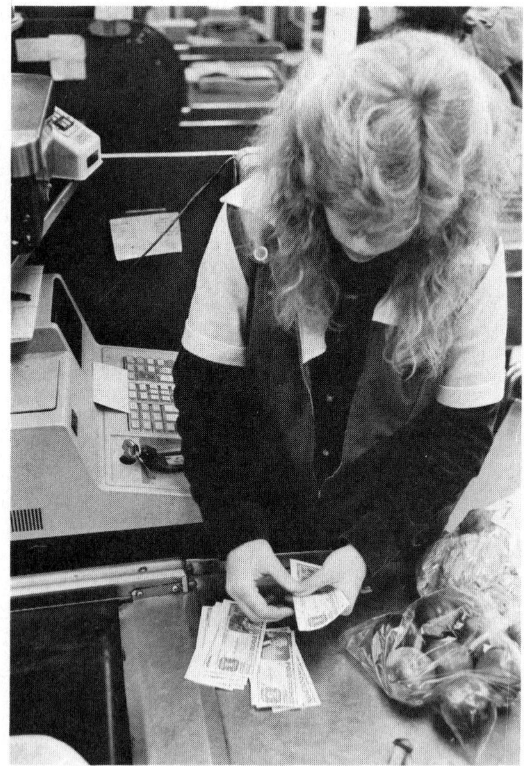

Almost 10 percent of the American population received food stamps in 1980. Since that time there has been some effort to cut back on the food stamp program.

(Mark Antman/The Image Works)

food stamp program.[73] In addition to a general opposition to such programs, the Reagan administration opposed the food stamp program because of a number of abuses associated with it. The major abuse here is that people have discovered that they can use food stamps to buy things besides the food for which they were intended. Other abuses include the counterfeiting of food stamps, administrators sending stamps to themselves via fictitious welfare clients, and drug pushers accepting food stamps in payment for drugs.[74] Again, however, we must not forget that many people were able to avoid hunger because of food stamps.

Medicaid

This program (along with its companion, Medicare, which was discussed in Chapter 7) was started in 1965 to help the poor pay their medical bills. Medicaid will pay for such things as doctor visits, prescription drugs, outpatient hospital services, lab tests and x-rays, dental treatments, inpatient hospital stays, such family planning services as abortions, and nursing home expenses.[75] By 1980 over $20 billion was being spent on Medicaid payments. Objections to this social welfare program seem to be less, although some concern is often expressed over unneeded procedures as well as Medicaid's role in driving up the cost of health care. The Reagan administration projects only minor cuts in this program.

Aid to Families

The most controversial federal welfare program is Aid to Families with Dependent Children (AFDC). The federal government's involvement with this program began in 1935 when it joined already existing state programs. It was originally intended to provide aid to widows with children. The entire character of the program has changed and today 80 percent of the payments go to single parents (almost entirely women) who have been deserted by their mates. In 1936 about a half million people received about $21 million in federal assistance, but by the early 1980s those numbers had grown to 11 million recipients of $7 billion in federal assistance.[76] It is worth noting that of these 11 million recipients, about three-quarters were children while the rest were the parents who were caring for them.[77] The Reagan administration hoped to cut this program by as much as $1 billion by eliminating many people from the welfare rolls and cutting payments to others. These cuts were undertaken even though most people on welfare do not abuse the system and most are not living in luxury. One study indicated that the purchasing power of the average AFDC benefit had actually *fallen* by 18 percent between 1973 and 1979. In Texas, the maximum cash welfare payment to a family of four in 1973 was $140 per month. In 1982 it had risen by *one* dollar to $141 per month, while the cost of living had doubled in that same period.[78]

The AFDC program has been subjected to a variety of critiques. First, it is said to encourage unwed women to have children since they know they can rely on funds from AFDC to support the children. Second, it supposedly encourages parents not to marry, or to separate if they are married, since a person must be single in order to qualify for benefits. Here is the way one welfare mother spoke of her husband:

> I love Earl . . . I'd be better off divorcing him and having him come back to live with me. It doesn't pay you to be honest today. If you're crooked, you can run around in a big Cadillac and have money coming out of your pockets.[79]

Third, it is thought to encourage unwed mothers to have large numbers of children since AFDC will increase its support. Fourth, it may lead recipients to hide alternative sources of income for fear of having

Local agencies also help the poor. Here a local church in Chicago sponsors a food giveaway program.
(AP/Wide World Photos)

their benefits cut or eliminated. Fifth, it is assumed to discourage parents from taking full-time jobs since they may earn little if anything more than they would on welfare. Finally, this is the area that most people have in mind when they complain about "welfare cheats," the kinds of people who drive expensive cars or who are able to take Hawaiian vacations while still receiving welfare payments. (While this latter group may be particularly nettlesome, there are clearly comparatively few people included in it.)

Myths About Welfare for the Poor

In spite of all of the attention devoted to federal welfare expenses, and the need felt by many to cut them, by many standards the United States spends comparatively little on social welfare programs. Let us look at three issues here. First, we will compare welfare and military expenditures. Second, we will compare U.S. expenditures on welfare to those in Europe. Third, we will attempt to show that there is actually far more money spent in the United States on "welfare for the rich" than on welfare for the poor.

Welfare vs. Military Expenditures

In 1980 the national defense budget was about $136 billion; by 1983 the military budget had risen dramatically to $212 billion.[80] This is part of a massive $1.6 trillion arms build-up in which arms procurement is supposed to grow by 16 percent per year through 1987 (compared to a growth rate of 14 percent during the height of the Vietnam war).[81] Thus, in peacetime with poverty and unemployment rates at high levels, the federal government has sought to *cut* welfare programs while simultaneously engaging in an unprecedented peacetime expansion of the military. This means that in recent years we have increasingly chosen guns over butter. Furthermore, there are enormous abuses within the defense sector. Revelations abound of cost overruns, useless weapons, cheating by government contractors, and poor quality control over weaponry. Whatever else one can say about the merits and liabilities of this defense buildup, it is clear that we have, at least in part, sought to expand the military by taking from the poor.

Welfare in Europe and the United States

Despite ongoing cutbacks resulting from economic recession, Western European societies continue to spend far larger sums of money on social welfare programs than the United States. As we have seen, on a variety of measures, European nations spend about twice as much as America on such programs.[82] Although some cutbacks can be anticipated in European welfare programs, they will remain far larger than comparable American programs. Furthermore, bear in mind that while European nations are scaling back their programs, the United States is doing the same, but from a comparatively much smaller base.

Welfare for the Rich and the Poor

Most of the complaints about welfare involve welfare payments to the poor. Although it is an unusual concept, there is such a thing as welfare for the rich (and the middle class), and it is entirely likely (exact figures are impossible to come by) that far more money is spent in the United States on welfare for the rich than on welfare for the poor. Welfare for the rich does not usually come in the form of a regular check from the government. Rather it comes in such forms as tax deductions for home ownership, a wide range of tax-deductible business expenses, and the like. The form that welfare for the rich is most likely to take is taxes not paid. One of the best known cases of this kind is the oil billionaire J. Paul Getty, who in the early 1960s was earning about $300,000 per *day*, but at the end of the year paid less in taxes than most manual workers, only a few thousand dollars. Computing what Getty should have paid without deductions, it can be argued that Getty had gotten what amounted to a $70 million welfare check from the federal government.[83] More generally, in 1980 a tax return which indicated an income of a million dollars or more was also likely to include itemized deductions of over one-half million dollars.[84] While multimillionaires like Getty are in an excellent position to exploit the tax system, most middle-class Americans are able to get, albeit on a far smaller scale, the same kinds of welfare payments from the government.

Not only is it likely that the rich and middle class get far more money in welfare payments than the poor, but the upper classes are actually praised for it while the poor are damned for their welfare payments. A. Dale Tussing makes this point by arguing that there are in fact two entirely different welfare programs in America: "One is well-known; it is explicit, poorly funded, stigmatized and stigmatizing, and it is directed at the poor. The other, practically unknown, is implicit, literally invisible, is nonstigmatized and nonstigmatizing and provides vast unacknowledged benefits to the non-poor—whether working class, middle class or well-to-do."[85]

SUMMARY

Part I: The Problem

1. Public consciousness of the problem of poverty has varied greatly throughout the twentieth century.

2. Despite problems in conceptualizing poverty, using the official government

poverty index we know that 34.4 million people, or about 15 percent of the population, were below the poverty line in 1982.

3. In recent years the number of people below the poverty line has been increasing.
4. The poor are disproportionately likely to be drawn from the following categories—children, the aged, fatherless families, the handicapped, and black Americans. The characteristics of the people in these categories make it such that poverty is a difficult problem with which to deal. There are no simple solutions to the problem of poverty.

Part II: Causes and Consequences

5. Poverty is built into the basic structure of capitalist society.
6. World-systems theory allows us to understand the division of the world into rich and poor nations.
7. Within the United States, Marxist theory helps us to understand the existence of poverty. However, the experience of many Western European countries makes it clear that poverty is not inevitable in capitalism.
8. The policies of the United States government have a profound effect on poverty. For example, an effort to deal with inflation by slowing down the economy will likely lead to more poverty.
9. Racism, sexism, and ageism in American society contribute to the high level of poverty in general, and the disproportionately high rate among the groups directly affected.
10. Problems within the family can contribute to poverty and, conversely, family life is profoundly affected by poverty.
11. Although poverty is clearly a problem that contributes to other social problems, poverty also performs various positive functions in society.
12. If we hope to deal with poverty, one of the things we must do is find alternatives to the various functions performed by poverty.
13. American culture contributes to the problem of poverty with its belief that individuals are to blame for being poor and are responsible for alleviating their own economic problems.
14. One of the main social-psychological results of being poor is the stigma and label associated with it. The poor are generally seen and treated as disreputable.
15. It is difficult to unravel the cause-and-effect relationship between poverty and psychological problems.
16. Various physiological factors, or at least the way these characteristics are treated by others, are related to poverty.
17. Poverty adversely affects individual health and lowers life expectancy.

Part III: Responses

18. The major responses to the problem of poverty in the United States are to be found in the welfare system that has evolved over the years. Among the most important components of that system are Social Security, the School Lunch Program, the Food Stamp Program, Medicaid, and Aid to Families with Dependent Children.
19. Although there are many complaints about the costs of welfare for the poor in the United States, we have recently been cutting welfare while increasing military expenditures; we spend far less on welfare than many Western European nations, and it is very likely that we spend far more money on welfare for the rich than welfare for the poor.

SUGGESTED READINGS

Blumberg, Paul, *Inequality in an Age of Decline.* New York: Oxford University Press, 1980. An analysis that anticipates an increase in inequality and poverty in the United States.

Gans, Herbert, "The Positive Functions of Poverty." *American Journal of Sociology,* 78, 1972, 275–289. An essay that demonstrates how one type of sociological theorist, a structural functionalist, approaches the problem of poverty.

Harrington, Michael, *The Other America: Poverty in the United States.* Baltimore, Md.: Penguin, 1963. A major work that in its time helped lead to many efforts in the 1960s to deal with the problem of poverty.

Simmel, Georg, "The Poor." In Donald Levine, ed., *Georg Simmel.* Chicago: University of Chicago Press, 1971, pp. 150–178. A surprising analysis of poverty by a classic sociologist.

FOOTNOTES:

[1]Godfrey Hodgson, *America in Our Time* (Garden City, N.Y.: Doubleday, 1976).

[2]Barry Bluestone and Bennett Harrison, *The Deindustrialization of America* (New York: Basic Books, 1982).

[3]Leonard Beeghley, "Illusion and Reality in the Measurement of Poverty," *Social Problems,* 31 (1984), 322–333.

[4]George Simmel, "The Poor." In Donald Levine, ed., *Georg Simmel* (Chicago: University of Chicago Press, 1971), pp. 150–178.

[5]United States Bureau of the Census, Current Population Reports (Series P–60, No. 140), *Money Income and Poverty Status of Families and Persons in the United States: 1982 (Advance Data From the March 1983 Current Population Survey)* (Washington, D.C.: U.S. Government Printing Office, 1983), p. 1; Spencer Rich, "U.S. Poverty Rate Rises to 15 Percent," *The Washington Post,* August 3, 1983, pp. A1, A14. See also, U.S. Bureau of the Census, *Statistical Abstract of the United States: 1984* (Washington, D.C.: U.S. Government Printing Office, 1983), p. 471.

[6]U.S. Bureau of the Census, *op. cit., Money Income and Poverty Status,* p. 3.

[7]Richard Titmuss, "Poverty vs. Inequality: Diagnosis," *The Nation,* February 8, 1965, pp. 130–133.

[8]U.S. Bureau of the Census, *Current Population Reports,* Series P–60, 105 (June 1977), p. 58; Series P–60, 121 (February 1980), p. 1.

[9]Spencer Rich, "Poor Hurt Most by Social Cuts, CBO Study Says," *The Washington Post,* August 26, 1983, pp. A1, A6.

[10]Hobart Rowen, "A Widening Gap Between Rich and Poor," *The Washington Post,* March 11, 1982, p. A29.

[11]Paul Blumberg, *Inequality in an Age of Decline* (New York: Oxford University Press, 1980).

[12]Rich, *op. cit.*

[13]David Matza and Henry Miller, "Poverty and Proletariat." In Robert K. Merton and Robert A. Nisbet, eds., *Contemporary Social Problems,* 4th ed. (New York: Harcourt Brace Jovanovich, 1976), pp. 642–673.

[14]Spencer Rich, "Up to 1.2 Million Elderly May Face Poverty," *The Washington Post,* March 28, 1982, p. A4.

[15]Spencer Rich, "Survey Shows Elderly Exceed Average Income," *The Washington Post,* August 19, 1983, pp. A1, A3.

[16]Idella Swisher, "Family Income of the Disabled," *Social Security Administration, Social Security Survey of the Disabled, 1966.* Report 13 (Washington, D.C.: U.S. Government Printing Office, 1970).

[17]William Ryan, *Blaming the Victim* (New York: Random House, 1971).

[18]Immanuel Wallerstein, *The Modern World-System: Capitalist Agriculture and the Origins of the European World-Economy in the Sixteenth Century* (New York: Academic Press, 1974); *The Modern World-System II: Mercantilism and the Consolidation of the European World-Economy, 1600–1750* (New York: Academic Press, 1980).

[19]Jim Brooke, "Kidney, Cornea Sale Flourishes in Brazil," *The Washington Post,* October 12, 1981, pp. A22, A23.

[20]*Ibid.*, p. A22.

[21]*Ibid.*

[22]*Ibid.*

[23]*Ibid.*, p. A23.

[24]Carlos Fuentes, "Rich Nations and Poor, Linked in Need," *The Washington Post,* October 18, 1981, pp. C1, C5.

[25]"A Survival Summit," *Newsweek,* October 26, 1981, pp. 36ff.

[26]Wallerstein, *op. cit.*, 1974, p. 15.

[27]Karl Marx, *Capital*, Vol. 1 (New York: International Publishers, 1867/1967).

[28]See, for example, Ben Agger, *Western Marxism: An Introduction* (Santa Monica, Cal.: Goodyear, 1978).

[29]"If You Think U.S. Social-Welfare Load Is Heavy," *U.S. News and World Report*, November 8, 1982, p. 46.

[30]*Ibid.* See also "Reassessing the Welfare State," *Time*, January 12, 1981, pp. 32–33.

[31]"The Welfare Crisis," *Newsweek*, July 25, 1983, pp. 48–51.

[32]*Statistical Abstract, op. cit.*, pp. 422, 485.

[33]*Ibid.*

[34]"Recession's Ill Wind Blows Inflation Down," *U.S. News and World Report*, January 10, 1983, pp. 45–48.

[35]William Julius Wilson, "The Black Underclass," *The Wilson Quarterly* (Spring 1984), 94

[36]Donald Bell and Diane Hill, "How Social Security Payments Affect Private Pensions," *Monthly Labor Review* (1984), p. 15–20; *Statistical Abstract, op. cit.* p. 384. The number covered by pensions goes up to 56 percent if we exclude farm workers and include government workers. (Spencer Rich, "Study Finds Pensions are Widespread, "*The Washington Post*, July 7, 1984, pp. F1, F2). If we look only at employees of medium and large firms, 84 percent of employees are covered by private pension programs. (Bureau of Labor Statistics, "Employee Benefits in Medium and Large Firms, 1981" [Washington, D.C.: U.S. Department of Labor, August, 1982], p. 7.)

[37]Peter Henle and Raymond Schmitt, "Pension Reform: The Long, Hard Road to Enactment," *Monthly Labor Review*, 97 (1974), 3–12; Fred J. Cook, "The Case of the Disappearing Pension," *The New York Times Magazine*, March 19, 1972, pp. 30ff; Lawrence Meyer, "Pensions: Many Pay, but Few Collect," *The Washington Post*, September 6, 1982, pp. A1, A10.

[38]Andrew Hacker, ed., *U/S: A Statistical Portrait of the American People* (New York: Viking Press, 1983), p. 184

[39]*Statistical Abstract, op. cit.*, p. 447

[40]Lillian Breslow Rubin, *Worlds of Pain: Life in the Working Class Family* (New York: Basic Books, 1976)

[41]Leonard S. Syme and Lisa F. Berkman, "Social Class, Susceptibility, and Sickness." In Peter Conrad and Rochelle Kern, eds., *The Sociology of Health and Illness* (New York: St. Martin's Press, 1981); Lee Rainwater, "The Lower Class: Health, Illness and Medical Institutions." In Irwin Deutscher and Elizabeth J. Thompson, eds., *Among the People: Encounter with the Poor* (New York: Basic Books, 1968); August B. Hollingshead and Frederick C. Redlich, *Social Class and Mental Illness* (New York: Wiley, 1958).

[42]Paul C. Glick and Arthur J. Norton, "Marrying, Divorcing, and Living Together in the U.S. Today," *Population Bulletin*, 32 (Washington, D.C.: The Population Reference Bureau, Inc., 1979); J. Richard Udry, "Marital Instability by Race, Sex, Education, and Occupation Using 1960 Census Data," *American Journal of Sociology*, 72 (1966), 203–209.

[43]Herbert Gans, "The Positive Functions of Poverty," *American Journal of Sociology*, 78 (1972), 275–289.

[44]Max Weber, *The Protestant Ethic and the Spirit of Capitalism*, Talcott Parsons (tr.) (New York: Scribners, 1958)

[45]Alexis de Tocqueville, *Democracy in America*, Vol. II. Phillips Bradley (tr.) (New York: Knopf, 1960)

[46]"Living Standards—U.S. Still Ranks High. *U.S. News and World Report*, December 20, 1982, pp. 52–53

[47]Robert Lane, *Political Ideology* (New York: Free Press, 1962)

[48]Matza and Miller, *op. cit.*

[49]*Ibid.*, p. 662

[50]John R. Coleman, "Diary of a Homeless Man," *New York*, February 21, 1983, pp. 25ff

[51]Judith Cummings, "Increase in Homeless People Tests U.S. Cities' Will to Cope," *The New York Times*, May 3, 1982, pp. 1, B13

[52]Alice Bonner, "The Drifters," *The Washington Post*, October 23, 1981, pp. B1, B13

[53]Coleman, *op. cit.*, p. 29

[54]*Ibid.*, p. 32

[55]*Ibid.*, p. 35

[56]Robert Coles, *Migrants, Sharecroppers, Mountaineers* (Boston: Little, Brown, 1971), p. 149

[57]Lu Ann Aday, Ronald Anderson, and Gretchen Fleming, *Health Care in the U.S.: Equitable for Whom?* (Beverly Hills, Cal.: Sage 1980).

[58]June Jackson Christmas, "How Our Health System Fails Minorities," *Civil Rights Digest*, 10 (1977), pp. 2–11.

[59]Aaron Antonovsky, "Social Class, Life Expectancy and Overall Mortality," *Milbank Memorial Fund Quarterly*, 45 (1967), pp. 31–73; Evelyn Kitagawa and Philip M. Hauser, "Education Differentials in Mortality by Cause of Death, United States 1960," *Demography*, 5 (1968), pp. 318–353.

[60]Marvin Wolfgang, "Criminal Homicide and the Subculture of Violence." In Marvin Wolfgang, ed., *Studies in Homicide* (New York: Harper & Row, 1967).

[61]Elmer Johnson, "Selective Factors in Capital Punishment," *Social Forces*, 36 (1957), pp. 165–169.

[62]M. Zeitlin, K. A. Lutterman, and J. W. Russell, "Death in Vietnam: Class, Poverty and the Risks of War," *Politics and Society*, 3 (1973), pp. 313–328.

[63]David J. Rothman, *The Discovery of the Asylum* (Boston: Little, Brown, 1971).

[64]Jay Mathews, "Shaken by Welfare Costs, California County Revives Poorhouse," *The Washington Post*, February 25, 1983, p. A2.

[65]Samuel Mencher, *Poor Law to Poverty Program* (Pittsburgh: University of Pittsburgh Press, 1967).

[66]Rothman, *op. cit.*

[67]Harold Wilensky and Charles Lebeaux, *Industrial Society and Social Welfare* (New York: Free Press, 1965).

[68]Hacker, *op. cit.*, pp. 177–178.

[69]Cited in Gregory Jaynes, "Food Progam's Advocates Fear Cutbacks Will Wipe Out Gains in Nutrition," *The New York Times*, September 18, 1981, p. D16.

[70]"Backing Down on Benefits," *Time*, October 12, 1981, pp. 32ff.

[71]"Cuts in Social Services-Main Impact Ahead?" *U.S. News and World Report*, October 25, 1982, pp. 55–56.

[72]Marjorie L. DeVault and James P. Pitts, "Surplus and Scarcity: Hunger and the Origins of the Food Stamp Program," *Social Problems*, 31 (1984), 545–557.

[73]"Backing Down on Benefits," *op. cit.*, p. 44.

[74]"The Stakes Get Higher in Food-Stamp Frauds," *U.S. News and World Report*, February 7, 1983, pp. 51–52.

[75]Hacker, *op. cit.*, p. 182.

[76]"Backing Down on Benefits," *op. cit.*, p. 44.

[77]Hacker. *op. cit.*, p. 189.

[78]Spencer Rich, "Welfare Benefits Form Crazy-Quilt Pattern Across U.S.," *The Washington Post*, January 30, 1982, p. A3.

[79]Walter Shapiro, "Jitters on a Welfare Line," *The Washington Post-Outlook*, September 27, 1981, p. C5.

[80]*Statistical Abstract of the United States*, *op. cit.*, p. 322.

[81]"Dangers in the Big Buildup," *Time*, March 22, 1982, pp. 50ff.

[82]"Reassessing the Welfare State," *Time*, January 12, 1981, pp. 32–33; "If You Think U.S. Social-Welfare is Heavy," *U.S. News and World Report*, November 8, 1982, p. 46.

[83]Philip M. Stern, "Uncle Sam's Welfare Program for the Rich," *The New York Times Magazine*, April 16, 1972, pp. 28ff.

[84]"When the Rich Fill Out Returns," *U.S. News and World Report*, November 15, 1982, p. 93.

[85]A. Dale Tussing, "The Dual Welfare System," *Society*, 9 (January-February, 1974), pp. 50–57.

IV

Problems of Human Progress

It is true that neither the ancient wisdoms nor the modern sciences are complete in themselves. They do not stand alone. They call for one another. Wisdom without science is unable to penetrate the full sapiential meaning of the created and material cosmos. Science without wisdom leaves man enslaved to a world of unrelated objects in which there is no way of discovering (or creating) order and deep significance in man's own pointless existence.

Thomas Merton

11
Problems of the Economy and in the Workplace

Our concern in this chapter is with some of the major problems found in the world of work. Those problems, as well as the work world in general, exist within an economy that has been rapidly changing. While producing many positive advances, those changes have also created a variety of difficulties for American workers. Before getting to those problems, we will examine the changing nature of work, specifically changes in the American labor force.

CHANGES IN THE LABOR FORCE

If we take the turn of the twentieth century as our starting point, it is clear from Table 11.1 that there have been enormous changes in the occupational structure of the United States.

Table 11.1 details the major changes in the labor force by occupational level. Table 11.2 examines the same changes, but seeks to clarify what has taken place by reducing the eleven occupational categories in Table 11.1 to four general types. In the following pages, we highlight some of the major changes reflected in these two tables.

The Decline of the Farm

One of the most striking changes in the American labor force, evident in Tables 11.1 and 11.2, is the remarkable decline in the number of people who work on farms or perform farm-related activities. These statistics indicate that in the last century America has moved from an agrarian economy to an industrial and, more recently, to a *postindustrial*,[1] service economy. As we can see from Table 11.2, the percentage of the labor force on the farm dropped from 37.5 percent in 1900 to below 3 percent in 1982, and it is forecast to go below 2 percent by 1995.

The decline in the number of farm work-

Table 11.1 Changes in Labor Force by Occupational Level

OCCUPATIONAL LEVEL	PERCENTAGE OF THE LABOR FORCE 1900	1930	1960	1970	1982	1995*
Professional, Technical, and Kindred Workers	4.3%	6.8%	10.8%	14.0%	17.0%	17.1%
Managers, Officials, Proprietors, except Farm	5.9	7.4	8.7	7.9	11.5	9.6
Clerical and Kindred Workers	3.0	8.9	14.1	16.9	18.5	18.9
Sales Workers	4.5	6.3	7.2	6.8	6.6	6.9
Private Household Workers	5.4	4.1	2.7	1.4	1.0	0.7
Other Service Workers	3.6	5.7	8.9	10.4	12.8	15.6
Craftsmen, Foremen, and Kindred Workers	10.6	12.8	13.8	12.9	12.3	11.6
Operators and Kindred Workers	12.8	15.8	17.5	16.3	12.9	12.1
Laborers, except Farm and Mine	12.5	11.0	5.1	4.2	4.5	5.6
Farmers and Farm Managers	19.9	12.4	3.9	1.7	1.5	1.1
Farm Laborers and Foremen	17.7	8.8	2.3	1.2	1.3	0.8
Not Reported	—	—	5.0	6.3	—	—
Total Percent	100.2	100.0	100.0	100.0	99.9	100.0
Employed Civilian Labor Force, Total Number (in thousands)	29,073	45,480	65,778	78,678	99,526	127,110

Sources: Percentages for 1900 and 1930 from Philip M. Hauser, "Labor Force," in Robert E. L. Faris, ed., *Handbook of Modern Sociology* (Chicago: Rand-McNally, 1964), p. 183. Percentages for 1960 and 1970 adapted from Constance Bogh DiCesare, "Change in the Occupational Structure of U.S. Jobs," *Monthly Labor Review* (1975), p. 24. Percentages for 1982 and total employed civilian labor force for 1930 through 1982 from *Employment and Earnings* (30) 1, (Washington D.C.: U.S. Department of Labor, 1983). Data for 1995 from George T. Silvestri, John M. Lukasiewicz, and Marcus E. Einstein, "Occupational Employment Projections Through 1995," *Monthly Labor Review* 106, 11 (1983), 37–49. Totals are rounded.
*The figures for 1995 involve projections.

Table 11.2 Changes in Labor Force by Occupational Group

OCCUPATIONAL GROUP	PERCENTAGE OF THE LABOR FORCE 1900	1930	1960	1970	1982	1995*
White-Collar	17.6%	29.4%	40.8%	45.6%	53.7%	52.5%
Service	9.1	9.8	11.6	11.8	13.8	16.3
Manual	35.8	39.6	36.4	33.4	29.7	29.3
Farm	37.5	21.1	6.2	2.9	2.7	1.9
Not Reported	—	—	5.0	6.3	—	—
Total	100.0	100.0	100.0	100.0	99.9	100.0

Sources: Data for 1900 and 1930 adapted from Philip M. Hauser, "Labor Force," in Robert E. L. Faris, ed., *Handbook of Modern Sociology* (Chicago: Rand-McNally, 1964), p. 183. Data for 1960 and 1970 adapted from Constance Bogh DiCesare, "Changes in the Occupational Structure of U.S. Jobs," *Monthly Labor Review* (1975), p. 24. 1974 statistics from *Handbook of Labor Statistics—1975—Reference Edition* (Washington, D.C.: U.S. Department of Labor, 1975), p. 41. Data for 1982 from *Employment and Earnings* (30) 1 (Washington, D.C.: U.S. Department of Labor, 1983), p. 157. Data for 1995 adapted frrom George T. Silvestri, John M. Lakasiewicz, and Marcus E. Einstein, "Occupational Employment Projections Through 1995," *Monthly Labor Review* 106, 11 (1983), 37–49. Totals are rounded.
*Figures for 1995 involve projections.

ers is partly due to technological advances that allow far fewer people to produce much more food. These factors forced many people in this century to leave the farm as the need for their labor declined precipitously. Needless to say, this disruption was a serious problem for many of them. People were not only pushed off the farms by a lack of work, but they were also attracted to the more urbanized industrial and service sectors.

The Rise of the Professions

Table 11.1 shows that the number of people in the professions and related occupations almost quadrupled between 1900 and 1982. This growth is but part of the more than tripling of the more general white-collar category (Table 11.2) during this period.

There are several reasons for the growth of the professional category, which encompasses a wide array of occupations, from established professions such as law and medicine, to semiprofessions such as school teaching and nursing, to a variety of technical occupations such as health therapists, computer specialists, and scientific technicians. One factor is the greater sophistication of our knowledge, techniques, and ma-

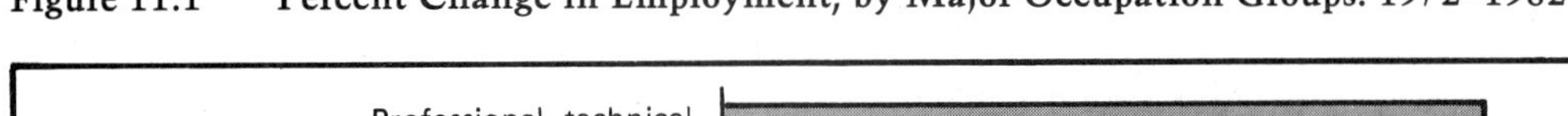

Figure 11.1 Percent Change in Employment, by Major Occupation Groups: 1972–1982

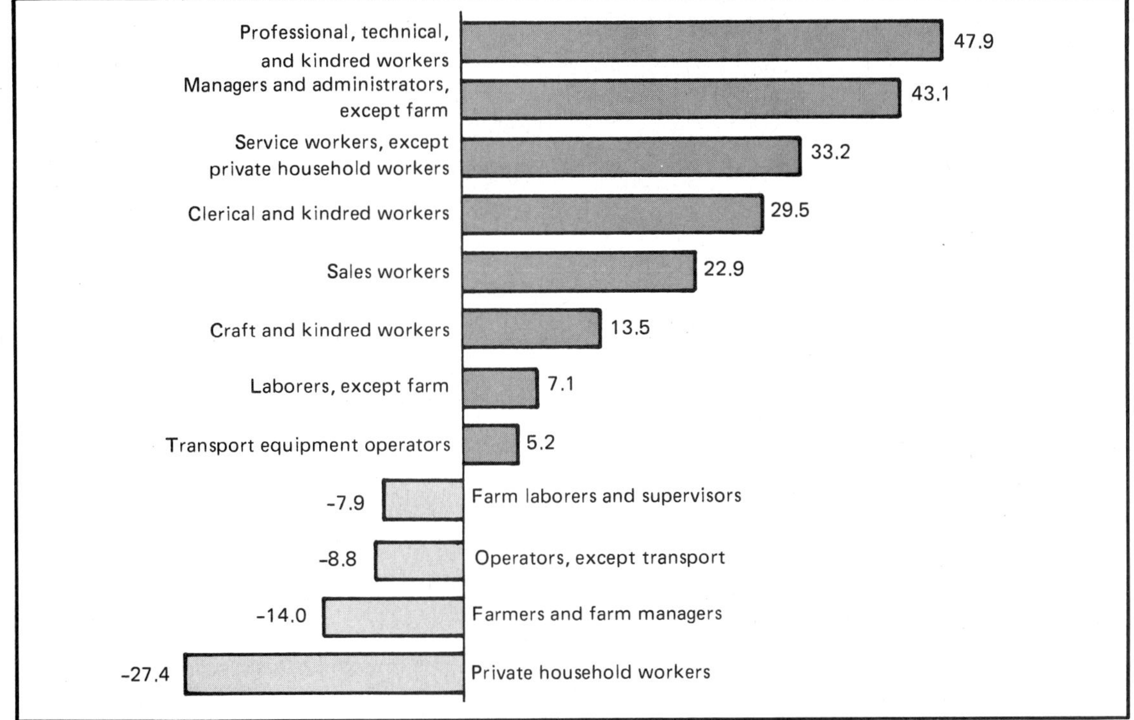

This figure provides information on changes in major occupational categories. Its most important conclusions are that white-collar and service sector employment grew, and declines were recorded among blue-collar and household workers.

Source: U.S. Bureau of the Census, Current Population Reports, Series P–23, No. 130, *Population Profile of the United States: 1982* (Washington, D.C.: U.S. Government Printing Office, 1983), p. 26.

chinery, which has led to a growing demand for technically trained personnel. A second factor is the increasing wealth and sophistication of the American population, which led them to demand more and more services from such diverse occupations as psychiatry, tax accounting, divorce law, and architecture. A third factor is the internal pressure from these occupations either to coerce their clients, or to create a desire within them, to use their services. Lawyers, for example, have helped make real estate transactions so complex that one is almost compelled to use their services in buying or selling a house.[2]

Finally, the growth of the professions is fueled by the growing number of occupations that are striving for and achieving (at least in their own eyes) the high status of the professional. Professional recognition is a desirable goal for many occupations because it carries with it gains in power, economic position, and prestige. Thus, many people, such as personnel managers, morticians, and librarians, are now actively seeking the professional label.

The massive expansion of professionalization has created a number of social problems, as Paul Starr has recently shown in his study of the history of the medical profession, *The Social Transformation of Medicine.*[3] Basically, Starr shows how medicine rose from "a relatively weak, traditional profession of minor significance"[4] in the eighteenth and nineteenth centuries to a position of sovereignty by the mid-twentieth century. One of the resulting contemporary problems is the extraordinary power of the modern medical profession and its willingness, indeed eagerness, to allow its authority to spill "over its clinical boundaries into areas of moral and political action for which medical judgment is only partially relevant and often incompletely equipped."[5] Moreover, the medical profession has been successful in turning "its authority into social privilege, economic power, and political influence."[6]

The Clerical Revolution

Within the white-collar category, managers and officials have almost doubled since 1900, but clerical workers have risen from 3 percent to about 19 percent of the labor force; the proportion of clerical workers has multiplied more than six-fold! Included in this category are such occupations as word processors, clerks, typists, stenographers, office-machine operators, and receptionists. Clerical work will continue to be, as it has been since 1970, *the single largest occupational category.*

A major reason for the massive growth of this occupational category is the proliferation of paper- and now computer-work in large-scale bureaucracies. Thus, the growth of white-collar work has been fueled by the growth of large bureaucracies and such technological changes as the development of the word processor.

In addition to helping to increase the number of people employed in white-collar occupations, bureaucratization has also radically altered the nature of such work. White-collar clerical work formerly brought with it higher prestige than blue-collar work.[7] The growing factory-like structure of many bureaucracies, however, has created problems for white-collar workers by making their occupations indistinguishable in many cases from blue-collar factory work. This trend is likely to continue, if not accelerate, as both blue-collar and white-collar work are altered in similar ways by the ongoing computer revolution.

Rise of the Service Occupations

While one of the basic types of service workers, private household workers (for example, maids), has declined dramatically in the twentieth century, the category of "other service workers" has almost quadrupled and will continue to grow rapidly in the next decade. In this category we find such occupations as counter workers in fast food restaurants, dishwashers, hospital orderlies, guards, janitors, and the like. The problem here is that many of the occupations in this fast-growing category require little education and few skills, pay low wages, and are dead-end jobs.

Decline in Blue-Collar Workers

In 1900 there were about twice as many people in manual, blue-collar occupations as in white-collar occupations, but as of 1982 white-collar workers dominated blue-collar workers by a better than five-to-three ratio. Actually, higher status blue-collar occupations such as foremen, craftsmen, and operators have increased their proportion of the labor force slightly. It is the lowest status blue-collar workers, laborers, who have borne the brunt of the decline in this category since 1900.

There are several reasons for the gradual decline in the number of blue-collar workers, especially laborers. Various technological advances such as automation and robotics[8] have begun to replace significant numbers of these workers. The decline of traditional "smokestack industries"[9] such as textiles, automobiles, and steel manufacturing has led to the loss of many manual jobs in those, and related, industries. The worldwide change in the economic balance of power has shifted many manual jobs out of the United States and into less developed nations. The problems these shifts have caused blue-collar workers, as well as problems intrinsic to the nature of that type of work, will be our major concern throughout this chapter.

PART I: THE PROBLEM

UNEMPLOYMENT, HEALTH AND SAFETY HAZARDS, ALIENATION

As is clear in the brief historical review above, people at all levels (professionals, managers, skilled craftsmen) within the work world are experiencing an array of problems. However, our focus in this chapter will be on the blue-collar, semiskilled, and unskilled occupations that are affected by some of the most serious problems. While these occupations experience a wide range of difficulties, we will focus in this chapter on three major problems: *unemployment, health and safety hazards* on the job, and the problem of *alienation* from work. While our focus will be on the nature of these problems within low-status occupations, it should be borne in mind that these problems are also found in higher-status occupations. However, they are far less ubiquitous and felt far less severely in high-status than low-status occupations.

Unemployment

One of the most extreme manifestations of a nation's economic problems is its unemployment rate.[10] As this is being written, the unemployment rate in the United States hovers around 7.5 percent and it was not too long ago that it stood at approximately 10 percent for more than a year—a rate that the nation had not seen since the early 1940s.[11] Traditionally, unemployment has most plagued those in semiskilled and unskilled occupations. And even though there has been some shift toward greater unemployment for white-collar workers, the rate for the lower-status blue-collar workers still far outstrips that for

Figure 11.2 Trends in the Labor Force: 1950–1982

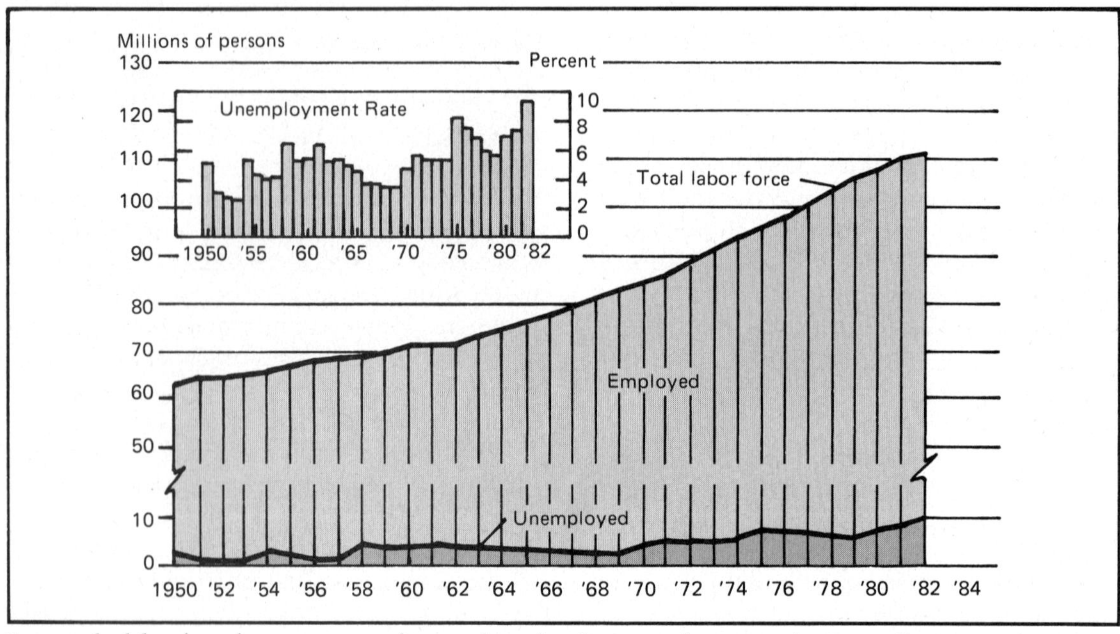

Even as the labor force has grown over the past three decades, so too has unemployment, albeit in a cyclical manner.

Source: U.S. Bureau of the Census, *Statistical Abstract of the United States: 1984* (Washington, D.C.: U.S. Government Printing Office, 1983), p. 404.

white-collar workers. For example, in March 1985 the unemployment rate for lower-level blue-collar workers (handlers, cleaners, helpers, laborers) was more than three times the rate for white-collar (clerical, administrative) workers.[12] Unemployment is also related to level of education which, in turn, is related to the status of one's occupation. Those with less than a high-school education (and therefore likely to find their way into semiskilled and unskilled occupations) have an unemployment rate that is double that of those with some college education and more than four times the rate for college graduates.[13] Race is also related to occupational status and rate of unemployment. Blacks are more likely to be in low-status occupations and they are more than twice as likely to be unemployed as whites.[14]

Health and Safety Hazards

Work kills, maims, and makes large numbers of people ill; work may be dangerous to your health.[15] Statistics are not easy to come by in trying to describe the dimensions of the problem of occupational safety and health. We know, for example, that there are about 100,000 cases of black lung disease among American coal miners and that about 4,000 people die from it each year. We also know that about 80,000 workers were exposed to radiation in 1980 and that as a result they run a high risk of contracting cancer. This constitutes an increase both in the number of people exposed and the amount of radiation to which each worker was exposed. In fact, the exposure rate has quadrupled since 1969.[16] Another major occupational hazard is working with asbestos, and it is estimated that a large number of the half million people who have worked with that substance can expect to contract cancer and other diseases. In a study conducted at a Bethlehem Steel shipyard, it was found that 86 percent of the workers showed at least some signs of lung damage.[17]

The total number of deaths and illnesses attributable to the workplace is far more difficult to estimate accurately. One source estimates 25,000 occupationally related deaths annually,[18] while another puts that figure at considerably less than 1,000.[19] The National Safety Council estimates that in 1980 13,000 people were killed and 2.2 million suffered disabling injuries in accidents on the job. It is also estimated that occupationally related diseases and illnesses kill an additional 100,000 people per year, and make almost 400,000 ill.[20] In terms of trends in occupational injuries and illnesses, one source reports a decline,[21] while another finds an increase, at least in worker perceptions of occupational hazards.[22] However, even the source that reports a decline contends that there were no less than 5.7 *million* occupational injuries and illnesses in 1978.[23] Thus, while there is a wide range in the estimates, there is little question that there are a great many injuries and illnesses associated with work in America.

Even though they demonstrate the existence of a major problem, there are a variety of reasons to believe that official statistics on death, illness, and injury associated with work greatly *under*estimate the dimensions of the problem. Most data on these matters are derived from employers who have a vested interest in *not* reporting large numbers of occupational injuries and illnesses. Many occupationally caused illnesses are almost impossible to differentiate from illnesses caused by factors outside the workplace (for example, cancer of various organs and parts of the body). Harmful exposure to cancer-causing agents can occur on and off the job, making the origin almost impossible to specify. Complicating matters still further is the fact that there is in almost all cases a time lag between exposure, onset of illness, diagnosis, and, if it occurs as a result, death. For example, those who were exposed to radiation as a result of atomic bomb testing in the 1950s are only now beginning to experience the effects. Lack of medical expertise on the relationship between work and health is another factor in the underestimation of occupationally related illness and death. Still another factor is the mobility of many workers. A worker may have been exposed to a hazard for a short time many years ago and changed jobs a number of times since. Hence it is difficult to link a current health problem to a past occupational exposure. Finally, it is clear that we are just beginning to learn about the relationship between various hazards and health problems. In the future, we will undoubtedly learn about many more health hazards on the job. Given all of the reasons for underestimating health hazards, it is clear that thousands die and millions are made ill each year by their jobs.

Occupational safety and health problems are *not* evenly distributed throughout the work world. Those in semiskilled and unskilled occupations are more likely to be injured or killed by *safety* hazards on the job than those in higher-status clerical, managerial, and professional positions. To put it more concretely, fork-lift trucks are far more likely to run over blue-collar than white-collar workers. Similarly, black lung disease is far more likely to affect coal miners than executives of coal mine companies. In 1978 blue-collar workers accounted for almost 80 percent of all job-related injuries but made up only about 40 percent of the workforce.[24] By contrast, white-collar workers of all kinds accounted for almost half the workforce, but little more than 10 percent of the injuries. To take one specific example, the vast majority of work-related amputations are experienced by blue-collar workers.[25]

Although blue-collar workers are more likely to be exposed to safety hazards, *health* dangers are more evenly spread throughout the occupational world. However, even here it is the manual worker who is more likely to be exposed to dangerous chemicals and substances of all kinds. On the other hand, stress-related problems on the job are not monopolized by blue-collar workers.

Alienation

In the preceding sections we have dealt with problems that for most semiskilled and unskilled workers are not day-to-day realities of their work lives. As great a problem as unemployment is, only about 14 percent of blue-collar workers are unemployed. Of the 86 percent who are employed, most are reasonably secure. Health and safety hazards affect a far larger proportion of the blue-collar workforce, but their impact is likely to be intermittent and invisible. For most blue-collar workers, indeed most of all types of workers, the biggest problems in the work world are traceable to the work itself.[26] *All* occupations are rife with problems for those who hold them. Since we cannot go into all these problems in this section, we will focus on one problem, *alienation*,[27] which is inherent in many occupations,[28] but is most characteristic of blue-collar workers who work in organizations, such as the automobile assembly-line worker.

Robert Blauner defines alienation in terms of its four major social-psychological consequences.[29] The first is *powerlessness*, or the feeling by individuals of being dominated by other people or objects, as well as the feeling of being unable to reduce or eliminate that control. *Meaninglessness* is people's inability to see their role in relation to other roles and their purpose in the organization. Third, alienated individuals suffer from *isolation:* they lack a feeling of belonging to the work situation and identification with the workplace. Finally, alienation involves a feeling of *self-estrangement*, which manifests itself in a lack of involvement in one's work. Self-estranged workers are unable to express their "unique abilities, potentialities, or personality." Additional consequences of self-estrangement include "boredom and monotony, the absence of personal growth, and a threat to a self-approved occupational identity."[30]

PART II: CAUSES AND CONSEQUENCES

In this section we will deal with the causes and the consequences of the three work-related problems that most plague low-status workers—unemployment, health and safety hazards, and alienation. The general logic of the analysis will be to move from macrolevel causes to more microlevel consequences of social problems.

SOCIOLOGICAL LEVEL

The Nature of Capitalism

Unemployment

Many observers argue, and the evidence seems to support their position, that un-

Table 11.3 Levels of Analysis: Economy and the Workplace

LEVELS	APPROPRIATE QUESTIONS	A PARTIAL SYNOPSIS OF PRESENT CONCLUSIONS
SOCIOLOGICAL	How is the nature of capitalism connected to work-related problems of unemployment, health and safety hazards, and alienation?	Capitalism has historically created and demanded at least some unemployment. Capitalists tend to be reckless of the health and safety of their employees in their search for profits. The basic structure of capitalism serves to alienate workers.
	How has the recent decline of American industry affected unemployment?	The decline of American industry, especially the "smokestack industries," has served to increase the unemployment rate.
	How are various social structures involved in the problem of health and safety hazards?	Certain occupations are inherently more hazardous. Employing organizations often take inadequate precautions. The federal government has tended to be lax in its control over hazardous working conditions.
	How are automated and robot technologies affecting the various work-related problems?	These technologies are greatly increasing the problem of unemployment, but they may serve to reduce health and safety hazards on the job as well as alienation.
	How is the dual labor market linked to these work-related problems?	Those in the secondary labor market are far more likely than those in the primary labor market to be confronted by unemployment, health and safety hazards, and alienation.
INDIVIDUAL	What is the impact of unemployment on the individual?	Unemployment is likely to be devastating psychologically for the individual. It is also likely to shatter many relationships. The individual is also likely to suffer a number of negative physiological reactions to being unemployed.
	What is the impact of alienation on the individual?	The worker is likely to be faced with feelings of powerlessness, meaninglessness, isolation, and self-estrangement.

(Continued)

Table 11.3 Levels of Analysis: Economy and the Workplace (*Continued*)

LEVELS	APPROPRIATE QUESTIONS	A PARTIAL SYNOPSIS OF PRESENT CONCLUSIONS
	What is the impact of health and safety hazards on the individual?	Obviously, the worker must cope with the fear of being injured. For some, the fear becomes reality and they must deal with the resulting physiological problems.

employment is a normal part of capitalist society. Unemployment tends to be highest during recessions and depressions and lowest during boom periods, but even then it never disappears. Karl Marx observed more than a century ago that one of the reasons unemployment is a continuous reality in capitalist society is that it is in the interest of the system, especially the capitalists who exploit it, to have what he called a "reserve army of unemployed."[31] Such a reserve army is useful to the capitalists in several ways. First, they can be quickly drawn into the labor force when the economy cycles up and moves into a boom period. Firms are able to expand productivity rapidly because

This farm auction in Illinois reflects a growing problem in rural America: the disappearance of the small farmer. The trend is part of an overall decline in farm employment.

(AP/Wide World Photos)

of this readily available pool of labor. Second, when the economy begins to turn downward toward a recessionary period, workers can be laid off or fired to cut costs, and they descend down into the reserve army where they generally wait until they are needed again as a result of an expanding economy. Third, a reserve army of unemployed serves to keep employees in line. Workers are well aware of the fact that if they earn the displeasure of their superiors, there are many unemployed people who would be more than willing to take their places, thereby relegating them to the reserve army of the unemployed. Although Marx's ideas are a bit dated, and we do not use his terminology ("reserve army of unemployed") today, his essential perspective remains valid—it *is* in the interest of capitalists to maintain at least some level of unemployment.

Such an explanation is useful in helping us understand the existence of unemployment throughout the history of capitalist America, but it does not help us understand the recent increase in the level of unemployment (not too many years ago a 4 or 5 percent rate of unemployment was considered a maximum acceptable level),[32] much of it seemingly quite intractable. In this context, we need to discuss basic changes in American industry, as well as the rise of the economies of other countries (for example, Japan) that have taken both business and jobs from the American economy. Before we do, however, we will need to address the relationship between capitalism and health and safety issues as well as alienation.

Health and Safety

To Marx, the capitalist is reckless of the health and safety of workers. In order to maximize profits, the capitalist is willing to ruin the health of workers and to thrust them into dangerous occupational situations. Among other things, the capitalist is willing to employ and exploit very young children, to work everyone as long as their endurance (and the law) will allow, and to employ them on tasks that are dangerous in the short run and unhealthy in the long run. For example, Marx uses material from a government report on pottery workers to show, among other things, that their work has led them to be "stunted in growth, ill-shaped, and frequently ill-formed in the chest; they become prematurely old, and are certainly short-lived."[33] In describing the manufacture of matches, Marx says: "Dante would have found the worst horrors of his Inferno surpassed in this manufacture."[34] Marx's conclusions about this issue are couched in his usual passionate rhetoric: "But in its blind unrestrainable passion, its were-wolf hunger for surplus-labour, capital oversteps not only the moral, but even the merely physical maximum bounds . . . . Capital cares nothing for the length of life of labour-power."[35] One of the reasons that the capitalist is insensitive to the health and safety needs of the proletariat is the reserve army of unemployed. Workers who are injured, made ill, or even killed by their work are easily replaced by new workers drawn from the mass of unemployed. Thus, the role played by capitalism in endangering worker safety and health is intimately related to its role in creating and sustaining unemployment.

Alienation

As was the case with unemployment and health and safety hazards, the starting point for any discussion of alienation is the work of Karl Marx.[36] In Marx's ideal world,[37] people work with nature to produce what they need to survive. They own and/or control the tools needed to make their products. They work in harmony with other people in a collective effort to produce their means of subsistence. They use and/or have control over that which they produce. Finally, they are able to express their distinctly human capacities in their work. In this ideal state, the workers are naturally interconnected to their productive activities and the means of production (tools and the like), their products, their fellow workers, and themselves.[38] It is this set of natural interconnections that is shattered, in Marx's view, by the *structure* of capitalist society.[39] In that society, the capitalist owns the resources needed to produce goods and services and the workers (proletariat) must sell their labor power to the capitalist in order to work with the "means of production." This means that the workers are separated from their products, as well as from the activities involved and the people they work with. The activities, as well as the labor of fellow workers, belong, like the product, to the capitalist. Since they no longer work for themselves, but for the capitalists, workers find themselves unable to express their distinctly human capacities in their work. It is the structural nature of capitalist society, the division between capitalists and workers, that lies at the root of alienation. Marx was well aware of the fact that alienation had adverse physiological and psychological consequences for workers, but his main concern was to describe the structural origins of alienation within capitalism. We will accept Marx's basic argument that alienation is traceable to the structures of capitalism and later discuss the consequences, primarily the psychological consequences, of alienation for blue-collar workers.

The Decline of American Industry and Unemployment

To some degree, health and safety hazards and alienation are inherent in the position of blue-collar workers within capitalist society. While unemployment is also intrinsic to capitalism, it is the case that the problem of unemployment has been heightened by the recent decline in American industry. The fact is that the decline of many American industries (or, as Bluestone and Harrison call it, "the deindustrialization of America"[40]), especially steel and autos, caused by internal problems and external competition, has been a major factor in the extraordinarily high unemployment rate to which we almost seem to have become accustomed. For example, employment in the steel industry dropped 36 percent between 1976 and 1982, from over 400,000 workers to less than 300,000 workers.[41]

A number of factors are involved in the recent rise in unemployment in America. The United States has been afflicted by aging industrial sectors, especially its smokestack industries. The inefficiencies of these outdated factories have, in turn, helped make it difficult for American industries to compete with foreign industries. On the other side, successes of foreign manufacturers on a variety of fronts have made them formidable competitors in the international marketplace. In recent years there has been an influx of legal and many illegal immigrants from Latin American and Far Eastern countries. These immigrants have taken jobs, primarily low-paying manual work, from native Americans.

Radios, TVs, and Video Recorders

It is important to underscore the role played by the failure of many American industries to compete with foreign industries in the rise in unemployment. One major example of this is the manufacture of radios and televisions. Once dominated by American firms, this industry is now controlled by Japanese companies as well as other Far Eastern manufacturers. An even more striking example is the video tape recorder industry. Invented in 1956 by an American manufacturer (Ampex), about 90 percent of all video recorders sold in the world are now manufactured in Japan, with the only competition being Philips, a Dutch manufacturer. The video recorders marketed in the United States under names like Zenith and RCA are *all* produced by Japanese manufacturers. Japanese firms were willing and able to undertake the long-term risks involved in producing a low-priced video recorder; American firms were not. Instead, Zenith and other American firms concentrated on products that guaranteed them short-term profits. In the end, the short-run rationality of these firms led to the long-term irrationality (for Americans) that it is Japanese workers and companies that are reaping the rewards of dominating the market for a product invented in America.[42]

Automobiles

However, the best-known example in this area is the success of the Japanese automobile industry. Much of this success is traceable to the skills and abilities of Japanese managers and workers. For the most part, they did not create new technologies, but rather adapted American technologies and simply used them more effectively and efficiently.[43] The success of Japan can also be traced to the failures of their American counterparts. American automobile work-

A sea of auto imports from Japan in Newark, New Jersey, illustrates the difficulties that American automobile companies have had in competing with the Japanese.

(J. P. Laffont/Sygma)

ers earned comparatively high wages and yet were characterized by high rates of absenteeism, sabotage, low productivity, and poor-quality work.

For their part, managers of American automobile firms (as well as those in many other industries) seem to have grown arrogant, contented, and unresponsive to the impending challenge from Japan. By the time that challenge actually materialized, management reaction was both too little and too late.[44] The incompetence of top-level American management was underscored by John DeLorean (one-time top executive at General Motors, creator of the DeLorean car, and indicted then acquitted in a cocaine conspiracy) in his critique of the top executives at GM:

> First and most importantly, there are a great many incompetent executives. . . . Most of our management mistakes today are not mistakes of commission, they are errors of omission. Missed opportunities—things left undone . . . we react rather than act. . . . Our inability to compete with the foreign manufacturers is more due to management failure than anything else. . . . The system and management are stifling initiative.[45]

There is little doubt that part of the blame for the failure of some American industries and, as a result, the unusually high rate of unemployment must be borne by top American management and their emphasis on short-run profitability rather than long-term growth.

Disinvestment

Another factor in the deindustrialization of America is what Barry Bluestone and Bennett Harrison call the "systematic disinvestment in the nation's basic productive capacity."[46] To maintain productivity, as well as to allow it to grow, industries must invest in basic plant and equipment. It is through this kind of industrial investment that the United States became the world's greatest economic power. However, in recent years, much of that money has been diverted from such productive investment. For example, instead of investing in new plants and equipment in the United States, corporations are investing in similar facilities in other countries. While this may be good for these other nations, and even for the corporations doing the investing, it is not good for the American economy and it certainly does not help the employability of the American worker. Another example of disinvestment is the many billions of dollars spent in recent years in the mergers of huge corporations. From the point of view of the economy as the whole, as well as the workers in it, these billions would have been far better spent in investment in productive capacity. Mergers, in themselves, produce no new factories, technologies, or jobs. They do, however, help pad the bank accounts of stockholders and top executives.

The success of Japanese industry (as well as that of other rising industrial states) *and* the failure of American industry have helped lead to the heightened level of unemployment in this country.

Occupations, Organizations, and the Government

We can specify a number of large-scale causes of safety and health hazards on the job, including the inherent nature of the occupation, the employing organization, the role of the federal government, and society as a whole. In emphasizing such large-scale causes, we do not mean to imply that individuals (for example, through carelessness on the job) may not at times cause such problems for themselves.

Occupations and Organizations

Danger of one sort or another is built into a wide array of *occupations* and while the hazards can be minimized, they can never be completely eliminated. Examples include construction workers laboring on the skeletons of rising skyscrapers; firemen dealing with a blaze; miners and the dangers of cave-ins; and police officers trying to apprehend criminals. *Employing organizations* often take improper precautions, do not supply workers with relevant information, supply defective or ineffective safety equipment, perform inadequate safety inspections, and refuse to admit that dangers exist.

The Role of the Government

In addition to tracing causes of health and safety hazards to the nature of the occupation and the employing organization, we can also place some responsibility with the government. The federal government has tended to be lax in terms of its control over hazardous work conditions. It was not until 1970 that comprehensive legislation on this matter was passed. The Occupational Safety and Health Act of 1970 recognized, for the first time, "the right of the government to inspect, cite, and penalize employers for infringements of the right of workers to labor under safe and healthy conditions."[47] The federal agency created in 1971 to deal with these problems was the Occupational Safety and Health Administration (OSHA). It is widely believed that OSHA was founded to mollify labor and that there was no real intention of dramatically altering health and safety conditions in the workplace.[48] However, the degree of its activity has been shaped by the philosophy of the president in power. During the Carter administration (1976–1980), OSHA tended to be very active. A number of improvements in occupational safety and health were made and workers grew more aware of, and knowledgeable about, hazards on the job. Under the Reagan administration "the agency has throttled down or off on many of its regulatory controls, shrinking the scope of work-place inspections and putting a hold on . . . health and safety standards the agency is supposed to produce."[49] In the first two years of the Reagan administration, the number of serious citations given to industry was halved and penalties levied dropped from twenty-five million dollars to five million dollars. Although some gains have been made over the years, the fact remains that major health and safety hazards remain and less rather than more is being done about them. A former official of the AFL-CIO sums up the problem: "you can have a carnage in the work place and no one cares. If we did, we'd have a program that works."[50]

Technological Change

Special and detailed attention must be given to the role of technological change in unemployment because we are now entering an era in which automation and robots are going to replace a large number of semiskilled and unskilled workers.[51] The modern industrial robot is a rather clumsy-looking machine, a combination machine tool and computer, that is already capable of performing the rather simple tasks formerly assigned to lower-level blue-collar workers. In the future, more sophisticated robots with the ability to "see" and with tactile senses will begin to replace more skilled workers.[52]

Industrial robots have a number of advantages over human workers including the fact that they are cheaper (it is estimated a robot can pay for itself in as little as two years); they do not complain, even on the jobs considered worst by human workers; they work faster; they never tire; they are accurate time after time; they are impervious to danger; they are not troubled by uncomfortable working conditions; and they are not bothered by depressingly monotonous tasks.

The big advance in robot technology is the adaptability of the newer robots. Many come equipped with a variety of sensing devices that allow them to recognize defects and adjust to handling misfed materials. Instead of being relegated to the junk heap, or being rebuilt, the new robots can simply be reprogrammed to handle new requirements. As a result of such advances, the emerging factory of the future will be one in which robots do an increasingly large share of the basic tasks while a skeleton labor force will be retained to oversee and maintain the robot workforce.

Management is drawn to robots because they are superior to human workers, especially in jobs involving simple manual tasks, and this will lead to higher levels of unemployment. We will be replacing more and more manual workers with robots, and in the process we will be creating factories with fewer and fewer workers.[53] However, it would be wrong to conclude that no people would be associated with factory work of the future. They will be there, but they will serve primarily in support functions.[54]

As attractive as robots are to employers, they are generally seen by workers, and rightly so in many cases, as a threat to them and their jobs.[55] Although workers may welcome robots for their ability to do dirty, dangerous, or repetitive jobs, they are feared more because of their potential for replacing many manual workers. The fear is that not only will such workers be replaced, but that millions of semiskilled and unskilled jobs will never be created. The fact is that robots are not simply an extension of previous technological advances, they are an entirely new technology. While all previous technologies required people to operate them, robots compete directly with humans and will eventually replace many of them.[56]

The potential impact of automation and robot technology on blue-collar work is staggering. Experts have suggested that eventually technology "may be refined to such an extent that most factory work could be carried out by robots and automated machinery."[57] Nearly "one-third of all manufacturing employment" could be eliminated by 1990, and sometime after that "it will become technically possible to replace all manufacturing operatives in the automotive, electrical-equipment, machinery, and fabricated-metals industry."[58] In the automobile industry, it is estimated that 20 percent of existing jobs will be eliminated by 1995. General Motors alone plans on having 14,000 robots installed and operating by 1990.[59] Overall, by 1990 about 200,000 robots are expected to be in operation in various industries.

Technological Change, Alienation, and Safety and Health

We have been concentrating on the effect of technological change on unemployment. While it is clear that advancing technology will increase unemployment, at least in the short run, it is likely to have a more positive effect on the problems of health and safety, as well as alienation. Many of the most dangerous and unhealthy jobs are likely to be among the first to be automated, with robots replacing human beings. This is clearly an advance for those workers who will no longer be required to work on such jobs. Similarly, we can anticipate that it is the most alienating jobs that will be automated in the near future. These are the simplest jobs—the ones on which it is easiest to replace a human being with a machine. Again, there is a gain here to those who will no longer be forced to perform such numbing tasks. It seems clear that we have a trade-off of problems here. Automation and robots will serve to reduce the problems of alienation and health and safety hazards, but at the cost of increasing unemployment.

Dual Labor Market

Another of the structures that can be related to the problems of unemployment, health and safety hazards, and alienation is the *dual labor market.*[60] The basic premise of the dual labor market theory is that there are two labor markets in the United States. One is the *primary labor market* that involves higher-status and higher-paying occupations. Included here would be such high-status occupations as those of scientists, executives, and managers. These occupations offer incumbents a considerable amount of job security. They tend to have comparatively lengthy career ladders associated with them so that incumbents can anticipate considerable mobility over the course of their work lives. These jobs are likely to require both a good deal of education and considerable training. In some cases, they may require specific educational credentials. People in such occupations often are allowed considerable discretion in how they do their work.

The other major component of the dual labor market is the *secondary labor market* encompassing lower-status, lower-paying, and more unstable occupations. These occupations require little in the way of education or training. Few skills are needed and there is little in the way of upward mobility; these are dead-end jobs. There is a high turnover rate since employers have little need to invest in such workers and the workers have little incentive to remain in a given job. Those who work on these kinds of jobs are likely to be given little or no discretion in their work. What they do is likely to be rigidly controlled by the external demands of supervisors and/or the technology on which they work. Included here would be the semiskilled and unskilled—the low-status occupations that have been discussed throughout this section.

There is little mobility between these two labor markets. Thus, those who start in the primary labor market are unlikely to sink into the secondary labor market. Conversely, those who begin their careers in the secondary labor market are unlikely to rise into the primary labor market. There are major structural barriers between these two labor markets. For example, the possession of advanced degrees and special credentials tends to separate those in the primary labor market from those in the secondary labor market.

Returning to our main concerns here, the point is that the dual labor market is related to the problems discussed in this chapter. Those in the secondary labor market are more likely to experience unemployment, health and safety hazards on the job, and alienation. This is not to say that these problems are nonexistent in the primary labor market, but that they are much less likely to be found there.

Having covered in this section a number of the macrolevel causes of unemployment, health and safety hazards, and alienation, we turn now to a discussion of some of the effects of these problems on individuals.

INDIVIDUAL LEVEL

Unemployment

Needless to say, unemployment usually has a devastating effect on individuals.[61] First, there is the obvious economic impact of being unemployed. Few people have the resources to weather more than a few months of unemployment comfortably. There is unemployment insurance, but that does not last forever. Some take odd jobs as busboys or janitors to help tide them over, but these are usually only temporary jobs. Then people start selling their possessions. The next step might be the sale of one's own blood in order to get a little money to continue on. Finally, when all else has failed, there is the public dole, welfare.

This brings us to the psychological effects of being unemployed. Since work is the central way of organizing life for most people, and a source of self-esteem for many, being unemployed is often a devastating psychological blow. Here is the psychological reaction of one factory worker to being unemployed:

> "My job was my whole life. That's all I did. It's unbearable now. Staying home is terrible. I can't go on like this."[62]

Reactions to unemployment may include grief, disbelief, shock, numbness, rage, and feelings of worthlessness. As these feelings mount, the unemployed worker may become mentally ill and be driven to a series of self-destructive behaviors—alcoholism, drug addiction, and suicide—as well as behaviors aimed at striking out at others, including spouse abuse, child abuse, theft and even murder.[63]

Pictured is a recently laid-off steelworker in a Pennsylvania unemployment office. Unemployment is almost always a devastating experience, especially in an industry like steel where the jobs may never be filled again.

(J. P. Laffont/Sygma)

Existing interpersonal relations are likely to be shattered by unemployment. Ties with former colleagues on the job may be broken, especially if the friends remain on the job. Friendship patterns outside the job also are likely to be sorely tested by the economic and psychological strains of unemployment. Even relationships with family members may well be adversely affected by being unemployed.

Finally, unemployment is likely to have adverse physiological effects on individuals. Unemployment can lead to heightened blood pressure with the result that there is an increased likelihood of heart disease. A number of other diseases have been related to unemployment, but while the likelihood of disease increases, the probability of getting medical help declines because of the loss of health insurance, as well as the unemployed person's inability to afford adequate medical help.[64] A decline in physical health could also be traced to poorer diets, less regular eating habits, poorer quality living arrangements, more time on the move, and the like. There are millions of stories like the following, but it will give the reader a feel for the physiological (and psychological) impact of unemployment:

> Jimmy Thomas, with nothing to do all day but watch television and sift through bills he is helpless to pay, became a compulsive overeater, out of sheer anxiety. 'I'm extremely on edge until 5 p.m.,' he says. 'That's when I know all the bill collectors have gone home'. . . . After two years of this, Jimmy Thomas's body has ballooned up to 309 pounds. He has high blood pressure and last August had a heart attack, though he is only 33. 'Some people drink—I don't drink,' he says. 'Some people use drugs—I don't use drugs. I use food.'[65]

Thus, the unemployed worker is likely to suffer economically, psychologically, interpersonally, and physiologically.

Alienation

Although most blue-collar workers are afflicted in varying degrees with alienation, the following discussion will focus primarily on the best example of this, the automobile assembly-line worker. Keep in mind, however, that workers in higher status occupations, such as professionals, semiprofessionals, and white-collar employees, also are confronted with alienation.

Automobile assembly-line workers perform their assigned tasks (tightening a bolt, fastening a fender, and the like) at set intervals and no variation is permitted. For eight hours or so each day the worker performs the same task again and again. Says one such worker: "What's there to say? A car comes, I weld it; a car comes, I weld it. One hundred and one times an hour."[66] A spot-welder on one automobile assembly-line describes his job this way:

> I stand in one spot, about two- or three-feet area, all night. The only time a person stops is when the line stops. We do about thirty-two jobs per car, per unit, forty-eight units an hour, eight hours a day. Thirty-two times forty-eight times eight. Figure it out, that's how many times I push that button.[67]

Respite from this kind of work comes when the line breaks down, an event many workers hope for and sometimes contribute to by sabotaging the machinery:

> Sabotage? . . . Last week I watched a guy light a glove and lock it in the trunk. We all waited to see how far down the line they'd discover it.[68]

As a result of the nature of the work and the reactions to it (like sabotage), the automobile assembly-line worker has been called the "classic symbol of the subjection of man to the machine in our industrial age."[69] In Blauner's estimation, it is the automobile assembly line in which "technological, organizational and economic factors" combine to produce the most alienating work environment.[70] More recently, a scathing critique of work on a French automobile assembly line concluded that such work is "destructive to health, reasonable existence, and human dignity."[71]

What is it about the assembly line that makes it such a nightmare for most people? In other words, what makes the assembly line so alienating?

Powerlessness

For one thing, assembly-line workers are almost totally powerless. They are unable to control the pace of the line, their superiors, or top management. The machines are set by the engineers and they are designed to get the maximum productivity from each worker. Once the speed of the line is determined, there is little workers can do to affect it. As a result, workers are unable to control their own pace of work. This is perhaps the most demoralizing aspect of the job, and it differentiates assembly-line work from almost all other occupations since both the rate of work and the kind of work are invariable and uncontrollable. There is some degree of powerlessness in virtually all occupations, but most workers have some control over pace and kind of work. Even the lowliest clerks can usually vary their own work pace and make their work more interesting by changing tasks from time to time.

The assembly-line workers are also characterized by an inability to control their immediate supervisors. For one thing, it is difficult for them to interact with their foremen. The combination of noise, job pressure, and the need for continual attention to the line makes it impossible to communicate with anyone. Even if assembly-line workers could communicate with their supervisors, they would have little chance of affecting their behavior. In fact, workers have few resources that can be used to gain something from their supervisors, for they have few skills and are easily replaceable. Their almost total unimportance to the organization further increases the assembly-line workers' sense of powerlessness. They lack even the power to leave the work scene occasionally because their absence would be noticed immediately. It is also hard for them to quit, especially in these tough times for the automobile industry, because they have few skills and would find it extremely difficult to find other positions.

Meaninglessness

For a variety of reasons, assembly-line workers tend to find their work meaningless. They are unable to see what their very specialized tasks have to do with the work of others on the line or with those who work at other levels in the organization. They are also unable to see what tightening a bolt has to do with the finished product (and in some cases they may not even know what the finished product is). Finally, the intrinsic nature of the job contributes to a feeling of meaninglessness. The work is so specialized, so uninteresting, and so unimportant that is difficult for anyone to derive any gratification from the work itself.

Isolation

The assembly-line workers' problems are compounded by their isolation. The noise and the demands of the line prevent interaction on the job, making it difficult for friendship groups to develop at the workplace. The workers are also isolated from white-collar workers and all levels of management. Both of these groups try to keep what they consider to be the proper distance from manual workers. Assembly-line work is usually found in large plants and their size also serves to inhibit the development of personal relationships. Huge cafeterias and parking lots are hardly conducive to the development of personal interaction.

Self-estrangement

Finally, those who work on the assembly line are particularly prone to self-estrangement. This means that the workers are simply unable to express their abilities in their work. The work is boring and monotonous, requiring continual attention but little skill or involvement in the task or in the employing organization. Hence they daydream, perhaps these days about robots that will rescue them from their jobs. Unfortunately, since they are lacking in skills and abilities, the assembly-line workers that are displaced by robots are going to find it difficult to obtain another job of any kind, let alone one better than the position they have.

Health and Safety Problems

Instead of offering generalizations about the effect of health and safety hazards on individual workers, in this section we look at the dangers confronting individuals in two types of low-status occupations.

Nightworkers

We do not often think of it, but nightwork can be particularly dangerous to one's health and safety. There are approximately 10 million people who work at times other than during the day. And the vast majority of those who work at night are in low-status occupations. They confront a variety of risks. Police on night patrol obviously face more danger than those who work during daylight hours. Taxi drivers are safer from robbers and muggers during the day, but are often driven to nightwork by the higher income. Beyond the safety risks, there are added health problems. Nightwork can disrupt the body's natural biological rhythms. Nightworkers tend to sleep less than dayworkers and the sleep that they do get tends to be less restful. Nightwork also often leads to disruption of eating habits, which causes loss of appetite and gastrointestinal ailments.[72]

Coal Miners

One of the most dangerous occupations is coal mining. The history of coal mining is dotted with cave-ins and explosions. In the 1940s, a thousand or more miners a year died in the mines. More recently, coal mining seemed to have grown somewhat safer with only 106 miners dying in accidents in 1978. In the 1980s, however, we have begun to see an upturn in accidents (over 150 deaths in 1981) as a result of increased levels of mining and a decline in governmental inspections. At the same time, citations for violations and civil penalties paid by mine owners dropped substantially.[73] In addition to the physical danger, remember that coal miners, as a result of the coal dust they inhale on the job, are subjected to very high rates of the debilitating, and often fatal, black lung disease, as well as a variety of other illnesses of the lung.

PART III: RESPONSES

In this section on responses to economic problems, we will follow the pattern employed in the preceding section. That is, we will begin with some macrolevel responses to the problems of unemployment, safety and health hazards, and alienation. Then, we will turn to a discussion to some of the ways in which individuals respond to these problems.

MACROLEVEL RESPONSES

The Socialist Alternative

A Marxist would argue that the solution to the problems of unemployment, health and safety hazards, and alienation (and many other problems as well) is comparatively simple—overthrow the capitalist system in which these are inherent problems and replace it with a socialist or communist system that has no such structural necessities. Few of the readers of these words would accept this solution since most tend to be committed to capitalism and critical of the alternatives. In any case, there is evidence of the continued existence of these problems in communist and socialist societies. More importantly, in those societies there seem to be other economic problems such as a lack of many consumer goods, long waits for some products, considerable inefficiency, and poor product quality. It *may* be that another economic system would be the solution to the problems discussed in this chapter, but few, at least at this point in our history, would consider such alternatives, let alone fight for one of them. Since such a massive overhaul seems unlikely, we need to consider some less extreme solutions to the problems of unemployment, health and safety hazards, and alienation.

Before moving to other responses, it should be noted that this critique of contemporary communist and socialist societies does *not* constitute an adequate critique of Marx's original theory. Contemporary socialist and communist societies are a long way from the ideal developed by Marx. Marx's image of an ideal communist society *would* constitute a much more adequate response to the problems discussed in this chapter. However, despite many efforts, no society has even come close to Marx's model.

Employee-Owned Companies

Despite the lack of any deep sentiment in America for socialism as a solution to the problem of unemployment, it is worth noting that there is increasing evidence, albeit still very limited, of grass-roots interest in a kind of socialistic solution—employee-owned companies. In 1976 there were less than 300 employee-owned companies in the United States, but by 1983 that number had grown to more than 5,000.[74] While most of these companies were either owned by the employees from the beginning, or had moved over the years in that direction, a significant number involve efforts by workers to buy the company and make it more profitable. Such efforts are primarily designed to avert unemployment, but it is also possible that employee-owned companies would be less dangerous, less unhealthy, and less alienating.

Invigorating the American Economy

If one rejects the idea of converting the United States from a capitalist to a socialist system, then the focus shifts to the issue of reforms that can be instituted within the American capitalist system. One of the most pressing needs is that the American economy do a better job of competing in the international arena. A more vigorous economy would reduce the level of unemployment, although it would seem to offer little hope either of improving health and safety conditions or reducing alienation. The need for an invigorated economy has come to be called by many experts the need for a new national *industrial policy.*[75] There are great differences among experts on what this national industrial policy should look like. Some see the need for greater government support of American industry, while others feel that the government is already too involved in supporting inept industries that might be better off being allowed to fail. Some, although not many, argue for an effort to revive traditional smokestack industries like automobiles and steel. Most believe that those industries have been lost, at least into the foreseeable future, to Japan, South Korea, Hong Kong, and even China. Thus, most of the attention seems to be focused on maintaining control over, and expanding upon, the so-called "high-tech" industries like computers, semiconductors, telecommunications, robotics, aerospace, and biotechnology. The best-known center of high-tech industry in the United States is "Silicon Valley" in California, but perhaps an even more hopeful model for the future of the United States is found in recent developments in New England.

The Renaissance in New England

As is well known, New England was, at one time, the center of the industrial revolution in the United States. It contained many of the early smokestack industries such as textiles and shoes. However, in the twentieth century New England underwent an economic decline that was to foreshadow what was to happen to the Midwest with its smokestack industries. By 1975 New England had the highest unemployment rate in the United States. However, it was at about that time that things began to improve. New England possesses some of the finest universities in the United States, and these universities acted as magnets for some of the early high-technology industries. While these new industries did not provide jobs for the semiskilled and unskilled workers who had been laid off by the smokestack industries, they did provide a whole range of new jobs for highly skilled technical, professional, and managerial workers. This has been the basis of an economic renaissance in New England, which can be said to have "become the Japan of the United States."[76]

Are High-Tech Industries the Answer?

Although this is certainly a success story, it is easy to overstate its significance. The fact is that while a few displaced workers were able to find jobs in these new industries, the vast majority were forced into lesser jobs, or out of the labor force altogether. Thus, the negative effects of the deindustrialization of the old New England factories continues to outweigh the gains made by the high-technology industries. More generally, the accepted view is that even if high-technology industries are enormously successful, they can never compensate for the declines in traditional industries. Further reducing the luster of high-tech industries is that they will face increasing competition from various sources, especially Japan and other Far Eastern countries. Beyond that, some cracks have already begun to appear in the image of unmitigated success that has accompanied high-tech industries. At this moment, some of the computer companies such as Texas Instruments and Atari are facing grave difficulties. In fact, Atari is shifting some of its jobs from Silicon Valley in California to Hong Kong and Taiwan and thousands of workers are losing their jobs. Could it be that the high-technology revolution has already run its course? Probably not, but it does seem unlikely that it will solve our economic woes, especially our unemployment problems. An AFL-CIO official said of this development: "It clearly indicates that the high-tech firms are also moving abroad and that they are no guarantee for absorbing the nation's jobless."[77]

In fact, a majority of the jobs into the 1990s will be available in the white-collar clerical, service worker, and professional categories.[78] Although millions of new jobs will open up in these areas, there is little hope that the factory workers laid off in the last few years will find their way into them. In most cases they lack the skills, education, training, life styles, or interpersonal

The growth of new and advanced technologies is radically altering clerical work.
(Charles Gupton/Southern Light)

abilities to succeed in many of these occupations. There is a need to develop a massive training program for these workers. Paraphrasing Karl Marx's famous revolutionary call, two authors said: "Workers of the Future Re-Tool! Nothing to Lose But Your Jobs."[79] While much more can and should be done, it is hard to envision a scenario in which the bulk of these displaced workers find their way into either high-tech industries or high-status occupations. This means that we are likely to find ourselves as a nation in which millions of ex-employees of smokestack industries are unable to find stable employment for the rest of their lives, except perhaps in low-status, low-paying service jobs like those in the fast-food industry. Since many of the workers laid off were and are the youngest in terms of seniority, we are likely to have to support these people with money, psychological counseling, medical aid, and the like for twenty, thirty, even forty years. Their children can be trained for new industries or high-status occupations, but they are likely to be part of a lost generation of American workers.

Managerial Reform

Management in both traditional smokestack industries and more contemporary high-tech industries is also going to have to play a significant role in reinvigorating the American economy. Management is going to have to become more competent and more farsighted in order for American industry to do a better job of competing in the international arena. Let us look at two recent and important efforts to outline needed managerial reforms—William Ouchi's *Theory Z*[80] and Thomas Peters and

Robert Waterman's *In Search of Excellence.*[81]

Theory Z

William Ouchi outlines a number of reasons for the success of Japanese industry. He emphasizes a variety of practices and policies that serve to give Japanese managers a long-run rather than a short-run perspective, as well as a broad-scale orientation rather than the narrow, specialist view that tends to characterize American managers. Thus, for example, the guarantee of lifetime employment (at least at the major Japanese firms) allows Japanese managers to think in terms of long-range success whereas American managers, who lack any such long-term employment guarantees, are forced to demonstrate success almost immediately. Furthermore, the Japanese policy of rotating managers among a variety of specialties tends to give them a wide-ranging perspective on the organization while the American practice of specialized managers gives them a much narrower perspective. Despite these and other advantages, Ouchi does *not* think that it is possible or desirable for American managers to emulate the Japanese model. Rather, he thinks that there are organizations in the United States that have developed practices that have many of the elements of the Japanese model, but which are better adapted to American culture. These organizations operate on the basis of what he calls "Theory Z" and he contrasts this to "Theory X," which dominates traditional American industry.

Ouchi sees Theory X as the approach that has gotten American industry into so much trouble. Among other things, Theory X stands for a high degree of specialization, an absence of long-term employment guarantees, rapid employee evaluation and promotion, short-term outlooks, an adversarial relationship between management and worker, managerial efforts to control and routinize work in the organization, a formal and bureaucratic structure, emphasis on monetary incentives to workers and profits for the corporation, and a corporate culture that emphasizes little more than maximizing income and profits.

In contrast, Ouchi argues that there are organizations that utilize an alternate approach, Theory Z, and as a result promise to be more successful in allowing American industry to compete in the international arena. These organizations encourage nonspecialized career paths with more mobility between managerial functions, longer-term employment guarantees, more measured evaluation and promotion, longer-term outlooks, greater trust between management and worker, respect for the subtleties involved in work in the organization, rather than efforts to control and routinize work, an informal and more clan-like organizational structure, an emphasis on nonmonetary incentives and organizational goals, and a strong and elaborate corporate culture that emphasizes such things as service to the customer and contributions to the larger society. The thrust of Ouchi's argument is that American industry would do a far better job of competing in the international marketplace if it replaced its traditional reliance on Theory X with Theory Z.

In Search of Excellence

Peters and Waterman also criticize traditional American managerial practices and they, too, argue that an alternative already exists within American industry. In their view there are "excellent" American corporations (for example, Delta Airlines, IBM, Hewlett-Packard, 3M) and what is needed is that traditional American industries alter their policies so that they more closely resemble those of the excellent companies.

The excellent corporations are those that have been able to be both large and continually innovative. A number of things have allowed these companies to prevent their large size from keeping them from being innovative. They have a bias for action rather than developing elaborate blueprints for action that may never materialize. This allows them to try out various ideas; they have a willingness to experiment. Excellent companies prize innovators, and they seek to foster, support, and protect them. They also respect lower-status workers within the organization. Workers are "seen as a source of ideas" and therefore as much more important than machines and other capital investments.[82] Excellent corporations are unified around a broad philosophy and value system; they are not simply motivated by profit maximization. Among the most important of these values is the need to serve the needs of the customer. While these organizations are tightly organized around such central values, they allow the workers within the organization considerable autonomy. There is a disinclination to proliferate top-level managers. In fact, excellent companies tend to have lean central managements and very simple organizational forms.

The models of the "excellent" and the Theory Z organizations are not the only ones available, but they illustrate the point that managerial reforms are needed if American industry is to compete more effectively in the world market. More competitive American industry is an answer to a number of specific problems, especially reducing the problem of unemployment.

Technological Change

As was pointed out earlier, technological changes such as automation and robotics that are serving to exacerbate such problems as unemployment may also help to reduce accidents and health hazards on the job, as well as the alienating conditions in the workplace. Automated technologies and robots will be taking over the most dangerous jobs in American industry. Many lives will be saved and many more injuries averted because of the employment of these technologies. Unfortunately, many of the long-term unemployed we are likely to encounter in the future might well welcome another chance at such dangerous occupations. In addition, those who will be able to avoid dangerous jobs might well be forced to replace them with the stress and tension of long-term and hopeless unemployment. Thus, they may end up substituting emotional problems for physical dangers.

While new technologies promise to eliminate some old dangers, they also threaten to confront workers with a whole new set of dangers. Increased use of nuclear energy, for example, is a clear danger to all of those who come into contact with it. One nuclear power plant accident could wipe out the gains from injuries prevented by substituting robots for humans on thousands of dangerous tasks.

It seems clear that with the coming of automation and robots, we will see the disappearance of a large number of the most alienating jobs in the United States in the next few decades. On the automobile assembly line, for example, most of the menial tasks now being performed by people will come to be performed by robots and other technologies. The classic symbol of alienated work, the automobile assembly-line worker (and many other assembly-line workers), will become a disappearing breed. This is not to say that all low-status, alienating jobs will be taken over by robots. Highly alienating jobs that employ relatively few people, or are found in relatively small organizations, are likely to be with us for some time to come. Beyond that, in other areas it has yet to be shown that the new technologies make work any less alienating. For example, will the modern office workers find typing on a word processor any less alienating than past workers found the pounding of typewriters?

Nevertheless, alienation exists throughout the entire occupational structure of capitalist society. Elimination of the most alienating jobs at the bottom of the hierarchy will leave the rest of the occupational structure untouched. Alienation, as it is manifested in feelings of powerlessness, meaninglessness, isolation, and self-estrangement, is likely to be with us as long as capitalism is with us.

Organizational Responses

Organizations such as corporations and governmental agencies are able to respond to the problems discussed in this chapter in various ways. For example, in the 1970s there was considerable interest among corporate managers in efforts to deal with the problem of alienation. This is much less significant in the 1980s since, for one thing, many blue-collar workers, who are the most likely to be alienated, are happy to have any job, even an alienating one. Thus they are putting much less pressure on management to deal with the problem. In addition, management now tends to see automation and robots as the evolving answer to alienation and is therefore unwilling to invest in programs to deal with the problem since many of these jobs are likely to be eliminated in the next decade or two. Nevertheless, we can expect management to continue to invest some time and money in such programs as *job enlargement*, which involves adding a number of activities to jobs in order to make them less alienating, *job rotation*, which involves rotating workers among jobs so that they are not as alienated by a single repetitive job, and the *democratization* of work, which involves giving the employees more of a say in how the job should be organized and performed.[83]

Various organizations may also respond to the problems of occupational safety and health hazards. At the minimum, what is required is greater vigilance and reform efforts by various governmental agencies, employers, and unions. Unfortunately, the federal government, at least at the moment, seems less, rather than more, interested in dealing with health and safety matters. Beyond that, there is little to indicate that employers and unions are doing any better today at dealing with threats to workers' health and safety than they have in the past.

Unions

The problems of unemployment, health and safety hazards, and alienation would *seem* to be the kinds of things that labor unions were created to deal with. Thus, the reader might ask why we have said so little up to now about the role of unions in responding to these problems. The answer is that the union movement in the United States is in such a weakened condition that it might be better thought of as a social problem itself, rather than as a solution to other problems. Membership in American labor unions peaked in 1953 with 25.5 percent of the labor force and it remained more or less at that level for more than a decade. However, in recent years the labor movement has begun to decline and in 1980 its membership dipped to under 21 percent of the labor force.[84] In the 1980s the decline has accelerated and by 1984 union membership was only 18.8 percent of the labor force.[85] In addition to a decline in membership, there also seems to be a significant decline in support for unions within the population as a whole.[86] Ongoing changes make the future prospects of the labor movement look bleak.

The strength of the labor movement has been, and continues to be, among blue-collar workers. The labor movement has been much less successful in organizing white-collar and service workers. In coming years the number of blue-collar workers is likely to decline and the number of white-collar and service workers to increase. Thus, the traditional base of the union movement will continue to erode and there are no signs of great inroads into the ranks of white-collar and service workers. Even within the blue-collar ranks, problems await union leaders. The greatest strength of unions within the blue-collar ranks has been in the smokestack industries, like autos and steel, and their continued decline is likely to mean fewer blue-collar members for the unions in the future. The kinds of workers (professionals, technicians, and scientists) who will be drawn to the high-tech industries have never been very receptive to unions and show no signs of changing their stance. Similarly, those drawn into the service industries have traditionally resisted unionization, and this area is likely to enjoy big growth. To take a striking example, McDonald's employs *three times* the number of people who work for U.S. Steel. Most of these are teenagers who work for relatively short periods of time while still in school. These workers are not readily available to the union movement. In addition, unions have never been very successful in certain areas of the country (for example, the South and Southwest), and that situation is not likely to improve significantly. This failure is made even more troublesome by the fact that these are the areas that are likely to experience major economic development in the coming decades. A number of companies (among them, IBM, DuPont, Polaroid, and Texas Instruments) have resisted unionization, as have many whole industries. Overall, in fact, the unions in recent years have been more involved in giving back past gains than they have been in winning new advances for their members.[87]

Thus, all of the trends seem to point in the direction of American unions growing able to do less, not more, to respond to such work-related problems as unemployment, safety and health hazards, and alienation. Even if unions are unable to do more in these areas, they still contribute to a mitigation of problems at work. The *threat* of unionization helps give workers in non-unionized firms higher pay and better working conditions. Were it not for the threat of unionization, there are employers who would want to roll back the gains of the last century and return to the kinds of adverse conditions that existed in the heyday of the Industrial Revolution. And unions have done things to aid the unemployed, make work safer, and reduce alienation. None of this is to say that unions have been ideal. In fact, unions have themselves created an array of problems for their members (for example, unresponsive leaders), management (via impossible demands), and the larger society (as a result of union corruption). Overall, one could say that unions have had some impact on reducing work-related problems and, despite some trends that threaten their current status, they could still play a positive role in the future in helping to cope with those problems.

Union-Management Cooperation

While unions may not be able to do much about the problems discussed in this chapter on their own, they might be able to contribute to solutions through an increase in cooperation between labor and management.[88] Historically, capitalism has been built on an adversary relationship between management and workers (and their unions). In a number of instances, unions and their members have come to realize that they have a vested interest in keeping the employing organization in business. Among other things, this may involve union and worker willingness to reduce future demands, cut back on past gains, cooperate with management in making production more efficient, serve in administrative positions, and even become stockholders in the corporation. Through such efforts, unions and workers hope to buttress their employing organization, thereby keeping people off the unemployment rolls. But these efforts must not be one-sided and management, too, must be willing to make concessions in order to mitigate work-related problems.

MICROLEVEL RESPONSES

In the preceding section we have examined a wide array of macrolevel responses to the problems of unemployment, hazards on the job, and alienation. In this section, we turn to some of the ways in which individuals and groups have sought to cope with these problems. However, although such efforts exist, individuals, or small groups of people, can do comparatively little about the kinds of problems discussed in this chapter. This is especially true of unemployment and health and safety hazards. Clearly, the basic causes of unemployment lie far beyond anything individual workers can affect. For example, unemployment is, as we saw earlier, built into the basic structure of capitalist society, as well as its inherent cyclical character. Obviously, the individual worker, or even groups of workers, can have little or no impact on such structural dynamics. The same can be said about health and safety problems, although it is possible to think of more things that workers can do (for example, wear protective garb, insist on safer working conditions) to protect themselves. It is in the area of alienation that we find more evidence of meaningful worker responses to problems. This is not to say that workers can affect the macrolevel causes of alienating working conditions, but they have been able to develop a variety of devices that serve to reduce, at least to some degree, the negative impact of alienation.

Given the likelihood of the continued existence of alienation, we are likely to see a continuation of efforts by individual workers, and groups of workers, to deal with it. There is a rich body of sociological research on such efforts,[89] which include restriction of output, evasion of company regulations and supervision, sabotage, playing games to make the work more tolerable, and exaggerating the significance of one's work. These efforts are never very successful since they do not deal with the basic sources of the problem—the nature of capitalist society, as well as the character of the occupations and organizations in which people work. Yet they allow people to survive in such work and that is not an insignificant accomplishment. The conclusion of this section, and this chapter, will deal with some of these efforts.

Restriction of Output

One way that groups of workers can exhibit their power, while striking back at management for creating alienating working conditions, is by banding together to limit their productivity so that it is below management's expectations and demands. The famous studies at the Hawthorne plant of the Western Electric Company in Chicago first brought these informal practices to the attention of the social scientist.[90] In one component of the study, an incentive system was employed based upon productivity. It was felt that tying pay to productivity would lead to higher output. However, the work group developed and successfully enforced an informal norm of what *they* defined as a "fair day's work" and it was below what the organization expected. The work group, its power over the members, and its ability to defy management were sources of satisfaction to workers and this satisfaction helped mitigate, at least partially, the negative effects of alienation.

Evading the Rules

Similar satisfactions can be derived from evading the rules of the organization. In one study of a machine shop, Donald Roy showed that workers evaded the rules by cheating, loafing, swindling, and conniving.[91] Roy was a participant observer in this study and he noted that "we machine operators did 'figure the angles,' we developed an impressive repertoire of angles to play and devoted ourselves to crossing the expectations of formal organization with perseverance, artistry, and organizing ability of our own."[92] The preeminent function of these activities is to enhance the meaningfulness of work for low-status workers. The informal group, its norms, its cohesiveness, and its efforts to beat the system all serve to ameliorate the negative effects of alienation.

Games Workers Play

In other studies, Roy examined informal group practices that are not aimed against management but do nevertheless serve to make work life more meaningful, less alienating.[93] Roy was interested in what prevented workers from "going nuts." In one study of the repetitive work of machine operators, he was concerned with devices operators used to find some meaning in this otherwise essentially meaningless occupation. Roy found that each worker tried to make a game out of his work and that the group as a whole developed a series of little games to help pass the work day. For example, during the morning "peach time" was announced, at which time one worker took out two peaches and divided them among four workers. Then there was "banana time." The same man who brought the peaches also brought one banana, which was supposedly for his own consumption. However, regularly each morning one of the workers would steal the banana and consume it gleefully while shouting "banana time!" The person who brought the banana would routinely protest, and just as regularly another worker would admonish him for protesting so vociferously. As the day progressed there were "window time," "fish time," and "coke time." Through these games workers on essentially meaningless jobs endeavored to make their work life more meaningful.

These, and other, responses by individuals and groups demonstrate that while people strive to cope with alienation, as well as other work-related problems, such efforts are ultimately futile since they fail to address the macrolevel causes of these problems. The implication is that these problems can only be meaningfully dealt with at the macrolevels from which they emanate. In fact, in a recent study, Michael Burawoy suggests that the kinds of worker activities described in this section succeed only in helping to support the capitalist system that is the basic cause of many of the problems.[94] Indeed, Burawoy argues that management actively participates in these games. The games are played within the limits of acceptable profit margins and help to support basic work rules. Worker activities of the types described in this section do not attack the basic causes of the problems; rather they serve to reaffirm them and to allow the worker to assent to them more willingly and less as the result of external coercion.

SUMMARY

1. The context for the discussion of work-related problems in this chapter is the changing nature of the American labor force, especially the decline of farm-related work, the rise of the professions, the boom in clerical occupations, and the decline in the lowest-status blue-collar jobs.

Part I: The Problem

2. The focus in this chapter is on three problems that are especially likely to confront semiskilled and unskilled blue-collar workers—unemployment, health and safety hazards, and alienation. Although these problems are particularly acute in blue-collar occupations, they are found throughout the occupational hierarchy.

Part II: Causes and Consequences

3. The nature of capitalism seems to demand a certain amount of unemployment, or as Marx put it, a "reserve army of unemployed." Capitalists also tend to be reckless of the health and safety of workers and the creators of alienating working conditions.
4. The recent decline of American industry, especially the "smokestack industries," has exacerbated these problems, especially unemployment.
5. Various large-scale structures are implicated in the health and safety hazards at work, including occupations, employing organizations, and the federal government.
6. Technological change, especially automation and robot technology, is exacerbating the problem of unemployment in blue-collar occupations.
7. The dual labor market is implicated in these problems since it is those who exist in the secondary labor market who are far more likely to experience them than those in the primary labor market.
8. At the individual level, unemployment is likely to have devastating psychological and physiological effects. The same can be said about alienation. More specifically, alienation leads to heightened feelings of powerlessness, meaninglessness, isolation, and self-estrangement. Health and safety hazards are obviously most likely to adversely affect individuals physiologically.

Part III: Responses

9. One response at the macrolevel to these problems is the creation of a socialist alternative to capitalism in America. However, the evidence is that existing socialist societies are not much more successful in solving at least some of the problems discussed in this chapter and they also serve to create other problems.
10. Efforts by employees to buy out companies on the verge of extinction would help with unemployment and perhaps reduce other problems as well.
11. Almost all of the problems discussed here, but especially unemployment, would be aided by a reinvigoration of the American economy.
12. Improvement in managerial practices, such as those employed in "Theory Z" and "excellent" companies, would also help improve the lot of American workers.

13. New technologies will reduce alienation and health and safety hazards, although they are likely to exacerbate the problem of unemployment.
14. Employing organizations can do a great deal to alleviate the problems discussed in this chapter.
15. Labor unions would seem to be an ideal aid in the solution of these problems. Unfortunately, the decline of the American labor movement has weakened their ability to be a significant positive force.
16. Greater cooperation between union and management could do much to reduce these problems.
17. At the microlevel, there are a variety of responses open to individuals and groups, including restriction of output, evasion of the rules, and games in the workplace.
18. However, individual responses such as these do not affect the macrolevel causes of the problems and may even serve to support the system that is causing them.

SUGGESTED READINGS

Annals, 470, November 1983. The entire issue of this journal is devoted to robotics and work.

Bluestone, Barry, and Bennett Harrison, *The Deindustrialization of America.* New York: Basic Books, 1982. An analysis of the decline of some American industries.

Ouchi, William, *Theory Z.* New York: Avon, 1981. Among other things, a discussion of the applicability of the Japanese model of management to American industry.

Peters, Thomas J., and Robert H. Waterman, *In Search of Excellence: Lessons from America's Best-Run Companies.* New York: Harper & Row, 1982. Suggestions for improving American business by deriving lessons from the best-run companies in this country.

Ritzer, George, and David Walczak, *Working: Conflict and Change,* 3rd ed. Englewood Cliffs, N.J.: Prentice-Hall. 1986. A basic text in the sociology of work.

Starr, Paul, *The Social Transformation of Medicine.* New York: Basic Books, 1982. An important study of the history of the medical profession and its changing power within society.

FOOTNOTES

[1]Daniel Bell, *The Coming of Post-Industrial Society.* (New York: Basic Books, 1976).

[2]Magali Sarfatti Larson, *The Rise of Professionalism: A Sociological Analysis* (Berkeley: University of California Press, 1977).

[3]Paul Starr, *The Social Transformation of Medicine.* (New York: Basic Books, 1982).

[4]*Ibid.*, p. 4.

[5]*Ibid.*, p. 5.

[6]*Ibid.*

[7]David Lockwood, *The Blackcoated Worker: A Study in Class Consciousness* (London: George Allen and Unwin, 1958).

[8]Robert Miller, ed., "Robotics: Future Factories, Future Workers," *Annals,* 470 (1983), entire issue.

[9]Barry Bluestone and Bennett Harrison, *The Deindustrialization of America* (New York: Basic Books, 1982).

[10]John A. Garraty, *Unemployment in History: Economic Thought and Public Policy* (New York: Harper Colophon, 1978).

[11]U.S. Department of Commerce, Bureau of the Census, *Statistical Abstract of the United States: 1984* (Washington, D.C.: U.S. Government Printing Office, 1983), p. 405.

[12]U.S. Department of Labor, Bureau of Labor Statistics, *Employment and Earnings,* 32 (April, 1985), p. 22.

[13]*Ibid.*

[14]*Ibid.*

[15]Jeanne M. Stellman and Susan M. Daum, *Work is Dangerous to Your Health* (New York: Vintage, 1973).

[16]Joanne Omang, "A-Worker Exposure Soars, Group Says," *The Washington Post*, September 5, 1981, p. A6.

[17]"Lung Damage Found in 86% of Ship Workers," *The Washington Post*, July 9, 1979, p. C2.

[18]Stellman and Daum, *op. cit.*, p. xiii.

[19]Harvey J. Hilaski, "Understanding Statistics on Occupational Ilnesses," *Monthly Labor Review* (1981): pp. 25–29.

[20]Patrick G. Donnelly, "The Origins of the Occupational Safety and Health Act of 1970," *Social Problems*, 30 (1982), 13–25.

[21]Hilaski, *op. cit.*

[22]Richard L. Frenkel, W. Curtiss Priest, and Nicholas Ashford, "Occupational Safety and Health: A Report on Worker Perceptions," *Monthly Labor Review* (1980), 11–14.

[23]Hilaski, *op. cit.*

[24]Norman Root and Deborah Sebastian, "BLS Develops Measure of Job Risk by Occupation," *Monthly Labor Review* (1981), 26–30.

[25]David P. McCaffrey, "Work-Related Amputations by Type and Prevalence," *Monthly Labor Review* (March 1981), 35–41.

[26]George Ritzer and David Walczak, *Working: Conflict and Change*, 3rd ed. (Englewood Cliffs, N.J.: Prentice-Hall, 1986).

[27]William A. Faunce, *Problems of an Industrial Society*, 2nd ed. (New York: McGraw-Hill, 1981), pp. 130–181.

[28]George Miller, "Professionals in Bureaucracy: Alienation Among Industrial Scientists," *American Sociological Review*, 32 (1967), 755–768; Leonard Pearlin, "Alienation From Work: A Study of Nursing Personnel," *American Sociological Review*, 27 (1962), 314–326; Louis A. Zurcher, Jr., *et al.*, "Value Orientation, Role Conflict, and Alienation From Work: A Cross-Cultural Study," *American Sociological Review*, 30 (1965), 539–548.

[29]Robert Blauner, *Alienation and Freedom* (Chicago: University of Chicago Press, 1964).

[30]*Ibid*, p. 26.

[31]Karl Marx, *Capital*, Vol. I (New York: International Publishers, 1867/1967).

[32]*Statistical Abstract: 1984, op. cit.*, p. 405.

[33]Karl Marx, *op. cit.*, p. 245.

[34]*Ibid.*, p. 246.

[35]*Ibid.*, pp. 264–265.

[36]Karl Marx. *The Economic and Philosophic Manuscripts of 1844*, Dirk J. Struik, ed. (New York: International Publishers, 1964).

[37]Isidore Wallimann, *Estrangement: Marx's Conception of Human Nature and the Division of Labor* (Westport, Conn.: Greenwood, 1981).

[38]George Ritzer, *Sociological Theory* (New York: Knopf, 1983), pp. 76–77.

[39]Bertell Ollman, *Alienation*, 2nd ed. (Cambridge: Cambridge University Press, 1976).

[40]Bluestone and Harrison, *op. cit.*

[41]Warren Brown, "Fading Muscle: Steel, Once Symbol of U.S. Might, Casts Shrinking Economic Shadow," *The Washington Post*, April 24, 1983, pp. F1, F5.

[42]Blumberg, *Inequality in an Age of Decline* (New York: Oxford University Press, 1980), pp. 122–25; Peter Behr, "Playing it Safe, and Losing Out," *The Washington Post*, January 17, 1982, pp. A1, A17; "How Zenith Lost Its Competitive, Creative Edge," *The Washington Post*, January 19, 1982, pp. C1, C10; "Serving Only the Present," *The Washington Post*, January 20, 1982, pp. D1, D10.

[43]William Ouchi, *Theory Z* (New York: Avon, 1981).

[44]J. Patrick Wright, *On a Clear Day You Can See General Motors* (New York: Avon, 1979).

[45]*Ibid.*, p. 261.

[46]Bluestone and Harrison, *op. cit.*, p. 6.

[47]Donnelly, *op. cit.*, p. 13.

[48]Kitty Calavita, "The Demise of the Occupational Safety and Health Administration: A Case Study of Symbolic Interaction," *Social Problems*, 30 (1983), 437–448.

[49]Kathy Sawyer and Pete Earley, "OSHA Befriends Industry, but Draws New Fire," *The Washington Post*, July 5, 1983, pp. A1, A12.

[50]*Ibid.*, p. A12.

[51]R. Miller, *op. cit.*

[52]Robert U. Ayres and Steven M. Miller, "Robotic Realities: Near-Term Prospects and Problems," *Annals*, 470 (1983), 28–55.

[53]Louis Ferman, "The Unmanned Factory and the Community," *Annals*, 470 (1983), 136–145.

[54]Gerald Nadler and Gordon H. Robinson, "Design of the Automated Factory," *Annals*, 470 (1983), 68–80.

[55]John Naisbitt, *Megatrends: Ten New Directions Transforming Our Lives* (New York: Warner, 1982), p. 29.

[56]Ayres and Miller, *op. cit.*

[57]Sar A. Levitan and Clifford M. Johnson, "The Future of Work: Does It Belong to Us or to the Robots?" *Monthly Labor Review*, 105 (1982), 11.

[58]*Ibid.*

[59]Gail Martin, "Industrial Robots Join the Work

Force," *Occupational Outlook Quarterly*, 26 (1982), 2–11.

[60]Rodney Hodson and Robert L. Kaufman, "Economic Dualism: A Critical Review," *American Sociological Review*, 47 (1982), 727–739; E. M. Beck, Patrick M. Horan, and Charles M. Tolbert, "Industrial Segmentation and Labor Market Discrimination," *Social Problems*, 28 (1980), 113–130.

[61]Underemployment (in this case, employment on jobs in which one is unable to use one's educational background) also has negative effects on workers. See Beverly H. Burris, "The Human Effects of Underemployment," *Social Problems*, 31 (1983), 96–110.

[62]*Time*, "Anguish of the Jobless," *Time*, January 18, 1982, p. 90.

[63]Bluestone and Harrison, *op. cit.*, pp. 63–66.

[64]Bluestone and Harrison, *op. cit.*, pp. 63–66.

[65]"Left Out," *Newsweek*, March 21, 1983, p. 34.

[66]Barbara Garson, *All the Livelong Day* (Harmondsworth, England: Penguin, 1977), p. 88.

[67]Studs Terkel, *Working* (New York: Pantheon, 1974), p. 159.

[68]Garson, *op. cit.*, p. 93.

[69]Charles R. Walker and Robert Guest, *Man on the Assembly Line* (Cambridge, Mass.: Harvard University Press, 1952), p. 9.

[70]Blauner, *op. cit.*, p. 182.

[71]John Calder, Introduction to Robert Linhart, *The Assembly Line*, Margaret Crosland, (tr.) (Amherst: University of Massachusetts Press, 1981), p. 10.

[72]Peter Finn, "The Effects of Shift Work on the Lives of Employees," *Monthly Labor Review* (1981), 31–35; David Margolick, "The Lonely World of Night Work," *Fortune*, December 15, 1980, p. 111.

[73]Ward Sinclair, "Mine Blasts: Budget Cuts Hit Safety Enforcement Like a Ton of Kentucky Coal," *The Washington Post*, February 15, 1982, pp. A1, A6, A7; Douglas B. Feaver, "Accidents Up, Citations Down in Coal Fields," *The Washington Post*, February 3, 1982, p. A21.

[74]Bluestone and Harrison, *op. cit.*; "When Workers Take Over the Plant," *U.S. News and World Report*, April 18, 1983, pp. 89–90.

[75]See, for example, Robert Reich, *The Next American Frontier* (New York: Times Books, 1983); Ira C. Magaziner and Robert B. Reich, *Minding America's Business: The Decline and Rise of the American Economy* (New York: Harcourt Brace Jovanovich, 1982).

[76]"Where the Jobs Are—and Aren't," *Newsweek*, November 13, 1981, p. 89.

[77]Martha M. Hamilton, "Atari to Fire 1,700, Shift Plants to Asia," *The Washington Post*, February 23, 1983), p. F4.

[78]Max L. Carey, "Occupational Employment Growth Through 1990," *Monthly Labor Review*, 104 (1981), 42–55.

[79]Pat Choate and Noel Epstein, "Workers of the Future Re-Tool! Nothing to Lose But Your Jobs," *The Washington Post*, May 9, 1982, pp. D1, D5.

[80]Ouchi, *op. cit.*

[81]Thomas J. Peters and Robert H. Waterman, *In Search of Excellence: Lessons from America's Best-Run Companies* (New York: Harper & Row, 1982).

[82]*Ibid.*, p. 15.

[83]Ritzer and Walczak. *op. cit.*

[84]George Ruben, "Organized Labor in 1981: A Shifting of Priorities," *Monthly Labor Review* 105 (1982), 21–28.

[85]Paul O. Flaim, "New Data and Union Members and Their Earnings," *Employment and Earnings*, 32 (1985), p. 13.

[86]"Labor's Unhappy Birthday," *Time*, November 16, 1981, p. 125.

[87]Frank Swoboda, "Many Unions Being Asked to Settle for Less To Avoid Big Job Losses," *The Washington Post*, January 10, 1982, p. H9.

[88]John Simmons and William Mares, *Working Together* (New York: Knopf, 1983).

[89]For a summary of this research, see Ritzer and Walczak, *op. cit.*, pp. 271–279.

[90]Fritz Rothlisberger and William J. Dickson, *Management and the Worker* (New York: Wiley, 1964).

[91]Donald Roy, "Efficiency and 'the Fix': Informal Intergroup Relations in a Piecework Machine Shop," *American Journal of Sociology*, 60 (1954), pp. 255–266.

[92]*Ibid.*, p. 257.

[93]Donald Roy, "'Banana Time': Job Satisfaction and Informal Interaction," *Human Organization*, 18 (1959–1960), 158–168; "Sex in the Factory: Informal Heterosexual Relations Between Supervisors and Work Groups." In Clifton Bryant, ed., *Deviant Behavior: Occupational and Organizational Bases* (Chicago: Rand McNally, 1974), pp. 44–66.

[94]Michael Burawoy, *Manufacturing Consent: Changes in the Labor Process Under Monopoly Capitalism* (Chicago: University of Chicago Press, 1979).

Hamlet: Ay, marry, why was he sent into England?

First clown: Why, because he was mad; he shall recover his wits there; or if he do not, 'tis no great matter there.

Hamlet: Why?

First clown: 'Twill not be seen in him there: there the men are as mad as he.

William Shakespeare

12
Problems in Health Care

Peter Conrad
BRANDEIS UNIVERSITY

All societies must deal with the problem of maintaining the health of their members. It is an essential social task, for if illness and disability become too widespread, a society may have difficulty functioning. In small, simple societies some type of healer often fulfills this role. Such a healer, sometimes known as a *shaman* or a witch doctor, takes a magico-spiritual approach to health and illness and attempts to cure disease by appealing to the gods or removing evil spirits from the body.

In more complex societies like our own, we also find "healers." In modern societies our healers, doctors and other health professionals, rely on science rather than magic as the source of their healing ability. In the past century, the scientific approach has lead to great progress in reducing suffering and disability from illness. There is little doubt that many diseases now have less detrimental effects and people live longer today than a hundred years ago.

With this progress, however, have come new problems. Although it often may seem that our healers, such as doctors, work on their own, they are enmeshed in a complex social network—the *medical care system.* In the past forty years this system has grown enormously and has itself become a major social problem for society. While enormous, rising costs are the most obvious problem, we can identify a number of distinct yet interrelated problems in health care.

PART 1: THE PROBLEM

Sick Care vs. Health Care

One of the overriding problems of our medical system is that the dominant orientation is one of *sick care* rather than *health care.* We have a system that treats people who are sick but does very little to promote health.

Sociologist Irving Kenneth Zola tells the story of a physician describing some of the problems with the sick-care orientation.

> "You know," he said, "sometimes it feels like this. There I am standing by the shore of a swiftly flowing river and I hear the cry of a drowning man. So I jump into the river, put my arms around him, pull him to shore and apply artificial respiration. Just when he begins to breathe, there is another cry for help. So I jump into the river, reach him, pull him to shore, apply artificial respiration, then just as he begins to breathe, another cry for help. So back in the river again, reaching, pulling, applying breathing and then another yell. Again and again, without end, goes the sequence. You know, I am so busy jumping in, pulling them to shore, applying artificial respiration, that I have *no* time to see who the hell is upstream pushing them all in."[1]

American clinical medicine devotes most of its energy to short-term, often Band-Aid solutions to sickness rather than attempting to focus on ways to improve health.[2]

The sick-care orientation is manifested in almost every aspect of the medical care system. Chronic illnesses like cancer, stroke, and heart disease have become the major diseases of our times. There is considerable evidence that as much as 90 percent of cancer is environmentally caused, yet the overwhelming amount of medical research monies are spent in an effort to find a cure for cancer rather than trying to prevent it.[3] Cancer is not atypical, since it has been estimated that 95 percent of all health costs go to medical care and only 5 percent go into prevention and health promotion. Our entire medical reimbursement system is set up to pay for sick care and not health care. One example of this is the payment structure of insurance companies. Health insurance policies generally provide coverage for most episodes of a serious illness, but do not pay for regular check-ups or preventative treatment. To the extent that individuals want "health care," they must seek and pay for it on their own.

The sick-care orientation pervades medical education.[4] Medical schools spend thousands of hours teaching doctors how to diagnose and treat disease, but a few dozen hours are spent teaching subjects like nutrition or positive health. This is due in part to the manifest mission of medicine—heal the sick—but it also reflects the reward structure of the medical profession. The most specialized physicians, such as cardiac surgeons, are embued with the greatest prestige and the highest incomes. Family practitioners and public-health physicians, who may be the most health-care oriented doctors, are considered less prestigious and have lower incomes.

Medicine with a health-care orientation has been overshadowed by the practice of sick care. With the exception of public-health measures, including sanitation, food and water regulations, and the like, little attention has been given to prevention and even less to health promotion.

The Medicalization of Society

In this century the domain of medicine has grown considerably: childbirth, sexuality, death as well as old age, anxiety, obesity, child development, alcoholism, drug addiction, homosexuality, among other human experiences, have been defined and treated as medical problems. This has expanded the realm of what we think of as sickness. Sociologists began to examine the process and consequences of the *medicalization* of society, especially the medicalization of deviant behavior.[5]

In our society an increasing amount of deviant behavior has become medicalized.[6] By the medicalization of deviance we mean the defining of a behavior as a medical problem or "treating" a behavior with a medical treatment. A classic example is hyperactivity in children. Hyperactivity, which is medically known as Minimal Brain Dysfunction (MBD) or Attention Deficit Disorder (ADD), is typified by a child who displays overactivity, fidgetiness, restlessness, impulsivity, aggressive-like behaviors, and an inability to focus or pay attention for any length of time. In other words, children who are troublesome to others. Most children diagnosed as hyperactive are identified by teachers in school because they are disruptive to the classroom.[7] The predominant treatments for hyperactivity are stimulant medications like Ritalin, Dexedrine, or Cylert. These drugs have the effect of helping children to focus better and reduce their "overactive" behavior. Research suggests that medications improve the behavior of 60 percent of children defined as hyperactive.

While it may be more humane to treat troublesome children as "sick" rather than "bad," and there is some evidence that children learn better when on medications, there is also a darker side to medicalization. First, it places the control of the problem in the hands of medical experts so that lay people can no longer evaluate the problem on an equal level. Second, it allows the use of powerful forms of medical social-control mechanisms, in this case psychoactive drugs, that could not be used if the problem were not medicalized. Third, it individualizes social problems; in this case, it focuses the problem and solution on the individual rather than the social situation (like the classroom or school). In other words, it decontextualizes the behavior from the situation in which it occurred; that is, it encourages people to see the behavior out of its context. Finally, it depoliticizes deviant behavior; that is, it removes any possible meaning from the behavior. This is similar to the labeling of Soviet dissidents as mentally ill, where the medicalization serves to neutralize the meaning of political protest and dissent, rendering it (officially, at least) as the ravings of madpersons. While with hyperactivity madness is not an issue, treating this behavior as a medical problem removes any meaning the behavior might have in the context of the social situations of school or family.[8]

A good example of medicalization that is a natural life event rather than deviance is childbirth. In the nineteenth century childbirth was largely a family event, taking place in the home and attended by lay midwives. Richard and Dorothy Wertz call it "social childbirth" and depict it as a woman-centered event.[9] With the increasing professionalization of medicine, doctors began to replace midwives. Doctors were able to obtain a virtual monopoly over birth through the passage of physician-backed laws restricting midwife practice and a transformation of middle-class women's views of birth. Physicians became increasingly interventionist in their childbirth practice partly due to their training (they felt they had to "do something") and their desire to use instruments "to establish superior status." They increasingly treated childbirth as a potentially pathological, rather than natural, event. In other words, childbirth entered the realm of sick care. This placed childbirth securely in the physician's workshop, the hospital, and encouraged an increasingly technological approach to birthing. Even the vocabulary and imagery changed. Midwives had "attended" births; physicians "delivered" babies.

In recent years we have seen a challenge to this monopolization with the rise of "lay midwives" and home births, but this only encompasses a small fraction of all births.[10] For the most part, childbirth is still medicalized under physician dominance, although the process has been more "humanized" through "natural" or prepared childbirth classes and the advent of hospital birthing rooms. Birthing rooms are usually nicely decorated hospital rooms that create a more homelike atmosphere for the birth and ostensibly encourage less medical intervention. But we need only look at the routine use of technology like fetal monitors and the astonishingly high rate of Caesarian births, approximately 25 percent of all births, to find evidence of the continuing medical dominance of childbirth.[11]

Although there has been some demedicalization in society,[12] such as the 1973 American Psychiatric Association decision not to classify homosexuality as an illness, the trend over the past century has definitely been toward the expansion of the medical domain.[13]

Women and Health

Women are large consumers of health care. They consistently have higher rates of morbidity, or sickness, than men, at least as measured by the utilization of medical care.[14] Traditionally, women have also visited doctors more often with their children, and an entire medical specialty, obstetrics-gynecology, is dedicated specifically to woman's reproductive health. In addition, since women, on average, live eight years longer than men, women are the vast majority of the elderly with medical problems.[15]

Clearly women have been major recipients of medical care. In the 1960s the women's movement began to demonstrate how medicine was a male-dominated institution and how sexism in health care affected women. Sexist practices eliminated the early dominance of American women (such as midwives) in providing health care for one another and thus contributed to women's ignorance about their own bodies and health needs.[16]

One of the major feminist criticisms of medicine has been the distorted picture medicine has painted of women. During the nineteenth century, organized medicine gained a strong dominance over the treatment of women, and proceeded to profess erroneous and damaging conceptualizations of women as sickly, irrational creatures who were always at the mercy of their reproductive organs.[17] We might say that medicine took a "womb-centric" view of women. It was believed that women were "fragile" and this led to a "cult of invalidism" among upper-class women in the nineteenth century. It became expected and fashionable for a woman of means to be weak and sickly. Sometimes medical authority was used overtly to "keep women in their place," as when numerous nineteenth-century physicians said women should not be allowed to get the vote because, if they had such responsibilities, their wombs would shrink and their brains would become oversized.[18] Needless to say, medicine did not invent sexism but it became an authoritative voice reinforcing stereotypes and the status quo.

While the grossest and most obvious medical biases have diminished, forms of sexism remain. One study in the 1970s demonstrated how medical textbooks in gynecology consistently described women "as anatomically destined to reproduce, nurture and keep their husbands happy." Women were depicted frequently as "frigid" and sexually unresponsive. One 1971 textbook read: "The traits that compose the core of the female personality are feminine narcissism, masochism and passivity."[19] Such reasoning reinforces the worst in gender stereotyping.

Women also took the medical profession to task for the dominance and control phy-

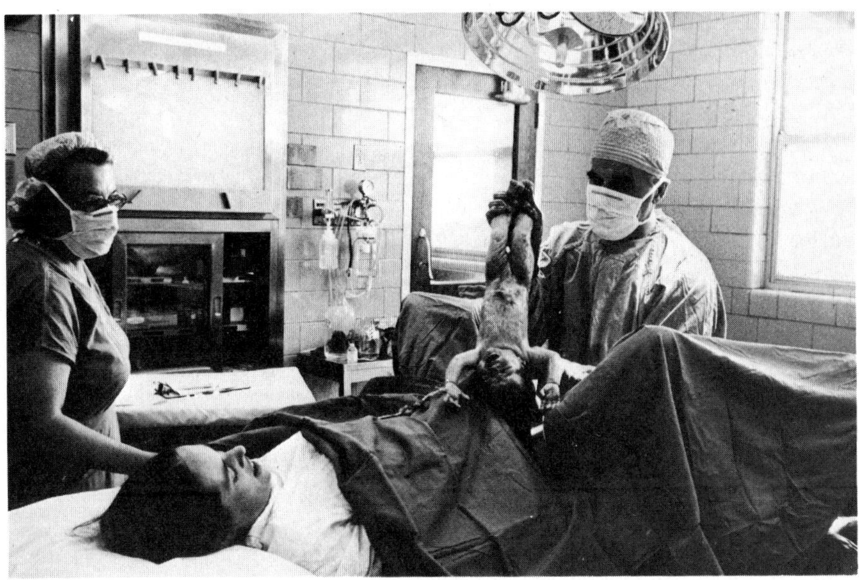

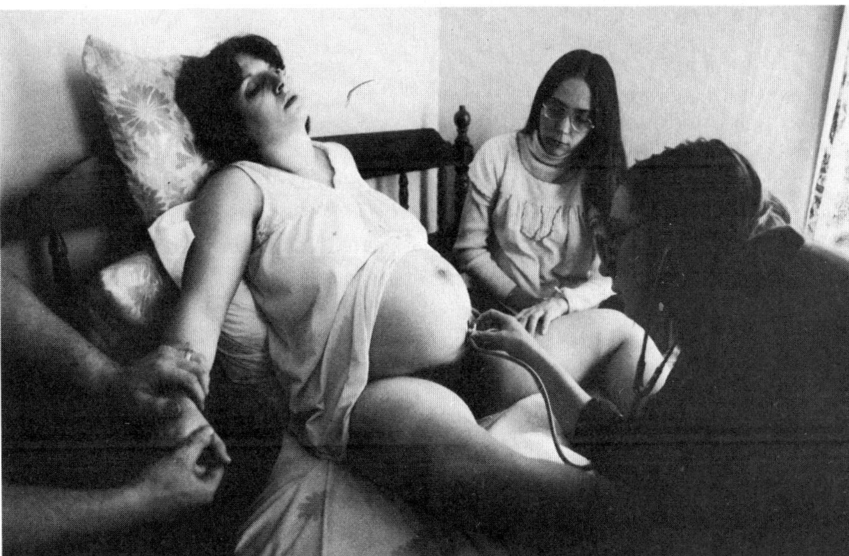

Childbirth is a good example of the medicalization of society. Over the years the medical profession took control over the childbirth process from midwives. However, in recent years there has been some rebirth in interest in midwives and in the demedicalization of medical care.

(Above, Bob Combs/Photo Researchers; below, Robert Eckert/The Picture Cube) sicians had over matters concerning women's health. Whether it was in terms of birth control, abortion, childbirth, or menopause, women were increasingly demanding the "right to control their bodies." This has spawned challenges about unsafe birth control pills, a strong movement supporting abortion as "a woman's right to choose," and pressure for more humane childbirth, including home birth.[20] Furthermore, critics have argued that women are more likely to have their life problems medicalized.[21] Two brief examples will suffice. Personal troubles like anxiety and life distress are common and suffered by many people. In the last few decades doctors have become involved in treating these "disorders," mostly with psychoactive medications. In 1979, 160 million prescriptions were written for tranquilizers, including 60 million for Valium alone. Sixty to 80 percent of these drugs were prescribed for women.[22] Recently menopause has become medicalized and many women are "treated" with estrogen replacement therapy.[23]

The health care occupational structure reflects the sexism of our social structure. (See Chapter 9 for more on gender inequality.) At the top end of the medical hierarchy, until the most recent years, over 90 percent of the doctors were male. At the other end of the hierarchy, 84.8 percent of the nursing aides, orderlies, and attendants were female.[24] This is not to mention nursing, which is 97 percent female. Beginning in the late 1960s, large numbers of women entered medical school and now make up almost 30 percent of medical school classes nationwide. Women who complete medical school tend to concentrate in certain, generally stereotypically "female," medical specialties, including pediatrics and psychiatry, and are underrepresented in the more prestigious and powerful surgical specialties.[25]

Women are becoming more conscious about their special problems in the health system and continue to struggle to regain some control of their bodies and health.

Accessibility and Inequality of Medical Care

If medicalization suggests that some people may get more medical care than might be necessary, it is also true that some people do not get all the care they need. For medical care to be useful to people it must be accessible. The use of medical services is called "utilizaton." Medical care in our society is not equally accessible and thus we can see variations in the utilization of services.

Twenty years ago it would have been even more obvious than today that poor people did not have equal access to hospitals and medical care. The poor needed to rely on public hospitals and charity wards when they needed medical attention. There was very unequal care in a "two class medical system"—one for those who had resources to pay, and one for those who did not.[26] With the passage of Medicaid, the federal-state program to pay for care for the medically indigent, and Medicare, the federal program for the elderly, it was believed that access to medical care would become more equal. In significant ways (payment for sick-care services, for example) access for disadvantaged groups has improved.

But discrepancies persist and affect the utilization of services. We can see this more clearly if we examine two types of services. Medical services can be seen as forming a continuum: on one pole is urgent or immediate care and on the other is elective or discretionary care. If we use hospitalization as a measure of immediately necessary care, we can see in Table 12.1 that the lower the income, the more hospital care people receive. On the opposite pole, we can consider regular dental check-ups as an example of discretionary care (after all, one is not going because one has a problem, but to find or prevent problems). Here we see that the lower the income, the lower the use of services. What can we make of this, even based on such limited data? For one thing, the poorer people more often get care at the hospital and stay longer. This may mean that they have more severe sicknesses than other people or they may use the hospital more for other reasons. On the other hand, poor people tend not to go for preventive or discretionary services, those that could prevent future problems. Notice that when the poor go for dental care, the only time they have higher utilization is when the visit is to have a tooth pulled or to have surgery, or, in our terms, an urgent service.

Research by Diana Dutton can help us understand this discrepancy better.[27] Dutton's research indicates that previous explanations of lower utilization by the poor of discretionary services—citing financial constraints and differences due to culture—were not adequate taken either alone or together to explain why poorer people do not use discretionary services as much as might be expected. Dutton examined a third explanation, one which takes medical care system differences into account. She suggests that poorer people use less discretionary services because the structure of the health system encourages them to use hospital outpatient depart-

Table 12.1 Utilization of Nondiscretionary and Discretionary Medical Services

NONDISCRETIONARY MEDICAL SERVICE: HOSPITALIZATION (1980)[1 2]			
INCOME	DISCHARGES	DAYS OF CARE	AVERAGE LENGTH OF STAY
less than $7,000	157.5	1457.8	8.4
$7000–9999	141.6	1270.4	8.2
$10,000–14,999	120.4	959.6	6.9
$15,000–24,999	111.2	782.9	6.5
$25,000 or more	102.4	714.1	6.0

DISCRETIONARY MEDICAL SERVICES: DENTAL VISITS (1971–1974)*			
INCOME	PERCENTAGE OF POPULATION 25–29 TO VISIT DENTIST	REGULAR CHECK-UP VISIT	VISIT FOR TOOTH PULLED OR SURGERY
less than $4,000	24.6	24.0	25.6
$4,000–6,999	32.5	30.2	15.1
$7,000–9,999	41.2	49.0	11.2
$10,000–14,999	45.6	50.9	10.1
$15,000 or more	61.5	61.3	5.0

[1]Number per 1,000 population
[2]Excludes deliveries

Source: *Health U.S., 1982* and *Health U.S., 1978*, Department of Health & Human Services (Washington, D.C.: U.S. Government Printing Office, 1983, 1979).
*Later data available in Dry Form.

ments and emergency rooms as primary providers. In part, this is because there are few primary care physicians in poor areas and hospital services are covered by Medicaid. There is strong evidence, for example, that nonwhites are twice as likely as whites to use a hospital emergency room as a source of care and are less likely to have their own physicians.[28] The lack of equal access to care is one reason blacks have poorer health than whites and why in 1976 the infant mortality rate among blacks was 26.2 per thousand compared to 13.3 among whites.[29]

Hospital providers deal largely with immediate and urgent care rather than preventive and discretionary care. This suggests that if we want to improve preventive services for underserved populations, we need to make some changes in the way in which our medical system delivers care.

Women are not the only group to be underrepresented in the medical profession. Blacks and minorities have also had difficulty breaking into the ranks of physicians. In 1970 only 2.2 percent of all physicians were black.[30] Although there has been a great deal of publicity about the impact of affirmative action in opening up medical opportunities for minorities, the number of blacks in the medical profession remains low compared to the population as a whole.[31] For example, the percentage of black applicants accepted to medical school decreased between 1970 and 1977.[32] Hispanics and Native Americans also have very small numbers of physicians. This then contributes to the problem of inaccessibility to medical services since physicians are unlikely to live and practice in central cities and rural areas, where a large portion of the minority poor reside.

The unequal distribution of doctors and medical services affects utilization as well as accessibility. Although number of physicians is only one particular measure, it gives us a sense of the unequal distribution of services. Rural areas have less than half the number of doctors per population than do urban areas. The number of physicians varies by region as well: for example, there are 228 doctors per 100,000 people in the Northeast while there are only 158 per 100,000 people in the South. One can find similar differences in numbers of nurses and hospital beds.[33] Recent research has shown that public and other urban hospitals are closing due to financial circumstances at an alarming rate.[34] Since most of their patients are poor and on public assistance, this decreases the access poor and minority patients have to the medical care system and creates further inequalities in health care.

Costs

Inequality and access to medical services, although still a problem, were the major public policy issues of the 1960s. In the 1980s by far the dominant policy issue in health care is the continuously rising cost of medical care.

In 1950 4.3 percent of the gross national product (GNP) of the United States was spent on health care, a total of about $13 billion. In 1983 the United States spent over 10.5 percent of its GNP, or over $350 billion, on health care. This is a twenty-six-fold increase in a little over three decades. Medical costs have been more than double the inflation rate for that period. And the spiraling of costs continues. It is likely that by 1990 health care costs will consume 12 percent of the GNP, or over $600 billion (see Figure 12.1). Many observers have raised serious questions about whether a society can afford to spend such a large part of its resources on health care. Others have questioned whether we are "getting our

Figure 12.1 Escalating Health Care Costs

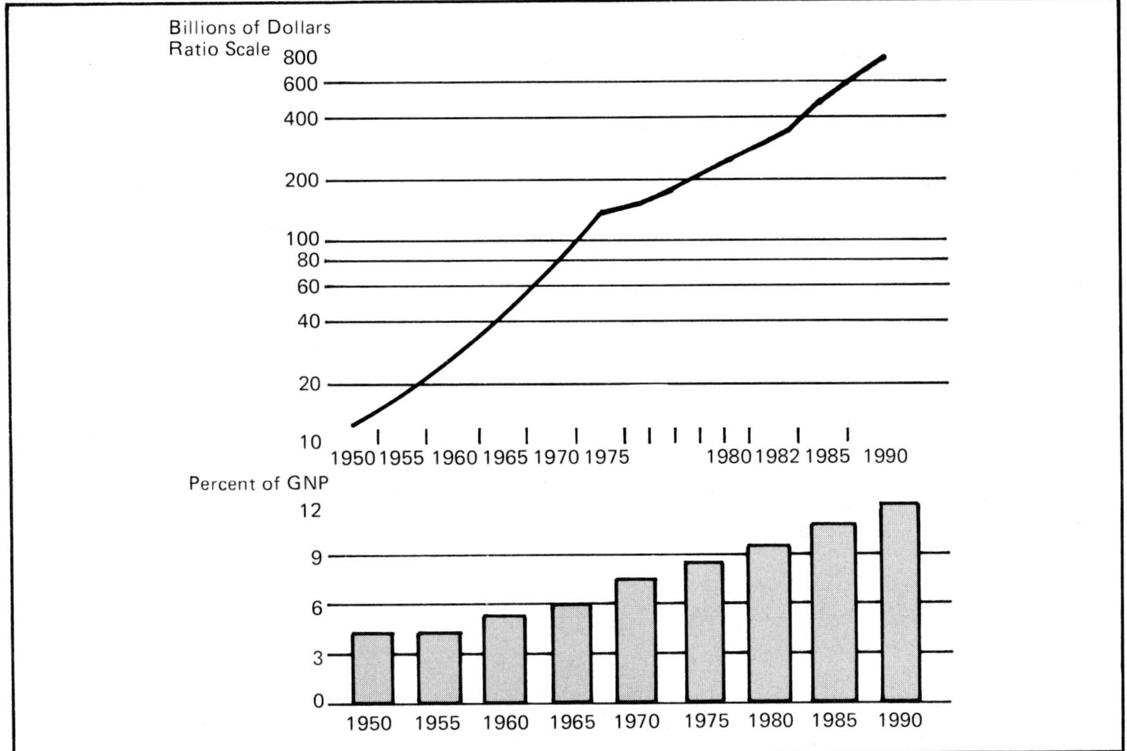

Health care costs have skyrocketed over the past three decades, and are likely to continue their upward spiral.
Source: The Conference Board, Inc., 845 Third Ave., New York, N.Y., 10022.

money's worth" or have reached a point of diminishing returns.[35] Most experts agree that these skyrocketing costs need to be controlled but are in disagreement on how this is to be accomplished.

One factor in the rising medical costs is our aging population (see Chapter 7). People are living longer and more people are growing old: the percentage of the population 65 and over in 1900 was 4 percent, in 1950 was 9 percent, and in 1980 was 11 percent.[36] Older people use health services more than the rest of the population since they are more likely to suffer from chronic illness. The elderly's health expenses are three times that of other adults. While it is true that as the population ages a society tends to spend more on medical care, this alone does not account for the spiraling health costs.

One of the largest expenditures for health care is hospital costs. In 1980 hospital costs were 40.3 percent of our total health care bill. And hospital costs have been rising at an extraordinary rate. For example, a semiprivate hospital room cost $23 in 1965. In 1985 it is expected to be $263, more than a 1000 percent increase in two decades (see Figure 12.2). All indications are that costs will continue to rise.

Figure 12.2 Hospital Room Charges

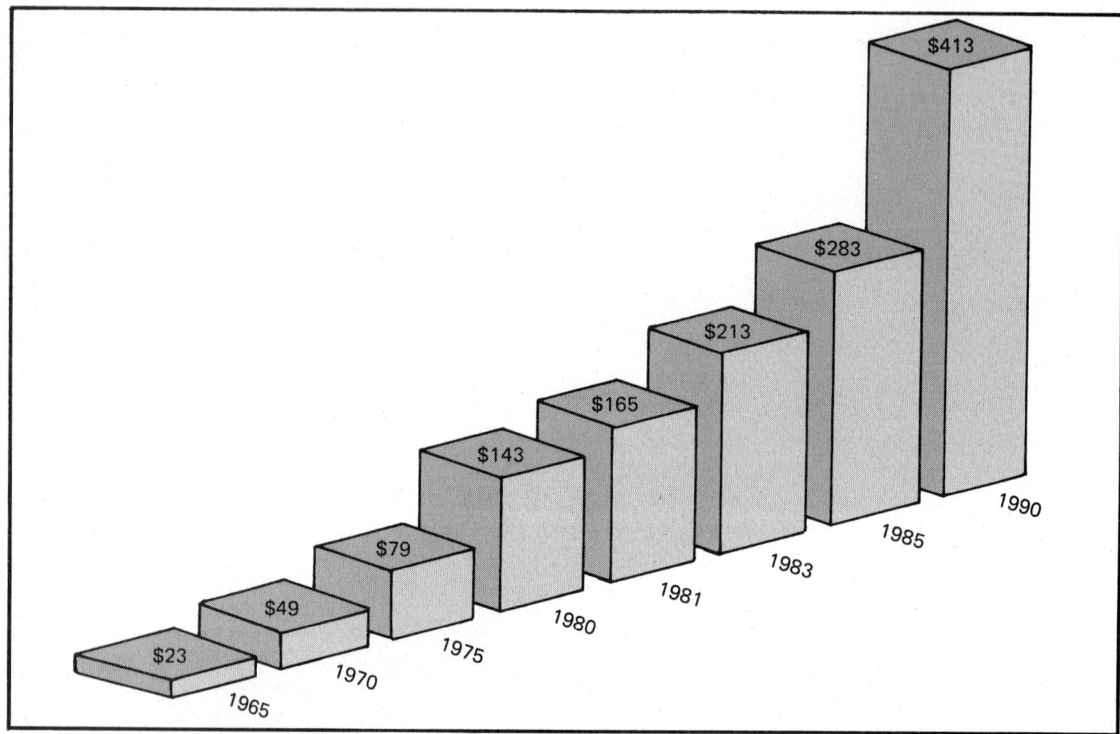

Hospital room charges have increased dramatically, and an even greater jump is predicted for 1985–1990.
Source: The Conference Board, Inc., 845 Third Ave., New York, N.Y., 10022.

A large part of the rising hospital costs comes from the increasing technological sophistication of medical care. Coronary care units, neonatal infant care units, CT (Computerized Axial Tomography) scanners, and the like are expensive forms of medical care. While sophisticated technology is certainly useful in many circumstances, it is not clear that the benefits of such technologies always outweigh their costs. In any case, once a new technology is in a hospital, it is likely to be used. Victor Fuchs calls this the "technological imperative," "the desire of the physician to do everything that he has been trained to do, regardless of the cost-benefit ratio."[37] Such a "can do-should do" ethic among medical professionals has contributed significantly to our cost crisis.

The way in which hospital care is paid for is also a factor in rising medical costs. For many Americans, although not all, hospital costs are partially paid for by "third-party payers." Third-party payers include Blue Cross/Blue Shield, the insurance industry, and government programs like Medicare and Medicaid. Third parties paid only 40 percent of hospital costs in 1950, while paying nearly 70 percent in 1980.[38] The rise of third-party payers has meant that the actual increases in hospital costs have not been apparent to most of us. We only know about them when we have an increase in insurance premiums or we read in the newspaper about the dangers of Medicare going bankrupt. Third parties have made some limited attempts to control costs (which will be discussed later), but the lack of cost controls has been a major contributor to increasing health costs.

How does the United States compare with the rest of the world in terms of rising health costs and health in general? While our health costs are among the two or three highest, using two common (albeit crude) comparative measures, the health of Americans does not rate among the top ten in the world. In 1973 the *life expectancy rate* was 67.56 for American males (ranked nineteenth) and 75.27 for females (ranked ninth) and the *infant mortality rate* (babies that die within the first year of life) was 16.7 per 1000 live births, which ranked fifteenth in the world.[39] This raises, again, the question of the cost effectiveness of our medical system. It is worth noting that these low rankings of the United States may also be related to the problem of inequalities in health care. If we look at the figures for white Americans only, our statistics come closer to the best in the world.

When we examine health care as a social problem we see a matrix of interrelated problems. While the issue of rising costs dominates the current political debates, the other faces of the health care problem remain important and in need of attention. In short, we have an extremely expensive medical care system that continues to deliver mostly sick care rather than health care. On the one hand, we have limited access to this system by some who need it. On the other hand, we can see the expansion of the system to include more medicalized human problems. For some groups, especially women and minorities, the structure of the medical system has created special and particular problems.

PART II: CAUSES AND CONSEQUENCES

SOCIOLOGICAL LEVEL

The causes and consequences of the health care problems we have just discussed are complex and interrelated. The causes of the problems can be found in both long-term trends and recent changes in health care. The professionalization of medicine, the fee-for-service system, and the increase in the numbers of the chronically ill have been central to health care in the United States at least since the turn of the century. The dominance of third-party payers, the dramatic increase in medical technology, and the influx of the corporate sector into medical care are all more recent developments. The consequences of the health care problems are not always clearly distinguishable from the problems themselves. Important consequences include the effects of higher medical care costs and the potential of cutbacks; the increasing domain and influence of medicine in society; the ethical issues created by the implementation of new forms of medical technology; the attention given to profitability when medicine comes to be seen as a business; and the difficulties patients have coping with chronic illness. We will examine all these issues in this section.

The Decline of Infectious Disease and the Rise of Chronic Illness

If we take a historic look at the extent and patterns of disease in Western society, we can see enormous changes and locate some of the roots of the sick-care orientation of medicine.[40] In the early nineteenth century the infant mortality rate was very high, life expectancy was short (approximately forty years), and life-threatening epidemics were

Table 12.2 Levels of Analysis: Health Care

LEVELS	APPROPRIATE QUESTIONS	A PARTIAL SYNOPSIS OF PRESENT CONDITIONS
SOCIOLOGICAL	What are some consequences of the sick-care orientation?	The sick-care orientation focuses on cure rather than prevention, which encourages expensive medical intervention.
	What are the key factors in the rising medical costs?	Fee-for-service creates an incentive for more and sometimes unnecessary care; the lack of cost controls by third-party payers, as well as increasing medical technology and our aging population, are also important.
	What are some consequences of medicalization?	Medicalization extends the sick role to more human problems but also decontextualizes the problem and encourages individual rather than social responses.
	What insight does the "limitations of modern medicine" argument give to our health care problems?	The argument contends that social factors were more significant than medical factors in the "conquest of infectious disease." Thus with chronic disease it is even more likely that social factors are significant in terms of etiology and prevention.
	How does the U.S. compare with other countries in terms of health?	While the costs of the U.S. health care system are among the world's highest, at least in measures like infant mortality and life expectancy, others rank higher.
	Would a national health insurance solve all the health care problems?	No, but it would increase accessibility, equity, and control, which are important. It would necessarily affect other aspects of the health care problem.
SOCIAL-PSYCHOLOGICAL	Why is the "sick role" concept no longer adequate to describe the experience of illness?	The sick role emerged from sick-care orientation and does not fully take into account the experience of chronic illness.

Table 12.2 Levels of Analysis: Health Care (*Continued*)

LEVELS	APPROPRIATE QUESTIONS	A PARTIAL SYNOPSIS OF PRESENT CONDITIONS
	Is the subjective side of illness important to health care?	Yes. Treatment of chronic illness needs to take patients' experiences into account. Self-help groups often build on subjective experience to create their alternatives and challenges to the health care system.

common. Infectious diseases, particularly those of childhood, were often fatal. Even at the beginning of the twentieth century, the annual death rate in the United States was twenty-eight per thousand (compared with nine per thousand today) and the causes of death were usually pneumonia, influenza, tuberculosis, typhoid fever, and various forms of dysentery.[41] Today we have "conquered" most of these infectious diseases; they are no longer feared and people in Western societies rarely die from them (although they are still prevalent in Third-World countries). In Western societies the major causes of death today are chronic diseases such as cancer, heart disease, and stroke, as one can see clearly from Figure 12.3.

Medicine is usually credited with the greatest victory over infectious diseases. After all, certain scientific discoveries such as the germ theory and medical interventions such as vaccinations and drug therapies had been developed and used to combat infectious diseases and, so the logic goes, they must have been responsible for reducing deaths from them. While this explanation has become the common wisdom, and indeed may seem quite reasonable from a casual reading of medical history, it is contradicted by some important social-scientific work.

In reaction against this medically centered view of history, Rene Dubos argued that it was social change in the environment rather than medical interventions that accounted for the reduction of mortality due to infectious disease.[42] He viewed the nineteeth-century campaign for clean water, air, and proper sewage disposal as particularly significant "public-health" measures. Thomas McKeown, in a detailed and rigorous study, showed that biomedical interventions were not the cause of the decline of mortality (that is, the death rate) in England and Wales in the nineteenth century.[43] This viewpoint has become known as the *limitations of modern medicine* argument and is now well known in public-health circles. The argument is a simple one: discoveries and interventions by clinical medicine (that is, medical care rendered by doctors to their patients) were not the cause of the decline of mortality for various populations. Rather, it seems that such social and environmental factors as (1) sanitation, (2) improved housing and nutrition, and (3) a general rise in the standard of living, were the most significant contributors. This does not mean that clinical medicine did not reduce people's sufferings or prevent or cure diseases in some people; we know it did. But social factors appear much more important than medical inter-

Figure 12.3 The Changing Contribution of Chronic and Infectious Conditions to Total Mortality (Age- and Sex-Adjusted) in the United States, 1900–1973.

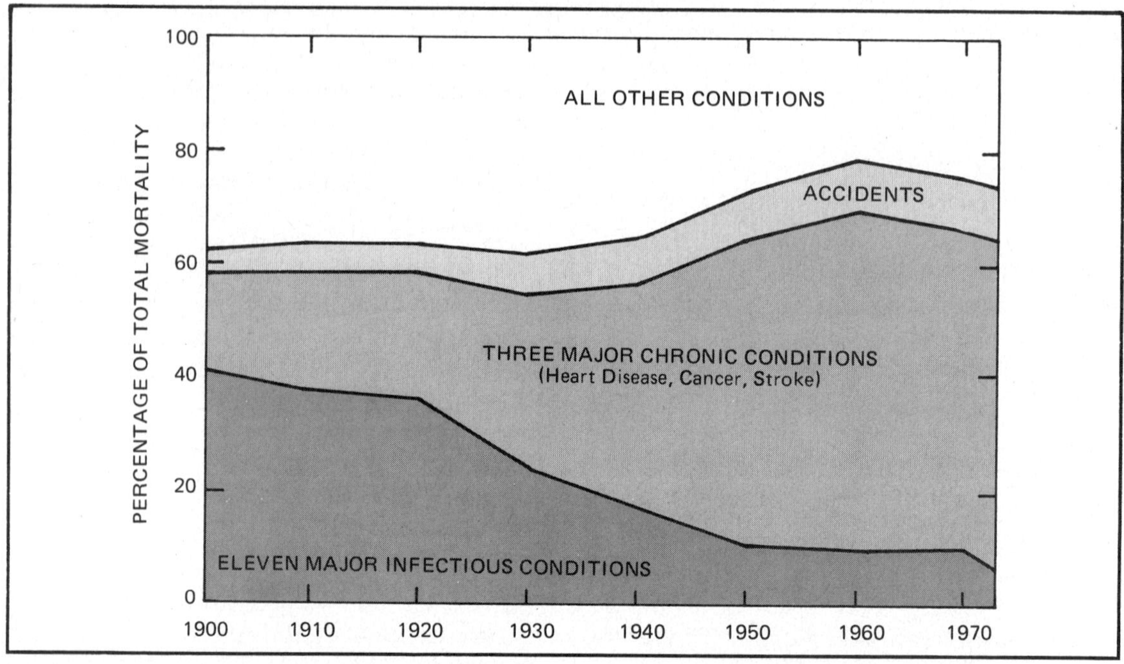

During the 20th century, infectious diseases have accounted for fewer deaths, while three chronic diseases have caused an increase in total mortality.

Source: J. B. McKinlay and S. M. McKinlay, "The Questionable Contribution of Medical Measures to the Decline of Mortality in the United States in the Twentieth Century." *Milbank Memorial Quarterly/Health & Society,* 55 (1977):405–428.

ventions in the "conquest" of infectious disease.

A more recent study by John McKinlay and Sonja McKinlay has elaborated upon this argument.[44] They examined nine infectious diseases in the U.S. from 1900 to 1973 and found that the mortality rates of all diseases except polio were declining *before* the medical intervention (vaccination or treatment) was introduced. (We can see several examples in Figure 12.4.) While some have criticized the specific examples presented[45] or argued that medical intervention has had a greater effect than these researchers suggest,[46] it is clear that this perspective underlines the need for a broader, more comprehensive approach to understanding disease and its control.

Since physicians and lay people alike saw medicine as the primary factor in the reduction of infectious disease, the medical model and its emphasis on "magic bullets"[47] reinforced "sick care" over a more broadly conceived "health care." And the increase of chronic diseases—which affect people for long periods of time and are often subject to long-term medical care—has contributed to the increasing costs of medical care.

Ivan Illich, a well-known author and social critic, takes the limitations of medicine argument to its logical, if extreme, conclu-

Figure 12.4 **The Fall in the Standardized Death Rate (per 1,000 Population) for Four Common Infectious Diseases in Relation to Specific Medical Measures, for the United States, 1900–1973.**

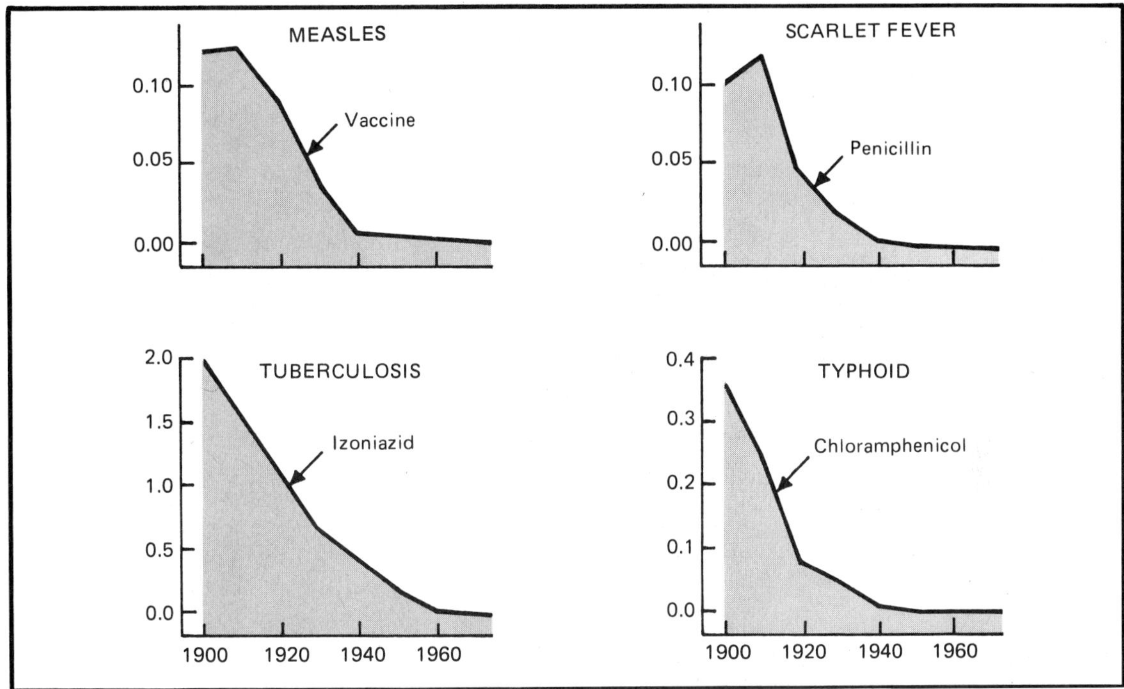

This figure shows that the decline of the death rate for four infectious diseases preceded the introduction of specific medical measures to deal with them. Underscored is the importance of social change in the reduction of the death rate and the tendency to overemphasize the role played by the medical profession and medical innovations.

Source: J. B. McKinlay and S. M. McKinlay, "The Questionable Contribution of Medical Measures to the Decline of Mortality in the United States in the Twentieth Century." *Milbank Memorial Quarterly/Health & Society,* 55 (1977):405–428.

sion. In his book *Medical Nemesis*[48] Illich argues that medicine is not only limited in its effect on health, it actually does more harm than good. He contends that medical care is either socially or clinically *iatrogenic,* that is, the diagnosis or treatment itself causes disease or disability. Illich connects the historical limitations of medicine with the development of a professional monopoly of medicine. He sees patients as more or less defenseless in the hands of the medical monopoly. Illich argues that we have given up our autonomy to medical professionals and that the only cure for "medical nemesis" is the deprofessionalization of medicine and the substitution of self-care. In short, he contends that we should abolish most of what we know as the medical profession. One need not accept Illich's radical view to accept the notion that social factors may be as important as biomedical factors in causing and preventing disease, or that the professional organization of medicine may be a significant cause of our health care problems. Undoubtedly some aspects of medical care are useful and important; the questions are which ones and under what circumstances.

The Professionalization and Monopolization of Medicine

Physicians have a professional monopoly of medical practice in America. This monopoly allows the medical profession an enormous control of all the affairs related to health and contributes to nearly all of the problems we have examined. Only physicians can legally practice medicine. It was not always that way. In the early nineteenth century various groups of "irregular" practitioners such as homeopaths, midwives, and botanical doctors competed freely for the "medical turf." How did one group of practitioners, allopathic or "regular" physicians (MDs), achieve their monopoly?

One line of thinking might argue that physicians achieved their exclusive rights of medical practice because of their superior scientific knowledge and clinical achievements. This argument suggests that people in the government recognized this expertise and therefore supported medical doctors' rights against other healers and quacks. But this does not seem to be the case. As we discussed above, the most significant improvements in the health status of the population came from social changes rather than clinical advances. In fact, in the early nineteenth century medicine was not a prestigious profession and physicians had a difficult time earning a living (something that seems very surprising today). Most had to supplement their medical work with another job, such as pharmacy or farming.[49] Medical techniques were rather primitive and limited until the twentieth century. "American colonial medical practice, like European practice of the period, was characterized by the lack of any substantial body of scientific knowledge."[50] As L. J. Henderson aptly observed, "Somewhere between 1910 and 1912 in this country, a random patient with a random disease consulting a doctor at random, had, for the first time in the history of mankind, a better than fifty-fifty chance of profiting from the encounter."[51]

The key to the MD-physicians' monopolization of medical care was the success of the American Medical Association (AMA) in consolidating medical power in its own hands. In 1847 a group of regular MD-physicians organized the AMA "to promote the science and art of medicine and the betterment of public health."[52] The AMA was also able to set and enforce standards and ethics over all medical practice and strive for exclusive professional and economic rights to the medical turf. Over a period of forty years, largely because of the AMA's politicking and the "cultural authority" physicians were developing, the AMA was able to gain state support, through licensing, for their exclusive rights over medical care.[53] This created a legally enforced monopoly of practice.

To control a professional monopoly one needs also to control the training of practitioners. In the early 1900s Abraham Flexner, a well-known educator, was hired by the Carnegie Foundation to evaluate the quality of medical schools in the United States. He found them to be largely inadequate. The Flexner Report on medical education was published in 1910 and it forced the closing of many weak medical schools and helped to place medical education under AMA professional control. One of the consequences of this was that it allowed the AMA to regulate the number of places in medical school. By limiting the number of places, an artificial "shortage" of doctors was created. The fewer the doctors, the smaller the number to share in the monopoly of practice. Fewer physicians meant that access to medical care would be limited, which especially affected the poor. It was only through federal intervention and support in the 1960s that the number of medical schools increased substantially and more doctors were trained.

The AMA was the crux of the regulars' attempt to "professionalize" medicine. As Magali Sarfatti Larson points out, professions organize to create and control markets.[54] Organized professions like medicine attempt to regulate and limit the competition, usually by controlling medical education and by limiting licensing. One consequence of this was the elimination of (mostly female) midwives' right to practice and severely limiting the number of women in medical training and practice. The regular physicians and the AMA set out to consolidate and control the market and they were successful.

The medical monopoly engendered a professional sovereignty and dominance unrivaled by other professions. This *professional dominance* gave physicians a monopoly of the "right" to knowledge, as well as the right to practice.[55] Physicians developed a dominance over other health workers—including nurses, pharmacists, and other professionals—and over the organization of their work. Physicians could set the standards for other medical workers' work and evaluate them as well. However, physicians themselves were "functionally autonomous." That is, physicians were insulated by their professional status from outside evaluation and generally free to regulate their own performance. It was very difficult for others to have legitimate ways of evaluating or criticizing physicians' work. The monopoly over medical practice includes the right to define what constitutes disease and how to treat it. This is a significant factor in the medicalization we discussed earlier. This professional medical sovereignty was not significantly challenged until the 1970s.[56]

In the past half-century medicine has become increasingly specialized. One consequence of this is that it has become much more difficult for people to find primary care (family) doctors. In 1929 only 25 percent of American physicians were full-time specialists; by 1969 the proportion had grown to 75 percent.[57] In 1950 there were 112,000 primary care practitioners; by 1973 there were only 50,000. With the demise of the G.P. (general practitioner) patients had a difficult time finding a family doctor and "housecalls" became an artifact of the past. This was especially true in rural areas, where physicians were few and difficult to reach. In the late 1960s, the AMA tried to upgrade general practice into its own specialty, family practice. Since that time the number of family doctors has increased significantly, but generalists like family doctors are not as prestigious as specialists and in some parts of the country there is still an unmet demand for primary care.

In the 1960s federal programs to expand medical schools increased greatly the number of physicians being trained. We are starting to experience the effects of the rising number of physicians. Between 1970 and 1990 an 80 percent increase in the number of physicians is expected—from about 325,000 to almost 600,000. Today there are about 500,000 doctors. There are some who argue that we are beginning to have a surplus of physicians,[58] which already seems to be true in certain specialties like surgery. Whether the increasing number of physicians will mean more accessible and better health care remains to be seen. It is also possible that as traditional medical specialties become saturated, doctors will expand into new medical turfs and we will see an increase in the medicalization of human problems. It is also possible that the high costs of medicine may limit the expansion of medical turf. Third-party payers may simply refuse to recognize or cover certain categories of life problems. The outcome is not yet clear.

Medicine in Capitalist Society

In a society with a capitalist economic system medicine, like any other service, is affected by the free enterprise system and the "profit motive." Until recent years policymakers showed little interest in the "business" aspects of medicine. But with the cost crisis of the past two decades, increasing attention is being paid to the financial structure of medicine.

The key element underlying the economic structure of medicine is the *fee-for-service* system. Fee-for-service means that a provider charges a fee for every service that is provided; for example, every office visit, lab test, surgical procedure, and so forth. Obviously the more services that are provided, the more fees that can be collected.

There are certain advantages for the delivery of medical care in a fee-for-service system. In an open market, fee-for-service would mean competition by providers and thus guarantee reasonable prices. Under a marketplace system, fee-for-services gives the providers incentive to be responsive to patients or they will go elsewhere for their medical services. Such a system should allow free choice for a provider and the patient as consumer. Finally, the fee acts as a screen and discourages patients from seeking unnecessary care.

But there are significant disadvantages to basing the financial structure of medical care on fee-for-service. First, when there is a medical monopoly there is no real competition, so medical costs do not follow the rules of the marketplace. What competition exists is among institutions within the medical system, leading to a duplication of services and a maldistribution of resources. Second, physicians define what the patient needs and then provide the service. Thus patients do not come to medical care as true consumers. They may come with a problem, but they do not come seeking a service and they rarely "shop around" for the best deal. Third, while the fee-for-service may screen out some demand for unnecessary medical care, it also may block some people from seeking medical care at all because of the cost and thus reduce the accessibility of services. Fourth, and perhaps most significant, fee-for-service puts the incentive in the wrong place. Rather than creating an incentive for prevention, fee-for-service provides incentive for more medical services ("sick care"), some of which may be unnecessary.

Fee-for-service is an important contributor to the problem that has been called "excess" or "unnecessary" surgery. While it is difficult to demarcate when poor judgment becomes unnecessary surgery, there is a consensus that between 15 and 30 percent of all surgery can be defined as unnecessary.[59] A 1974 Congressional report estimated that there were 2.4 million unnecessary operations in the United States, resulting in 11,900 avoidable deaths and a cost of $3.9 billion. It seems that the largest amount of excess surgery is found in such procedures as hysterectomies, tonsillectomies, hemorrhoidectomies, gall bladder removals, and most recently, Caesarian sections.[60] It appears that fee-for-service practice is an important contributor to this phenomenon, by creating "incentives" for unnecessary services. There is some evidence that salaried physicians (who do not work on a fee-for-service basis) perform less surgery. An interesting comparison is the fact that the United States has twice as many surgeons as Great Britain and twice the amount of surgery per population. Recent programs calling for "second opinions" for elective surgery have been somewhat successful in reducing the problem, although it has not been eliminated.

The predominance of the fee-for-service system in the context of a medical monopoly has been a major contributor to the current health care cost crisis.

A second important element in the cost crisis is the emergence of the *third-party payers* of medical care and the lack of instituted cost controls. As differentiated from direct or out-of-pocket payments, third-party payments are those made through some form of insurance, charity, or government program (hence the term "third-party"). The major forms of third-party payments in the United States are private health insurance (including Blue Cross/Blue Shield) and federal Medicaid and Medicare programs. The proportion of our health care bill paid by third parties has grown significantly in three decades: in 1952, 32 percent of personal health care costs were paid by third parties; by 1982 it was up to 68 percent.[61] Over 80 percent of the American people are covered by some government or private insurance (although sometimes only for hospital costs). The government and the insurance industry have become central in financing health care in this country.

There are considerable social and medical benefits from having third parties pay for medical care. These include the notion that people do not have to worry about most hospital and medical care costs when they become sick, making first-rate medical care available and affordable to much of the population and protecting families against costs of an expensive and long-term illness.

However, the dominance of third-party payers has also contributed to our health care problem. Since most health insurance is provided by employers for employees or the government for the poor and elderly, people tend not to act as "consumers" of medical care. In fact, in these cases people usually do not even choose their insurance programs. Moreover, the providers often bill the insurance company directly and the patients are involved only when the insurance does not cover a certain procedure. Most insurance policies only cover care received in a hospital, thus providing disincentives for less expensive outpatient or home care. Even more importantly, until recent years third-party payers paid whatever the doctor or hospital asked; any "reasonable and customary" fee. Medical costs continually rose and the insurance industry paid the fees and raised the insurance premiums. There were no checks on efficiency or cost-benefit ratios and little incentive to control spiraling costs. It is only in the last decade that the insurance industry seriously tried to limit medical costs. Finally, over 200 million Americans have some type of private medical insurance. A very large proportion of these are written by commercial insurance companies (such as Aetna, Prudential, Equitable Life, etc.) that sell health policies as part of their insurance business. A certain portion of these health costs are defined as part of these companies' earnings or profits, contributing to rising health costs.[62]

The most recent trend in health care has been the *corporatization* of medical services. Fueled by the rise of third-party payments and the increase in the number of physicians, there has been a significant expansion of the number of for-profit institutions in medicine.[63] Arnold Relman, editor of the prestigious *New England Journal of Medicine,* calls this the "new medical-industrial complex" and warns about its threat to professional medical care.[64] Foremost in the new medical-industrial complex are proprietary nursing homes, large investor-owned hospital "chains" (such as Humana and Hospital Corporation of

America), and the walk-in emergi-centers that are springing up all over the suburban landscape. These are all privately owned corporations that are in the medical business because they believe it is profitable. Their promoters claim they can provide service equal to the "nonprofits" to needed markets with better business efficiency, thereby saving costs. One recent study in California, however, suggests costs and patient charges are higher in investor-owned hospitals.[65] Some critics express concern that since these facilities are businesses first, they will put profits before patients. For example, they may drop unprofitable (but needed) services and use intensive marketing to increase the use of unneeded (but profitable) services. While potential exists for some cost savings here, there is also the possibility of increased costs and decreased services in the name of good business.

Corporatization is a complex issue. As sociologist Paul Starr points out, the corporate entry into medical care is a threat to the professional sovereignty and dominance of physicians.[66] If this is correct, control of medical care will be largely taken out of the hands of the medical profession. As the balance of power in medicine changes, it will shift some of the priorities and problems as well. It is difficult to predict exactly how this will turn out.

The Growth of Medical Technology

Along with the rise of specialized medicine and the corporate influence, there has been a significant growth in the uses of technology in medicine. With our increasing knowledge, we are able to bring more and more technological solutions to medical problems. Some of these have literally been life-savers. They have, however, also brought with them a new set of problems.

Technological innovations such as CT scanners, hemodialysis machines, electronic fetal monitors, and neonatal infant care units, have transformed medical care. These medical technologies contribute enormously to the cost of medical care, although they are usually justified by claims of saving lives or reducing maladies. But medical technologies are often adopted before they are adequately tested and become "standard procedures" without sufficient evidence for their efficacy.[67] Some expensive technologies, such as cardiac care units, have become widely adopted despite high costs and contradictory evidence about their effectiveness.[68] The "technological imperative" in medicine, which leads to a "can do-should do" ethic, encourages the extensive use of new technologies.

Life-saving medical technological solutions are of course beneficial, but they can be very expensive. Let us briefly look at the example of hemodialysis machines. Before the advent of dialysis machines, people with end-stage renal disease (kidney failure) would die. With this technology people can receive a 4- or 5-hour dialysis treatment 3 times a week and continue to live their lives. (Most hope eventually to obtain a kidney transplant and get off dialysis treatment.) Continued dialysis treatment, however, is very expensive at about $25,000 a year. In 1972 end-stage renal disease (and dialysis treatment) became the only disease of the nonelderly to receive Medicare funding. When the law was enacted in 1972 only 40 patients per million were receiving hemodialysis treatment; by 1980 there were over 200 patients per million. The cost of treating these roughly 50,000 patients for this one disease is $2 billion.[69] No doubt, even with its discomforts, dialysis is a miracle treatment for sufferers of end-stage renal disease. But can we as a society afford to use all expensive technologies for all diseases? It seems clear that as much as we might like to, we will not be able to (unless there is a major reorientation of government policies, such as drastic reduction of the military budget). Imagine, for example, the advent of a readily usable "artificial heart," a technology that really is not very far away. Assuming it costs $50,000, will everyone with heart disease be able to get one? And who will pay for it? If such technologies are limited, how will we decide who gets one? Is age the criteria? Social worth? Ability to pay for it? In Great Britain, where the government pays for all health care, dialysis is only begun on patients under 55 years old.[70] How will we "ration" expensive and lifesaving technologies in a society with limited resources? If we do nothing, we implicitly "ration" in favor of those who have the resources to pay for it. Clearly, some difficult questions lie ahead in relation to costs and, to a degree, accessibility.

Neonatal infant care units (NICUs) are housed in most major medical centers. They are complex high-technology centers that allow physicians to "salvage" (the medical term) infants who would otherwise die. Some of these infants are simply very premature babies with very low birth weight.[71] Physicians in NICUs currently initiate very aggressive interventive treatment at birth in order to save the infant. "In spite of vigorous treatment, however, the survival rate for these tiny infants is relatively low and among survivors the neurological outcome is often poor. The very low birth weight infant is susceptible to brain injury, which may result in handicaps such as mental retardation and cerebral

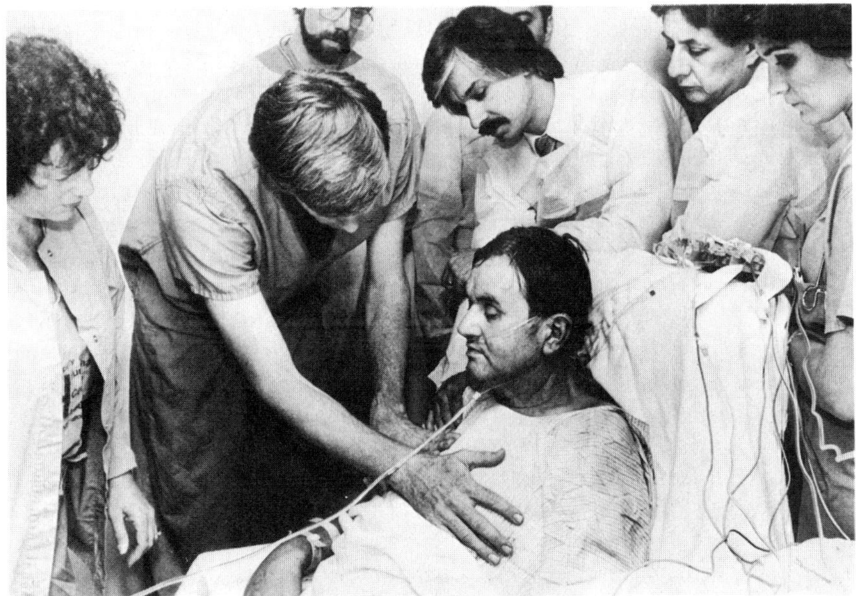

William Schroeder was one of the first artificial heart recipients. While dramatic, the issue is whether society can afford such technological marvels. If not everyone who needs one can get an artificial heart, how do we decide who receives one?

(William Strode/Sygma)

palsy."[72] The estimated cost of the NICU medical interventions for these low birth weight babies is $238.5 million or about $67,842 to produce a survivor.

Beyond fueling health costs, new technologies can create other dilemmas. We have already mentioned the possibility of rationing certain expensive interventions. In other cases, people may want *less* treatments. For example, some parents and interested parties have raised questions about whether doctors in NICUs should be "salvaging" some of these infants—many of whom may be severely disabled if they live. They question what kind of life these infants will have, even if they survive. This has on occasion pitted parents against those who support medical intervention. Parents are concerned with the "quality of life" a severely disabled child will have when he or she grows up as well as the enormous cost (social and economic) of supporting the child through his or her lifetime. Raising the quality of life issue brings us directly to the social-psychological dimensions of health care. What are the consequences of health care for peoples' lives?

SOCIAL-PSYCHOLOGICAL LEVEL

The Sick Role and the Experience of Illness

As the types of diseases in society change from infectious to chronic, so does our understanding of the social-psychological experiences of illness. When sociologist Talcott Parsons developed the concept of "the sick role" in the 1950s, he had in mind acute forms of illness (typically infectious diseases) where people become sick, are treated, and fully recover.[73] To a degree, this focus resulted from the dominant "sick-care" orientation of our medical system. Parsons argued that in order to prevent the potentially disruptive consequences of illness in a group or society, there exists a set of culturally shared roles and norms which he called "the sick role." In his formulation the sick role has two benefits and two obligations. The benefits are that (1) the sick person is exempted from normal social responsibilities, at least to the extent it is necessary to get well and (2) the individual is not held responsible for his or her condition and cannot be expected to recover by an act of will alone. The obligations are that (1) the person must recognize that it is undesirable to be ill and want to recover and (2) the sick person is obligated to seek and cooperate with "expert" advice, generally that of a physician. There have been numerous criticisms of the sick-role concept, but only a few need concern us here.

Today, with chronic illness as the most prevalent form of disease, the sick-role model no longer adequately describes the experience of sick people. Conditions like diabetes, multiple sclerosis, and arthritis do not necessarily improve with time or medical care, so people must learn to live with them. Even diseases like cancer and heart disease are long-term conditions. People with these kinds of chronic illness often are not accorded the sick-role exemptions Parsons suggested. For example, they cannot be expected to recover and thus are not always relieved of normal social responsibilities. Sometimes people are blamed for their disease. Illnesses such as leprosy, epilepsy, and venereal disease carry a stigma that is a type of blame. And the rates of "noncompliance" with medical regimens suggest that not all patients regularly follow doctors' orders.[74] This does not mean that the concept of the sick role is wrong—only that it is limited to certain types of illnesses under certain conditions. We all know that there are ways in which we can obtain social exemptions by using the sick role; for example, a note from a doctor certifying illness may allow us to miss an important exam without penalty.

One of the consequences of the increasing medicalization has been the extension of the sick role to more human problems. This has at least conditionally legitimated some forms of deviance. For example, if alcoholics are accorded this sick role, they are not blamed (or, at least, are blamed less) for their drinking and are deemed in need of treatment rather than punishment. While in this case the sick role may contribute to an alcoholic's recovery, medicalizing deviance also has the social consequences discussed earlier.

To better understand the experience of a chronic illness, a few sociologists have attempted to develop a more subjective or "insider's" account of what it is like to be sick.[75] This view focuses on the sufferer's perspective and examines management strategies, interactions with others, and the effect of illness on identity and self.

For example, a recent study developed a sociological interpretation of what it is like to have epilepsy.[76] One aspect of the study examined how people handled the potential stigma of others knowing they had epilepsy. This problem is of some concern to people with epilepsy because they are frequently discriminated against in a number of ways (denied employment, driver's licenses, insurance, and sometimes interpersonally as well). Thus a large proportion of people with epilepsy are "in the closet." Contrary to what one might think, people with epilepsy do not always conceal the fact that they have epilepsy, but carefully parcel out information about it. They sometimes go to great lengths to conceal their disorder and lie about it to achieve practical ends, such as getting a job. But they also reveal information about it in certain situations. The authors call these strategies "instrumental" and "therapeutic" telling. Instrumental telling is usually for a specific purpose, such as when a person wants to reduce the fear and confusion others might have should they witness a seizure. For example, a college student might tell a roommate not to worry if a seizure occurred; "just make me comfortable and keep me from hurting myself by falling." Therapeutic telling involves sharing important facts about oneself, similar to letting out something that one has been holding back. For example, one woman told the researchers that in her whole life she had never told anybody other than her parents and doctor that she had epilepsy. Although she had had only two seizures in her life, she thought epilepsy was the worst thing in the world. She said: "It just seems so weird now that I've—because I'm talking to you about it. It's really not so bad. You know, it hasn't affected me that much, but no one wants to talk about it. . . . [Talking about epilepsy] makes me feel I'm not so bad off."[77]

Disclosing such a secret selectively to supportive and nonjudgmental others can help "banish the ghosts" that flourish in secrecy and isolation. Controlling information about a potentially discreditable part of self, either by concealing or revealing it, is an important strategy in managing epilepsy and perhaps other conditions as well. Significantly, it is an attempt by sufferers to gain some control over their illness.

Professional dominance and the medicalization of society have contributed to the common perception that the "objective" aspects—diagnosis, medical treatment—of illness are the only significant ones. With the predominance of chronic illness, we can begin to see a shift from sick care to health care. In this context it becomes increasingly important to pay more attention to the subjective side of sickness. Sufferers expend a considerable amount of time and energy managing their illnesses and everyday "health care." When subjective experience is shared with others, it can precipitate the development of the types of self-help movements we discuss in the next section.

PART III: RESPONSES

Since health care has become a major public issue, there have been numerous attempts to address its problems. In the 1960s the federal government set out to develop programs to improve access to and equality of medical care. In the 1970s the government shifted its focus toward controlling costs, in part by encouraging new and innovative methods of delivering medical care. In the 1980s, the government has attempted to reduce medical costs by cutting back expenditures, resulting in some new problems of access and inequality. The rise of self-help movements has challenged aspects of medicalization and has struggled for reforms in the medical care of women. The new initiatives in health promotion may in a small way begin to neutralize the sick-care orientation. The continuing social responses to health care in our society make it a particularly dynamic and changing problem.

Governmental Actions

Since just after World War II, when Congress passed the Hill-Burton Act, which supported hospital building and expansion, the federal government has been increasingly involved in the shaping, and to a degree the financing, of the delivery of medical services.

The largest federal commitment came under the Johnson administration in 1965 in the forms of Medicare and Medicaid (officially, Titles 18 and 19 of the Social Security Act). With the advent of these programs, the federal government became a major factor in health care financing and reimbursement. Medicare was an expansion of the Social Security system and was intended to improve access to services for the elderly by paying for most of their health bills. Medicaid was aimed at the "medically indigent" and was part of the 1960s "war on poverty." It was a joint federal-state program that was to help make medical care accessible to the poor. Before 1965 the federal government paid about 10 percent of all medical expenditures. By 1982 it paid for nearly 30 percent of health care costs, or $87 billion. The federal contribution to Medicare alone had risen from a couple of billion dollars in 1965 to $52 billion in 1982 and it is still rising.

The Medicare-Medicaid response has had a number of consequences. Medicare has provided basic medical insurance coverage for 99 percent of Americans over 65.[78] While there are still significant out-of-pocket expenses, this widespread coverage is a stark contrast when compared with the lack of coverage of the elderly prior to 1965. Medicaid has been much less comprehensive. Because it is a federal-state matching program, coverage varies from state to state. While the poor receive more coverage than before Medicaid, because of severe restrictions of eligibility about 60 percent of the poor are not covered by Medicaid. Utilization of services has increased under Medicaid so that the poor, who have higher rates of sickness than the nonpoor, visit medical services more frequently than other groups.[79] Because the broadest coverage of Medicaid is for women and dependent children, its major impact has been on maternal and child health.

Although federal programs have surely helped some sick people and reduced inequality and inaccessibility of medical services, their effect is limited. Under the Reagan administration there were a number of cutbacks in these programs. But, even before these cutbacks, Medicare covered less than half the elderly's health expenses, and Medicaid covered only a third of that of the poor.[80] And, we must note, there are over 25 million Americans with no insurance at all.[81]

The intent of Medicare and Medicaid is certainly worthy, even if the results are limited. But these programs also created new problems. They put billions of new dollars into the health system with no cost controls, so it was clear by the 1970s that Medicare and Medicaid were fueling escalating health costs. Some people were reaping enormous profits from the system, especially owners of shoddy nursing homes and so-called "Medicaid mills." Tightening restrictions eliminated the worst offenders, but medical costs continued to soar.

In the early 1970s, the federal government began to mandate a series of programs aimed at reducing costs, especially with Medicare. In 1972 utilization review boards—hospital-based committees—were instituted to review the appropriateness of medical utilization. These were followed by Professional Standard Review Organizations (PSRO), which were intended to monitor both quality and cost of care. In the middle 1970s, the nation was divided up into dozens of Health System Agencies (HSAs), which were to be regionalized health-planning agencies. HSAs attempted to limit uncontrolled hospital and technological growth by requiring a "certificate of need" approval before there could be any new investment over $100,000. There were even attempts to put a "cap" (ceiling) on the total amount that could be allocated to a program. While a few cost-control programs had limited effects in specific situations, overall the federal attempt to control costs so far has been a failure.

The newest federal attempt to control costs is a complex reimbursement system called "diagnostically related groups" (DRGs). Mandated in 1984 for Medicare, this program replaces the fee-for-service system with a form of "prospective reimbursement" where the government will pay only a specific amount for a specific medical problem. The prices of 467 specific diagnoses are established in advance. Medicare will pay no more, no less. If a hospital spends less than the set amount, it is allowed to retain the difference. The hope is that hospitals will have the incentive to be efficient and save money. The concern is that patients will get poorer treatment.

Costs remain a critical problem. With the aging population and rising medical costs, the threat of bankrupting the Social Security system looms on the not-so-distant horizon.

Health Maintenance Organizations

In the 1970s a new form of medical organization came into prominence: the health maintenance organization or HMO. While a number of programs began in the 1950s (for example, Kaiser-Permanante in California and the Health Insurance Plan of Greater New York), it was only when the federal government began to support them in the 1970s that HMOs really started to flourish. HMOs are designed to modify the fee-for-service system (thus reducing costs) and to shift the emphasis in medicine toward "health care." They are essentially a "prepaid group practice." Subscribers pay a yearly fee to belong to an HMO and in turn the HMO provides all necessary medical care. HMOs reverse the traditional incentive: instead of an incentive for providing "sick care" because it is reimbursable, these organizations have the incentive to keep people healthy and out of the hospital. HMOs can be seen as an alternative to the traditional fee-for-service system and as a means for controlling health care costs.

There are several forms of HMOs, but their major characteristics include:

1. A defined population of enrolled members;
2. Payments (by members) determined in advance for a specific period of time and made periodically;
3. Services provided to a patient by HMO physicians for essentially all medical needs, with reference to outside specialists controlled by HMOs; and
4. Voluntary enrollment by each individual or family.[82]

HMOs vary in their organization. Most are multispecialty practices with anywhere from four to over a hundred physicians. Physicians are usually paid by salary rather than on a fee-for-service basis. In many HMOs patients choose their own medical provider—a doctor or nurse practitioner—but some require patients to see whatever doctor is available. Nearly all require patients to see a doctor within the group, if available. For example, a pregnant woman would have to choose one of the obstetricians associated with the HMO. While this limits choice, clients do not seem to find it a major problem. There is little evidence of lower quality care in HMOs; in fact, there is even some suggestion that care is better.[83]

By 1983 there were over 250 HMOs in operation, enrolling about 12 million people. Some are nonprofit and others are corporately sponsored. (To a small degree the latter may contribute to the corporatization of medicine.[84]) There are some suggestive figures about HMOs. A recent national survey reported that HMO subscribers spent only half as many days in the hospital as those who have traditional health insurance.[85] A review of all studies of HMOs suggests that they tend to save money compared to conventional insurance coverage—ranging from 10 to 40 percent in savings.[86] It is not yet clear whether HMOs may attract a self-selected population of younger and healthier people, which would partially explain the cost savings, but the results so far are impressive.

HMOs are perceived as a major answer to health care problems, including cost, accessibility, and sick care. And the early results are promising. But HMOs need to be expanded beyond their relatively small, largely middle-class base to cover more people before they will truly make an impact. It may be especially important to have them expanded to include various underserved groups, including poor, elderly, and rural populations. The future potential of HMOs to affect our health care problems is considerable.

The Rise of Self-Help Groups

Self-help and mutual aid groups have a long history in Western society.[87] Since the 1960s we have seen the emergence of thousands of self-help groups. Among other things, these groups have presented a challenge to the increasing medicalization of human problems and in a specific and important way, made a unique contribution to women's health.

Self-help groups can take several forms. One way of looking at them is in terms of their relationship to the medical profession. In this sense we can see groups as having an adjunct, alternative, or advocacy orientation. We separate these orientations only for clarity of discussion; in actuality many groups share all three orientations.

Adjunct self-help groups include those groups of people who band together for mutual support and information exchange. Their work parallels and supports that of the medical profession. Examples include Emphysemas Anonymous, Mended Hearts (heart surgery), stroke clubs, the International Larynectomee Association, epilepsy groups, and Reach for Recovery (mastectomy). These are not social clubs per se but are organized to give services that do not otherwise exist.[88] They share the unusual benefit of bringing together new and isolated sufferers with "people who have been there."

Some self-help groups seek to provide an alternative to the care given by the medical profession. One of the best examples of this is the Women's Health Movement, especially as it existed through the 1970s. This is one of the most widespread and successful self-help groups in recent years. Many feminists concluded that medical services, particularly gynecological care, were not sensitive to women's needs and were demeaning to them. In an unusually large variety of locations, women organized their own women's health centers and gynecological clinics. They trained women to do their own gynecological exams and helped women do them for each other.[89] While the clinics usually had medical back-up, they were able to provide sensitive and humane services by themselves. This was also true with birth control and birthing care.

One of the great triumphs of the Women's Health Movement was a book entitled *Our Bodies, Ourselves* by the Boston Women's Health Collective.[90] Now in its third edition, this book has sold millions of copies and has been translated into several languages. The book includes lay explanations of medical knowledge about health problems of women presented in clearly written language and an attractive format. While it is often critical of the medical profession's treatment of women, the main goal of the book is to provide information so that women can make better decisions about their health. In addition to demystifying the body and medical problems, this book served as a guide to self-help, reaching many more women than the clinics were able to serve.

Health knowledge and self-help abilities were *empowering* to women who began to challenge professional dominance and attempted to gain more control over their health. It was clearly a grass-roots response to the women's health issues discussed earlier. In recent years, although many of the self-help clinics have diminished due to funding problems, the Women's Health Movement has continued to provide alternative information and has emerged as an important advocacy group for women's health issues.

Self-help groups can become advocates for their members both in terms of the medical profession and society at large. The handicapped in our society have long been a "hidden minority."[91] In the 1970s disabled and handicapped people began demanding their rights. The legal keystone to this disability movement is the 1973 Rehabilitation Act, which prohibited discrimination against "otherwise qualified handicapped" individuals "under any program or activity receiving Federal financial assistance." The far-reaching implications of this have led some to call it "the civil rights act of the handicapped."[92]

A major part of the disability self-help movement is the Independent Living Movement, early examples of which were located in Berkeley, California, and Boston. In addition to raising consciousness about architectural barriers and discrimination against the handicapped, these two centers provide a wide range of services, primarily managed by disabled people themselves. These include peer counseling, attendant care, referral, training in independent living, advocacy services, health maintenance, housing referral, and wheelchair repair. Similar centers have sprung up around the country.[93] By its lobbying, public relations, and open advocacy, the disability movement has changed the world in which many disabled people live and has succeeded in changing parts of society (and medical care) to make life for disabled people more like that of the able-bodied.

There are, of course, some limitations to self-help groups. They alone cannot solve our health care problems, since the problems are deeply rooted in the structure of society and the medical system. With a few exceptions, such as the Women's Health Movement and the disability movement, most of the groups take an individual rather than a social structural approach to self-help. That is, they feel it is enough to help their individual members rather than to change problematic aspects of society. This limits their vision of the possibilities of change. Self-help groups reach only a small group of people. They tend not to have mass appeal and attract mostly middle-class people.[94]

Nevertheless, health-oriented self-help groups have made a powerful impact on health care in America. They provide support and services where there were none; they have challenged and altered aspects of the medical profession and medical care; they have directly questioned the medicalizaton of society; they continue to demonstrate that not all health care needs to be mystified and professionalized; and perhaps most significantly, they have empowered people to see that health care is something that they can affect and even control.

Health Promotion and Prevention

Along with the popular interest in fitness and health in our society (for example, jogging, health foods, health clubs) has come a new interest in health promotion and disease prevention. Much of this interest stems from the emergence of chronic disease as the major health problem and the lack of success of the traditional medical approach in preventing these diseases.

There is accumulating evidence that aspects of people's *life style* have an effect on health and the risk of disease and that modification of one's life style can promote health and reduce risk. Leon Breslow and his associates have conducted research into the "causes" of health in the same way others have studied the causes of disease. After following a sample of nearly 7,000 adults for over five years, they showed that life expectancy and health are significantly related to seven fundamental health habits:

1. Eat three meals a day at regular times and don't snack;
2. Have breakfast every day;
3. Engage in moderate exercise two or three times a week;
4. Get adequate sleep (7 to 8 hours a night);
5. Don't smoke;
6. Keep weight moderate;
7. Drink no alcohol or only in moderation.[95]

These health habits have a cumulative effect. A person with six or seven of these habits would be likely to live *eleven* years longer than someone with three or less.

The movement toward health promotion got a big boost with the 1979 publication of the Surgeon General's report on disease prevention and health promotion, *Healthy People*.[96] The report recognizes the "limitations of modern medicine" and highlights the importance of behavioral and social factors in health. It deemphasizes the role of physicians in controlling health activities and argues persuasively for the need to turn from "sick care" to prevention. It suggests that people adopt better diets, with more whole grains and less red meat, sugar, and salt; stop smoking; exercise regularly; keep weight down; seek proper prenatal and postnatal care; and so forth. Importantly, it sets specific goals that the nation should achieve by 1990 (reduce infant mortality from 12 per thousand to 9 per thousand, for example). In some circles *Healthy People* was deemed a revolutionary report, more significant than the 1964 Surgeon General's report on smoking. On the one hand, the report officially legitimates the centrality of social and behavioral factors in caring for our health. On the other hand, some have criticized the report for overemphasizing individual life style rather than social structural changes.[97] Ideally health could be promoted on all fronts: societal, life style, and biomedical.

One of the most interesting innovations in health care has been the emergence of corporate health promotion or "wellness" programs in the workplace.[98] A recent study of California employers with more than 100 employees found that 21.1 percent (N = 424) of the employers developed corporate wellness programs sufficiently to offer four or more health promotion activities,[99] including smoking cessation, nutrition and weight control, exercise/fitness, stress management, and the like. Major corporations, including Lockheed, Control Data, Metropolitan Life, Johnson and Johnson, IBM, Pepsico, and the Ford Motor Company, among many others, have developed programs they deem successful.

Business pays an enormous part of health costs through health insurance benefits—an estimated $77 billion in 1983. General Motors, for example, spends more on health insurance than on steel.[100] Not

Many corporations have recently set up facilities to encourage their employees to exercise and stay fit.

(David Burnett/Woodfin Camp & Associates)

surprisingly, one of the major goals of corporate programs is to control health costs, specifically by keeping workers healthier and reducing hospitalization. Other goals include decreasing absenteeism, improving worker morale, and increasing productivity. Some early results are promising, particularly in terms of reducing cardiovascular risk of stroke or heart attack. Numerous companies claim dramatic increases in fitness, reductions in the number of smokers, and success in improving nutrition and controlling weight.[101] One recent careful study found that worksite programs can produce substantial reductions in hypertension, a major risk factor for cardiovascular diseases.[102]

Most of these life style approaches to health promotion are relatively new and it will take many years before we know how effective they are in decreasing the need for health care and controlling costs. Health promotion is no panacea for our health problems, but it is a beacon for innovative approaches to health.

National Health Care Policies

Ultimately, when we talk about solutions to health care problems, we need to confront national health care policies. The United States is the only major Western industrialized nation without some type of national health insurance. National health insurance (NHI) is a program in which the government pays for the health care of its citizens, usually from tax revenues. Congress has regularly considered such programs in the past. From the turn of the century onward, dozens of proposals for NHI have been proposed and defeated. These defeats were influenced by the AMA's lobbying, the fear of "socialized medicine," and the concern with how much NHI would cost taxpayers. So many major bills were introduced in Congress in the 1970s that experts predicted we would have an NHI program in place by 1980.[103] With the advent of the Reagan administration and a more conservative Congress, there has been little concern for developing NHI.

Let us briefly look at two other medical systems for examples of how other Western societies have responded to the health problem. In 1948 Great Britain reorganized its system into a National Health Service (NHS).[104] A NHS program goes even further than an NHI: the government not only finances medical care but actually controls and operates the system. The NHS is a public system of medicine: hospitals, clinics, physicians, and other medical personnel work under the auspices and control of the Ministry of Health. The fee-for-service system has been eliminated. The NHS is financed by progressive tax revenues, with essentially no cost to the patient at the time of services, and physicians are paid in yearly stipends. This has reduced the "profit motive" in medicine and allowed the government to influence the system directly. It is a good example of what is often called "socialized medicine."

During its thirty-year development, the NHS managed admirable accomplishments, including: (1) eliminating financial barriers to access; (2) making the system more rational and equitable; (3) providing care on a community level with community-based physicians; (4) maintaining a high level of medical care quality; and (5) controlling costs. The final point deserves elaboration. The NHS seems to be more cost-effective than the largely private American system. Great Britain spends about 6 percent of its gross national product on health whereas America spends over 10 percent. Specifically, the British government spent only about $300 per citizen per year in 1978 for health care, compared to

American expenditures of $863 per person for all public and private health care during the same year.[105] And, by most measures, the health status of the populations are almost equal. Moreover, there is evidence that the NHS delivers care more equitably.

There are also problems with the NHS. The British have controlled costs by "rationing" medical services. While all necessary medical care is more or less available (with a few specific exceptions such as not beginning dialysis if a patient is over 55), patients who want elective services must "queue up" for them. There are in fact two- and three-year waiting lists for some elective medical care. Doctors, especially community-based general practitioners, have expressed dissatisfaction over their high patient loads, lower medical status, and relatively low salaries (especially when compared to the astronomical earnings of American physicians). And, in recent years, the NHS has felt the constraints of tight governmental fiscal policies. Overall, however, most sources report a high level of satisfaction with the NHS in Great Britain.

Closer to home, the Canadian medical system provides some interesting lessons. Canada is a country rather similar to the United States, although with a much smaller population. Between 1947 and 1971, Canada gradually introduced a national health policy that guaranteed medical care as a right for everyone. The form of NHI adopted by Canada is financed out of a progressive income tax and results in an increased equity in health services and a remarkable control of health costs. Before the NHI health costs in Canada and the U.S. were about the same. The NHI policy, implemented by the Canadian provinces, has been able to control health expenditures at about 7 percent of GNP while the U.S. has soared to 10 percent. Canada's cost for a health insurance system that covers everyone (as opposed to the fragmented American system that excludes over 10 percent of the population) is over $100 per person *less* than the U.S.[107] This impact comes from lowering administrative costs, removing profitability from selling health insurance, and being able to set controlling costs as a national priority.[108] Canada, although implementing a progressive financing system, has still maintained a fee-for-service, private enterprise orientation in the delivery of medical care. From all indications the health status of Canadians is equal to or better than that of Americans.

A major response to our health care problems eventually must be to develop a single system of medical care in the United States. It will more likely resemble an NHI than an NHS. This alone will not solve all health care problems,[109] but should make strides toward increasing equity by covering all Americans and by reducing costs through consistent and system-wide controls. Given the current political climate of reducing governmental social expenditures, however, it may be a few more years before a national American health policy becomes a reality.

SUMMARY

Part I: The Problem

1. The orientation of our medical system is one of *sick care* rather than health care, focusing our attention on curative rather than preventative solutions to health problems.
2. Over the past century, the domain of medicine has expanded to include a vast array of human problems, including childbirth, hyperactivity, and various forms of deviant behavior. The la-

tent consequences of *medicalization* may well outweigh the manifest benefits.

3. Numerous "women's problems" have been medicalized and certain aspects of medicine's structure and ideas have been deemed to be sexist and detrimental to women.
4. The poor continue to have unequal access to medical care, especially discretionary and preventative services. Recent cutbacks may exacerbate these inequities.
5. Health care costs have skyrocketed in the past 20 years, so now health care consumes 10.5 percent of the GNP. Increasing medical technology and "third-party payers" are part of the problem, as is our aging population. There is some question about how much a society can afford to pay for health care and whether we are getting "our money's worth."

Part II: Causes and Consequences

6. The rise of chronic illness is a major cause of our health care problem, in part because it requires an examination of complex etiologies.
7. Physicians' *professional monopoly* of medical practice has encouraged medicalization and made control of costs difficult.
8. In a capitalist society, a *fee-for-service* system can turn medical care into a profitable commodity, increasing costs, expanding the medical domain, and encouraging sick care. The role of third-party payers and corporatization is significant here.
9. The growth of medical technology has provided some life-saving solutions to medical problems but has also fueled rising costs and raised new questions about ethics and accessibility.
10. The technological orientation of modern medicine has given short shrift to the social-psychological aspects of illness. The subjective side of illness has been ignored in medicalized and sick-care orientations; with the predominance of chronic illness, it is increasingly important to pay attention to the subjective experience of illness.

Part III: Responses

11. The government has attempted to increase accessibility in a variety of ways, especially with Medicare and Medicaid, and in recent years has been unsuccessfully attempting to develop policies to control costs.
12. Health Maintenance Organizations (HMOs), a form of prepaid group practice, are a major new way of delivering medical care, reversing the traditional "sick-care" incentives and hopefully reducing costs.
13. Self-help and mutual aid groups have emerged as alternatives for people with chronic illness and as challenges to medicalization, professional dominance, and, most particularly, the medical treatment of women.
14. As a challenge to the sick care orientation, and to a lesser degree to control costs, considerable attention has recently been paid to various new forms of health promotion.
15. While the United States does not have national health insurance, there are important lessons to be learned from systems like those of Great Britain and Canada that could lead to changes in national policy.

SUGGESTED READINGS

Conrad, Peter, and Rochelle Kern, eds., *Sociology of Health and Illness: Critical Perspectives,* 2nd ed. New York: St. Martin's Press, 1985. A wide-ranging collection of sociological articles on the social production of disease and the medical care system.

Friedson, Eliot, *Profession of Medicine.* New York: Dodd, Mead, 1970. An excellent sociological analysis of the organization and dominance of the medical profession in America.

Starr, Paul, *The Social Transformation of American Medicine.* New York: Basic Books, 1982. This comprehensive sociohistorical analysis of the development of American medicine won the Pulitzer Prize.

U.S. Department of Health, Education and Welfare, *Healthy People: The Surgeon General's Report on Health Promotion and Disease Prevention.* Washington, D.C.: U.S. Government Printing Office, 1979. This primer on health promotion presents a great deal of material in an easily accessible style.

Waitzkin, Howard, *The Second Sickness.* New York: Free Press, 1982. This book presents a Marxian critical analysis of the dilemmas of health care in the United States.

NOTES

[1]Quoted in John McKinlay, "A Case for Refocusing Upstream: The Political Economy of Illness." In Peter Conrad and Rochelle Kern, eds., *Sociology of Health and Illness: Critical Perspectives* (New York: St. Martins, 1980), p. 613.

[2]*Ibid.*

[3]Samuel Epstein, *The Politics of Cancer* (New York: Doubleday, 1979).

[4]Robert Coombs, *Mastering Medicine* (New York: Free Press, 1978).

[5]Irving Kenneth Zola, "Medicine as an Institution of Social Control," *Sociological Review,* 20 (1972), 487–504; Eliot Freidson, *Profession of Medicine* (New York: Dodd, Mead, 1970).

[6]Peter Conrad and Joseph W. Schneider, *Deviance and Medicalization: From Badness to Sickness* (St. Louis: Mosby, 1980).

[7]Peter Conrad, *Identifying Hyperactive Children* (Lexington, Mass.: Heath, 1976).

[8]Peter Conrad, "The Discovery of Hyperkinesis: Notes on the Medicalization of Deviant Behavior," *Social Problems,* 23 (1975), 12–21.

[9]Richard Wertz and Dorothy Wertz, *Lying-In* (New York: Free Press, 1977).

[10]Barbara Katz Rothman, *In Labor* (New York: Norton, 1981).

[11]William Ray Arney, *Power and the Profession of Obstetrics* (Chicago: University of Chicago Press, 1982).

[12]Renee Fox, "The Medicalization and Demedicalization of American Society," *Daedalus* (Winter 1977), 9–22.

[13]Peter Conrad and Joseph W. Schneider, "Looking at Levels of Medicalization," *Social Science and Medicine,* 14A (1980), 75–79.

[14]Constance Natanson, "Sex, Illness and Medical Care: A Review of Data, Theory and Method," *Social Science and Medicine,* 11 (1977), 13–25.

[15]Ingrid Waldron, "Why Do Women Live Longer than Men?" *Social Science and Medicine,* 10 (1976), 349–362.

[16]Barbara Ehrenreich and Deirdre English, *For Her Own Good* (New York: Doubleday, 1978).

[17]G. J. Barker-Benfield, *Horrors of a Half-Known Life* (New York: Harper & Row, 1976); Wertz and Wertz, *op. cit.*

[18]Peter Gabrial Filene, *Him/Her/Self: Sex Roles in Modern America* (New York: Harcourt Brace Jovanovich, 1974).

[19]Diana Scully and Pauline Bart, "A Funny Thing Happened on the Way to the Orifice: Women in Gynecology Textbooks," *American Journal of Sociology,* 78 (1973), 1045–1051.

[20]Suzanne Arms, *Immaculate Deception* (Boston: Houghton Mifflin, 1975).

[21]Catherine Kohler Reissman, "Women and Medicalization: A New Perspective," *Social Policy,* 14 (1983), 3–18.

[22]Muriel Nellis, "Hooked, Women and Prescription Drugs," *The Boston Globe Magazine,* January 13, 1980, pp. 10–12.

[23]Francis B. McCrea, "The Politics of Menopause: The Discovery of Deficiency Disease," *Social Problems,* 31 (1983), 111–123.

[24]Department of Health, Education and Welfare, *Decennial Census Data* (Washington, D.C.: U.S. Government Printing Office, 1970).

[25]Jill Quadagno, "Occupational Sex Typing and Internal Labor Market Distributions: An Assessment of Medical Specialities," *Social Problems,* 23 (1976), 442–445.

[26]See Anselm Strauss, *Where Medicine Fails* (New Brunswick, N.J.: Transaction Books, 1972).

[27]Diana B. Dutton, "Explaining Low Use of Health Services by the Poor: Costs, Attitudes or Delivery Systems?" *American Sociological Review,* 43 (1978), 348–368.

[28]Department of Health and Human Services, *Health, United States, 1981* (Washington, D.C.: U.S. Government Printing Office, 1981).

[29]Wornie Reed, "Suffer the Children: Some Effects of Racism on the Health of Black Infants." In Peter Conrad and Rochelle Kern, eds. *op. cit.*, pp. 314–326.

[30]Department of Health, Education and Welfare, *Decennial Census Data for Selected Health Occupations: United States, 1970, op cit.*

[31]Jerry Weaver and Sharon Garret, "Sexism and Racism in the American Health Care Industry: A Comparative Analysis," *International Journal of Health Services,* 8 (1978), 677–703.

[32]Hal Strelnick, "Bakke-ing Up the Wrong Tree," *Health/PAC Bulletin* 11 (1980), p. 3.

[33]U.S. Department of Health and Human Services, *Third Report to the President and Congress, On the Status of Health Professions in the United States* (Washington, D.C.: U.S. Government Printing Office, 1982).

[34]Alan Sager, "The Reconfiguration of Urban Hospital Care: 1937–1980." In Ann L. Greer and Scott Greer, eds., "Cities and Sickness," *Urban Affairs Annual Review,* 26 (1983), pp. 55–98.

[35]John McKinlay and Sonja McKinlay, "Observations on the Proposition that the Health of the Population is Improving." Unpublished manuscript, Boston University, 1976.

[36]National Center for Health Statistics, *Health, United States, 1983* (Washington, D.C.: U.S. Government Printing Office, 1983), p. 89.

[37]Victor Fuchs, *Who Shall Live?* (New York: Basic Books, 1974), p. 60.

[38]National Center for Health Statistics, *op. cit.*, 1983, p. 186.

[39]Victor W. Sidel and Ruth Sidel, *A Healthy State* (New York: Pantheon, 1983).

[40]Some parts of this section are adapted from Peter Conrad and Rochelle Kern, eds., *op cit.*, pp. 10–11.

[41]Eric J. Cassell, *The Healer's Art* (New York: Penguin, 1979), p. 72.

[42]Rene Dubos, *Mirage of Health* (New York: Harper & Row, 1959).

[43]Thomas McKeown, "A Historical Appraisal of the Medical Task." In G. McLachlan and T. McKeown, eds., *Medical History and Medical Care: A Symposium of Perspectives* (New York: Oxford University Press, 1971), pp. 29–55. See also John Powles, "On the Limitations of Modern Medicine," *Science, Medicine and Man* 1 (1973), 1–30.

[44]John B. McKinlay and Sonja M. McKinlay, "The Questionable Contribution of Medical Measures to the Decline of Mortality in the United States in the Twentieth Century," *Milbank Memorial Quarterly/Health and Society,* 55 (1977), 405–428.

[45]Paul Starr, *The Social Transformation of American Medicine* (New York: Basic Books, 1982), p. 464.

[46]Sol Levine, Jacob J. Feldman, and Jack Elinson, "Does Medical Care Do Any Good?" In David Mechanic, ed., *Handbook of Health, Health Care and Health Professions* (New York: Free Press, 1983), pp. 394–404.

[47]Dubos, *op. cit.*

[48]Ivan Illich, *Medical Nemesis* (New York: Pantheon, 1976).

[49]William G. Rothstein, *American Physicians in the 19th Century: From Sects to Science* (Baltimore: Johns Hopkins University Press, 1972).

[50]*Ibid.*, p. 27.

[51]H. L. Blumgart, "Caring for the Patient," *New England Journal of Medicine,* 270 (1964), 449–456.

[52]Quoted in Rodney Coe, *The Sociology of Medicine,* 2nd ed. (New York: McGraw-Hill, 1978), p. 204.

[53]Starr, *op. cit.*

[54]M. S. Larson, *The Rise of Professionalism* (Berkeley: University of California Press, 1977).

[55]Eliot Freidson, *Professional Dominance* (Chicago: Aldine, 1970).

[56]Starr, *op. cit.*

[57]Stanley J. Reiser, *Medicine and the Reign of Technology* (New York: Cambridge Unversity Press, 1978).

[58]Starr, *op. cit.*

[59]R. S. McCleery and L. T. Keelty, *One Life-One Physician: Inquiry into the Medical Profession's Performance in Self-Regulation* (Washington, D.C.: Public Affairs Press, 1971).

[60]Duane Stroman, *The Quick Knife* (New York: Kennikat Press, 1978).

[61]National Center for Health Statistics, *op. cit.*, 1983, p. 186.

[62]Thomas Bodenheimer, Steven Cummings, and Elizabeth Harding, "Capitalizing on Illness: The Health Insurance Industry," *International Journal of Health Services,* 4 (1974), 583–598.

[63]Starr, *op. cit.*, pp. 420–449.

[64]Arnold Relman, "The New Medical-Industrial Complex," *New England Journal of Medicine*, 303 (1980), 963–970.

[65]Robert V. Pattison and Hall M. Katz, "Investor-Owned and Not-for-Profit Hospitals: A Comparison Based on California Data," *New England Journal of Medicine*, 309 (1983): 347–353.

[66]Starr, *op. cit.*

[67]John McKinlay, "From a 'Promising Report' to a 'Standard Procedure': Seven Stages in a Career of a Medical Innovation," *Milbank Memorial Fund Quarterly/Health and Society*, 59 (1981), 374–411.

[68]Howard Waitzkin, "A Marxian Interpretation of the Growth and Development of Coronary Care Technology," *American Journal of Public Health*, 69 (1979), 1260–1268.

[69]Robert L. Berg and Daniel B. Ornt, "End Stage Renal Disease: How Many, How Much?" *American Journal of Public Health*, 74 (1984), 4–5.

[70]Henry J. Aaron and William B. Schwartz, *The Painful Prescription: Rationing Hospital Care* (Washington, D.C.: The Brookings Institution, 1984).

[71]Carson Strong, "The Tiniest Newborns," *The Hastings Center Report*, 13 (February 1983), 14–19.

[72]*Ibid*, p. 14.

[73]Talcott Parsons, *The Social System* (New York: Free Press, 1950).

[74]Gerry V. Stimson, "Obeying Doctor's Orders: A View from the Other Side," *Social Science and Medicine*, 8 (1975), 97–104.

[75]Anselm L. Strauss and Barney G. Glaser, *Chronic Illness and the Quality of Life* (St. Louis, Mo.: Mosby, 1975).

[76]Joseph W. Schneider and Peter Conrad, *Having Epilepsy: The Experience and Control of Illness* (Philadephia: Temple University Press, 1983).

[77]*Ibid*, p. 159.

[78]Karen Davis and Diane Rowland, "Uninsured and Underserved: Inequities in Health Care in the United States," *Milbank Memorial Fund Quarterly/Health and Society*, 61 (1983):152.

[79]*Ibid*, p. 157.

[80]Starr, *op. cit.*, p. 374.

[81]Davis and Rowland, *op. cit.*, p. 152.

[82]Ernest W. Seward and Scott Fleming, "Health Maintenance Organizations," *Scientific American*, 243 (1980), p. 47.

[83]Harold S. Luft, "Health Maintenance Organizations." In David Mechanic, ed., *Handbook of Health, Health Care and Health Professions* (New York: Free Press, 1983), p. 32.

[84]J. Warren Salmon, "The Health Maintenance Organization Strategy: A Corporate Takeover of Health Services Delivery," *International Journal of Health Services*, 5 (1975), 609–624.

[85]Luft, *op. cit.*, p. 32.

[86]*Newsweek*, May 9, 1983, p. 29.

[87]A. H. Katz and E. I. Bender, "Self-Help Groups in Western Society: History and Prospects," *Journal of Applied Behavioral Science*, 12 (1976), 265–282.

[88]Zachary Gussow and George Z. Tracy, "The Role of Self-Help Clubs in the Adaptation to Chronic Illness and Disability," *Social Science and Medicine*, 10 (1976), 407–414.

[89]Sheryl Ruzek, *The Women's Health Movement* (New York: Praeger, 1978).

[90]Boston Women's Health Book Collective, *Our Bodies, Ourselves* (New York: Simon and Schuster, 1980).

[91]Sonny Kleinfeld, *The Hidden Minority* (Boston: Atlantic-Little Brown, 1979).

[92]Gordon DeJong, "Defining and Implementing the Independent Living Concept." In Nancy M. Crewe and Irving K. Zola, eds., *Independent Living for Physically Disabled People* (San Frasncisco: Jossey-Bass, 1983), pp.. 4–27.

[93]*Ibid.*.

[94]Jennie J. Kronenfield, "Self-Care as a Panacea for the Ills of the Health Care System: An Assessment," *Social Science and Medicine*, 13A (1979), 263–267.

[95]N. B. Belloc and L. Breslow, "The Relation of Physical Health Status and Health Practices," *Preventive Medicine*, 1 (1972), 409–421.

[96]U.S. Department of Health, Education and Welfare, *Healthy People: The Surgeon General's Report on Health Promotion and Disease Prevention* (Washington, D.C.: U.S. Government Printing Office, 1979).

[97]Peter Conrad and Lynn Schlesinger, "Beyond Healthy Habits: Society and the Pursuit of Prevention." Unpublished manuscript, 1980.

[98]Rebecca S. Parkinson *et al.*, *Managing Health Promotion in the Workplace* (Palo Alto, Cal.: Mayfield, 1982).

[99]Jonathan E. Fielding and Lester Breslow, "Health Promotion Programs Sponsored by California Employers," *American Journal of Public Health*, 73 (1983), 538–542.

[100]Andrew J. J. Brennan, "Health Promotion: What's In It for Business and Industry," *Health Education Quarterly*, 9 (1982), 9–19.

[101]Conference on "Wellness in the Workplace," Long Beach, California, May 1984.

[102]Andrea Foote and John C. Erfut, "Hypertension Control at the Work Site," *New England Journal of Medicine*, 308 (1983), 809–813.

[103]Richard J. Margolis, "National Health Insurance—The Dream Whose Time Has Come?" In Peter Conrad and Rochelle Dern, eds., *op. cit.*, pp. 486–501.

[104]See Rosemary Stevens, *Medical Practice in Modern England* (New Haven, Conn.: Yale University Press, 1966).

[105]Patrick Malone, "British Medicine/American Medicine: Leaning Closer but Still an Ocean Apart," *New Physician*, 28 (1979), 20–24.

[106]Aaron and Schwartz, *op. cit.*

[107]Sidney S. Lee, "Health Policy, A Social Contract: A Comparison of the United States and Canada," *Journal of Public Health Policy*, 3 (1982), 293–302.

[108]Theodore R. Marmor, "Canada's Path, America's Choices: Lessons from the Canadian Experience with National Health Insurance." In Ronald Numbers, ed., *Compulsory Health Insurance* (New York: Ballinger, 1982).

[109]John Ehrenreich and Oliver Fein, "National Health Insurance: The Great Leap Sideways." In Peter Conrad and Rochelle Kern, eds., *op. cit.*, pp. 502–508.

arrested 9/13/68 suspicion of first degree murder
041307
died 9/9/68 multiple gunshot wounds
Defend me from my friends; I can defend myself from my enemies.
Marechal Villars

13 *Urban Problems*

Richard S. Krannich
UTAH STATE UNIVERSITY

Many of the social problems discussed throughout this book are frequently identified as "urban problems." For instance, concern about crime in the United States is often focused specifically upon urban crime patterns. This should come as no surprise, since crime statistics show that both the absolute number of crimes reported and the crime rate are higher in large cities than in small towns. Available evidence suggests a similar situation regarding patterns of illegal drug traffic, illegal gambling, prostitution, and other forms of social deviance. Problems involving minority group relations with the white majority have also been identified with urban settings, due largely to the concentration of nonwhite populations in America's large cities and the periodic occurrence, especially since the 1960s, of violent and destructive rioting in the slums of many cities in the United States. Another frequently identified "urban problem" is that of poverty, reflecting the concentration of economically disadvantaged populations in many urban centers.

In a sense, these and numerous other social problems are justifiably viewed as urban problems, simply as a consequence of the fact that large portions of the populations of the United States and other advanced industrial societies are concentrated in urban places. Using the U.S. Census Bureau's definition of an *urban area* as either an incorporated (that is, legally defined) municipality with 2,500 or more residents or unincorporated but populous and densely settled "urbanized" areas, approximately 75 percent of all Americans live in urban areas. In fact, a majority of Americans live in or close to a relative handful of the nation's largest cities. Approximately three-fourths of the U.S. population lives within the boundaries of *Standard Metropolitan Statistical Areas* (SMSAs), which are areas within or immediately surrounding a large city or set of cities with a population of 50,000 or more residents. Nearly half of the nation's population is concentrated in metropolitan areas with 1 million or more residents.[1] [Although such patterns reflect the fact that the United States is among the world's most highly urbanized societies, other advanced industrial nations such as Canada, Great Britain, and Japan exhibit similar levels of population concentration. Moreover, developing societies such as Mexico are rapidly becoming urbanized as greater proportions of their populations come to reside in cities. In fact, it is predicted that by the year 2000 one-half of the world's population will be located in urban areas.[2]

In light of these patterns, it is not surprising that many social problems are identified with urban areas. Most of us live and work in urban areas, and we experience and react to a wide range of social problems in the context of the urban social environment. However, there is more to urban social problems than the simple fact of urban residential concentration. By conventional definition *urban places* are characterized by large, densely settled, and socially heterogeneous populations residing in a highly altered "built" environment. In addition to these basic defining characteristics, urban areas are characterized by large, distinctive social, economic, political, and cultural dimensions. The presence of diverse ethnic and social class groups in urban centers and the emergence of such new *urban subcultures* as the contemporary "punk" phenomenon contribute to a social mélange observed nowhere else. Urban economic structures increasingly reflect the role of cities as the administrative "nerve centers" of modern societies. As a result, there is a considerable concentration of political and economic power in urban centers due to the location of major government agencies, multinational corporate headquarters, and national media organizations in a relative handful of the world's largest cities. Under such conditions there emerge some social problems that seem to be specifically urban in character. The remainder of this chapter is focused upon the nature and sources of these uniquely urban problems and our societal responses to them.

PART I: THE PROBLEM

QUALITY OF LIFE IN THE CITY

Western cultures have long exhibited ambivalence about city life. The writings of numerous philosophers and social critics, including Aristotle, Rousseau, and Thoreau, contain numerous references to the assorted "evils" associated with the urban social milieu. This antiurban sentiment has been especially evident in America,[3] and was transformed into a central theme in the political ideology of the nation by Thomas Jefferson, who once wrote, "I view great cities as pestilential to the morals, the health, and the liberties of man." In contrast with European societies, where there appears to be a more positive orientation toward city life, this antiurban orientation has been recurrent in American philosophy, literature, and political thinking,[4,5] reflecting a dominant cultural bias that has influenced our perceptions of and responses to urban problems.

Social analysts and critics, echoing the English philosopher Thomas Hobbes, have frequently concluded that "the quality of life in the larger American cities is . . . solitary, poor, nasty, brutish, and short."[6] Attitudes expressed by the American public generally reflect such notions. For example, public opinion polls have repeatedly indicated that a substantial majority of American adults would prefer not to live in a large city.[7] In essence, American culture has placed a high value on an idealized notion of a "human-scale community" in which intimacy, trust, honesty, cooperation, and congeniality would be expected to flourish.[8] From the point of view of most Americans this "human scale" of community life is the antithesis of what is encountered in large cities.

In all fairness, however, it should be recognized that such imagery is largely a reflection of a partially inaccurate idealization of the qualities of small-town life. Although small towns may provide a setting for greater social intimacy, mutual trust, and cooperation, they also have been characterized as socially suffocating and oppressive. A lack of public privacy, restrictive social conservatism, and rigid pressures for conformity to local norms and expectations are some of the trade-offs that may accompany the human scale of small-town living. Small towns have often been found to be *closed communities* in which there may be little room for new ideas, new avenues of political involvement, new ways of life, or even the full social acceptance and integration of new residents.[9]

In terms of such objective indicators of quality of life as income, employment opportunity, housing quality, and health, rural areas actually exhibit lower overall levels of well-being than are evident in urban America.[10] In addition, the overall quality of life has been found to vary substantially among the nation's cities. In an analysis combining an assessment of economic, political, environmental, health and education, and social characteristics of U.S. metropolitan areas, one researcher identified 16 percent of all SMSAs as "outstanding" in terms of overall quality of life. Among those were such places as Hartford, Connecticut; Minneapolis-St. Paul, Minnesota; Nashville, Tennessee; and Portland, Oregon. Another 24 percent were rated as "excellent," 21 percent as "good," and 21 percent as "adequate." Only 18 percent of all SMSAs were classified as "substandard." Among these were Birmingham, Alabama; Jacksonville, Florida; San Antonio, Texas; and Philadelphia, Pennsylvania.[11]

Nevertheless, Americans continue to cling to a romanticized and somewhat unrealistic set of values that idealize the merits of small-town life and are highly critical of the urban social environment. If anything, the emergence and recognition of widespread urban problems during the twentieth century have intensified our cultural tendencies to find fault with the social characteristics of urban life. Especially since the 1960s, considerable public attention has been focused upon numerous events that, in the aggregate, have been described as the "urban crisis." In recent years American cities have been confronted by racial strife, neighborhood deterioration, physical decay, air and water pollution, traffic congestion, urban sprawl, fiscal collapse, and a host of other interrelated problems. These and other indicators of an "urban crisis" reflect the apparent failure of urban social structures adequately to meet the needs of a growing and changing society.

Congestion and Crowding

Many urban problems exist as direct consequences of the concentration of vast numbers of people in relatively limited geographic areas. Yet, despite our cultural biases regarding the conditions of population concentration, people have been living in cities for thousands of years, apparently adapting with much success. However, the number of persons living in and around some major contemporary urban centers is almost unimaginable. For instance, the

Table 13.1 Population Densities in Selected U.S. Standard Metropolitan Statistical Areas and Central Cities, 1980

	PERSONS PER SQUARE MILE	
	SMSA DENSITY	CENTRAL-CITY DENSITY
Atlanta	467.5	3,244.4
Boston	2,232.1	11,978.6
Dallas-Fort Worth	357.3	2,250.0
Los Angeles-Long Beach	1,837.2	6,462.5
New York	6,599.4	23,416.0
Washington, D.C.	1,089.3	10,132.3

Source: U.S. Bureau of the Census, *1980 Census of Population, Vol. 1: Characteristics of the Population, Part 1: U.S. Summary* (Washington, D.C.: U.S. Government Printing Office, 1983).

population of New York City alone is over 7 million; and over 9 million people live in the greater New York metropolitan area. The metropolitan Chicago area population exceeds 7 million; and approximately 7.5 million people live in the Los Angeles metropolitan area. Although these cities are atypical in terms of their large population size, it is important to note that as of 1980 the U.S. Census had identified 318 Standard Metropolitan Statistical Areas—areas surrounding and integrated with cities or sets of cities with populations of at least 50,000. This is in striking contrast with the fact that in 1800 there were only 6 American cities with populations of over 10,000 persons.

Accompanying such population concentrations are some inevitable problems of urban crowding and congestion. In some American central cities the residential population density is over 20,000 persons per square mile.[12] Moreover, each day the population swells even more as residents from surrounding cities, suburbs, and towns commute to factories, offices, and stores in major urban centers. In the resulting congestion many daily activities such as shopping, going to lunch, driving to and from work, and finding places to park, to which nonurbanites may give little thought, can become far less than routine simply due to the fact that there are thousands of others simultaneously pursuing their own daily activities.

Transportation

One particularly obvious problem related to urban congestion is that of urban transportation. For many urban workers the journey to and from work requires an enormous investment of time and energy. Commuters, especially those who must travel from suburban areas, may spend two, three, or more hours a day just going to and from their homes to the workplace. Those who choose to drive private automobiles encounter massive traffic jams, substantial risks of involvement in traffic accidents, and limited access to downtown parking. Researchers have observed numerous examples of aggression and violence triggered by urban traffic congestion, including fistfights, stabbings, and shootings by angry and frustrated motorists.[13] In addition, the quantity of energy resources expended by private commuter vehicles represents both

New York City's subways have come to symbolize the problems of urban public transportation.
(Jim Kalett/Photo Researchers)

a major financial outlay for individuals and a significant contribution to the national dependence on scarce petroleum reserves.

Despite the presence of various forms of public transportation services in most large cities, most Americans continue to rely almost exclusively on private automobiles for their transportation into and around urban areas. Those who choose to utilize such public transportation alternatives as buses, trains, and subway systems may encounter crowded facilities and limited service areas. Moreover, many cities have been unable to modernize or expand and upgrade their public transportation systems as service needs have changed, resulting in continued dependence on inadequate services and unreliable equipment. Public transportation remains relatively underdeveloped in most U.S. cities, although expanded urban mass transit could be cheaper, faster, and more energy efficient, and could help to reduce urban congestion and sprawl.

Environmental Deterioration

Other direct consequences of congestion include a variety of environmental quality problems that threaten the health and safety of urbanites. Due in large part to automobile emissions, many American cities continue to experience serious air pollution problems that frequently threaten human health. Although Los Angeles is most frequently mentioned as a city known for its smog problems, air-quality emergencies occur periodically in many large cities, often forcing people with respiratory ailments to stay indoors or seek medical attention. Studies have documented the fact that there are serious health hazards associated with urban air pollution, with some researchers suggesting that higher rates of lung cancer and some other life-threatening diseases are directly related to urban air-pollution problems.[14] Air pollution also contributes to rapid discoloration and even physical erosion of buildings and monuments, often irreparably damaging important and valuable city structures.

Grave concerns are also beginning to emerge about the quality and indeed the saftey of drinking water supplies in many urban areas. Industrial wastes, urban sewage effluents, and contaminated runoff from urban streets and parking lots all are entering the nation's culinary water sources at disturbing rates. In one study of eighty American cities, the U.S. Environmental Protection Agency found that at least one of six major toxic chemicals being investigated was present in the drinking water of all of the eighty cities.[15]

In addition, noise pollution generated by motor vehicle traffic, air traffic, construction equipment, and other machinery has become a problem in some urban places. Social impacts of high noise-pollution levels include a variety of effects on physical and mental health and on social behavior. High noise levels contribute to annoyance and general irritation.[16,17] In addition, some studies have documented the fact that some urbanites in high-noise areas are unable to establish normal sleep patterns.[18] Research has also suggested increased psychological stress related to noise-induced tension.[19] Other apparent effects of urban noise include altered patterns of social interaction as people retreat from social activities in high-noise settings where it may be difficult to carry on a simple conversation.[20]

The deterioration of the city has become a familiar sight throughout the United States.

(Sepp Seitz/Woodfin Camp & Associates)

Urban Blight and Housing Problems

An additional form of urban environmental deterioration involves the physical decay of the man-made or "built" environments in many urban centers. In most cities, major downtown area structures have been in place for years, often for well over a century. Inevitably such structures begin to show signs of deterioration as a result of age and limited maintenance. However, in some cities the deterioration has become so extensive that vast tracts of urban territory have become virtual wastelands. *Urban blight* is evident throughout the United States, reflected in abandoned homes and apartment buildings, collapsing and empty warehouses, factories, and offices, boarded-up store-fronts, deteriorating roads and bridges, littered empty lots where buildings once stood, and unsafe and substandard housing still occupied by millions of disadvantaged city dwellers. The immediate visual impacts of such physical deterioration are obvious. Even if we were to consider only the lack of esthetic value created by such conditions, the impacts of urban blight on social well-being would merit concern and attention.

However, the impacts of such deterioration of the built environment go far beyond the purely esthetic. For instance, vast areas of urban housing are literally collapsing. During the 1970s the problem of low-income housing worsened: average rental costs increased at twice the rate of increase in income levels, and millions of low-income housing units were eliminated as a result of demolition or renovation into more costly middle-class homes.[21] In many of those which remain, residents are exposed to a variety of health and safety hazards: children continue to be poisoned by eating chips of lead-based paint peeled from walls; hundreds die each year as a result of fires in dilapidated and overcrowded tenement buildings; children fall to their deaths from unscreened upper-story apartment windows; and each winter the newspapers carry reports about impoverished urban residents who have died from hypothermia in unheated homes and apartments.

Unfortunately, the relative scarcity of more adequate low-income housing supplies in American cities has resulted not only in the continued residential occupation of deteriorating structures but often in extreme residential crowding. The U.S. Census Bureau has reported that approximately 80 percent of all occupied housing units in the central cities of American metropolitan areas are in "undesirable" neighborhoods that are characterized by physical decay, overcrowded residences, and high crime. Substandard urban housing areas are generally characterized by household density levels (that is, the average number of persons per room in the housing unit) that substantially exceed levels considered adequate to allow some individual privacy. More importantly, research has begun to uncover detrimental social and psychological effects of substandard residential conditions, especially high household densities.[22] In particular, high household density has been linked with heightened levels of frustration and resulting aggressiveness, possibly as a result of the lack of privacy and the irritability that can arise when there is no place in which to be alone. As a result, persons living in high-density urban households tend to exhibit greater levels of family violence, a general impairment of social relations among household members, and withdrawal from social interactions.[23,24]

The Urban Fiscal Crisis

Despite a widespread recognition of these and other serious urban problems of congestion and decay, many cities are relatively powerless to attempt even to treat the symptoms, much less to identify and resolve the basic sources of urban blight. One major reason for this inability to respond is the fact that many major American cities continue to experience grave financial problems. Quite simply, the money available to cities in the form of tax revenues, municipal bond revenues, and urban assistance monies transferred from state and federal government programs is often not sufficient to meet even the everyday demands on urban governments.

The provision of such necessary services as police and fire protection, public utility service, public transportation, and road maintenance programs, sanitation, and so forth is necessary to support the urban residential population base. In addition, these services are also needed to meet the demands of the enlarged population that enters major city areas each day to work, shop, and seek services and entertainment.[25] In order to meet these needs, city administrations require vast economic resources to operate equipment, maintain facilities, and employ municipal workers.

Unfortunately, many cities have been unable to meet even these daily service provision needs, at least not at levels considered by most analysts to be adequate and sufficient for the requirements of the urban population. Instead, a process of retrenchment has occurred across urban America as service levels are cut and fiscal austerity programs implemented. In the move to cut expenditures, a wide array of public services and programs have been reduced or eliminated, often involving not only such "nonessential" components as recreational and cultural programs but also critical safety services such as police and fire protection.

In some highly publicized instances, major urban centers—primarily those in the northeastern industrial states—have approached fiscal collapse as a result of their inability to meet financial obligations. For instance, New York City was forced to the brink of bankruptcy in 1975 when revenues declined to the point that the city was unable to meet payroll and loan-interest expenditure requirements. Only an emergency bail-out program, implemented by the state and combined with drastic cuts in city services and payrolls, averted a financial calamity. Similar crises have also occurred in Cleveland, Philadelphia, Boston, and other major urban centers. Although bankruptcy has been averted in these cities, the costs in terms of unemployment among city employees and reduced expenditures for social welfare programs, education, public facilities improvements and maintenance, and a host of other programs have been severe. Under such conditions there is little chance for cities to turn attention and funds toward resolution of the problems associated with the congestion and urban physical deterioration outlined earlier.

The problems discussed thus far are by themselves reason enough for public concern about the quality of life in urban America. Indeed, it is these problems of congestion, urban blight, and fiscal distress that have been the focus of most public and policy attention directed toward the issues of the urban crisis. However, it is important not to focus our attention solely on these obvious examples of the urban dilemma, for they are in many ways only the reflections of more fundamental social problems that lie at the very heart of the contemporary urban crisis.

Problems of Social Organization in Urban Areas

American cities have increasingly become the homes of an urban *underclass.* Many urban areas, particularly the central-city areas of major metropolitan centers, have experienced population shifts resulting in a substantial concentration of low-income residents in central-city areas. Traditionally disadvantaged populations, in particular nonwhite Americans, are heavily concentrated in urban centers. For example, racial minority populations comprise over one-half of the population in Washington, D.C., and, according to the 1980 Census, approximately three-fourths of all black Americans live in the central cities of the nation's urban areas.

One indicator of the extremity of the problems of urban poverty is the growing number of destitute and homeless people who are struggling to survive in many urban centers. In contrast to the stereotypical conception that such individuals are only the hard-core skid row bums, the urban homeless include "winos, the insane, the unemployed, Vietnam veterans, (and) the new poor."[26] As a consequence of high unemployment rates, along with the forced closure or reductions in the programs of such publicly funded facilities as mental health treatment centers and halfway houses, the numbers of urban homeless have risen sharply in recent years (in part due to the deinstitutionalization of the mentally ill discussed in Chapter 4). For example, one recent analysis indicated that in Philadelphia the number of homeless who received emergency family housing increased fivefold between 1981 and 1983. In Detroit the number of homeless increased by an estimated 50 percent in just one year.[27] In these and many other cities there is a growing population of residents whose "home" is an abandoned building, a highway underpass, a sheltered store-front alcove, or an exposed steel grate above a heat ventilation duct. A recent event in Salt Lake City graphically illustrates the problems encountered in this search for shelter. In early 1984 budget shortfalls forced the closure of an emergency housing facility. Soon thereafter it was discovered that a group of homeless people had established residence inside of a toppled smokestack in the heart of a fenced and abandoned industrial area that has been identified as among the most hazardous radioactive waste sites in the nation. Their willingness to ignore the signs posted to warn of dangerous radioactivity reflects the desperation of the urban homeless.

Poverty, unemployment, underemployment, discrimination, and a blighted physical environment can combine to breed a sense of despair, frustration, and anger among many urban dwellers. The incidence of crime, aggression, and violence tends to increase under such conditions, perhaps partly as a response to frustration,[28] partly as a result of attempts to obtain a livelihood when more conventional opportunities for success are blocked,[29] and partly due to the relative inability of the disadvantaged to protect themselves from being victimized by unscrupulous others. As a result of these and other social conditions the rates for virtually all categories of crime are higher in urban places than in rural areas.

In light of such conditions, it is of little surprise that urbanites tend in general to express heightened levels of distrust of others.[30,31] In particular, city dwellers appear to avoid involvement with unknown others in the "public" sphere of everyday urban life.[32,33] Among the consequences of such avoidance and distrust are a reduced willingness to intervene on behalf of others. Social scientists have cited numerous examples of situations in which bystanders witnessing a crisis or crime have failed to provide help or assistance.[34,35] One widely cited example, which occurred in New York City, involved the murder of Catherine Genovese, who was stabbed by her attacker repeatedly over an extended period of time in a residential neighborhood. Despite her calls for help and the fact that thirty-eight neighbors admitted witnessing at least part of the attack, none came to her assistance or even called for police assistance until after she had been killed.[36] A more recent example was the 1983 gang-rape of a woman in a bar in New Bedford, Massachusetts. Despite the presence of numerous patrons other than the several rapists, none intervened. Only after the victim ran naked into the street did a passing motorist provide assistance and summon the police. Although such highly sensational occurrences are relatively infrequent, and are not limited only to large cities, they do vividly reflect an apparent pattern of reduced social involvement among many urban residents. In part, this appears to result from a tendency for people to experience a sense of reduced personal responsibility when there are numerous others present and the responsibility to take action is "diffused" among them.

Another dimension of this distrust of others is fear of crime, which according to some analysts has become a more widespread social problem than crime itself.[37] Residents of large cities tend to be substantially more fearful of being victimized by crime than are persons who live in smaller cities and towns.[38,39] Although this pattern may, in part, reflect a reasonable response to higher urban crime levels, evidence indicates that for many urbanites the fear of crime has come to exert an irrational and paralyzing effect, resulting in withdrawal from public involvement and interactions. In some instances, urban residents become literal prisoners in their own homes as they seek a safe haven from an outside environment perceived as hostile and dangerous.[40] In describing the ways in which some urban dwellers have responded to perceptions of "urban danger," one researcher has provided the following illustrations:

> One young Chinese woman never returns home alone on foot after dark. When she arrives by car, she honks her horn to alert her parents and then dashes the twenty feet to her door. A white man cautiously packs his suitcases into his car under cover of darkness before he leaves for a trip to escape being noticed by potential burglars. A middle-aged black woman sneaks surreptitiously from her home at 6:00 A.M. to do her laundry before the neighborhood youths gather in the laundromat to visit and smoke. She is anxious not to leave her home vacant, even for a few minutes, as an invitation to the burglars she constantly fears.[41]

In general, it is often suggested that the social and psychological well-being of urban dwellers suffers as a result of the conditions of city living. Although the evidence to support such a conclusion is neither extensive nor consistent, some studies have reported data indicating that urban residents tend to experience isolation from social contact with their neighbors.[42,43] Urbanites also have been found to exhibit relatively high rates of psychological disturbance and distress.[44] Although the evidence of such mental health effects also is not consistent,[45] one observer has concluded that "the incidence of neuroses and personality disorders is considerably higher in large urban settings, due to the terrifically harsh, intensively individualistic, highly competitive, extremely crude, and often violently brutal social life of the big city."[46] Clearly, this emotionally charged description of the evils associated with urban life reflects an antiurban bias, and indeed the available evidence suggests that the incidence of psychological disturbance is at most only modestly associated with urbanization. However, even if such patterns are not typical of the majority of city dwellers, they suggest that many people do find it difficult to adapt successfully to the demands and conditions of urban life. For that component of the population, the very experience of living in cities may give rise to problems that require our attention.

PART II: CAUSES AND CONSEQUENCES

SOCIOLOGICAL LEVEL

Early Urban Settlement Patterns

To understand fully the social forces that have helped cause the range of urban problems discussed in the preceding section, we must begin with a review of early urban settlement and development patterns. The ways in which the core areas of contemporary urban centers developed and ultimately expanded are important historical sources of many contemporary urban problems.

In America, most early cities were located at coastal port areas or along major waterways, permitting access to water transportation and shipping facilities. Eventually the development of steam railroad technologies permitted the emergence of major inland urban centers. In both cases, however, the characteristics of water- and steam-based industrial technol-

Table 13.2 Levels of Analysis: Urban Problems

LEVELS	APPROPRIATE QUESTIONS	A PARTIAL SYNOPSIS OF PRESENT CONCLUSIONS
SOCIOLOGICAL	How is "invasion-succession" related to urban problems?	More advantaged urbanites tended to move to the suburbs, leaving the city to the poor and disadvantaged.
	Has the movement of large numbers of people to the suburbs mitigated problems in the city?	No. In general, this movement has served to expand and intensify a variety of urban problems.
	Who were the people who were most likely to flee the city?	The white middle class. The result has been racial enmity between the city and suburbs and a decline in the urban tax base.
	What has been the effect of the movement of major industries and businesses out of the city?	There has been a decline in jobs, tax revenues, and in places where urban residents can do business.
	How do urbanites react to danger in the city?	Urbanites are conscious of the danger around them and many of them are victimized in a variety of ways. Some withdraw to the relative safety of neighborhoods and homes.
	How do urbanites react to environmental disruptions?	To the degree that they can, urbanites withdraw from these problems as well.
	What are the effects of residential congestion and density?	Although there are mixed results, the bulk of the evidence is that the effects are negative in a variety of ways.
	Are the individual and social-psychological effects of the city all negative?	No. The city is a source of individuality, nonconformity, and tolerance of differences.
	What is the economic situation in many American cities?	The cities are suffering from a declining tax base at the same time that the demands on them for services are increasing.
SOCIAL-PSYCHOLOGICAL AND INDIVIDUAL	What is the view held by the "social disorganization" theorists?	They see a variety of historical forces leading to social disorganization in the city. This, in turn, is related to a variety of individual problems, as well as difficulties in social relationships.

(Continued)

Table 13.2 Levels of Analysis: Urban Problems (*Continued*)

LEVELS	APPROPRIATE QUESTIONS	A PARTIAL SYNOPSIS OF PRESENT CONCLUSIONS
	Do all sociologists accept the view of the city as being characterized by social disorganization?	No. A number of sociologists have come to emphasize the positive characteristics of the city. There are sectors of the city that demonstrate persistent social organization and personal integration.

ogies, and the limited daily range of early means of personal transportation, necessitated a highly concentrated pattern of settlement and development. Businesses that depended on being highly accessible to customer populations were located in the most central areas of the city. Industries also tended to be situated in relatively central locations due to the need for access to water- and rail-shipping facilities and the limited transferability of steam power to locations far from the source of power generation.

Early urbanites relied primarily upon walking or horses to get from their homes to business and manufacturing areas of the city. Consequently, initial residential development occurred in areas immediately adjacent to the central business and manufacturing areas. The appearance of streetcar and trolley systems eventually expanded the reasonable daily commuting range, permitting modest geographical expansion of settlement areas into less central locations. Nevertheless, American urban centers continued to be characterized by highly concentrated development patterns until well into the twentieth century. The appearance and eventual widespread availability of the automobile greatly reduced the *friction of space* that had kept urban development and residential settlement confined to areas near the original city centers.

The forces of urban concentration combined with the growth pressures of expanding urban populations to result in the dense structural development patterns still evident in American city centers. The demands for access to central-city areas, especially for business locations, contributed to high urban land prices, necessitating maximum utilization of available central-city land area. Once all available land was utilized, expansion of business facilities was accomplished by building upward. Multistory buildings and, ultimately, massive skyscrapers appeared, which permitted ever-greater levels of activity in a constant central-city land area, but simultaneously created commercial-area densities that resulted in considerable central-city congestion.

Residential development pressures also were important in the emergence of typical city expansion patterns. During the latter part of the nineteenth century, the populations of American cities were swelled by vast waves of European immigrants. This influx reached a peak during the early years of the twentieth century, with over 9 million immigrants arriving in the United States between 1901 and 1910.[47] The vast majority of these new Americans flowed into major urban industrial centers, resulting in unprecedented rates of city growth and providing a source of labor for American industry during a period of rapid expansion.

The rapid urban growth that resulted from the flow of immigrant populations into American cities forced some outward expansion as available land areas near the city centers became fully occupied. Settlement patterns typically involved the concentration of ethnic minorities in older, less desirable city housing areas, while more established residents, especially those of the growing urban middle class, moved into newer housing around the urban periphery.

Even after the flow of immigrants to America was restricted by government-imposed immigration quotas, American cities continued to swell. During the first half of the twentieth century, internal migration patterns reflected a large-scale shift of the American population from rural areas to urban centers. New farming technologies began to reduce the need for human labor in rural agricultural areas. Simultaneously, the rapid expansion of American industry created increased demands for labor in urban areas, attracting many formerly rural residents to the nation's industrial cities. The flow of rural to urban migrants replaced the flow of European immigrants as a major source of urban population growth.

Invasion and Succession

The pressures for expansion and development in major urban centers therefore continued unabated as new urban migrants located in older neighborhoods, and more established and economically advantaged urbanites relocated in newer residential neighborhoods around the outer periphery of the expanding cities. Urban sociologists have described this process as one involving first the *invasion* of existing city areas by a new population group. As the invasion proceeds, the former occupants of the area begin to leave for other areas of the city, and are increasingly replaced by members of the immigrating groups. Ultimately there occurs a *succession* from one land occupation pattern to another as the transformation is completed and the character of the neighborhood shifts to reflect the predominance of the new population.

Underlying this process of invasion and succession in the expansion of American cities are some forces of change that have important implications for contemporary urban problems. In the first place, the segregation first of ethnic immigrant populations, later of formerly rural migrants, and most recently of racial minorities into the oldest, most crowded, and deteriorated urban residential neighborhoods is a reflec-

Table 13.3 Percent of the U.S. Population in Rural and Urban Areas, 1790–1980

	PERCENT RURAL	PERCENT URBAN
1790	94.9%	5.1%
1850	84.7	15.3
1900	60.4	39.6
1920	48.8	51.2
1940	43.5	56.5
1960	30.1	69.9
1970	26.4	73.6
1980	26.3	73.7

Source: U.S. Bureau of the Census, *1980 Census of Population, Vol. 1: Characteristics of the Population. Part I: U.S. Summary* (Washington, D.C.: U.S. Government Printing Office, 1983).

tion not only of the relative initial economic disadvantages of the immigrating populations but also of our cultural tendencies to discriminate against minorities. In essence, urban residential settlement patterns have demonstrated the efforts of the established, largely white, urban, middle and working classes to avoid residential proximity to, or contact with, minority populations.

The cultural integration of many European ethnic minorities has gradually blurred the lines of discrimination and prejudice, although there remain major ethnic enclaves in many urban centers. In contrast, racial minority groups, especially black migrants from the rural South, are more obviously distinguishable from the dominant white population than European ethnic populations, and have therefore been more likely to be restricted to highly segregated urban residential neighborhoods. The result has been a concentration of racial minority populations in the most deteriorated urban slum areas. The continued concentration of racial minorities in many older central city areas is only one consequence of these urban settlement and expansion patterns.

Forces of Outward Expansion

The forces of urban population growth and concentration inevitably exerted pressures for the outward expansion of cities, resulting in a gradual enlargement of urbanized land areas. However, the constraints of transportation accessibility to central-city areas continued to exert centralization pressures, at least through the initial decades of the twentieth century. The emergence of widespread private automobile ownership in the 1920s and 1930s substantially altered these patterns and greatly extended the distance that could separate the urban core from residential areas on the urban periphery.

By reducing the friction of space, which had forced the concentration of urban commercial activities and populations into relatively limited geographic areas, automotive technology gave rise to new processes of outward metropolitan expansion and extended areas of urbanized development. This shift from centralization to dispersion involved not only population location patterns but also reflected the increased flexibility of businesses to locate in areas beyond the traditional central-city locations.

The most obvious repercussions of the *transportation revolution* involved massive shifts of American population from central-city urban residential districts to suburban residential communities beyond the traditional boundaries of the urban periphery. Although some outward shifts of residential populations began to be noticed as early as the 1920s and 1930s, suburbanization remained of limited scope and importance until after World War II. Then, the combined effects of widespread automobile ownership and new and expanding urban expressway systems permitted the rapid growth of sprawling suburban housing areas, often in areas quite detached from the central city.

Although the decentralizing effects of automotive technology were probably inevitable, it is important to note that, unlike the United States, suburbanization in European nations has been far less extensive and has not tended to result in the widespread sprawling suburban expanses typical of contemporary America.[48] In many ways the unique nature and timing of American suburbanization may be attributed to the actions and decisions of key political *power brokers,* including both government officials and powerful business elites. For example, the emergence of federal programs to subsidize the development of extensive urban-area expressways and the interstate highway system resulted in new rapid-access highways that made it feasible for urban workers to live far from city centers. Research by Robert Caro has documented how decisions imposed by a small elite in New York City resulted in a metropolitan highway system that fixed the future shape of the city.[49] More recently, Peter Marcuse has described the effectiveness of a politically powerful "highway lobby" in preventing the development of a modern urban mass transit system in Los Angeles.[50]

Similar observations may be made concerning a variety of housing policies and programs that also have encouraged the highly dispersed form of outward urban expansion evident in the United States. Postwar federal housing policies, including in particular the availability of Federal Housing Authority (FHA) and Veterans Administration (VA) mortgage-loan programs, were especially influential in their contributions to the rapid expansion of American suburbs. These programs emerged partly in response to pressures exerted by powerful housing development interests and real estate speculators who stood to gain from the highly profitable expansion of development into previously undeveloped and inexpensive areas around the established urban periphery. Consequently, such programs primarily subsidized the development of low-density, single-family housing in outlying suburbs rather than multifamily housing in urban centers. Moreover, in the late 1940s and early 1950s there were hundreds of thousands of Americans who had delayed marriage or the birth of children during the war years and were then in search of family housing. This created a serious housing shortage in many urban and metropolitan areas, spurring the demand for new family housing supplies. These circumstances gave rise to an unprecedented shift of the American population from urban residential locations into newly developing suburban communities. Whereas in 1940 only an estimated 17 percent of Americans lived in suburbs,[51] over one-half of the U.S. population is now classified as suburban.[52,53]

The repercussions of suburbanization and the broader trend of outward expansion of urban-area populations and activities have been enormous. Despite the sprawl of suburban areas and the relatively low suburban residential population densities that have resulted, the problems of central-city congestion have not diminished. It is true that central-city population growth has slowed as a result of suburbanization, with some central cities actually sustaining overall population declines in recent years. However, the effective urban-area population surrounding large cities has continued to expand as growth shifts to suburban communities and even into more remote *exurban* communities beyond the suburban periphery.

In some areas this pattern of expanded urban regional population surrounding major metropolitan centers has resulted in widespread areas of continuous urban and suburban development. When such vast tracts of relatively high population density and continuous urban development result in the interpenetration of two or more regional metropolitan centers, the resulting expanded urbanized region is referred to as a *megalopolis*. Referred to by the U.S. Census Bureau as *Standard Consolidated Areas,* there are currently thirteen such areas in the U.S. Examples include the eastern seaboard urbanized area stretching from Boston to Washington, D.C., the northern industrial tier megalopolis including Chicago and Cleveland, and the

California coastal strip between San Francisco and San Diego.

The concentration of a majority of the American population in these expanded urban and metropolitan regions has simply intensified the problems of congestion and urban environmental distress discussed previously. Transportation congestion becomes even more widespread as central-city areas are inundated by literally millions of people who live in surrounding suburban and exurban communities but who continue to rely upon major metropolitan centers as the organizational hubs of commerce, administrative services, and industry. The sprawling urban expanses surrounding major metropolitan centers have increased the extent to which land areas are paved over, air is polluted, and water supplies contaminated.

Selective Decentralization of Population

The trends of urban expansion and decentralization from original city centers have occurred throughout the U.S., Canada, Great Britain, Japan, and other advanced industrial societies. As noted above, the phenomena of outward expansion have had some important repercussions in their own right. However, the greatest impacts of the decentralization process have derived from the fact that shifts of population and commercial activities out of central cities have occurred selectively, involving specific types of population and business. In fact, it may be argued that the most critical dimensions of the contemporary American urban crisis are direct consequences of the selectivity of urban decentralization.

The traditional processes of residential invasion and succession have frequently involved the segregation of economically disadvantaged and minority populations in older, less desirable urban areas. Concurrently, these processes have involved the shifts of more economically advantaged populations into newer and more desirable housing areas farther from the original city center. The selectivity of this process has been especially apparent in the case of suburbanization, which overwhelmingly has involved the movement of white middle-class and upper-middle class populations from city neighborhoods to predominantly or even exclusively white suburban communities.

Coinciding with the continued migration of domestic and foreign minority populations into city centers, the large-scale suburban transfer of the white middle class has been described quite accurately as a *white flight* from an increasingly nonwhite urban social environment. The magnitude of these shifts is reflected in the increasing proportions of nonwhite residents comprising the populations of many major urban centers. Urban America has come to exhibit a pattern of increasingly sharp spatial stratification between the predominantly white middle- and upper-middle-class suburban and exurban communities and urban-center populations that are disproportionately comprised of minority group members and other economically disadvantaged populations. Data from the 1980 Census indicate that over 85 percent of all black Americans reside in urban areas, with about 76 percent in central cities. In contrast, only 25 percent of white Americans live in urban central cities. Although recent data do indicate modest increases in the movement of black and other minority populations into some suburban areas, the pattern of racial and ethnic minority concentration in urban centers persists. Indeed, data suggest that recent black suburbanization exhibits "a familiar pattern of segregation and inequality," perpetuated by "economic inequality, racial prejudice, the local organization of government, (and) local housing markets."[54] This spatial stratification contributes not only to the maintenance of societal problems of minority discrimination but also to specifically urban problems of physical decay, poverty, and fiscal distress.

The selectivity of the shifts of urban population into suburban and exurban locations has involved not only racial differentiation but also related socioeconomic differentiation. The exodus of middle- and upper-middle-class populations from urban residential areas has contributed to an increasingly sharp economic distinction between deprived and economically disadvantaged urban populations and relatively advantaged suburban populations. In fact, the ability of a few major urban centers such as Portland, Oregon, Minneapolis-St. Paul, and Seattle successfully to confront some of their major problems and reconstruct deteriorating central-city areas may be attributable in part to the fact that, in comparison with less successful cities, they have experienced a less dramatic flow of middle-class populations out of the city.

In fact, a majority of impoverished Americans reside in metropolitan areas of the nation, with most urban poverty concentrated among blacks and other ethnic and racial minorities.[55] Undoubtedly these racial and socioeconomic divisions underlie many of the problems of class-based conflict evident in many cities. Indeed, it is in urban centers such as Los Angeles, Miami, Detroit, Cleveland, Boston, and New York, where there are large socially and economically disadvantaged central-city populations, that problems of street violence and destructive riots have been most frequent. The presence of such class inequalities and conflicts may contribute substantially to the inability of some cities to address their problems effectively. Animosity and conflict encourage a more rapid movement of businesses and middle-class residents out of cities, and create a social climate of hostility and distrust that inevitably impedes cooperative involvement by various urban factions in jointly confronting important needs and problems.

The conditions of urban poverty are reflected by and indeed contribute to some of the problems of physical decay in many urban neighborhoods. Areas of deteriorated and substandard housing persist as impoverished urbanites find themselves unable either to relocate in better but more expensive housing, or to invest heavily in home improvements and renovation efforts. Slum housing conditions are also perpetuated by the exploitative practices of some absentee landlords who own and manage deteriorating residential rental housing units but fail to reinvest sufficient amounts of money to provide for either minimal property maintenance or improvements.[56]

Selective Decentralization of Commerce

Compounding the problems of urban poverty has been the fact that the selective outmigration of urban-center populations has been accompanied by a simultaneous selective outmigration of urban business and industry. Manufacturing industries in particular have rapidly abandoned major traditional industrial city locations for suburban, nonmetropolitan, and even international locations in search of cheaper land, lower taxes, lower labor costs, less stringent pollution control requirements, and reduced transportation congestion.[57] Between 1970 and 1979, there was a 24 percent increase in manufacturing employment in nonmetropolitan locations in the United States, compared to only a 3.9 percent increase in metropolitan locations. This reflects a continuation of trends of industrial relocation to nonmetropolitan areas that first became widespread during the 1960s.[58]

Similar patterns of change have occurred in many nonmanufacturing industries as well. Both public and private sector service and administrative activities have exhibited shifts toward suburban and nonmetropolitan areas that coincide with the redistribution of population.[59] In particular, there have been major shifts of retail business out of central-city areas, reflecting both the suburbanization of their customer populations and the extensive development of large-scale suburban shopping centers and malls.[60]

From the viewpoint of some observers such relocation trends reflect a natural and adaptive process, with economic activities gradually being redistributed to maintain efficiency and productivity and to insure an optimal balance between commercial location and the needs of the populations.[61] However, an alternative orientation suggests that such relocations reflect choices made by powerful corporations to maximize profitability, regardless of the human costs of unemployment and economic distress that result when a major employer closes down or shifts locations. The increased ability and willingness of major corporations to be mobile has left labor unions and cities in a weakened bargaining position. Corporate threats to relocate have forced wage concessions, tax reductions, and less stringent enforcement of pollution-control requirements as urban communities attempt to prevent further economic decay.

Clearly, the selective shifts of business and commercial activities out of major urban centers have had serious repercussions for urban areas. As noted earlier, migration has resulted in contemporary patterns of urban population composition that reflect a disproportionate concentration of a less educated, less skilled, and primarily blue-collar labor force in urban centers. In contrast, suburban-ring communities have become the residential setting of a better-educated, primarily white-collar population. The shifts of business and industry have been somewhat conflicting, however, resulting in increasingly limited employment opportunities among the central-city urban workforce. Job opportunities in manufacturing, retail services, and other industries with relatively low-skill labor requirements have tended to shift out of urban centers over the past several decades. In contrast, highly technical and specialized administrative and professional management enterprises have remained concentrated in central-city locations.[62] What has resulted is a mismatch between the characteristics of the labor force in urban centers and the distribution of employ-

Table 13.4 Changes in the Suburban Black Population in Selected American SMSAs, 1970–1980

	BLACK PERCENTAGE OF SUBURBAN POPULATION	
SMSA	1970	1980
Atlanta	11.4%	19.1%
Boston	1.7	2.5
Chicago	4.0	6.4
Cleveland	3.7	8.2
Denver	0.4	2.1
Houston	5.1	5.4
Kansas City	0.7	1.5
Los Angeles	4.3	7.1
Miami	4.6	6.4
Minneapolis	0.2	0.7
New York	9.3	12.7
Philadelphia	12.4	15.4
Salt Lake City	1.1	0.9
Seattle	0.4	1.0
Washington, D.C.	7.1	14.7

Source: Derived from John R. Logan and Mark Schneider, "Racial Segregation and Racial Change in American Suburbs, 1970–1980," *American Journal of Sociology*, 89 (1984): 874–888.

ment opportunities provided by the types of business that have been less prone to decentralization. Consequently, the number of barriers encountered by lower-class urbanites attempting to escape the traps of unemployment, underemployment, and poverty have tended to increase.

Deteriorating Tax Bases and Growing Service Demands

In combination, these forces of population and industrial redistribution represent the key contributors to the emergence and persistence of major fiscal problems in American cities, and to the resulting inabilities of many urban centers to combat the problems of blight and physical deterioration of the built environment. The departure of higher income populations for the suburbs has reduced the amount of personal income tax revenues available to cities. Put simply, the urban center populations left behind by the shift of the white middle class toward suburbia tend overall to enjoy far lower income levels, resulting in lower income tax payments. Similarly, the loss of central-city manufacturing and commercial enterprises has led to a reduction both in locally collected corporate income tax revenues and in sales-tax collections. In addition, the deterioration and often the abandonment of urban buildings and facilities have resulted in declines in property values and therefore in property tax revenues, which often comprise a major component of urban governments' local revenue sources.

In the face of a deteriorating tax base, urban centers are often unable to meet the fiscal demands of public service provision. Unfortunately, the patterns of demographic and industrial location have actually operated to increase the levels of demand for many central city services. The disproportionate urban concentration of impoverished and low-income populations contributes to increased levels of need for a wide range of locally funded and administered public assistance and social welfare programs. For instance, the levels of need for a variety of low-income housing, welfare aid, occupational training, and counseling programs expand as the number of low-income residents increases. In addition, levels of crime and violence are higher in areas of urban poverty, necessitating greater allocations of resources for police and other law-enforcement and public safety services.

Research findings also have demonstrated that levels of demand for central-city public and private services increase as a direct function of suburban population growth.[63] In essence suburban populations make daily use of a wide range of publicly funded city services such as public transportation systems, safety services, traffic control and highway maintenance programs, and so forth. As the commercial and organizational service centers for both central-city and suburban populations, major cities bear a disporportionate share of the fiscal costs of providing services that are required and used by an expanded urban area population, a large proportion of which resides in and pays taxes to suburban municipalities. Consequently, the gap between service demands and resource availability continues to widen, and the ability of city administrations to respond to urban blight and other dimensions of the urban crisis deteriorates.

SOCIAL-PSYCHOLOGICAL AND INDIVIDUAL LEVELS

Urban Alienation and Social Isolation

The sources of such social-psychological and individual problems in the city as alienation, distrust, hostility, fear, isolation, and stress are less readily identified than are the sources of blight and fiscal collapse. However, sociologists have long argued that the transition from traditional and predominantly rural societies to more modern, highly urbanized societies is accompanied by fundamental shifts in the nature of social relations. Many sociologists have tended to trace social-psychological and individual problems in the city to "urban social disorganization." In the next few pages we will look at the work of some of these sociologists.

Gemeinschaft and Gesellschaft

Among the most prominent early sociologists to address this possibility was Ferdinand Tönnies (1855–1936), who described the contrast between *Gemeinschaft* and *Gesellschaft*.[64] Relations identified as *Gemeinschaft* were characterized as involving intimate, face-to-face primary associations, with individuals bound together into highly unified social wholes by shared values, interests, and beliefs. In contrast, *Gesellschaft* relations were described as reflecting the rational, individualistic pursuit of private goals, impersonality, and superficial social ties. Although Tönnies argued that *both* forms of relations could occur simultaneously, he also linked the existence of *Gemeinschaft* with small, traditional rural communities, and *Gesellschaft* with the forces of modernization and urbanization.

Mechanical and Organic Solidarity

Similar observations regarding the distinctiveness of urban social life were set forth by a number of early sociologists. Of particular importance was the distinction made by Émile Durkheim (1858–1917) between traditional societies exhibiting *mechanical solidarity*—integration based on shared sentiments and a limited division of labor—and more modern, urban societies organized on the basis of an *organic solidarity* derived from social and economic diversity and differentiation.[65] Although Durkheim suggested that social order could be facilitated by the organic solidarity of modern urban industrial societies, he also observed the potential for such conditions to foster disruption in the patterns of social life. In particular, rapid social and economic changes were identified as conditions that may accompany urbanization and modernization and that can contribute to the collapse of common norms, leading to *anomie* and social disorganization.

Size, Density, and Heterogeneity

Undoubtedly the most influential theoretical discussion of social relations in urban places was developed in the 1930s by an American sociologist, Louis Wirth. He argued that as a direct consequence of the size, density, and heterogeneity of the population in urban settings, social relations inevitably become superficial, transitory, and impersonal. According to Wirth, the large number of persons in cities makes it impossible for people to interact on a personal or "primary" basis. As a result, urbanites presumably are socially isolated, withdrawn, and alienated, exhibiting *anomie* as described by Durkheim. Wirth observed that the results of such conditions included "personal disorganization, mental breakdown, suicide, delinquency, crime, corruption, and disorder."[66] In essence, Wirth set forth a "determinist" framework, suggesting that a uniquely urban style of social relationship and personality resulted from, or was determined by, the size, density, and heterogeneity that characterize cities.

The Urban Personality

Another component of this traditional *urban disorganization* perspective is the contention that the presence of numerous and diverse *social stimuli* in cities may create a condition of *stimulus overload* for city residents. The sociologist Georg Simmel (1858–1918) concluded that the inability to respond adequately or fully to all of the sights, sounds, and persons encountered in the urban environment necessitates a selective withdrawal from other people and events that are not of direct relevance or immediate importance to the urban individual.[67,68] Simmel described a unique *urban personality*, characterized by detachment, individualism, and aloofness from others. Such characteristics may partially explain observations of abnormally high rates of social deviance and social withdrawal in urban settings. In the presence of literally thousands of others, the aloofness and blasé attitude described by Simmel may be an important adaptive response individuals use to preserve their privacy and individuality. However, it may also make it easier for them to step around a person slumped unconscious on the sidewalk or to observe a shoplifter or mugger without comment or intervention.

Criticisms of the Urban Disorganization Theorists

Despite the widespread acceptance of this *urban social disorganization* perspective, numerous critics have argued that Wirth's account of urban social life reflects an inaccurate and biased point of view. In the first place, some sociologists have noted that Wirth partially misinterpreted the theories of Tönnies and Durkheim. Both of those early theorists recognized that close, primary associations characteristic of *Gemeinschaft*, or mechanical solidarity, could coexist with the more impersonal and anonymous conditions of *Gesellschaft*, or organic solidarity. In contrast, Wirth set forth an "either-or" perspective in which urban life was depicted as inevitably impersonal and alienating.[69]

Other critics have taken issue with the suggestion that there is anything about urban residence that inherently leads to social disorganization in the manner suggested by Wirth. For example, Herbert Gans suggested that observed differences between the attitudes and behaviors of urban and nonurban dwellers do not reflect the influence of the urban environment per se. Rather, he argued that any differences that appear to distinguish urban social relations reflect the composition of the urban populations. In essence, what Gans suggested is that appearances of greater "social disorganization" among urbanites reflect the effects of social class and related social and demographic characteristics. In particular, Gans observed that anomie, alienation, and the personal "pathologies" identified by Wirth as characteristic urban problems were to be found primarily among deprived, socially and economically disadvantaged groups concentrated in inner-city areas.[70]

In contrast, other segments of the urban population have been found to exhibit strong group attachment and normative integration. For example, Gans observed that inner-city "ethnic villagers" tend to emphasize kinship ties, strong primary group attachments, and little anonymity. Such findings are supported by those of numerous other researchers who observe a persistence of social involvement and integration in a variety of inner-city neighborhoods. Such studies as William F. Whyte's *Street Corner Society*,[71] Elliot Liebow's *Tally's Corner*,[72] Gerald Suttle's *The Social Order of the Slum*,[73] and Elijah Anderson's *A Place on the Corner*[74] have repeatedly documented an internal social order and integration in even the most distressed of urban neighborhoods. The operation of such social organization was described by Anderson in his study of the social milieu of a South Chicago neighborhood bar:

> The people who frequent Jelly's bar and liquor store have come to create their own local, informal social stratification system. People come to

Jelly's to be sociable, but also to compete for social recognition and regard. For most, Jelly's is their place to be somebody; for group members are important to one another.[75]

In attempting to account for the development of such ties in the face of the ostensibly "disorganizing" forces of city life, and to explain observed patterns of heightened "deviance" such as crime, drug use, and homosexuality in large cities, Claude Fischer has developed a *subcultural theory* of urbanism.[76] This approach suggests that population size, density, and heterogeneity do in fact contribute to uniquely urban forms of social life. However, Fischer argues that, rather than creating alienation and anomie, such conditions enhance the likelihood that there will be a *critical mass* of nonconforming and unconventional individuals who, on the basis of their shared unconventionality, will tend to interact. Out of the interaction there may arise unique, often deviant, urban subcultures. To find evidence of such subcultures in major urban centers one need look no further than the 1950s "beatniks" of Greenwich Village, the 1960s "hippies" of San Francisco's Haight-Ashbury, the highly visible and politically potent gay community in San Francisco, and the contemporary "punkers" of London. These and other unconventional urban subcultures may be labeled as "deviant" from the perspective of the conventional culture. However, their emergence suggests that, at least in some ways, the urban social environment may actually contribute to social organization rather than fostering only disorder.

Perceptions of Urban Danger

Despite these observations of persistent social organization and personal integration among urban dwellers, it is also important to recognize that some of the problems identified by Wirth and others are real. One possible source of at least some of the problems associated with distrust and alienation is the perception of the urban social environment as dangerous, hostile, and threatening. In light of the pervasive conditions of blight and urban poverty, it would seem inevitable that many urbanites would experience feelings of frustration and powerlessness, contributing to a withdrawal from social involvement.

In addition, for at least some urbanites, the social environment is indeed a source of personal, physical danger. The highest rates of reported crime occur in inner-city

Table 13.5 Criminal Victimization Experience and Fear of Crime in the U.S. by City Size (1983 Data)

CITY SIZE	PERCENT REPORTING BEING A VICTIM OF CRIME AT LEAST ONCE DURING THE PRECEDING 12 MONTHS	PERCENT INDICATING FEAR ABOUT WALKING ALONE AT NIGHT IN THE AREA AROUND THEIR NEIGHBORHOOD
1,000,000 or more	28%	56%
500,000–999,999	32	49
50,000–499,999	27	54
2,500–49,999	21	40
Under 2,500, or rural	20	29

Source: Derived from a national sample survey reported in the *Gallup Report*, No. 210 (March, 1983), 3–9.

districts, and there is substantial evidence that official crime reports in these areas grossly underestimate the actual incidence of criminal occurrences. In spite of a greater concentration of police activity and patrols in urban slum neighborhoods, impoverished slum residents are the most highly victimized sector of the urban population. As one noted urban sociologist has observed, "the presence of many policemen does not prevent a high crime rate in an area of social disorganization."[77]

Many urban residents have responded to these "hostile world" conditions by a withdrawal into the relative safety of their own localized neighborhoods.[78,79] As Suttles found in his studies of a Chicago slum neighborhood, the perception of a threatening and unsafe urban social environment may result in the development of local *defended neighborhoods.* These are usually urban slum areas in which residents may know and trust one another but present a hostile response to outsiders. To observe this phenomenon one needs only to walk through the central-city neighborhoods of Chicago, the Bronx, or Los Angeles and notice the territorial claims of the graffiti-covered building walls, the informal interactions and sidewalk gatherings among local residents, and the hostile, often threatening response presented to outsiders. In fact, the presence of urban street gangs in many slum neighborhoods may be viewed, in part, as a reflection of this "defended neighborhood" response. Each neighborhood-based gang stakes out its own "turf," thereby establishing physical and social boundaries that effectively close off the neighborhood from the unfamiliar and hostile realm of the "outside world."[80]

Another way in which some urbanites respond to the perception of a threatening, hostile, and unpleasant urban milieu is by withdrawal into the isolation of their homes, which come to represent a "haven" from that external world.[81] Such responses frequently characterize the responses of individuals attempting to preserve their security in the face of real or perceived dangers of criminal victimizations. As noted earlier, urban residence is highly associated with fear of crime, a fact attributable only in part to a higher incidence of most crimes in urban areas. In fact, it has been observed that the perception of personal danger in the community may bear little relationship to either the actual crime rate or personal experience with criminal victimization.[82] It is this perception of hostility and danger that forces some urbanites to withdraw behind locked doors.

Effects of Environmental Disruptions

As mentioned in an earlier section of this chapter, urban residents are frequently the victims of a variety of environmental disruptions that degrade the quality of both the physical environment and the social environment. High levels of air-borne pollution threaten physical well-being, and may give rise to social withdrawal as residents seek the haven of closed doors and filtered air. Noise pollution has also been discussed previously as an environmental disruption that may have physically and psychologically damaging effects on many urbanites.

Thus, retreat into the home may reflect not only a withdrawal from the dangers of crime and violence, but also an attempt to buffer the impacts of visual blight, noxious exhaust fumes, and excessive levels of noise. For instance, research has shown that in neighborhoods bisected by streets with high traffic volumes, residents are less likely to interact with or even know their neighbors, remaining instead in the privacy and isolation of their homes in an effort to avoid noise, exhaust fumes, dust, and congestion.[83] Under such circumstances it should come as no surprise if we also observe the effects of social withdrawal and anonymity identified by urban disorganization theories as among the most critical problems of urban life.

Effects of Residential Congestion and Density

Urban housing conditions, especially those characteristic of low-income areas, may also contribute to a reduced quality of life and a breakdown of social relations. Numerous social scientists have suggested a relationship between abnormal and pathological behaviors, interactional breakdowns, and urban density. In some cases such suggestions are mere conjecture, or are derived from observations of pathological abnormalities among rats and other animals subjected to extreme crowding under experimental conditions.[84] However, there have also been numerous social-science studies of the hypothesized relationship between social disorganization and density. Some studies have examined relationships between area density, or the "outside" density of population in a given neighborhood or area, and such indicators of social pathology as crime rates for particular districts, the incidence of suicide, and numbers of admissions to mental health institutions. Although some of these studies have indicated greater rates of social and psychological disturbance and disorganization in high-density areas, overall findings have been inconsistent and inconclusive.[85]

However, more recent studies that focus carefully on the effects of crowding on individuals have more consistently demonstrated a relationship between density and the disruption of social relations. High *outside density* in city neighborhoods appears to result in reduced levels of interactions among urban neighbors.[86] In addition, high within-household or *inside density* accompanying the crowding of many household members into relatively small living areas has been shown in several investigations to contribute to reduced levels of personal satisfaction and to increased family conflict. Other observed effects of extreme residential crowding include reduced physical health and a general impairment of social relations.[87,88,89]

Positive and Negative Consequences of Urbanism

Although the existence of such patterns is not inconsequential, in general most urban dwellers seem both well-integrated and capable of successfully adapting to the conditions of urban life. Urban residents do appear to be proportionately less involved with their neighbors than are residents of small towns, but in general are not socially isolated from or unacquainted with their neighbors. More importantly, urban residents appear to exhibit more far-reaching social network ties, which increase the number and range of available social contacts.[90] Such evidence appears to raise serious questions about the degree to which social isolation and anonymity are widespread or pervasive among the urban population.

It is self-evident that in any large city a given individual will encounter a far greater number of unfamiliar "strangers" than would be the case in a small-town environment, and that proportionately few of those encountered will be personal acquaintances. This fact, plus the fact that urban areas characteristically exhibit great social heterogeneity as a result of the concentration of diverse subcultural groups in large cities, may contribute to some heightened levels of social withdrawal and detachment. In the public sphere of urban life, individuals are in constant contact with others who are not only strangers in the sense of a lack of acquaintance, but who are also often perceived as "strange" in the sense of being distinct in terms of racial, ethnic, social-class, and other subcultural characteristics.[91,92] Such phenomena as heightened levels of distrust, fear, and hostility toward others may be explained in large part by such perceptions.

In the public sphere of urban life, personal estrangement, intergroup conflict, and lack of willingness to help or otherwise intervene on behalf of others do appear to characterize the social milieu. However, such social "costs" are accompanied by some important positive consequences as well. For example, the urban social environment provides a setting in which individualism and nonconformity can flourish with only limited infringements on personal freedom. Unlike small towns, where privacy is limited and social sanctions against nonconformity may be swift and harsh, urban centers provide a milieu in which a wide range of unconventionality is tolerated.

Constant exposure to social diversity, as well as a tendency to avoid confrontation or interference with urban "strangers," gives rise to a context in which personal freedom of action and expression is more readily attained. This pattern of urban tolerance has been referred to as the *culture of civility*.[93] In general, social scientists have observed a tendency among urbanites to more or less ignore and tolerate others whose actions or appearances they may neither understand nor approve of, so long as those others in turn leave them alone. One

Cities bring very different kinds of people into close proximity to one another.
(Michael Weisbrot/Stock, Boston)

need only stand on a busy streetcorner in San Francisco or any of a variety of other cities, and observe the peaceful public coexistence of corporate executives, punk rockers, publicly homosexual couples, middle-aged hippies, prostitutes, police officers, and an incredible array of other highly diverse individuals, to see evidence of this civility and tolerance.

In contrast to the relative anonymity of the "public" sphere, social relations in the "private sphere" of contacts with kin, friends, coworkers, and other primary and quasi-primary relations provide a locus for involvement, intimacy, and social integration, thereby contributing to the social and psychological well-being of a majority of urban residents. Such ties provide most urbanites with a highly supportive "personal community" comprised of friends, coworkers, kin, and even neighbors. However, widespread access to private or public transportation, the separation of residence from places of employment and recreation, and realtively high rates of residential mobility have broadened the horizons of these social networks. As a result, for most urban residents their personal communities are not constrained by the boundaries of the neighborhood or the localized community area, allowing the selection of social partners and groups on the basis of shared interests rather than just physical proximity.[94,95] The bottom line to this discussion is that, in general, most urban residents do not appear to experience abnormal stress or alienation, and in terms of their networks of personal relations most appear to exhibit substantial social integration.

In spite of the integration enjoyed by most urbanites, however, a majority also express a sense of public anonymity and distrust of others. Thus, we may conclude that at least in selective ways the urban social environment does impinge upon social relations. The disruption of social relations does not appear to occur to the extent that widespread social breakdown occurs, yet many urbanites are uncomfortable and dissatisfied with many attributes of the urban experience. Indeed, a majority of Americans respond somewhat negatively to the urban environment. This is reflected by residential preference surveys indicating that approximately three-fourths of the adult population would prefer not to live in large cities.[96] At a minimum, such findings reflect the widespread ambivalence of our culture toward the conditions of modern urban society, and the failure of our cities to provide a social or physical environment that is generally contributive to the satisfaction and well-being of all urban residents.

PART III: RESPONSES

Although the preceding discussion has focused upon key urban problems primarily affecting American cities during the 1970s and 1980s, an attempt has been made to demonstrate that many of our contemporary urban problems have evolved over many years and are the products of fundamental and widespread processes of social change. Clearly, then, our current urban problems have not appeared out of thin air, but are long-standing and have been sources of public concern and policy attention for years.

Urban problems per se are not new, nor are efforts to accomplish urban reform. However, the degree of public recognition of the deteriorating conditions of urban America appears to have expanded since midcentury. Consequently, there has been a proliferation of policies and programs emanating from federal, state, and local governmental agencies, as well as private organizations, all in some way directed toward the resolution of the urban crisis.

Federal Housing and Urban Renewal Programs

In terms of program scale and financial commitment, a long tradition of federal government programs designed to improve urban housing conditions and alleviate urban blight represent the most visible, and at the same time perhaps the most controversial, of American responses to the urban crisis. Extensive federal government involvement in the replacement of substandard and deteriorating urban housing with new public housing facilities began during the Great Depression of the 1930s. However, the real emergence of the federal government as a major force affecting urban redevelopment responses began after World War II with the passage of the Housing Act of 1949.

Designed to address urban deterioration in a broad-based manner, this legislation incorporated both a continued emphasis on the provision of public housing funding and an additional new focus upon *urban renewal* efforts. This added component of the federal urban rehabilitation effort called for removal of deteriorated inner-city buildings and facilities. Urban renewal involved the condemnation and purchase of deteriorated and blighted areas by city governments, primarily with the use of federal urban renewal funds. Once purchased, all buildings in the renewal areas were ordinarily leveled. After land areas were completely cleared, the final step in the renewal process was to be accomplished by the sale of the vacant land to private developers at greatly reduced prices, whereupon new privately built housing and commercial buildings would be constructed.

The goals of urban renewal efforts included both the rehabilitation and development of old and deteriorating downtown commercial centers and the replacement of urban slum housing with an expanded supply of adequate housing for all income groups. In contrast with these grand objectives, the consequences of federal urban renewal programs have most often been substantially less positive and generally ineffective. Part of the reason for the overall failure of urban renewal and reconstruction programs has to do with the ways in which programs were implemented and managed. Implementation of federally sponsored urban renewal and public housing programs has generally been accomplished under the direction and control of local city government. In many cases, city administrations simply used renewal programs as mechanisms for improving the conditions of downtown business districts. Powerful urban business interests were often able to influence urban redevelopment efforts in ways that served the interests of the "land-based elite," comprised largely of downtown property owners, real estate speculators, and land development companies.[97] Most projects were more oriented toward improving the profitability of downtown businesses and protecting central-city property values than toward resolving the problems of physical decay in impoverished slum neighborhoods. In addition, the private developers who have purchased renewal tracts are motivated by financial profit rather than concerns about social reform. As a result, most have developed business offices or higher priced residential complexes rather than less profitable low-income housing.

Political manipulations by urban business interests directed federal urban renewal programs so that vast expanses of deteriorated slum housing were leveled. Such efforts operated to create a "buffer" between the downtown commercial area and impoverished residential areas. Most frequently, the bulldozed housing areas were replaced not with new low-income housing but with public facilities, commercial and industrial buildings, rental housing designed primarily for middle- and upper-income groups, and even parking lots and vacant lots. As a result of such redevelopment patterns, the overall supply of low-cost urban housing has actually declined in many cities where urban renewal programs have been implemented. Indeed, the "hidden agenda" behind many urban renewal programs could be described as an effort by city decision makers to prevent or slow the movement of higher income urbanites and businesses to the suburbs, while simultaneously pursuing a program of "Negro removal" to force blacks and other minority and low-income populations out of areas adjoining the central business districts.

In the words of one analyst, urban renewal programs can best be described as the "federal bulldozer."[98] Condemnation and clearing of urban slums have seldom resulted in the construction of either public or private low-income housing. Quite often no reconstruction occurred, leaving many central business districts surrounded by a vacant and unoccupied urban wasteland. During the 1950s only about 6 percent of new housing constructed in conjunction with urban renewal was designed for low-income residents.[99] Even after public recognition of such problems forced a redirection of urban renewal efforts, such patterns continued to predominate. Indeed, one analyst reported that in the late 1960s fewer than one-third of the housing units destroyed by urban renewal were replaced by new housing units, and that less than 10 percent of those new units consisted of low-income housing.[100]

It is ironic that the consequences of these urban renewal and redevelopment policies include a worsening of the urban housing problems they were initially designed to improve. Reduced supplies of existing low-income housing have forced greater crowding into the remaining available units. Housing costs have increased as levels of demand for low-cost housing further exceeded already inadequate supplies. In addition, established neighborhood-based social ties have been destroyed as impoverished residents of urban slum areas were forced from their homes by the federal bulldozer. Despite the obvious problems of urban slums, many such neighborhoods are characterized by a sense of "community" and cohesive social ties among those residing there. Consequently, the effects of forced dislocation accompanying urban renewal contribute to substantial personal grief and depression for many of those forced to move. In addition, a majority of those forced to move have received little or no assistance either in finding new housing, in bearing the financial burdens of moving, or in affording generally higher rates of rent.

Public Housing Projects

The predominant approach to the provision of low-income public housing as part of urban renewal and other related federal urban redevelopment programs has resulted in additional failures. In those relatively few instances when renewal funds were directed to the development of low-income housing facilities, the result has often been the construction of large, multistory, high-density "project" housing. Unfortunately, such designs generally fail to accommodate such social needs as the capacity for adult supervision of children playing outside, the provision of common areas where informal socializing can occur, or the feasibility of mutual support for and surveillance of "defensible space" by relatively small groups of residents.[101] Seldom has public housing been designed to replace the preexisting single family homes and smaller multiunit apartments that were destroyed. Unfortunately, the high visibility of massive public housing projects, plus the implementation of residency requirements, which frequently restrict their availability to all but the most severely impoverished and disadvantaged, have created a setting of social stigma and failure for those relocating into such projects.

In many cases, major low-income public housing projects have gradually been abandoned by residents attempting to escape from poor physical design characteristics, high rates of crime and personal victimization, and rapid deterioration due to vandalism, limited maintenance, and neglect. One highly publicized example involved the Pruitt-Igoe high-rise housing project in St. Louis. Completed in the mid-1950s, this project won an award for architectural design excellence. However, the project failed miserably in providing a safe and secure living environment. Cost-cutting decisions left the facility with uninsulated steam pipes, screenless windows, no public restroom facilities, and few common areas for social gatherings. Vandalism and a lack of adequate maintenance led to the rapid physical deterioration of the facility. The original plan for a racially mixed residential population quickly gave way to a population comprised only of the hard-core poor who were unable to move elsewhere. Due in part to the small number of adult male residents, as well as to design characteristics that failed to provide for "defensible space," rape, robbery, muggings, and assaults became commonplace, forcing many residents to retreat into the relative

This is the demolishing of the infamous Pruitt-Igoe housing complex in St. Louis. It was seen as a symbol of the failure of low-income public housing projects.

(Paul Okrassa)

security of their apartments. By 1973 the entire project was abandoned and demolished by the city housing authority after all other efforts to resolve problems of crime, violence, and physical deterioration had failed.[102]

In sum, urban renewal and other related federal programs have failed to resolve the basic problems of urban blight. Some successes have been noted, particularly in terms of the reconstruction and upgrading of some downtown commercial areas and facilities. However, efforts to rectify the problems of substandard and deteriorated urban slum housing via either private or public means have failed. The existence of urban slums does not result simply from the gradual aging and deterioration of formerly adequate housing, but from the pervasive effects of poverty and discrimination, which force the disadvantaged into whatever housing is available.

Other Efforts

Attempts to resolve the problems of blighted urban slums by treating only the symptoms of physical decay are destined to fail unless they are combined with broad-based changes to remove the sources of urban poverty. Some urban redevelopment programs, notably the Model Cities program of the 1960s, Head Start programs, and federal direct subsidy programs for purchases and rental of low-income housing, have attempted to focus some attention on the social sources of the urban crisis. However, these too have tended to result in more failures than success, and most such programs have faltered and eventually been abandoned as their goals remained unattained. Other programs, such as the 1974 Urban Housing Act program, have been of limited success due in part to questionable implementation strategies. The 1974 Act included a Community Development Block Grant Program designed to revitalize distressed urban areas. Originally, it was intended that block grant funds would be allocated only if the area was a slum or blighted area, if the use of funds would benefit low- to moderate-income families, and if there existed a demonstrated need for housing. However, in many cases only the first of these eligibility criteria was considered in allocating funds, often resulting in a redevelopment effort that addressed physical blight but ignored the needs of low-income residents.

In light of the failure of past and present federal government strategies to accomplish urban redevelopment, the Reagan administration has attempted to redirect federal urban policies while simultaneously reducing direct federal involvement in urban redevelopment efforts. In lieu of providing funds intended primarily for subsidized low-income housing, new federal programs call for a substantial reduction in expenditures, with available funds distributed directly to "qualified" poor to permit them to rent living quarters. Unfortunately, such policies ignore the fact that there is a substantial and growing shortage of low-cost urban housing. Put simply, the provision of rent money will not improve housing conditions among the poor if the supply of low-income housing remains inadequate. This limitation, along with funding cuts, has led some critics to describe the Reagan housing program as a step backward rather than a means of improving the situation.

In terms of efforts to encourage urban economic recovery, the Reagan administration has proposed the development of *enterprise zones* in selected depressed urban areas. Rather than relying on federal grants or other intervention strategies, this program is designed to offer tax credits, regulatory relief, improved public services, and other incentives to encourage the location of small businesses in the urban enterprise zones. Unfortunately, most analysts are pessimistic about the ability of this program either to "prompt investors to flock to the inner cities" or to transform the character of depressed and blighted inner cities.[103] In any case, the Reagan administration proposals have as yet had little impact on the trend of urban decay. Thus, urban America continues in the 1980s to experience decay, blight, inadequate housing, and a concentration of the nation's poor. Such conditions reflect the failure of past and present federal responses in the form of urban redevelopment programs to accomplish the goals of revitalizing urban centers.

Localized Urban Revitalization Responses

Many cities have engaged in localized efforts to respond to various dimensions of the urban crisis. Often linked with federal programs, cities have created their own public urban development agencies. These local agencies not only plan and direct urban redevelopment efforts but also actively pursue and attempt to attract business and industry back into the central cities. Many American cities are actively promoting revitalization and attempting to erase their images as "dying" and outmoded remnants of the past. Incentives, ranging from access to locally administered loans and grants to tax reductions to zoning variances, are offered as bait to the pool of businesses and industries in search of new locations.

Urban Megastructures

Overall there is little evidence that such efforts have met with much success. However, in some cities there have been impressive renovations of central-city business districts. Massive complexes incorporating large urban hotels, offices, and shops under the roof of a single megastructure have appeared in many large cities, including Detroit, Philadelphia, Boston, and Atlanta. Other cities have adopted similar if less grandiose strategies, replacing old and deteriorating central business district structures with new urban center shopping malls, civic centers, and the like. For example, a complex of grain elevators once used by the Quaker Oats Company in Akron, Ohio, became the centerpiece of Quaker Square, a new central-city shopping and office complex. A similar effort was un-

The Renaissance Center in Detroit was constructed in such a way that it was physically separated from the distressed areas around it. The result was that it highlights the distress rather than contributing to its improvement.

(John R. Maher/EKM-Nepenthe)

dertaken in Salt Lake City, where an old trolley car station and maintenance facility was transformed into the Trolley Square complex of shops and restaurants. Although supported and often funded in part by public redevelopment programs, many of these downtown renovation efforts have proceeded partly or completely through the investment of private funding. Such private involvement in urban redevelopment reflects the fact that not only city governments but also urban landowners, businesses, and corporate enterprises with urban center offices and headquarters have an important stake in reversing the trends of urban deterioration and collapse.

Evidence regarding the success of such efforts, and particularly of the gigantic urban megastructures, reflects mixed results. Although such structures are physically impressive and do present a more revitalized image than the structures that they have replaced, many such projects are experiencing serious financial difficulties and have failed to attain full occupancy of office and store space.[104] Moreover, it can be argued that such facilities simply erect new physical barriers between blighted urban neighborhoods and the shops and offices frequented by the middle and upper classes. For example, Detroit's Rennaissance Center sits in the midst of one of that city's most distressed areas, yet is so effectively isolated from the homes and businesses of surrounding neighborhoods that it has been referred to as "Fort Detroit." By creating a virtual "fortress" in the midst of urban blight, such developments may even contribute to the further deterioration and decay of downtown commercial activity. Smaller shops and businesses unable to afford to locate in the new megastructure facilities may find themselves isolated from shoppers who have turned their attention to the enclosed comfort and relative security of the new complexes.

Despite the hope that central-city megastructures and similar large-scale physical reconstruction projects might exert a "catalytic" effect on the revitalization of urban centers, such responses appear unlikely. Critics have observed that such projects fail to meet the needs of the central-city population and, in fact, reflect just one more example of the attempt by powerful political and financial interests to erect barriers between themselves or their clientele and the urban poor. However, critics have noted that, ironically, these facilities also are largely irrelevant to the vast numbers of suburban commuters. Well-to-do suburban and exurban residents may occasionally turn to the city for shopping and entertainment, but ordinarily prefer to leave the problems of the city behind and return to their outlying homes at the end of the day. Without a broader-based regeneration of urban business and population, these large urban commercial complexes may provide little in the way of an impetus for broad-based urban redevelopment and reform. Moreover, they direct attention away from the broader problems of poverty, unemployment, and underemployment, selective depopulation, and central-city decay.[105]

Taxing Commuters

In light of the limited success of these and other programs to retain or attract business, industry, and middle-class populations back into urban centers, some cities have adopted alternative responses in an effort to resolve the fiscal pressures of a declining tax base and expanding service provision needs. For instance, the implementation of wage taxes collected on the basis of place of employment rather than place of residence has allowed some cities to generate additional tax revenues from suburban and exurban commuters who work in central-city locations.

Annexation

Another approach, which represents an attempt by city government to capture a larger share of the taxes paid by those living beyond city limits, is *annexation.* Although such efforts often give rise to bitter political conflict, a number of large cities have successfully expanded their boundaries to annex surrounding unincorporated and even incorporated areas. When successful, this outward relocation of city limits can provide some fiscal relief in the form of the collection of additional tax revenues from residents in the newly added city areas. However, the opportunities for such actions are so limited that annexation cannot be considered an effective response to the urban fiscal crisis in most American cities.

Coordinated Approaches

A different local governmental response to the problems and costs of providing public services has been the creation of multicity or even metropolitan-area service authorities to provide for the service needs of a more widespread urban-area population. Traditionally, each of the many separate urban and suburban municipalities is highly urbanized and metropolitan areas have assumed independent responsibility for the funding and management of a wide range of public services, each attempting to provide for the needs of their separate populations. The high costs and inefficiencies of this multijurisdictional approach to the provision of safety services, municipal utilities, sanitation, libraries, and other public service programs have been widely recognized. In response, coordinated planning and service districts, encompassing several or many communities, have been created in a number of areas to fund and provide public services more effectively. Although broad-scale coordinated service provision is hindered by the concerns of local communities about maintaining their identities and political autonomy, such programs have become increasingly commonplace and represent a response that is likely to be adopted more widely in the future. One obvious example of such an approach is the organization of a coordinated government entity in Dade County, Florida, that encompasses the Miami metropolitan area. Another highly successful example of this coordinated approach to metropolitan government is Toronto, Canada. Indeed, Toronto represents a contemporary urban success story, where physical reconstruction has been combined with a progressive approach to social improvements to create a widely acclaimed improvement in the quality of city life.

Grass-Roots and Individual Responses

Most urban problems reflect the operation of large-scale forces of social change, which helps to explain their resistance to solution even by massive federal and local urban assistance and redevelopment efforts. Under such circumstances, it might seem that efforts by smaller private citizen groups and individuals to respond to urban problems would be hopelessly ineffective. Nevertheless, there are numerous examples of local grass-roots efforts that at least on a small scale have improved the quality of the urban experience for their participants and others.

For instance, John Palen has described the successes of Chicago's "Fifth City" community organization.[106] This cooperative grass-roots organization, located in an impoverished and predominantly black west-side slum area, conducted a fairly extensive housing rehabilitation effort. That effort not only provided for improved low-income housing opportunities, but simultaneously regenerated a sense of community identification, participation, and pride seldom observed in middle-class neighborhoods, much less in urban slum areas. Other authors and observers have documented a wide range of accomplishments of similar grass-roots neighborhood and community action organizations.[107,108] Another illustration of such efforts involves a project now underway in Salt Lake City. A group of local artists working with city planners is attempting to combine municipal low-income housing redevelopment with the establishment of a new inner-city "community" of artists' residences, studios, retail outlets, parks, and other facilities.

The specific objectives and goals of such organizations are frequently oriented toward some specific local problems such as housing deterioration, inadequate maintenance of rental properties by absentee landlords, discriminatory rental and employment practices, neighborhood crime problems, and so forth. The successes of such local organizations are seldom as impressive as those of the Fifth City organization, and in many cases their successes have been short-lived. However, the latent consequences of such organizations may be more important than their degree of success in attaining specific goals. In many ways such grass-roots efforts reflect extremely effective responses to the forces of urban alienation and anonymity discussed previously in this chapter. The organization of neighborhoods by such groups can instill a sense of purpose and identity among local residents, contributing to heightened participation in local life, greater social involvement, and a sense of mutual interdependence and cooperation.

What may result from such developments is the emergence of *community* in the sense of shared feelings of belonging and commitment to a common purpose. In some urban neighborhoods this pattern of social involvement and participation has appeared as an unplanned consequence of organizational efforts to pursue some more concrete program goals collectively. In others, especially some traditional ethnic neighborhoods, this spirit of community appears to reflect a cultural emphasis on close-knit neighborhood life. In still other urban neighborhoods the intentional pursuit of a close-knit community experience has resulted in the selective movement of people who share a commitment to social involvement and mutual participation into specific urban areas, giving rise to what some sociologists have called the *"contrived community."*[109]

These kinds of community-building responses provide enhanced opportunities for social integration. In addition, a majority of urbanites appear to adapt to the relative public anonymity of urban life by developing extensive private social ties beyond the local neighborhood. Even when ties with neighbors are limited, personal social networks involving others from within and often far beyond the city provide most urbanites with ample opportunities for social attachment and social support.[110,111]

Gentrification

In spite of such responses and adaptive behaviors, American businesses and population continue to flee the nation's urban centers. Some large urban areas do continue to experience new commercial and residential growth and development in central cities, but such patterns are largely limited to a relative handful of cities such as Houston and Phoenix in the Sun-Belt regions of the South and Southwest. Elsewhere, some very limited patterns of upper-class movement into areas of older but high-quality renovated urban housing have been observed. This process of *gentrification* in some older urban neighborhoods has received considerable attention in recent years. Both federally subsidized residential-mortgage and home-improvement loan programs, and loans provided by private financial institutions, have contributed to the gentrification phenomenon, since relatively few low-income residents can qualify for the financing needed for extensive renovation. Although gentrification can be viewed as one avenue for revitalizing the social and economic climate of urban centers, it has also been identified as a source of additional problems. In particular, gentrification has resulted in the displacement of substantial numbers of the urban elderly and other low-income residents, and has contributed to a further decline in the supply of low-cost urban housing. Despite the fact that such residential redevelopment has had these effects in some urban areas, gentrification does not appear to reflect extensive return migration to urban centers by the upper-middle class.

Continued Migration from the Cities

In fact, the most widespread contemporary response to the urban crisis appears to be a continuation of now-established patterns of movement away from city centers. Beginning in the late 1960s and becoming widespread during the 1970s, internal migration patterns in the United States, as well as in Japan and some highly urbanized European societies, shifted unexpectedly. In the past, migration had disproportionately involved a movement into metropolitan areas. Even though population shifts had involved a departure of many residents from central-city areas, the vast majority of those moving had remained in the suburban communities and smaller cities and towns immediately surrounding the nation's large cities. However, in the 1970s and 1980s, proportionately more people are moving into more remote nonmetropolitan areas.[112] This nonmetropolitan migration turnaround may be explained in part by the corresponding shifts of diverse industrial and commercial activities from urban locations to nonmetropolitan areas. In addition, Americans appear more willing and able to act upon their preferences to live in small-town environments than has previously been the case.

A Final Word

In a sense, these patterns of population and industrial redistribution reflect the individual choices of hundreds of thousands of people to respond to the problems of urban areas by leaving them behind. If such choices continue to be widespread, even greater problems of urban abandonment, class-based geographic stratification, and urban economic and physical deterioration may be anticipated. Thus, in the aggregate, our individual patterns of response may ultimately contribute to the perseverance of many of the urban problems that prior policies and programs have been unable to eliminate.

In an age of decentralization, massive efforts to revitalize some large urban centers may in fact be counterproductive. As outgrowths of historical forces of industrialization and modernization, traditional forms of organization in central-city areas may in some ways represent a dysfunctional remnant of the past, no longer responsive to the contemporary forces of social change. As such, it could be argued that at least in some central cities our efforts to stem the tide of urban decline can at best simply delay the inevitable.

Nevertheless, we remain a predominantly urban people. Major urban and metropolitan centers continue to dominate as the commercial and organizational nerve centers of large and complex societies. Cities are also a haven for the social variability and innovativeness that contribute to the emergence of new ideas and new directions of social change. Cultural variety and freedom for its expression are closely identified with urban life. Consequently, suggestions that we abandon efforts to resolve our urban problems and allow the "urban dinosaurs" to fade away of their own accord are unacceptable.

Instead, our responses must be redirected. "Band-Aid" approaches that emphasize superficial improvements and confront only the outward symptoms of the urban crisis have failed miserably, and will continue to fail. Moreover, programs that attempt to "restore" urban centers in a manner that emphasizes the centralized retail and service functions of the past are unrealistic in the face of contemporary patterns of residential and commercial location. Future efforts must instead focus response directly on such basic problems as urban congestion, poverty, and discrimination, and other root causes of our continuing urban crisis.

SUMMARY

1. Many of the problems discussed throughout this book may be thought of as primarily urban problems.

Part I: The Problem

2. Accompanying population concentrations in the city are some inevitable problems of urban crowding and congestion.
3. Public and private means of transportation in the cities cause people an array of problems.
4. The deterioration of environmental quality in the cities threatens people's health and safety.
5. Many buildings in the cities are deteriorating and for many the housing that is available is inadequate in a variety of ways.
6. Many American cities are suffering from grave fiscal crises.
7. The city is characterized by high levels of poverty, unemployment, underemployment, discrimination, and urban blight. These, in turn, cause a sense of despair, frustration, and anger among urban dwellers. The latter, in turn, are related to distrust of others and fear of crime.

Part II: Causes and Consequences

8. The major causes and consequences of problems in the city need to be seen in the context of the history of the city.
9. The process of invasion-succession, whereby new urban migrants locate in older neighborhoods replacing more established and advantaged groups, is related to a series of urban problems. For example, new migrant groups are relegated to the oldest, most crowded, and deteriorated urban environments.
10. The forces of outward expansion of the city, especially suburbanization, have tended to expand and intensify the problems of congestion and urban environmental distress.
11. The movement out of the city has been selective and there has been a tendency for those who are better off economically to flee the city. This has tended to leave the city as a center of poverty.
12. Many major industries and businesses have left the city leaving an insufficient number of jobs, especially the low-skill jobs for which many poor urbanites could qualify.
13. The redistribution of population and industry has left the cities with declining tax bases. Making things more difficult is the fact that the cities find themselves needing to provide more services with fewer funds.

14. Urban alienation and isolation is often traced to social disorganization in the city. Although many sociologists see these problems stemming from social disorganization, there are some who emphasize the positive characteristics of the city and their salutary effects on individuals and their social relationships.
15. Urbanites both perceive and experience considerable danger in the city.
16. Many city dwellers also experience physical, psychological, and social problems as a result of ecological deterioration.
17. Although there is some contradictory evidence on this issue, crowding and congestion in the cities have at least some negative effects on city dwellers.
18. On the positive side, it should be noted that the city contributes to more individualism, freedom, and nonconformity. Urbanites seem to have a greater tolerance of diversity.

Part III: Responses

19. The most visible efforts to cope with urban problems have come from the federal government. The best known of the government's programs was urban renewal. In general, urban renewal efforts were not successful and they often caused more problems than they solved. Efforts to redirect these federal programs in the 1980s have had little impact on the continued decline of many cities.
20. Less often noted have been local efforts to deal with urban problems. The most visible of these efforts have been the megastructures like Detroit's Renaissance Center. Although there have been local successes, many of these efforts have run into a series of difficulties.
21. There are some examples of small, private groups that have had some success in improving the cities.
22. While there is some evidence of urban revival in the process of gentrification, the major response of people to the urban crisis is a continuation of their tendency to move out of the cities.

SUGGESTED READINGS

Banfield, Edward C., *The Unheavenly City Revisited.* Boston: Little, Brown, 1974. A controversial discussion of urban problems. Banfield questions both the conventional wisdom regarding the nature and sources of the "urban crisis" and the capability of administrative planning and programs to resolve most urban problems.

Berry, Brian J. L., and John D. Kasarda, *Contemporary Urban Ecology.* New York: Macmillan, 1977.A broad-ranging review of historical and contemporary patterns of urban and metropolitan development and expansion. Includes discussions of suburbanization and its effects, and a comparative examination of international urbanization processes.

Fischer, Claude S., *The Urban Experience.* New York: Harcourt Brace Jovanovich, 1976.An important source of information on the physical and social context of urban life; sets forth the subcultural theory of urbanism.

Gans, Herbert J., *The Levittowners.* New York: Pantheon, 1967.A modern classic provides an in-depth analysis of the origins and backgrounds of residents in a new suburb, the nature of suburban life, and suburban politics.

Karp, David A., Gregory P. Stone, and William C. Yoels, *Being Urban.* Lexington, Mass.: D. C. Heath, 1977.One of the best treatments of urbanism, including a discussion of the historical roots of classical theories of urbanism.

Michelson, William, *Man and His Urban Environment.* Reading, Mass.: Addison-Wesley, 1976.An examination of the patterns of urban and suburban residence, with a valuable discussion of stages in life cycle and social class as factors affecting ways of life.

Suttles, Gerald D., *The Social Construction of Communities.* Chicago: University of Chicago Press, 1972.An explanation of how and why urban slum neighborhoods come to exhibit a strong social cohesiveness and "sense of community."

Whyte, William F., *Street-Corner Society.* Chicago: University of Chicago Press, 1943.A classic study of the structure and organization of an urban street gang, documenting the ability of the gang to create an enduring order in the urban slum.

FOOTNOTES

[1]U.S. Bureau of the Census, *1980 Census of Population. Vol. 1: Characteristics of Population. Part 1: U.S. Summary* (Washington, D.C.: U.S. Government Printing Office, 1983).

[2]Lester R. Brown, "The Limits to Growth of Third World Cities," *The Futurist* (December 1976).

[3]Thomas Bender, *Toward an Urban Vision: Ideas and Institutions in Nineteenth Century America* (Lexington: University Press of Kentucky, 1975).

[4]Morton White and Lucie White, *The Intellectual Versus the City* (New York: Mentor, 1962).

[5]Leo Marx, *The Machine in the Garden* (New York: Oxford University Press, 1964).

[6]Kirkpatrick Sale, "The Search for Community." In K. Finsterbusch and G. McKenna, eds., *Taking Sides,* 3rd ed. (Guilford, Conn.: Dushkin, 1984), p. 82.

[7]Gordon Dejong and Ralph Sell, "Population Redistribution, Migration and Residential References," *Annals,* 429 (1977), pp. 130–144.

[8]K. Sale, *op. cit.*

[9]Henry Fairlie, "The Idealization of Village Life." In K. Finsterbusch and G. McKenna, *Taking Sides, op. cit.,* pp. 89–94.

[10]Paul Eberts, "Social Indicators of Well-Being." In D. Dillman and D. Hobbs, eds., *Rural Society in the U.S.: Issues for the 1980s* (Boulder, Colo.: Westview, 1982), pp. 284–295.

[11]Ben-Chieh Liu, *Quality of Life Indicators in U.S. Metropolitan Areas* (New York: Praeger, 1976).

[12]U.S. Bùreau of the Census, *op. cit.*

[13]Charles J. Holahan, *Environmental Psychology* (New York: Random House, 1982), pp. 195–235.

[14]*Ibid.*

[15]John Carey, "Water: Is it Safe to Drink?" *National Wildlife,* 22 (1984), pp. 15–17.

[16]Craig R. Humphrey and John A. Krout, "Traffic and the Suburban Highway Neighbor," *Traffic Quarterly,* 24 (1975), pp. 593–613.

[17]Holahan, *op. cit.,* pp. 133–137, 164–169.

[18]Donald Appleyard and Mark Lintell, "The Environmental Quality of City Streets: The Residents' Viewpoint," *Journal of the American Institute of Planners,* 38 (1972), pp. 84–101.

[19]Holahan, *op. cit,* pp. 164–165.

[20]Kurt Finsterbusch, *Understanding Social Impacts* (Beverly Hills, Cal.: Sage, 1980), pp. 195–220.

[21]"Homeless in America," *Newsweek,* January 2, 1984, pp. 20–29.

[22]Holahan, *op. cit.,* pp. 195–235.

[23]Mark Baldassare, "Effects of Household Density on Subgroups," *American Sociological Review,* 46 (1981), pp. 110–118.

[24]W. Gove, O. Galle, and M. Hughes, "Overcrowding in the Home," *American Sociological Review,* 44 (1979), pp. 58–80.

[25]Brian J. L. Berry and John D. Kasarda, *Contemporary Urban Ecology* (New York: Macmillan, 1977).

[26]Colman McCarthy, "Three Days Down and Out in Chicago," *The Nation,* March 5, 1983, pp. 257ff.

[27]"Homeless in America," *op. cit.*

[28]Leonard Berkowitz, "Whatever Happened to the Frustration-Aggression Hypothesis?" *American Behavioral Scientist,* 32 (1978), pp. 691–708.

[29]Robert Merton, *Social Theory and Social Structure,* rev. ed. (Glencoe, Ill.: Free Press, 1968).

[30]Stanley Milgram, "The Experience of Living in Cities," *Science,* 67 (1970), pp. 1461–1468.

[31]Claude S. Fischer, "The Public and Private Worlds of City Life," *American Sociological Review,* 46 (1981), pp. 306–316.

[32]Lyn Lofland, *A World of Strangers* (New York: Basic Books, 1973).

[33]Fischer, *op. cit.*

[34]Bibb Latane and John M. Darley, "Bystander Apathy," *American Scientist,* 67 (1969), pp. 244–268.

[35]Milgram, *op. cit.*

[36]*Ibid.*

[37]Frank Clemente and Michael Kleiman, "Fear of Crime in the United States: A Multivariate Analysis," *Social Forces,* 56 (1977), pp. 519–531.

[38]*Ibid.*

[39]Gary R. Lee, "Residential Location and Fear of Crime Among the Elderly," *Rural Sociology,* 47 (1982), pp. 655–669.

[40]Lee Rainwater, "Fear and the House-as-Haven in the Lower Class," *Journal of the American Institute of Planners,* 32 (1966).

[41]Sally E. Merry, *Urban Danger: Life in a Neighborhood of Strangers* (Philadelphia: Temple University Press, 1981), p. 3.

[42]Jacqueline Zito, "Anonymity and Neighboring in an Urban High Rise Complex," *Urban Life and Culture,* 3 (1974), pp. 243–263.

[43]Stanley Gutterman, "In Defense of Wirth's 'Urbanism as a Way of Life,'" *American Journal of Sociology,* 74 (1969), pp. 492–499.

[44]Leo Srole, "Urbanization and Mental Health: Some Reformulations," *The American Scientist,* 60 (1972), pp. 576–583.

[45]Stephen D. Webb, "Mental Health in Rural and Urban Environments," *Ekistics,* 266 (1978), 37–42.

[46]K. Sale, *op. cit.,* p. 83.

[47]J. John Palen, *The Urban World* (New York: McGraw-Hill, 1975), pp. 41–63.

[48]David Popenoe, *The Suburban Environment* (Chicago: University of Chicago Press, 1977).

[49]Robert A. Caro, *The Power Brokers* (New York: Knopf, 1974).

[50]Peter Marcuse, "Mass Transit for the Few." In J. Scherer, ed., *Focus: Urban Society* (Guilford, Conn.: Dushkin, 1978), pp. 130–137.

[51]Wilbur C. Hallenbeck, *American Urban Communities* (New York: Harper, 1951), p. 202.

[52]Sylvia F. Fava, "Beyond Suburbia," *Annals of the American Academy of Political and Social Science,* 422 (1972), 11–24.

[53]Diana DeAre and Larry Long, "Meet the Average American." In K. Finsterbusch, ed., *Sociology 84/85* (Guilford, Conn.: Dushkin, 1984), pp. 186–189.

[54]John R. Logan and Mark Schneider, "Racial Segregation and Racial Change in American Suburbs, 1970–1980," *American Journal of Sociology,* 89 (1984), p. 888.

[55]Daniel P. Moynihan, "Poverty in Cities." In L. K. Lowenstein, *Urban Studies* (New York: Free Press, 1977), pp. 164–178.

[56]Joe R. Feagin, *Social Problems: A Critical Power-Conflict Perspective* (Englewood Cliffs, N.J.: Prentice-Hall, 1982), pp. 380–413.

[57]Rodney A. Erickson, "Nonmetropolitan Industrial Expansion: Emerging Implications for Regional Development," *Review of Regional Studies,* 6 (1976), pp. 35–48.

[58]Gene F. Summers, "Industrialization." In D. Dillman and D. Hobbs, eds., *Rural Society in the U.S.: Issues for the 1980s, op. cit.,* pp. 164–174.

[59]Rainwater, *op. cit.*

[60]Berry and Kasarda, *op. cit.*

[61]*Ibid.*

[62]*Ibid.*

[63]*Ibid.*

[64]Ferdinand Tönnies, *Gemeinschaft and Gesellschaft* (Community and Society), Charles P. Loomis, (ed. and trs.) (East Lansing: Michigan State University Press, 1957).

[65]Émile Durkheim, *The Division of Labor in Society,* George Simpson (trs.) (New York: Free Press, 1964).

[66]Louis Wirth, "Urbanism as a Way of Life," *American Journal of Sociology,* 44 (1938), pp. 1–24.

[67]Georg Simmel, "The Metropolis and Mental Life." In K. Wolff, ed. and trs., *The Sociology of Georg Simmel* (New York: Free Press, 1950), pp. 409–424.

[68]Milgram, *op. cit.*

[69]Thomas Bender, *Community and Social Change in America* (New Brunswick, N.J.: Rutgers University Press, 1978).

[70]Herbert J. Gans, "Urbanism and Suburbanism as Ways of Life: A Reevaluation of Definitions." In A. Rose, ed., *Human Behavior and Social Processes* (Boston: Houghton Mifflin, 1962).

[71]William F. Whyte, *Street Corner Society* (Chicago: University of Chicago Press, 1955).

[72]Elliot Liebow, *Tally's Corner* (Boston: Little, Brown, 1967).

[73]Gerald Suttles, *The Social Order of the Slum* (Chicago: University of Chicago Press, 1968).

[74]Elijah Anderson, *A Place on the Corner* (Chicago: University of Chicago Press, 1978).

[75]*Ibid.,* p. 207.

[76]Claude S. Fischer, *The Urban Experience* (New York: Harcourt Brace Jovanovich, 1976).

[77]Palen, *op. cit.,* p. 143.

[78]Suttles, *op. cit.*

[79]Gerald D. Suttles, *The Social Construction of Communities* (Chicago: University of Chicago Press, 1972).

[80]Suttles, *op. cit.*, 1968.

[81]Rainwater, *op. cit.*

[82]Richard Krannich, Thomas Greider, and Ronald Little, "Rapid Growth and Fear of Crime: A Four Community Comparison." Paper presented at the Annual Meeting of the Western Social Science Association, San Diego, April 1984.

[83]K. Finsterbusch, *op. cit.*, 1980.

[84]J. B. Calhoun, "Population Density and Social Pathology," *Scientific American*, 206 (1982), pp. 139–148.

[85]Holahan, *op. cit.*

[86]Mark Baldassare, "The Effects of Density on Social Behavior and Attitudes," *American Behavioral Scientist*, 18 (1975), pp. 815–825.

[87]O. Galle, W. Gove, and J. McPherson, "Population Density and Pathology: What are the Relations for Man?" *Science*, 176 (1972) pp. 23–30.

[88]Gove *et al.*, *op. cit.*

[89]Baldassare, *op. cit.*, 1981.

[90]Claude S. Fischer, *To Dwell Among Friends: Personal Networks in Town and City* (Chicago: University of Chicago Press, 1982).

[91]Fischer, *op. cit.*, 1981.

[92]Lofland, *op. cit.*

[93]Howard Becker and Irving Horowitz, "The Culture of Civility." In J. Walton and D. Carns, eds., *Cities in Change* (Boston: Allyn & Bacon, 1977), pp. 199–205.

[94]Fischer, *op. cit.*, 1982.

[95]Melvin Webber, "Ordering Diversity: Community Without Propinquity." In L. Wingo, ed., *Cities and Space: The Future Use of Urban Land* (Baltimore, Md.: Johns Hopkins Press, 1963).

[96]DeJong and Sell, *op. cit.*

[97]Harvey Molotch, "The City as a Growth Machine: Toward a Political Economy of Place," *American Journal of Sociology*, 82 (1972), pp. 309–332.

[98]Martin Anderson, *The Federal Bulldozer* (Cambridge, Mass.: MIT Press, 1964).

[99]*Ibid.*

[100]William Ryan, *Blaming the Victim* (New York: Knopf, 1971).

[101]Holahan, *op. cit.*

[102]Palen, *op. cit.*

[103]Edward C. Banfield, "The Zoning of Enterprise," *The CATO Journal*, 2 (1982), 339–349.

[104]William G. Conway, "The Case Against Urban Dinosaurs," *Saturday Review*, May 14, 1977, pp. 12 ff.

[105]*Ibid.*

[106]J. Palen, *op. cit.*

[107]Saul Alinsky, *Rules for Radicals* (New York: Random House, 1967).

[108]Suttles, *op. cit.* 1968.

[109]Suttles, *op. cit.* 1972.

[110]Fischer, *op. cit.* 1982.

[111]Barry Wellman, "The Community Question: The Intimate Networks of East Yorkers," *American Journal of Sociology*, 84 (1979), pp. 1201–1229.

[112]John M. Wardwell, "The Reversal of Nonmetropolitan Migration Loss." In D. Dillman and D. Hobbs, eds., *Rural Society in the U.S.: Issues for the 1980s*, *op. cit.*, pp. 23–33.

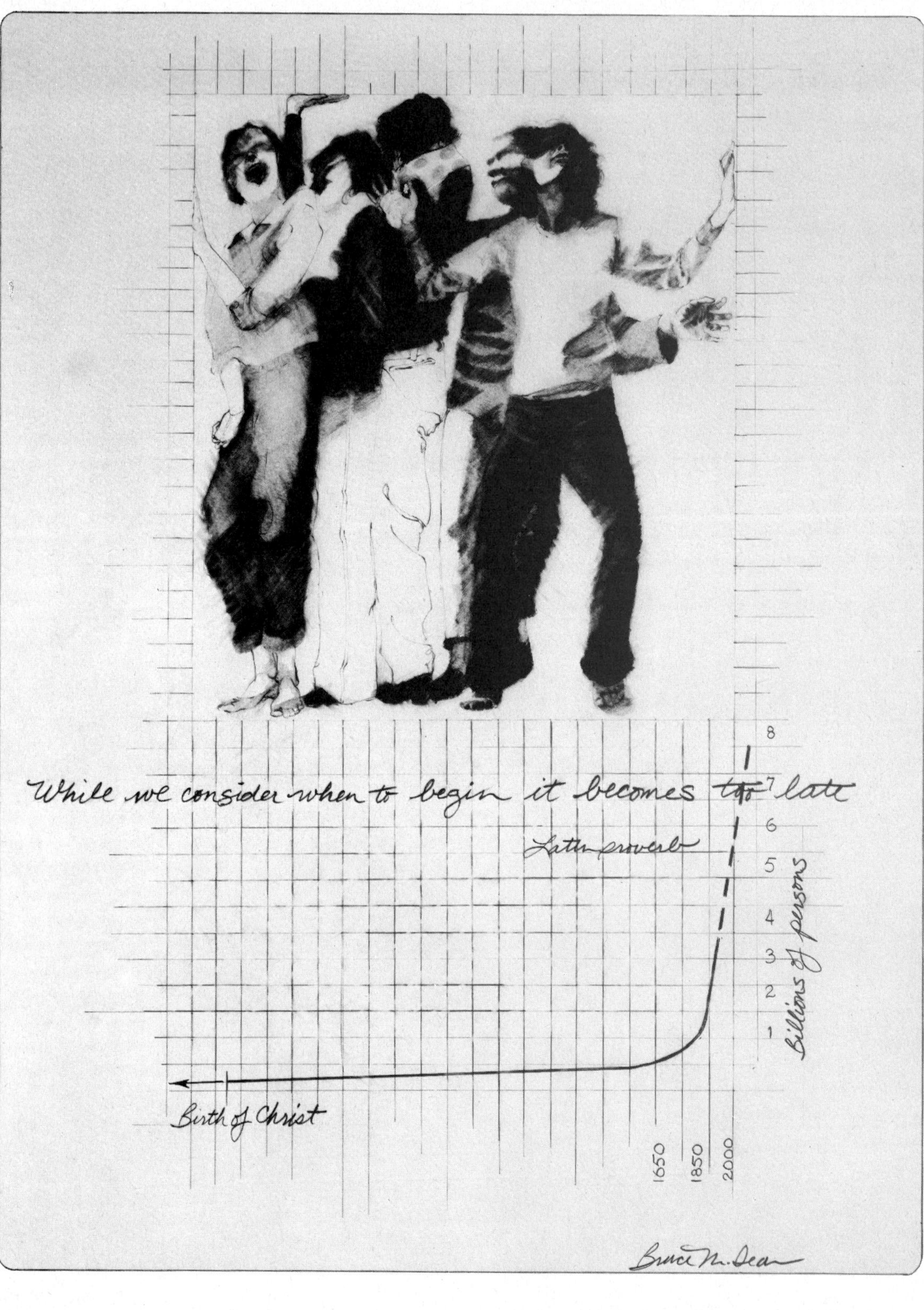
While we consider when to begin it becomes too late
Latin proverb
8
7
6
5
4
3
2
1
Billions of persons
Birth of Christ
1650
1850
2000

14 *Population Problems*

Although population growth has been controlled to a large degree in the United States, for the world as a whole it continues to be among the most serious (if not *the* most serious) social problems facing humankind. It has already badly strained the social and material resources of many nations. Should present trends go unchecked for even a few decades longer, population growth will have dire consequences.

For most of human history, population grew so slowly that it hardly appeared to grow at all. Kingsley Davis estimates that roughly 10,000 years ago, the entire human population totaled only about 5 million people.[1] Growth was so slow that the population would have doubled only about once every 60,000 years. As recently as 1750, population growth was still so slow that it would have taken 1,250 years to double. Today, the world population is growing by 83 million people a year,[2] doubling once every 40 years, and there are nearly 4.8 billion people on earth.[3] According to one estimate, 9 percent of everyone who *ever* lived is alive today.[4]

Another way to understand population growth is to realize that even after perhaps millions of years of existence, the population of the world numbered only about 300 million in the year A.D. 1000.[5] In all of its history to that date, the human population had only managed to grow to a total that is not much larger than the combined populations of the United States and Canada today. To put it differently, it now takes the world less than four years to add 300 million people to its total population. What once may have taken millions of years, now takes less than four years—and that time period is likely to grow shorter in coming years.

When we project today's population growth rates beyond the immediate future, the results nearly defy comprehension. For

Figure 14.1 Population Growth from 8000 B.C. to the Present

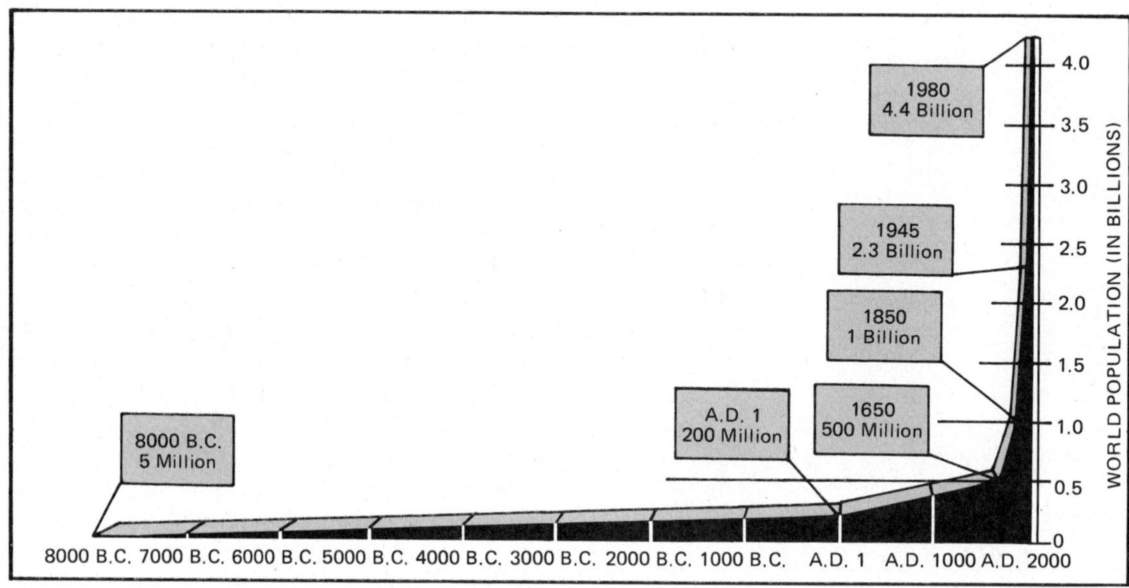

The chart shows world population growth since 8000 B.C. If stretched all the way back to the beginning—298000 B.C.—in this scale, the line would be an invisibly thin one.

Source: The New York Times, October 6, 1981, p. C1.

example, if the present growth rate held, there would be 168 *billion* people on earth 200 years from now. Or, to offer an equally incredible example, at its present rate of growth, the population of Mexico will climb from 76 million people today to over 1 *billion* people by the year 2100. Can you imagine Mexico with a population over one-fifth the size of today's world population, with as many people as currently live in the world's first "demographic billionaire," China?[6]

Obviously such populations for the world as a whole, and for Mexico in particular, are not only inconceivable—they are impossible. Long before any such numbers could be reached, calamity would overtake us. Such projections merely show how close calamity is. That is why Paul Ehrlich, in a now-classic book, spoke of a "population bomb" quietly ticking away and threatening soon to blow us up.[7]

In this chapter we outline the dimensions of the population peril and explain why it has occurred. Why, after thousands of years of infinitesimal increase, did human population explode? Finally, we explore means of averting cataclysmic population growth.

PART I: THE PROBLEM

Most of you have grown up with warnings about the dangers of the population explosion. Although these warnings no longer apply to developed countries like the United States,[8] in the less industrially developed countries, population growth continues unabated, and there are no prospects

Table 14.1 World Population: 1884–1984

YEAR	POPULATION (IN MILLIONS)
1884	1,514
1890	1,564
1900	1,650
1910	1,805
1920	1,860
1930	2,070
1940	2,295
1945	2,402
1950	2,526
1955	2,757
1960	3,037
1965	3,354
1970	3,696
1975	4,066
1980	4,432
1984	4,760

Source: Leon F. Bouvier, "Planet Earth 1984–2034: A Demographic Vision," *Population Bulletin*, Vol. 39, No. 1 (Washington, D.C.: Population Reference Bureau, Inc., 1984), p. 11.

in sight that it will be halted. In the long run, growth in these nations may be as serious a problem for Americans as would have been a continuation of our own population growth. We are all inhabitants of a single planet. If starvation, plague, political chaos, and ecological ruin occur on a massive scale in various parts of the world, they will cause severe problems for people everywhere.

The Population Explosion

Two factors enter into population growth. First is the *rate of natural increase*,[9] which is the net difference between the annual number of births and deaths divided by the total population. When we say that a population is growing at a rate of 3.1 percent a year (Bangladesh's present rate), it means that there are more births than deaths each year—enough to make the total population 3.1 percent larger at the end of a year than it was at the beginning of the year. Perhaps that does not sound like a great deal of growth; however, at that rate, the population will double in about 22 years. In other words, the population of Bangladesh (currently 99.6 million) will be about 245 million in less than four decades.[10]

A second factor in population growth is the *absolute size* of the population that is growing at a particular rate. If the population is small, doubling it does not add a large number of people to the world population. Obviously, doubling a population of a million (Oman's population today) only results in a population of 2 million, but a doubling of a population of a billion (roughly China's current population) adds another billion to the total. Bear in mind that doubling results in *exponential growth*. When even a tiny population continues at a rate of growth that causes it to double every few years, it will rapidly become a huge population. For example, if a nation of 4 million people began to grow at 3.5 percent per year (thus doubling every 20 years), in 20 years its population would be 8 million, after 40 years it would be 16 million, after 60 years it would be 32 million, after 80 years, 64 million, and, after a century of that rate of growth, the nation would have a population of 128 million people—32 times more than when the growth began. Human populations have recently undergone this kind of explosive growth. The speed with which such redoubling produces astronomical totals has caused social scientists to speak of a *population explosion*, for such change is more like an explosion than like simple expansion. The arithmetic is inescapable. The future it promises threatens to come upon us very rapidly.

Such dire projections for the future continue to be accurate, despite the fact that the world's rate of population growth has slowed a bit. As a result of this slowing, the United Nations has lowered its estimate of the world population in the year 2000 from 7.5 billion to 6.1 billion people.[11] In spite of the slowdown in growth, there is still great cause to worry about the future because the absolute increase in population (as a result of a larger and larger base) is larger in each succeeding year. For example, in 1970 there were about 3.7 billion people in the world, a growth rate of 2.1 percent per year, and an addition to the total of about 75 million each year. In 1983, with a population of about 4.7 billion and a lower growth rate of 1.8 percent a year, there are 85 million people being added each year, an absolute increase of 10 million per year over the early 1970s. About 75 percent of the total population of the world lives in less developed nations where the population is doubling every 32 years.[12]

Population and the Developing Nations

It is difficult to avoid doomsday rhetoric when describing population trends in economically less developed countries—a world encompassing most of Africa, Latin

Figure 14.2 World Population Growth, 1950–2000

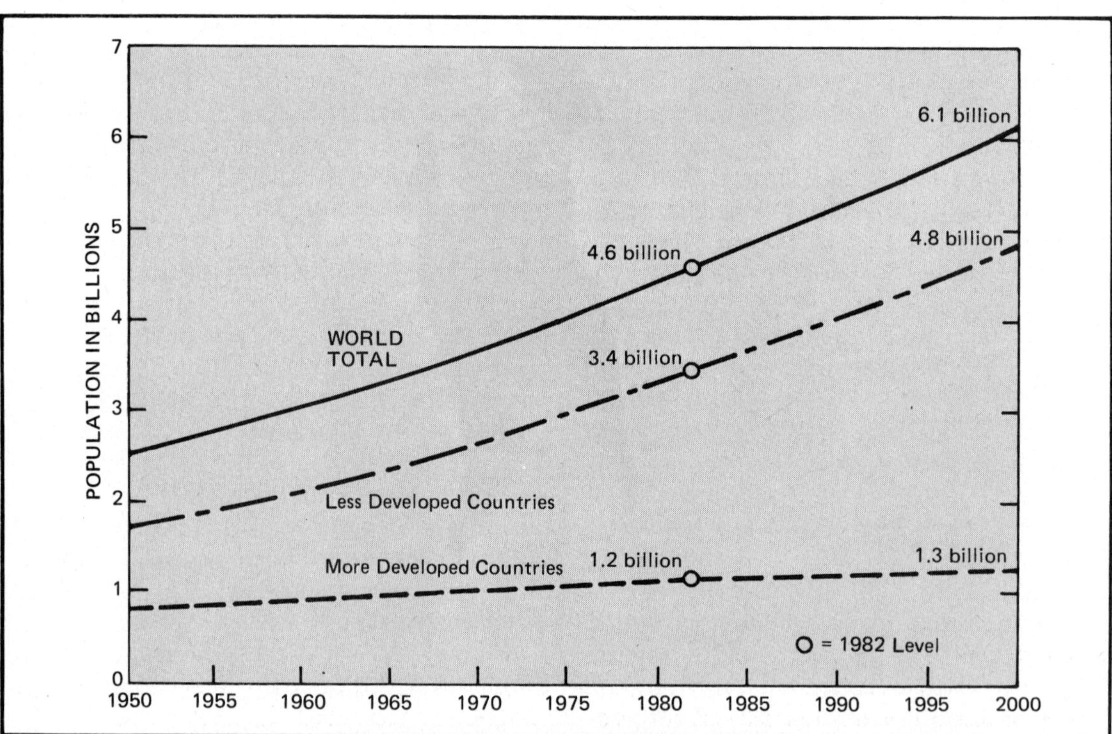

Less-developed nations will continue to account for most population growth through the year 2000.

Source: Nancy Yinger, *et. al.*, "Third World Family Planning Programs: Measuring the Costs," *Population Bulletin*, Vol. 38, No. 1, p. 50.

America, and Asia. Population growth means not only future prospects of horrid dimensions but has already caused great hardships, suffering, and social chaos.

The Cities

The most often used examples of these problems are the conditions in such Third-World cities as Manila, Caracas, and especially Calcutta. Although we will give some examples from one of these cities, bear in mind that these cities are swelled by rural migrants who have come to the city in search of a better life. In other words, the migrants perceived these cities to be more promising than the rural areas in which they lived. Consider but a few examples of urban problems in Calcutta caused, at least in part, by massive population pressures:

—Calcutta has been described as "a nightmare of crowds, of poverty, of organized and unorganized violence, of maimed beggars, of pavement dwellers, of pot-holed and ill-lighted streets."[13]

—The population density of Calcutta in 1921 was already equal to that of present-day Manhattan, and it has since more than tripled.

—Each year there is an influx into the city of "bursting, milling, grimy, disease-ridden, illiterate, unskilled, detribalised hordes."[14]

—It has been estimated that 600,000 people sleep on the street each night.

—Rudyard Kipling, about a century ago, described the city of Calcutta, then only a tenth of its present size, in this way:

> As the fungus sprouts chaotic from its bed,
> So it spread . . .
> And above the packed and pestilential town
> Death looked down.[15]

We need not project imaginary future catastrophes to warn of the population peril in the less developed world. They are already at hand.

The relationship between urbanization and population growth is clear in a nation like Mexico. Mexico's population is presently growing at a rate of 2.6 percent per year. At that rate, it must double every 27 years. The growth rate is not countrywide, however. It is in the cities that we find a disproportionate amount of population

Table 14.2 World's Ten Largest Urban Agglomerations: 1984

RANK	URBAN AREA	POPULATION (IN MILLIONS)
1.	Tokyo/Yokohama	21.3
2.	Mexico City	18.8
3.	New York metropolitan area	18.2
4.	Shanghai	17.0
5.	Sao Paulo	14.5
6.	Beijing	14.1
7.	Los Angeles/Long Beach	10.8
8.	Greater Buenos Aires	10.7
9.	Rio de Janeiro	10.2
10.	Seoul	9.9

World's Ten Largest Urban Agglomerations: 2034

RANK	URBAN AREA	POPULATION (IN MILLIONS)
1.	Mexico City	39.1
2.	Shanghai	38.8
3.	Beijing	34.5
4.	Sao Paulo	32.4
5.	Greater Bombay	30.6
6.	Dacca	29.2
7.	Calcutta	28.9
8.	Jakarta	26.8
9.	Madras	23.3
10.	Tokyo/Yokohama	19.3

Source: Leon F. Bouvier, "Planet Earth: 1984–2034; A Demographic Vision," *Population Bulletin,* Vol. 39, No. 1 (Washington, D.C.: Population Reference Bureau, Inc., 1984): 13, 22.

growth. In 1972 the urban population of Mexico was 33 million out of a total population of 54 million people. By 1979, the total population had risen to 69 million, of which 46 million were in the cities.[16] Thus, the vast majority of Mexico's population growth during the 1970s occurred in urban areas. A significant factor in this is the high level of migration from the farms to the cities, fueled by the high rural birth rate.

Urbanization in less developed nations (like that taking place in Calcutta) tends to be different from the urbanization that took place in industrialized societies. In the latter, urbanization took place as a result of mechanization and increasing productivity of the farms, which created a surplus rural population with little to do on the farms and few ways to earn a livelihood. Furthermore, there was the parallel process of industrialization that took place, at least initially, primarily in the cities and created a compelling need for urban labor. In contrast, in less developed nations the move to the cities is primarily a function of *rapid population growth* that is far beyond what the farms and plantations can support or use for labor. People in less developed countries are driven to the cities because there are too many people in rural areas and the competition for survival is fierce. The city seems to be a source of salvation, or at

Population growth has led to horrible living conditions in many urban areas in developing countries. The above is a scene in Manila in the Philippines.

(Charles Steiner/Sygma)

least it appears to offer some means of livelihood. However, there is not as much industrialization in these cities as there was in the cities of developed nations, and the result is that many are thwarted in their hope for improvement in life conditions. Most of the migrants to the city are able to do little more than swell the ranks of the squatter population.

Fertility and the Family

In general, one can say that the population explosion in less developed nations is having a powerful impact on the family, in some cases even forcing a modification of its basic structure, as well as pressing many families ever deeper into poverty.

Until recently, less developed nations were still fundamentally rural societies, so the extended family was the norm.[17] Population pressure has tended to change that. Less developed societies are, as we saw above, rapidly becoming urban. And, uprooted from its rural surroundings, the *extended family* system is generally being replaced by *nuclear family* life. While a nuclear family is made up of husband, wife, and their children, an extended family tends to be much larger and includes three generations living in one household or in close proximity. The poorest people in most of the less developed countries are often uprooted from their extended family ties—and from all the support and protection that such families afford—and thrust into the city to live in extreme privation—often within the fragile capsule of the nuclear family.[18] Furthermore, because of poverty, they lack many of the resources that nuclear families have in industrialized countries. For example, they cannot afford life and disability insurance to replace the protection once provided by the extended families against the death or disability of the breadwinner. And, because of the poverty of their societies, nuclear families in less developed nations cannot rely on the state to provide for their old age or for the education of their children[19] as can nuclear families in most industrialized nations.

Furthermore, unlike nuclear families in industrialized nations, those in less developed countries have *high fertility*. Consequently, the family must support large numbers of children. Yet, because women are so burdened by frequent pregnancy and child-rearing, and because the extended family with its potential support is weakened in the city, they find it difficult to enter the labor force to increase the family income.[20]

Thus, whereas the modern American family frequently has few children and two employed adult members, the nuclear family in less developed countries like Mexico (at least until very recently) has many children and only one adult able to work (and often he is unable to find work). As a result, many families send their children out to work at an early age to help support the family. Unlike child labor on unmechanized farms, however, child labor in the city has low productive value, so children earn very little. Furthermore, child labor tends to impede long-range economic development because it interferes with education. Consequently, the new generation has no higher levels of skills to offer an industrializing economy than did their forebears from the farms. Under such conditions, as one might expect, the family displays signs of breakdown.

Fertility and Society

It is not only the family that can experience problems under the burden of exploding population; the same could be said of whole societies. We mentioned earlier that at its present rate of population growth, Mexico would have 1 *billion* people by about the year 2100. However, that population size is highly unlikely to occur, for life in Mexico would become impossible long before that number could be reached. If the population is not checked by lowered fertility, it is likely that it will be checked by death through famine, disease, and perhaps internal strife. In the following sections, we examine two ways in which fertility threatens less developed societies: by overtaking economic limits and by causing political chaos.

Economic Limits

The goal of many less developed nations is *development.* Like the industrialized nations, they too would like the fruits of modern life—relief from arduous manual labor, good housing, education, abundant food and clothing, and all the goods that represent an improved quality of life. Although many less developed nations would like to have these characteristics, few of them accept everything about developed nations. Many such nations have come to reject many characteristics of developed nations (for example, rampant materialism, destruction of the environment, exploitation of other nations) while, at the same time, accepting the general goal of becoming more developed. Among the cruelest ironies for developing nations is that the very aspects of modern technology that are most easily adopted by less developed nations are the ones that have caused their populations to explode. This rapid population growth, in turn, has canceled out many of their efforts to develop economically.

It is not the case that most less developed nations have stagnant economies. Most of them are undergoing economic development at a rapid rate—in fact, many of their economies at present are growing more rapidly than those of the industrialized nations. However, their population growth literally consumes these gains about as rapidly as they occur. To illustrate the point, suppose a nation is increasing the value of the goods and services it produces by 3.5 percent per year. At that rate, the economy would double its productivity in twenty years. But, if its population is also growing by 3.5 percent per year, there will be absolutely no increase in the goods and services available per person. Thus, although the economy would grow, the lives of individuals would not improve at all.

We can, once again, illustrate this phenomenon with the example of Mexico.[21] Mexico's total national income increased, in large part because of the booming oil business, by a rather startling 163 percent between 1960 and 1976. During the same period, however, the population increased by a third with the result that the increase in per person income was roughly 54 percent. Thus, it could be said that the growth in the population consumed 67 percent of the total improvement in national income. In contrast, during the same period national income in the United States rose by less than half the increase in Mexico, 73 percent. However, since population growth was much lower in the United States, only a third of that increase was eroded by population increase. Thus, the per capita income in the United States rose by 49 percent, almost the same as the increase in Mexico, although the economy had improved only half as much as the Mexican economy.

Although the economies of less developed countries may grow, sometimes dramatically, the lives of average citizens may not improve much. In fact, it may be that the wealthier members of these societies absorb most of the improvement with the lower classes as bad, or perhaps even worse, off than they were before the improvement in the economy. Thus, the outlook, even with economic growth, is not all that bright for less developed countries. It would be even worse if economic growth should slip *below* population growth because the stan-

Figure 14.3 Latin American Birth, Death, and Natural Increase Rates and Total Population: 1960–2025

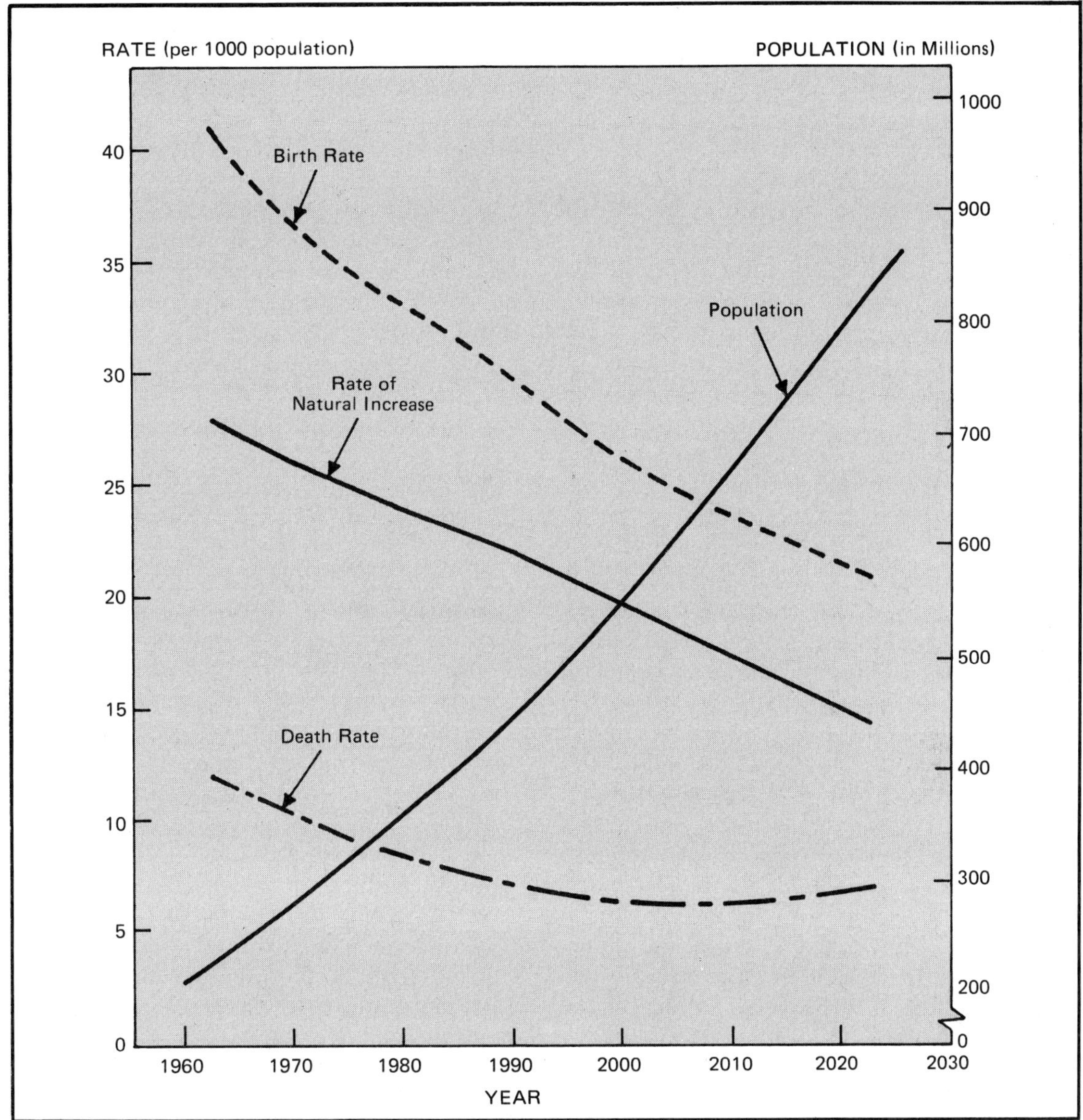

In spite of the decline in the birth rate and the overall decline in the death rate, the population of Latin America will continue to grow.

Source: Leon F. Bouvier, "Planet Earth: 1984–2034—A Demographic Vision," *Population Bulletin*, Vol. 39, No. 1, p. 9.

dard of living in such a case would deteriorate despite economic development. This state of affairs is what less developed nations now face. Most of their economic growth is used to keep their already dismal standard of living from getting even more depressed.

Exponential population growth is not simply a treadmill that prevents poor nations from achieving greater economic development. The situation is even worse than that: the constant expansion of their economies, which is necessary simply to sustain their present population growth, cannot continue indefinitely. Productive capacities are not endlessly expandable. As we will see in the following chapter on ecological problems, land, air, water, forestry, minerals,[22] food,[23] and other vital resources are limited. Considering these limited productive capacities, we see only calamity in the near future for less developed nations. Very soon their economic expansion will encounter these limits. And, with no gains in production to be eaten up by the expanding population, there will be progressively less for people who already live on the edge of survival.

Indeed, it is estimated that 60 percent of the people in the less developed world already suffer from malnutrition, with consequent widespread physical and mental retardation. One person in five is eating so little as to be slowly starving to death.[24] Yet, several decades from now, these same nations will have twice as many mouths to feed. As you read this chapter, it is *already too late* to prevent millions of people from starving to death.

Political Chaos

Within developing nations, rapid population growth can cause political disorder. Rapidly growing populations are also young populations. Families have large numbers of children, and thus at any given moment children tend to outnumber adults. In such societies, there are also disproportionately high numbers of young adults. Hence, the economies must grow very rapidly in order to provide an increasing number of jobs to absorb these waves of young people, many of whom are being forced and/or attracted to the city in search of a better life. Thus, the jobs to be provided need to be largely urban jobs. But economies rarely can expand rapidly enough to create enough jobs; therefore, there is growing unemployment, especially among young adults. As this process continues, there is increasing danger that these unemployed masses will engage in political unrest in an effort to improve their lot.[25]

The population explosion also threatens *international* political stability. As the conditions worsen in less developed countries, the continued relative well-being of the developed nations is likely to increase the antagonisms between rich and poor nations. At present, the poor nations are also poor militarily, but that could change in the future as less developed nations acquire nuclear bombs. (China exploded a nuclear bomb in 1964, and India exploded its first bomb in 1974.) More threatening, at least for the foreseeable future, is the possibility that the major powers may be lured into the internal problems of less developed nations. The fear, of course, is that problems within such nations could escalate into a nuclear confrontation between the United States and the Soviet Union. Therefore, the population explosion may imperil life not merely in poor nations but in all nations.

Furthermore, this situation is only likely to grow worse, since the population in developing countries is younger and therefore a larger proportion has its childbearing years ahead of it. In the developing world, about 38 percent of the population is under

15 years of age, while the comparable figure is 23 percent in developed nations.[26]

The Population Problem in Developed Nations

The population explosion occurred much earlier in the developed nations than in the less developed nations discussed above. The acceleration began sometime in the seventeenth century. Europeans consequently became an increasingly larger proportion of the world's population. Kingley Davis reports that in 1650, northwestern Europeans, living in Europe and overseas, made up 18 percent of the world's population. By 1920, they made up 35 percent.[27] Recently, however, the growth of European and other industrialized populations has slowed greatly, while growth in less developed, non-European countries has become rapid. The decline in birth rates in industrial nations was briefly reversed during the post-World War II baby boom but has since declined. In fact, the birth rate in the United States has recently reached *replacement level,* which means, all other things being equal, that the next generation will be no larger than the present one. Contrary to popular opinion, we have *not* achieved *zero population growth,* since the total growth is still being enhanced by immigration. The net result of this reduction of population growth among Europeans, as well as Europeans living overseas, is that this group accounted for only about 20 percent of the world's population by the 1970s.[28]

Although sheer population increase is not a problem in developed countries, a variety of demographic problems *do* continue to exist. For example, large families are an economic burden in modern developed societies. An income that affords average comfort to a family of four may leave a family of eight in dire poverty. Since it is poor families that are likely to have large numbers of children, this problem tends to be largely restricted to the lower classes. Although too many children still burden the poor, large families are no longer the trend in developed countries. Instead, it is *low fertility* that is causing problems for the family in developed countries.

Low Fertility and the Family

Some of the unprecedented stresses and strains on modern marriages can be traced to the low fertility rate. A large number of marriages end in divorce, and those that do not last only an average of seven years. One factor in this is that the role of wife and mother (and therefore husband and father) has changed considerably, since women now bear fewer children and are still young when they stop bearing children. Women can therefore be less dependent upon their husbands because they now are able to take a job outside the home and because divorce does not leave them with a house full of children to support. For men, by the same token, divorce does not mean the financial difficulty it once meant.

The major functions of the family unit (aside from affection and companionship) have always been economic and reproductive. However, because income now primarily comes from jobs rather than from property, the family is no longer as vital for the transmission of wealth. And, because women are now much more able to earn their own living, they are no longer as economically bound to the family. In such circumstances, a massive decline in fertility of the kind the industrialized nations are experiencing greatly reduces another support for continuation of family units. Little wonder that the family is showing so many signs of fragility. As we have seen, this is quite different from the impact of large

Figure 14.4 Average Number of Children Ever Born to (or Expected by) Birth Cohorts and Annual Total Fertility Rate, White Women: 1800–1982

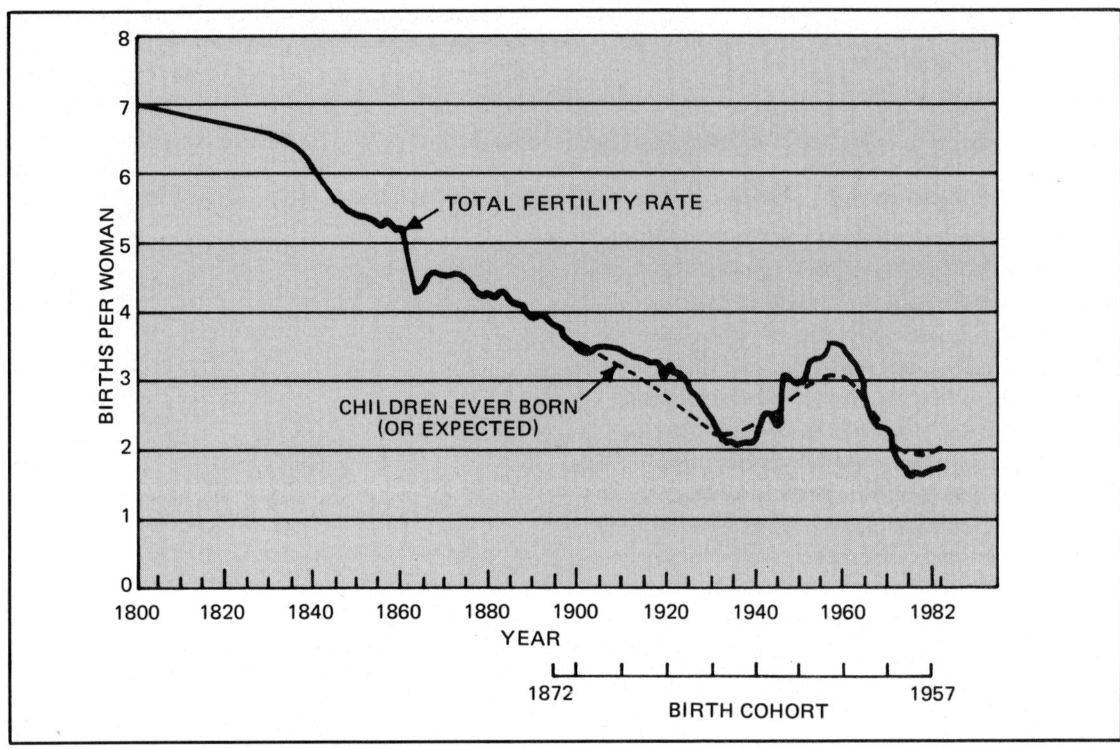

The average number of children born per family has declined steadily since 1800, from seven to two. There was a minor variation in this pattern in the 1950s when the number briefly rose to three.

Source: Arland Thornton and Deborah Freedman, *The Changing American Family*, 38 (1983), p. 13.

family size that at present characterizes less developed nations.

It is appropriate to go into a bit more detail on the increasing tendency for women to enter the labor force in the United States (and other industrialized nations) and the impact of this on family and childbearing.[29] In Chapter 9 we detailed the statistics on the dramatic increase[30] of females in the labor force. Our concern here is with the impact of being employed on fertility, and research has consistently shown that the fewer children a woman has, the more likely she is to work outside the home. The issue, however, is whether women keep their family size low in order to have time and energy for work, or whether women who have fewer children (for whatever reasons) have more time for work. Although both of these things are likely to be true, at least in part, the important conclusion is that for whatever reason, work and fertility are inversely related among women. And this, in turn, means that since more women are working, there is a decline in their fertility. And, this decline in fertility is having adverse effects on the stability of the family unit.

Migration

While low fertility rates may be causing some problems for developed countries, perhaps the major demographic problems in such countries are traceable to high levels of international migration; especially, large numbers of people coming from less developed countries to developed nations.[31] In the case of the United States, restrictions on legal immigration mean that large numbers of people from less developed countries enter the United States illegally. The vast majority of these illegal aliens, perhaps as high as 80 or 85 percent, come from Mexico. In the late 1970s and early 1980s about 1 million deportable Mexican nationals were apprehended each year, but many of these may have been repeat offenders. Whatever the actual numbers of those apprehended, there are somewhere between 3.5 and 6 million illegal aliens in the United States today.[32] The problem is that most of these people entered the country with few if any resources, and their illegal status virtually guarantees that they will remain at the bottom of American society. They represent a substantial drain on the American economy and the source of a wide range of social problems.

The general problem of migration from less to more developed countries is likely to continue to accelerate as more and more people are forced to leave countries like Mexico as a result of continuing disparities in economic conditions in the two types of nations. Further exacerbating the problems in the developed countries is the fact that these illegal immigrants tend to have a much higher birth rate than the indigenous

A major population problem in industrialized countries, such as the United States, is illegal immigration.

(J. P. Laffont/Sygma)

population. Thus, their numbers will swell rapidly, as will their drain on the economies of developed countries.

Fertility and American Society

Except for the problem of illegal immigration discussed above, the population explosion has already delivered its major blows to American society. In the over 200 years since 1776, our population has increased by over 100 times. This immense population growth has caused many massive changes in the scale on which we live. We are a nation of large cities and large organizations, and we urgently need to learn how to manage and humanize life on such a scale. Furthermore, many of our social problems arise from the size, complexity, and impersonality of our society, especially of our cities. Troubles that once could be dealt with by friends or family are now often transformed into public problems because so many people do not have family or friends who are able to help them. To be neighborly today often means little more than contributing to charity fund drives.

For American society as a whole, perhaps the major impact of a large population is the burden it (and its accompanying life style) places on the ecological life-support systems (see Chapter 15). More people require more food, use more mineral resources, consume more water, pollute more air, and in other ways make more and more demands on the physical environment. Even if our population does, as is anticipated, increase to 275 million before it stabilizes, we will almost certainly find ways to support such numbers. We may well have to give up consuming so much and reduce the material level of our lives, but our growth has certainly not guaranteed disaster for the United States. However, the same cannot be said about population growth in less developed nations. If disaster comes, for us and for the rest of the world, it seems more likely that it will stem from the calamitous consequences of population growth in less developed nations.

PART II: CAUSES AND CONSEQUENCES

What has caused the dramatic population explosion in developing nations? Since population growth is mainly reducible to two basic factors of births and deaths (the third, in- and outmigration, will not concern us here), the issue is what causes an increase in births and/or a decrease in deaths. At one level, the obvious answer is that we are mainly dealing with changes in individual behavior. But at another, deeper level, we are most concerned with the large-scale structures and forces that are leading people to live longer, to have more children, and ultimately to have births far outstrip deaths. We will get to these macrolevel causes, but before we do, and as an introduction to them, we need to look at the history of population growth in developed countries, specifically the dramatic change that took place in the mid-seventeenth century in northern Europe. This development may be seen as a precursor, at least in part, to ongoing population changes in less developed nations. Thus, we will be looking at some of the theorizing done, at least initially, on seventeenth-century Europe, but our ultimate objective will be to discuss the relevance of this theory to the contemporary scene, particularly in the less developed nations.

The Malthusian Theory of Population

At the beginning of this chapter we pointed out that for most of human history, populations grew very slowly. Then suddenly, in the mid-seventeenth century, northern European populations began rapid growth. It is in this context that we need briefly to examine the work of the English economist and clergyman, Thomas Malthus (1766–1834).[33]

Malthus argued that human populations could easily increase exponentially; that is, he recognized the arithmetic of population explosions. He observed that human populations did not (in his time or earlier) seem to follow an exponential pattern of growth, and he wondered why. In his famous book, *An Essay on the Principle of Population,* first published in 1798, he argued that population growth followed a cyclical pattern. Malthus pointed out that every so often populations do begin to grow exponentially, in geometric increases (2, 4, 8, 16, 32, and so on). However, the supply of resources, principally food, that are necessary to sustain life do *not* increase exponentially. Resources increase arithmetically (2, 4, 6, 8, 10, and so forth). Thus, populations quickly outstrip the supply of resources. At this point, positive checks on population growth occur. Growth is cut off, Malthus claimed, by certain checks, including starvation, disease, and war.[34]

According to Malthus, death periodically intervened to halt exploding populations. His theory focused on three main elements—goods production, fertility, and mortality. He argued that when *production* increases and there are more goods (such as food and clothing) per person, *mortality* declines (people are healthier), and thus a population grows. Malthus pessimistically believed that humans are incapable of restraining their *fertility* and thus would *always* reproduce up to the limits of production. When this occurs, goods per capita decline past the danger point and mortality rises rapidly to halt population growth. In

One of the most pressing problems today is how to respond to the boom in population in developing countries and the bleak future awaiting millions of children.

(William Campbell/Sygma)

this process, obviously, the weakest and poorest members of society are those most likely to die. (About fifty years later, Charles Darwin found in Malthus's theory of human population cycles the general mechanism for the "survival of the fittest," a concept that permitted him to form his general theory of biological evolution.)

At the time that Malthus wrote, his theory seemed to fit the facts of population changes. For example, the population of England seemed to have followed this cyclical pattern for some centuries. Improvements in agricultural production were invariably followed by rapid population growth and, then, as these gains were eaten away by growth, inevitably *Malthusian checks,* such as famine and plague, appeared and cut back the population. About the time that Malthus's theory was published, however, this vicious population cycle appeared to have been broken.

Demographic Transition Theory

Malthus's theory depended on fertility remaining high while fluctuations in mortality periodically permitted population increases or population decreases. But as the Industrial Revolution gathered headway, several unexpected things happened. Industrialization permitted a previously undreamed of rate of growth in productivity. Industrial nations were able to support vast populations in comparison with populations of medieval times. Industrialization revolutionized agriculture. Farm production rose incredibly. And the wealth generated by manufacturing permitted importation of large amounts of food and raw materials. All of these advances enabled people to live longer and healthier lives.

This change in mortality is part of what is called the *demographic transition.*[35] In one of the formulations of this theory, Davis did not fundamentally dispute Malthus but merely pointed out that Malthus's theory seemed applicable only to the preindustrial (less developed) societies of his time. Malthusian theory did not fit what was happening in seventeenth-century Europe and it does not explain what is occurring in modern developed *or* developing nations. Rather, it is modern demographic transition theory that has supplanted Malthusian theory as the major explanation of the relationship between fertility and mortality in modern societies.

Kenneth Kammeyer and Helen Ginn have broken down the processes involved in the demographic transition into three stages:

> Stage 1—A premodern stage of economic development in which the birth rate and the death rate are both high. Population size is stable.
>
> Stage 2—The beginnings of modernization and economic development. The death rate is dropping but the birth rate remains high. Population size is growing.
>
> Stage 3—Modernization and economic development are well advanced. The birth rate is low, approaching, or reaching the low level of the death rate. The population is stable or growing very slowly.[36]

The major stages of the demographic transition are depicted in Table 14.3.

SOCIOLOGICAL LEVEL

Social Structural Factors

Implicit in the discussion of demographic transition theory as it applies to industrialized societies of the past are a series of macrolevel causes of this change in population growth. One major factor is clearly *industrialization,* which we can define as large-scale changes in economic and social organization resulting from changes in production methods; from production of goods by

Table 14.3 The Three Stages of the Modern Demographic Transition

STAGE	DEATH RATE	BIRTH RATE	POPULATION GROWTH RATE
1. Agricultural	High	High	Low
2. Transition	Low	High	High
3. Final	Low	Low	Low

Source: Adapted from Kenneth C. W. Kammeyer and Helen L. Ginn, *An Introduction to Population*, 2d ed. (Homewood, Ill.: Dorsey Press, 1986).

hand to production of goods by power-driven machinery centered in factories. With industrialization, people moved from agricultural life, where having many children was a benefit, to industrial life, where children became more of an economic burden than a benefit. Related to industrialization was another related macrolevel factor, *urbanization.* With industrialization, people moved out of rural areas and into the cities. With little or no land to be worked in the cities, there was

Figure 14.5 The Modern Demographic Transition (as Modeled on the Western European Experience)

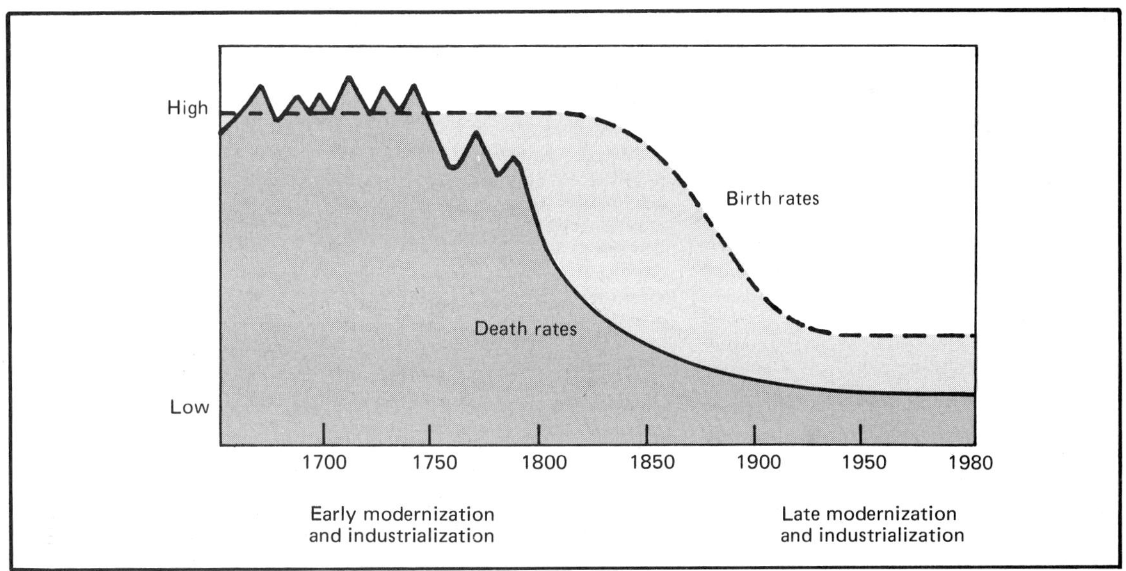

Here we can see that death rates declined before birth rates in Western Europe during the modern era, causing a rapid increase in population. This sudden jolt in demographics has evened out as the birth rate in Western Europe has dropped to the same low levels as the death rate.

Source: Adapted from K. C. Kammeyer and Helen L. Ginn, *An Introduction to Population*, 2d edition (Homewood, Ill.: Dorsey Press, 1986).

again less need for large numbers of children. Thus, the large-scale processes of industrialization and urbanization combined to help lead to a decline in the birth rate. Over a number of years, people began to have fewer children in the industrialized countries.

There is a third factor implied in the demographic transition in industrialized societies, and that is improved *sanitation, nutrition, and health-care systems* that helped lead to a decline in the death rate. At first, the changes were brought about by comparatively simple improvements in diet, living conditions, water supplies, and housing. For example, when a sewer system was built in London, the death rate went down since disease-carrying elements were removed from the city environment.[37] Industrialization, and the applications of industrial principles to farming, helped increase the available food supply. Accompanying urbanization and industrialization was a great improvement in educational facilities. Scholars learned more about proper nutrition, and that knowledge was conveyed to the masses via the educational system or popular communication media.[38] All of these factors, and many others, helped contribute to the decline in the death rate by, in particular, a reduction in the infant and early childhood mortality rates, as well as deaths attributable to a wide range of communicable diseases.

Less Developed Countries

We have seen that population grew rapidly in some nations because of their rapid economic growth. The Malthusian checks were held in abeyance because agricultural and industrial productivity kept up with population growth. Eventually, declines in fertility also helped break the vicious cycle that afflicted preindustrial times. However, this explanation cannot account for present population explosions in less developed nations. These nations are *not* heavily industrialized, and their population growth has *not* been caused by changes in their economic conditions.

The central factor in the demographic transition in the industrialized nations was a decline in the death rates while the birth rates remained high. In modern, less developed nations the big difference is that the decline in the death rate has taken place much more rapidly. What took a century or two in industrialized countries has occurred in a few decades in the nonindustrialized countries. While their mortality rates have undergone a substantial decline, their birth rates have remained high. The result is an unprecedented increase in the populations of less developed countries.

How do we account for this dramatic change? Industrialization cannot be the answer. The same is true of urbanization since less developed countries are not as urbanized as the developed countries. And these countries have not been notably successful in developing their own health, sanitation, and medical care systems. However, what they have been successful in doing is importing medical, technical, and scientific expertise from the developed nations. Thus, they have been able in a very short period greatly to reduce infant mortality, childhood diseases, communicable diseases of all types, and the like. In addition, they have imported modern technology to improve sanitation. Other technologies also have been imported that enable them to increase the food supply and improve its quality. Now all of this is not to say that the less developed countries have been able to approach the developed nations in any of these areas, but they have been able to improve things so quickly that their population has grown dramatically. In a sense, we could say that the major macrolevel factor in the demographic transition in today's less developed countries is the *modernity* of the Western world and its willingness to share a variety of its most important developments with the less industrialized nations. Less developed countries have been able to enjoy at least some of the benefits of modernization without going through the process themselves.

It is paradoxical, but the future of nonindustrialized nations, as well as the rest of the world, has been imperiled by one of our noblest achievements—the ability to reduce the heavy and persistent early death and infant mortality rates that long afflicted human societies.[39] By exporting various medical and scientific discoveries and practices, such as vaccines and insecticides, the industrialized countries have played a central role in helping nonindustrialized countries cut their death rates almost miraculously.

These scientific innovations developed slowly in the industrialized world and only gradually lowered death rates. Meanwhile, productivity rose and family fertility adjusted to changed conditions. But in the less developed nations, scientific and medical technology has sometimes literally fallen from the sky, changing mortality rates almost overnight. Take the incredible case of Ceylon (now Sri Lanka).[40] The death rate there was cut in half in one year (from 1946 to 1947). What happened? The countryside was sprayed with DDT to kill mosquitoes and other insects. In consequence, malaria and several other serious diseases declined greatly. The DDT was imported, as were the experts who ran the operation. The Ceylonese played little or no part in this program that changed their mortality dramatically. Nor did this program have an impact on their fertility. Thus, large numbers of infants and children survived who would have perished otherwise. This added to the population and accelerated its growth. Although this process went on for years, the birth rate in Ceylon did eventually begin to decline, but not before there had been a massive population increase.[41]

Transforming Guyana's Environment

To take another example, environmental conditions were also responsible for a high mortality rate in the Latin American nation of Guyana. Swamps and marshlands supported malaria-bearing mosquitoes, impure water supplies caused diarrhea and stomach disorders, and lack of sanitation in homes and towns promoted tuberculosis and other diseases. Even when these conditions are not fatal, they weaken people, reduce their resistance to infections, and generally increase their risk of death.

Figure 14.6 shows mortality rates from five major causes of death in Guyana from 1911 to 1960.[42] These five causes (tuberculosis, diarrhea and enteritis, nephritis, malaria, pneumonia and bronchitis) accounted for about one-half of the deaths in

Figure 14.6 Mortality Rates by Disease in Guyana

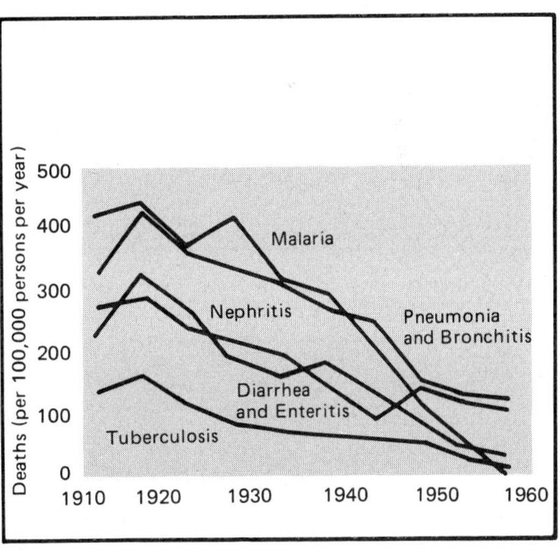

The above graph shows how communicable diseases affected the death rate in nonindustrial societies. After the introduction of modern medicine and widespread vaccination campaigns, the death rate in Guyana and nations with similar development patterns declined precipitately.

Source: J. R. Mandle, "The Decline in Mortality in British Guiana, 1911–1960," *Demography*, 7 (1970), 301–315.

that country between 1911 and 1936, but in the late 1950s, these five causes accounted for only one-fourth of the deaths. Such diseases as nephritis, pneumonia, and bronchitis, for example, are directly related to environmental conditions. These infectious diseases often accompany a disease, such as diarrhea, that is actually one of the environmental group. In fact, the incidence of infectious diseases increases as the environmental diseases become prevalent, especially in unhealthy bodies that have little resistance to infection. A population in poor health supports infectious diseases. The decline of these diseases contributes strongly to lower death rates.

As Figure 14.6 indicates, malaria was the most serious cause of death in Guyana until the early 1940s. At this point it began to decline sharply, and by the late 1950s it had virtually disappeared as a cause of death. The related infectious disease, nephritis, also declined sharply over this period. Getting rid of malaria was a central factor in the fall of the death rates not only in Guyana but also in numerous other countries in Asia, Africa, and Latin America.[43] The key to the eradication of malaria is the elimination of the mosquito that carries the disease. The elimination of malaria was accomplished not by using hospitals and doctors or treating the population but by operating on the environment in which the population lives. Two general methods were used. Prior to World War II, the swamps and stagnant waters in which the mosquito develops were drained and filled. In the postwar period, DDT became available, and its use is responsible for the subsequent rapid disappearance of the disease.

The high death rates from diarrhea and enteritis in Guyana and many other nations of Latin America, Asia, and Africa are a result of water supplies severely polluted with human wastes. The more careful disposal of waste and the gradual improvement of water supplies contributed to a 50 percent decline in the death rates from diarrhea and enteritis. The general improvements in sanitation also had the effect of lowering the death rates from tuberculosis and other diseases. By 1960, mortality had fallen to one-third the level of 1920.

The major diseases in Guyana were essentially controlled by environmental intervention. It should be noted, however, that infant mortality was greatly reduced through educational programs directed at mothers.[44] Similarly, the targets in developing areas of the world in the post-World War II period were the water supplies and the minds of young mothers. In most regions the mosquito, too, was a target. As Figure 14.6 demonstrates, the effects on the mortality rates were spectacular.[45]

However, death in nations like Guyana has only taken a holiday. Had the population stabilized in these nations, their reduced mortality rates might have been permanent. But, as their population growth soars, it is obvious that low mortality is temporary. Hence, the next economic reverse they encounter—from drought, crop blight, raw material shortage, or civil strife—may produce considerable mortality in many less developed nations. The Malthusian checks lurk off stage.

Cultural Factors

The above discussion focuses on various macrolevel, structural factors (such as industrialization, urbanization, development of health and sanitation systems, medical advances, improved technologies) in population growth. These factors, in a variety of ways, lead to a decline in the death rate and, before it can be counterbalanced by a decline in the birth rate, a dramatic increase in the population. Beyond social structural factors, there are also cultural factors that play important roles in population growth.

The introduction of the cultural dimension allows us to begin to deal with the paradox that the birth rate in less developed countries tends to remain high despite the hardships that the population increase causes. Why do people not see the dangers of the growing population and adjust their behavior so that population growth is reduced? There is obviously no simple answer to this question. For example, one factor may be the ignorance of people not only about the situation in society, but even about various birth-control measures. However, our focus here is the norms, values, and traditions of developing societies that help maintain high levels of fertility.[46]

One relevant set of values is that which deals with age of marriage, sexual relations, and childbearing. Many less developed nations have cultural systems that support an early age for all of these activities. Obviously, the earlier people marry, have sexual relations, and begin childbearing, the more children they are likely to have.

Idealization of the Large Family

Another important factor is the tendency to idealize the large family. The large-family ideal derives from the long experience of high rates of infant and child mortality. To be assured that one son would survive to continue the family line, to take over the father's land or trade, and to care for parents in their old age, parents had to have two or three sons. Because only about one-half of the infants born are male, rather high fertility was required to achieve these objectives. Although the abrupt decline in mortality levels in the underdeveloped nations has made it possible to achieve these objectives with smaller families, the time-honored ideal of a large family persits.

The traditional agricultural economies of less developed nations are also frequently supportive of the large-family ideal. Because children are able to perform useful, productive agricultural work, they contribute to the household income from an early age. However, as the children grow into adulthood, problems arise. If more than one son should survive, the family plot must be divided, or some of the sons must seek employment elsewhere. With levels of mortality low, as they are today, surplus population results from high fertility levels in less developed countries.

Pronatalism and Familism

All of this is related to the cultural phenomena of pronatalism and familism. *Pronatalism* is the strong positive value a society places on having children. *Familism* is the high value an individual or a couple puts on producing offspring. Tellingly, pronatalism and familism are not restricted to the cultures of less developed nations, but are characteristic as well of such developed countries as the United States. In studies of fertility conducted in the United States in the last twenty years, it has been shown that the values of pronatalism and familism have been so prominent and pervasive that almost every young married couple simply assumed they would have children, often as soon as possible after marriage. Many couples felt a moral responsibility to have children.[47]

In spite of pronatalism and familism, the United States has been able to control population growth, but the same cannot be said for less developed countries. In those countries these values continue to impel large numbers of couples to have large numbers of children.

Sex Roles

Another important value system related to population growth involves the definition of *sex roles* within the society. Specifically, it is traditional notions of sex roles (especially those for women) that contribute to population growth. Traditionally, of course, women are expected to have children and to stay home and raise them. In addition, there are a series of related sex-role ideas about women such as that they are supposed to be emotional, passive, nurturant, sympathetic, sensitive, compassionate, and concerned about others. Perhaps the best summation of these characteristics is to say that in accord with traditional sex roles women are expected to be *maternal.* And being maternal means, above all else, bearing and raising children. The traditional male sex role also serves to increase population growth since the man is expected to protect, and provide economic support for, the family as a whole and the children in particular.

Although sex roles are certainly changing dramatically in the United States, strong elements of traditional sex-role expectations remain in force. In the less developed countries, traditional sex roles are an even more potent force.

The crux of the cultural problem is that rapid changes in the conditions governing mortality have occurred without significant changes in the cultural traditions of these societies. For thousands of years, human culture has developed to insure sufficient fertility. Suddenly, these customs, values, marriage patterns, and sexual practices have become dysfunctional. The population explosion has occurred so rapidly that traditional cultures have not been able to adjust to it. It is important to recognize that the developed nations never had to cope with the demands for such rapid change. Mortality changes in the industrial nations occurred gradually. Indeed, declining mortality was simply one aspect of wholesale social change. The whole culture of industrializing nations gradually became modern. Thus, there was time for the family to change with the changing times. By contrast, the arithmetic of the population explosion overtook less developed nations before they could hope to develop an adequate response. Indeed, even if less developed nations could somehow change their value systems immediately, it would already be too late for many of them to avert serious consequences.

INDIVIDUAL LEVEL

The structural and cultural forces outlined above do not in themselves produce babies. It is the actions (or inactions) of individuals, men and women, that affect the birth rate (and, to a large degree, the death rate as well). The point is that these actions are shaped to a large degree by these forces. Thus, we can say that various structural and cultural forces coalesce to keep the birth rate unduly high in developing nations. Similar structural and cultural factors serve to reduce the death rate. Faced with the need to cut population growth, developing societies could either try to reduce the birth rate or increase the death rate. Since policies to increase the death rate are unthinkable in most cases, national policies are usually aimed at cutting the birth rate. Thus nations often try to make structural or cultural changes aimed at reducing the birth rate. It is here, however, that they often encounter the independent significance of individual thought and behavior. That is, despite these large-scale changes many people continue to have large numbers of children.

One of the most telling indicators of the persistence of a long-standing individual behavior is the resistance of individuals in less developed countries to the use of contraceptives. The use of contraceptives is urged by officials and contraceptives are produced and disseminated, often free of charge. In spite of this, large numbers of people do not use these contraceptives and hence do not limit their family size. To be fair, contraceptives are not readily available in some areas of Latin America, Asia, and Africa. Even when contraception is available and its availability is known, however, there is all too often a pervasive pessimism regarding its effectiveness. People tend to view the claims made about contraception with suspicion. Traditional societies rarely had effective means of controlling natural events of any sort, and the belief that such control is beyond human capacity is rather strong.[48]

The result of this is that contraceptive use in less developed countries is much lower than such utilization in developed countries.[49] In a worldwide fertility survey, data from 29 developing nations (including Senegal, Nepal, and Costa Rica) were compared to those from 16 developed countries (among them, Spain, Yugoslavia, and the United States). About one-third of currently married and fecund (that is, able to bear children) women, or their husbands, in developing countries use some form of contraception. The use of contraception in such countries ranged from a low of 3 percent in Nepal to a high of 71 percent in Costa Rica. The average for developing nations was approximately 32 percent. In contrast, the overall average for contraceptive use in developed nations was 72 percent with only three countries in which contraceptive use was less than 60 percent.[50]

There is also the issue of *when* people in less developed nations use contraceptives. If they use contraceptives *after* a very large family has been created, they are less effective as a population control mechanism than if contraceptives are used from the beginning of marriage, or at least after one or two children have been born. There is some evidence that contraceptives are likely to be used, if they are ever used, *after* a large number of children have already been born.[51]

Thus, it is clear from these data that individuals make a crucial difference. They may be impelled to take certain actions by structural and cultural forces, but they may well be immune to, or able to resist, those pressures for quite some time.

PART III: RESPONSES[52]

We will deal with several different responses to the problem of the population explosion, but first we need to analyze two very different orientations (the "doomsday" response and the view that people are "the ultimate resource") that lead to the conclusion that *no* response is required.

The "Doomsday" Response

The dawning in the 1960s and 1970s of the realization that there was a massive population problem in the world led many analysts and lay people to the conclusion that the crisis was inevitable and unavoidable. They believed that a "doomsday" would come, when human life would collapse under the strains of overpopulation. Some even predicted the exact year when it would happen. For example, William and Paul Paddock, writing in 1967, predicted widespread famine by 1975.[53] They described their vision by using the metaphor of a locomotive approaching a mudslide:

> Nothing can stop the locomotive in time. Collision is inevitable. Catastrophe is foredoomed. . . . The locomotive roaring straight at

Table 14.4 Levels of Analysis: Population

LEVELS	APPROPRIATE QUESTIONS	A PARTIAL SYNOPSIS OF PRESENT CONCLUSIONS
SOCIOLOGICAL	What social structural factors are related to the "demographic transition"?	The three main factors are industrialization, urbanization, and improvement in sanitation, nutrition, and health care systems.
	How do we account for the present population "explosion" in less developed countries?	Their birth rates have remained high while their death rates have undergone a substantial decline. The decline in the death rate is primarily attributable to the importation of improvements in sanitation, nutrition, and health care systems from developed nations.
	What cultural factors help account for population growth?	There are various cultural factors that contribute to high population growth, including support for an early age of marriage and childbearing, a high value placed on large families, pronatalism (the strong, positive value placed by society on having children) and familism (the high value an individual or a couple places on having children).
	How does an emphasis on traditional sex roles in the culture affect population growth?	An emphasis on traditional sex roles tends to contribute to population growth. For example, traditional women are expected to be maternal and to stay home and bear and raise children.
INDIVIDUAL	How do individuals in less developed countries tend to react to efforts to alter their propensity to have large numbers of children?	Individuals in less developed nations tend to resist such programs. Thus, efforts to get them to use contraceptives often fail. And there is evidence that even where contraceptives are used, they tend to be utilized *after* people have already had a large number of children.

us is the population explosion. The unavoidable landslide across the tracks is the stagnant production of food in the underdeveloped nations, the nations where the population increases are the greatest. . . . The collision is inevitable. *The famines are inevitable.*[54]

Although there have been widespread food shortages, and even considerable starvation, there has been nothing like the cataclysm forecast by the Paddocks. Although no cataclysm has yet occurred, there are those who continue to believe that it is coming. Those who accept such a view clearly feel that no meaningful response to the population problem is possible since the crisis is inevitable.

People as "The Ultimate Resource"

At the opposite end of the spectrum, but also believing that no response is necessary, are those who argue that population growth leads to the improvement in living conditions, *not* their deterioration. One, Julian Simon, even argues that population growth leads to more plentiful supplies of natural resources, *not* to their depletion.[55] Simon argues that more people means more minds to apply themselves to the issue of how to expand resources and greater stimulation of various activities aimed at such expansion. This view is based on history that shows that in the past population growth has been associated with more not fewer resources. Because of this history, the best prediction is that it will continue to be true in the future. Thus, no response is needed to the population problem or, more accurately, there is little or no need to lower fertility.

Needless to say, the kind of counterintuitive position enunciated by Simon has been subjected to much criticism.[56] For example, it is argued that Simon's is a long-run view (the population problem will be resolved in sixty years, or so), but in the interim many people may die, and many lives made intolerable by problems derived from the population explosion. Furthermore, there is certainly no guarantee that our past successes will be repeated in the future. Can we afford to sit back and do nothing and wait to see whether Simon is right and the past repeats itself in the mid-twenty-first century?

Thus the doomsayers see an insoluble problem and those who view people as the "ultimate resource" see the problem tending to resolve itself in the long run, but both share a tendency to favor inaction. However, they are in the distinct minority; most observers favor some sort of action to stem the population explosion, although as we will now see they differ greatly on the nature of the solution.

"Economic Development Is the Best Contraceptive"

This response seems self-explanatory, but it takes various forms. The best known is the perspective associated with various socialistic and communistic orientations. The basic idea is that the real problem is the maldistribution of wealth within, and especially between, nations. What is needed is a series of revolutionary activities designed to redistribute the wealth. Once the wealth is redistributed, many of the problems of overpopulation will disappear because they are more traceable to inadequate resources in less developed countries than they are to too many people in those countries. However, it is questionable whether there is enough wealth in the world to provide for an adequate life style for everyone and even if there is now, it is highly unlikely that there will be enough wealth for the burgeoning populations of the future. This is not to say, however, that a redistribution of the wealth will not help the problems of overpopulation; the lot of the hungry masses in developing countries could certainly be improved by a more equitable world system. Relatedly, socialist-communist policymakers may argue that a redistribution of wealth may lead people in developing countries to have fewer children and that would go a long way toward helping solve the population problem.

There is also a more conservative variant of this approach that is based on the essentials of the demographic transition theory. That is, in the later stages of the transition in Europe, economic development led to structural and cultural changes which, in turn, led to a decline in fertility. That is, there is a belief that what happened in Europe to reduce fertility is directly and firmly related to socioeconomic development and that the same process will reoccur in the high growth, less developed countries of the world today. There is an extreme form of this approach that comes close to Simon's orientation, which argues that we should just let demographic transition take its course and it will bring with it economic development, macrolevel changes, and, ultimately, a decline in fertility.[57]

The Family Planning Approach

Whenever most people think of responses to the population crisis, they think of what is generally called the "family planning" approach. For many years, this has been the most direct and visible effort to respond to this problem. We can see family planning as involving three basic elements. First, there is an effort to provide people with knowledge and information about reproductive physiology and contraceptive techniques. Second, there is the actual provision of contraceptive devices and techniques. Finally, there is a propaganda campaign that supports the acceptability of contraception as well as the ideal of a small family.

One thing to be noted is that this is largely a micro-oriented approach in which the goal is to change individual behavior directly. There is little effort to alter large-scale structures and the culture. These are striking omissions since, as we have seen, the major causes of the population explosion have been at the macrolevel. Not only is this an individualistic approach, but it is also a voluntaristic one since there is no effort to coerce people into using contraceptives or to limit their family sizes. In fact, there is often the assumption, supported by evidence in some locales, that many couples already want fewer children than they actually end up having. Thus, family planning is seen as simply giving many people what they already want and for that reason, and others, there is no need to coerce them into using family planning; they will eagerly embrace it.

The family planning approach has come under attack over the years from a number of quarters. Various religions have opposed contraception, at least for a time, and the official Roman Catholic Church position has remained steadfastly opposed to it. Early nineteenth-century feminists opposed contraception because they feared a conspiracy to decrease their offspring and then to force them into the low-paid sector of the labor force. Ironically, most modern feminists favor contraception *because* it will help free them of the burdens of child-bearing so that they can enter the labor force earlier and stay in it longer and more continuously.[58] Some socialist-communist thinkers oppose directing family planning programs at developing nations because they may be used as a means of limiting their power so that they can be controlled and subjugated more easily.

However, the most vehement attacks on family planners in recent decades have come from those demographers who accept a "societalist approach"[59] and therefore see such individualistic and voluntaristic programs as ineffective in dealing with what is most basically a macrolevel problem.[60]

The Societalist Approach

The societalist approach begins with the assumption that all societies, their cultures, and many of their social structures are all set up to make sure that new children will be brought into the population and cared for in various ways. The structures, values, and norms of society tend to encourage, even in some ways coerce,[61] people to have children. Thus, if fertility is to be lowered, it must be done by changing the structures and culture of societies that encourage and, at times, coerce, people into procreation. Let us look at two of the ways that society pressures people into having children, as well as the ways in which these pronatalistic pressures can be reduced.

The Role of Women

Generally, as we saw earlier, it can be argued that in a variety of ways many societies coerce women into having children. In one study of nineteenth-century Europe it was found that in societies where women were very subordinate to men, family planning was not adopted as quickly as in societies where there was less of a power differential between the sexes.[62] These societies tended to have cultural and structural constraints that led women to resist family planning and therefore to have higher fertility levels. Culturally, women tended to be considered important only for their ability to bear and rear children. These cultural beliefs affected both women and men. Structurally the system of sexual stratification left women in a weak position and therefore unable to take advantage of family planning programs. A more specific structural problem for women in such societies was that they tended to be isolated from formal communication networks, as well as the educational system. Therefore they tended not to be in the situations in which they could get new and sophisticated ideas on various things, including family planning. Even if they could get such information, their position at the bottom of the sexual stratification system would make it difficult for them to do anything about it in light of the likely opposition of males to any change in a system that worked so well for them.

The policy implications of this case are fairly obvious: the status of women must be improved if we hope to do anything about high fertility. The cultural system needs to be altered so that men and women are similarly valued. The view that women should stay in the home needs to be changed and equal access for both sexes to the labor force should be a cultural value. The system of sexual stratification requires an overhaul so that men and women have equivalent power and status. Women need to be integrated into the educational system and other communication networks for many reasons—including getting the skills and abilities needed to succeed in the work world, getting information about available careers, to say nothing of obtaining information on the range of family planning programs available to them.

The Economic Value of Children

It has been noted throughout this chapter that there is a traditional belief that children are an economic asset to their parents. Although this view is much less strongly held in urban society, it continues to be widely believed in agricultural areas and societies. The belief is that children can work in the fields while the parents are still comparatively young and then when the parents have aged, the children can provide economic and physical security for them. These beliefs can be altered by a variety of structural changes. Compulsory education would force parents to look for alternative sources of labor. Child labor laws that limit the amount of time a child can work can have the same effect. The evidence is that when changes like these are made, fertility declines. A social security system would reduce the need for parents to produce children to provide for them in their old age. Adequate police or safe retirement centers could replace the need for the child to provide physical security for aged parents. The trend toward urbanization is a structural change that has the effect of reducing the need for having large numbers of children. Ultimately, the norms and values of society need to be altered so that those who have fewer children are more prized than those who have large numbers of children. These are the kinds of macrolevel changes that are favored by the societalists and there is much to recommend their view, given the importance of macrolevel factors in causing the population crisis. It makes sense to seek a solution at the same level at which the major causes of the problem are found.

Ultimately, structural and cultural changes, if they are to be successful, must impact on the motivations and actions of individuals. However, individuals can be recalcitrant. What do we know about the effect of macrolevel changes on the individual? In answering this question, it is useful to turn to the recent history of China, where a massive macrolevel effort has been undertaken to alter individual motivation and behavior. How successful have the Chinese been?

China: A Model Societalist Approach?

As we have already seen, China has the largest population on earth, recently surpassing the 1 billion mark.[63] Since the official population was almost 550 million in 1949 (the year that the Communists gained power), the population almost doubled in a little over three decades. One cause of this growth was a dramatic drop in the death rate.[64] It might also be presumed that the other major cause was a high, or even increasing, fertility rate. However, the evidence is that the Chinese have been quite successful in cutting the fertility rate and that population growth would have been much greater were it not for that. As we will see, the success of China's efforts can be traced to its focus on societal-level factors.

When the communists took power they did not at first try to reduce fertility, but a series of actions did have that consequence. Among these were efforts to break down the partiarchal family system and to move women into positions of political and economic importance. This improvement in the relative status of Chinese women would, according to both theory and previous practice, have the effect of decreasing fertility. Additionally, the Marriage Law of 1950 was enacted with the goal of eradicating the age-old Chinese custom of marrying off (or selling) very young daughters. This law raised the legal age of marriage (to eighteen for women and twenty for men) and was later supplemented by a propaganda campaign aimed at convincing people to marry later and thereby reduce their fertility.

In 1954 China began to take direct action to decrease fertility and by 1957 a nationwide family planning program was in full swing. It was a classic program, combining the distribution of contraceptive devices, educational programs on reproductive physiology, and a propaganda campaign extolling the virtues of small families.[65] This, combined with societal changes, seems to have been successful in reducing fertility in the mid-1950s.[66] However, in the late 1950s and through the 1960s several political upheavals in China caused interruptions in the family planning programs with the result that fertility levels returned to, and in some years exceeded, those of pre-1954 China.

A new stage in China's population program began in 1971 with official adoption of three reproduction norms that can be summarized concisely as "later, longer, and fewer"—later marriage, longer spacing between children, and fewer total children.[67] Specifically, China's leaders asked people to delay marriage until their middle or later twenties. While the legal age of marriage was still 18 and 20 for women and men respectively, there was much pressure on young people to wait until they were much

China has sought to cope with its population problem by developing a wide-ranging campaign to encourage one-child families.

(J. P. Laffont/Sygma)

older. (In 1980, the legal age of marriage was increased to 20 for women and 22 for men.) There was also pressure to have at least three-year intervals between children and to have no more than two or three children. "Birth planning" committees were set up to oversee this program and couples wishing children made their requests to these committees. When approval was granted, by means of a "planned birth card," the couple could then go on to have a child. In addition to this kind of control, there were incentives, such as paid vacations, for couples who opted to have surgery to avoid future conceptions. In some areas of China, there were much more pronounced rewards and punishments for controlling fertility. Food, clothing, and even income were granted or withheld when couples met, or failed to meet, family-size objectives.

However, the most dramatic and widely publicized stage in China's fertility control program began in 1979 when the "one child" campaign was launched.[68] Since China's birth rate had gone up dramatically in the 1960s when the early family planning program was abandoned, a large cohort of potential new parents was moving into its childbearing years in the 1980s. Chinese leaders believed that if this large cohort produced even two children per couple, their plans for economic development would be endangered.

Although there is some variation by region, the most characteristic form of this new program is the agreement by a couple, after they have had their first child, to have only the single child. When they do, they are issued a "one-child certificate." Such a certificate yields a variety of benefits to the parents, including government stipends, extra living space, additional paid maternity leave, supplementary pensions; the children are given priorities in terms of future educational and occupational opportunities.[69]

The success of this one-child program is by no means assured, but there are a number of factors that indicate that it may well work. However, there is one overarching factor that may make it possible for China to achieve what many would have thought to be a demographic miracle a quarter century ago. That factor is the set of societal and cultural changes made by China over that period that have reduced individual motivations for childbearing. Some changes were made to help ensure the success of the revolution (the breakup of the patriarchal family), some were made for ideological reasons (greater equality for women, increased age at marriage), and many of the others were made specifically to reduce motivations for fertility. In this latter category, the Chinese have recognized that people often have children because they provide economic security in old age. Providing extra income and supplementary pensions for couples who agree to have only one child is a pointed counterbalance to this age-old motivation for having more children. The official Chinese goal is to achieve zero population growth by the year 2000. That may not be achieved, but, if the present policies are continued and even strengthened, the Chinese may well come reasonably close to their objective. Whatever the future reality, the Chinese have already demonstrated that fertility declines can be achieved by strong government policy, a concerted family planning program, and societal and cultural changes that reduce the motivations for childbearing.

Although the Chinese program has been a great demographic success, and promises even greater successes in the future, a caution should be noted. Such a program requires considerable state control over the individual and intrusion into the lives of individuals. Many Americans, given our democratic traditions, could not accept such intrusions. However, in many less developed societies the choice may be between such authoritarian control and rampant population growth. This entire chapter has been devoted to the grave dangers of such population growth. But various less developed nations will have to address the question of whether coping with the population problem is worth the amount of authoritarianism such a program may require.

SUMMARY

Part I: The Problem

1. The explosive growth in the world's population, largely attributable in recent years to developing countries, constitutes a major problem for everyone.
2. In developing countries, the impact of the exploding population is most felt in the cities.
3. Population growth in developing countries has led to an increase in the nuclear family and to higher levels of poverty within such families.
4. The growth of the economies in less developed countries is unable to keep up with the booming populations.
5. Rapid population growth is related to political chaos within developing countries, as well as the danger of international conflict.
6. Within developed countries today, the greatest problems result from low,

rather than high, fertility. For example, low fertility has caused strains in the modern family.

7. For developed countries, large numbers of illegal aliens constitute a major demographic problem.
8. Although the population explosion has all but ceased in developed countries, there are still large populations in these countries placing great strains on the environment.

Part II: Causes and Consequences

9. The explosive growth in population associated with the demographic transition is related to a variety of sociological causes such as industrialization, urbanization, and improvement in sanitation, nutrition, and health care.
10. The recent, unprecedented growth in the population of less developed countries has been the result of the ability to import modern advances in science and medicine in order to cut death rates dramatically while birth rates remain high.
11. Cultural factors are especially important in helping us understand the paradox of birth rates remaining high in less developed countries, despite the hardships caused by such a population increase.
12. Among the cultural factors encouraging high birth rates are pronatalism, familism, and beliefs about traditional sex roles.
13. Ultimately, individual action and inaction make a key difference in population growth.
14. Individuals in developing countries tend to persist in long-standing practices and to resist changes such as efforts to get them to make greater use of contraceptives.

Part III: Responses

15. There are two views that argue that no response to the population explosion is possible or needed. In one, the "doomsday" perspective assumes that catastrophe is inevitable, with the result that any response is useless. In the other, the view that people are an "ultimate resource," there is the sense that more people will lead to expansion at various levels in society.
16. One response to the population problem is to focus on economic development as the best way of coping with a growing population.
17. Another is the family planning approach that focuses on limiting population growth through the dissemination of contraceptives.
18. The societalist approach focuses on the need to change the larger structure and culture of society in order to be able to reduce the pronatalistic forces acting on individuals.
19. Contemporary China is cited as a model of a successful societalist approach to limiting population growth.

SUGGESTED READINGS

Bouvier, Leon, "Planet Earth 1984–2034: A Demographic Vision," *Population Bulletin*, 39. Washington, D.C.: Population Reference Bureau, 1984. A demographer looks at some dimensions of population change in the next half century.

Council on Environmental Quality and the Department of State, *The Global 2000 Report to the President*, Vol. I. Harmondsworth, Middlesex, England: Penguin Books, 1982. An important government report that deals with population and ecological problems.

Jones, Landon Y., *Great Expectations: America*

and the Baby Boom Generation. New York: Ballantine, 1980. An economic, social, and cultural examination of the effects of the "baby boom" generation on American society.

Weeks, John R., *Population: An Introduction to Concepts and Issues,* 2nd ed. Belmont, Cal.: Wadsworth, 1981. A basic introduction to demography.

Yuan Tien, H., "China: Demographic Billionaire," *Population Bulletin,* 38. (Washington, D.C.: Population Reference Bureau, 1983.) A look at the problems and prospects of population growth in China.

FOOTNOTES

[1]Kingsley Davis, "The World's Population Crisis." In Robert K. Merton and Robert Nisbet, eds., *Contemporary Social Problems,* 4th ed. (New York: Harcourt Brace Jovanovich, 1976), pp. 265–303.

[2]Leon F. Bouvier, "Planet Earth 1984–2034: A Demographic Vision," *Population Bulletin,* 39 (Washington, D.C.: Population Reference Bureau, 1984), p. 4.

[3]Population Reference Bureau, *1984 World Population Data Sheet* (Washington, D.C.: Population Reference Bureau, 1984).

[4]John Noble Wilford, "9 Percent of Everyone Who Ever Lived is Alive Now," *The New York Times,* October 6, 1981, p. C1.

[5]John D. Durand, "Historical Estimates of World Population," *Population and Development Review,* 3 (1977), 253–296.

[6]H. Yuan Tien, "China: Demographic Billionaire," *Population Bulletin,* 38 (Washington, D.C.: Population Reference Bureau, 1983).

[7]Paul R. Ehrlich, *The Population Bomb* (New York: Ballantine, 1968). For the alternative view that the population bomb is nothing more than a "dud," see Donald Bogue and Amy Ong Tsui, "Zero Population Growth," *The Public Interest,* 55 (1979), 99–113.

[8]Bouvier, *op. cit.*

[9]This is not the same as the overall rate of growth, which, in addition to births and deaths, also includes migration.

[10]Population Reference Bureau, *1984 World Population Data Sheet, op. cit.*

[11]Bouvier, *op. cit.*; Pranay B. Gupte, "U.N. Lowers Estimates of Population in 2000," *The New York Times,* June 13, 1982, p. 4.

[12]Bouvier, *op. cit.*, p. 11.

[13]Harold Lubell, cited in Peter Wilsher and Rosemary Righter, *The Exploding Cities* (New York: Quadrangle, 1975), p. 22.

[14]*Ibid.*, p. 22.

[15]*Ibid.*, p. 19.

[16]United Nations, *Demographic Yearbook: 1981* (New York: United Nations, 1983), p. 193.

[17]This is a broad generalization with a number of exceptions. For example, rural Cambodians have traditionally had a nuclear, not an extended, family system. See, for example, J. Van Deusen, C. Coleman, and L. Khoa, "Southeast Asian Social and Cultural Customs: Similarities and Differences, Part 1," *Journal of Refugee Settlement,* 1 (1981), 20–40.

[18]We must be careful not to overstate this. Many families in cities in less developed countries are extended because migrants from rural areas are often headed toward a relative's home in the urban area. Furthermore, many such urban families are often unable to afford to do anything but let extended family members live in the same house.

[19]M. Cain, "Perspectives on Family and Fertility in Developing Countries," *Population Studies,* 36 (1982), 159–175.

[20]However, there is some evidence that this now may be changing. In a recent study in Mexico there is evidence that the family is being "reextended" in the city with family members providing such supports as day care that would allow women to go to work. S. Smith, "Women's Work, Fertility and Competing Time Use in Mexico City." In J. Simon and P. Lindert, eds., *Research in Population Economics,* Vol. III (Greenwich, Conn.: JAI Press, 1981), pp. 167–187.

[21]John R. Weeks, *Population: An Introduction to Concepts and Issues,* 2nd ed. (Belmont, Cal.: Wadsworth, 1981), p. 231.

[22]Council on Environmental Quality and the Department of State, *The Global 2000 Report to the President,* Vol. I (Harmondsworth, England: Penguin, 1982).

[23]Lester R. Brown, "World Food Resources and Population: The Narrowing Margin," *Population Bulletin,* 36 (Washington, D.C.: Population Reference Bureau, 1981).

[24]Robert Heilbroner, *An Inquiry into the Human Prospect* (New York: Norton, 1974).

[25]Davis, *op. cit.*

[26]Bouvier, *op. cit.*, p. 11.

[27]*Ibid.*

[28]Weeks, *op. cit.*

[29]Linda J. Waite, "U.S. Women at Work," *Population Bulletin,* 36 (Washington, D.C.: Population Reference Bureau, 1981).

[30]*Ibid.,* p. 3.

[31]Bouvier, *op. cit.,* pp. 8–10.

[32]Cary Davis, Carl Haub, and JoAnne Willette, "U. S. Hispanics: Changing the Face of America," *Population Bulletin,* 38 (Washington, D.C.: Population Reference Bureau, 1983), p. 27.

[33]We will return to Malthus's ideas, as well as the work of those (the neo-Malthusians) who worked in this tradition, in the following chapter on ecological problems.

[34]Thomas R. Malthus, *An Essay on Population* (New York: Augustus Kelley, 1798/1965).

[35]Although the basic ideas certainly precede them, Frank Notestein and Kingsley Davis both published articles in 1945 that laid out some of the basic dimensions of demographic transition theory. See Frank Notestein, "Population—the Long View." In T. W. Schultz, ed., *Food for the World.* (Chicago: University of Chicago Press, 1945); Kingsley Davis, "The World Demographic Transition," *Annals of the American Academy of Political and Social Science,* 237 (1945), 1–11.

[36]Kenneth C. W. Kammeyer, *An Introduction to Population* (San Francisco: Chandler, 1971); Kammeyer and Helen Ginn, *An Introduction to Population,* 2nd ed. (Homewood, Ill.: Dorsey Press, 1986). Forthcoming title.

[37]Thomas R. McKeown and R. G. Record, "Reasons for the Decline in Mortality in England and Wales During the Nineteenth Century," *Population Studies,* 16 (1962), 94–122.

[38]One of the key points here is that death rates were declining *before* medicine began to make an important contribution. See Chapter 12 for further discussion of this issue.

[39]This, however, is not to say that there is today anything approaching equality between developed and developing countries in this area. In some sub-Saharan African countries the infant mortality rate approaches 1 out of 5 while in a developed country like Sweden it is 1 per 100. See Cristine Russell, "Study Finds 1 in 10 Babies Worldwide Die Before 1st Birthday," *The Washington Post,* December 13, 1981, p. A16.

[40]Davis, *op.cit.,* 1976.

[41]U. S. Bureau of the Census, *Country Demographic Profiles—Sri Lanka* (Washington, D. C.: U. S. Government Printing Office, 1977).

[42]Jay R. Mandle, "The Decline in Mortality in British Guiana, 1911–1960," *Demography,* 7 (1970), 301–315.

[43]Kingsley Davis, "The Amazing Decline of Mortality in Underdeveloped Areas," *American Economic Review,* 46 (1956), 305–318.

[44]Mandle, *op. cit.*

[45]It is also important to point out that the decline in death rate simultaneously meant an improvement in the health of the population. Improved health, in turn, is related to improved fecundity and the birth rate actually increases, at least for a time. The statistics here in the case of Guyana are interesting.

[46]Judith Blake, "Coercive Pronatalism and American Population Policy." In Charles Westoff and Robert Parke, eds., *Social and Demographic Aspects of Population Growth and the American Future* (Washington, D.C.: U.S. Government Printing Office, 1972); Kingsley Davis, "Population Policy: Will Current Programs Succeed?" *Science,* 158 (1967), 730–739.

[47]Lee Rainwater, *Family Design: Marital Sexuality, Family Size and Contraception* (Chicago: Aldine, 1965).

[48]J. Mayone Stycos, *Human Fertility in Latin America: Sociological Perspectives* (Ithaca, N. Y.: Cornell University Press, 1968).

[49]Robert Lightbourne, Jr., Susheela Singh with Cynthia P. Green, "The World Fertility Survey: Charting Global Childbearing," *Population Bulletin,* 37 (Washington, D.C.: Population Reference Bureau, 1982).

[50]*Ibid.,* p. 31.

[51]Michael Bamburger and Margaret Earle, "Factors Affecting Family Planning in a Low Income Caracas Neighborhood," *Studies in Family Planning,* 2 (1971), 175–178.

[52]Part III of this chapter draws heavily on the written work of Kenneth Kammeyer. He is, in reality, the author of this part and coauthor of the entire chapter.

[53]William Paddock and Paul Paddock, *Famine 1975! America's Decision: Who Will Survive?* (Boston: Little, Brown, 1967).

[54]*Ibid.,* p. 9.

[55]Julian Simon, *The Ultimate Resource* (Princeton, N.J.: Princeton University Press, 1981).

[56]See, for example, "Review Symposium on Julian L. Simon, *The Ultimate Resource,*" *Population and Development Review,* 8 (1982), 163–177.

[57]Nicholas J. Demerath, *Birth Control and Foreign Policy: The Alternatives to Family Planning* (New York: Harper & Row, 1976).

[58]Linda Gordon, "Why Nineteenth-Century Feminists Did Not Support 'Birth Control' and Twentieth-Century Feminists Do: Feminism, Reproduction and the Family." In Barrie Thorne and Marilyn Yalom, *Rethinking the Family: Some Feminist Questions* (New York: Longman, 1982), pp. 40–53.

[59]Demerath, *op.cit.*

[60]Blake, *op. cit.*; Davis, *op. cit.*, 1967.

[61]Blake, *op. cit.*

[62]John Knodel and Etienne Van de Walle, "Lessons from the Past: Policy Implications of Historical Fertility Studies," *Population and Development Review*, 5 (1979), 217–245.

[63]Tien, *op. cit.*

[64]Judith Bannister and Samuel H. Preston, "Mortality in China," *Population and Development Review*, 7 (March 1981), 98–110.

[65]H. Yuan Tien, *China's Population Struggle: Democratic Decisions of the People's Republic 1949–1969* (Columbus: The Ohio State University Press, 1973).

[66]P. C. Chen and A. Kols, "Population and Birth Planning in the People's Republic of China," *Population Reports*, Series J. 25. (Baltimore: Johns Hopkins University Press, 1982).

[67]H. Yuan Tien, ed., *Population Theory in China* (White Plains, N.Y.: M. E. Sharpe, 1980).

[68]Leo Goodstadt, "China's One-Child Family: Policy and Public Response," *Population and Development Review*, 8 (1982), 37–58; Chen and Kols, *op. cit.*; Tien, *op. cit.*, 1982.

[69]Chen and Kols, *op. cit.*

and there arose a smoke
out of the pit, as the
smoke of a great furnace
and the sun and moon
were darkened by reason
of the smoke of the pit.
revelation 9:2

15 *Ecological Problems*

The earth's *biosphere*—the surface layer of the planet and the surrounding atmosphere—sustains all life. Land, air, water, and energy are all fundamental to the existence of living organisms. Problems have arisen because human beings have followed an evolutionary course in which they and their technologies, cultures, and societies have come increasingly to strain the ability of the biosphere to sustain life on earth.[1] In a mere 20 or 30 thousand years, little more than a pulse beat on the geological time scale, humans and the larger structures they have created have so drastically depleted and poisoned the basic life-support systems of the planet that they now threaten the future of the human species and perhaps all of life itself.

PART I: THE PROBLEM

Many of our ecological problems are traceable to the ever-present, but continually burgeoning, need for energy. In order to satisfy their need for energy, people have been forced to cut down trees for firewood, dig mines in order to get coal and uranium, and drill wells to gain access to oil. Many of these resources will be depleted in a relatively few (by geological standards) years. And the depletion of the fossil fuels (coal, oil) we burn in immense quantities contributes mightily to the fouling of available air and water in the biosphere.

In addition to depleting and fouling our natural resources at an alarming rate, we are also actively poisoning the land, the air, and the water on which we are dependent for our survival. Some of this poisoning is as a result of the burning of the fuels that we require for our energy needs. But not all of the poisoning of the biosphere is traceable to these sources. Note the following cases, many of which will be drawn upon later in this chapter:

—In the 1940s and 1950s the Hooker Chemical Company dumped tons of toxic chemicals into the Love Canal in upper New York State. The chemicals eventually seeped around and into houses on the canal's banks on the outskirts of Niagara Falls. Studies began to show a high incidence of such things as cancer and birth defects among those living in residences near the canal. Eventually, the residents were relocated, the area was declared a disaster area, and many millions of dollars of local, state, and federal money were spent in an effort to clean up the area.[2]

—Among the chemicals dumped into the Love Canal was dioxin, one of the most toxic and carcinogenic substances in existence. More recently dioxin has caused the United States literally to *buy* the town of Times Beach, Missouri, for almost $37 million and to ask its 2,500 residents to pack up and leave. The cause of the problem was the spraying in 1971 of oil containing dioxin to control dust on the roads. In December 1982, the Environmental Protection Agency (EPA) performed tests that revealed dioxin levels in the town *100 times* the level considered to be harmful. The residents had apparently been living with such levels for eleven years.[3]

—The major accident in 1979 at the Three Mile Island nuclear power plant in Pennsylvania and several other recent alarms have alerted many people to the grave dangers associated with a full-scale nuclear accident,[4] as well as related problems such as the difficulties involved in disposing of nuclear wastes.

—The Asarco copper-smelting plant in Tacoma, Washington, employs 575 people, pumps $35 million per year into the local economy, and unfortunately also pumps large quantities of arsenic, a cancer-producing poison, into the atmosphere. Joggers

One of the great ecological disasters of modern times occurred in Bhopal, India, in 1984 when a gas leak from a Union Carbide plant killed and injured thousands of people.

(Baldev/Sygma)

complain that they can literally taste the air on windless days.[5]

In December 1984, a deadly gas, methyl isocyanate, used to make pesticides escaped into the air from the Union Carbide plant on the outskirts of Bhopal, India. Many of those who lived adjacent to the plant died almost immediately, while by the end of the week following the accident about 2,500 people had died. Many others died in the following weeks and months from the after-effects of the gas. Countless others experienced health problems such as blindness and paralysis.[6]

Long before modern society and its technological marvels, people were depleting and poisoning the biosphere. Chopping down trees and burning the wood served to deplete and poison the environment. What is different today is that there are many more of us and we possess an infinitely greater ability to affect the biosphere adversely. As William Ophuls points out, we must remember that even though our *ecosystem* has the capacities to repair, maintain, and regulate itself, there are *limits* to these abilities.[7] While the system has been able to develop the ability to handle certain problems (for example, the replenishment of a forest after a fire), there are a variety of modern problems with which nature has not yet been able to cope, and with which it may never be able to deal. For example, there are as yet no natural adaptations to high levels of radiation or synthetic chemicals and nature may not have the time to develop adequate adaptations to these and other problems. As Ophuls concludes: "the essential message of ecology is *limitation:* there is only so much the biosphere can take and only so much it can give, and this may be less than we desire."[8] In the following pages we look at various aspects of the biosphere and the ways in which we are severely testing their limits.

Air

We inhabit the bottom of a vast ocean of air. Into this precious atmosphere, all the nations of the world pour billions of tons of poisonous gases and particles each year. However, it is the United States which is, by far, the greatest air polluter. The major source of this pollution is modern forms of transportation. Other significant sources are stationary fuel consumers, such as home furnaces, as well as industrial production.

It would seem that with vast quantities of air, our use of the skies as industrial dumping grounds would have little immediate effect. However, the circulatory systems of the skies do not necessarily distribute pollutants uniformly. Atmospheric pollution is primarily the problem of industrial and industrializing areas of the world, and its effects are felt most severely in regions that do the polluting. For example, the arsenic produced by the Tacoma, Washington, copper-smelting plant discussed above pollutes only a limited geographic area. In spite of this, it seems clear that there is the likelihood of both wide-range and long-range danger from air pollution.[9]

Smog

All the heavily industrialized and densely populated areas of North America experience moderate to severe air-pollution problems. Although the atmosphere above Los Angeles county is somewhat less polluted on the average than that of New York or Chicago, that area has severe pollution problems with *smog*—a mixture of fog and automobile and industrial fumes. Los Angeles has a severe smog problem because frequently the air above it does not circulate, so pollution builds up. The city rests between the ocean and the mountains. The problem arises because air infused with the pollutants from cars, industries, and homes tends to become trapped and stagnant.

The climate and topography of Los Angeles, and Southern California in general, produce frequent *temperature inversions.*[10] Such inversions occur most often in warm climates where the sun heats the upper layers of the atmosphere. Normally, air heated by the warmer temperatures of the earth will rise above the colder air masses at higher altitudes. This upward movement of air carries pollutants in the surface air into the upper atmosphere, where winds disperse them over a wide area. In a temperature inversion, the upper air is warmer than the lower air and the pollutants therefore stay in the surface air, often increasing to intolerable concentrations. Winds sweeping across flatlands or oceans will usually mix the air even where temperature inversions exist. But mountains that surround cities built in valleys (such as Los Angeles) trap the layered air within the valleys and prevent wind from entering the valleys.

Over the years, Los Angeles became the prime example of the automobile city, a settlement composed of hundreds of suburban centers connected by a complex system of auto routes. It had no well-developed central city where dense areas of population could support the development of large-scale mass transit. Unfortunately, this dependency on auto transport has seriously endangered the skies over Los Angeles, as well as other rapidly growing American cities, to say nothing at this point of the energy demands of automobile transportation.

While Los Angeles still has a smog problem, it seems to have improved since its worst levels in the 1950s. However, the problems are still at their worst in the heat of August and September when the area looks, as described by one traveler, "like a bowl of chicken gravy."[11]

Carbon Dioxide

While smog is a very well known air quality problem, difficulties created by the increase in carbon dioxide—CO^2—in the atmosphere are much less well known, but perhaps even more serious.[12] Carbon dioxide is found naturally in the atmosphere, but in the last century the level of carbon dioxide has increased by 15 percent and it is currently growing by 0.4 percent a year. Major sources of the increases in carbon dioxide are the burning of fossil fuels and deforestation.[13] Carbon dioxide plays a central role in determining the temperature of the earth's atmosphere. An increase in carbon dioxide can lead to a warming of that atmosphere. This, in turn, would lead to changes in the climate throughout the world with potentially dramatic effects on crops, livestock, food supplies, rainfall, coastal flooding, and the like. The warming of the climate would enlarge the desert areas of the world and reduce the area suitable for agriculture. The rise in ocean levels could lead to coastal flooding and possibly the evacuation of coastal areas. Ultimately, the ability of large numbers of people to survive could be adversely affected by increasing levels of carbon dioxide.[14]

Ozone Depletion

Another more recent concern is the depletion of the ozone level in the atmosphere that protects us from hazardous levels of solar radiation.[15] A major factor in this is the fluorocarbons that are released from aerosol sprays, refrigeration equipment, and various industrial processes. Fluorocarbons have a very long life span and as they make their way into the upper atmosphere, they act to deplete the ozone layer. The result of this is believed to be an increase in ultraviolet radiation, and higher levels of such radiation are related, among other things, to increases in skin cancer. The projected depletion in the ozone layer will lead to approximately 300,000 additional cases of skin cancer in the United States each year and perhaps over 1 million additional cases among Caucasians around the world. Fluorocarbon-induced ozone depletion is related to other problems as well, such as dangers to plants and animals and a cooling of the earth's atmosphere.

Water

The availability of water has always established the limits of human population density. Many ancient civilizations flourished and declined in accordance with their supplies of water. Millions of people have faced death from drought in areas like the sub-Saharan region of Africa. The *carrying capacity* of world regions—that is, the ability of the environment to support a human population of a given size and at a particular level of cultural development—still depends in large part on the abundance of water.

The amount of water that can be diverted from natural flows is limited, and the availability of such water is not keeping pace with population growth around the world.[16] Thus, portions of the United States and the rest of the world suffer from chronic water shortages, and much of the rest of it will experience the same fate unless we stop wasting available resources.

In addition to a lack of water, there is the problem of the pollution of a wide array of bodies of water. Although some corporations have moved to deal with pollution by developing modern water-treatment systems, a significant problem remains. Even with the best of these treatment systems in industry, there is still the problem of *thermal pollution*—or returning water that is too warm into the lakes and feeder rivers. Because warm water dissolves less atmospheric oxygen, raising the water temperature seriously endangers a body of water's oxygen supply and kills many forms of aquatic life.

Eutrophication—the depletion of a water system's oxygen supply and the subsequent choking of other aquatic life by algae—is a key process in understanding the effects of human population on natural water systems. The balance of life in a lake, river, or ocean depends above all on the supply of oxygen dissolved in the water and the proper levels of available nitrogen and phosphorus. When industry pours water heated by the excess energy of production into a natural waterway, the oxygen-carrying capacity of the water system decreases. Over time, the various life forms that inhabit the water system begin to die off and the water system itself may eventually die.

Acid Rain

A form of pollution that has received a great deal of attention in recent years is *acid rain.*[17] Acid rain is literally rain containing too much acid, especially nitric and sulfuric acid. All rain has some acid in it that is derived from natural processes like volcanic eruptions, forest fires, and the bacterial decomposition of organic matter. However, the problems we are encountering today are not primarily traceable to these natural sources, but rather to power plants, factories, smelting plants, and auto emissions. It is estimated that 90 to 95 percent of the acid rain in the northeastern United States comes from such man-made sources.[18] The primary villain seems to be the tall smokestacks belonging to a large number of electric utilities and industries in the midwestern and eastern United States. These smokestacks give off various acids, as well as such toxic metals as mercury and cadmium. These emissions mix with the water vapor in the atmosphere, chemical reactions occur, and ultimately acid rain is formed. While these acidic deposits usually come down in the form of rain, they also can be found in hail, snow, dry particles, and fog.

Acid rain, of course, falls on both land and water. On land, it is absorbed into the earth where it breaks down minerals and ultimately robs plants of the nutrients they need to survive and grow. Eventually, the acid in the ground (along with the toxic metals) seeps into bodies of water where it joins the derivatives of acid rain that have fallen directly into the water. The effects are not immediate and dramatic. Said one aquatic scientist: "You don't see massive destruction . . . Things just quietly disappear."[19] Over time aquatic life is slowly killed or its growth stunted. As lakes and rivers grow increasingly acidic, they turn "oddly clear and bluish."[20] Eventually the body of water ceases to be able to support anything but the most primitive forms of life.

Some areas are able to resist acid rain because they are rich in alkaline limestone that buffers, or neutralizes, the acid. Thus, the damage is not felt uniformly. It is eastern Canada that is hardest hit by acid rain. Not only is Canadian ecology vulnerable to this problem, but it is also on the receiving end of the kind of pollution from the United States that is conducive to the creation of acid rain. As Canada's Environment Minister put it: "We are at the end of a gigantic geographical exhaust pipe."[21] It is estimated that if nothing is done, Canada will lose 48,000 lakes by the end of the twentieth century.

Although action is clearly needed, caution is also called for. One of the ironies of the acid rain problem is that it is in part attributable to an effort in 1970 by the Environmental Protection Agency to deal with the smog problem by ordering industrial plants to increase the height of their smokestacks. However, these new smoke-

Pollution has effectively destroyed many bodies of water.
(Jeffrey D. Smith/Woodfin Camp & Associates)

stacks had several *unanticipated consequences.* Because pollutants were being emitted higher into the atmosphere, they could be carried much farther distances by the winds. In addition, the pollutants were injected so high that they could remain up there longer, thereby making it more possible for the needed chemical reactions to take place.

The Oceans

Although it is not its exclusive concern, the United States, with its lengthy coastlines, has a deep interest in the health of the oceans. While 70 percent of the earth's surface is ocean water, the vital resources of energy and oxygen, which make those seas come alive with plant and fish life, are concentrated in thin bands along the major continental shorelines and at the polar regions of the planet. These waters, however, are the most accessible to human use and abuse. The industralized nations, especially the United States, are adversely affecting these areas by indiscriminately dumping industrial wastes and human sewage in them.[22] In addition to worry over intentional dumping, there is also concern about accidental spills and discharges, especially of crude oil, due to routine vessel maintenance of ships at sea.[23] Among the short-term results are despoiled beaches, dead fish, and declining bird populations. Even graver dangers are anticipated in the future.

Concern about damage to the oceans led to the passage of the Clean Water Act in 1972. As a result of the controls placed on ocean dumping, some progress seems to have been made. Despite the gains, the oceans are certainly not out of danger. In addition to better controls on dumping, environmentalists are more optimistic about the ocean's ability to purge itself, or adapt to pollution.[24]

Land

Modern society is not only responsible for a fouling of the air and the water, but also the land ("soil degradation"[25]) on which we live and on which we depend for so much.

Poisoning the Land

We have already encountered several examples of the way in which we are poisoning our lands—Love Canal, Times Beach, and the like. Of course, the land, air, and water are interrelated, with the result that the pollution of one often leads to the pollution of the others. Indeed, one of the great concerns in the pollution of the land is that the underground reservoirs that are so important to us may ultimately be befouled. Contaminants (for example, petrochemicals) that were disposed of years ago, presumably safely, are now beginning to show up in some of our deeper wells.

The greatest threat to the land is the chemicals we are producing at a very high rate (about 1,000 new ones per year). There are about 50,000 chemicals currently on the market and many of them have been a great boon to society. However, about 70 percent of them have been classified by the Environmental Protection Agency as definitely or potentially hazardous to human health. One government survey concluded that virtually every person in the United States, indeed the world, carries the adverse effect of one or more of these chemicals. It is estimated that in the United States alone almost 80 billion pounds of hazardous chemical wastes are generated each year and that about 90 percent of it is *not* being handled in a safe manner. The result is that dangerous chemical wastes turn up in a wide array of places and have adverse effects on large numbers of people.

Pesticides

Much of our recent attention has been focused on toxic wastes, but a related and longer-term concern has been the dangers of pesticides. The attention of the nation in the early 1960s was drawn to these dangers by Rachel Carson in her classic book, *Silent Spring.*[26] While recognizing the problems caused by insects, Carson warned us of the dangers to ourselves and our habitat posed by pesticides. Pesticides (and herbicides) are, of course, chemicals that are used to cope with the threats to crops and timber caused by pests and weeds. Although some pesticides have been banned or tightly controlled, the fact is that pesticide/herbicide usage has doubled since Carson wrote in the early 1960s.[27] It was estimated that over $4 billion were spent in 1982 to keep our farms and forests lush and green. Ironically, in spite of all the effort devoted to, and all the money spent on, dealing with pests, there is about as much crop loss to pests today as there was in the early 1940s when the agriculturalists in the United States first began the rush to herbicides. It would appear that many insects have adapted to the poisons and grown immune to them.

Although insects may have found ways of adapting to pesticides, the same cannot be said of humans. Farm workers exposed to these chemicals may come down with cancer, nerve and brain disorders; their offspring may have birth defects; and for females there may be a greater likelihood of miscarriages. More generally, the chemicals poison the soil, forests, streams, lakes, oceans, air, and even a good portion of the food supply. The result is that traces of these pesticides are commonly found in people who never go near a farm or forest.

Although the worst of the pesticides (DDT, aldrin, parathion) have been tightly regulated in the United States, American chemical companies have been shipping these and other chemicals to Third-World countries.[28] Exemplifying the dangers, here is a quote from a Brazilian environmentalist: "I can send any 15-year-old to the store to buy ten drums of products so lethal that skin contact is sufficient to kill a person."[29] These chemicals also threaten Americans, since some of these agricultural products find their way back into the United States.

Garbage

The mountains of garbage produced by modern society are having an unprecedented effect on the environment. One of the causes of this disaster is the movement of our society away from reusable, recyclable products to a "throw away" ethic. We have produced mountains of often almost indestructible junk, some of which will be with us for centuries. The needs of mass consumption in the United States produce *16 billion* pounds of trash *a day.*[30] While wastes from food and other necessities are justified, much of the rest (such as disposable cartons, packages, wrappings, plastic and styrofoam cups, and so on) is not.

But as unsightly and destructive as these leftovers of mass consumption may be, they do not usually have the deadly consequences of some of our other refuse. The toxic and nuclear waste products from the industrial processes that produce the goods for mass consumption are often dangerous and deadly; some, for all practical purposes, will be with us forever. Once they have been created and have worked their way into the environment (which some inexorably will), their harmful effects will reach all forms of life for many, many years.

Nuclear Waste

The most widely feared wastes are the radioactive materials produced by nuclear

Oil spills and mountains of garbage are two types of ecological disaster.
(Cathy Cheney/EKM-Nepenthe)

power plants[31] and nuclear weapon-making. The United States now has over 100 million gallons of high-level radioactive waste, of which about three-fourths is derived from the production of nuclear weapons.[32] This amount is likely to grow in coming years with the proposed dramatic increase in nuclear weapons. Whatever the amount, fission byproducts may remain dangerous for from 600 to 500,000 years![33] Furthermore, it must always be remembered that there is no safe level of radioactivity. Whenever anyone is exposed to *any* dose of radioactivity, the probability that cancer or genetic defect will occur is increased. Complicating matters is the fact that we as yet have no adequate means of transporting or disposing of nuclear wastes and those that we do have are plagued by problems such as leaky tanks.

Energy

The intermittent shortages of gasoline, fuel oil, and electrical power in the United States, Japan, Europe, and other industrialized nations (and many less developed countries as well) since 1973 were predicted by ecology-minded scientists decades ago. Of course, students of population have long been aware that increases in population soon outstrip increases in resources, particularly the food resources from farm production. But the consequences of our reliance on fossil fuels to satisfy the ever-increasing energy demands of modern society did not become generally apparent until the 1950s. For example, in 1954 a geophysicist, Harrison Brown, outlined the problems facing the world community due to population pressure, industrial pollution, and potential shortages of food and raw materials. Perhaps his most significant findings related to the depletion of the earth's energy resources.

> Consumption of the earth's stores of fossil fuels has barely started, yet already we can see the end. In a length of time which is extremely short when compared with the span of human history, and insignificant when compared with the length of time during which man has inhabited the earth, fossil fuels will have been discovered, utilized, and completely consumed."[34]

Earl Hayes sees an end to the exponential growth of energy consumption in the United States, with energy growth essentially ceasing as we approach the year 2000.[35] At current rates of consumption, which can only *underestimate* the world-wide demand for energy, world-wide deposits of petroleum will be 90 percent exhausted by the year 2030. Deposits of coal throughout the world will be 90 percent exhausted in the year 2400.[36]

Nuclear Power

For some years, a great deal of faith was placed in nuclear power plants and their ability to provide the power needed by society as the power sources discussed above begin to disappear. However, the accident at the Three Mile Island nuclear power plant on March 28, 1979, as well as later revelations of problems in many other nuclear plants, helped blunt the movement toward nuclear power in this country.[37] Fears and protests sparked by the accident at Three Mile Island have been important, but other factors such as construction delays have also wreaked havoc with the industry. However, it is likely that the biggest problems facing the nuclear power industry are economic in character. For one thing, such plants are extremely expensive to build and costs have escalated over the years. For another, demand for electricity has leveled off as a result of consumer conservation efforts impelled by the high cost of energy. As a result of these factors, there is little impetus these days to move in the direction of expensive and potentially dangerous nuclear energy. This had led one expert to write of "giving up on nuclear power" and "phasing out nuclear power over the next couple of decades."[38]

The Ecosystem

In a memorable speech to the United Nations World Conference on Environmental Problems, India's then Prime Minister Indira Gandhi summed up the fundamental concept of the ecosystem: "Life is one and the world is one and all these questions are interlinked." The concept of an *ecosystem* was further developed by one of the major figures in the history of the study of ecology, Barry Commoner, in his book *The Closing Circle.*[39] Commoner's essential point is that human beings inhabit a world of ecological relationships in which each part of the environment is intimately linked to all others. When any natural element in the complex equation of natural balances is disrupted, many others will also be modified with potentially tragic consequences. The very basic life-support systems that we have briefly discussed are not independent entities, so we cannot study these systems by reducing them to their constituent elements and properties. Rather, we must always study the relationships among these elements—the complex ways in which changes in one element may have far-reaching effects on other elements.

Table 15.1 Energy Options for the Future*

KIND OF ENERGY, EXTENT OF USE, AND SOURCES	HOW THE ENERGY IS RELEASED	ADVANTAGES	DRAWBACKS
Fossil fuels In widespread use. Coal, petroleum, or natural gas. Found in certain portions of the earth where animal and plant remains have decayed into fossil fuels.	The fuel is burned to boil water and produce steam. The steam is then used to generate electricity.	The technology is well developed and can easily be improved by new techniques. Likely to provide three-fourths of all electricity even in the twenty-first century.	Considerable thermal and air pollution. All fossil fuels will run out in the next few hundred years. Coal mining is very damaging to the environment.
Nuclear (fission) Used in industrialized countries and only occasionally. Uranium and other radioactive metals. Found in certain areas of the earth. Metals that are more abundant may be used if breeder reactors are perfected†	The atoms of the fuel are split (which releases energy) in a chain reaction. The heat produced by the reaction is used to boil water and produce electricity in the same manner in which the heat from fossil fuels is used.	Essentially no air pollution and in improved models, perhaps slightly less thermal pollution than present power generation produces. *If* breeder reactors prove practical, fuel supply is nearly unlimited.	How to dispose of radioactive wastes is a problem. Conventional nuclear reactors will run out of fuel early in the twenty-first century. Breeder reactors may not be practical. They can also be used to manufacture nuclear weapons.
Thermonuclear (fusion) Method of power use is hypothetical. Hydrogen or lithium. Hydrogen is found in seawater, and lithium in certain rocks.	The atoms of the fuel are fused (which releases energy) into pairs. To begin this reaction requires great heat and energy (usually a small fission "bomb"). The heat produced by the reaction is used to boil water and produce electricity in the same manner in which the heat from fossil fuels is used.	In one version, the fuel supply (a form of hydrogen) is almost limitless. Air pollution is absent, redioactive waste is essentially absent, and thermal pollution is probably minimal.	No one knows whether fusion power can be made to work. If it can, the only limiting factor is possible thermal pollution of the earth's atmosphere.
Geothermal Used occasionally. Masses of very hot rock that can extend from several hundred feet to several miles beneath the earth's surface.	Holes from the earth's surface to the hot rock underneath allow water occurring naturally underground that is heated by the hot rock to rise to the surface in the form of very hot water or steam. Holes can also be drilled from the surface to the hot rock, and water can then be forced down to be heated and rise as steam. The steam is used to produce electricity in the same manner as when fossil fuels are used.	The energy is free. No air pollution.	Suitable sites may be scarce, and drilling and site preparation costs may be high. If deep-lying salt water is used as a heat source, saline pollution may be a problem. Thermal pollution probably would be severe.
Solar power Used occasionally. Sunlight (due to thermonuclear reactions in the sun).	Sunlight is focused upon a molten salt or some other medium. The medium transfers the heat to boil water to produce electricity in the same manner as when fossil fuels are used.	The energy is free and very abundant. No air pollution. Even today, solar house heating might be cheaper then electric heating in the United States.	Even though desert, very large areas of land would be required to absorb enough sunlight to be practical for large-scale use. Solar power is impractical in climates that are not sunny. It may affect climate adversely and create thermal water pollution.

*We have omitted some sources of power that are unlikely to have a major impact, such as windmills, tidal generators, and hydroelectric power.
†Using uranium as a raw material, breeder reactors make more fuel than they consume.

PART II: CAUSES AND CONSEQUENCES

SOCIOLOGICAL LEVEL

In this section our main focus will be on the role played by various macrostructures and institutions (which we inhabit) in creating and sustaining various ecological problems. This is not to absolve individuals who commit innumerable ecological crimes. However, the view here is that most of these individual acts are traceable to larger structural and cultural causes. We will begin with a discussion of some of the major macrolevel causes and then turn, more briefly, to some of the individual physiological causes and effects of ecological problems. We begin with five main macrolevel causes of ecological difficulties—population growth, technology, urbanization, the capitalist economic system, and cultural values.

Population Growth

Nowhere are the consequences of population growth so profoundly felt as in the ecological system. Through their sheer numbers, humans are having an unprecedented impact on life-support systems. Furthermore, the economic growth required to sustain such numbers has greatly amplified this impact. With previously undreamed-of power billions more people are now acting upon nature to alter and even destroy it.

Neo-Malthusian Pessimism

Of the many social scientists concerned with the ecological problems of continued population and economic growth, those taking the gloomiest view of the future are often called *neo-Malthusians.* The name indicates that they hold updated but similar views to those of Thomas Malthus, who, as we saw in the previous chapter, believed that human populations tended to expand rapidly but were periodically checked by disease and famine.

In more modern times, the human race seemed to have found the means to overcome this brutal fate. Some advanced nations, like the United States, have been able to slow population growth, but the major advances have been made by overcoming the harsh checks on the human race. We conquered plagues and greatly reduced mortality. And we developed the means to produce food in incredible amounts. The neo-Malthusians argue, however, that the age-old checks of famine and disease still await us. Rather than removing these natural checks on growth, we merely raised them to a much higher level or postponed them for a longer time.

The Club of Rome

The most prominent group of neo-Malthusian scientists is the *Club of Rome,* which is devoted to studying the interplay of economic, political, natural, and social factors on a global scale.[40] One of their computer models shows that if present growth trends continue,[41] resources will soon become inadequate to maintain industrial output; pollution will increase, further eroding our resources; and food production will decline for lack of fertilizers and other essential resources. These changes, the Club of Rome predicts, will gravely decrease the earth's capacity to support human life and will result in catastrophic famines and increases in disease. These effects will prompt the outbreak of social disorders. Thus, the population will be sharply reduced through the old, brutal Malthusian checks. Furthermore, *both* industrial and population growth must be cut back considerably if this grim future is to

Table 15.2 Levels of Analysis: Ecology

LEVELS	APPROPRIATE QUESTIONS	A PARTIAL SYNOPSIS OF PRESENT CONCLUSIONS
SOCIOLOGICAL	How does population growth affect ecological problems?	In general, the larger the number of people, the more negative the effect on the ecological system. Some effects of overpopulation are depleted resources, inadequate food supplies, rising carbon dioxide levels, and more ozone depletion.
	How does the interaction of technology and population growth affect ecological problems?	Large populations tend to require technologies that are more likely to be harmful to the environment.
	Are many modern ecological problems traceable to technological advances?	Yes. There are many examples including acid rain, dangerous pesticides, the risk of nuclear accidents, and chemical pollution.
	How does urbanization affect the environment?	The high population density of cities tends to place a great strain on the ecosystem.
	What is the relationship between capitalism and ecological problems?	There is a danger in the capitalist system that the need to be competitive forces the capitalist to take actions (for example, the development of energy-intensive technologies) that serve to heighten the damage to the environment.
	Given the ecological problems attendant to capitalism, does the answer lie in moving toward a socialist alternative?	Socialist countries have not done a much better job of protecting the environment. In fact, the source of the problem may be industrialization, which is common to both modern capitalist and socialist societies.
	What American cultural values contribute to our ecological problems?	Among the American values that contribute to actions that adversely affect the environment are dominating nature, progress, and materialism.

(Continued)

Table 15.2 Levels of Analysis: Ecology (*Continued*)

LEVELS	APPROPRIATE QUESTIONS	A PARTIAL SYNOPSIS OF PRESENT CONCLUSIONS
INDIVIDUAL	Is the individual best seen as a cause of ecological problems, or as the victim of ecological problems caused by larger structural and causal forces?	The individual is largely the victim of ecological problems caused by macrolevel forces.
	What is the "tragedy of the commons" and how does it relate to ecological problems?	Most people take actions that work to their personal advantage even though those actions may work to the (ecological) detriment of the group as a whole. To put it another way, the individual's gain from helping to solve the (ecological) problem would be less than he/she would stand to lose by changing his/her behavior.
	What is the impact of various ecological problems on individual health?	There is a long list of health problems asssociated with ecological problems, including hunger, cancer, emphysema, and birth defects.

be averted. Unchecked, either form of growth will produce the predicted collapse of the world system.

Not only do many scholars accept the basic conclusions of the Club of Rome's pessimistic model,[42] but so, at least implicitly, does a large segment of the American public. This is best summarized in a report by Daniel Yankelovich and Bernard Lefkowitz on their survey of a wide variety of studies of American attitudes.[43] Their basic conclusion is that Americans are in the process of changing from post-World War II optimism to a much more pessimistic, apprehensive, and limited conception of the future.

Not everyone accepts the grim predictions of the Club of Rome. For example, a group of British scientists argued that the main reason the Club of Rome model projects a collapse of the world system is that it assumes resources will be depleted.[44] But, the British group argues, past history has shown that new resources are continually being discovered and that technologies for developing such resources are constantly being improved. Thus, there is no reason to assume that resources will soon be depleted. It seems more likely, the British group argues, that exploration and scientific discoveries will continue to keep resources growing faster than the population, thereby preventing the Malthusian catastrophe.

This challenge to the assumption that resources will not continue to outstrip population growth was severely hurt by the world-wide energy crises of the 1970s. This demonstrated the difficulty of assuming that the future will simply resemble a continuation of the past. The fact that for the past one hundred years we have been able to develop new resources faster than we have depleted the old ones does not prove that we will continue to be able to do so. Any lag in new scientific breakthroughs or a decline in new natural resource discoveries would justify the Club of Rome's projection of a decline in resources.

The Global 2000 Report

Although somewhat more muted, a more recent, U.S. government report, *The Global 2000 Report to the President,* like the Club of Rome report, comes to a pessimistic conclusion about the demographic, ecological, and economic future of the world.[45] It foresees burgeoning populations, especially in developing nations, while increases in income will generally fail to keep pace with the population explosion. The result will be a worsening situation in developing countries and an increasing gap between the rich and poor nations. Food production is projected to increase, but not enough to be of much help in the poorest nations. Among other things, the report also anticipates significant deforestation, water shortages, increasing strain on energy sources, growing problems traceable to rising carbon dioxide levels, more ozone depletion, and the like. What makes the report so striking is that the authors themselves feel that it has an optimistic bias; it *underestimates* the dimensions of the population and ecological problems.

Population and Technology

We turn next to the role of technology in causing ecological problems, but before we do the point should be made that population and technology are often seen as *competing* explanations of ecological problems. While people like Paul Ehrlich and John Holdren focus on the role of population,[46] others like Barry Commoner, Michael Corr, and Paul Stamler argue that "the predominant factor in our industrial society's increased environmental degradation is neither population nor affluence, but . . . technological changes."[47] While there is much merit in both positions, the view adopted here is that population growth and technology should be seen as *interacting* causes of ecological problems. The fact is that there is a tendency for larger populations to require technologies that not only require more energy, but are also likely to be more harmful to the environment. For example, the greater demands on agriculture lead to the need not only for more energy to produce the food, but also the greater use of highly destructive pesticides. For another example, the greater need of a larger population for energy leads to a move away from relatively scarce petroleum and in the direction of the increased use of polluting coal and dangerous nuclear energy.

Technology

Many of the ecological disasters discussed early in this chapter are traceable, at least in part, to modern technology. Acid rain is traceable to modern factories and to the newer and higher smokestacks that were supposed to reduce pollution. The near-disaster at Three Mile Island, and the continuing danger of nuclear accidents, is traceable to modern nuclear technology. The Love Canal and Times Beach, Missouri, were abandoned because of modern chemicals, especially dioxin. The killer fog in London in December, 1952, in which more than 5,000 people died,[48] and the smog associated with, but not restricted to, Los Angeles are traceable to modern means of transportation and manufacture.

It would be accurate to say that some of these problems were the result of ignorance—human ignorance of the complexity of ecological systems. Back in the 1950s, there was much less awareness of these potential dangers. Rachel Carson, in her book *Silent Spring*, was one of the first to alert the public to the ecological dangers posed by modern technology. However, Carson did not warn against technological change per se, but attacked its indiscriminate use.

In the years since *Silent Spring*, ecologists have increasingly turned their attention to the unanticipated consequences of new technologies. Barry Commoner has provided a good overview of the ecological problems caused by indiscriminate application of new production technologies:

> New production technologies have replaced old ones. Soap powder has been displaced by synthetic detergents; natural fibers (cotton and wool) have been displaced by synthetic ones; steel and lumber have been displaced by aluminum, plastics and concrete; railroad freight has been displaced by truck freight; returnable bottles have been displaced by nonreturnable ones . . . . On the farm . . . fertilizer has displaced land. Older methods of insect control have been displaced by synthetic insecticides, such as DDT, and for controlling weeds the cultivator has been displaced by the herbicide spray. Range-feeding of livestock has been displaced by feedlots.[49]

Each of the technologies that Commoner reviews has contributed to the affluence of the American population, and many have come to be considered necessities of the American style of life. But feedlots for the increased production of beef also greatly concentrate animal waste, and consequently the nitrate runoff, in local streams. Synthetics such as nylon and plastic require large investments of energy and do not degrade back into the ecosphere. An entire continent has been bulldozed and graded to allow for comfortable travel in private automobiles, which creates pollution.

While technology clearly causes ecological problems, this does not mean that we ought to do away with it. The problem of technology is not so much in its products or its methods as in the cultural process whereby they are applied. This has led to the nearsighted application of a solution to a problem without regard for its effects outside a narrow set of goals. Clearly, we need to do a better job of understanding the ecological effects of technological changes and preventing their worst effects.

Up to this point, we have discussed the two causes of ecological damage that are most frequently cited by those outside of the social sciences—population growth and technology. However, it is the contribution of sociology (and other social sciences) that there are other aspects of society that may be as important, or even more important, causes than population and technology. It is to some of these that we now turn.

Urbanization

Many with deep concerns about the ecology of the earth are inclined to place the blame for present problems upon city life. The basic view is that the high density of the urban population places enormous strains on the ecosystem. A few million people spread across a Rocky Mountain state have much less of an impact on the environment than the same number of people crammed into Manhattan. Thus, the basic problem in the cities is not population per se, but population density and the resulting increased intensity of all sorts of activities that serve to affect the environment adversely.[50]

Although there are few who would dispute the negative effect of large numbers of people in small urban areas, there are disputes over what is wrong with cities as well as the alternatives to them. One of these might be called the *nostalgia view.* It pines for a return to a simple life style patterned after the ways of simple horticultural people. According to this view, humans went wrong when they lost personal touch with nature and the natural life, and they must once again learn to live in close harmony with nature. The second school might be called the *humane-city approach.* It takes for granted the necessity for large-scale technical societies and is concerned to structure modern cities to make them more habitable and less ecologically harmful. It will be clear that the second view has more merit, although it might be possible to live in the city *and* remain close to nature.

The Nostalgic View

In this view, the problems of modern society have led to romantic recollections of the past. This view is especially pronounced in the comparisons some people make between environmental problems of contemporary life and the more natural relationship of simple societies to their environments. It is true that horticultural societies and hunting-and-gathering bands lived at the top of an elementary natural food chain, subsisting on animal and plant life. Thus, the natural order of things influenced their way of life more than they influenced the plant and animal world. However, it is not at all clear that such groups had less profound environmental impact because they were "in tune" with nature and more respectful of it. It seems more to the point to say that simple societies lacked the numbers and the technological capacity to damage nature more than they did.

In fact, anthropological and archaeological evidence suggests that agricultural methods used by inhabitants of simpler societies were often destructive of the natural environment. Centuries ago, primitive tribes in New Zealand and Africa slashed and burned to clear fields and then moved on when the land fell unproductive after several growing seasons.[51] The huge denuded tracts of land eroded, the forests never returned. Indeed, it was not modern society that in Biblical times chopped down the forests of the Middle East and turned the area into an arid waste.

The point is not to blame simpler societies for being hard on the environment but to realize that *human culture is not natural* (in the sense that animal life is). Human culture involves the ability to act upon nature, to shape and modify it in ways that enhance the prospects of human existence. The nostalgia for simpler life styles is actually a rejection of human culture. From the day the first human used a club to increase the power of his blows, humans were no longer natural. A true return to nature would necessitate giving up all inventions, including fire and digging sticks, and returning to a life like that of the wild chimpanzee. For anything short of that is only a question of degree—how much and what kind of culture—for all culture is unnatural.

Some versions of the nostalgia for simpler times, especially popular in the late 1960s and early 1970s, advocate a return to rural subsistence farming, to rural communes. But such a way of life is hardly a sensible alternative for large numbers of people to the problems of modern times. Given today's huge number of people, returning to such a primitive way of life is either fantasy or nightmare. It is a fantasy to think a simple agricultural life is possible, given present population size. Even if it were possible, the return to such a life would be a nightmare; it could be purchased only at the cost of billions of lives—for only a fragment of the population could be supported by a nonindustrial economy. We cannot learn how to preserve our economy by simply copying simple societies. Their people know less about the problem than we do. Modern people must solve this modern ecological crisis for themselves. That means finding modern solutions, although as we will see later in the chapter, some of these modern solutions may involve adopting smaller-scale technologies.

The Humane-City View

If rural communes or other attempts to return to the simple life are not solutions to our present problems, it is nonetheless clear that modern urban life creates social problems. To paraphrase the great architect, Frank Lloyd Wright, if the salvation of civilization requires that we raze the cities, then the prospects for civilization are dim indeed. We cannot abandon city life. Our only alternative is to modify it and make it more humane.

Changing the cities is the primary aim of modern urban architects and planners. Urban ecologists have begun a battle to bring nature back into the cities, through the preservation, creation, and effective use of open space. Other social engineers and planners are trying to design cities in ways that make them less vulnerable to congestion and decay. While changing the cities is the goal in the industrialized nations, preventing cities from becoming the center of ecological disaster is the goal in nonindustrialized countries. Urbanization is just beginning to occur on a broad scale in these nations and the objective is to avoid ecologically disastrous and totally artificial environments for the people. But unless Third-World nations attain the capital necessary for city planning and economic and social development, increasing numbers of urban dwellers will be forced to live in desperate urban squalor.

Capitalism

Since the United States is characterized by a capitalist economic system *and* by a number of severe ecological problems (among them, smog, toxic wastes, and acid rain), a linkage is often made between the two. That is, there is a belief that the capitalist economic system is a significant cause of ecological difficulties.[52] Charles Anderson states this in very wide-ranging terms: "advanced capitalism [i]s a form of social organization [that] is incompatible with human viability upon the earth."[53] This perspective is particularly characteristic of a number of Marxist social scientists. The thrust of their argument is that capitalists focus almost exclusively on increasing the size of their business and their profits. This means that they will take any and all actions that increase profits with little consideration for peripheral matters such as the impact of those actions on the environment. For their part, the consumers in the American capitalistic economy have developed a life style that leads them to use too much energy, consume too much of the earth's wealth, and litter their country with debris. This propensity to consume is slavishly fostered by the capitalists who find in it the route to higher and higher profits.

The Treadmill of Production

Along the same lines of explanation, but somewhat more specific, is Allan Schnaiberg's idea of the "treadmill of production" within capitalist society.[54] In brief, the *treadmill of production* operates in the following manner: Workers are forced to sell their labor time in order to earn enough income to satisy their consumption needs. For their part, the capitalists, in order to create profits for themselves and employment and income for their employees, are driven to create and expand production.

However, over time, the capitalist is forced by the need to keep up with competitors to replace workers with more efficient advanced technologies. In order to keep an adequate supply of consumers for their goods, capitalists must also create new jobs for the growing population, as well as for the people laid off as a result of technological advances. Production continues to expand, and this, in turn, yields more profits to the capitalist. These higher profits are, as before, plowed back into the enterprise in the form of still more advanced technologies. This, in turn, leads to expanded production that must be consumed by new consumers and/or more highly paid workers. The imagery of a treadmill makes it clear that both capitalists and workers are *forced* into various actions by the operation of the system. It is the basic process of competition within capitalism that is the main motor force of this treadmill. The speed of the treadmill picks up as capitalism develops, with the result that there is more and more damage to the environment. The quest for more production and higher profits leads capitalists to substitute energy-intensive (and typically heavily polluting) technologies for labor, with increasingly negative effects on the ecosystem. Thus, Schnaiberg, following Marx, places the blame for these problems on the system and not on the greed and insensitivity of individual capitalists. To put it in reverse, the altruistic capitalist who is sensitive to the environment would quickly be driven out of business by the dynamics of the capitalist system.

The Socialist Alternative

The records of most existing socialist countries are not noticeably better than that of the United States. Whatever their ideology or their economic organization, all nations, as they undergo industrialization, seem to impose the same blight upon life-support systems. Thus a number of rivers in the Soviet Union are terribly polluted by wastes from factories along their banks. Eastern European industrial cities are plagued by smoke and dust in their air, and oil on the Caspian and Black seas has seriously threatened the fishing and tourism industries there. Of course, one might argue that none of the contemporary socialist countries lives up to the ideal of socialism, but that argument would equally apply to contemporary capitalist nations. Although, in theory, the ideal socialist society is supposed to inflict less damage on the environment than one run on the principles of capitalism, the problems encountered in both types of societies are quite similar.[55] Thus, it seems difficult to argue that capitalism in itself is a distinctive cause of ecological problems. Rather, the major factor seems to be the industrialization that is characteristic of *both* contemporary capitalism *and* socialism.[56]

Cultural Values

We turn now to the role played by the American value system in the creation of a wide range of ecological problems. Although we will focus on American values, it should be made clear that these values predate American society and have long been characteristic of the Western world.[57] William Catton and Riley Dunlap define this *dominant Western world view* in terms of people feeling separate from and somehow above nature.[58] In more recent years, this has developed into an arrogance toward nature. Thus, it could well be argued that the dominant Western view has become anti-ecological and that is nowhere more true than in the United States.

Let us look at some of the specific dimensions of American culture that are in line with this anti-ecological perspective. For example, rather than living in harmony with nature or submitting to nature, Americans have placed the most value on *overcoming or dominating nature.* It has long been said, with some pride, that Americans came from other lands and "tamed the continent." They did not leave the land as they found it; they transformed it. Relatedly, we have placed a high value on *progress.* Americans tend to believe that there should be progressive improvement in the life of their society and that the future should hold still further improvement.[59] Usually progress means greater technological success in creating machines, buildings, communications systems, and so on. It is only in the last few years that some people have begun to question the ideas of "bigger and better" and "upward and onward."[60] *Materialism* is also an important American value. People want more and more things and believe their right to have them grows out of their ability to wrest them from the environment. These and other American values combine to lead Americans to exploit and ultimately abuse their environment with little or no regard for negative ecological effects. The fact is that as a culture we regard progress, material goods, and control over nature as far more important than we do the ideal of living in harmony with nature. We have only begun in recent decades to deal with ecological problems because we have been forced to do so. That is, the ecological problems that we created have begun to threaten our health and even our lives with the result that we have been reluctantly forced to address them. However, we still do not place much of a positive value on a healthy and thriving environment. Were we to have such a value, we would do much more to prevent and solve ecological problems than we are now doing. Thus, a significant factor in ecological difficulties is our value system, and major changes await a reordering of that value system. Until such a reordering occurs, we are likely to do little more than respond to each ecological crisis as it arises.

INDIVIDUAL LEVEL

Most of this part of the chapter has been devoted to the macrolevel causes of ecological problems—population growth, technology, urbanization, capitalism, and cultural values. The individual is seen as being impelled by these forces to behave in ways that are destructive of the environment. Although the individual is largely a victim of these larger structural and institutional forces, it would be wrong to absolve individuals of all responsibility. Ultimately, we all are reckless of our environment in innumerable ways. We litter the countryside, we keep our houses too cool (or too hot), we use too many appliances, we drive more than we need to, we eat more than we have to and we eat many of the wrong things, and we do little about the ecological damage that surrounds us. Thus individuals play a *causal* role in ecological problems and they can act to reduce those problems.

The Tragedy of the Commons

One of the best explanations of the role individuals play in the destruction of the environment is the so-called *tragedy of the commons.*[61] In general, an individual is driven to take those actions that work to his/her advantage, even if those actions work to the detriment of that which the group as a whole has in common. The individual gets to keep all of the gains from his/her personal actions while the negative effects are shared by everyone. This idea can be applied to a number of areas including damage to the ecosystem. Most generally, workers and capitalists engage in a variety of actions that serve to profit them even though they may hurt the environment. Each worker and capitalist gets to keep all of their personal gains while the damage they do to the environment is shared with everyone in society. Thus, they are unwilling to give up their personal gains for their small proportion of the gain that would accrue to the collectivity were they to give up, or change, their actions.

The majority of Americans are very materialistic and consumption-oriented. They are enjoying a variety of benefits that they are reluctant to surrender. They are, however, also very conscious of the negative impact many of their actions are having on the environment. However, when they think about acting to stop these actions, they find themselves in the "commons dilemma." That is, they would have to give up a series of very personally profitable actions in order to solve a problem that impacts on everyone. Their gain from helping solve the problem is far less than what they stand to lose. Thus, the "tragedy of the commons" helps us understand why individuals damage the environment and why they continue to inflict that damage knowingly.

Impact on Individual Health

However, it is our main contention that individuals are far better seen as victims of larger structural forces than they are as causes of our ecological woes. To illustrate this we will briefly review a few of the adverse effects on individual physiology caused by ecological problems.

The single best source on the issue of environmental threats to individual health is Erik Eckholm's *The Picture of Health.*[62] We cannot and need not go into all of the details in Eckholm's work, but we can enumerate just a few of the health problems produced by environmental problems:

- Famine leads to undernutrition and ultimately starvation, mainly among the poor members of less developed countries.
- Deficiency in vitamin A is the leading cause of childhood blindness in many developing countries.
- The affluent diet in industrialized Western nations has led to increased incidences of such diseases as coronary heart disease, diabetes, and bowel cancer.
- Chest cancer has been linked to the inhaling of asbestos fibers.
- The depletion of the ozone layer is likely to increase the rate of skin cancer attributable to sunlight.
- Cancer has been linked to exposure to radioactivity from various sources, including nuclear weapons and power plants.
- An estrogen, DES, given to mothers beginning in the 1940s has been linked to vaginal cancer in their daughters.
- Tobacco smoke has been linked to cancer and other diseases in smokers *and* those who live with smokers.
- Air pollution from cars and industries seems to be related to emphysema.
- Vietnam veterans exposed to Agent Orange claim that they are suffering from higher rates of such diseases as cancer and neurological problems, as well as birth defects in their children.

To be fair, not all of the linkages between environmental problems and health have been proven scientifically. In many cases it is difficult to unravel relationships between exposure and disease. Among other things, many years are likely to pass between exposure and contraction of disease and in the interim the individual has undoubtedly been exposed to many other potentially hazardous elements. Nevertheless, it seems safe to say that future research is far more likely to uncover links between environment and disease than it is to disprove such relationships.

The focus throughout this section has been mainly on the large-scale causes of ecological problems. Although each of them has been discussed separately, it is important to reiterate the point that all of these causes are interrelated.[63] Thus, we do not accept the views of those who argue for the overriding importance of one or another of these causes. In trying to cope with ecological problems, it would be best to address all of these causal factors by, for example, reducing population growth, using technologies that are less destructive of the environment, discouraging increasing urban population concentrations, regulating the excesses of the industrial world, altering some of our most basic beliefs, and trying to encourage pro-ecological behavior among individuals.

PART III: RESPONSES

Preservation and Conservation

Concern for the natural environment has always been a minority position in the United States. As we have seen, ours is a culture in which the themes of mastery over nature and the transformation of the earth by an industrious citizenry have been extremely powerful values. For generations our people have reveled in the seemingly inexhaustible bounty of the land. The defenders of nature have always had tough going against this cultural grain. Nevertheless, the large-scale destruction of the nation's forests and wildlife and the massive land-grabs of the Industrial Revolution were never without their critics. The contemporary environmental movement in the United States has its origin in the *preservationist* philosophies and politics of early nineteenth-century intellectuals such as John James Audubon and James Fenimore Cooper.[64] These advocates of the natural environment focused their attention particularly on the goal of preserving tracts of wilderness to ensure for future generations the experience of virgin forests and undeveloped natural vistas. The nineteenth-century preservationist movement did achieve many of its goals. For example, the National Parks and many of the state park systems in the United States and Canada would probably not have been created without the intervention of these preservationists against the land developers and forest exploiters.[65] In the period between the two World Wars, however, the movement waned. Until the 1960s environmental-action groups tended to remain scattered and weak; their influence in the halls of government was generally uncertain. On the other hand, the Great Depression did bring new levels of awareness of environmental problems in rural America. The severe problems of erosion, drought, and dust-bowl formation in the late 1920s and early 1930s produced *conservationist* policies in the New Deal administrations of Franklin Roosevelt. In response to the grinding poverty of large sections of the nation, where decay of the environment was depriving millions of rural people of their livelihoods, the federal government created the Civilian Conservation Corps and instituted other land improvement measures on a scale that had never been attempted before in this country.

TVA

The culmination of the conservationist movement in the New Deal era was the creation of the Tennessee Valley Authority (TVA) in 1933.[66] Originally designed to provide flood control and electrical power to the rural inhabitants of the Tennessee River basin, the project became the model of the articulation of developmental and conservationist goals through federal intervention in regional planning. It included efforts to control floods, soil erosion, and afforestation, as well as the elimination from agricultural use of marginal lands and the diversification of industry. Although the project remains the nation's greatest experiment in regional development and grassroots planning, many of its lofty goals appear to have been subverted. For example, local communities seemingly grew less involved in project decisions. Although extremely important, one lesson of TVA and other governmental efforts is that the environmental movement should be wary of putting too much faith in governmental commissions.

The 1960s and 1970s

From 1960 to 1970, the environmental movement in the United States experienced a period of marked growth and enthusiasm that was stimulated by the increasing visibility of pollution and environmental decay in the cities, which gave the lie to the unprecedented affluence of the period. At the same time, the American public, more mobile than ever before after the steep increase in automobile sales after World War II, set out in cars to experience for itself the grandeur of the continent. Visits to state and national parks increased dramatically, and while the amount of park land increased, it did not come close to keeping pace with the increase in visits. As a result, people who saw the parks for the first time were likely to see "a crowded and semiurbanized environment."[67] Some needed little more than a frustrating visit to an overcrowded park to convince them that this country had little open and usable space left.

The environmental groups that expanded during this period (for example, the Wilderness Society, the Sierra Club, and the Audubon Society) were primarily middle class with a commitment to the protection of wilderness and wildlife, but often neglectful of the problems of the poor, the city bound, and those in underdeveloped nations, for whom economic development is the saving hope.[68] Although some effort was made to broaden their interests and their constituency, the environmental groups remain largely middle class in orientation.

As was true of many other social issues, the late 1960s and early 1970s marked a heightening of interest in ecological issues. Earth Day 1970, a nationwide observance of concern for the environment by university students, environmental groups, the mass media, and political leaders throughout the nation, was a central event in the growth of the environmental movement in the United States and throughout the world. For the first time in its history, the Gallup Poll in 1970 recorded "the environment" among the country's major problems. The 1970s marked a decade of considerable public and governmental concern with environmental issues.

In response to intense political pressure from many segments of society, Congress passed a series of environmental measures. These included the Clean Air and Water Act (1968) and the National Environmental Protection Act (NEPA, 1970), which established the Council on Environmental Quality. NEPA also established the procedures for environmental review by requiring Environmental Impact Statements for all projects involving the use of federal lands and federal funds. Parallel legislation was passed in most states and some, such as Oregon and Vermont, passed even more stringent controls over the packaging industry to ensure the recycling of bottles and cans. Environmental law became firmly established in the nation's law schools, and the membership lists of the Sierra Club, the National Wildlife Federation, and the Audubon Society, as well as ecology action groups, swelled as never before. These groups exerted considerable power in society as exemplified by their successful effort to force the government into shelving plans to build a supersonic transport plane.

However, events of the early 1970s, especially the oil crisis, seemed to overtake the environmental movement very quickly. As people struggled to find gasoline to commute to their jobs, legislators throughout the nation hurried to suspend environmental standards. Congress passed emergency legislation to construct the Alaska pipeline, although few congressmen were confident that the environmental impact of the project on the delicate tundra of the North Slope had been adequately assessed. In spite of such setbacks as these, the environmental movement survived the 1970s only to face an even greater challenge in the 1980s in the form of the Reagan administration and its Department of the Interior.[69]

The 1980s

The conservative Reagan administration came into power in 1980 with the belief that it had a broad mandate to cut back on federal involvement in environmental protection. In addition, it operated with the view that concern for the environment had gone too far and was having an adverse effect on various businesses and on the economy as a whole. The Reagan administration argued for a better balance of economic and environmental interests, although many felt that it tilted in the direction of the interests of big business. In any case, it came into power with an orientation that stood in direct opposition to the momentum that had built up over the previous decade for greater federal involvement in coping with ecological problems. Reflecting his desire to change direction, President Reagan appointed conservative James Watt as Secretary of the Interior. Reagan's first Secretary of the Interior believed that the Department had been biased in favor of "blind preservation" and against the interests of business. One of the Secretary's first acts was a highly symbolic turning of the bison on the department's seal so that it faced right rather than left. Many of the department's later acts were true to the symbolism as it freed large amounts of land for oil, gas, coal, and geothermal exploration; relaxed strip mining controls; streamlined rules on environmental impact statements; almost completely halted national park acquisitions; sought to sell off government lands; tried (but failed) to open wilderness land to oil and gas exploration; and proposed to release the entire outer continental shelf of the United States for offshore oil drilling.

The EPA

Also characterizing the early 1980s were changes in the Environmental Protection Agency (EPA). The EPA had been set up in 1970 and over the years had developed the following as its basic mission:

> To enforce federal laws to control and abate pollution of oil and water, solid waste, noise, radiation and toxic substances; administer the Superfund for cleaning up abandoned waste sites, and award grants for local sewage-treatment plants.[70]

During the Carter administration (1976–1980), the EPA had been staffed by people dedicated to protecting the environment even if their actions had an adverse effect on business. The EPA was, needless to say, very active during those years. When President Reagan took office he began replacing Carter appointees with those committed to turning responsibility for the environment back to local communities and industry. In a short period of time, the director of EPA had "demolish[ed] the nation's environmental management capacity."[71] There was a significant drop in the number of cases handled by EPA as well as in its budget. Finally, EPA was rocked by a scandal which, among other things, made it clear that it was not fulfilling its mandate to protect the nation's environment.

The Courts

However, there is more to the environmental movement than the federal government. The courts at various levels have made a series of decisions that at times have furthered the interests of the environment, while at other times their decisions have cut the other way.[72] One can anticipate a continuation of important judicial decisions in coming years. However, in the early 1980s there was a shift in the relationship between the federal government and the courts. In the 1970s, the EPA tended to initiate legal action, while in the early 1980s there was a decline in government-initiated litigation. In response, it is likely that various environmental groups will take up the slack and initiate more court action. Although the impetus may be different, the courts will continue to be very involved in environmental matters.

Social Movements

Another important response to environmental problems has been a variety of social movements. We can get a feel for the importance of these movements by examining the specific cases of the pro- and anti-nuclear power social movements.

Bert Useem and Mayer Zald are concerned with the development of the pro-nuclear power social movement.[73] Most social movements begin outside the political structure and, if they are successful, become a pressure group *within* that structure. However, the pro-nuclear power movement is unusual in that it followed the opposite course of losing power within the government and then forming a social movement in an effort to regain that power.

In the 1960s and into the 1970s the pro-nuclear power group exerted considerable influence on government policy, and it pushed it in the direction of expanding nuclear power. However, during this period an anti-nuclear power movement developed and gained considerable momentum. Useem and Zald define this movement as "the organized, collective effort that tried to stop the use of nuclear fission to generate electricity, by closing down existing plants, halting the construction of new plants, and implementing strict safety standards for the disposal of radioactive waste and the operation of nuclear reactors."[74] In reaction, at least in part, to this movement, the government began to lose its enthusiasm for the nuclear industry as is reflected in such things as stricter safety regulations, tightened environmental restraints and, since 1977, a moratorium on the building of new nuclear plants. As it lost its influence over government policy, the pro-nuclear group moved toward two distinct social movements, one based in industry and the other in local communities. In other words, a pro-nuclear power social movement emerged as a countermovement in response to the success of the anti-nuclear movement. Although the pro-nuclear power social movement had some successes, it was ultimately unable to stem the tide running against the nuclear industry.

While Useem and Zald are concerned with the pro- and anti-nuclear power social

cial movements on a national level, Edward Walsh is interested in the rise of a more local anti-nuclear social movement in the wake of the 1979 accident at the nuclear plant at Three Mile Island in Pennsylvania.[75] This is an unusual social movement in that it was neither created by marginal members of society, nor was it the product of a series of long-simmering grievances. Instead, it was precipitated virtually overnight in previously conservative middle-class communities surrounding Three Mile Island. Many of these people had been evacuated immediately following the accident. When they returned home, the residents found the threat of a badly damaged reactor that had come very close to a meltdown, large amounts of radioactive water and gas in the reactor in need of cleanup, and a company that was anxious to get its remaining undamaged reactor on-line as soon as possible. Although there were some anti-nuclear organizations in place in the area prior to the accident, the social movement exploded almost immediately after it and the area came to be described as a "hotbed of activism."[76] This activism was kept alive by continuing efforts to open the undamaged reactor and to clean up the damaged one. The local movement has also been aided by the existence of the national anti-nuclear power social movement.

The point here is that social movements at a national and a more local level represent a continuing method of responding to ecological problems. In addition to the scope of their operations, these movements differ in whether they are long-standing responses to long-running problems, or whether they develop rapidly as a result of ecological crises.

The Future

It is clear that our ecological problems are not going to disappear on their own. In fact, left alone, existing problems are likely to increase and new ones will come to the fore. What can be done? At one level, it is clear that it is going to take considerable effort at the national and international levels. Many ecological problems affect large portions of the United States, as well as many other parts of the world. Some ecological problems (for example, the deterioration of the ozone layer) are truly international. Solutions therefore require governmental and legislative efforts that are national and international in scope. Furthermore, money, lots of money, is required. Thus, at the national level, government interest, laws, and money are needed, but more is obviously needed than efforts by the federal government.

Changing Values

At another level, we need a reorientation of American culture, a reorientation that may already be underway. Basically, we need to move away from a system that values things growing constantly bigger and better. We are no longer able to master and subdue all that surrounds us. Rather, we must learn to live more harmoniously with our environment. We need to learn to value and protect our environment rather than seeing it as something to be exploited, raped, and despoiled. Most importantly, we need to accept the idea that we are approaching the limits of what the environment can yield to us. At best, we can expect a steady state, at worst a marked decline in our style of life. Rather than valuing an ever-growing society, we have to accept what Lester Brown calls a "sustainable society."[77] We need, in other words, to focus on, and invest in, resources that we can renew rather than the current propensity to exploit such nonrenewable resources as coal and oil.

Changing Technology

Finally, we need to say a word about technology. There is a tendency to look to-

The anti-nuclear movement was mobilized by the 1979 accident at the Three Mile Island reactor in Pennsylvania.

(Jim McHugh/Sygma)

ward science to provide us with an elaborate new technology that can solve all our problems, or at least the problems that exist within a specific domain, in a single stroke. With the coming decline of coal and oil, there was a tendency to look to nuclear energy as the technological solution to the problem. However, our recent history has indicated that nuclear energy is not only not the answer, but may be another, even greater, problem. Thus, many observers have argued that we should move away from looking for solutions in such grand, and potentially dangerous, technologies.

The alternative has come to have a variety of labels, including the search for *appropriate,*[77] *soft,*[79] or *human*[80] technologies. Here is the way Denton Morrison describes the differences between the traditional hard technologies and the increasingly attractive soft technologies:

> The existing hard energy systems are based mainly on nonrenewable fuels (oil, natural gas, coal, uranium) and involve large-scale, complex, centralized social organization and hardware. In contrast, soft energy systems are based on renewable resources (the sun and its derivatives) and involve smaller-scale, simpler, less centralized social organization and hardware.[81]

In fact, Morrison sees a focus on soft technology as a key ingredient in the new softening, or increasing realism, of the environmental movement. Gone is the enthusiasm and radicalism of Earth Day and the environmental movement of the early 1970s. In its place is a more realistic environmental movement of the 1980s in which a focus is on the much humbler soft technologies and soft energy sources.

International Scope

Finally, it must be understood that environmental problems are not restricted to the borders of the United States; indeed, ecological problems are often international in scope. It matters very little that the inhabitants of North America and other highly modernized areas of the planet may be comfortable in a reasonably stable natural environment, if the majority of the world's people are suffering. The earth's life support systems know no international boundaries. People in the poor lands are tied by the tightest ecological bonds to people in rich lands. Pollution of the air and seas by industrialized countries adversely affects everyone. Conversely, poverty and starvation in the less developed nations impact on the industrialized nations and promise even greater effects in the future because of their ability to destabilize nations and ultimately international relations. Thus people in the United States must act to solve international ecological problems not only for the well-being of others, but ultimately for their own well-being.

SUMMARY

Part I: The Problem

1. Pollution of the *air* includes smog, increase in carbon dioxide levels, and depletion of the ozone layer.
2. Among the problems related to *water* are lack of an adequate water supply in a number of areas of the world, as well as various forms of pollution including thermal pollution, eutrophication, acid rain, and the dumping into the oceans of waste and oil.
3. On the *land* we discussed such problems as its poisoning with various chemicals, pesticides, garbage, and nuclear waste.
4. Among our *energy* problems are the emerging shortages of fossil fuels, as well as the various difficulties besetting the nuclear power industry.
5. Although we discussed problems associated with air, water, land, and energy separately, it must be remembered that they are all part of the *ecosystem.*

Part II: Causes and Consequences

6. One major cause of our ecological problems is the huge demands placed on the environment by the burgeoning *population.*
7. Large populations are likely to require advanced *technologies* that use large amounts of energy and are destructive of the environment.
8. The process of *urbanization* creates ecological problems by concentrating large numbers of people in limited areas.
9. *Capitalism* clearly causes serious ecological problems, but it appears that the *socialist* alternative constitutes little, if any, improvement.
10. The *culture* of America (and the Western world in general) encourages environmental problems because of its antiecological orientation.
11. Individuals cause ecological problems by, among other things, acting in their self-interest rather than the collective interest (i.e., "the tragedy of the commons").
12. People suffer a variety of adverse health consequences as a result of the range of ecological problems.

Part III: Responses

13. The roots of current efforts to respond to ecological problems can be found in past preservation and conservation movements.
14. The 1960s and 1970s were peak decades in the effort to clean up the environment.
15. The 1980s have been a decade of retrenchment in federal interest in dealing with ecological problems.
16. While the federal government has retrenched, the courts and a variety of social movements have taken over a more active role in dealing with ecological problems.
17. The future will require a change in the anti-ecological character of our culture and the development of alternative, more human technologies.

SUGGESTED READINGS

Carson, Rachel, *Silent Spring.* Boston: Houghton Mifflin, 1962. An important book in its day, which warned of the dangers of pesticides.

Catton, William R., Jr., *Overshoot: The Ecological Basis of Revolutionary Change.* Urbana: University of Illinois Press, 1980.

Commoner, Barry, *The Closing Circle.* New York: Knopf, 1971. Another classic work on ecological problems.

Humphrey, Craig R., and Frederick R. Buttel, *Environment, Energy and Society.* Belmont, Cal.: Wadsworth, 1982. A sound overview of ecological issues.

Schnaiberg, Allan, *The Environment: From Surplus to Scarcity.* New York: Oxford University Press, 1980. A useful, but difficult, recent analysis of ecological problems that has become known for its focus on the causal role played by the "treadmill of production" in capitalist society.

Schumacher, E. F., *Small Is Beautiful.* New York: Perennial Library, 1973. A cult classic in its day, which is now recognized for its championing of small and more human technologies.

FOOTNOTES

[1]William R. Catton, Jr., *Overshoot: The Ecological Basis of Revolutionary Change* (Urbana: University of Illinois Press, 1980).

[2]"The Poisoning of America," *Time,* September 22, 1980, pp. 58ff.

[3]"The Toxic-Waste Crisis," *Newsweek,* March 7, 1983, pp. 20–24.

[4]"Atomic Power: 40 Years Old and Under a Cloud," *U.S. News and World Report,* December 6, 1982, pp. 58–59.

[5]"Tough Decision for Tacoma," *Time,* July 25, 1983, p. 25.

[6]"India's Night of Death," *Time,* December 17, 1984, pp. 22–31.

[7]William Ophuls, *Ecology and the Politics of Scarcity* (San Francisco: Freeman, 1977), p. 29.

[8]*Ibid.* p. 43.

[9]Philip Nobile and John Deedy, eds., *The Complete Ecology Fact Book.* (Garden City, N.Y.: Doubleday, 1972).

[10]Louis J. Battan, *The Unclean Sky* (Garden City, N.Y.: Doubleday, 1966).

[11]"Cleaner Air and Water," *U.S. News and World Report,* February 28, 1983, p. 32.

[12]Melinda Cain, "Carbon Dioxide and the Climate: Monitoring and a Search for Understanding." In David A. Kay and Harold K. Jacobson, eds., *Environmental Protection: The International Dimension* (Totowa, N.J.: Allanheld, Osmun, 1983). pp. 75–100; G. M. Woodwell, "The Carbon Dioxide Question," *Scientific American,* 238 (1978), 34–43; Council on Environmental Quality, *Global Energy Futures and the Carbon Dioxide Problem* (Washington, D.C.: Council on Environmental Quality, 1981); Department of State, *The Global 2000 Report to the President* (Harmondsworth, England: Penguin, 1982).

[13]Woodwell, *op. cit.*

[14]*Ibid.*, p. 43.

[15]Thomas B. Stoel, "Fluorocarbons: Mobilizing Concern and Action." In Kay and Jacobson, eds., *op. cit.*, pp. 45–74, *Global 2000 Report, op. cit.*

[16]Bruce K. Ferguson, "Whither Water? The Fragile Future of the World's Most Important Resource," *The Futurist* (1983), 29–36.

[17]"Acid Rain, A Year Later," *Science* (July 5, 1983), 241–242; "Emission Control Will Control Acid Rain," *Science* (July 15, 1983), 254.

[18]"Acid Rain, A Year Later," *op. cit.*

[19]Cass Peterson, "The Border War Over Acid Rain," *The Washington Post*, September 27, 1982, p. A4.

[20]"Storm over a Deadly Downpour," *Time*, December 6, 1982, p. 84.

[21]*Ibid.*, p. 85.

[22]Robert McManus, "Ocean Dumping: Standards in Action." In Kay and Jacobson, eds., *op. cit.*, pp. 119–139.

[23]Alan B. Sielen and Robert J. McManus, "IMCO and the Politics of Ship Pollution." In Kay and Jacobson, eds., *op. cit.*, pp. 140–182.

[24]"Can the Sea Purge Itself?" *Newsweek*, August 31, 1981, p. 68.

[25]John Lawrence Hargrove and Janis Callison, "Soil Degradation: New Concerns but Uncertain Prospects." In Kay and Jacobson, eds., *op. cit.*, pp. 217–239.

[26]Rachel Carson, *Silent Spring* (Boston: Houghton Mifflin, 1962); Frank Graham, Jr., *Since Silent Spring* (Boston: Houghton Mifflin, 1970).

[27]Ward Sinclair, "America's Pesticide Use Raises New Safety Fears." *The Washington Post*, January 30, 1983, pp. A1, A8, A9.

[28]"Pesticides' Global Fallout," *Newsweek*, August 17, 1981, pp. 53, 55.

[29]*Ibid.*, p. 53.

[30]Arthur Purcell, *The Waste Watchers* (Garden City, N.Y.: Anchor, 1980), p. 10.

[31]S. Jacob Scherr, "Radioactive Waste Disposal: The Quest for a Solution." In Kay and Jacobson, eds., *op. cit.*, pp. 101–118.

[32]Walter Pincus, "Nuclear Waste Problem Just Keeps Growing," *The Washington Post*, October 26, 1981, p. A8.

[33]Scherr, *op. cit.*, p. 102.

[34]Harrison Brown, *The Challenge of Man's Future* (New York: Viking, 1954).

[35]Earl T. Hayes, "Energy Resources Available to the United States, 1985 to 2000," *Science* (January 19, 1979), pp. 233–239.

[36]Hubbert, cited in Craig R. Humphrey and Frederick R. Buttel, *Environment, Energy and Society* (Belmont, Cal.: Wadsworth, 1982), p. 143.

[37]Lester Brown, *Building a Sustainable Society* (New York: Norton, 1981); "Legacy of Three Mile Island," *Time*, March 24, 1980, pp. 58–62.

[38]Brown, *op. cit.*, pp. 73, 81.

[39]Barry Commoner, *The Closing Circle* (New York: Knopf, 1971).

[40]Donella and Dennis Meadows *et al.*, *The Limits of Growth* (New York: Signet, 1972).

[41]On the other hand, if present population and industrialization levels are stabilized, the Club of Rome predicts a rosier future.

[42]For example, see Rufus E. Miles, *Awakening From The American Dream: The Social and Political Limits to Growth* (New York: Universe Books, 1976), p. 223.

[43]Daniel Yankelovich and Bernard Lefkowitz, "The Public Debate on Growth: Preparing for Resolution," *Technological Forecasting and Social Change*, 17 (1980), 95–140.

[44]H. S. D. Cole *et al.*, eds., *Models of Doom: A Critique of the Limits of Growth* (New York: Universe Books, 1973). For a summary of the debate around the Club of Rome report, see Humphrey and Buttel, *op. cit.*, Chapter 4.

[45]*The Global 2000 Report to the President, op. cit.*

[46]Paul Ehrlich and John P. Holdren, "Impact of Population Growth." In Parker G. Marden and Dennis Hodgson, eds., *Population, Environment, and the Quality of Life.* (New York: Wiley, 1975), pp. 40–50.

[47]Barry Commoner, Michael Corr, and Paul J. Stamler, "The Causes of Pollution." In Marden and Hodgson, eds., *op. cit.*, p. 67.

[48]Louis J. Batten, *The Unclean Sky* (Garden City, N.Y.: Doubleday, 1960).

[49]Commoner, *The Closing Circle, op. cit.*, p. 144.

[50]Amos H. Hawley, *Urban Society: An Ecological Approach* (New York: Ronald, 1971), p. 245.

[51]William Burch, *Daydreams and Nightmares* (New York: Harper & Row, 1971).

[52]Charles H. Anderson, *The Sociology of Survival: Social Problems of Growth* (Homewood, Ill.: Dorsey, 1976); Stephen Cotgrove, *Catastrophe and Cornucopia: The Environment, Politics and the Future* (Chichester, England: Wiley, 1982).

[53]Anderson, *op. cit.*, p. 6.

[54]Allan Schnaiberg, *The Environment: From Surplus to Scarcity* (New York: Oxford University Press, 1980).

[55]Robert Heilbroner, *An Inquiry Into the Human Prospect* (New York: Norton, 1974).

[56]Cotgrove, *op. cit.*

[57]Lynn White, Jr., "The Historical Roots of Our Ecologic Crisis," *Science*, 155 (1967), 1203–1207.

[58]William R. Catton, Jr. and Riley E. Dunlap, "A New Ecological Paradigm for Post-Exhuberant Sociology," *American Behavioral Scientist*, 24 (1980), 15–47.

[59]Miles, *op. cit.*

[60]E. F. Schumacher, *Small is Beautiful: Economics as if People Mattered* (New York: Harper & Row, 1976).

[61]Garrett Hardin, "The Tragedy of the Commons," *Science*, 162 (1968), 1243–1248.

[62]Erik P. Eckholm, *The Picture of Health* (New York: Norton, 1977).

[63]Lettie M. Wenner, *One Environment Under Law: A Public-Policy Dilemma* (Pacific Palisades, Cal.: Goodyear, 1976), p. 130; see also, Lettie M. Wenner, *The Environmental Decade in Court* (Bloomington: Indiana University Press, 1982).

[64]Roderick Nash, *Wilderness and the American Mind*, 3rd ed. (New Haven, Conn.: Yale University Press, 1967).

[65]David Potter, *People of Plenty* (Chicago: University of Chicago Press, 1954).

[66]Philip Selznick, *T.V.A. and the Grass Roots* (New York: Harper & Row Torchbooks, 1966).

[67]James McEvoy, "The American Concern with Environment." In William Burch, ed., *Social Behavior, Natural Resources and the Environment* (New York: Harper & Row, 1972).

[68]Craig R. Humphrey and Frederick R. Buttel, *op. cit.*, pp. 130ff.

[69]Bil Gilbert, "Inside Interior: An Abrupt Turn," *Sports Illustrated*, September 26, 1983, pp. 66ff.

[70]"The EPA: An Agency Reeling Under Siege," *U.S. News and World Report*, February 28, 1983, p. 24.

[71]Jerry Adler, "'Ice Queen' Under Fire," *Newsweek*, February 21, 1983, p. 24.

[72]Wenner, *op. cit.*, 1982.

[73]Bert Useem and Mayer N. Zald, "From Pressure Group to Social Movement: Organizational Dilemmas of the Effort to Promote Nuclear Power," *Social Problems*, 30 (1982), 144–156.

[74]*Ibid.*, pp. 145–146.

[75]Edward J. Walsh, "Resource Mobilization and Citizen Protest in Communities Around Three Mile Island," *Social Problems*, 29 (1981), 1–21.

[76]*Ibid.*, p. 14.

[77]Lester R. Brown, *Building a Sustainable Society* (New York: Norton, 1981).

[78]Rice O'Dell, *Environmental Awakening: The New Revolution to Protect the Earth* (Cambridge, Mass.: Ballinger, 1980).

[79]Denton E. Morrison, "The Soft, Cutting Edge of Environmentalism: Why and How the Appropriate Technology Notion is Changing The Movement," *Natural Resources Journal*, 20 (1980), 275–298.

[80]E. F. Schumacher. *Small Is Beautiful* (New York: Perennial Library, 1973).

[81]Morrison, *op. cit.*, p. 275.

16
Militarism and International Political Economy

Robert J. Antonio and Patrick J. Akard
UNIVERSITY OF KANSAS

More than five years after the 1979 military coup, approximately 45,000 people have died in El Salvador.[1] This figure includes not only insurgents and government soldiers, but thousands of innocent persons caught between the warring factions. Thousands more have been kidnapped, tortured, and killed by right-wing, paramilitary death squads. The violence, destruction, and economic upheaval is so extensive that it is difficult to express in "objective" terms. Before the conflict, El Salvador's "economic-social standing" (based on social indicators of health, education, and welfare) was already among the lowest in Latin America. In this poor region, only Haiti (one of the world's poorest nations) was ranked substantially below El Salvador.[2] During the first three years of the war, El Salvador's gross domestic product declined by over 25 percent, much of its infrastructure (bridges, roads, public utilities, and the like) was damaged or destroyed, and at least $1 billion was lost due to capital flight.[3] Rich Salvadorans deposited their money ($2 to 5 billion) in banks in Switzerland and the United States.[4] Indeed, the war wrecked an already weak economy and impacted disproportionately on the large peasant underclass.

El Salvador is a highly inegalitarian, agricultural society. An oligarchy monopolizes the nation's wealth, land, and military power. This group enjoys a living standard comparable to the privileged classes in the most developed societies. In contrast, peasants who harvest coffee and other crops tend to be propertyless and live close to starvation much of the year.[5] Peasant life is plagued by infant mortality, malnourishment, disease, disfigurement, official arbitrariness, and elite violence. The overarching powerlessness, insecurity, harshness, and tenuousness of life cannot be easily comprehended by the average North American.

Following the 1979 coup, the new Salvadoran regime promised to steer a middle course between oligarchy and radical egalitarianism.[6] However, promised land reforms were only partially completed and did not erode the iron grip of the oligarchy.[7] Authentic reformists were eliminated and in two years (1980–1982) about 25,000 people were killed.[8] The conflict became a full-scale war between U.S.-backed government forces and a front of several guerrilla factions. In the United States, public debate raged over whether the struggle was a result of communist subversion or a reaction to poverty and exploitation. Meanwhile, Salvadorans continued to suffer.

The conflict in El Salvador is a microcosm of three interrelated problems that dominate international relations: Cold War tensions between the United States and the Soviet Union; political instability and military conflicts in the Third World; and world poverty and economic underdevelopment. This chapter deals with these issues in the context of militarism and its relation to world political economy (that is, the world distribution of power and resources, and the struggles over them). To deal with such a broad and complex subject in one chapter, it is necessary to focus on a limited number of contributing factors. Emphasis will be primarily on the United States and its political-economic relations with the Third World, and East-West tensions as they impact on these relations. The connection between the Soviet Union and its satellites cannot be analyzed here, though this is a crucial issue in the debate on international conflict. The type of dominance exerted by the U.S.S.R. over its clients reflects its perceived geopolitical interests more than the process of world capitalist development. This important story is part of the present world crisis, but is beyond the scope of this chapter. For similar reasons, the important relations between

Many people have died in the conflict in El Salvador.
(Claude Urraca/Sygma)

the developed industrial economies of Western Europe, Japan, and the United States cannot be included in the discussion below.

Unlike previous chapters, the major factors examined here are all at the sociological, or macro, level. This is due to the nature of the subject matter, and to avoid making an already complex set of problems more difficult. However, the data presented below will allow the reader to draw clear implications about the consequences of world political and economic problems for the individual and social-psychological levels of analysis.

PART I: THE PROBLEM

The Roots of the Cold War: The "Communist Threat" and U.S. Interventionism after World War II

At present, Central America is the focus of U.S. attention, but during the last forty years Southeast Asia, Africa, and the Middle East have all shared center stage. The desire to "contain" the "communist threat" emerged immediately after World War II and was fueled by growing Soviet dominance in Eastern Europe as well as the victory of Mao Zedong in China. In 1950, a then top-secret memorandum (NSC-68) from the National Security Council expressed the strategy of postwar US foreign policy.[9] The U.S.S.R. was portrayed as being animated by a drive toward expansion and total domination, and was supposedly already entertaining ideas of a war against the United States and its allies. Therefore, the Soviets needed to be "contained": the memorandum outlined a plan for a massive U.S. military buildup, extensive military assistance for U.S. allies, covert economic, political, and psychological warfare to foment "unrest and revolt" in strategic Soviet "satellites," development of "internal security" agencies at home, broadening of foreign intelligence operations, and a reduction of expenditures for everything but defense and foreign assistance.[10] NSC-68 was a powerful rationale for policy already in place. In 1947, the Truman Doctrine committed the U.S. to the role of "international policeman." As Godfrey Hodgson has stated:

> The Truman Doctrine contained the seeds of American aid, economic or military, to more than one hundred countries; of mutual defense treaties with more than forty of them; of the great regional pacts, alliances and unilateral commitments: to NATO, to the Middle East, to the Western Hemisphere, and to Southeast Asia. It justified fleets of carriers patroling the Mediterranean and the South China Sea, nuclear submarines under the polar icecap, air bases in the Thai jungle, and police advisors in Uruguay and Bolivia. In support of it, an average of a million soldiers were deployed for twenty-five years in some four thousand bases in thirty countries. It contained the seeds of a habit of intervention: clandestine in Iran, Guatemala, Cuba, the Philippines, Chile and the CIA alone knows where else; overt in Korea, Lebanon, the Dominican Republic, Laos, Cambodia and Vietnam. "From Korea to Berlin to Cuba to Vietnam," Senator Fulbright has written, "the Truman Doctrine governed America's response to the Communist world. Tactics changed from 'massive retaliation' to 'limited war' and 'counter-insurgency' but these were variations on a classic formulation that few questioned."[11]

For forty years, public opinion in the United States has been mobilized successfully against the U.S.S.R. and its allies. The sense of urgency about the Soviet threat and the willingness to stem it militarily have oscillated. However, the perceptions of the Soviet Union as the main threat to world stability and the interests of the United States have never been seriously shaken. And, certain Soviet policies have upheld these perceptions. The repression of internal dissidents, persecution of Soviet Jews, military interventions (especially in Hungary [1956], Czechoslovakia [1968], and Afghanistan [1979]), the destruction of the Polish workers' "Solidarity" movement (early 1980s), and widespread assistance to Third-World insurgency movements have perpetuated Cold War sentiments. Moreover, the Soviet Union made a stunning recovery from the destruction and depopulation that occurred during World War II, becoming one of the world's largest economies and the second leading military power. This power provides a rationale for large-scale U.S. military spending and military aid to repressive anti-Soviet regimes.

The Nuclear Threat

In this Cold War context, the superpowers have carried on an expensive and dangerous arms race since the end of World War II. By 1983, the U.S. had 29,000 nuclear weapons and the U.S.S.R., 17,400 (Great Britain, France, and China had much smaller nuclear forces). Moreover, nuclear weapons are deployed by the United States in at least 15 countries and in submarines throughout the world.[12] The U.S. and U.S.S.R. innovate continuously more sophisticated weapons systems. Advances in offensive weapons stimulate new means of defense that generate further advances in offensive weapons (see Figure 16.1). The nuclear arms race produces an ever-growing stockpile of increasingly lethal weapons. The perceived need for "deterrence" results in the superpowers accumulating far more nuclear weapons than are necessary to destroy each other completely (see Figure 16.1).[13] The speed and complexity of the new missiles have sharply reduced reaction time to attack, increasing the chance for accidental war. In 1983, the Reagan administration proposed a space-based satellite, missile defense system, as well as an assortment of new "space age" offensive nuclear weapons.[14] The administration said it needed $25 billion simply to complete feasibility studies of the new system. Moreover, deployment would require revision of treaties that forbid such systems.[15] The U.S.S.R.'s military appropriations are secret, but it is safe to assume that they are continuing their arms build-up as well.

In the early 1980s, the United States was unwilling to negotiate seriously about a new arms control treaty, and the position of the Soviet Union also hardened. This raised public fears and consciousness about the dangers of nuclear war. The growing anti-nuclear movement became increasingly vocal about the threat of war. In the West, large protests (in 1982) responded to the planned installation of U.S. Cruise missiles in Europe. A tamer version of this movement developed in some Eastern bloc countries (even Communist leaderships were fearful about new Soviet missile deployments on their soil).

Concern about a nuclear holocaust was stirred further by scientific findings that a full-scale nuclear war would cause a "nuclear winter" (of world-wide subzero tem-

Figure 16.1

The figure shows actions and reactions in the development of nuclear weapons. For each weapon listed, we see who developed it first and when the weapon was matched by the opposing side. We also see the enormous increase in the destructive power of nuclear weapons (as of 1983) in comparison to all munitions used during World War II.

Source: R. L. Sivard, *World Military and Social Expenditures, 1983* (Washington, D.C.: World Priorities, 1983), pp. 14, 18.

Action ⇄ Reaction
in the Nuclear Competition

US 1945	atomic bomb	1949 USSR
US 1948	intercontinental bomber	1955 USSR
US 1952	thermonuclear bomb	1953 USSR
USSR 1957	intercontinental ballistic missile (ICBM)	1958 US
USSR 1957	man-made satellite	1958 US
US 1960	submarine-launched ballistic missile (SLBM)	1968 USSR
US 1966	multiple warhead (MRV)	1968 USSR
USSR 1968	anti-ballistic missile (ABM)	1972 US
US 1970	multiple independently-targeted warhead (MIRV)	1975 USSR
US 1982	long-range cruise missile	198? USSR
US 1983	neutron bomb	198? USSR
US 198?	anti-satellite weapon	198? USSR

A single square above represents the TNT equivalent of the munitions used in World War II. An estimated 3 million tons were used in that war. The block of squares represents the TNT equivalent of today's world stockpile of nuclear weapons. Estimated at 16,000 million tons of TNT, these weapons alone have over 5,000 times the destructive power of World War II.

Increasingly modern missiles have heightened the danger of nuclear war.
(T. Zimberoff/Sygma)

peratures), ending humanity as well as most other life on the planet.[16] Also in 1983, the American television movie, *The Day After* (an explicit and horrifying, yet understated, portrayal of the aftermath of a nuclear war in the small city of Lawrence, Kansas), frightened people in the many nations where it was shown. Despite the growing fear of war, weapons technology continues to advance, as does the nuclear stockpile.

Militarism and the Less Developed World

Both the capitalist and Communist blocs compete for increased influence in the resource-rich, less developed world. The resulting struggle for economic and political dominance, combined with internal instability, stimulates militarism, interventions, and warfare. Both superpowers arm client states, sometimes encouraging military conflicts. For many less developed nations, "modernization" means militarization—in 1983, 56 of 114 developing countries were at least partially under military control and, in a majority, official violence against the public is commonplace.[17] Much Third-World wealth is drained by military purchases instead of being invested in economic development and social welfare. For example, the People's Republic of China is third (of 142 nations) in military spending but ninety-first in social-economic standing.[18] China has made great strides in feeding and housing its populace. But how much greater could the gains have been if its military spending were sharply reduced? In 1982, military expenditures of the developed countries "were 17 times larger than their extensions of aid to countries in need."[19] What if this spending ratio were reversed?

Central Economic Problems in the Less Developed World

The potential for conflict due to militarization and simmering East-West tension is magnified by widespread poverty and deprivation. The economic problems of less developed countries (LDCs) are the subject of extensive debate, with theorists emphasizing one or more of the following problems.

Poverty, Inequality, and Life Chances

In much of the less developed world, life is short, brutal, and oriented toward mere subsistence. Ruth Leger Sivard stated that:

> Among the poorest fifth of the world population, the average life is 21 years shorter than among the richest fifth. . . . Diets in terms of basic nutrients contrast sharply. The poorest fifth eat only half as much protein. In calories they consume less than the average minimum requirements, while the richest eat considerably more than they need. Among the poorest, three in five do not have safe water. They have a seventh as many physicians, and less than one-third as many teachers for their children. One baby in eight dies before his first birthday. Three adults in five cannot read.[20]

Two billion people, mostly in LDCs, have yearly incomes of less than $500, 600 million are without full employment, and 400 million suffer from hunger and malnutrition. Life expectancy reflects the gap between nations: at birth it is 76 years in Iceland and Japan compared to 40 in Afghanistan, Kampuchea, and Ethiopia. However, as Sivard aptly pointed out: "Between the poor and the rich [nations], the gap is even broader in the quality of life than in the length of it."[21]

However depressing, these data understate poverty in developing nations. Ruling elites and professional classes are better off than the masses, and their condition inflates the aggregate figures. For example, in El Salvador there are 3,160 persons per physician (compared to 270 in the U.S.S.R. and 520 in the U.S.).[22] This is a poor ratio. However, the physicians serve the rich, while most peasants have little or no access. Similar differentials exist on other indicators—such as infant mortality, protein intake, education, and income (see Figure 16.2).

Figure 16.2 The Development Gap, 1980

	Richest fifth of world population	Poorest fifth of world population
GNP per capital ($)	9,469	206
Govt. education exps. per cap ($)	497	6
Teachers per 1,000 school-age pop.	40	12
Women in total univ. enrollment (%)	43	27
Adult literacy (%)	97	42
Govt. health exps. per cap ($)	432	2
Physicians per 10,000 people	21	3
Life expectancy (years)	74	53
Infant deaths per 100 births	2	12
Calories per cap as % of requirements	134	90
Protein supply per cap (grams)	99	48
Population with safe water (%)	96	39

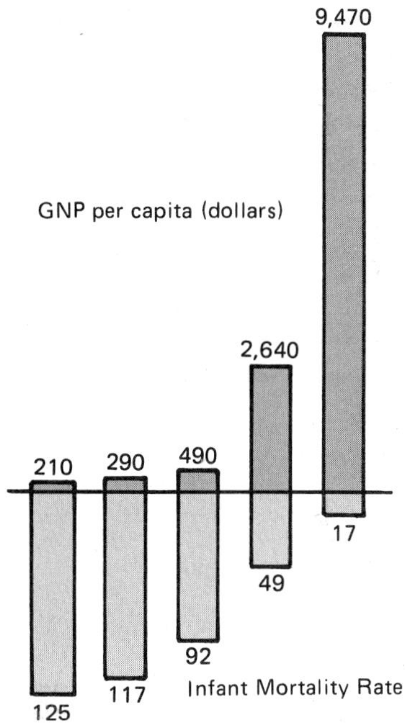

A number of measures showing the enormous gap between the richest and the poorest fifths of the world's population are illustrated here. Also it can be seen from the second part of the figure that the higher a nation's Gross National Product, the lower its infant mortality rate.

Source: R. L. Sivard, *World Military and Social Expenditures, 1983* (Washington, D.C.: World Priorities, 1983), p. 25.

Backwardness

Poverty goes hand-in-hand with backwardness. For example, the top fifth of nations in gross national product ($9,470 yearly, per capita) have an infant mortality rate of 17 (per thousand live births) while in the lowest fifth ($210) the rate is 125.[23] LDCs have little industrial capacity, primitive technology, low agricultural productivity, a poorly developed infrastructure, and, overall, too little capital, technical, and human resources. Much of the labor force is unskilled and illiterate (in Somalia, Ethiopia, Upper Volta, and Yemen Arab Republic less than 10 percent of the population is literate[24] and in more than one-third of the world more than one-half the population is illiterate). Again, quantitative data present only a partial picture of backwardness. Daily life is full of discomforts. Public utilities and motorized transportation, when they exist, are often unreliable. The delivery of basic goods and services is unpredictable and often fails completely.

Traditional social and religious institutions sometimes hinder technical advancement, educational efforts, and public-health measures. Social organization is characterized by inefficiency, excessive red tape, and widespread corruption. Personal ties, social status, and bribes govern rather than law. Tribal conflicts with ancient origins sometimes prevent the delivery of services, undermine equal opportunity, and contribute to power struggles and coups. Backwardness presents a maze of impediments to everyday life. Some problems appear to have simple solutions ("why don't they eat the sacred cows?"), but even the most "irrational" facets may be connected to an underlying logic of power and privilege, reflecting impervious religious, class, caste, and/or clan ties. These vast problems promote a feeling of pathos that undermines initiative and improvement. Although distorted, this "feeling" often reflects the objective material and social constraints on change.

Dependency

LDCs are politically, militarily, and economically dependent on advanced societies and their banks. For example, between 1971 and 1982, the foreign debt of developing countries grew from $90 billion to $626 billion.[25] Many debtor nations had to borrow even more from the same banks or the International Monetary Fund (IMF) just to make interest payments and prevent defaults. In the early 1980s, world recession reduced the demand for many Third-World products and raw materials. Loans made in the 1970s were based on assumptions of steady demand and inflating prices. The result was a world debt crisis that threatened the major banks and the entire capitalist world economy.

Loans from First-World banks and the U.S.-dominated IMF come with provisos that require austerity measures: slashing health, education, and welfare expenditures (which are already funded at a minimal level). Also, the measures frequently raise the price of basic foods and goods necessary for subsistence. In 1984, violent rioting in the Dominican Republic was a response to IMF-related government price increases on "all imported goods and many basic foodstuffs."[26]

A crucial source of economic growth for developing nations is direct investment by foreign (multinational) corporations. However, this entails costs as well as benefits. Third-World investments by industrial nations aim at extracting resources and/or the exploitation of cheap labor. They do not promote "even development" and self-sufficiency. "Development" sometimes means the destruction of native industries and agriculture, causing the importation of goods that were formerly produced or grown domestically. Third-World subsidiaries of multinationals have introduced advanced technologies, provided capital, and increased employment opportunities. However, the multinationals operate according to criteria of profitability, not the welfare and productive needs of the host country. They sometimes interfere with domestic politics (for example, the U.S.-based ITT corporation's involvement in the military overthrow of Salvadore Allende, the democratically elected Marxist President of Chile).[27] Frequently, multinationals help perpetuate authoritarian regimes and extreme class disparities to maintain a compliant labor force and low wages. When political order breaks down, the host nation may face an abrupt withdrawal of resources.

Political, military, and economic dependency are intertwined in most underdeveloped nations. Aid comes at the cost of political and military favors—as, for example, accepting political interference, housing military bases, or fighting proxy wars.

PART II: CAUSES AND CONSEQUENCES

Few analysts dispute the existence of the social, political, and economic problems outlined above. But there is far less consensus on their causes and consequences. This section considers a number of competing perspectives on East-West conflict, Third-World political instability, and Third-World underdevelopment. The debate on these issues is complex for a variety of reasons. First, like the other social problems dealt with in this book, the ideological orientation of the observer affects what he or she chooses to view as a "problem," what facts are selected as "causes," and what consequences are emphasized or ignored. This is especially true when international political or economic problems are perceived in the context of the Cold War. There is a tendency to seek simplistic, monocausal explanations for events that are in reality quite complex and variable from one country to the next. For this reason, competing theoretical or ideological *pre*suppositions regarding underdevelopment and world political conflicts have been introduced below.

There is also a problem concerning the relationship between political and economic factors. Though international political events and economic conditions interact and are clearly interrelated, the two spheres are also partially independent; the degree of relative autonomy is a subject of much debate. In the Third World, for example, poverty and underdevelopment are breeding grounds for discontent that may lead to overt political conflict. In the United States, there is a clear relationship between militarism and the domestic economy, reflected in the recent debates on the federal budget. These interrelations seem to require that the subjects be dealt with together. On the other hand, no single orientation can adequately deal with both spheres. The multiplicity of political and economic problems in specific regions of the world cannot be explained with reference to a single "causal" model. Because of their interrelationship, both underdevelopment and world political conflict are discussed in this section. But due to the complexity and substantial independence of these conditions, they will be taken up separately below.

APPROACHES TO DEVELOPMENT AND UNDERDEVELOPMENT

The United States has suffered from two severe recessions since the early 1970s, resulting in hardship and "sacrifices" on the part of many citizens. In this era of belt-tightening, one might ask why we should focus on the economic problems of the developing world when we have so many of

Table 16.1 Levels of Analysis: Militarism and International Political Economy

LEVELS	APPROPRIATE QUESTIONS	A PARTIAL SYNOPSIS OF PRESENT CONCLUSIONS
SOCIOLOGICAL	What do modernization theorists see as the causes of the problem of underdevelopment?	Less developed nations are seen as impeded by traditionalism, archaic institutions, and their lack of resemblance to modern capitalist societies.
	What do dependency theorists see as the causes of the problem of underdevelopment?	They emphasize exploitation of less developed nations by modern capitalist societies.
	What are some of the key ways in which development can occur?	Although there is disagreement over the details, it is clear that the following are crucially involved in the process of development: involvement in world trade, receipt of foreign aid, direct foreign investment, population control, and increased productivity (especially agricultural).
	What are some of the factors involved in current East–West political and military instability?	Insecurity in the U.S. over its erosion of power and its actions (e.g., arms build-up) to compensate for it. On the other side there is Soviet expansionism and its insecurity over the U.S. arms build-up.
	How does East–West instability impact on stability in the Third World?	Clearly U.S.–Soviet competition is involved in the conflict in places like Nicaragua and El Salvador, but there are also many indigenous problems and elements contributing to the instability in the Third World.

Table 16.1 Levels of Analysis: Militarism and International Political Economy (*Continued*)

LEVELS	APPROPRIATE QUESTIONS	A PARTIAL SYNOPSIS OF PRESENT CONCLUSIONS
	Does U.S. military spending contribute to the development of the American economy?	Yes, in some ways, but the overall evidence is that it does more economic (and social) damage—"guns" rather than "butter," windfall profits to a small number of large companies, outrageous costs and cost overruns, a "brain drain" to defense industries, etc.

our own. Indeed, President Reagan outlined an "America first" economic plan prior to a well-publicized conference on North-South relations, arguing that "no American contribution can do more for development than a growing, prosperous U.S. economy."[28] Before considering Third-World poverty and underdevelopment, we should ask why this is a crucial issue for the United States at this particular moment.

There are two ways to answer. The first is the "humanitarian" response: as the richest nation in the world, the United States has a moral duty to work toward the alleviation of poverty, hunger, and suffering. But there are also several "pragmatic" reasons for stressing the urgency of the development issue. For example, the economic interests of the United States and other developed nations are increasingly intertwined with those of the Third World. Not only is dependence on developing nations increasing for crucial raw materials such as tin, zinc, and especially oil; these nations are also a growing source of inexpensive consumer goods (clothing, electronic equipment), and a major market for U.S. capital goods and agricultural products. Developing nations purchased 37 percent of all American exports in 1980, more than the European Economic Community, Eastern Europe, Japan, and Australia combined.[29] Over a third of the total income from the foreign investment of U.S. firms comes from developing countries.[30] Geopolitical interests must also be considered: the costs of social and political unrest that accompany poverty and deprivation (including possible exploitation of unrest by the other superpower). Even beyond humanitarian arguments—which are formidable in their own right—the developed nations cannot afford to neglect the problems of developing economies.

Even if there is agreement on the importance of economic progess in the Third World, there is no consensus on the primary causes of underdevelopment, or even on what changes would (or should) constitute development. While this subject has been dealt with in a variety of ways, two basic competing approaches may be distinguished. From one perspective, often referred to as the "modernization" approach, there is a set of universal "stages" or general characteristics through which any "modernizing" or "industrializing" society must pass. This means that the categories used by the classical social theorists to explain the earlier European transition from agrarian feudalism to industrial capitalism may also aid in understanding the problems of developing countries today. Other theorists, however, stress the qualitatively *different* situation of contemporary Third-World nations, whose development must occur in an established world economy dominated by the already-industrialized nations. From this "dependency" perspective, the problem is not simply "industrialization"—a technical issue—but *capitalist* development, which entails unequal and exploitative relationships between economies with more or less power in the international marketplace. The difference between these two general orientations is crucial, for one sees the extension of capitalism into the Third World as the *solution* to problems of underdevelopment, while the other views this process as the major *cause* of these problems.

Modernization Theory

Sociologist Talcott Parsons[31] developed a theory of modern society which argued that as societies grew more complex ("structurally differentiated") occupational roles became more specialized, explicitly defined, and reliant upon the mastery of particular technical skills. With modernity, placement on the basis of tribal, clan, family, and friendship ties declines as a result of intensified demands for training, experience, and merit. "Traditionalism" and "ascription" are replaced by "universalism" and "achievement." Parsons envisioned "modernization" as an evolutionary process in which societies move away from tradition, hierarchical power, and inequality and toward a system based on education, democracy, and equality of opportunity. The modern system functions effectively because it stresses "objective" evaluation of merit rather than arbitrary ascriptive characteristics. Parsons considered the United States to be the "lead society" and virtually equated modernization with the development of contemporary American values, socioeconomic organization, and technology.

Parsons's views reflected the fact that in the 1950s and early 1960s, the United States *appeared* on the verge of overcoming the problems of class conflict, bureaucracy, and social integration. The modernization theorists who built on Parsons's views remained in the orbit of postwar optimism but were generally more moderate in their claims about how far development and differentiation had advanced. However, the core themes of modernization theory remained closely tied to Parsons's general scheme. In the 1960s, "modernization" was generally treated as a sort of "Americanization" process.

Parsonsian-type "modernization" theory flourished in American sociology during the 1960s.[32] However, it was not confined to sociology, but was current throughout the social sciences. For example, economist and presidential adviser, W. W. Rostow,[33] described stages of economic modernization; political scientists David Apter and Samuel Huntington[34] addressed political modernization, and psychologist David McClelland[35] stressed motivational aspects of modernization. Most importantly, these ideas informed public policymaking and sometimes were invoked to justify the U.S. role in the Third World.[36]

Some General Features of Modernization Theory

While there are some differences over specific elements of the development proccess, most theories of modernization are informed by the following general assumptions:

1. Backwardness is largely a result of internal conditions. Although such external factors as technology transfers, foreign trade, and foreign aid contribute to development, modernization ultimately reflects the level of social differentiation, which is, in turn, shaped by the degree of traditionalism.

2. Values and ideas are the most important (though not exclusive) determinants of development. Overturning traditional attitudes and instituting modern beliefs are the main means to transform material and political structures.[37]

3. Modernization cannot be instantly created by revolutionary means. The processes of valuative change, social differentiation, and consequent technological growth *evolve* gradually.[38]

4. Modernization theory is not consistent with radical egalitarianism. Modernization requires a social hierarchy, though one increasingly based on achievement and merit. The "best" people must be attracted to the most difficult roles and motivated to perform competently. Differences in income serve this purpose. Modernization theorists realize that existing hierarchies have strong ascriptive elements, but believe that long-term evolution is toward purely merit-based differences in wealth. LDCs are behind in this evolutionary process.

5. Though most modernization theorists do not refer to the United States as the "lead society," they retain a profile of attributes from capitalist industrial societies (the U.S., Japan, and Western Europe) as the baseline against which less developed nations are measured. The list of characteristics[39] reflects rather directly concrete aspects of capitalist systems. Often, the very definition of development necessitates U.S.-style capitalism, representative "democracy," and capitalist cultural traditions.

Dependency and Modern Marxist Theories of Development and Underdevelopment

Karl Marx argued that European capitalism was based not only on the exploitation of its own workers, but also on colonial extraction from Asia, Africa, and the Americas. In the early twentieth century, a broader theory of "imperialism" began to take shape due to the efforts of the early British critic of imperialism, John Hobson, and by the radical Marxists V. I. Lenin and Rosa Luxemburg. They contended that capitalist states were driven by the threat of stagnation and economic crisis to search for new markets for their industrial products and for capital investment. Direct political control over colonies guaranteed windfall profits in both of these areas. Marx believed that imperialistic expansion would stimulate universal capitalist industrialism, world-wide proletarian revolution, and, eventually, world socialism. However, in the mid-twentieth century much of Asia, Africa, Latin America, Southern and Eastern Europe remained underdeveloped agricultural societies, despite the fact that anticolonial struggles after World War II had largely ended the old direct political form of colonialism. Dependency theory emerged in the 1960s in part as a revised Marxist response to these new conditions, and as a rebuttal to modernization theory.

André Gunder Frank,[40] a major proponent of dependency theory, contended that underdevelopment comes neither from traditional values nor from archaic institutions but is a direct product of capitalist urban centers draining the wealth out of the less developed hinterlands. In his view, underdevelopment is a direct product of capitalist development and expansion: the advanced capitalist nations profit from enduring subordinate satellites. As we saw in Chapter 10, Immanuel Wallerstein[41] coined the term "world-system" in portraying the history of capitalism as a process whereby the "core" capitalist powers use their superior state and military structures to insure a steady extraction of surplus from the less developed "periphery" and "semi-periphery."[42]

Dependency theorists such as Frank and Wallerstein maintain Marx's concern for international economic exploitation, but reject his belief in the ultimately progressive consequences of imperialism. Other recent neo-Marxists[43] are critical of dependency theory but still stress dependent relations and neocolonial exploitation. These thinkers build more directly on Marx's theories. They do not emphasize as strongly the enduring nature of backwardness. Marxists disagree about the pattern and consequences of capitalist development in the less developed world. In partial opposition to the dependency theorists, certain Marxists argue that peripheral nations must first adopt more capitalist traits before they can escape the control of the "core." They believe that autonomy requires an adequately developed economic base and that a strong state apparatus with nationalist goals could force foreign investors and firms (for example, through taxes, laws, export-import restrictions) to contribute to indigenous capitalist development.[44] The hope is to establish a national capitalist class and capital accumulation process that would set off the dynamic of growth. However, such differences should not be exaggerated because all Marxist scholars emphasize dependency and exploitation.

Some General Features of Dependency Theory

1. Dependency analysts stress external conditions as the cause of underdevelopment. Dependency is imposed from the outside by the world capitalist system and the activities of the particular nations, corporate units, and capitalists who dominate it.

2. The dependency approach emphasizes material conditions more than beliefs and values. Dependency is enduring backwardness due to external exploitation and control over a nation's labor force, capital, and political structure. National resources become the basis of surplus profits for foreign capitalists instead of being used to benefit the indigenous population. The pattern of development is determined by capital, not the people. Foreign interests provide economic, political, and military support that keeps client elites in power, a flow of wealth leaving the country, and the working class and/or peasantry poor. The consequent low wage structure subsidizes consumerism in the rich nations. A radio or suit produced in an LDC costs less, but has been made by poorly paid workers under poor working conditions. Importation of labor-saving machinery is minimized if it competes with inexpensive labor, since such "development" would reduce profits. Finally, the low cost of labor encourages a migration of industrial production to the periphery and semi-periphery that increases unemployment and reduces the price of labor in the core. Thus, the capitalists benefit at home as well as in the Third World.

3. Dependency analysts reject evolutionary gradualism. Less developed nations must overcome hierarchies, elites, and state-military structures that perpetuate the drain of surplus to the core. The structure of privilege, power, and coercion does not whither away nor is it willingly abandoned by the elite. This does not mean that a military regime can *only* be removed by force—as exemplified by the peaceful transition away from Argentina's military government in 1983. However, the new Argentine leadership did not institute revolutionary changes in the economy nor depose the healthy factions from their positions of power. Given the brutal nature of many Third-World regimes, insurgency cannot be ruled out as a means of change.

4. Dependency analysts are not utopians, calling for the complete elimination of all hierarchy. On the other hand, they reject the claims that development produces a social hierarchy based increasingly on training, merit, and competence. Instead, they assert that these ideals are an ideology that legitimates a military and class hierarchy. The dependency position is egalitarian in that it assumes that Third-World inequality could and should be sharply reduced. Dependency analysts also argue that voting means little when the populace is illiterate and impoverished and parties representing them are forbidden. The thrust of the dependency position is that authentic democracy is impossible without social equality.

5. The dependency approach does not view capitalist society as the inevitable model for development. On the other hand, neither does it invoke Communist bloc models. Most dependency theorists are also highly critical of the Soviet Union and its relations with its own satellites. The dependency approach stresses autonomy and the use of national resources to better provision the indigenous populace. The political perspective of these thinkers is to the Left of modernization theorists. However, their political models vary: they range from social democracy to more traditional state socialist positions.

Modernization or Dependency Theory?

Alejandro Portes[45] argues that modernization theory is in a state of "almost complete exhaustion." The emphasis on values as the key determinant of underdevelopment, the almost exclusive stress on internal conditions, and the implicit ideological biases were all criticized in the later 1960s and 1970s in light of events in Vietnam, Chile, and other Third-World countries that seemed to contradict this viewpoint. On the other hand, dependency theory has also been attacked as an ideology or as Third-World "rhetoric"; in its extreme form it "has become a *deus ex machina* explanation" for all that goes wrong in these societies.[46] The dependency position views development/underdevelopment as following an international logic of capital; this sometimes results in insensitivity to relevant internal conditions, differences between nations, and noneconomic factors (though this is changing).[47] Finally, the dependency position does not explain the type of political and economic dominance that occurs in the state socialist bloc.

One solution to the weaknesses of the two approaches might appear to be a synthesis of some kind. This would be difficult, however, given their contradictory assumptions and propositions. On the other hand, the deficiencies of each require consideration of certain factors to which the other attends. A more adequate approach to dependency and backwardness must explain internal as well as external factors, focus on deal as well as material interests, and capture historical particularities as well as effects of the world capitalist dynamic. Certain aspects of the two approaches are not inherently contradictory. For example, even Marxist regimes have discovered the impediments that traditional world views and attitudes pose to the establishment of modern means of production and administration. Destructive tribal conflicts and parochial beliefs have contributed to misery and backwardness all over the Third World. But as will be shown below, more elements from dependency theory are consistent with the historical facts than is the case with the modernization approach. Further, the egalitarian assumptions of dependency theory are in line with the aspirations of many Third-World peoples. Thus any new framework is likely to be constructed largely on the remains of the dependency perspective. However, it will likely contain some elements formerly associated with modernization theory. It must avoid the overly broad and sometimes vague generalizations of both modernization and dependency theory. It must also be based on more sufficient historical support than either of its precursors.

THE ECONOMICS OF DEVELOPMENT

Some Preliminary Issues

Before examining the empirical evidence on the causes of underdevelopment in the Third World, some preliminary issues must be addressed. The first concerns the definition of the problem: just what is *development*? That is, what are the primary goals toward which proposed solutions are directed? In the 1950s and early 1960s, economists usually defined "development" in aggregate terms such as certain annual percentage increase in GNP or per capita income, which did not take the distribution of national income into account. For sociologists interested in "modernization," another key indicator was the level of industrial development, measured, for example, by the decline of agriculture's share of production and employment relative to manufacturing and services. Programs with increases in GNP or rapid "industrialization" as their primary targets were advocated, and implemented with some success in a number of developing nations.[48]

By the mid-1960s, an increasing number of theorists called for a new definition of "development." Earlier modernization theorists had emphasized the "trickle-down" benefits of growth. In this view, growing GNP meant more production, which generated more jobs for a larger number of people, higher incomes, urbanization, and a generally improving standard of living. The problem with this view is that industrialization and aggregate economic growth does not *in itself* eliminate hunger, poverty, and unemployment. While growth may be a *necessary* condition for the elimination of Third-World poverty, it is not *sufficient.* The historical tendency in most rapidly industrializing nations has been that of *unequal* development and the emergence of a *dual* economy: a small, urban industrial sector providing better jobs and incomes, and promoting education for a middle-class minority; and a large, stagnant rural agricultural sector in which the bulk of the population remains.[49] Further, the capitalization of land formerly used for subsistence farming, rapid urban migration of peasants, and increased use of *capital*-intensive technology, which has historically accompanied industrialization, can actually make matters much worse by generating vast pockets of unemployed urban poor.

These inequalities do not appear to be transitional, as earlier modernization theorists had expected, but chronic. Inequality has actually been increasing within developing nations.[50] This observation led to a new definition of "development" in which the primary goal was the elimination of poverty (measured by such factors as unemployment, food consumption, and the distribution of income) and the increase in life chances for as *many* people as possible.[51] Thus the *distribution* of income, employment opportunities, health care, education, and so on, becomes an issue in any discussion of development, beyond the simple question of aggregate economic growth. However, this poses another problem for policy advocates, as Hans Singer and Javed Ansari point out:

> For the developing countries, there remains the dilemma that, on the one hand, GNP growth is essential to provide the resources, and probably also the potential preconditions, for a non-violent redistribution of incomes, while at the same time emphasis on GNP growth has inherent tendencies to solidify and accentuate existing inequalities.[52]

Complicating the picture further is the fact that those in policymaking positions—whether native elites, multinational banks or corporations, or international lending agencies like the IMF—often look with disfavor upon egalitarian programs that might reduce private profit.

Another factor complicates any discussion of Third-World underdevelopment. There is a tremendous *diversity* among developing countries. The Third World includes a vast array of nations with different problems and needs. Problems relating to politics, agriculture, or population are much different in sub-Saharan Africa than in Latin America or Southern Asia. Further, it is now necessary to distinguish *truly* low-income nations like Bangladesh (with a per capita annual income of $90) from "middle-income" or "newly industrializing countries" (NDCs) like Brazil or Taiwan. The former are sometimes referred to collectively as the "Fourth World": nations with staggering poverty, few resources, and little hope for sufficient economic growth in the near future. The nations in the Organization of Petroleum Exporting Countries (OPEC) also represent a separate category: developing nations that experienced a sudden astronomical increase in export income from 1973 until the world recession of the early 1980s. While there are still development problems in the oil-exporting nations, they do not suffer from the acute shortage of capital that characterizes other Third-World economies.

With these distinctions in mind, the (non-socialist bloc) world economy can be characterized by four major trends since World War II. First, there has been a *convergence* of the economies of the developed nations. The postwar dominance of the United States has given way somewhat with the rapid renewal of the economies of Western Europe and Japan. On the other hand, there has been a pattern of *divergent* growth (1) between developed nations and the Third World; (2) between the LDCs and NDCs *within* the Third World; and (3) *within* the national economies of each developing nation, reflecting dualistic development.[53] These differences within and between nations should be kept in mind when discussing policy options, for they may well be the source of fundamental conflicts of interest.

Promoting Development: Competing Perspectives

A crucial obstacle to development in most non–oil-producing Third-World countries is a shortage of capital for productive investment. For a number of reasons, such as the small number of individuals or business enterprises with significant surplus funds, the level of indigenous savings required for sustained growth is inadequate. Time is also a crucial constraint. For social, political, and humanitarian reasons, Third-World nations cannot afford the luxury of a gradual, long-term process of capital accumulation as occurred in the earlier industrializing nations. Thus international sources of investment funds may be crucial. These are primarily export earnings; foreign aid such as grants and loans from developed nations or international agencies; and direct investment in the domestic economy by foreign enterprises such as multinational corporations. In addition to the source of new capital, the proper method of its application is also the focus of debate. What combination of factors (capital, labor, available resources, and technology), and in what industries, are most likely to stimulate favorable growth?

Some of the most important arguments between development theorists concern the following key issues.

World Trade and Underdevelopment

As dependency theorists often point out, there may be a difference between what LDCs *should* do and what they *can* do, given their weak position in the world economy. This is immediately apparent when considering trade policy. Export earnings are perhaps the most desirable source of external income for development. Trade deficits, where more money is flowing out for imported goods than is received through exports, are serious problems for most non–oil-producing LDCs. Economists have long debated what kind of trade policy best reduces trade deficits and promotes Third-World development. In the traditional view, the way to maximize growth and productivity both within nations and for the world economy as a whole, was to minimize trade barriers—that is, promote free trade between nations (the corollary to "laissez-faire" within nations). Each country would benefit from its own "comparative advantage" in resources, labor power, geography, and so on. The market would induce them to concentrate on those goods that they could produce most efficiently and thus sell competitively. This "free trade" approach continues to be advocated by many today, including the Reagan administration.[54]

Unfortunately, as dependency theorists emphasize, the ideal of free trade bears little resemblance to reality. Third-World countries have long been plagued by a number of disadvantages in their trade relations with developed nations. Being underdeveloped, they have had to import costly manufactured goods (especially capital goods like heavy machinery) from industrialized nations, while relying on the export of one or a few *primary commodities* (raw materials or agricultural products like coffee or cocoa) to pay for them. Nearly half of all Third-World countries earn 50 percent or more of their export receipts from a single primary commodity.[55] In the traditional view, there is nothing wrong with this, since by emphasizing those resources in which they have a relative advantage, Third-World countries accumulate cash for more extensive development. In reality, however, dependence on a primary commodity export has stifled growth. It leaves the exporting nation very vulnerable to unpredictable fluctuations in the world market for their particular export commodity—even if it is oil, as Mexico has recently discovered. In addition, except for energy resources, the demand for primary products grows much more slowly than that for manufactured goods as the world economy expands. There has also been a steady deterioration of the *terms of trade* between developed and developing countries; that is, the relative prices of imported versus exported products. This is because the prices of most manufactured goods have increased historically in relation to the prices of most primary products. Other factors have also undermined the Third-World position, such as the development of synthetic substitutes for such crucial primary exports as rubber and cotton.

This situation led many development theorists to call for new strategies that would both diversify Third-World economies and make them more independent of developed nations. In the 1950s and early 1960s, a strategy of *import-substitution industrialization* (ISI) was carried out by a number of Latin American countries on the recommendation of the United Nations' Economic Commission on Latin America (ECLA). Their argument was that "free trade" and the "international division of labor" valued by many economists actually retarded Third-World growth. They called for protective tariffs on industrial imports to promote *internal* industrial development of products for domestic consumption, thereby reducing dependency on imports. The import-substitution strategy failed, however, and, if anything, increased dependency. For one thing, the main beneficiaries of the new policy were foreign firms that were invited in to set up production facilities due to their possession of capital and technological know-how, and granted liberal tax and investment incentives.[56] Also, while some formerly imported consumer products were now produced domestically, there was a much greater need for imports of even more expensive capital goods—machinery, spare parts, and raw materials for the new domestic industries. As Raúl Fernández[57] notes, "the real substitution . . . was of one type of imports for another." Finally, there was a crucial barrier to sustained growth due to the very limited internal markets for the new domestically produced products.

The failure of import-substitution industrialization, due to limited internal markets among other factors, led to the emergence of a different strategy that would take advantage of the much larger markets of developed nations while still promoting industrial development. This strategy—*export-oriented industrialization* (EOI)—would also adhere to the classical principles of trade by taking advantage of a major internal resource—a general abundance of cheap labor—to produce certain labor-intensive manufactured goods for export such as textiles, apparel, shoes, and consumer electronics. Middle-income developing countries like Brazil, Taiwan, and South Korea had relative success through this type of development; ironically, even to the point of provoking protectionist measures for certain industries by the U.S. and other industrial nations. The share of U.S. manufactured imports from developing countries increased from 15 percent in 1965 (around the time of disillusionment with ISI and promotion of EOI) to 24 percent in 1977.[58]

Does this mean that Third-World nations now support open trade and free market solutions? In spite of recent success, many development theorists are cautious about the effects of export-oriented industrialization as it is currently being implemented. To begin with, only a limited number of LDCs, with key political, geographical, economic, or demographic advantages, have been able to get export-oriented industrialization off the ground. Second, while one of the problems of ISI has been overcome—the limited market for consumer goods—others have not. Participating LDCs are still dependent on the First World for imports of capital goods, and on outside sources for financing. Indeed, the largest international debts owed to banks, governments, and international agencies are held by these newly developing countries that borrowed heavily to finance industrialization projects. Finally, the U.S. retains numerous protective barriers against manufactured goods from the Third World. These barriers are even higher for Japan and Western Europe; their removal is a crucial prerequisite to Third-World industrialization.[59]

The above reservations are important. But, from the standpoint of eliminating world poverty, the observation made earlier is even more crucial: industrialization and a growing GNP do not in themselves eliminate poverty. Past development strategies have been oriented toward the markets of the industrial nations, relying on their (capital-intensive) technologies, capital, and methods of organization. They have therefore tended to increase inequality and perpetuate dualism. Export-led development is certainly better than no development at all. It has succeeded in generating capital, stimulating growth, and raising the standard of living in a limited number of developing countries. But those theorists for whom elimination of poverty and deprivation for as *many* people as possible is the goal are critical. They argue for options more appropriate for the broad-based needs of the specific developing economy in question, rather than those of international capital. From this perspective two problems in particular have been inadequately addressed in recent years: hunger and unemployment. It follows that any adequate theory of development must deal with the problem of agricultural self-sufficiency and develop strategies for industrialization that maximize absorption of the surplus population.

These issues have led to what is sometimes called the "appropriate technology" response. From this perspective, when growth alone is the primary goal, export-oriented industrialization requires use of the most up-to-date methods of production to be competitive in the world market. This external orientation has led to the adoption of large, centralized, and capital-intensive production techniques that do little to alleviate widespread underemployment or promote rural development. The problems are exacerbated when the actual producers are foreign multinationals, who make production decisions based on their own needs and technological preferences—including the purchase of expensive equipment from their own subsidiaries. A more appropriate strategy might include the promotion of the more localized light industry, even handicrafts, that would maximize the use of abundant labor supplies while establishing the economic base for later development of large-scale industry.

In this discussion of economic policy, it is important to remember the political dimension. Policy means little without the power to put it into practice; a crucial question concerns who is doing the decision-making. It is for this reason that many Third-World theorists stress the need for political and economic independence from the "core" countries, and their multinational corporations, banks, and international agencies. Unfortunately, the latter have the capital, markets, and technical know-how. Further, within Third-World countries there are competing classes with divergent interests: for example, an urban bourgeoisie that benefits from rapid, Western-oriented industrialization, and a rural peasantry that does not. This is often reflected in struggles for political power, as we have seen. Even a state with the best interests of its own people at heart must walk a precarious line between competing parties both within and without the nation. Too much emphasis on policies for stimulating growth and attracting foreign capital may lead to popular unrest by the have-nots; a policy that is too egalitarian may cause the haves to pack up and leave, taking their resources with them.

Foreign Aid: Catalyst or Obstacle to Development?

Many feel that outside assistance is essential, at least in the short term, for development to continue, no matter what the specific policy advocated. But if external assistance is necessary for Third-World development, then *how much* is needed, *what kind*, and *from whom*? These questions are the focus of the current debate on foreign aid. There are a number of different types of financial assistance received by developing countries. Aid may be *bilateral* (between two individual nations) or *multilateral* (mediated through international agencies such as the International Monetary Fund [IMF] or World Bank). It need not be public: the fastest-growing sources of assistance to developing nations are loans from multinational banks in developed nations. Aid may be economic or military. It may be general, or restricted to specific uses (for example, for specified development projects, or the purchase of products from the donor nation). It may also take the form of outright grants, or loans that require repayment with interest.

The arguments on international aid are similar to those on domestic welfare programs. A number of theorists argue for massive increases in the level of financial assistance by rich nations to the Third World.[60] These advocates note that while the absolute amount of assistance from developed nations has increased to some extent, the amount relative to total GNP has actually fallen steadily since the 1960s.[61] The U.S. spends only .23 percent of its GNP on development assistance—thirteenth out of the seventeen Organization for Economic Cooperation and Development (OECD) donor countries.[62] Ideal target rates by advocates range from .7 percent to 1.0 percent of the GNP of developed nations.

Apart from the *amount* of aid given to Third-World countries, the way in which it is administered has also been criticized. Important multilateral organizations like the IMF and the World Bank are dominated by the developed nations, since representation is based essentially on the size of financial contribution. As noted earlier, these agencies often require severe austerity measures by the recipient nations before loans are approved; or restrict aid to Western-style development projects that may be innappropriate for the specific needs of the country. This has led many Third-World countries to call for a greater voice in such organizations, or even the creation of new international economic agencies with more democratic representation. In response, the developed capitalist nations refuse to provide funds without guarantees that such assistance will not be used for projects detrimental to the international capitalist system. The capitalist nations, of course, feel that capitalist development is in the best interests of *developing* nations as well as their own. Not all Third-World representatives agree.

"Conditionality" is even more important in the case of bilateral aid, where economic need may be less important than political orientation. At the 1981 Conference on North-South relations in Cancún, Mexico, President Reagan made it clear that the era of "massive American handouts" was over, and that preference would be given to (1) "friendly" governments based on U.S. security interests (that is, anticommunist); and (2) policies promoting "economic freedom"[63]—that is, capitalism.

As with the debate on domestic welfare programs, critics of increased aid argue that it often fosters increased dependency and stifles internal sources of innovation and investment.[64] Many dependency theorists would agree with conservatives that this has been the case historically. But like radical critics of welfare liberalism, they argue that the system of international economic assistance was never meant to foster the economic autonomy of Third-World nations, but to keep them in the fold.

The Effects of Direct Foreign Investment

There are also sharp disagreements on the effect of the other important source of external funding, direct foreign investment. Most of the controversy concerns the organizational structure in which such investment occurs. Most foreign investment in developing countries occurs through the establishment of subsidiaries of multinational corporations (MNCs)—also called transnational corporations (TNCs)—and the resulting transfer of capital and technology. The rapid expansion of MNCs from their home countries in the "core" to local production facilities in other nations is the crucial structural feature of the postwar international economy. For some, it means that we must revise all traditional thinking on the nature of the international economy and international trade. Bernadette Madeuf and Charles-Albert Michalet make this case as follows:

> [T]he new international order basically reflects a radical transformation of the position of the industrialized economies of the world. They are no longer restricting themselves to the export of goods. They are now, increasingly, also exporting branches of industry. Direct international investment is to be added to, and sometimes replaces exports. . . . The original way in which TNCs operate is leading to a radical change in the nature of international trade . . . there is an increasing proportion of exports and imports . . . which can no longer be analyzed in terms of movement from one country to another. For it is, in fact, movement from one productive unit of a TNC to another—between subsidiaries of parent companies. . . . Nation States are in fact trading less and less with each other. Trade flows are captured by TNCs and transformed into internal movements in which products replace goods to the extent that certain types of subsidiaries may be regarded simply as workshops.[65]

In their view, the call for "free trade " in the international marketplace is mere rhetoric, since they see "the replacement of the world market by the planned structures of TNCs."[66]

What effect does multinationalization have on Third World development? Theorists who argue that investment by MNCs has a positive effect on development cite correlations between the levels of such investment and growth rates. Such findings are correct, but have little relevance for the debate on multinationalization. There is little disagreement that direct investment by MNCs can raise aggregate measures like GNP, levels of savings, or manufacturing growth rates. The debate concerns the qualitative effects; "the fundamental economic and social meaning of development as it relates to the diverse activities of MNCs."[67]

Proponents of multinationalization point out that foreign investment is essential for Third-World development. While it may be profitable for the corporations concerned (otherwise they would not be there), it also "fills the gaps" between available domestic funds, technology, and skills, and that necessary for growth. MNCs provide jobs and wages that would not be there otherwise; they may also be the most important source of tax revenue to the state. Thus promotion of Third-World development should include policies that encourage foreign investment, since all parties benefit.

Critics of this position argue that multinationalization has had a number of harmful effects on developing countries, at least as it has occurred in the past. Even the economic benefits may be questioned. The importation of technology, capital, and management skills may actually impede local innovation and business activity, since small domestic firms have little chance of competing. What domestic savings are available for investment will also likely go to the MNCs, where profits are higher and risks fewer. While there may be short-term benefits with the initial investment, the net effect on foreign exchange earnings may be negative in the long run due to the necessary importation of intermediate products and capital goods, and the repatriation of profits to the home company. Public revenue may also be less than expected, since MNCs are often lured by attractive tax concessions and liberal investment allowances.

Even more important for critics are the social and political effects of MNCs on host countries. While some segments of the population do undoubtedly benefit, the fruits are not equally distributed. Centralized, capital-intensive enterprises may also employ inappropriate technology, given the needs of the population as a whole, producing inappropriate products and generating consumption habits out of line with the limitations of a developing economy. Most serious of all are the instances where MNCs, whose yearly sales may dwarf the total GNP of the host country, have used their economic power to interfere with the internal politics of the nation—from obtaining tax concessions to overthrowing governments.

Those who support open encouragement of foreign investment, and those who advocate the complete nationalization of foreign holdings and/or restrictions on foreign investment, represent the two extreme responses. In the middle are most development theorists, who recognize foreign investment as a vital source of much needed capital and technology, and who argue for various compromise positions involving cooperation between MNCs and host governments in ways that are mutually beneficial. Given their current relative position, this may require strengthening the bargaining power of host nations. Some Third-World theorists argue that this means reducing dependence upon the multinational corporation for capital and technology. This might be done through international development banks for direct investment in the projects of developing countries (presumably less dominated by the developed countries than is the World Bank) and greater promotion of research, development, and the transfer of technological information through *international* agencies such as those affiliated with the UN, rather than through the activities of private corporations.

Population, Agriculture, and Development

When Americans consider Third-World poverty, the image that comes to mind is often that of teeming masses with little or nothing to eat. This is certainly accurate in many cases, as the data noted earlier show. But the problems of population and agricultural self-sufficiency are more complex than they appear at first glance. The initial inclination is to define the problem as one of numbers: not enough food—too many people. But an adequate response should also consider crucial qualitative issues, such as the distribution of world food supplies and peoples, and the distributional effects of previous development policies.

The "population explosion" is indeed a serious problem in the Third World. It is a relatively recent phenomenon; ironically the result of one of the few products of Western industrialization—medicine and health care practices—that have had a significant "modernizing" effect. While mortality rates are still high in comparison with those of developed nations, there has been a definite convergent trend.[68] Unfortunately, modern birth control has had a lesser impact. (For more on this see Chapter 14, especially the section on demographic-transition theory.) Those who argue that population control is the first essential step in combating world poverty have a strong case. In the last few decades, economic growth rates in the developing countries have matched those of the industrial nations; yet the gap in per capita income has widened due to differences in the population growth rate.[69] Higher growth rates also mean that a different age structure exists in the Third World. Over one-half the population is under fifteen in the LDCs, as opposed to one-quarter in the developed world.[70] Among other things this means that those adults who can work have more mouths to feed. While sociologists in the United States are increasingly concerned with the problems of the elderly, the immediate reality in the Third World is that of starving children.

The obvious response to this problem is rapid dissemination of birth control education and assistance. This usually requires overcoming social, cultural, or religious barriers. Some even view forced (versus voluntary) family planning as a necessary, if distasteful, option, especially in light of the success of obligatory family planning in China.

Few dispute the need for birth control in the Third World. But some theorists stress that *underdevelopment*, not *overpopulation*, is the real source of Third-World poverty. Rather than emphasizing the factor of "too many people," the argument is reversed: if adequate development took place, the population problem would take care of itself. Per capita income would increase and population growth rates decline as they eventually did in the earlier industrializing nations. The distributional issues are also important. For example, the developed nations have one-third of the world's population but consume 80 percent of its resources. Adjustments in the international pattern of unequal consumption would certainly improve the situation of most developing countries. There are also the previously mentioned internal distributional problems tied to rapid, Western-style industrialization: unequal distribution of new income and rapid rural-urban migration that amasses too many people in too small an area—with too few resources. This might call for a policy of development more appropriate to the needs of the developing country, which would generate a more balanced distribution of income and a more "natural" spatial distribution of the population. Some who stress the need for "appropriate" development first have even suggested that the "population problem" is a contrivance of First-World theorists to avoid the real causes of dependency and underdevelopment[71]—a means of "blaming the victims" for their difficulties.

There are significant parallels between the discussion of overpopulation and that of agricultural development in the Third World. For both problems, the obvious solutions evoke numbers and technology. In the latter case the problem is inadequate food supply, and responses include application of modern techniques to raise the very low level of productivity of Third-World agriculture. But as with population, the real situation is more complex. There is a general consensus that the direct and immediate supply of food from the First World is a necessity for those poorest nations where starvation is epidemic. But long-term responses that would help the Third World feed itself are more complicated.

Since humans must eat before they can do anything else, it would seem that any strategy of development would begin with the problems of food production. But despite much discussion of the possibilities of modern seed and chemical fertilizer in fostering a "green revolution" in the Third World, actual output was not substantially increased. Moreover, in the 1950s and early 1960s, development theory's emphasis on urban industrialization often meant the neglect of the agricultural sector. This was even the case among the educated in the Third World itself, where agricultural studies has traditionally been a low-prestige area in comparison to the urban professions or government service. This situation is being rectifed today, but it is an important reason why agricultural output remained stagnant in the Third World—even *declining* in southern Africa—while GNP began to grow in the 1960s and 1970s.[72]

The first step toward eliminating world hunger is a drastic improvement in agricultural output, which in turn requires a substantial increase in the productivity of both land (more yield per acre) and labor (more output per worker). This is not as easy as it sounds. To begin with it is difficult to transfer agricultural techniques from developed to developing nations. Differences in climate, soil, and seasonal conditions may mean, for example, that the latest methods from the United States may not be applicable in a particular developing country. Even when proven techniques are available there are other obstacles to be considered. Biological and chemical improvements of the land or new seed strains are promising means of increasing output. But this may require overcoming the suspicion of the peasant farmer. What may appear to be stubborn traditionalism from our perspective is actually a justifiable fear of experimentation, given the peasant's extremely tenuous hold on subsistence. Other "improvements" may have broader socioeconomic limitations. Mechanization, for example, can increase agricultural output tremendously, as the U.S. experience has demonstrated. But where capital is scarce and the individual units of land are small, large-scale mechanization may not be economically feasible. On the other hand, even its successful implementation could generate other problems such as increasing an already high level of unemployment as farm workers are displaced. It should be remembered that agriculture is not just an "industry," but a way of life for the vast majority in the Third World. As with industrial development, it is dangerous to focus exclusively on quantitative goals without considering the qualitative effects of change.

Since agricultural development is perhaps the most pressing problem of all in the Third World, it is worthwhile to note briefly the differences between developing countries. Agriculture is an issue in which it is misleading to lump all Third-World countries together. Even beyond the obvious variation in growing conditions, there are the different social, political, and demographic factors from one developing country to the next. In sub-Saharan Africa agricultural production is carried out mainly on small family farms. Many African nations have potentially cultivatable land that is undeveloped. The size and productivity of family farms is limited by the lack of capital and technology, and the corresponding reliance on hand labor. Population is also a factor, but with a twist: there are often labor shortages during harvest season that limit the area of cultivation. In this context, education and the introduction of modern techniques would be most directly beneficial. Increasing output per worker would not immediately threaten large-scale displacement of the rural population.

The situation is different in Asia. There is a reliance on primitive farming techniques, which means low productivity, and the basic unit is the small subsistence farm. However, in Asia overpopulation is a much greater problem. There is not enough land for the rural population, which means that peasant families are confined to tiny parcels that they may be forced to share with others. Tenant farming and heavy financial indebtedness are also important aspects of peasant life. The perpetual state of debt to landlord or moneylender is another factor limiting the activity of the individual peasant farmer. In this context, solutions must include expansion of farm size to improve efficiency and allow the use of modern production methods, without simultaneously displacing large numbers of peasants with nowhere else to go.

In Latin America, the basic problem is not so much the amount of land available as its distribution. While significant land reform has taken place in a few countries (Mexico, Bolivia, and Cuba), most of Latin America remains in a semifeudal condition in which 1.3 percent of the landowners own 71.6 percent of the land.[73] The majority of peasant producers live on tiny plots *(minifundios)* that may or may not provide subsistence, while the rich minority own vast tracks of land *(latifundios)* worked by peasants who must supplement their limited incomes. In spite of their size, most latifundios are quite inefficient, since their owners have little direct need to increase productivity. Where they are worked intensively, it is generally in the large-scale production of export crops like coffee, which does little to improve the condition of the peasantry.

In Latin America, agricultural reform must include providing those with the motivation to increase productivity beyond subsistence with enough land to do so. But it is here that agriculture is most directly a political problem. Patterns of land ownership have not emerged for purely economic reasons, but are based on a long tradition of power and privilege. Attempts to change this tradition have usually resulted in violent confrontation, as we have seen.

Economic development in the Third World is an extremely complex issue. We have been able to consider only a few of the major problems in the preceding discussion. A major complicating factor is the political nature of economic decisions; abstract theories of development are implemented in concrete situations by groups with practical power, whose interests may conflict with the interests of other groups. This is perhaps the appropriate point at which to consider world poverty in the broader context of international political conflicts, which so often shape our perception of Third-World problems.

EAST-WEST CONFLICT AND THIRD-WORLD INSTABILITY

The 1970s and the U.S. "Inferiority Complex"

During the 1970s, some proclaimed a long-term erosion of U.S. power compounded by more recent major policy failures and a "loss of nerve." The loss of the Vietnam War generated the "Vietnam syndrome," an alleged tendency toward isolationist disengagement even when vital national interests were at stake. The 1973–1974 oil crisis produced long gas lines and quickly doubled the price of fuel and heating oil. The success of the OPEC oil cartel contributed to runaway inflation, which caused economic hardships and reduced living standards of lower- and middle-class Americans throughout the middle and later 1970s. By 1978, the dollar reached its nadir against major European currencies; few Americans could afford European travel, European exports sold at premium prices, and U.S. servicemen stationed in Europe were reduced to near poverty. From 1977 to 1980, U.S. productivity (which had been slowing for over ten years) ceased its postwar pattern of growth and fell 0.5 percent per year.[74] The competitiveness of U.S. industry declined and many American goods lost their reputation for quality and reliability (for example, U.S. autos were consistently outperformed by most Japanese and many European models). The United States continued to be the largest and richest economy, but intensifying international economic competition and growing dependency on expensive, imported raw materials increased the nation's sensitivity to its status in the world. *Business Week* writers pronounced the "decline of U.S. power."[75]

"America's inferiority complex" peaked with the fall of the Shah of Iran. He was a recipient of much U.S. military aid, but little attention was given to the brutality of his regime and existence of internal forces opposed to "Westernization." American intelligence sources did not comprehend the weakness of the regime until the revolutionaries reached the palace gates. The U.S. supported the Shah until he fell and then failed in its attempt to replace him with a "moderate" successor. American embassy officials were later taken hostage (after President Carter permitted the exiled Shah into the United States for medical treatment) and an embarrassing attempt to rescue them failed. The American public felt it was powerless to protect itself even against "second rate" powers.

This perceived loss of power was a major factor in the election of Ronald Reagan in 1980. Moreover, these conditions provided a stage for Reagan's massive enlargement of the military budget,[76] return to strident "containment" rhetoric, and increasing reliance on force in foreign affairs (military interventions in Lebanon and Grenada, expanded military aid for repressive Central American regimes in El Salvador, Honduras, and Guatemala, and even *overt* CIA assistance to counterrevolutionaries ["contras"] attempting to overthrow Marxist Nicaragua). There are parallels between these events and an earlier period in American history between 1948–1950, in which the civil war in Greece, the "loss" of China to the Communists, the first Soviet A-bomb, and the Korean War led many Americans to feel that we had "lost control" of world affairs. Many have argued that strong U.S. Cold War sentiment grew out of these earlier frustrations.[77] Perhaps a similar effect has taken place in the 1980s.

The Expansion of Soviet Hegemony?

Many believe that the U.S. has caved in to the U.S.S.R. Since the 1950s, conservatives have argued that the Soviets have been toppling the "dominoes" and slowly moving toward world hegemony. The events of the 1970s were seen as the culmination of this process. But before designating Soviet expansionism as the most important source of conflict, it is necessary to consider some facts on the relative influence of the West versus the Soviet bloc. Criticism of the "domino theory" does not require a defense of Soviet policy.

First, it is not clear that the United States and its allies disengaged. Between 1945 and 1975, the U.S. and Western Europe were responsible for 79 percent of all military interventions compared to 6 percent for the communist nations,[78] although conflicts and interventions by communist regimes have increased in recent years and some have been among the most bloody (for example, the Pol Pot government in Kanpuchea killed 2 million people in four years).[79] Ninety-five percent of the interventions occurred in the developing countries where the contest for world dominance is hottest.[80] Between 1950 and 1980, the U.S.

trained more than 411,000 military personnel from developing countries, more than nine times the number trained by the Soviet Union. Most of these personnel came from repressive military regimes.[81] In the last thirty years, U.S. covert actions helped bring down the governments in Iran, Guatemala, Vietnam, and Chile, and influenced events in many others.

The United States did not drop out of the international scene during the latter 1970s. For example, the U.S. still vastly outspent the U.S.S.R. in foreign aid: in 1978, the U.S. spent about $5.5 billion compared to the U.S.S.R.'s $900 million.[82] The U.S. exported slightly less than $8 billion worth of arms to developing countries as opposed to the Soviet Union's $4 billion. U.S. military expenditures increased throughout the mid-1970s—procurement (spending for maintenance goods and for foreign military sales) rose from $45.8 billion in 1976 to $69 billion in 1979.[83] Though Soviet military strength has grown rapidly, the U.S. had higher military expenditures and remained the leader in sophisticated military hardware.[84] Finally, despite the economic dislocations of the middle and later 1970s, the U.S. GNP was still over twice as large as that of the U.S.S.R.. The U.S. continued to impose economic sanctions on the Soviet bloc, its allies, and potential allies (through boycotts, embargoes, tariffs, political riders to "most favored nation" trade status, and manipulations of U.S.-dominated world economic institutions such as the International Monetary Fund and the World Bank). Economic leverage remained a most effective instrument of American policy throughout the 1970s.

The general point is that the United States has not retracted or weakened. Instead, the world changed! The undisputed world dominance that the U.S. enjoyed after World War II is gone. The United States now competes with Soviet military power, European and Japanese economic power, and new assertions of autonomy from many developing nations throughout the world.

The tendency to see the world in black and white, "East-vs-West" terms leads many Americans to interpret any loss of American influence as a corresponding Soviet gain. But this is not the case; indeed, the Soviet Union has recently suffered some serious foreign policy setbacks.[85] A 1980 study of Soviet geopolitics published by the Center for Defense Information reached the following conclusions:

> Outside Eastern Europe, Soviet influence has lacked staying power. Inability to accumulate influence in foreign countries over long periods is a dominant feature of Soviet world involvement.
>
> Starting from a very low base of political, economic, and military involvement, the Soviets have increased their influence around the world. Starting with influence in 9 percent of the world's nations in 1945, they peaked at 14 percent in the late 1950s, and today have influence in 12 percent of the world's nations. Of the 155 countries in the world today, the Soviets have influence in 19.
>
> The Soviets have been successful in gaining influence primarily among the world's poorest and most desperate countries.
>
> Soviet foreign involvement has to a large extent been shaped by indigenous conditions, and the Soviets have been unable to command loyalty or obedience.
>
> Soviet setbacks in China, Indonesia, Egypt, India, and Iraq dwarf marginal Soviet advances in lesser countries.
>
> Temporary Soviet successes in backward countries have proved costly to the Soviet Union. They provide no justification for American alarmism or military intervention. U.S. policies should emphasize our nonmilitary advantages in competition for world influence.[86]

The above observations do not reduce the danger of the East-West conflict, or justify

Soviet incursions. Nor do they reflect the great degree of political and military control exerted by the Soviet Union along its borders in Eastern Europe and Afghanistan. But they do suggest that a growing number of nations are independent of *either* U.S. or Soviet domination. It may also mean that recent instances of Soviet aggression are a reaction to perceived "failures" and "loss of control" much like our own.

The Arms Race and the "Window of Vulnerability"

In the early 1980s, the United States engaged in the largest peacetime military build-up in its history, intensifying an arms race that had never really slowed during the "era of détente" between 1970 and 1976. There are a number of social, political, and economic factors behind the present build-up, but the main justification is an old one: the United States is "falling behind" the Soviets. The Soviets were estimated to be spending more for general defense, generating an increasing military "spending gap."[87] Even more threatening, however, was the increase in the number, power, and accuracy of Soviet ICBMs (intercontinental ballistic missiles), which according to some gave them the ability to wipe out our own land-based missiles in a "first strike." For some this signified an increasing "window of vulnerability" in our defenses.[88] Similar arguments were made about tactical nuclear weapons and conventional forces to justify broad, across-the-board increases in all U.S. military programs.[89]

The history of U.S. arms policy urges caution when considering these claims. The past is replete with various "periods of peril" in which wild exaggerations of Soviet strength and Cold War scare tactics justified rapid arms build-ups.[90] For example, NSC-68 justified massive increases by claiming the Soviet Union would have 200 atomic bombs by 1954. This was a vast overestimation, and neglected to note that they had no adequate means of *delivering* the bombs to American targets.[91] In 1954 and 1955 the delivery system itself was the center of controversy when a strategic "bomber gap" was declared. This was based largely on the misperception of American diplomats in Moscow during the May Day parades. What they took to be a large number of new long-range bombers flying in display over the city turned out to be a very small number—the whole Soviet force—continually circling overhead. An "emergency" build-up continued anyway, and by 1961 there was a bomber gap: the U.S. had 600 long-range strategic bombers to the Soviet's 190.[92]

One of the most famous "periods of peril" concerned the "missile gap" that was the focus of the 1960 presidential race between Kennedy and Nixon. American sensitivity to this issue, in the wake of the Soviet launching of Sputnik in 1957, may have cost Nixon the presidency. After the elections, the new Defense Secretary Robert McNamara found that the Russians did not have the 1000 ICBMs they were said to have, but 50! The U.S. accelerated production of a whole new generation of missiles anyway.[93]

These facts are not presented to lay the blame for the arms race solely on the United States. There has been mutual distrust, overreaction, and steady acceleration of armaments on both sides. The Soviets have relentlessly sought to catch the U.S., and reached what they considered to be rough parity by the mid-1970s. Currently each side has certain advantages in the "strategic balance" (see Tables 16.2, 16.3, 16.4). The Soviets have more delivery vehicles, but the U.S. has more warheads; they have many more land-based ICBMs, but we have much greater numbers in nearly invulnerable air- and submarine-

Table 16.2 World Nuclear Weapons

	US	USSR	UK	FRANCE	CHINA	TOTALS
Strategic	10,000	7,400	192	80	4	17,676
Intermediate	1,300	3,500	96	18	200	5,114
Tactical	17,700	6,500	158	165	100	24,623
Total:	**29,000**	**17,400**	**446**	**263**	**304**	**47,413**

Strategic—*capable of intercontinental distances and/or intended for use against the enemy's homeland.*
Intermediate—*range or combat radius of 1,500 miles or more.*
Tactical—*all other shorter range or battlefield systems, including land mines and artillery shells.*
Weapons—*warheads and bombs*
Source: Ruth Leger Sivard, *World Military and Social Expenditures 1983* (Washington D.C.: World Priorities, 1983), p. 15.

launched forces.[94] A new controversy has recently emerged concerning the European deployment of U.S. medium-range Cruise and Pershing II missiles. The Soviet Union sees this as a new and dangerous first-strike threat, with deadly accurate missiles six minutes from Moscow. The U.S. argues that this is a defensive measure to counter the European deployment of Soviet medium-range SS-20s. The arms race may soon enter a new level of escalation with the development of space-based weapons systems.

The Causes of Third-World Instability

Most observers of Third-World conflicts recognize that there are numerous sources of tension, including poverty, rapid social and economic transformation, and political confrontations from within and without. Disagreements occur on which factors are primary. The recent debate over El Salvador exhibits a fundamental cleavage between those who emphasize Soviet intervention, and others who consider poverty and U.S.-supported military regimes as the most important factors.

The U.S. government portrays El Salvador as a victim of expansionary communist totalitarianism. According to President Reagan, "Central America has become the stage for a bold attempt by the Soviet Union, Cuba, and Nicaragua to install communism by force throughout this hemisphere."[95] His contention was that the Salvadoran rebels are fed by a direct flow of arms and aid from conquest-oriented Soviet surrogates—Cuba and Nicaragua

Table 16.3 Strategic Nuclear Forces of the Superpowers

	US			USSR		
	LAUNCHERS	WEAPONS		LAUNCHERS	WEAPONS	
	NUMBER	NUMBER	% OF TOTAL	NUMBER	NUMBER	% OF TOTAL
Land-based	1,047	2,147	21	1,398	5,496	74
Sea-based	544	4,960	50	904	1,592	22
Bombers	241	2,892	29	150	300	4
Total	**1,832**	**9,999**	**100**	**2,452**	**7,388**	**100**

Source: Ruth Leger Sivard, *World Military and Social Expenditures 1983* (Washington D.C.: World Priorities, 1983), p. 15.

Table 16.4 European Theater Nuclear Forces

	NATO								WARSAW PACT	
	US		UK		FRANCE*		TOTAL		USSR	
	LAUNCHERS	WEAPONS	LAUNCHERS	WEAPONS	LAUNCHERS	WEAPONS	LAUNCHERS	WEAPONS	LAUNCHERS	WEAPONS
Strategic	**[48]**	**[576]**	**64**	**192**	**80**	**80**	**144**	**272**		
Sea-based	[48]**	[576]**	64	192	80	80	144	272	—	—
Intermediate	**156**	**312**	**48**	**96**	**18**	**18**	**222**	**426**	**1,748**	**3,663**
Land-based	—	—	—	—	18	18	18	18	606	1,236
Sea-based	—	—	—	—	—	—	—	—	57	57
Bombers	156	312	48	96	—	—	204	408	1,085	2,370
Tactical	**1,127**	**1,127**	**108**	**158**	**165**	**165**	**2,400**	**5,450**	**2,676**	**2,676**
Land-based	277	277	—	—	42	42	319	319	773	773
Bombers	850	850	108	158	123	123	1,081	1,131	1,603	1,603
Other	na		na		na		1,000†	4,000†	300†	300†
Total	**1,283**	**1,439**	**220**	**446**	**263**	**263**	**2,766**	**6,148**	**4,424**	**6,339**

**France maintains liaison with the Allied command, but does not formally commit her forces to NATO.*

***Poseidon subs assigned to the NATO command are shown here but not included in the theater total. They appear above in the table for strategic forces.*

†Partially estimated.

Source: Ruth Leger Sivard, *World Military and Social Expenditures 1983* (Washington D.C.: World Priorities, 1983), p. 15.

(both nations deny the U.S. accusations). This is seen as part of a pattern of "international terrorism" aimed at destablizing non-Marxist regimes and promoting communist insurgency. From this perspective, U.S. support of the Salvadoran regime is ultimately a defensive response to threats to U.S. military security and economic interests.

The first priority of U.S. policy is to support friendly regimes against "communist" insurgents. Second, authoritarian leaderships are officially encouraged to "democratize" (have elections) and reduce human rights violations. The hope is for the eventual emergence of a popular, anticommunist government with long-term stability. The U.S. has not typically reduced aid to anticommunist regimes simply because they are repressive. But this has been justified by distinguishing "authoritarian" from "totalitarian" (communist) regimes. Authoritarian systems, once stabilized, are said to evolve toward democracy with the proper assistance, while communist systems are inherently totalitarian and can never lead to a more democratic system once in place.[96]

On the other hand, critics claim that extreme economic and social inequalities are the primary source of Third-World conflicts. Moreover, they assert that U.S. military aid tends to increase inequalities and strengthen the oligarchs. Critics generally see insurgent "liberation movements" as primarily nationalist responses to inequality and consequent political repression, rather than being rebellions directed by the Soviet Union. However, they argue that U.S. support for ruling elites leaves insurgents no option but to seek political models and military aid from non-Western and Marxist-Leninist sources.[97] This perspective rejects the distinction between authoritarian and totalitarian regimes, arguing that authoritarian systems often remain so and that democratizing trends in Leftist regimes are overlooked. It is claimed that the U.S. isolates these regimes economically, fosters militarism, and promotes dependency on the Soviet bloc.

Critics also argue that elections in "authoritarian" regimes are "public relations campaigns" designed to demonstrate that the regime is deserving of continued U.S. support.[98] As Vietnam demonstrated, even "small" wars are extremely costly economically, politically, and in lives. There U.S. participation must be defended vigorously at home; the issue of "democracy" helps justify the costs.

The Salvadoran leadership conducted "democratic" elections in 1982 and 1984. Despite guerrilla threats and attacks, the vast majority of eligible voters went to the polls (percentage turnout was higher than in any recent United States election!). For the most part, the U.S. news media applauded them as "fair" elections. But critics note that the media did not stress the absence of the Left opposition in the elections. Also unreported were the facts that voting was compulsory in El Salvador and that identity cards were stamped at the polls. The card must frequently be shown to public and to military officials.[99] The critics claim that Salvadorans were forced to vote and "choose" from only right-wing candidates. Moreover, the high illiteracy rate (35 percent), censorship, violence, and climate of intimidation made a truly democratic election impossible. Finally, despite the elections, the military still rules and the oligarchy remains in place.

The Consequences of Militarism on the U.S. Economy

The anticommunism of the early 1950s was a rationale for large-scale increases in military spending. As early as NSC-68, policymakers argued that military spending

"Democratic" elections in El Salvador are not the same as such elections in the United States.
(Claude Urraca/Sygma)

would stave off the communists and "stimulate" the economy.[100] This is called "military Keynesianism," after the British economist J. M. Keynes, who in the 1930s called for state "regulation" of the economy and, particularly, increased state spending to stimulate economic demand and growth. Keynes, however, stressed primarily nonmilitary spending. Between 1950 and 1951, the U.S. military budget increased from $14 billion to $34 billion and its share of the gross national product jumped from 5.1 percent in 1949 to a high of 13.2 percent in 1952. After the Korean War, it declined somewhat (to the 7-to-9 percent range) as a percentage of GNP, but expenditures grew in real dollars.[101] The growth of military spending was accompanied by sustained economic growth from 1950 to 1965.[102] The production of "guns and butter" seemed to be mutually reinforcing.

During the first two decades after World War II, the United States enjoyed an enviable position in the world economy. The major capitalist countries and the Soviet Union had been ravaged by war and were rebuilding. The U.S. emerged with its economy and military intact: its technology, goods, and the dollar dominated world markets and the result was unparalleled affluence. But by the middle 1960s, other industrial nations (especially Japan and West Germany) were becoming highly competitive and U.S. economic growth slowed considerably. The U.S. was "bogged down" in Vietnam and President Johnson did not raise taxes to pay for the war. As a result, his Great Society program (of increased spending on health, education, and welfare) was reduced and eventually junked. In roughly three years, the Vietnam build-up increased military spending from $50 billion to $78 billion.[103] This caused higher deficits and inflation, as well as an imbalance in foreign trade (the U.S. was importing increasingly more than it was exporting).[104] This began the 1970s cycle of economic problems and minimal growth.

Despite some debate about the topic,[105] there is much evidence that military spending does economic and social damage. In the 1970s, Seymour Melman[106] described the waste of resources and its inflationary effects on the economy. Military research and production drains scientists, engineers, skilled workers, and capital from other sectors. High profits and pay in military industries create scarcity and increased costs for competing consumer industries. *Much* lower military expenditures allow Japan and West Germany to devote their material, capital, and human resources to market-oriented production. In 1982–1983 the U.S. "spent more than twice as much on military as on civilian research"—this is the obverse of Western Europe.[107] As Lester Thurow[108] states, American scientists and engineers have the "choice" between "designing a new missile with a laser guidance system or . . . designing a new toaster." Military jobs not only pay more, but focus on "cutting-edge" intellectual and technical problems.

A small minority of fortunate producers benefit greatly from American military spending. These are among the largest U.S. firms; seventeen of the top twenty-five defense contractors were in *Fortune*'s 80 largest firms.[109] The top thirty-three military contractors control slightly more than 50 percent of all military contracts.[110] Furthermore, "cost plus" contracts protect military producers from inflation and other cost increases. They are not strapped by the cost-efficiency considerations of other firms; added costs are simply passed on to the government and taxpayers. In the military industries, vast underbidding on contracts followed by large cost-overruns is commonplace. Because suppliers know that military contractors are often careless in managing costs, outrageous overcharges for apparently trivial tools, parts, and materials sometimes occur. In 1983, the public was outraged to learn that the Pentagon paid $110 for a 4-cent diode, $44 for a 17-cent light bulb, and $727 for an $8 electrical plug.[111]

Military contracting provides *publicly funded* windfall profits for a privileged sector of industry. Furthermore, military contracting is often in high-tech industries that employ much capital but few people. Therefore, military production generates fewer jobs than it eliminates through its competition with other industries. A 1984 study demonstrated that in the early 1980s military contracting contributed to the loss of "1.52 million jobs, with factory, clerical and sales workers bearing the brunt of the loss." The associated "brain drain" has diverted one-third of all scientific and engineering work to the defense industry.[112]

Research on defense spending (1939–1968) demonstrated that "guns" are purchased at the expense of "butter." Capital is drawn away from the production of consumer durables and revenue is siphoned off from health, education, and welfare.[113] Even though it can stimulate certain sectors of the economy, military spending must be paid for by the public. It is a form of consumption that reduces the availability of resources for improving the average person's quality of life. In the early 1980s, the U.S. embarked on one of the largest peacetime military build-ups in history.[114] In 1983 and early 1984, government military outlays provided a stimulus to a very depressed economy operating far below its industrial capacity. However, the build-up also produced gigantic federal deficits, generated fears of a future economic crisis, and caused drastic cuts in already reduced health, education, and welfare benefits. In 1982, the number below the poverty line rose to over 34 million people, up from the less than 32 million below the poverty level in 1981.[115] (See Chapter 10 for more on poverty.)

PART III: RESPONSES

Responses to Underdevelopment: Enduring Questions

Many of the possible responses to world poverty and underdevelopment were noted in the previous section, since a discussion of the causes of these problems call forth corresponding solutions. As has been shown, proposals reflect the interest or bias of the observer, and vary depending on what one thinks needs to be done, and for whom. However, any adequate discussion of possible solutions must first answer the following questions:

1. Perhaps the most fundamental question is reflected in the debate between "modernization" and "dependency" theorists. Are the obstacles to "development" primarily *internal,* reflecting the level of education, social differentiation, and so on, or are there *external* constraints that stem from the location of less developed countries in the structure of the world economy? An even more basic question: Is *capitalism* the cause of or the solution to world poverty and underdevelopment?

2. What do we *mean* by "development"? Is our primary goal an increase in aggregate growth rates or GNP, or is the *redistribution* of resources (within or between nations) the most pressing problem? Can we afford to consider the *quality* of life for the *majority* of Third-World peoples, and would this approach *necessarily* contradict a more quantitative orientation?

3. Once general goals (including our definition of "development") are decided on, what *specific* policy measures are required for their implementation? This requires asking questions about the relationship between particular LDCs and the world economy. Does development require *free trade,* or are certain protectionist policies more beneficial? Is foreign aid a stimulus or impediment to development? How should it be administered? What is the role of multinational corporations in the economies of Third-World nations? In proposing specific policy recommendations, the *differences* between developing countries must be remembered, as illustrated in the previous discussion of population and agriculture.

4. Any discussion of policy recommendations must further ask: *Who* decides, and *in whose interests* are these decisions made? Many Third-World theorists have called for a "new international economic order" that would increase the representation of LDCs in international lending agencies and decrease their dependence on the developed world. But as noted above, those who control the world's resources are unlikely to give up their power to determine how they are used. Further, there are policy disagreements *within* Third-World nations—sometimes violent disagreements—for example, between factions that benefit from Western-oriented development and those that do not. These competing interests must be clearly identified.

5. Is the current world economic situation a "zero-sum game"? That is, will progress in developing nations require solutions that adversely affect other interests? Or, are there possible solutions in which all parties benefit?

Responses to Third-World Political Instability

There is near unanimous agreement that economic problems are a major source of discontent and unrest in the Third World. The preceding questions about underdevelopment are relevant, then, in discussing social and political upheavals in developing countries. However, it is also generally recognized that revolutions do not emerge mechanically from economic conditions. The nature and degree of political conflict depends on the specific relations between the classes struggling for power in a given country. Moreover, any struggle that threatens the political status quo must also be seen in its relation to the precarious East-West balance of power, if for no other reason than that it is perceived this way by the superpowers. There are no "insignificant" revolutions in Moscow or Washington.

Responses to Third-World instability naturally vary with one's definition of the problem. As noted earlier, explanations fall along a continuum between those emphasizing *internal* sources of unrest and those that stress external pressures. But disagreements cannot always be solved by an "objective" determination of the source of unrest, for value judgments are involved as well. There are disagreements on whether political uprisings are progressive or subversive. On the other hand, stability is not in itself the basis for positive evaluation, since it may be the result of severe repression by those in power.

The position of the Reagan administration has consistently been that Third-World conflicts are the product of communist subversion. While acknowledging indigenous social and economic problems, the administration sees the primary stimulus as outside agitation. This view is exemplified in the recent report by Reagan's "bipartisan" (actually hand-picked) Commission on Central America headed by former Secretary of State Henry Kissinger, which concluded that "whatever the social and economic conditions that invited insurgency in the region, outside intervention is what gives the conflict its present character."[116] Since the problem is construed in military terms—as an invasion by outside aggressors in league with internal collaborators—the response has been military as well. "Friendly" governments are to be protected through the supply of arms and other military assistance.

Another important element in the administration's approach to Third-World conflicts is the interpretation of these conflicts as part of the general East-West confrontation. The incursions in Latin America are seen to represent Soviet probes to test our strength and our will as a superpower. In the words of the Kissinger report, "Our credibility worldwide is engaged. The triumph of hostile forces in what the Soviet Union calls the 'strategic rear' of the United States would be read as a sign of U.S. impotence."[117] Political instability in the Third World is thus linked to the vital security interests of the U.S.

As noted earlier, those who interpret Third-World conflicts in such universal terms often do so out of a professed fear of communism. In this view (exemplified in the NSC-68 document discussed above) the communist doctrine, and the Soviet power that propagates it, allow no room for compromise; nothing short of world conquest will do. While such a doctrine would not be swayed by moral argument, the Soviets do

The U.S. (and the USSR) is a military presence in many less developed nations.
(El Koussy/Sygma)

understand the threat of counterforce. This is the basis of "containment" and "peace through strength."

Recent American policy has been criticized for its support of repressive right-wing regimes in the name of anticommunism. This has been defended by administration officials as an unfortunate but necessary choice to avert a much greater evil. Following an argument by former UN Ambassador Jeane Kirkpatrick,[118] "traditional" authoritarian regimes such as those of pro-U.S. governments in Central America are products of history, which may be liberalized with the proper assistance, providing that external threats are checked. Communism, however, is seen as *inherently* totalitarian and can never lead to a *more* democratic system once in place.[119]

There are a number of criticisms of this response to Third-World conflicts. One might be called the "pragmatic" critique: as Vietnam and numerous other examples have shown, military solutions are increasingly less effective in preserving American influence in the Third World. John Sewell and John Mathieson, who are by no means complacent about recent acts of Soviet aggression, nevertheless conclude that

> [T]he use of military power to achieve American objectives in the Third World may no longer be generally applicable. A recent study identified 215 incidents in which U.S. forces were used for political purposes since the end of World War II (185 of these were in the Third World) and concluded that the use of military force to achieve political objectives has primarily a short-run effect and is no substitute for long-run diplomacy.[120]

Unfortunately, diplomatic solutions are difficult if the problem is defined in terms of a universal threat to democracy. Eldon Kenworthy[121] argues that based on public statements and recent actions, the Reagan administration is simply incapable of believing that a government can be both Marxist and in any way nonaligned. This, he argues, is the real reason for its repeated rejection of attempts by Nicaragua to enter into negotiations, in spite of pleas to do so by Mexico and the Contradora Group of moderate Latin American nations.[122] Similarly, the Kissinger Commission rejected any solution in El Salvador that involves sharing political power with the rebels, since such a move "would be only a prelude to a takeover by the insurgent forces."[123]

Critics argue that perceptions that mask complex internal problems and call for black or white responses may accomplish precisely the opposite of what is intended by driving reformers, insurgents, or newly formed radical governments into the Soviet camp.[124] Abstract, doctrinaire responses do not often consider unique social, political, and economic conditions that may relate to unrest. Indeed, the "facts" may be used selectively to fit perceptions. American assistance to El Salvador "promotes democracy" while Soviet aid to Nicaragua "is a new kind of colonialism."[125] The point is the need to be conscious of our own "selective perception" of events.

In general, those who advocate a more flexible response to Third-World conflicts do not deny the existence of Soviet interest or Soviet presence in these situations. The difference is in the emphasis on the internal sources of conflict that provide potential opportunities for external influence. These sources include widespread poverty and deprivation, political repression, and social inequality. From this perspective, policy should be geared toward "preventive medicine": strategies for promoting economic development; or support for regimes that work to reduce massive inequities and increase democratic participation. Critics of this view argue that such a "human rights" basis for foreign policy, as put forward during the Carter administration, proved unrealistic and led to our "loss" of Iran and Nicaragua.[126] Advocates counter that Carter's "human rights" policy was limited and inconsistent in practice. They also argue that with "friends" like the former Shah of Iran or Anastasio Somoza (assassinated president of Nicaragua), who needs enemies? Or rather, who needs a universal enemy like the Soviets, since we generate a plethora of enemies of our own who see the U.S. precisely in this light.

U.S.-Soviet Relations: Détente or Deterrence?

Because direct conflict between the superpowers would threaten the annihilation of the human race, there is general consensus on the need for "peaceful coexistence," whatever one side thinks about the other. This prompted the cold warrior, Richard Nixon, to a more pragmatic foreign policy of détente in the early 1970s, which made possible a limited (and temporary) thaw in East-West relations. In recent years, however, there has been a general disillusionment with this strategy. Many have argued that conciliatory attitudes by the U.S. merely allowed the Soviets to gain the upper hand in the world balance of power. This view was cogently expressed by President Reagan:

> So far détente has been a one-way street which the Soviet Union has used to pursue its own aims. I know of no leader of the Soviet Union, since the Revolution and including the present leadership, that has not more than once repeated in the various Communist congresses they hold, their determination that their goal must be the promotion of world revolution and a one-world Socialist or Communist state, whichever word you want to use. Now, as long as they do that and as long as they, at the same time, have openly and publicly declared that the only mo-

> rality they recognize is what will further their cause, meaning they reserve the right to commit any crime, to lie, to cheat in order to obtain it, I think that when you do business with them—even in détente—you keep that in mind.[127]

More sophisticated versions of this argument have been put forth by a number of foreign policy analysts. Helmut Sonnenfeldt,[128] for example, sees the number of Soviet "thrusts" in the world in the late 1970s, culminating in the invasion of Afghanistan, as due to the absence of countervailing power that resulted from the U.S.'s post-Vietnam hesitancy.[129] Soviet incursions should have been expected, he argues, since historically they have only negotiated seriously when they have "perceived adverse trends in the balance of forces."[130] This view that the Soviets will only respect the threat of countervailing force is the justification for our current military build-up.

The policy of the United States toward the Soviet Union has never been based on trust. But there have been different approaches to easing East-West tensions in the past. Michael Klare[131] distinguishes two competing orientations that have coexisted within the U.S. foreign policy establishment, which he dubs the "Prussians" and the "Traders." The Prussians see a strong global military presence as the fundamental prerequisite for containing Soviet expansion. The Traders, on the other hand, feel that to maintain U.S. hegemony, we should use our top weapon—economic superiority. In this view, the expansion of world trade and the establishment of closer economic ties with the Soviet Union and its satellites would provide a foundation for peaceful coexistence based not on "trust," but on solid economic interests.

The latter view was shared by President Roosevelt, who had hoped to integrate the Soviet Union into the new world economic order that was being planned at the end of World War II. This Trader strategy was abandoned in the Truman administration with the Cold War and the policy of containment. The Prussian orientation has dominated U.S. policy since that time, with limited exceptions during the later Nixon, Ford, and early Carter administrations (the era of détente). It has been aggressively advocated in the last few years in response to perceived Soviet political and military escalations. From this perspective, the only response that will "stabilize" East-West relations is one that reasserts the U.S. will to actively protect its interests in the world, and match any build-up in Soviet armaments.

Very few argue that U.S.-Soviet relations can or should depend on mutual trust. But critics of current U.S. policy contend that a more realistic portrait of Soviet perceptions is needed. For example, the U.S.S.R. has always claimed that its policies have been defensive reactions to external threats. Given their history of invasion by foreign powers (in particular by Germany in World War II), they were sensitive to what they saw as their encirclement by hostile forces after the war. For this reason, they claim that a buffer zone in Eastern Europe is essential for their national security. The Soviets also point to China on their southern border, a threat made more ominous by the recent improvement in relations between China and the United States. Further, while they admit to a build-up of both their conventional forces and their nuclear arsenal, they argue that this was only a reflection of their determination to achieve parity with the U.S. in a race in which they have been far behind in most of the postwar period. Even the invasion of Afghanistan in 1979, an event that generated more widespread condemnation than any other Soviet action of recent years, is said to have been "misunderstood" and falsely portrayed in the West. Jonathan Steele gives us the Soviet version of events in that country:

> In April 1978 a national-democratic, anti-feudal coup had toppled the regime of King Daoud. The new government wanted to modernize a backward, primitive society rapidly. Unfortunately it went too far, too fast. In its impatience it managed to alienate part of the masses who should have been on its side. As internal resistance mounted, with the help of arms supplies secretly channelled to the rebels by the United States and China, the danger of counterrevolution increased. After several appeals for help from the Afghan government, the Soviet Union decided to send in about 85,000 troops.[132]

These arguments should sound familiar to those acquainted with similar U.S. justifications for intervention in Third-World nations.

Critics of the confrontational strategy do not generally advocate blanket acceptance of the Soviet line. Most also condemn the use of coercion and military force by the Soviet Union against neighboring countries, as well as within its own borders. However, in their view, expressed Soviet concerns cannot be treated as mere propaganda. Rather, any response that is to succeed at easing East-West tensions must take their very real feelings of insecurity into account. Past U.S. policy has given the Soviets as little reason to trust us as we have to trust them. Policies that emphasize (with much public fanfare!) the reassertion of U.S. political and military dominance may only reinforce Soviet fears and make

President Reagan and Mikhail Gorbachev, General Secretary of the Soviet Union's Communist Party, head the leading nations in the arms race.
(Philippe/Ledru/Sygma)

them less willing to negotiate. Steele,[133] for example, disagrees with the views of analysts like Sonnenfeldt. In his view, détente was possible *because* the Soviets had achieved a rough parity with the U.S. According to Steele, the Soviets took détente as a sign that the U.S. was finally willing to accept them as an equal superpower. From their perspective, current policies represent a withdrawal of that recognition.

Avoiding Armageddon

In the nuclear age, the prevention of war between the superpowers is perhaps the most fundamental problem we face. Recent policy has emphasized strategic imbalances that must be redressed quickly if catastrophe is to be avoided. But as past experience has shown, the justified view that we face a period of peril can be used to different ends. Critics of the strategy of confrontation also argue that we are running out of time. But in their view, the crucial question is not whether there are gaps in the destructive capabilities of one superpower or another, but whether such gaps have any meaning today in a world where the two major powers have the capability of obliterating each other fifty times over. In their view, what is essential is serious and immediate negotiations toward arms *control*, regardless of what one side thinks of the other's doctrines or politics.

Writing for the Union of Concerned Scientists, Daniel Ford and his associates[134] enumerated five basic principles that they argue must be accepted before serious arms negotiations are possible:

1. Both sides have relatively equivalent arsenals sufficient to deter attack. Thus nothing is gained by enlarging stockpiles of weapons.

2. The idea that a technological "breakthrough" could give one side the upper hand is fruitless given current capacities for destruction.

3. The most recent technological innovations have increased "first strike" capacity that may be used in times of crises—and thus may also generate computerized "launch on warning" strategies that greatly magnify the dangers of malfunction or misunderstanding.

4. Both sides have massive overkill potential and can therefore feel secure and afford some flexibility at the bargaining table.

5. Both sides must abandon their pursuit of new weapons systems.

Recent innovations promise an especially dangerous escalation. Cruise missiles are very mobile and extremely hard to detect. Space-based antisatellite or antimissile systems threaten to open a whole new "frontier" in arms escalation. This has led a number of arms-control advocates to call for an immediate bilateral freeze on the production and deployment of nuclear weapons. Ford and his associates[135] see a number of advantages in such a step:

—A freeze at current levels of nuclear armaments would be equitable to both countries.

—The freeze would prevent the deployment by both sides of any more of the new weapons now under development with first-strike capability—especially Cruise missiles on both sides.

—A freeze would halt plans that would drastically escalate the arms race by placing nuclear war-fighting systems in outer space.

—Such an agreement could be adequately verified through satellites and other means of surveillance, and in fact would be much easier to verify than a limited numerical reduction.

Not all observers agree that these assumptions are valid. Even those who support a resolution of this type point out that it is only a first step. Long-term solutions would have to provide mechanisms for easing tensions in political "hot spots" such as the Middle East or the borders between Eastern and Western Europe, perhaps through the revitalization of the U.N. Security Council or establishment of other international peace-keeping organizations to prevent localized conflicts. (For suggestions, see The Independent Commission on Disarmament and Security Issues, 1982.[136]) But, in the case of nuclear weapons, the technology is rapidly outstripping the capacity of humans to keep it under control. For many the costs of one mistake call for a bold first step.

SUMMARY

1. This chapter deals with militarism and the internationsl political economy by focusing on three interrelated problems that dominate international relations: Cold War tensions between the United States and the Soviet Union; political instability and military conflicts in the Third World; and world poverty and underdevelopment.

Part I: The Problem

2. The problems dealt with in this chapter are introduced with particular reference to:
   a. The emergence of a perceived communist threat and resulting U.S. interventionism and policy of "containment" after World War II, which in turn resulted in a dangerous and expensive arms race and the possiblity of nuclear annihilation.
   b. The growth of militarism and political instability in the less developed Third World in the context of Cold War tensions between the superpowers.
   c. The tremendous economic problems that magnify and interact with political tensions, including poverty and inequality, backwardness, and dependency on the developed world for political, military, and economic assistance.

Part II: Causes and Consequences

3. Even beyond humanitarian concerns, the U.S. and other developed nations have an interest in the health of Third-World economies, given our increasing political and economic interdependence.
4. Two general conceptual orientations to the problem of development can be distinguished. The *modernization* approach focuses on the internal obstacles to development (social, cultural, or technical), while *dependency* theory emphasizies external constraints imposed on underdeveloped economies due to their position in the international capitalist system.
5. Views on the causes or consequences of underdevelopment also depend on one's definition of *development*—for example, whether quantitative criteria, which emphasize aggregate growth rates, are used; or qualitative concerns, which deal with distributional issues.
6. One major problem in industrializing nations is *unequal* development and the emergence of a *dual economy*, which may actually increase inequality as growth occurs. The divergence *between* Third-World economies (as between truly underdeveloped and

"newly developing" nations) also complicates the picture and must be taken into account.

7. There are differences of opinion on the relationship between *world trade* and underdevelopment; for example, on the issue of free trade. This is reflected in the emergence of alternative trade strategies such as import-substitution and export-oriented industrialization, and responses that emphasize employment of appropriate technology.
8. There is also disagreement on the role of *foreign aid;* for example, on whether it is a necessary catalyst for development, or perpetuates dependency and underdevelopment.
9. A similar debate exists over the value of direct investment by *multinational corporations* in developing nations.
10. A number of crucial questions concern the relationship between *population, agriculture,* and *underdevelopment* in the Third World. For example, are the problems primarily quantitative (too many people, not enough food)? Should overpopulation be viewed as a *cause* or an *effect* of underdevelopment? Given the great differences in conditions and needs among nations, each case must be considered individually; there are no universal causes or solutions.
11. A number of unique historical events threatened American self-esteem and culminated in a U.S. inferiority complex in the 1970s, which was the context in which Americans viewed world events, including relations with the Third World and the Soviet Union.
12. This included the general perception of the expansion of Soviet power and influence in the world as a major cause of East-West tensions. Evidence suggests, however, that the U.S.S.R. has suffered a decline in world hegemony as well as the U.S.
13. Both superpowers have engaged in destabilizing arms build-ups that increased Cold War tensions. Earlier build-ups in the U.S. have been justified by exaggerating the power of Soviet forces. There is a rough parity between the superpowers today, with both possessing the ability to destroy the world many times over.
14. Disagreements exist over the primary cause of political instability in the Third World. While some point to internal poverty, inequality, and repression as major factors breeding discontent, others emphasize Soviet-inspired subversion.
15. Whatever the justification, there is evidence that militarism has a number of negative consequences for the U.S. economy.

Part III: Responses

16. Responses to the problem of underdevelopment depend on one's answer to the crucial questions introduced in the text, including: (a) Are the obstacles to development primarily internal (modernization theory) or external (dependency theory)—*caused* by capitalism or *alleviated* by it? (b) What *is* "development"? (c) *Who* decides what policies to apply, and in *whose interests* are they carried out?
17. Responses to Third-World political stability also vary depending on the definition of the problem. Those who see the problem as one of communist insurgency often pose military solutions, while those who see poverty or internal repression as major factors favor social reforms, economic aid, or other nonmilitary measures, which may include dealing with rebels where they are a factor.
18. A similar distinction exists between

those who favor *détente* and those stressing the need for *deterrence* in U.S.-Soviet relations. From the latter perspective, recent conciliatory overtures by the U.S. have merely been used by the U.S.S.R. to better their own position. Some critics of the hard-line "Prussian" response favor a "Trader" strategy, which employs the *economic* (versus military) dominance of the U.S. in developing closer ties with the Soviets.

19. The ultimate "social problem" is the threat of nuclear annihilation. An increasing number of individuals, groups, and nations have argued that a necessary first step in the reduction of this threat is a mutually verifiable freeze on the production of nuclear armaments. Such organizations as the Union of Concerned Scientists have outlined arguments for such a freeze based not on "trust" between superpowers, but on logical and possible steps that would preserve the security of both, while reducing the possibility of holocaust.

SUGGESTED READINGS

Brandt Commission (Independent Commission on International Development Issues), *Common Crisis North South: Cooperation for World Recovery.* Cambridge, Mass.: MIT Press, 1983. An extensive follow-up to an earlier examination of the problems of the underdeveloped world and its relationship to the developed nations, headed by former West German Chancellor Willy Brandt.

Ford, Daniel, Henry Kendall, and Steven Nadis (for the Union of Concerned Scientists), *Beyond the Freeze: The Road to Nuclear Sanity.* Boston: Beacon Press, 1982. A critical history of the arms race, emphasizing the irrationality of past and current policies, and providing some alternative strategies for reducing the danger of nuclear conflict.

Hodgson, Godfrey, *America in Our Time.* New York: Vintage Books, 1978. A comprehensive account of the key social, political, and economic factors shaping American ideology and consciousness from World War II to the early 1970s.

Independent Commission on Disarmament and Security Issues, *Common Security: A Blueprint for Survival.* New York: Simon and Schuster, 1982. A relatively nonideological examination of the military aspects of the East-West conflict.

Kirkpatrick, Jeane, "Dictatorships and Double Standards," *Commentary,* November 1979, pp. 34–45. A classic statement of the conservative view of political upheavals in the Third World by the Reagan administration's former Ambassador to the UN.

Melman, Seymour, *Pentagon Capitalism.* New York: McGraw-Hill, 1970. A critical examination of the nature, practices, and costs of defense spending in the United States.

Singer, Hans and Javed Ansari, *Rich and Poor Countries.* London: George Allen and Unwin, 1982. A well-known account of the problems of underdevelopment from a Third-World perspective, with a wealth of factual information.

Weiner, Myron, ed., *Modernization: The Dynamics of Growth.* New York: Basic Books, 1966. A collection of articles which favor the modernization approach to development.

Wilber, Charles K., ed., *The Political Economy of Development and Underdevelopment.* New York: Random House, 1973. Important essays by authors sympathetic to Marxian and/or dependency approaches to underdevelopment, and critical of mainstream modernization theory.

FOOTNOTES

[1]ECA *(Estudios Centroamericanos),* "El Salvador 1984," *NACLA Report on the Americas,* XVIII (1984), 13.

[2]Ruth Leger Sivard, *World Military and Social Expenditures 1981* (Leesburg, Va.: World Priorities, 1981), pp. 28–29.

[3]"El Salvador: It May Be Too Late for Talks," *Business Week,* May 23, 1983, p. 62.

[4]Walter LaFeber, "How We Make Revolution Inevitable," *Nation,* January 28, 1984, p. 70.

[5]*Ibid.,* p. 69.

[6]ECA, *op. cit.,* p. 14.

[7]Janet Shenk, "El Salvador," *NACLA Report on the Americas,* XV (1981), 15–16.

[8]ECA; *op. cit.,* 14.

[9]Jerry W. Sanders, *Peddlers of Crisis* (Boston: South End Press), 1983, pp. 23–50.

[10]U.S. National Security Council, "NSC-68: A Report to the National Security Council, April 14, 1950." In Thomas H. Etzold and John Lewis Gaddis, eds., *Containment: Documents on American Policy and Strategy, 1945–1950* (New York: Columbia University Press, 1978), pp. 435–436.

[11]Godfrey Hodgson, *America in Our Time* (New York: Vintage, 1978), p. 32.

[12]Ruth Leger Sivard, *World Military and Social Expenditures 1983* (Washington, D.C.: World Priorities, 1983), pp. 14–18.

[13]Daniel Ford, Henry Kendall, and Steven Nadis (for the Union of Concerned Scientists), *Beyond the Freeze: The Road to Nuclear Sanity* (Boston: Beacon Press, 1982), p. 12.

[14]The Union of Concerned Scientists, "Reagan's Star Wars," *The New York Review of Books,* April 26, 1984, pp. 47–52.

[15] "'Crisis at the Doorstep' Prompted Move to Aid El Salvador, Reagan Says," *The Kansas City Star,* April 15, 1984, p. 5A.

[16]Carl Sagan, "Nuclear War and Climatic Catastrophe, Some Policy Implications," *Foreign Affairs,* 31 (1983), 257–292.

[17]Sivard, *op. cit.,* 1983, p. 11.

[18]*Ibid.,* p. 23.

[19]*Ibid.,* p. 23.

[20]*Ibid.,* p. 25.

[21]*Ibid.,* p. 26.

[22]*Ibid.,* p. 36.

[23]*Ibid.,* p. 23.

[24]*Ibid.,* pp. 38–40.

[25]*Ibid.,* p. 24.

[26]"29 Dead After Second Day of Rioting over Prices," *The Kansas City Times,* April 25, 1984, p. A3.

[27]See *NACLA Latin America and Empire Report,* Special issue on Chile, 7 (1973), entire volume.

[28]"Third World: Uncle Sam's Tough New Stand," *U.S. News and World Report,* October 26,1981, p. 23.

[29]*Ibid.,* p. 23.

[30]John Sewell and John Mathieson, "North-South Relations." In Joseph Pechman, ed., *Setting National Priorities: Agenda for the 1980s* (Washington, D.C.: Brookings Institution, 1980), p. 511.

[31]Talcott Parsons, *The Social System* (New York: Free Press, 1964); *The System of Modern Societies* (Englewood Cliffs, N.J.: Prentice-Hall, 1971).

[32]Berthold F. Hoselitz, *Sociological Aspects of Economic Growth* (Glencoe, Ill.: Free Press, 1960); Alex Inkeles, "The Modernization of Man." In Myron Weiner, ed., *Modernization: The Dynamics of Growth* (New York: Basic Books, 1966), pp. 138–150; Alex Inkeles and David H. Smith, *Becoming Modern* (Cambridge, Mass.: Harvard University Press, 1974); S. N. Eisenstadt, "Social Change, Differentiation, and Evolution," *American Sociological Review,* 29 (1964), 375–386; S. N. Eisenstadt, *Modernization, Protest and Change* (Englewood Cliffs, N.J.: Prentice-Hall, 1965); A. R. Desai, ed., *Essays on Modernization of Underdeveloped Societies,* 2 vols. (Bombay, India: Thacker, 1971).

[33]W. W. Rostow, *The Stages of Economic Growth: A Non-Communist Manifesto* (London: Cambridge University Press, 1960).

[34]David Apter, *The Politics of Modernization* (Chicago: University of Chicago Press, 1965); Samuel P. Huntington, *Political Order in Changing Societies* (New Haven, Conn.: Yale University Press, 1968).

[35]David G. McClelland, "The Impulse of Modernization." In Myron Weiner, ed., *Modernization: The Dynamics of Growth* (New York: Basic Books, 1963), pp. 28–39.

[36]André Gunder Frank, "Sociology of Development and Underdevelopment of Sociology." In James Cockcroft, André Gunder Frank, and Dale L. Johnson, eds., *Dependence and Underdevelopment: Latin America's Political Economy* (Garden City, N.Y.: Anchor, 1972), pp. 322–397.

[37]Alejandro Portes, "On the Sociology of National Development: Theories and Issues," *American Journal of Sociology,* 82 (1977), 68–77.

[38]*Ibid.*, pp. 65–66.

[39]Inkeles and Smith, *op. cit.*, pp. 17–32.

[40]Frank, "The Development of Underdevelopment," *op. cit.*, pp. 3–17; "Economic Dependence, Class Structure, and Underdevelopment," *op. cit.*, pp. 19–45.

[41]Immanuel Wallerstein, *The Modern World-System* (New York: Academic Press, 1976); *The Capitalist World Economy* (Cambridge: Cambridge University Press, 1979); *The Modern World-System II* (New York: Academic Press, 1980).

[42]Anthony Brewer, *Marxist Theories of Imperialism: A Critical Survey* (London: Routledge and Kegan Paul, 1980), pp. 165–167.

[43]Emmanuel Arghiri, *Unequal Exchange, A Study of the Imperialism of Trade* (London: New Left Books, 1972); Samir Amin, *Unequal Development* (New York: Monthly Review Press, 1974); *Accumulation on a World Scale* (New York: Monthly Review Press, 1976); P. P. Rey, *Les Alliances de Classes* (Paris: Maspero, 1973).

[44]Thomas Weisskopf, "Imperialism and the Economic Development of the Third World." In Richard Edwards, Michael Reich, and Thomas Weisskopf, eds., *The Capitalist System* (Englewood Cliff, N.J.: Prentice-Hall, 1978), p. 507.

[45]Portes, *op. cit.*

[46]*Ibid.*, p. 77.

[47]Alejandro Portes, "From Dependency to Redemocratization: New Themes in Latin American Sociology," *Contemporary Sociology*, 13 (1984), 346–349.

[48]Hans Singer and Javed Ansari, *Rich and Poor Countries* (London: George Allen and Unwin, 1982), p. 19.

[49]*Ibid.*, p. 52.

[50]Michael Todaro, *Economic Development in the Third World* (New York: Longman, 1981), p. 64.

[51]*Ibid.*, pp. 70–72; Singer and Ansari, *op. cit.*, p. 29.

[52]Singer and Ansari, *op. cit.*, p. 249.

[53]*Ibid.*, pp. 19–20; Sewell and Mathieson, *op. cit.*, pp. 502–504.

[54]"Third World . . .," *U.S. News and World Report*, *op. cit.*

[55]Todaro, *op. cit.*, p. 339.

[56]*Ibid.*, p. 375.

[57]Raúl Fernández, "Third World Industrialization: A New Panacea?" *Monthly Review*, 31 (1980), 12–13.

[58]Sewell and Mathieson, *op. cit.*, p. 507.

[59]Brandt Commission (Independent Commission on International Development Issues), *Common Crisis North South: Cooperation for World Recovery* (Cambridge, Mass.: MIT Press, 1983), pp. 101–118.

[60]*Ibid.*, pp. 152–156.

[61]Todaro, *op. cit.*, p. 408.

[62]Sewell and Mathieson, *op. cit.*, p. 525.

[63]Third World . . .," *U.S. News and World Report*, *op. cit.*, p. 20.

[64]Garrett Hardin, "The Toughlove Solution," *Newsweek*, October 26, 1981, p. 45.

[65]Bernadette Madeuf and Charles-Albert Michalet, "A New Approach to International Economics," *International Social Science Journal*, 30 (1978), p. 256.

[66]*Ibid.*, pp. 256–257.

[67]Todaro, *op. cit.*, p. 402.

[68]*Ibid.*, p. 163.

[69]Singer and Ansari, *op. cit.*, p. 49.

[70]Todaro, *op. cit.*, p. 165.

[71]*Ibid.*, p. 173.

[72]*Ibid.*, pp. 254–255.

[73]*Ibid.*, p. 260.

[74]Lester Thurow, "How Reagan Can Wreck the Economy," *The New York Review of Books*, May 14, 1981, p. 6.

[75]Bruce Nussbaum *et al.*, *The Decline of U.S. Power* (Boston: Houghton Mifflin, 1980).

[76]Thurow, *op, cit.*

[77]Hodgson, *op. cit.*, pp. 34–47.

[78]Ruth Leger Sivard, *World Military and Social Expenditures 1980* (Leesburg, Va.: World Priorities, 1980), p. 9.

[79]Sivard, *op. cit.*, 1983, pp. 21–22.

[80]Sivard, *op. cit.*, 1981, p. 8.

[81]*Ibid.*, p. 9.

[82]Sivard, *op. cit.*, 1980, p. 24.

[83]Emma Rothschild, "Boom and Bust," *The New York Review of Books*, April 3, 1980, pp. 31–34.

[84]Sivard, *op. cit.*, 1981, pp. 36–37.

[85]"U.S. Foreign Policy in the 1980s," *Monthly Review*, 31 (1980), pp. 1–12; Richard Feinburg and Kenneth Oye, "After the Fall: U.S. Policy Toward Radical Regimes," *World Policy Journal* 1(1983), 206–211; Jonathan Steele, "The Soviet Union: What Happened to Détente?" In Noam Chomsky, Jonathan Steele, and John Gittings, eds., *Superpowers in Collision: The Cold War Now* (London: Penguin, 1982), pp. 60–64.

[86]"U.S. Foreign Policy in the 1980s," *Monthly Review*, *op. cit.*, p. 3.

[87]Ford *et al.*, *op. cit.*, p. 35.

[88]Robert Johnson, "Periods of Peril: The Window of

Vulnerability and Other Myths," *Foreign Affairs*, 61 (1983), pp. 952–953.

[89]James Fallows, "The Great Defense Deception," *The New York Review of Books*, May 28, 1981, p. 15.

[90]Johnson, *op. cit.*

[91]*Ibid.*, p. 959.

[92]Ford *et al.*, *op. cit.*, p. 18.

[93]*Ibid.*, pp. 19–20.

[94]*Ibid.*, pp. 6–12; Leon Sigal, "Warming to the Freeze," *Foreign Policy*, 48 (1982), 54–65.

[95]"Crisis at the Doorstep . . . ," *op. cit.*, p. 5A.

[96]Jeane Kirkpatrick, "Dictatorships and Double Standards," *Commentary*, November 1979, p. 44.

[97]LaFeber, *op. cit.*, pp. 69–72.

[98]Edward S. Herman and Frank Brodhead, *Demonstration Elections: U.S.-Staged Elections in the Dominican Republic, Vietnam, and El Salvador* (Boston: South End Press, 1984).

[99]Jack Spence, "The Great Salvador Election Blitz," *NACLA Report on the Americas*, XVII (1983), pp. 11–15.

[100]U.S. National Security Council, *op. cit.*, pp. 437–438.

[101]Gabriel Kolko, *Main Currents in Modern American History* (New York: Harper & Row, 1976), pp. 317–319; Tom Riddel, "Militarism: The Other Side of Supply," *Economic Forum*, XIII (1982), pp. 49–70.

[102]Thurow, *op. cit.*, p. 6.

[103]Bruce M. Russett, "Who Pays for Defense?" In Frank N. Trager and Philip S. Kronenberg, eds., *The National Security Education Program* (Lawrence: University Press of Kansas, 1973), p. 450.

[104]Hodgson, *op. cit.*, pp. 244–260.

[105]David Gold, "Fewer Jobs, Slower Growth: Military Drains the Economy," *Dollars and Sense*, 93 (1984), pp. 6, 8; James M. Cypher, "A Drop Not a Burden: U.S. Economy Relies on Militarism," *Dollars and Sense*, 93 (1984), pp. 7, 9, 17.

[106]Seymour Melman, *Pentagon Capitalism* (New York: McGraw-Hill, 1970).

[107]Sivard, *op. cit.*, 1983, p. 12.

[108]Thurow, *op. cit.*, p. 6.

[109]"Directory of the Top 500 Industrial Corporations," *Fortune*, May 2, 1983; Department of Defense, *100 Companies Receiving the Largest Dollar Value of Prime Contract Awards. FY 1982* (Washington, D.C.: U.S. Government Printing Office, 1983).

[110]Department of Defense, *op. cit.*

[111]"Spare-Parts Bills Jar the Pentagon," *Newsweek*, July 25, 1983, p. 69; Orr Kelly, "Why Pentagon Pays $44 for a Light Bulb," *U.S. News and World Report*, August 1, 1983, p. 29.

[112]Mike McNamee, "Study: Defense Reduces Jobs," *USA Today*, April 9, 1984, p. 1B.

[113]Russett, *op. cit.*

[114]James M. Cypher, "Ideological Hegemony and Modern Militarism: The Origins and Limits of Military Keynesianism," *Economic Forum*, XIII (1982), pp. 1–20; Riddel, *op. cit.*; Thurow, *op. cit.*

[115]U.S. Bureau of the Census, Current Population Reports (Series P-60, No. 140), *Money Income and Poverty Status of Families and Persons in the United States (Advance Data From the March 1983 Current Population Survey)* (Washington, D.C.: U.S. Government Printing Office, 1983), p. 1.

[116]"Kissinger's Rescue Plan," *U.S. News and World Report*, January 23, 1984, p. 22.

[117]*Ibid.*

[118]Kirkpatrick, *op. cit.*

[119]*Ibid.*, p. 44

[120]Sewell and Mathieson, *op. cit.*, p. 501.

[121]Eldon Kenworthy, "Central America: Beyond the Credibility Trap," *World Policy Journal*, 1 (1983), 181–200.

[122]*Ibid.*, pp. 190–191.

[123]"Kissinger's Rescue Plan," *op. cit.*, p. 23.

[124]Kenworthy, *op. cit.*, p. 192.

[125]*Ibid.*, p. 192.

[126]Kirkpatrick, *op. cit.*

[127]Quoted in Steele, *op. cit.*, p. 46.

[128]Helmut Sonnenfeldt, "The Soviet Challenge." In Joseph Pechman, ed., *Setting National Priorities: Agenda for the 1980s* (Washington, D.C.: The Brookings Institution, 1980), pp. 348–380.

[129]*Ibid.*, p. 351.

[130]*Ibid.*, p. 349.

[131]Michael Klare, "The Traders and the Prussians," *Seven Days*, 1 (March 1977), pp. 32–33.

[132]Steele, *op. cit.*, pp. 56–57.

[133]*Ibid.*, pp. 43–45.

[134]Ford *et al.*, *op. cit.*, pp. 85–87.

[135]*Ibid.*, pp. 90–91.

[136]Independent Commission on Disarmament and Security Issues, *Common Security: A Blueprint for Survival* (New York: Simon and Schuster, 1982).

Appendix
Review of Basic Sociological Concepts

Concepts may be defined as abstract generalizations developed and used by sociologists to summarize and to order meaningful aspects of the social world. More concretely, a concept is a word or a phrase that stands for some important part of reality. The concept "happy" stands for an individual's good feelings, smiling face, and all-around good humor. Instead of saying all that, and more, about a person, all we need to say is that the person is happy. In this Appendix we will define some of the most important concepts in sociology, including heredity, socialization, adult socialization, nonreflective response, reflective action, mind, self-concept, personality, role, group, primary group, secondary group, reference group, deviant behavior, crime, social structure, culture, value, subculture, and society. A basic understanding of these concepts and how they interrelate should give the student a good sense of the sociological perspective as it is employed throughout this book.

All attempts to understand humanness must start at the beginning, with the fertilized ovum and its genetic content, for much of what we are, and especially much of what we can become, is limited by biological factors.

For a long time, social science paid little attention to biology because during the late nineteenth century there had been too much reliance on biological explanations of social behavior. Recently, however, the work of some biologists has been recognized as vital to a comprehensive social science. Furthermore, a number of sociologists, called *sociobiologists,* have come to concentrate on the role of biological factors in social behavior.

There are at least three major ways in which biology is critically important to the social-science understanding of human behavior. First, whatever else they may be, humans are biological organisms, and the particular kind of organism they are has implications for social science. Second, many of these important biological characteristics are passed from one generation to the next through *heredity*, the genetic transmission of characteristics from parents to offspring. Finally, the line dividing humans and animals, once thought to be quite firm, has become blurred as we have learned more from *ethology*—the scientific study of animal behavior.

Every so often, the media report tragic cases of children who have been locked away in attics or closets and who have been raised in virtual solitary confinement by deranged parents or guardians. When found, such children appear to be extremely mentally defective—they cannot speak and usually they are not even toilet trained. These *feral* children—the word literally means wild, or untamed—have had only their genetic resources to draw on in order to become human. Not one of these children has ever become normal, but those who lived long enough have shown considerable ability to learn. Their condition was caused by being cheated and deprived of the opportunity to learn to be human.

Like lions and gorillas, human infants must learn a great deal; otherwise, they will be human in physical form only. The process through which this learning occurs is *socialization.* When an individual has become adequately human, we say he/she has been properly *socialized*—made social. In this sense, humanity is a social product. We learn who and what we are through the socialization process. Children locked away in attics do not become human; they remain, at most, potentially human.

If the essence of humanness is to be social, it is also to be continually responsive to those around us; in fact, the socialization process never ends. Hence, socialization occurs beyond childhood and it is even possible to think meaningfully of ongoing *adult socialization.* Throughout life, we are placed in new circumstances that require us to learn new ways of behaving—we go to school for the first time, move to a new school, take a new job, get married, become parents, move, retire, and so on—all of which require us to become somehow new. Consequently, human beings are always vulnerable to being poorly socialized and are therefore vulnerable to learning inappropriate behavior. Because socialization is so crucial to humanness, occurs throughout the entire life cycle, and can, and often does, go wrong, it is a major focus of sociology.

One of the basic assumptions of sociology is that the human being who is being socialized is capable of both nonreflective responses *and* reflective actions. People share *nonreflective responses,* or automatic, unthinking responses to external stimuli, with lower animals. But unlike lower animals, humans are also capable of *reflective action,* which refers to what an individual does on the basis of conscious thought and prior consideration. As Karl Marx put it long ago: "What distinguishes the worst architect from the best of bees is this: that the architect raises his structure in imagination before he erects it in reality."[1] While nonreflective responses indicate that the actor reacts more or less blindly to his or her environment, reflective action involves a creative act on the part of the actor. People are not merely passive responders to external stimuli, but they are also active creators of their own senses of social reality.

The idea that people are capable of reflective action implies another critical sociological concept, the *mind.* This refers to the thinking process by which an individual is able to interact with himself or herself. Thus, to the sociologist the mind is not viewed as a physical entity, but as a mental process. By interacting with themselves—by thinking—individuals are able to evaluate the variety of stimuli aimed at them and to decide whether they will respond. The mind allows human beings to postpone a response to external stimuli until they have had time to think through how they wish to respond. People can not only select the stimulus to which they will respond, but they can also choose how they will respond. Individuals can consider various responses in their minds before choosing the one they think is best suited to a particular situation. Human beings are *not* slaves to the stimuli stemming from their external environment.

People respond not only to external stimuli, but also to themselves. Through socialization, as well as interaction with other people, people develop a *self-concept.* This means that people have attitudes toward themselves just as they have attitudes toward all of the things around them. One's self-concept is shaped early in life through the childhood socialization process. Children become aware of who and what they are on the basis of how initially parents, and later many others, define them. However, the self-concept is not set in childhood, but is constantly subject to revision as people move through the various stages of the life cycle. Nevertheless, young people do develop relatively enduring modes of thinking, feeling, responding, and behaving; in other words, they develop a *personality.*

One of the fundamental outcomes of socialization is the ability to play social *roles.* A role is a set of expectations applied to a particular social position (such as child, student, friend, worker, spouse). These expectations define how any particular individual holding the position is supposed to act. Put another way, they are a set of *norms,* or generally accepted rules, about what a person should or should not do when holding a particular position in society. Those around you expect you to behave in certain ways if you are to be regarded as playing the role properly. Being judged a normal, competent, mature person depends on having learned to play assigned roles properly. A disruptive student, alcoholic father, negligent mother, or brutal friend is not fulfilling his or her role.

Through the experience of playing several different roles, we learn to take the roles of others and, from that vantage point, learn to shape our behavior to fit others' expectations of us. Not all humans learn to take the roles of others well. Some of us learn to play our roles well, others to perform them poorly. Thus, some of us form favorable conceptions of ourselves, and some of us are damaged along the way and are inadequately or inappropriately socialized.

Despite the fact that we have a fairly consistent set of expectations about how all persons in any given position should behave, we recognize that people, given their varying personalities, will differ in how they actually behave. For example, some people show considerable anxiety about the adequacy of their behavior in whichever role they are playing—at work they seek constant reassurance that they are doing an adequate job, and at home they seek reassurance that they are good spouses or responsible parents. Thus, a person's behavior represents a blend of role performance and personality.

It is obvious that roles are social. Because roles exist only in relationship to other roles and depend on a shared consensus about how they ought to be performed, roles are properties of groups. It is the group that both socializes us into roles and defines what roles are. Furthermore, groups are collections of roles. Thus, without roles there is no group; without groups there are no roles. The role associated with the position of father, for example, is meaningless outside the context of a group called the family. You cannot say what expectations you have about fathers without saying how someone in that role should relate to others in the roles associated with the positions of mother and child.

Not every bunch of people who happen to be in the same place at the same time is a group. People waiting to cross a street or passengers in an airplane are not groups, they are *aggregates* or *collectivities.* Social scientists restrict the use of the concept of a *group* to a collection of people who are involved in some organized and recurrent pattern of interaction. A group consists of some recognized set of roles and norms. Furthermore, groups are oriented toward some set of goals, whether these involve winning a game or enjoying friendship. Because of shared goals and recurrent interaction among members, groups have at least a vague notion of the boundary that distinguishes members from nonmembers. To be a group, a collection of people must perceive that they share collective existence and common purposes.

Social scientists have found it useful to distinguish among several types of groups. Most important is the distinction between primary and secondary groups as well as the idea of a reference group. *Primary groups* are characterized by intimate relations among members and a strong sense of group membership. Typical examples of primary groups are families, street gangs, play groups, and social clubs. Primary groups are the usual scene of socialization as well as our "private lives," and because of our intimacy with, and our long exposure to them, they serve as primary sources of identity. *Secondary groups* are characterized by less personal relationships among members and demand only a limited part of our loyalties and feelings. In secondary groups, relationships are based more on calculation and utility than on sentiment. We tend to take part in such groups because of what they do for us, not because of what they mean to us. Typical examples are work groups, civic organizations, and college classes that never gather except for their specific function.

Reference groups are those groups to which people refer in order to make comparative self-judgments. Individuals evaluate themselves according to the standards and values of their reference groups, and they orient their behavior, either positively or negatively, toward these groups. Sometimes people have negative as well as positive reference groups. Various activities may be disdained because they are associated with a group that the individual holds in contempt. Young people, for example, may avoid certain activities because adults engage in them.

Every group has agreed-upon norms, or rules, and the members are the source of enforcement of those norms. A major part of socialization in both childhood and adulthood, as people move from one group to another, is learning what the norms are and conforming to them. Groups have considerable power to make members conform to their norms—from withholding approval to beating up, banishing, or otherwise severely punishing those who transgress.

We are here stressing the power of groups to socialize people by inducing them to conform, to observe the norms, and to fulfill their roles. The power of the group, however, is limited. Although most people conform most of the time, not everyone does so all of the time. Failure to conform is *deviant behavior.* Deviance may consist of minor violations of norms or role performances that may be overlooked, but sometimes other group members take deviance seriously and punish the deviant or try to prevent recurrence of the behavior.

Ordinarily, social scientists are primarily interested in major acts of deviance; in acts that are regarded as serious transgressions. They have focused on explaining why serious acts of deviance occur—homicide, robbery, delinquency, alcoholism, drug addiction, spouse abuse, child abuse, rape, and the various bizarre behaviors associated with mental illness. Such acts are of major importance to a great number of people in society, as demonstrated by the existence of formal agencies specifically meant to stymie such acts. These acts are frequently not simply deviant but are against the law, they are *crimes*. Society has decided that it cannot or will not tolerate such behavior and turns to social scientists for aid in finding ways to prevent it. These forms of deviance may be considered *social problems*.

However, not all social problems involve deviance. For example, poverty is not typically caused by failure to conform to group norms. In fact, most of the problems discussed in this book do not involve deviance. Furthermore, even those problems that do involve deviance cannot be wholly understood by analyzing human behavior. In order to be able to explain most forms of deviance,as well as most other social problems, we must raise our sights from human behavior to a higher level of analysis—the nature and operation of social structure, culture, society, as well as the international arena.

Social scientists must work on both the microscopic and macroscopic levels of analysis. A good portion of their study is directed toward understanding individual thought and action or relatively small groups. Study at this level is often called *microscopic analysis* because it is close to the individual (think of the microscope). But a considerable amount of social-science study asks how social structures, culture, society, and even intersocietal relations operate. Here, social scientists adopt a very broad perspective in which the individual recedes to a dot and very large features of the social world come into view. Study at this level is called *macroscopic analysis*. Attempts to fashion complete answers to what causes a given social problem always involve both micro and macro considerations.

The starting point for all macrosocial analysis is understanding the distinction between two fundamental sociological concepts: social structures and culture. We may define *social structures* as relatively permanent patterns of specialized roles, groups, procedures, and activities through which fundamental social activities are performed. Through the economic structure, the economy, for example, the society produces and distributes valued goods and services. Through its political structure, a society coordinates and organizes its activities, especially those involving goals, and makes decisions about goals and means. Societies also need to maintain some degree of commitment of members of society. Religious structures help do this by integrating societies, legitimating existing social arrangements, providing a sacred sense to social norms and values, and giving members of society a shared set of solutions to questions of ultimate meaning. Throughout this book we have examined problems within various social structures (for example, health care, the economy, and the international political economy), the role played by various structures in causing deviance (crime, alcoholism and drug addiction, and mental illness), and other social problems (poverty, racism, sexism, ageism, family and sexual violence, urban decay, the population explosion, and ecological disaster).

In addition to possessing an array of social structures, all societies also possess a *culture*. To put it simply, culture is a people's way of life. More specifically, culture may be defined as the entire complex of ideas and material objects that the people of a society need and use in carrying out their collective life. The culture encompasses knowledge and beliefs, technologies, language, and, most importantly, norms and values. We have already encountered the idea of norms in discussing groups. Not only do groups have such rules, but so does the larger society; these are the cultural norms. *Values* may be defined as a culture's generally accepted standards of desirability. Norms and values are often intimately related. Values define desirable objectives, while the norms define the rules to be adhered to in achieving those goals. Thus, in American society we value economic success and we have a variety of norms about the proper ways for achieving it.

In many ways, culture is synonymous with civilization. Culture is that complex pattern of living that humans have evolved. Culture is learned. And the process of socialization is the process of passing on the culture to the next generation. Culture and society are interdependent. Without culture there is no society; culture exists only as an aspect of society.

In addition to the culture of the society, there are also a number of subcultures within any society. A *subculture* is a culture within a culture—a group of people that has developed or maintained its own distinctive set of beliefs, norms, values, and the like. These may be at variance with those of the larger society, or they may be at variance with those of other subcultures, or both. In the area of social problems, we are most concerned with criminal, delinquent, and drug-abuse subcultures: subcultures that are at considerable variance with the culture of the society as a whole. Encompassing both social structures and culture is a society. American society, for example, encompasses both a culture (and many subcultures) and a large number of social structures. We may define a *society* as an aggregate of people who are united by social relationships and who are relatively self-sufficient and self-sustaining, who live in a definite physical location, and who have so existed for a relatively long time. At the most macroscopic level, sociologists are interested in *intersocietal,* or international, relations.

The concepts defined and outlined in this Appendix are employed explicitly and implicitly throughout this book.

FOOTNOTE

[1]Cited in Frederick Bender, ed., *Karl Marx: The Essential Writings* (New York: Harper Torchbooks, 1972), p. 360.

INDEX

Italicized page numbers refer to key terms and their definitions.

ABOUT THE AUTHOR

George Ritzer is Professor of Sociology at the University of Maryland. He is the author of numerous books, especially in the areas of sociological theory and the sociology of work, and he has published many articles in the leading journals in the field. Professor Ritzer has held a Fulbright-Hays fellowship, been Fellow-in-Residence at the Netherlands Institute for Advanced Study, and was selected as Distinguished Scholar-Teacher at the University of Maryland. Born in New York City, Professor Ritzer received his Ph.D. from Cornell University. He is married, has two children, and is an avid tennis player.